THE DIARY OF JOHN LONGE
(1765–1834)
VICAR OF CODDENHAM

The Revd John Longe MA (1765–1834), vicar of Coddenham-cum-Crowfield. A copy of the silhouette hangs in the clergy vestry of St Mary's Church, Coddenham.

THE DIARY OF JOHN LONGE
(1765–1834)
VICAR OF CODDENHAM

Edited by

MICHAEL STONE

General Editor

RICHARD WILSON

The Boydell Press

Suffolk Records Society
VOLUME LI

A Suffolk Records Society publication
First published 2008
The Boydell Press, Woodbridge

ISBN 978–1–84383–357–4

Issued to subscribing members for the year 2007–2008

The Boydell Press is an imprint of Boydell & Brewer Ltd
PO Box 9, Woodbridge, Suffolk IP12 3DF, UK
and of Boydell & Brewer Inc.
668 Mt Hope Avenue, Rochester, NY 14620, USA
website: www.boydellandbrewer.com

A catalogue record for this book is available
from the British Library

This publication is printed on acid-free paper

Printed in Great Britain by
Antony Rowe Ltd, Chippenham, Wiltshire

CONTENTS

Revd John Longe.
Coddenham, Suffolk.

ILLUSTRATIONS

PREFACE

'The means of information within a given limit is preferable to works of much greater merit, from a distant quarter'. So wrote an antiquary in 1792 in opening the history of his locality.[1] The present volume hardly moves out of Suffolk and its given limit is the life of one man in the locality of Coddenham-cum-Crowfield in the middle of our county. John Longe first interested me because I lived for nearly seven years in the village of which he had been vicar, in sight of his parsonage house, and of the parish church of St Mary in which he and I led worship two centuries apart. Through his writings, he then vividly revealed himself to me as a fine example of a gentleman-parson of a very different age. This volume is part of a longer journey. My first connection with his villages resulted from the invitation of the diocesan bishop to serve three parishes including Coddenham, and then in a wider cluster including Crowfield. I soon met Sylvia Bickers and Sally Garrod, pillars of Coddenham Village History Club and I thank them for introducing me to John Longe, whose family archive had been occasionally consulted but without sustained exploration, and for their steady support. I undertook post-graduate research on different aspects of Longe's life, parish ministry and social contribution, first for an MA degree by dissertation with the University of Essex, and then more briefly within the Institute of Continuing Education at the University of Cambridge. Any academic rigour that I gained is attributable to supervision by Professor John Walter and Frank Grace.

I have enjoyed throughout the genial friendship of Nicholas Longe, direct descendent of John, who readily lent me material. I have been encouraged by the general interest of my colleagues in the Suffolk Local History Council, including the photographic skill of Philip Pantelis, supplementing the unfailing helpfulness of the search-room staff at Suffolk Record Office, Ipswich. More recently, the learned enthusiasm of Professor Richard Wilson as General Editor and especially of David Dymond and David Sherlock as successive patient Co-ordinating Editors, all acting on behalf of the Suffolk Records Society for this present project, have carried me through. Another gratifying aspect has been the number of casual and often unexpected connections that have come from my having read the volumes previously published by Suffolk Records Society, edited by such resounding names as John Blatchly (xxiv), Norman Scarfe (xxx), Jane Fiske (xxxii, xxxiii) and T.C.B. Timmins (xxxix).

I wish also to thank those to whom I have turned for advice in specific areas: John Ridgard, Ted Cockayne, David Cubitt, Brian Pateman and Nick of Cosimedia, as well as those the substance of whose help has been remembered but the source forgotten. Among many encouragers has been my historian son David, whose volume

1 John Mastin, 'The History and Antiquities of Naseby (1792)' in C. Vialls and K. Collins (eds), *A Georgian Country Parson: the Rev. John Mastin of Naseby* (Northampton, 2004), p.75.

on medieval agriculture beat mine to publication by several furlongs. Finally, I thank my wife Esme for patient acceptance of the implications within domestic life of the study that has lain behind this work and her encouragement from first to last.

Michael Stone
Melton, Woodbridge

ABBREVIATIONS

Ag. Hist. Rev.	*Agricultural History Review*
BA	Bachelor of Arts
Bart or bt	baronet, a member of the lowest hereditary order
Coll.	College
d.s.p	died (*decessit*) without issue: (see *s.p.*)
DD	Doctor of Divinity, a higher university degree
dw	penny-weight, one-twentieth of an ounce troy, as in silverware
FRS	Fellow of the Royal Society
Hon.	Honourable, title of the child of a nobleman
HT	*History Today*
IJ	*Ipswich Journal*
JEH	*Journal of Ecclesiastical History*
JP	Justice of the Peace, magistrate
MA	Master of Arts
MB	Bachelor of Medicine
MD	Doctor of Medicine
NRO	Norfolk Record Office
ODNB	*Oxford Dictionary of National Biography* (in 60 volumes), 2004
P&P	*Past & Present*
PC	perpetual curate: see glossary
PSIAH	*Proceedings of the Suffolk Institute of Archaeology & History*
R.	rector, incumbent of a parish, usually the highest stipend
Rt Revd	Right Reverend, title of a bishop, the titular head of a diocese
s.p.	*sine prole*, without issue
SPCK	Society for Promoting Christian Knowledge
SPG	Society for the Propagation of the Gospel
SR	*Suffolk Review*, the journal of Suffolk Local History Council
SRO(I)	Suffolk Record Office, Ipswich branch
UEA	University of East Anglia
V.	vicar, incumbent of a parish, usually with stipend lower than a rector
Ven.	Venerable, title of an archdeacon, a senior diocesan post under the bishop
Very Revd	title of a dean, as of a cathedral, but also of Hadleigh

INTRODUCTION

The Church of England, 1790s to 1830s

The Reverend John Longe exercised ordained ministry as a vicar from 1794 to 1834 through a challenging period of change in state, society and church. The after-shocks of the French Revolution were not confined to that country, for right across Western Europe the grip of the old regime was weakening. In England this was a period crucial in the development of institutional religion, and thus of the clergy.

There were many occasions of anxiety in the nation at large. For nearly the whole of twenty-two years Britain was expensively engaged in war with France. For two periods within this time south-eastern England was in daily fear of armed sea-borne invasion. Wartime prosperity for farmers was not shared by rural labourers, but the sharp post-war depression affected all. In a series of civil uprisings in East Anglia between 1814 and 1831 impoverished countrymen were confronted by military force. Property owners not only faced groups of determined agitators, but were also vulnerable to furtive incendiarism. All levels of society experienced poor harvests and volatile prices with resulting bank collapses and ever-rising poor-rates. Many farmers and landowners were suspicious of the scientific advances that would have improved their yields and their profits, and unappreciative of legislative attempts to protect the agricultural interest. Although the changes comprising the 'Industrial Revolution' were mild by comparison with those experienced in more northern regions, they were transforming local towns such as Ipswich, where already slums were developing.[1]

Religion remained for most people the context for everyday life.[2] Through the eighteenth century the institutional church had appeared secure, even imposing, for sacred church and secular state had been seen as two sides of the single coin.[3] The *Book of Common Prayer* being part of the law of the land, church-goers regularly prayed for the sovereign, head both of church and (with Parliament) of state.[4] In the 1790s few challenged this theoretical identity or the political usefulness of the established church that seemed to justify its privileged position. Government needed the stability that the church was encouraging, at a time when un-churched societies abroad were in violent revolution. Steadiness was valued, idealism was suspect. It seemed vital for the equilibrium of society that the established church should preach

1 Frank Grace, *Rags and Bones: a Social History of a Working Class Community* (2005), pp.40–51.

2 Religion, though becoming detached from daily living, was still part of the thought process of the majority: C.J. Somerville, 'The Secularisation Puzzle', *HT*, 44, no.10 (1994), p.14.

3 Frances Knight, 'From Diversity to Sectarianism: the Definition of Anglican Identity in Nineteenth Century England' in R.N. Swanson (ed.), *Unity and Diversity in the Church* (Oxford, 1996), pp.377–88; G.M. Ditchfield, *The Evangelical Revival* (1998), p.94; Peter Virgin, *The Church in an Age of Negligence: Ecclesiastical Structure and Problems of Church Reform, 1700–1840* (Cambridge, 1989), p.43; R.A. Soloway, *Prelates and People: Ecclesiastical Social Thought in England 1783–1852* (1969), pp.45–51.

4 The *Book of Common Prayer* is still part of the law of the land, although fewer Anglican services today include a prayer for the queen.

moral obedience, deference and restraint. Ironically, it was the lack of restraint in response to radical writers such as Tom Paine that pushed frightened moderates into alliance with the privileged. Some preachers even claimed that the existing social structure with its marked hierarchy was divinely ordained.

Nevertheless, for all its imposing appearance, the established church was damaged by a combination of secular changes associated with the rapid growth in urban population. As both active dissent and total non-attendance grew, profound weaknesses in the church were increasingly acknowledged. In the 1790s, however, structural reform of the church was hardly a live issue, for vested interest is a powerful conservative force. Clergy holding richly endowed posts felt threatened; lay patrons defended the monetary and social value of their advowsons. Spiritual renewal across the nation was unlikely to be led from a bench of bishops, appointed to be politically active, although a minority in the House of Lords. With Convocation long suppressed, only lay-controlled Parliament could change the law. In the earlier years of the new century the problem was simply too deep and complex for substantive legislation. Consolidated in 1817, earlier tentative legislative attempts addressed only symptoms, leaving Suffolk's country parishes little affected.

For most people in rural areas what was real was local, as personified in their resident parson. Despite the circulation of much information and more rumour, only the more dramatic national events came to their notice and those often from the pulpit. The great *theoretical* strength of the established church was that no parish was without its social and moral leadership. However, for many parishes the clergyman was simply not 'there', at best merely a visitor. When duty was delegated by an absentee to a succession of curates, both continuity and authority suffered. Many parsons who were resident lived in grand parsonage houses with social aspirations to match, and were thus socially distanced from the humble cottagers they existed to serve. A lay patron was free to present a man possessing neither vocation nor aptitude, for the taking of holy orders by a young man of good appearance required little of either. Once beneficed, an incumbent could shelter behind his legal freehold, for his bishop had no control over the sources of his income and little effective sanction against neglect of office.

The central ground of the church, better designated orthodox than high church, was solidly held by bookishly pious clerics, benevolent in a paternalistic way. This steady core of the established church sympathised with neither Roman Catholicism nor those few extremists later called 'Anglo-Catholics' nor the evangelical wing. This set of comfortable attitudes was shared by lay gentlemen, even those living in a more shallow and self-indulgent style.

On the financial side the established church had a massive total income, but its distribution was massively unequal.[5] At the lower end the expectation of a comfortable livelihood had outstripped the income of many a rural incumbency, for in 1802 nearly half the livings in England were valued under £85 per annum, and unbeneficed clergy earned even less.[6] Plurality was one perhaps inevitable result, but steps taken to increase income in other ways also tended to distract from pastoral duties. Some assisted in neighbouring parishes, others took boarding pupils, or farmed more extensively than the glebe. William Kirby of Barham took private pupils, as did the diarist William Jones who grumbled that his comfort was compromised. Benjamin

[5] Reliable financial figures were not then available to refute extravagant critical speculation, by such as the authors of *The Black Book* (1820–23) and *The Extraordinary Black Book* (1831).

[6] C.K. Francis Brown, *A History of the English Church 1800–1900* (1953), pp.17–19.

Newton needed to travel to supervise his estates. Holland, vicar and diarist, earned fees deputising for absentee incumbents nearby. Skinner resented that the business of farming took him from enjoyment of his studies. Mastin not only enjoyed farming but was in demand as a consultant land agent. Even Woodforde had to supervise his Norfolk 'farming man'.[7]

Both ceremonial and enthusiasm were suspect, and theology and spirituality muted. Country clergy, though understating these facets of religion, did mostly fulfil their perceived role as advocates of law-abiding behaviour in a shared faith that was public and corporate. Young people learnt the catechism, but by rote. Humble rural folk felt a positive sense of belonging, centred on the parish church and its burial ground. Nevertheless, they were quietly tenacious of alternative beliefs: timeless fears, hopes and taboos.[8] However much the parson castigated such beliefs as superstition, at best he achieved an uneasy mix of his orthodox teaching with it.

In most country districts, as distinct from fast-growing towns, church attendance continued under the influence of habit and custom, but even here conformity and deference were weakening and dissatisfaction growing. As early as 1800, the clergy of Lincolnshire reported alarming apathy among agricultural labourers.[9] Tithe negotiations and confrontation with farmers, the leaders of parish society, were potentially destructive of good pastoral relations. Many clergy benefited from improved farm yields, and consequent rising status, but this distanced them from their people. Charity was dispensed paternalistically, the vicar exercising judgment to give or withhold. A patronised recipient might mask negative feelings with a show of deference, but resentment found outlets both dramatic and insidious. Clerical justices increased substantially in numbers from the 1780s and elevation to the county bench increased the likelihood of painful confrontation within the parish.

Generalisations need a measure of adjustment. A committed clergyman and his wife, by patient example and simple good works, could exercise significant influence for good. There were such men and women. The divine was indeed seen to be involved in daily life. The conforming majority seldom lacked respect for such divine engagement, in a world not yet minutely explained by scientists. The spiritual and sacred aspect of life had not diminished into the personal concern of a minority, to be invoked by others only at times of crisis. Increasingly from the 1790s some church ministers contributed the positive aspects of evangelical influence, though rural ministry was the last to benefit. Education, in the limited sense of instilling a simple moral God-given code, was regarded as another instrument of order and stability. The Sunday School movement, largely sustained by those of evangelical belief, encouraged a competing response among the orthodox in 1811 in the forma-

7 Sundry passages in O.F. Christie (ed.), *The Diary of the Revd William Jones 1771–1821* (1929); C.P. Fendall and E.A. Crutchley (eds), *The Diary of Benjamin Newton 1816–18* (Cambridge, 1933); Jack Ayres (ed.), *Paupers and Pigkillers, the Diary of William Holland 1799–1818* (Stroud, 1984); H. and P. Coombs (eds), *Journal of a Somerset Rector 1803–34, John Skinner* (Oxford, 1984), p.349; C.Vialls and K. Collins (eds), *A Georgian Country Parson: the Rev. John Mastin of Naseby* (Northampton, 2004); John Beresford (ed.), *The Diary of a Country Parson 1758–1802* (Oxford, 1924–31), 5 vols. The Parson Woodforde Society's project to publish the whole extant diary is now complete.

8 Bob Bushaway, 'Tacit Unsuspected but still Implicit Faith', in Tim Harris (ed.), *Popular Culture in England c.1500–1850* (1995), pp.189–215; James Obelkevich, *Religion and Rural Society: South Lindsey 1825–75* (Oxford, 1976), pp.259–310. In his rich Suffolk narrative books, George Ewart Evans disclosed that much alternative belief survived into the early twentieth century.

9 Soloway, *Prelates*, p.232.

tion of 'the National Society for the Education of the Poor in the Principles of the Established Church'. The title reveals much.

Things moved on. War unified the nation, but the peacetime years after 1815 were times of want and anti-climax, breeding demands for reform and change. Rioting (however defined) was frequent, and full-scale revolution seemed possible. Lacking a proper police force the government resorted to repression, with which the church was damagingly identified. Writers defending the church seemed swamped by contrary forces. Cartoonists and radical journalists like William Cobbett were moulding popular opinion to new heights of anti-clericalism. Even moderate politicians began to query the virtual monopoly of the established church, while friendly voices urged the wisdom of limited concessions.

Earlier, the country might seem to have been delivered from 'pagans, papists and puritans', but these elements, though incompatible, were fighting back in coalition.[10] Although religious 'voluntaryism' had in the 1790s been unfairly associated with strident political radicalism, Methodism in maturity showed its positive aspects and Old Dissent also increased confidently. In the villages, being visibly committed to a minority dissenting congregation was a price paid more readily.[11] Roman Catholics, few in Suffolk, were considered to lack that quality of Englishness associated with the established church, but sustained pressure from religious minorities for removal of disabilities succeeded in 1828–29.[12] When the Whigs were returned to power it seemed that an unstoppable process would bring about the disestablishment of the Anglican church.

The year 1830 was one of substantial and widespread turmoil. Triggered by hunger rather than by political radicalism, the 'Swing Riots' troubled some twenty counties in south and east England.[13] Governments came and went. When the House of Lords rejected the second Reform Bill in 1831 the bishops were a popular target.[14] Old-style orthodox churchmen, no longer complacent, now saw their cherished principles breached from several directions. Stirrings in the world of science, in the field of geology for example, were undercutting contemporary Christian assumptions.[15] Encouraged by these new forces, politicians in Parliament openly planned to re-allocate ecclesiastical endowments. The Reform Act did in the event prove an anti-climax, but moderate Tories accepted some equalising of church endowments, if only to deter more sweeping changes. Announced in mid-1832 and driven by Bishop Blomfield, the Ecclesiastical Revenues Commission was (in re-named and permanent form) ultimately to produce much improved use of resources.

Within the embattled church allegiances were hardening: those holding evan-

10 Robert Southey's memorable descriptive words (1824): Sheridan Gilley, 'Nationality & Liberty, Protestant & Catholic: Robert Southey's Book of the Church', in Stuart Mews (ed.), *Religion and National Identity* (Oxford, 1982), p.415.

11 See Appendix A for the 1851 census, for dissenting success locally. See also Knight, 'From Diversity', p.382, and Chris C. Park, *Sacred Worlds: an Introduction to Geography and Religion* (1994), p.71.

12 G.I.T Machin, *Politics and the Churches in Great Britain 1832–68* (Oxford, 1977), p.22; John Wolffe, *The Protestant Crusade in Great Britain 1829–60* (Oxford, 1991), pp.14–16, 22–4; Richard Brown, *Church and State in Modern Britain 1700–1850* (1991), p.427.

13 E.J. Hobsbaum and Rude, *Captain Swing* (1969), p.11.

14 Robert Towler and A.P.M. Coxon, *The Fate of the Anglican Clergy* (1979), pp.6–7; J.H. Bettey, *Church and Parish* (1987), p.110.

15 William Smith's *Geological Map* (1815) and Charles Lyell in *The Principles of Geology*, 3 vols (1830–3). In archaeology the implications of John Frere's brilliant observations in Suffolk (1797) were long unrealised: *PSIAH* XXXIX, part 2 (1998), pp.268–9, and part 4 (2000), pp.541–2.

gelical beliefs were forming into a party and the old orthodox high church defended its position by use of patronage.[16] It was secular 'interference with God's church' that triggered a demand from a group of Oxford academics for loyalty to an idealised Anglicanism. Within a few weeks of Keble's Assize Sermon at Oxford in the summer of 1833 others were meeting at Hadleigh, in shared concern to combine theological learning with personal holiness. Their writings were to give them the name Tractarians.

Meanwhile, in 1833 the state was active in several spheres previously regarded as the province of the church: by its first grant for education; by a Factory Act; in outlawing slavery abroad; and soon in a radically amended Poor Law. Some concerns of Dissenters were addressed and persistent calls for tithe reform led to compulsory commutation into cash payments, whilst respecting rights of property. These developments were enough to lower the temperature, for few in Parliament were radical. Although hardly foreseeable in 1833, the Church of England retained its established status, however nominally. Britain escaped revolution.

Introducing John Longe of Coddenham

This was the context in which, from 1797 until his death in 1834, John Longe ministered as vicar of Coddenham-cum-Crowfield, a comfortable benefice in central Suffolk (plates 2 and 3). He came into that living by a series of chances and the exercise of patronage, both typical of his time.[17] By both upbringing and temperament he valued traditional ways. Longe was one of many clergy of orthodox Anglicanism, perhaps high in theology but restrained in liturgical practice, before Oxford Tractarians formed a self-consciously holy ecclesiastical grouping. Already aged thirty-five when the nineteenth century opened, Longe's style was formed as a gentleman in the previous century. Like many contemporaries he was ill at ease with open enthusiasm in worship; like many who enjoy material prosperity he valued and defended the status quo.

Longe provides an excellent example of the well-to-do clerical Justice of the Peace, as much engaged in local administration as in matters spiritual. His standards were of his time, though these would satisfy neither his Victorian successors, nor the evangelical minority of his generation. He was most comfortable with those like-minded gentlemen, both laymen and clerics, whose secular interests and lifestyle he shared. In an age when many parish clergy of means absented themselves from their parishes Longe must be credited with living in his parsonage house and fulfilling for his parishioners the duties they expected of him. He met these obligations with the aid of a succession of assistant curates, whose modest salaries he could well afford. Alongside many aspects of a life of ease, he actively contributed in public service to the good, as he saw it, of his fellow men. These factors dictated the style of his ministry, physically present in his parsonage, but distanced from his parishioners. Although Longe's adult life began in privilege and good fortune, the following years brought family tragedy and conflict. His older age was marred both by physical illness and by the painful passing of familiar ways. Whether he is aptly described as 'John Bull in a dog-collar' will be considered below.[18] A loyal Englishman, Longe

16 Clive Dewey, *The Passing of Barchester* (1991), pp.1–6, for the organised use of patronage.

17 For Longe's early years to 1796 see below in introduction to Diary of 1796.

18 Dr John Ridgard used this phrase in a talk to a group in Suffolk, but does not claim to have coined it. For silhouette see frontispiece.

impresses as conventional and reliable, ordered and controlled. He was fatherly to his household and his parishioners but any subordinate daring to show lack of deference would find him distinctly impatient. Having formed a view he would fight to uphold it and his confrontational style extended to conflict with his squire.

In concentrating on one specific man the aim of this volume is to illustrate the working of the rural church within the wider county scene. The use of previously unpublished material casts a steady light on the public social ways of a clerical gentleman, securely established within a substantial benefice.[19] Longe conformed to the mores of an English gentleman in his home life, his parochial ministry and his wider public offices. Financially, all rural benefices were funded from two main sources of income, both derived from land *within* the parish, namely tithes and the cultivation of the glebe. Apart from the poorest parishes aided from Queen Anne's Bounty, no income flowed in from external sources. Offerings and fees were tiny. Since the first part of Longe's incumbency, up to 1813, coincided to his benefit with a period of prosperity for Suffolk farming, the income yielded from the fields of Coddenham and Crowfield was substantial. In 1826 the annual income of the benefice (as distinct from his private income) totalled over £936. In an official report, averaged over three years ending in 1831, this substantial figure was even exceeded, shown as £1,009.[20] Roughly half of this income was entitlement to tithe which Longe negotiated into a cash 'composition'. For a tenant farming tithe-payer, its substantial scale is clear from a calculation sometimes used: one-quarter of rent of arable, plus one-seventh of rent of pasture. For the period 1797 to 1815, Longe's annual tithe income fluctuated between just below £400 and £577 and in one later year rose above £650.[21] Although his benefice was only a vicarage the greater tithes had been added by the earlier benefactor Balshazar Gardemau. Few Suffolk livings equalled that amount.[22] Longe was businesslike and successful in collecting his tithes, although not always without conflict.[23] The other church income derived from land held with the benefice. Although the ancient Coddenham glebe comprised less than thirty scattered acres, to this had been added in the mid-eighteenth century land and property within the substantial Gardemau trust.

Longe also had a life interest by way of private family income, from farms he and his wife Charlotte had been willed, mostly by Nicholas Bacon. The church lands and the private lands together totalled 833 acres. Of this, Longe's own farm of 125 acres, worked by a bailiff plus four others, showed a large profit of £555 in 1800 from a mixed system of about three-fifths arable and two-fifths pasture. The rest of the land was leased to tenant farmers at a total annual rental, by best estimate in 1826–27, of £675. Moreover, Longe enjoyed dividends on investment funds

19 For a selection of primary sources, see pp.285–88. The Longe archive is SRO(I) HA24/50/19/ with the 6 pocket-books at /4.3(1)–(6). For an example see plate 8.

20 The Report of the Commissioners appointed to enquire into the Revenues of the Established Church, presented to Parliament in June 1835. The Suffolk material is accessible in A. Page, *Supplement to the Suffolk Traveller* (1844), p.1026. Details of Longe's 1826 income were listed in a case for the opinion of counsel. SRO(I) HA 24/50/19/3.19.

21 Tithe records are scattered throughout the archive, but see bundle at SRO(I) HA 24/50/19/4.5(17).

22 A Suffolk example of single-minded increasing of tithe income, up 131 per cent (1791–1817): John Leroo at Long Melford. See A. Tindal Hart, *The Country Priest in English History* (1959), pp.121–2.

23 Efficiency in the actual collecting of tithes varied. Jones knew he was defrauded: Christie, *Jones*, p.171; Thirkens, in 1828 collecting a mere quarter, feared being harassed to death: Eric J. Evans, *Tithes and the Tithe Commutation Act* (1978), p.3; the Revd George Parker was shot dead in 1806 after tithe antagonism: John Houghton, *Parsons through the Ages* (Milton Keynes, 2002), pp.23–9.

forming a further part of the Bacon inheritance.[24] Taxes, rates and diocesan dues only slightly reduced this gross income, totalling by Longe's reckoning in the year 1826 £116 14s. 7d. He had also an obligation to maintain the fabric of the chancel, the vicarage and other church property, at an average annual cost he calculated as £164 0s. 0d.[25] In comparison with this net income, at this time farmworkers were receiving no more than 10 shillings a week. The largest stipend he paid a graduate curate, other than his own son, was a not ungenerous £100 plus cottage. Financially, Longe was more comfortably placed than all but a very few of his clerical colleagues in Suffolk. Longe's responsibility as vicar was within the geographical boundaries of Coddenham with its adjacent hamlet of Crowfield in mid-Suffolk.

Longe also took some part in the social life of Ipswich, the ancient borough town eight miles away, where agricultural engineering was newly added to its historic role as trading centre for its rural hinterland. Even before the large dock was completed in 1842 its population rose from 11,277 in 1801 to 20,201 in 1831. During the French wars thousands of military personnel were stationed there, affecting the social scene.[26] Although larger than Bury St Edmunds in the western half of the county, Ipswich struggled in vain to emulate Bury's cultural life and elegance. Halfway between these two major towns lay Stowmarket, linked to Ipswich in that pre-railway age both by turnpike and by the River Gipping, recently rendered navigable. By virtue of its central location, Stowmarket was the 'neutral' venue for county-wide meetings of gentry. Coddenham village lay between Ipswich and Stowmarket, within easy distance of both by horseback, gig or carriage. Longe was not socially isolated.

Of the thirty-seven parishes within Bosmere and Claydon Hundred, Coddenham with its 1801 population of 653 ranked joint second in population with Bramford, behind Needham Market. The more isolated hamlet of Crowfield (population 250) had a reputation for being backward and lawless. The population of both rose in the next thirty years by an appreciable 40 per cent. Coddenham was no longer a centre of communication as in Roman times, for the turnpike from Ipswich via Stowmarket to Bury St Edmunds ran on the further side of the Gipping valley and the Norwich turnpike which forked from it at Claydon passed through only the fringe of Coddenham parish. Despite the absence of coaching traffic, the tradesmen of Coddenham served several surrounding parishes by the network of minor turnpiked roads and local lanes. Coddenham was a valley village, with separate upland hamlets at Coddenham Green and Crowfield. Much of Coddenham parish (2,719 acres) and the whole of Crowfield (1,721 acres) lay on the boulder clay which stretches north to the Waveney valley. Although this had been within Suffolk's dairying region, by 1837 three-quarters of Coddenham was arable following the need for crops during the French wars (see maps in illustrations 1, 4 and 5).[27]

The big house locally was Shrubland Park, owned by the Bacon family for two

24 Although some of this wealth came from Charlotte's father, none came from Longe's father who, being a younger brother, was modestly situated.

25 This average for repairs was too low, since Longe's estate later accepted a dilapidations deduction.

26 G.R. Clarke, *The History and Description of the Town and Borough of Ipswich* (1830), pp.192–3; Peter Bishop, *The History of Ipswich, Triumph and Disaster* (1995), pp.100–3; Robert Malster, *A History of Ipswich* (Chichester, 2000), pp.118–22; Frank Grace, 'Economy, Government & Society in Ipswich c.1500–c.1830' in Robert Malster and Neil Salmon (eds), *Ipswich from the 1st to the 3rd Millennium* (Ipswich, 2001), p.24.

27 SRO(I) FDA66/A1/1a: Tithe Apportionment 1837; Arthur Young, *General View of the Agriculture of the County of Suffolk* (1813, reprint of 1969), p.199.

centuries. When Nicholas Bacon sold most of the estate in 1788 to the Middletons of Crowfield and on his death gave substantial status and land to the Longes, he created divided ownership and leadership, which (as is shown below) contributed to lack of harmony. Sir William Middleton owned almost two-thirds of Coddenham parish, plus most of Crowfield, and many families depended on him for employment and housing, although his personal influence was somewhat weakened by his frequent absence in London and Italy.[28] The new hall stood just outside Coddenham parish, but the old hall and much of Shrubland Home Farm lay within. Longe's social standing was nevertheless secure with a substantial 24 per cent of Coddenham, alongside only two smaller owner-occupier farmers.[29] Longe resided in the vicarage for thirty-seven years, contributing Christian ministry, both in his duties within St Mary's church itself, and in his relationship with his curates, vestry members and parishioners. He was involved in traditional ways with the poorer elements in the parish, through the administration of its charities and the management of his endowed school. Like any parson, he then had his relationship with the wider church and all the time he was exercising his role as a gentleman in county society.

Church life: the services

The Restoration settlement rendered obligatory throughout England the use of *The Book of Common Prayer* of 1662. Morning and Evening Prayer, similar in structure, were unvaried and impersonal. To these were added either a sermon or catechism teaching and perhaps other set liturgy. Public baptisms, churchings and burials were usually conducted on a Sunday too.[30] Attendance being a matter of duty and social conformity, spiritual uplift was thought inappropriate. As with thousands of country churches at that time, the style of worship at Coddenham was austere. Only when strong feelings were engaged on national occasions of thanksgiving or fasting, would emotions be aroused.

At Coddenham, in accordance with the desire of bishops for two services a Sunday in rural churches ('double duty'), Longe provided both morning and afternoon service, the latter being the better attended.[31] In 1801 Longe met the request of parishioners at Crowfield for weekly rather than fortnightly services.[32] Double duty in both town churches at Bungay was, for example, the subject of a campaign in 1830.[33] Weekday services were held at Coddenham only in Lent and in Easter week. Longe recorded his own involvement in precise language. When he 'preached', with no other clergyman present, he both led the service and delivered a sermon, whereas when he 'officiated', he read the Prayer Book office ('officium') without sermon.[34] Holy Communion was 'administered'. Other services he merely 'attended', sitting

---

28 The Middletons were in 1842–3 employing as farm staff alone between 42 and 56 regular males, plus another 44 seasonal day labourers, plus casual harvest women. M.J. Stone, 'Shrubland Farm Labour Book', unpublished paper, from primary source in the private archive of Lord de Saumarez.

29 SRO(I) FDA66/A1/1a: Tithe Apportionment.

30 Infant baptism would have been important to Longe as an orthodox churchman but the sources consulted are silent on his views. Much national controversy was later.

31 Only from 1838 did bishops have power to order the holding of two services: T.C.B. Timmins (ed.), *Suffolk Returns from the Census of Religious Worship of 1851*, SRS xxxix (1997), p.xx.

32 NRO DN/VIS 38/8: the 1801 Visitation Return: an example of pressure, albeit diluted in scale.

33 Ethel Mann and Hugh Cane (eds), *An Englishman at Home and Abroad 1829–62* (Bungay, 1996), p.11: John Barber Scott's diary entry for 2 January 1830.

34 How far Longe composed his own sermons is considered below.

in his pew in the chancel. After some initial experimenting Longe settled to taking duty personally and preaching at Coddenham once each Sunday, alternately morning and afternoon.[35] He attended the other Coddenham service (without sermon), led by his curate, who was also required to take the Crowfield service at alternating times.[36]

Periodic ill-health reduced Longe's ability to take services, for example for nearly eighteen months in 1826/27, for which he arranged a variety of cover. His sons Robert and Henry deputised for him, in addition to their duties elsewhere.[37] He engaged the elderly schoolmaster Mr Betham to assist him at Crowfield, but this arrangement proved unsatisfactory.[38] Longe's curate took extra duties and neighbouring clerics helped. One wet Sunday, Longe cancelled service at Coddenham at short notice, and the same on Christmas Day. Another time he walked down to his church with difficulty, and 'read prayers only', and on a further winter afternoon he 'suffered much from fatigue and cold afterwards'.[39] Despite this, in 1827 Longe took forty-three Sunday services, at only three omitting his sermon.[40] When aged sixty-five Longe sustained the usual service pattern by employing a second permanent curate, himself attending at Coddenham in his pew. Only when one curate was away did Longe lead and preach and not after April 1833. On his visit to Norfolk that Michaelmas, he received Communion, possibly for the last time.[41] He died the following spring.

Although there is no register identifying the leadership of Sunday services, one can draw some conclusions from surviving marriage-banns books, signed by the officiating minister on three Sundays. At first, at Coddenham Longe alternated with his curate as above, but this ratio later fell slightly and then at the age of sixty-two he 'retired' from active taking of services. At Crowfield he was present on fewer occasions. This evidence corroborates his diary entries.

In each of Longe's two churches, Holy Communion was administered four times a year, the practice of the time in rural Suffolk. By holding this service at one church a few days after the relevant festival, Longe was able to celebrate at both.[42] The diary record suggests that he valued this sacrament. For example, even in a year when through ill-health he took few other services he administered Communion at Coddenham on three of the 'sacrament Sundays', missing the fourth only through being away. On recovery from lengthy illness, Longe personally celebrated Communion at Eastertide in 1833 at both his churches and moreover donated a communion flagon to Crowfield.

Regarding numbers of those attending church, there was little recording nationally in Longe's time. In 1813 and 1820, the *communicant* numbers at Coddenham reported to the bishop were 'about 100 usually'. Later in his life, Longe's diary gives aggregate numbers of communicants at his two churches between 90 and 116. Generally, however, communicants were substantially fewer than those attending

---

35 Although the diary is often silent, Longe recorded officiating on 21 Sundays at Crowfield in 1798, but only 16 at Henley and Coddenham together. He relinquished the Henley living in June that year.

36 As suggested by the 1798 diary.

37 These facts are recorded in the diary throughout the period.

38 Diary: 5, 24 Nov. 1826.

39 Diary: 10 Dec. 1826 to 25 Feb. 1827 and 20 April 1827.

40 Diary: 1827 *passim*.

41 Diary: 29 Sept. 1833. Because his village church was frequently damp and cold Parson Woodforde did not even attend Sunday service for the last seven years of his life.

42 Again the diary evidence supplements general statements in visitation returns.

all services, as is confirmed nationally by the 1851 census.[43] We are warned by historians not to judge as spiritual indifference either the smaller number of communicants or the infrequency of the service, for which several reasons are suggested, long after Puritan influence waned. Some thought it only for the educated or especially holy, or as death approached. Ironically, reception was deterred by belief as to its potency, coupled with fear of unworthy reception.

An important part of parish ministry consisted in 'surplice duties': baptisms, marriages and burials. Although incomplete, records confirm the impression given by the diaries that Longe delegated many services to his curates, a trend that increased in the 1820s, although he was able to continue other interests, both public and domestic.[44]

Just as the visual focus in most East Anglian churches at this time was the three-decker pulpit, so the sermon delivered from its top deck was the climax. Indeed some laymen absented themselves when no sermon was to be given. After reading the office the parson donned gown in place of surplice to emphasise that he was now addressing the people rather than offering worship to God. For Longe this was his prime opportunity to give his non-reading parishioners basic Christian teaching and moral influence. After his earliest years Longe probably read from the pulpit from published collections of sermons which were readily available. The carefully considered words of an eminent divine were widely considered superior to the untested opinion of a country parson. Contemporary preachers often merely encouraged their hearers passively to accept their lot. Duty was paramount. The personally devout George Horne, when bishop of Norwich, preached that social inequality was the divine will, not to be questioned. Even the evangelical Hannah More was heard to exclaim: 'From liberty, equality and the rights of man, good Lord, deliver us.'[45] In this matter, preachers might follow Archdeacon Paley, whose text book was current orthodoxy when Longe was an undergraduate, but they sometimes went further, promising heavenly reward for submissiveness and threatening eternal punishment for its absence.[46]

We know something of Longe's preaching from a list of sermons he started as a young man under his father.[47] Longe's parishioners were expected to accept deferentially their need to remain content under a benevolent deity. Since law-abiding conduct was of course in the interests of the materially privileged, Longe might be accused of exercising social control, but this was an age still reacting against the religious excesses and violent division of the seventeenth century. Longe was typical in using the Bible as the basis of his teaching. More aggressively, he preached 'against Dissenters etc.' shortly after local Wesleyans had built their chapel. He liked to use seasonal themes at New Year, Trinity Sunday and harvest, noting significantly when these sermons were freshly written. He once preached on the crime of murder coupled with the perils of drunkenness, and as the congregation had been smaller than usual, he repeated it the following Sunday. One surprising subject was a comparison of Christianity with 'Paganism, Judaism & Mohammedanism'. Week by week Longe was preaching orthodox Christianity as then perceived, in an attempt to drive out 'agricultural superstition', the tenets of an ancient sub-Christian folk-

43 Extracts are given at Appendix A.
44 The three types of register are available at SRO(I) on microform, referenced by parish name.
45 A neat summary of widespread fear of the effects of the French Revolution.
46 This stick-and-carrot approach was not limited to later Victorian 'hell-fire' preachers.
47 SRO(I) HA 24/50/19/4.5(2). A transcript of this catalogue of Longe's sermons is given at p.171.

culture retained by many Suffolk farm-workers, and its illogical combination with what they heard from the pulpit.[48]

Parish clergy received invitations, not universally welcome, to speak on special occasions elsewhere. In 1794, Longe preached at the bishop's visitation in St Mary-le-Tower church, Ipswich, turning to his father for assistance in composing his sermon.[49] On the Coronation anniversary in 1797, Longe preached at Norwich cathedral in the presence of the bishop and dean.[50] Later, he twice wrote to the bishop to be excused giving charity sermons although on other occasions he preached for the clergy widows and orphans charity.

Specially composed prayers were circulated to parish clergy for use on national occasions. This practice, underlining concern for the monarchy and the closeness of church and state, also presupposed belief in the efficacy of corporate prayer. The nation gave thanks for the recovery of King George III. In the troubled war years from 1793 to 1800, national fast days were observed. In contrast, general thanksgiving was observed for naval victories, for relief from the horrors of invasion and for the Peace of Amiens in 1802. When war resumed, military successes on land and sea were similarly marked. In peacetime, the nation was publicly thankful on royal occasions and responded appropriately at the time of the Swing Riots and in the cholera epidemic.[51] The only scripts of sermons surviving among Longe's papers were written following naval victories: in 1798 after Aboukir Bay (the Nile) and in 1805 after Trafalgar. On such occasions enthusiasm was permissible and Longe intermixed flowery language with biblical and liturgical phrases. The behaviour of undisciplined French soldiers to civilians was 'disgracefully cruel', contrasting with the vigilance and bravery of our fleets and armies under the blessing of God.[52] He did not omit to preach the duty of obedience in response to God's loving care.

Although music is an important part of public worship today, Timmins wrote of Suffolk that 'nearly one fifth of the churches … had no music or singing at all in 1852 despite the efforts of individual incumbents to introduce simple psalmody'.[53] At Coddenham, however, a rustic choir with instrumentalists led singing of the psalms from the west gallery long before then. Longe made an annual donation specifically to improve the standard of psalm singing. In 1817, to replace other instruments, he commissioned a London professional to supply and instal a pipe organ.[54] Longe heavily subsidised both the organ and the inaugural concert and later arranged both organ-tuning and the installing of additional pipes. He started a children's choir, encouraging them with both singing lessons and treats at the vicarage.[55] Longe was musically ahead of his time.

An important task of parish clergy was to instruct both children and young

48 Obelkevich, *Religion* and George Ewart Evans, generally. Ian Dyck, *William Cobbett and Rural Popular Culture* (Cambridge, 1992), *passim*.

49 No.48 in Longe's catalogue and confirmed in the diocesan record: NRO DN/VSC/14/28.

50 Diary: 22 Sept. 1797.

51 SRO(I) HA24/50/19/4.5(1): Longe kept a number of these circulated printed prayers.

52 SRO(I) HA24/50/19/4.5(3). These two sermons, closely written on quarto, run to 19 and 12 sides.

53 Timmins, *Census 1851*, p.xix. By 1851 the days of the church band were over and chanting was led by Sunday School children. Longe admits no problems with those who tried to lead music in worship, such as plagued clerical diarists generally.

54 SRO(I) HA24/50/19/4.5(18) and (19). See also David Allen, 'The Vanished Barrel Organ of Coddenham Church', PSIAH XXXVIII, part 4 (1996), pp.442–54. As this was a dual organ, Longe chose the hymn tunes to be set on the barrel, Handel being his clear favourite.

55 Diary: 4 Jan. 1826. The robed choir singing from the chancel was a later development.

servants, though it was a problem to secure their attendance. At Coddenham, children were from 1801 taught to read after church, in a Sunday School maintained by voluntary contributions as well as in the village day-school.[56] Longe assured the bishop that children were catechised in Coddenham every Sunday.[57] In 1813 there were twenty-four children in Coddenham Sunday School and thirty-two at Crowfield, which lacked a day-school.[58] Both establishments were 'in connection with' the newly formed National Society and the clergy used their books, including Lewis's *Exposition* with those 'sufficiently qualified to profit by it'.[59]

In Norwich diocese, which in Longe's time (and until 1837) included the whole county of Suffolk, confirmation was held only at seven-year intervals. The bishop's secretary, in notifying the incumbent of the local venue and date, required him to instruct those aged fourteen and upwards.[60] Longe accordingly preached on confirmation, announced his arrangements for final instruction and invited candidates to come to the vestry after service. In addition to exercising control and instilling appropriate attitudes, he had to judge the readiness of each for this step, beyond mere ability to recite the catechism. On six weekdays before the occasion Longe personally examined the candidates in the vestry, young men and women separately, giving each approved candidate a 'ticket'.[61] The age range of candidates, from fourteen to twenty-five, resulted partly from the passage of seven years since the bishop's last visit. In 1813 Longe presented seventy-one young people, twenty-two male and forty-nine female. He gave them as presents Adams' *Advice* and Novell's *Sermon*. In 1820, there were 107 candidates, seventy-nine from Coddenham and twenty-eight from Crowfield.[62] Waggons conveyed them the eight miles to Stowmarket, again young men and women separately.[63] On the day, having handed in his list, he would wait with his candidates until called: in the churchyard (if fine) or in an adjoining house if not. From the viewpoint of the candidates, being 'bishop'd' was probably memorable for the wrong reasons.[64] The touch of the bishop's right hand was more valued than his left. Dissenters might request confirmation with no intention of transferring allegiance. What was intended by clergy as the gateway to regular quarterly reception of Communion, was for the youngsters a graduation.

There was a strong sense in many rural parishes at this time that the church 'belonged' to the community rather than to the incumbent. Even so, the fabric of Coddenham church (other than the vicar's chancel) was in a poor state in Nicholas

56 The school routine is dealt with below.

57 NRO DN/VIS 38/8, 43/6, 49/3, 60/6: 1801, 1806, 1813, 1820 (Coddenham). If this was indeed so it was unusually conscientious, despite the requirements of Canon 59 and the rubrics. R. O'Day, 'Clerical Renaissance' in G. Parsons (ed.), *Religion in Victorian Britain*, I (1988), p.199: by 1821, catechising was usual only in Lent and just before confirmation. William Cobbett claimed that catechising no longer existed in 1835. Tindal Hart, *Country Priest*, p.45.

58 See s.13 of the 1820 Visitation Return, p.175 below. It appears that here Sunday School was for the younger children whereas urban practice provided Sunday education for older (working) children.

59 1820 Visitation Return, as above. First published in 1700, this simple book on the catechism by a Kent parish priest had by 1812 run to forty-two editions: Jeremy Gregory 'Eighteenth Century Reformation: the Pastoral Task of Anglican Clergy after 1689' in John Walsh *et al.* (eds), *The Church of England c.1689–1833: From Toleration to Tractarianism* (Cambridge, 1993), p.72.

60 NRO DN/VIS/60/6: at each centre, on one day the confirmation and then the bishop's visitation.

61 Diary: 15–29 April 1827.

62 SRO(I) HA 24/50/19/4.5(12) and (20).

63 Diary: 10 May 1827.

64 Solemnity and propriety were rare. F. Brown, *English Clergy*, p.101. At Manchester the bishop confirmed about 8,000 at a single session (1812); another bishop confirmed a similar number at six venues in six days (1825); in Cambridge there were distressing scenes (1833).

Bacon's last years.[65] Since the Shrubland family had links also with Barham and Crowfield, their interest was diluted.[66] In 1805, soon after Longe's institution, work was done in the tower by a variety of tradesmen and a bell and the clock were repaired in London.[67] The pulpit was moved to the east end of the nave, from its previous position down the church, as favoured by earlier Puritans.[68] It is reasonable to see the leadership of Longe in all this. In the chancel Longe gave personal attention to the large and dominant east window, instructing Mr Yarrington of Norwich to replace the old painted glass to Longe's design, which incorporated some old heraldic glass.[69] The detail of that design has survived.[70] In the three main lights were the arms of eighteen successive owners of Shrubland Park up to the last of the Bacons, but *excluding* the Middletons who succeeded them. In the dominant position in the centre at the top was a newly made device of Longe himself. Longe could hardly have conceived a more telling memorial, and indeed insult, and we learn much of his character thereby.

Church life out in the parish

A curate was the employee of the incumbent, not of the wider church, although all were supposed to be licensed by the bishop. Longe drew curates from his own degree in society, often sons of his friends.[71] Since university education was non-vocational, in his first ordained post a young man needed such practical training as was regarded as appropriate, quoted as reason for the modest stipend.[72] Then, with the experience gained, a curate hoped to move on to a living of his own, though those less well connected or educated, might spend all their lives as curates, depicted by contemporary novelists as poor earnest men.[73] Graduating in unprecedented numbers, the number of potential curates exceeded the unchanged number of posts in the diocese, leaving many to scrape a living by short contracts even Sunday by Sunday, whilst awaiting a long-term post.[74] Well-intentioned legislation to protect curates proved powerless in practice.[75]

Before the 1830s many curates were deputising for incumbents who resided elsewhere, either in another living, or in leisured retirement. Longe's situation was unusual; he was legitimately responsible for two churches, could well afford a curate

65 SRO(I) FAA/2/54: the Archdeacon's General Court Book listed for the nave and tower at Coddenham a substantial amount of disrepair, whereas the chancel was in good order.

66 A memorial or a dedicated window for the Middletons is present in each of the three churches.

67 SRO(I) FB 37/E1/2: churchwardens' book: the tradesmen employed included a goldsmith (presumably for gold-leaf) and chair-bottomer (who worked with rushes).

68 For example, Ramsholt, largely unrestored, has its Jacobean pulpit in mid-nave.

69 Diary: 23 Sept., 12 Oct. 1831. Longe designed his window to include some old and seventeenth-century glass with Shrubland coats of arms (probably then in store). He supplemented this with new.

70 Davy visited again later, in July 1843, SRO(I) microfilm J400/3, p.220. This work was replaced in late Victorian restoration and the glass has disappeared. Also John Blatchly (ed.), *A Journal of Excursions through the County of Suffolk: David Elisha Davy, 1823–44*, SRS xxiv (1982), p.229.

71 Pettiward, Howes, Colvile and Wenn were all sons of Longe's friends.

72 Fifty years ago it was quite usual for solicitors to pay a graduate articled clerk (comparable to a curate in his first post) only a few pounds a week, in view of the practical training he was receiving.

73 That non-graduates could gain a secure position is illustrated by John Mastin of Naseby, son of a husbandman, who left school aged twelve but ultimately held three livings: Vialls and Collins, *Georgian Country Parson*, pp.1–5.

74 Curates were not the only ill-paid parish clergy, for many livings yielded a tiny income.

75 For example Sir William Scott's Act of 1803.

and had an attractive parsonage-house for himself. His curate gained experience with the benefit of supervision and was provided with a cottage in Coddenham rent-free plus an annual salary between £60 and £100. Longe had one full-time curate during most of his ministry, adding a second after ill-health forced his own retirement. Most of his curates moved after a few years to their own living, but significantly remained in friendly contact with Longe.[76] All curates lacked security: on becoming vicar at Coddenham in 1797, Longe dismissed Mr Pettiward, having engaged Mr Howes.[77] One of Longe's curates (Roberts) having searched unsuccessfully for ten months, left voluntarily before finding a living.[78]

Other arrangements were of limited scope and casual nature. One second curate was employed by the week, until he secured a living nearby.[79] Aged Mr Betham, a local schoolmaster, was another engaged on a casual basis when Longe was indisposed, but proved unsatisfactory. A third received a guinea per Sunday until succeeded by young Henry Longe, who travelled to and from Woodbridge.[80] Influence or at least connection was the key to preferment. Although the patron did not abandon all judgment in favour of the first comer, speed was advisable when news of a potential vacancy was received.[81]

In Norwich diocese at this time, little general visiting of parishioners by clergy was expected. Unlike William Kirby at Barham and Richard Cobbold at Wortham, Longe limited his visiting to those he chose for social reasons, delegating to his curates such general pastoral visiting as was considered appropriate.[82] In 1838, the next bishop was to expect much more.[83] Longe himself had exercised 'best practice' as a young curate at Coddenham, visiting labourers where there was sickness in the household, praying and reading with them and leaving tracts with those who could benefit. In neat columns in an exercise book he recorded appropriate data, ownership of bible and prayer-book and church attendance. Significantly, this written record lasted only a few weeks.[84] Out in the parishes, it was curates who related to poorer parishioners, rather than the socially elevated vicar, a man still regarded with awe, although deference was probably lessening.[85] Christianity remained important in life even if respect for the established church was diminishing.

One danger in attempting generalisation is to idealise rural society before the

76 Virgin, *Age of Negligence*, p.284: only about 20 per cent of curates nationally found a living within five years. Longe appointed curates with above-average connections. See notes on people (p.260).

77 Diary: 22 March, 18 June 1797. Mr Pettiward, curate during the interregnum and related to the squire of Great Finborough, soon acquired a family living.

78 Diary: 12 Nov. 1826, 9 Sept. and 2–4 Oct. 1827.

79 Diary: 9 Oct. 1831: Mr Treadway went on to Otley.

80 Diary: 31 March, 1 April 1833: Taylor was to 'take one part of the duty' at Coddenham, the regular curate taking the other service there, plus one at Crowfield.

81 Diary: 24, 26, 30, 31 Dec. 1831: Longe wrote to Norwich on Christmas Eve and received the reply on Boxing Day.

82 This is admittedly a conclusion drawn from silence. Kirby compiled a record over fifty-five years on the poor in his parish (SRO(I) FB35/3a/1). Frank Grace, 'A Census of the Poor: Barham in 1830', *SR* 38 (2002), pp.26–34. In north Suffolk, Cobbold memorably painted dozens of his poor parishioners, in naïve style, accessible in Ronald Fletcher (ed.), *The Biography of a Victorian Village: Richard Cobbold's account of Wortham, Suffolk* (1977).

83 For the contrast between the expectations of the two bishops compare the Visitation queries: NRO DN/VIS/ up to 1838, which for Coddenham are /65/11.

84 The book measures 5 by 17 inches. After twenty-three entries, the pages are ruled but otherwise blank. Does one draw conclusions from that particular silence?

85 Deference or its absence is difficult to substantiate. See Howard Newby, *The Deferential Worker* (1977), *passim*, with much material drawn from Suffolk.

Industrial Revolution, say half a century earlier, a danger from which Cobbett was not immune. In fact, in the hearts of many Suffolk labourers the church's ministry had been rejected before Longe's time, an attitude frequently masked, for a measure of deference paid a dividend in material aid and charity. True deference is more than mere silence plus outward conformity, the typical expedient of the powerless Suffolk countryman in the face of the powerful. Such was the context in which Longe exercised his ministry, aware in his last years that anti-clerical feeling was becoming more general.

The classic eighteenth-century theory of relationship between national church and state was reflected in miniature at parish level. Both secular and church life were under the jurisdiction of the incumbent and the elected churchwardens, with the parish vestry. As vicar, Longe was *ex officio* responsible, even if absent from the vestry chair for a particular meeting. Although oversight by local JPs was, apart from crime, limited to secular civil matters, the circle was completed when the incumbent was himself magistrate. To fund its functions the vestry raised a rate adjusted quarterly, based on a schedule of rateable values. The major responsibilities were to the poor of the parish (see below) and maintenance of nearly seven-and-a-half miles of parish roads plus the parish's length of the Ipswich–Norwich turnpike.[86] Longe would inspect any physical encroachment along the roadsides.[87] He personally supervised road repairs on occasion, and arranged an improvement to employ labourers then without work.[88] A plan to replace a ford with a bridge led to conflict with Sir William Middleton. On other expenditure, the parish paid out of rates both modest items such as maintenance of the communal well, regular contributions for the relief of poor prisoners and occasional items such as a bounty for a militia substitute.

The precise position of the parish boundary (of nearly twenty miles) was vital both to Longe as tithe owner and to the vestry as rating authority. The Rogationtide perambulation was a community activity, followed by shared refreshment.[89] The diary shows that about seventy people took part in 1826.[90] Longe once needed to go out again, with an old inhabitant to check a doubtful stretch of boundary.[91]

The functioning of the parish under the incumbent, its officers and vestry has become well known through the publication of transcribed records. One custom alleged by Coddenham, that Crowfield should contribute one-third of the expense of maintaining the fabric of the large building of St Mary's, understandably caused friction. By later legislation, 'daughter' hamlets could be made to pay for both churches, but only for twenty years.[92] Coddenham records confirm the usual picture, of petty expenses reimbursed both to unpaid officers and to modestly salaried parish clerk and sexton, paid extra for duties beyond the routine. Others were paid for tolling the bell, keeping order during service and church cleaning.[93] All this was under the supervision of Longe as vicar, with the two churchwardens.

86 HA 24/50/19/4.5(20): a survey by chain of all Coddenham roads was made in 1830.

87 Diary: 25 April 1826.

88 Diary: 25, 29 April, 20 Dec. 1831.

89 SRO(I) FB37/E1/2: churchwardens' book. Longe paid half from May 1798. The cost was at that time met by half from the vicar, one-third from Coddenham rates and one-sixth from Crowfield rates.

90 Diary: 5 May 1826.

91 Diary: 22 May 1798.

92 Vestries Acts, 1818, 1819.

93 Churchwardens' records: SRO(I) FB37/E2–7. Overseers' book: SRO(I) FB37/G1. Other payments were for mole-catching and trapping sparrows.

The established church was not without competition. Despite the marked national growth of Methodism, the locality was stronger in Independents and Baptists, the old Dissent.[94] As the established church was so comprehensive Longe concluded complacently that Dissenters were of extreme religious views and their activities might be loftily disregarded so long as they were peaceable.[95] Despite the building of two dissenting chapels in Coddenham and Crowfield, Longe seemed not to realise to what extent the local influence of his own established church was weakening, as would later be shown in the 1851 census.[96] His visitation returns give the view Longe relayed to the bishop, but his diary is almost silent.[97]

Conventicle Licences, needed for public worship anywhere outside the buildings of the established church, reveal that separate congregations competed locally.[98] Bitterness between them surfaced when the Wesleyans built a fine new chapel in Coddenham in 1823 but failed to raise a congregation. They offered the chapel at auction, but withdrew it when the highest bid came from their rivals, the more successful local Independents. At a second auction the Independents secured the chapel by subterfuge through a respected farmer bidding for them, but not recognisable as their representative. Surprisingly, this was a Coddenham churchwarden.[99]

In his visitation returns Longe consistently reported that there were no Roman Catholics in his parishes. Nevertheless he had strong views, for reasons that today seem extreme. On the long-standing issue of Catholic Emancipation he recorded the defeat in a full House of Commons of a motion designed to remove penalties and disabilities.[100] Longe's disapproval of recusants was indicated when one November 5th he directed his curate to use the patriotic protestant service.[101]

Within the Church of England, evangelicalism as a distinct form of Christianity was growing in influence and credited by many with raising standards. Finding little in common with them, orthodox clergy accused them of unfashionable enthusiasm and of favouring only like-minded parishioners. Evangelicals in turn accused the mainstream clergy of neglecting duty for worldly and distracting interests. There was little mutual comprehension. One of the few evangelicals who served in rural mid-Suffolk, John Charlesworth, ministered for thirty years from 1814 as rector of Flowton, a small parish six miles from Coddenham. His sympathetic biographer claimed that he raised his parishioners from degradation to decency but, more controversially, Charlesworth disregarded custom and etiquette, drawing into his ministry hearers from neighbouring parishes.[102] Longe simply ignored evangelical clergy, mixing outside the parishes with men like himself.

94 For the attendance on census-day in 1851 at Coddenham and Crowfield see Appendix A.

95 Longe enjoyed an assured position in the Anglican heartland of rural Suffolk. Compare the vituperation of incumbent diarist John Skinner in his coal-mining area: Coombs, Skinner, *passim*.

96 Appendix B compares references in the Conventicle Register with Longe's reports to his bishop. As his catalogue of sermons shows (transcript at p.171), Longe once preached against Dissenters.

97 Diary: 11, 12 Oct. 1797. Even this exception does not disclose Longe's attitude.

98 NRO DN/DIS/4/1 and 2.

99 See without detailed attribution G. Sydenham, 'Glimpses of Congregational Church Life during the 18th and 19th Centuries', *SR* 3, no.6 (1968), p.208.

100 Diary: 5 March 1827, one of Longe's longer entries, suggesting the strength of his feelings.

101 Diary: 5 Nov. 1826. The political aspects are noted in the text below.

102 John P. Fitzgerald, *The Quiet Worker for Good: John Charlesworth* (1865), passim.

The Parish poor, young and old

Throughout Longe's ministry there was substantial poverty in Suffolk as elsewhere.[103] As outlined later in this introduction he was for many years a director of the house of industry at Barham, to which parishioners were from time to time admitted. Parish rates were the basic source of funding both there and within the home 'out-relief'. Although ex officio chairman of vestry, Longe distanced himself from the actual allocation of rate relief, which is not here examined. As vicar, Longe supplemented that provision by dispensing aid funded by voluntary giving.[104] Some funds came from the generosity of past benefactors, some from recent legacies, some from the living including himself.[105] Both giving and dispensing were at best motivated by Christian concern, at worst a vehicle of manipulation. The typical reference to 'deserving' poor introduced subjective distinctions. Alms given at Communion by ancient injunction were after service distributed by Longe to the poor who were present, or whose absence was explained to his personal satisfaction.[106] Winter was particularly difficult. Bread was distributed. Each January Longe would open a subscription list for coals for the poor, himself subscribing £5. In January 1831 Longe with others augmented the bequest of Sir William Middleton. Another winter, to arrange distribution of blankets, Longe with his curate met the young Sir William and Lady Middleton at the village shop which supplied them. As a subscriber to the newly founded county General Hospital at Bury St Edmunds, Longe nominated a patient for admission, a labourer's young wife with cataracts.[107]

Compulsory poor rates and voluntary charity both had their place, but there was also the desire to encourage habits of self-help and thrift, through 'clubs'. At Christmas 1831 the distribution from the village shop organised by Lady Middleton with Mrs Longe was for members of the village clothing club.[108] Thrift was achieved also through friendly societies and savings banks. Longe was a trustee of at least one Coddenham Friendly Society.[109] He and other local gentlemen supervised the management of Coddenham Saving Bank.[110] He noted once that the balances totalled £14,092 2s. 10d., a very substantial sum.[111] One local friendly society drew their credit balance in the saving bank on Christmas Eve.[112] As late as 1833 Longe was continuing this administrative work, as was expected of him in his paternal role as vicar.[113]

Charity was not exclusively local but also operated in the form of 'briefs' for selected hard cases, circulated by the Lord Chancellor's secretary. He once alleged neglect by wardens and omissions by clergy (a tactful distinction) to publish briefs

103 Some background on attitudes towards poverty is given at Appendix C.

104 In the first six weeks of the year 1831 Longe's diary has entries on ten separate days relating to the financing and distribution of coals, blankets and other relief to the poor of Coddenham.

105 Gardemau charitable funds (mentioned at p.xxxii and p.177n.) were supplemented later by other giving. In his own will Longe left £100 for the local resident poor: see below, p.225.

106 The distribution is recorded in visitation returns, noted above.

107 Diary: 5 Sept. 1833.

108 Diary: 21 Nov. 1831.

109 Diary: 16 July 1827.

110 Founded shortly after the Act in 1818 to serve the area around: White's *Directory of Suffolk*, 1844.

111 Diary: 19 March 1827.

112 Diary: 24 Dec. 1827.

113 Diary: 4 March 1833. SRO(I) 106/13/2 refers both to the Saving Bank of the Hundred, and to Friendly Societies based at Coddenham Crown (three) and Crowfield Rose.

when received.[114] The system was soon replaced, to benefit three charities of the established church in turn, by the annual 'king's letter'. A collection at Coddenham church door after a service was customarily supplemented by Longe's own substantial donation, to make a round figure.[115]

Locally, thirty children of the poor were educated at Coddenham Free School, founded and endowed by Lady Catherine Gardemau of Shrubland Park half a century before Longe's time, of which by virtue of his office he was a trustee.[116] The supporting endowment was rent from a farm at Mendlesham, though in later years the trustees needed subscriptions from clergy and gentry to provide adequate income. There were originally two schoolrooms, later combined to a single hall 54 feet long by 15 feet 6 inches wide, but separate porches were retained for girls and boys. There were also a parlour, backhouse, pantries and back-yards.[117] The master was required to read morning and evening prayer daily with the children and each Saturday morning to teach the catechism and psalms. Saturday afternoon was free but on Sunday all were to attend church with him twice, assembling at the school. Four holidays a year totalled six weeks. Hours were from eight o'clock until four or five o'clock according to season, with an hour's mid-day break. Of the ten weekday sessions, boys were to have seven for reading and three for writing and arithmetic, and girls (by attending one less of each) had time for sewing and knitting with the master's wife. Reading was taught in the Bible and *Book of Common Prayer*, supplemented only as the trustees chose.[118] No child was admitted under the age of six and none continued after twelve (boys) and fourteen (girls). Repeated misconduct or irregular attendance meant expulsion, but parents sometimes removed children for the sake of their earning power, however small.[119]

Apart from one note when a young curate, there is no evidence that Longe taught in the school or even attended sessions, a task he probably delegated to his curate.[120] By 1833 only young Sir William Middleton and the Revd William Kirby of neighbouring Barham remained as trustees with Longe. They sometimes reached decisions informally but each spring they met to approve the annual accounts and to worry over the farm rent. Management of the school seems to have occasioned Longe no great commitment of time but the record of meetings is patchy.

In 1810, before formation of the National Society, in response to the rising child population locally it was decided to enlarge the school from thirty places (the original foundation) to fifty. This was made possible by improved farm rents in pros-

114 SRO(I) HA24/50/19/4.5(11). See also M.J. Stone, 'The Week's Good Cause? The Royal or Church Brief', *Parson Woodforde Society Quarterly Journal* xxxvii, no.3 (2004), pp.4–7.

115 Diary: 13, 25 Nov. 1831 (for the SPG); Diary: 20, 22 Jan. 1833 (National Society for the Education of the Poor). The third charity was the Incorporated Church Building Society. The practice ended in 1853.

116 Lady Catherine (Montague), daughter of the 1st earl of Sandwich, when widow of an earlier Bacon had married the vicar, the Revd Balshazar Gardemau. The school continued until the 1970s.

117 SRO(I) FB37/L2/1: the book combines records of the rents received from Mendlesham Farm, school expenditure accounts and some short minutes. SRO(I)HA24/50/19/4.5(20) gives a later plan.

118 SRO(I) HA24/50/19/4.5(20): School Rules and Regulations (undated). Longe's contemporary James Cooper (1765–1839) was master of the school for thirty years from 1802. One pictures the children walking 'in crocodile' to the church, over a half-mile distant.

119 School accounts book (note 116). In general, working-class children left school about the age of ten even in the 1840s: David Wardle, *English Popular Education 1780–1970* (Cambridge, 1970), p.43.

120 Many clergy were active in the school-room at this time. Anthony Russell, *The Clerical Profession* (1980), pp.184–200. For Henslow see S.M. Walters and E.A. Stow, *Darwin's Mentor* (Cambridge, 2001), pp.180–7. For contrast, consider Skinner's conflict with the lady of the manor in Somerset.

perous war years, but the ambitious decision was soon to be regretted since from 1815 'the low price of corn and the pressures of the times' forced a rent reduction. Surprisingly, the trustees neither provided additional funds themselves nor raised funds from local donors. Instead, they curtailed and then suspended the children's customary Easter gift of clothing, purchased from local tradesmen. When all could not be provided with clothing, they introduced an element of control by rewarding behaviour and attendance or, as one might say, depriving offenders.[121] The earlier gift of hats, bonnets and tippets, was more austerely replaced by shoes and worsted stockings.

In 1816, having placed the school into 'connection with' the National Society, the trustees introduced the financially attractive Madras system. Of two rival methods, the National Society had adopted the one pioneered in India by an Anglican army chaplain, Dr Andrew Bell. An instructor came from Ipswich for a week to assist in the change.[122] It was claimed that one adult could instruct a thousand children, but dramatic results were achieved at a cost: by reducing teaching to the mechanical repetition of facts, such as the dates of monarchs and multiplication tables. The master instructed selected older children, who then led smaller groups. Minutely sub-divided lessons were tested, and everything was competitive, with small honours and minor humiliations.[123] However fashionable, the system seems doubly unsuitable for a village school of fifty pupils. There is no evidence at Coddenham of conflicting religious opinions on education, such as broke out in Somerset.[124] The trustees were not however totally autonomous since the wider church periodically sent in inspectors and the state introduced registration of charitable trusts in an attempt to check financial abuse. Longe delivered the required statement to the court and produced the school documents to commissioners.[125]

The wider church

Longe's concern for educating the children of the poor was not confined to Coddenham and Crowfield. Nationally such education was seen as a church matter and the established church was spurred into action in 1811 by provision made by other Christian bodies, whose Sunday Schools were achieving some results with children who worked six days a week. More was clearly needed, fuelled by a desire to encourage social stability and application to work. Others saw reading as the gateway to scriptural faith and wanted it to be Anglican. In the contemporary manner of such initiatives, a group of orthodox Anglican gentlemen founded and funded on a voluntary basis the National Society. In Suffolk on 25 February 1812 a meeting was held of the nobility, gentry, clergy 'and others' to form a new county body, the title of which echoed that of the National Society.[126] The specific aim was to give

121 School accounts book (note 116), *passim*.

122 This cost a fee plus board and lodging: School accounts book (note 117).

123 Wardle, Popular Education, pp.85–7.

124 Anne Stott, 'Hannah More and the Blagdon Controversy, 1799–1802', JEH 51/2 (2000), pp.319–46.

125 Diary: 19, 22 Oct. 1827.

126 The full title was 'The National Society for the Education of the Poor in the Principles of the Established Church throughout England and Wales'. Attendance at Stowmarket was so numerous that the venue had to be hastily changed from the King's Head to the parish church: Peter Northeast, 'The Provision of Elementary Education in Nineteenth Century Rural Suffolk', *SR* 5, no.2 (1981), p.90.

poor children a church education. To meet the pressing need in the two biggest Suffolk towns new schools were founded there and existing village schools were to be supported. Under the bishop's patronage a general committee of forty was set up, half clergy (including Longe) and half laymen.[127] East and west sub-committees followed. Longe was actively involved in this way for the rest of his life, but no record survives of his theoretical views on the style of such education.[128]

If we may judge from the 44-page annual report of 1824 the Suffolk Society flourished.[129] However, of the total 9,257 children in all the schools, more than half attended on Sundays only. The two pairs of central schools at Ipswich and Bury, with rolls totalling 525 boys and girls, enjoyed 64 per cent of the annual expenditure. The balance provided minor assistance for 152 rural schools 'connected with' the Society. The income came mostly in subscriptions from nearly 300 gentlemen, although parents in the town schools contributed their pence. As chairman of the eastern sub-committee Longe regularly attended meetings right up to 1833.[130] In that year the state first breached the principle of *laissez faire*, with small grants for new school buildings through the two societies nationally, a grant that was to increase forty-fold within twenty-six years.

This voluntary county society existed separately from the diocese, a somewhat shadowy entity. Norwich diocese (Norfolk and Suffolk), in number of parishes second only to Lincoln, was served by some 1,100 parish clergy. Secure in their freeholds, they felt little sense of identity with the diocese, which in the 1820s was still known for irregularity and slackness of administration.[131] For effective control much depended on the personal qualities of each bishop. The energetic Edward Stanley succeeded Henry Bathurst only after Longe's death.[132] George Horne (1790–92) had been noted for devotion rather than pastoral skill. Charles Manners Sutton (1793–1805) was primarily a royal courtier at Windsor. His successor, another aristocrat, Henry Bathurst (1805–37), continued in office until his death at the age of ninety-two. Amiable by nature, he was criticised as weak and lazy and casual towards ordinand selection.[133] When Longe coached his own youngest son Henry for ordination as deacon in 1826 he found him 'very deficient in his preparation' only ten days before the ordination exam. Within a week Henry was duly ordained in Norwich cathedral.[134]

Bishops delegated the conduct of diocesan administration to archdeacons and other staff, themselves residing for months in London to sit in the House of Lords. Parish clergy seldom saw their bishop but Dr Bathurst increased the distrust among

---

127 SRO(I) FAA/15/1: the Minute Book of the Suffolk Society from 1812. No women were included.

128 Wardle, Popular Education, pp.80–8. Some believed that education was a vital influence for good but others were convinced that the power of original sin required application of the rod.

129 SRO(I) HA24/50/19/4.5(1): Coddenham then had 50 weekday places, with 16 more on Sundays.

130 Diary: 5 Feb. 1833.

131 R. Arthur Burns, 'A Hanoverian Legacy: Diocesan Reform in the Church of England *c.*1800–33' in Walsh *et al.*, *Church of England*, pp. 265–82; G.F.A. Best, *Temporal Pillars* (Cambridge, 1964), p.239: Norwich's 'notoriously decrepit administration'.

132 Longe's respected friend Kirby held the revived post of rural dean later primus inter pares.

133 Copious material on Bathurst exists, from an uncritical work by his son, Henry Bathurst, *Memoirs of Bishop Bathurst, Lord Bishop of Norwich*, 2 vols (1837), to R.G. Wilson's comment that the diocese was dubbed 'the Dead See': 'The Cathedral in the Georgian Period 1720–1840' in Ian Atherton *et al.* (eds), *Norwich Cathedral – Church City & Diocese 1096–1996* (1996), pp.576–614.

134 Diary: 27, 30 April; 17, 31 May; 2, 11, 18 June; 2 July; 1 Nov. 1826. For a detailed account of an ordination examination (in Lincoln diocese) see Vialls and Collins, *Georgian Country Parson*, pp.28–9.

his parish clergy, almost unanimously Tory, by being sturdily Whig, notably in crucial debates on emancipation and reform between 1828 and 1833.[135] However, Longe had friendly, if deferential, dealings with Dr Bathurst and even bought an engraved portrait of him. A bishop made his visitation progress in early summer to a series of centres to meet his clergy and churchwardens and conduct confirmation. In Norwich, as has been noted, the interval was over twice the theoretical three years and even then might be undertaken by an episcopal colleague.[136] Visitation was preceded by a set of questions for incumbents to address in writing.[137] In his first visitation notice Bishop Bathurst admitted that 'he was very much unacquainted' with Norwich diocese.[138] When similarly questioned churchwardens in laconic replies revealed no irregularity in the conduct of Longe's parishes.[139]

As administrative machinery in the diocese, episcopal visitations were supplemented by archdeacons, but they could not have effective personal knowledge of so many parishes, and also lacked effective sanctions to secure amendment of either clerical conduct or physical defects in buildings. They worked in two distinct ways. 'Generals' were held at centres twice a year when the clergy, sometimes with their churchwardens, would gather to worship and hear a sermon, receive the archdeacon's charge, conduct some business, including payment of their diocesan dues, and dine.[140] Longe's friend Mr Parker, in his sermon in 1826, 'very properly repelled the charge of those both in and out of the church who accuse (us) of not preaching the Gospel'.[141] The non-evangelical clergy were on the defensive. Secondly, the archdeacon visited parishes with his registrar by appointment to inspect church fabric, goods and ornaments, parsonage houses, and churchyards.[142] Longe's ill-health led him to delegate his duties in 1833 for Berners' visitation.[143]

On taking up his incumbency Longe indicated his orthodox churchmanship by joining two societies: for the Promotion of Christian Knowledge (SPCK) and the Propagation of the Gospel (SPG).[144] At that time, there were no 'hard-edged' parties, but in Longe's lifetime those of evangelical vision within the Church of England did develop in that sense. Moreover, an Oxford group appealed to the spiritual and holy among educated clergy. At this later time, Longe attended a gathering of clergy in Ipswich when 'Mr Rose of Hadleigh preached a very superior discourse.'[145] H.J. Rose, a leading high-church figure, was speaking shortly *after* Keble's Assize Sermon in Oxford, which some take as the start of the Oxford Movement, and just *before* the crucial Hadleigh Conference he himself hosted. Incidentally, Longe expressed surprise on another meeting of this county clergy charity on reading that

135 E.R. Norman, *Church and Society in England, 1770–1970* (Oxford, 1976), pp.79–88. Yet the otherwise isolated Skinner was actively befriended by his bishop. See over a score of references in five years up to 1833, in Coombs, Skinner.

136 1806, 1813, 1820 and 1827, but relevant diocesan records from 1827 have not survived.

137 For one visitation return of Coddenham and Crowfield (that of 1820) see p.175 below.

138 Henry Bathurst had previously held livings in Norfolk in plurality. Woodforde collected his tithes.

139 The returns of 1820 from churchwardens of Bosmere survive. Churchwardens are still today required to answer archdeacon's articles of enquiry annually and to receive him on visitation.

140 Woodforde's diaries (in fully transcribed form) convey the feel of these occasions.

141 Diary: 21 April 1926.

142 Canon Law stipulated three-yearly visits, but all England and Wales were covered by a mere fifty-eight men. Frances Knight, *Nineteenth Century Church and English Society* (Cambridge, 1995), pp.167–9.

143 Diary: 4 June 1833.

144 Diary: 7 Dec. 1797 (SPCK); several times Longe records paying annual subscriptions to SPG.

145 Diary: 18 July 1833. The promise of H.J. Rose was unrealised for he died at an early age.

he had himself been elected a vice-president and auditor. He was getting forgetful, and the duties must have been light, for he had noted in his earlier diary this indication of his status among the county's clergy.[146]

Georgian gentleman

The sequence of events that led Longe to his comfortable benefice is summarised below. He was extraordinarily fortunate, for Coddenham had long been a good living. Whereas many Suffolk parishes had no fit parsonage house, he was able to move with his household into the grand and spacious vicarage built in 1775 by the Bacons in its little park above Coddenham, his home for the next thirty-seven years. It was furnished in a style which any Trollopean archdeacon would have recognised with approval (plates 6 and 7).[147]

The main three-storey house with basement measured 50 feet wide by 45 feet deep. The service area was at lower ground floor level, and those quarters for children and servants not on the top floor were accommodated in the two-storey annexe at the west end, which with its enclosed store-yard measured 102 feet frontally with thirty windows. Shortly after succeeding his father thirty-seven years later, Longe's son Robert, considering the mansion too large, was to remove both the attic floor and the annexe.[148]

John and Charlotte were comfortably established and seemingly secure, with four sons and a daughter and a household of servants (see below). While her children were still under fifteen, however, Charlotte died of an asthmatic condition. Five years later Longe married Frances Ward, eight years his junior, whom he had known from his Norfolk days.[149] Longe was able to send all four sons away to school and then to Cambridge. Painful events ensued. His eldest son died aged twenty and a little later his beloved daughter Charlotte married Robert Martin Leake, then an army major, of whom Longe did not approve. Five days after the wedding, Charlotte wrote to her father from Norfolk: 'I trust nothing will prevent our happy meeting at Coddenham.'[150] A third sadness came to Longe, when the wife of his eldest surviving son John separated herself from him, alleging cruelty. They were childless. By contrast, Longe's second son Robert, having married the daughter of neighbour and friend, the Revd Charles Davy, remained in Suffolk after his ordination and his father had the pleasure of knowing four grandchildren.[151] Henry, who was also ordained, married after his father's death. Very much a family man, Longe continued the pattern of his own youth in Norfolk, both with his own sons and all his life with his younger brother. Longe's correspondence with Charlotte was affectionate, but he remained distant from his son-in-law.

---

146 Diary: 30 Aug. 1831, 27 Aug. 1833.

147 I owe this phrase to Prof. Richard Wilson in informal communication. The substantial facilities of the vicarage are given in four inventories, transcribed below (pp.210–23). Reference has been made to a transcript prepared by a group of students of Suffolk College under Dr John Ridgard: see 'Raphaels seven, Bings of Port five': SRO(I) qs 92 LON.

148 NRO DN/FCB 6: faculty of December 1836. The detached stable-block was demolished later.

149 For the Ward family tree, see p.lx. Frances was the daughter of Col. Ward of Salhouse Hall.

150 For the Longe family tree see p.lix. The marriage was conducted at Coddenham by a family friend with twelve signing witnesses (including John Longe). The correspondence tends to support the local tradition that Charlotte eloped, returning for that ceremony: SRO HA24/50/19/4.2(1).

151 Charles Davy is not to be confused with David Elisha Davy, the antiquary.

Longe's social life in Suffolk was active, at least until ill-health forced him to curtail it. Among parishioners he significantly found very few he thought to be of his own social standing, but his diary is full of the names of gentry and clergy with whom he and his wife exchanged dinners and calls. His friends were from a fairly narrow social band: gentlemen whom he met in his public duties, militia officers during wartime and clergy of his own social degree and churchmanship.[152] Clergy of means and education shared lay gentlemen's sensitivity to social distinctions and status.[153] Longe did invite to the vicarage his farm tenants and their wives, but this was limited to one evening a year. Also annually, he entertained the farmers to tithe dinners at the Crown Inn. The Crown was also the venue for monthly dinner meetings of Coddenham book club in which Longe took a leading part. This combination of social and literary interest was characteristic of gentlemen clergy in addition to more specialist academic interests.[154]

Longe does not record the pleasures of the table as Parson Woodforde did, but he does note receiving gifts of venison from the nearby Helmingham estate, dragging his own fishponds for the table and shooting on his own land. 'Status' food was a frequent gift, despatched miles by coach.[155] In keeping with the contemporary style, Longe's cellar was stocked to a degree rare today. He ordered wines from Lisbon by the hogshead (about 300 bottles), shipped in hampers into Ipswich. A bill from one London supplier was equal to seven months' salary for his curate. It may reasonably be supposed that Longe's ill-health was connected with these pleasures, for gout disabled him in later years, along with 'oppression on the chest'.[156] He also brewed twice a year, often using malt from his own barley. His men-servants were allowed three pints a day, plus a reasonable quantity of small beer.

The historian must be sensitive to the social implications of leisure activities, which reinforced status. Indeed, to have leisure time was almost the definition of a gentleman.[157] Because the duties generally expected of them were so modest, parish clergy were free to exercise talents in other spheres of life.[158] By cultivating intellectual pursuits other than theology, gentlemen clergy confirmed to the world their culture and classical education, inevitably maintaining the gulf between them and nearly all their parishioners.[159] William Kirby of Barham was a world-famous

152 Parson Woodforde considered even the more prosperous farmers as below his own degree. See R.L. Winstanley, *Parson Woodforde: Life and Times of a Country Diarist* (Bungay, 1996), p.120. See also Jane Austen's *Emma*. Some of Longe's friends are named in the notes on people (p.260 below).

153 Evangelical clergy after Wilberforce evangelized 'those who counted' in society: Ford K. Brown, *Fathers of the Victorians: the Age of Wilberforce* (Cambridge, 1961), pp.49–70. The evangelical aspects are dealt with below.

154 See illustrations on p.ix and John Blatchly, *Some Suffolk and Norfolk Ex Libris* (2000), pp.16–19 for John Longe's book-plate and for Crabbe's derogatory verses about book clubs. A book club might have a membership equal in number between clergy and laymen, as at Ixworth: Jane Fiske, *The Oakes Diaries: Business, Politics and the Family in Bury St Edmunds, 1778–1800*, SRS xxxii (1990), p.274. For details of administration of a book club, see P.J. Foss and T. Parry (eds), *A Truly Honest Man: Diary of Joseph Moxon, 1798–9* (Macclesfield, 1998), pp.35, 62, 71, 88, 106.

155 For example, Fiske, Oakes Diaries, II, p.41: a turtle was sent 'very lively' from Liverpool in high summer on the coach roof, arriving dead at Bury St Edmunds four days later.

156 For medical matters see Appendix D (p.234).

157 John Rule, *Albion's People: English Society 1714–1815* (1992), p.41.

158 Other high-profile Suffolk-born clergy of the time included George Crabbe the poet (1754–1832), and Bishop Blomfield (1786–1857).

159 Jane Austen criticised clergy not for absence of education, but for any lack of manners, because it cast doubt upon their moral code. Irene Collins, *Jane Austen and the Clergy* (1994), pp.35–8, 93, 143.

entomologist without any suggestion that he neglected his parish. J.S. Henslow was pastorally successful at Hitcham whilst being a distinguished scientist at Cambridge. The interests of most gentlemen extended into the scientific world. Longe observed eclipses through his telescope, as well as recording temperatures and taking an interest in the weather as any gentleman-farmer would.[160] Contemporary popular interest in archaeology drew both genuine clerical scholars such as William Stukeley and more eccentric practitioners like John Skinner.[161] At Coddenham, Roman finds in the parish led to Longe contributing to *The Gentleman's Magazine*.[162]

An interest in local history claimed many clergy.[163] In Suffolk the well-known antiquary David Elisha Davy stayed with Longe on his excursions.[164] Other clerics nationally, as diverse as Thomas Malthus, Sydney Smith and Gilbert White of Selborne, are remembered for their specific contributions. There were of course graduate clergy who had little interest in such matters, of whom Norfolk parson Woodforde is an example. Alongside his wide reading Longe's antiquarian studies were well-known to similar enthusiasts, with several of whom he corresponded. His researches were by no means confined to his own property rights and the title to his advowsons. For example he treasured (and declined to lend) the Temple manuscripts, which came into his possession on Nicholas Bacon's death.[165] Longe was also characteristically tenacious in obtaining from the Record Commission official volumes of local records for public display in Ipswich.[166] Demonstrating both his own connection with Ipswich and his proud links with the Bacons, Longe gave to the borough a portrait of Nathaniel Bacon, compiler of the *Annals* (1654) a highly rated history of the town.[167] In addition to his reading with the book club, Longe purchased books regularly, including classical authors, making space for them by selling surplus ones back to his Ipswich bookseller. One invoice names *Burke's Peerage*, and then a markedly contrasting volume by the Caroline divine Jeremy Taylor, *Holy Living and Holy Dying*.[168] Such a breadth of interests rather than specialisation may be taken as typical of better-off Georgian clergy.

Gentlemen clergy also engaged in outdoor pursuits. Unlike some of his clerical contemporaries, Longe did apparently not hunt but in his younger days he would fish and occasionally go coursing.[169] He made gifts of game to friends who had no expanse of land. The practice of shooting in those days was to take a walk carrying a gun, probably with a companion and one's pointers, rather than to join an organised

160 Longe had his reflecting telescope 'improved' in London: SRO(I) HA24/50/19/4.2(1).

161 Skinner (the diarist) was convinced that *Camulodunum* was sited in Somerset, over 150 miles away, rather than at Colchester.

162 *The Gentleman's Magazine* (April 1825).

163 County histories of Cambridgeshire (Cole), Leicestershire (Carter), Somerset (Collinson) and Dorset (Hutchins) were all compiled by clerics: Houghton, *Parsons*, pp.1–8; Bettey, *Church and Parish*, p.113.

164 Diary: 8, 9 Aug. 1827. Davy, famous Suffolk antiquary, never proceeded from deacon to priest. For one account, see Blatchly, *Davy Journal*, p.95, who also at p.95n. draws attention to Longe.

165 Twice, loan of these manuscripts was requested. Diary: 24 July 1831 (by Sir William Betham, on behalf of Mr T.P. Percival); 5 Oct. 1831 (by Bishop Bathurst on behalf of Mr J.L. Peregrine Courtnay). Nicholas Bacon's mother was from the Temple and Grenville families of national statesmen. No attempt has been made to trace and view these manuscripts, here un-named.

166 SRO(I) HA24/50/19/4.4(7) includes Longe's correspondence with the intermediary in this campaign: his MP, Charles Tyrell. See also note 221 below for diary dates.

167 Diary: 31 Dec. 1831. The Puritan Bacon was Town Clerk, Recorder and MP for the borough.

168 SRO(I) HA24/50/19/4.5(21): a bundle including this 1830 invoice.

169 Among clerical hunting men, one extreme figure was 'Tally Ho!' Hanmer, popular in his parish, charitable to the poor and a good preacher, but chronically in debt: Houghton, *Parsons*, p.41.

party with beaters.[170] Longe continued very fond of his dogs and valued their loyalty. He took great interest in the large garden at the vicarage, buying shrubs and plants from Suffolk nurserymen and occasionally employing contractors from the village as well as his gardener on works of re-construction. He proudly measured the girth of a cedar.[171] His melon-pit was important to him.[172] His enjoyment of showing his estate to visitors suggests fashionable competition in these gardening activities, a mark of respectability.[173]

A gentleman's household in Longe's time required for both comfort and prestige a team of servants. By 1811 Longe's wealth enabled him to build up a domestic and outdoor staff of eleven, excluding farm servants. As paterfamilias he kept a firm hold on his household.[174] He discharged one butler, saved another from debtor's prison and parted with two others after altercations. His housekeeper by contrast stayed twenty-two years into her old age, but a cook and three other female servants left together, unwilling to accept the more rigorous style of her successor. Satisfactory cooks were notoriously difficult to find and keep. One became pregnant by the gardener, some offended by their 'temper', and the work of others was unsatisfactory. Away from Longe's oversight, a long-serving maid soon showed unacceptably quick temper to newly married Charlotte. Young kitchen-girls and servant-boys mostly stayed a year or so before leaving for a 'superior' place. At the vicarage the post of footman and groom was combined, though the skills were different. Longe discharged two. Experienced staff were found from further afield, but younger ones came from local families. It was a close and hierarchical life 'below stairs' and clashes between servants were inevitable. By contrast, the gamekeeper stayed in Longe's service for thirty-seven years, the coachman for at least twenty.[175] The wages for Longe's eleven servants totalled the large sum of about £200 a year, with a further £40 or so for livery and other clothing, but the greatest expense was in bed and board, which in 1813 Longe valued at 4 shillings a day. That cost alone for ten servants would total £730 annually, at a time that Longe's curate, a kind of superior servant, received only £70 a year plus a cottage.

The modern observer must not assume that a gentleman living in rural mid-Suffolk was isolated. He could travel freely, in Longe's case mostly limited to East Anglia by choice.[176] In the matter of national news, far from ignoring the wider world, Longe kept abreast of current affairs by reading journals and newspapers,

170 Shrubland shooting parties were more organised (M.J. Stone 'Shrubland Farm Labour Book', unpublished), but by no means on the scale of the later nineteenth century.

171 Diary: 16 July 1833. That owners of extensive gardens were planting the fashionable cedar is evidenced by the survival of so many mature trees today. An example is Barking Rectory.

172 A melon-pit was a symbol of status, because of the cost of cultivation. See diary 10 May 1796.

173 Not all clergy were models of respectability like Longe. For examples of clergy in court for drunkenness, conspiring in a false prosecution and poaching, see Pamela Horn, *The Rural World 1780–1850* (1980), p.151 and Clive Emsley, Crime and Society in England 1750–1900 (1996 edn), pp.180–4. For examples of other unacceptable behaviour see Houghton, *Parsons*, p.40, Roy Porter, *English Society in the Eighteenth Century* (1990 edn), p.298 and Woodforde's diary:18 June 1802.

174 Of clerical diarists, both Holland and Skinner had frequent servant difficulties. Winstanley, *Woodforde*, devotes a chapter to 'Servants and servant problems'. See Longe's Servants' Wages Book (1811–22), with additional material (pp.178–209); also, M.J. Stone, 'Below Stairs, or the Servant Problem: the Vicarage at Coddenham in the Early Nineteenth Century', *SR* 39 (2002), pp.2–8.

175 Gamekeeper James Scoggin died in 1837, aged seventy-seven. His tombstone (at Coddenham) records thirty-seven years of faithful service to John Longe. He was forgiven the death of a favourite dog: diary 27 Dec. 1826.

176 For details of his travel and mode of transport see Appendix E.

subscribing in 1830 not only to the *Ipswich Journal* and *Norfolk Chronicle* but also to *Quarterly Review*, *The Gentleman's Magazine* and *Theological Review*.[177] He frequently met and talked with like-minded friends and colleagues. He occasionally noted royal and national affairs in his diary.[178] He sometimes had a personal interest in naval news, for the famous Admiral 'Broke of the Shannon' was son-in-law of Sir William Middleton of Shrubland Park, and Longe also knew Broke's sons who were involved in the naval battle at Navarino Bay (Greece).[179] Longe's interest in the wider world of public affairs did not, however, mean that he overlooked those nearer home.

Conflict

For centuries, the payment of tithe was a source of confrontation on both principle and amount and the annoyance was not all on one side. In attempting to preserve harmonious relations with parishioners for whom they were pastorally responsible many incumbents accepted less than their due, both reducing their own income and prejudicing their successors and their patrons. Such concession was not Longe's business-like style. He recorded all transactions after settling terms of composition into cash. If dissatisfied, he was capable of threatening sanctions, either to revert to taking the tithe in kind or, more menacingly, to lease the right to a third party, whose professional collector was likely to be ruthless. From once being appropriate for financing the established church, tithes had in practice become a deeply flawed system. That was not the fault of Longe, but his style of negotiating for his dues was bound to prejudice pastoral relationships even in prosperous farming conditions. In the depressed decades from 1815 the situation was doubly difficult.

Longe did not merely confront but also engaged in litigation with his own parishioners. By the 1820s, poor rates were a greater claim on men of property than any tax or duty and the key factor in sharing that burden was the rateable value allotted by the parish vestry. Clergy justifiably considered it unfair that their tithe income was rated as capital.[180] Where that tithe was settled by composition, in the absence of specific agreement between the parties that the amount payable was net ('not subject to diminution'), the payee had to bear the rates on it. When a Norfolk case drew attention to the rating of tithes from Midsummer 1822 Coddenham's vestry demanded from Longe the full assessment.[181] Longe considered suing each occupier for the rates but counsel's opinion pointed to his lack of evidence. His over-optimism continued, as he still refused to pay, conceding only when summonsed to appear before his fellow magistrates sitting at the Crown in Coddenham. The wrangle damaged his relationship with farmers and other leading residents.[182]

177 Receipts: a bundle at SRO(I) HA24/50/19/4.5(21).

178 Diary: 5 Jan., 8 Aug. 1827.

179 Diary: 10 Nov. 1827. See E.L. Woodward, *The Age of Reform 1815–70* (Oxford, 1938), pp.208–9.

180 Alan Haig, *The Victorian Clergy* (1984), p.302.

181 Revd Dr Bulwer v. Inhabitants of Cawston. The rateable value of Longe's tithe in 1823 was over double that of his substantial house and land in possession. He bitterly compared his burden with a valuation favouring the squire, Sir William Middleton. SRO(I) HA24/50/19/4.5(20).

182 Most of the vestry members at Coddenham were tithe-payers, which must have sharpened the conflict. SRO(I) HA24/50/19/3.21, /4.4(4), /4.5(13), /4.5(16), /4.5(17) and /4.5(20). Views on the principle of rating tithes were expressed by correspondents to the local press: *Norfolk Chronicle*, 20 April, 25 May, 1 June, 8 June 1822; *IJ*, 2 May 1822 (and earlier 17 July 1818).

The manner in which Longe conducted himself in a number of other confrontations reveals much about his character. The mischief to the community was obvious when squire and parson in uneasy duality of leadership failed to work together harmoniously.[183] Most of these disputes related to land. Sir William claimed as manorial waste some strips between Longe's land and the public road and his men began felling trees. He also claimed right of way through one of Longe's farms for carting woodland timber. The conflict was public knowledge, not least because Longe gathered statements from local inhabitants and damage to the community was thus hardly reduced by the parties agreeing to private arbitration. The award in due course gave neither party clear victory.[184]

Another cause of conflict related to a mile-long track through Shrubland Park, linking Coddenham village most directly with the turnpike (plate 5). Without consultation with Longe, who had land accessed from it, Sir William decided it was 'unnecessary' and took steps to close it. Having shown that Admiral Uvedale of Bosmere Hall had used it with his carriage, Longe secured a court order expressly reserving his rights in perpetuity.[185]

Tithes unsurprisingly led to prolonged litigation between Longe and Middleton. The generosity of Balshazar Gardemau in giving rectorial tithes in Coddenham parish did not extend to Crowfield, where Sir William was proprietor of these 'great' tithes. He had orally agreed, claimed Longe, that hay ranked for vicarial tithe by long-established parish custom. Sir William relied on general law in claiming otherwise, but he was confronted by the zeal of an antiquary. Longe filed a bill in Chancery against both him and his principal tenant and put in train extensive enquiries: of registrars and librarians in Norwich, London (the Exchequer, First Fruits Office and Tower of London) and Oxford (the Bodleian Library) and even planned to approach the Vatican. He went back to 1220; he summarised tithes received since 1631 and he found an early relevant case.[186] Interrogatories were administered to local witnesses by a commissioner sitting at Coddenham Crown.[187] The conditional finding in London referred one issue to Suffolk assizes. There Longe secured the verdict he wanted: 'the jury took half a minute to decide'. The chancery master in London then settled detailed wording of the order. After seven years Longe was vindicated.[188]

There were other areas of concern. Sir William in his old age expressed the wish to be buried, not at any of the three local churches with which he was connected, but in his 'chapel', the only building left standing of the recently demolished Old Hall, just within Coddenham parish. Longe needed to satisfy himself that this building had consecrated status. Having searched his own considerable records without result, Longe asked the bishop's secretary for advice. Even if Longe was tactful in conveying the unwelcome news when received, the baronet's son did not

183 See Owen Chadwick, *Victorian Miniature* (London, 1960), p.151 and *passim*, for an account of such disharmony in a Norfolk village. Woodforde had a happy relationship with his squire: Winstanley, Woodforde, p.218. For a Coddenham example of later conflict between baronet and vicar (Robert Longe), see: M.J. Stone, 'Diverting Drama', *SR* 32 (1999), pp.2–19.

184 SRO(I) HA24/50/19/3.7: the full written award of the Master of Downing College, Cambridge.

185 SRO(I) HA24/50/19/4.5(19): Longe's papers. SRO(I) 106/5B/1; Quarter Sessions order.

186 Longe summarised the position to his bishop in the 1820 Visitation Return: p.175.

187 Detailed examination of witnesses of fact in the locality before an impartial lawyer commissioned for the purpose: the practice is still occasionally used today in appropriate circumstances.

188 SRO(I) HA24/50/19/3.21, and 4.5(13), and 4.5(16), and 4.5(22) (Longe's notes and calculations). The award of costs against the farmer suggests that he was in collusion with Middleton.

accept it. This led, immediately after Sir William's death, to Longe repeating icily to the son, that there was an 'insuperable objection to fulfilling the wishes of the deceased'.[189]

Another conflict arose on the death of Sir William, since his son as tithe-payer at Crowfield was alleging a modus, whereas Longe claimed as valid a more recent agreement for composition. Longe took legal advice but did not live to see the matter resolved.[190] There was a further tithe dispute in the neighbouring parish of Barham where Sir William claimed (of the incumbent, the gentle William Kirby) a wider definition of the area at Shrublands exempt from tithe as demesne. As patron there Longe did have a legitimate interest since the capital value of his advowson was calculated on the income of the living. Relying on ambiguity in a terrier among his own records of nearly a century earlier, Longe advised his friend to file a bill in the Exchequer, offering to bear half the costs. His papers contain no record of the outcome.[191]

Whether Longe was by nature contentious must be left to opinion but conflict was not confined to the Middletons alone. He was earlier in contention with Samuel Kilderbee, a relative of his wife, Charlotte. In 1798, to raise funds to purchase a Coddenham farm, Longe and his co-trustee decided to sell a more distant farm. As the sale could not be achieved simultaneously, Mr Kilderbee provided a bridging loan on the security of Longe's bond. Despite the stated date, Longe thought that repayment was to await actual completion of sale. When the sale was delayed, however, Kilderbee demanded immediate repayment. First naïve and then suspicious, Longe accused him of unethical behaviour and Longe's father had to intervene before the matter was resolved.[192]

In families of the status of the Bacons and of the Temples from which Nicholas Bacon's mother came, many heirlooms passed down to descendents by operation of law. Despite the generosity of Nicholas Bacon, Longe had to identify those items which then belonged to others and to despatch them. It was a situation that could easily lead to misunderstandings, and a lengthy process.[193] Longe sent sixty-two packages to Moor Park.[194] Two separate instances of minor conflict ensued. Over two months after the main consignment, and with no preamble discernible from the diary, Longe despatched 'the picture of *Roman Charity*'.[195] A month later he received letters, one of which occasioned him 'great uneasiness'.[196] A few days later Longe received his *copy* of that picture back again, suggesting that he may have

189 Diary: 17 March to 6 April, 7 Aug. 1827; SRO(I) HA24/50/19/4.5(13) and (29). See also Davy SRO(I) J400/3, Tom Williamson, *The Landscape of Shrubland Park* (Clare, 1997), p.3 and both Tom Williamson, 'Shrubland before Barry' and John Blatchly, 'The Terra Cotta Trail' in Harper-Bill *et al.* (eds), *East Anglia's History*, pp.128, 135, 190–1.

190 A modus, being an earlier fixed-sum agreement ignoring price inflation, operated harshly against the tithe-owner, who would try to have it annulled. The unfortunate effect of Lord Tenterden's Act (1832) was to rush parties into confrontation. See Eric J. Evans, *The Contentious Tithe 1750–1850* (1976), p.121. Diary: 17 May, 14 June, 24 Aug. 1833.

191 Diary: 9 July 1833.

192 Diary: 17 May, 26, 28 July, and then the resolution from 1 to 24 Dec. 1798. SRO(I) HA24/50/19/4.2(1). The surname of Kilderbee, town clerk of Ipswich, is familiar from two Gainsborough portraits.

193 Longe despatched items in 1796 (diary, 22 Nov. 1796) and was still discussing two years later.

194 Diary: 21, 30 March, 9 April 1798. Moor Park, Farnham (Surrey) was the seat of the Temple family. Nicholas Bacon's mother, Dorothy, daughter and co-heir of John Temple, was grand-daughter of the statesman Sir William Temple of Sheen, 1st baronet.

195 Diary: 16 July 1798.

196 Diary: 17, 18, 19 Aug. 1798.

confused a copy with an original.[197] A further difficulty is revealed in November 1798, which suggests that Longe was accused of having improperly retained gems that were family heirlooms and lawyers became involved.[198]

Longe inherited one dispute from Bacon, who had been claiming glebe status for six acres of land. Small plots in different ownership were intermixed, with the situation further complicated by Bacon's diversion of a road. Longe having typically researched the history, complained that a boundary tree had been removed and took advice from his London lawyer, Dr Windus. He was advised that his case was weak and he considered buying the disputed land from these claimants if the price were reduced. It was fourteen years later, following two deaths, that he was admitted to these copyhold lands.[199]

The Longe family estate at Spixworth (Norfolk) passed in 1812 from Longe's childless cousin Francis to his widow Catherine, with next reversion to Longe's eldest son John. Both Francis and Catherine in turn were short of funds. Wishing to protect the estate for his son, Longe lent her the large sum of £5,000, but still she was in difficulties. Members of the Longe family were in 1820 sued as beneficiaries in reversion, probably as guarantors on another loan, by one Birch. Catherine took desperate steps: she dismissed servants; she tried to sell a farm; she attempted to borrow on security of her interest; she began to fell oak trees for sale. Led by Longe, his son commenced injunction proceedings in Chancery, but the impecunious Catherine died, aged seventy-four. A complicated settlement of both cases was negotiated, but young John could receive only an encumbered inheritance.[200]

Mental illness in landed families often led to conflict. Nicholas Bacon's manic-depressive condition was not Longe's only contact with mental illness, though he had known neither Nicholas's brother John, nor their father who ended his days in a 'madhouse'. Longe was one of 106 witnesses in the nationally celebrated case of The King v. Barlee & others at Chelmsford Assizes. The question at issue was whether Mrs Barlee, confined in the infirmary of Ipswich Gaol for contempt of court, was a lunatic as alleged by her estranged husband and others. Longe gave evidence that when he visited her there in his capacity as a magistrate she appeared to be of sound intellect. Since the opposite view prevailed, the defendants were acquitted of making criminally false charges. Although he knew members of the Barlee family socially Longe gave his evidence on oath without favour.[201]

Again, conflict through insanity arose for Longe in his capacity as trustee of a deceased parishioner, Mrs Sleorgin of Henley Hall, whose grand-daughter Miss Croasdaile was well-known to him. She was at odds with her father over his refusal to take any action for her brother, who had returned to Suffolk after military service in India in a disordered mental state. Supported by Longe and his fellow magistrate the Revd Dr John Chevallier who specialised in such matters, Miss Croasdaile

197 Diary: 26 Aug. 1798. A picture of that name, by Smart after Domenichino, was later at the vicarage. This was probably John Smart, a minor Ipswich artist. See Appendix F and notes on people below.

198 Diary 2, 3, 8, 15 Nov. 1798. The full situation is not revealed.

199 SRO(I) HA24/50/19/4.5(15): glebe papers and diary 31 Dec.1798.

200 The main source comprises bundles of papers: SRO(I) HA24/50/19/3.21 and 5.2. The complexity is confusing and includes a West Indies estate. In one action four members of the related Howes family were made parties. One lender was Catherine Longe's father, Militia Colonel George Duckett MP. Diary entries are at 4 March, 18 Nov. 1826, 18 April, 26 May 1827.

201 For the diary summary, see 7–11 March 1826, and for more extended coverage Chelmsford Chronicle, 10 March and *IJ*, 11, 18 March 1826.

pressed to place her brother in secure residential care. Provision was found at Dr Wright's Lunatic House near Norwich, but only at the expense of any remaining relationship with Mr Croasdaile, who threatened Longe with court proceedings. In fact, Longe appears to have acted well in a difficult situation. The Croasdailes also wanted Longe to relinquish his position as trustee, which he ultimately did for the widowed Mrs Croasdaile.[202]

Conflict could also arise within his own family. Longe had never had a good relationship with his son-in-law, Major Robert Martin Leake. On Longe's death substantial property (in which he enjoyed a life interest under Nicholas Bacon's will) would pass to his four children, with Martin Leake representing daughter Charlotte. Thereafter the interests were confined within an entail, on which substantive future changes could be made only with Longe's agreement. As early as 1826 two unrelated issues were under discussion. First, a substantial part of the value of the trust related to the two advowsons and it was desirable to have advance agreement involving valuation.[203] The Barham advowson would not come to the Longes during the lifetime of Kirby, but he was older than Longe. Longe was not to know that Kirby would live to the age of ninety, by which time it would not benefit Henry personally, by then settled elsewhere.[204] Secondly, Leake and Charlotte had no children and he was anxious that the entail should be barred. Longe accused Martin Leake of 'very unhandsome conduct' in treating the subject 'in a very uncandid and indelicate manner'. Longe ensured stalemate by taking no positive step; unfriendly silence lasted until after his death four years later.

These examples of conflict might suggest a pattern of unwillingness to settle matters privately. A generous judgment would be that Longe felt keenly the responsibilities of trusteeship, protecting the estate for the sake of his successors. The more critical assessment would conclude that he was personally over-zealous in defence of his property rights and resented the Middletons in particular. On either view, it is hard to avoid the conclusion that these confrontations rendered his parochial ministry less effective.

Party politics

Although there was no Tory party in the modern sense, most parsons shared Tory values, standing for public order and continuity, buttressed by the established church and loyalty to the Crown. Among bishops, Henry Bathurst of Norwich was rare in holding Whig political views. The Tory grouping of politicians enjoyed power in government from the time of Pitt the Younger until 1830.[205] All the greater was the

202 SRO(I) HA 24/50/19/5.1, 5.2 and 5.3: papers relating to both aspects of the Croasdaile case. Diary 17 March, and from 7 Nov. to 22 Dec. 1826; also diary 4 April, 30 July 1831, 19 June 1833.

203 In 1833 Longe took counsel's opinion on whether he could resign the living and immediately present his son to succeed him. He was advised that this was legal, subject to the bishop's consent, provided there was no contract yielding benefit to either party: SRO(I) HA24/50/19/3.22. It was not done.

204 There is more than one valuation. In one (HA24 50/19/3.20) the Bacon farms (over 468 acres) were valued at £18,802 15s. 10d. The two advowsons were valued at £8,345, though elsewhere at £12,026. Exactly what agreement was reached after Longe's death (or indeed with regard to the entails) is unclear.

205 For Parliamentary representation in Suffolk and Ipswich see Appendix G. For other local material see Clarke, History of Ipswich, passim, Gwyn Thomas, 'Parliamentary Constituencies' in Dymond and Martin, *Historical Atlas*, pp.30–1 and David Warnes and John Blatchly, *Bribery Warehouse* (Ipswich, 1986).

shock to Longe and like-minded colleagues when Earl Grey was able to form his Whig administration in that year.

Longe's interest in politics had begun early, when he went to Ipswich with his vicar, Nicholas Bacon, before polling in the borough election of 1796, despite having no vote there, to support their parishioner William Middleton. They were again in the town both for the declaration of the result and at a large dinner afterwards, to commiserate with Middleton on his defeat.[206] Thirty years later, Longe still followed Ipswich politics, noting the 'Yellow' victory, and in the following year celebrations by the 'Blues', when the earlier result was overturned.[207] The division into 'Blues' and 'Yellows' lasted between elections and throughout social and economic life. In Ipswich, Longe used the Tory inn (the Great White Horse), read the 'Blue' local newspaper and patronised the 'Blue' bank.[208] In the county, in an exclusively Tory gathering on nomination day, so different from disputed Ipswich elections, any third candidate was dissuaded from standing.[209] Again with Nicholas Bacon in 1796, young Longe attended, and continued in later years to take the greatest interest in the efforts of Sir William Middleton to gain a seat when a baronet.[210]

Pitt the Younger and Charles James Fox had died in 1806 but memories of their views still polarised rival interests nationally in the early 1820s. Longe was a member of a small Tory group in the county, keen 'to cement and strengthen the good old cause', by forming a Suffolk Pitt Club.[211] 'Since opponents were exerting themselves', he wrote in July 1820, 'it was particularly necessary for "the Loyal Party" to be active and vigilant.' About 200 gentlemen met in 1821, resolved to dine annually and voted Longe onto the new committee. Twice that number dined in August, in a temporary structure near the Great White Horse. A year later similar numbers of diners again required a 'booth', in the garden of the Angel hotel in Bury.[212] However in 1823 the violence of party politics having subsided, as Longe and his colleagues acknowledged, they did not repeat this function. Longe's involvement is nonetheless a good example of his active work at county level in a cause in which he so passionately believed.

Neither the absence of a contest in the county election nor the alleged fading of partisan support prevented excited celebration in 1826. After giving early breakfast to local freeholders, flourishing his new blue tasselled flag with evident enjoyment, Longe led them to the edge of Ipswich where a large gathering met Sir Thomas Gooch. The subsequent progress was harmonious and respectable.[213] Later that day, at the 'Blue' dinner in Ipswich, Longe showed his 'ultra' views on Roman Catholics. Having at first looked in vain for criticism of proposed Catholic Emancipation, he noted with satisfaction the sustained reception given to an after-dinner toast to 'the Protestant ascendancy' which amounted to the same thing.[214]

---

206 Diary: 16, 28 May, 23 June 1796.

207 Diary: 12, 17 June 1826, 18 April 1827.

208 Diary: *passim*.

209 Diary: 31 May 1796.

210 Middleton never obtained a county seat: see Appendix G.

211 SRO(I) HA24/50/19/4.4(8): Longe's standard letter for the short-lived Pitt Club and other material.

212 See Fiske, *Oakes Diaries*, pp. 266, 276 for both dinners.

213 Diary: 20 June 1826. Note the length and enthusiasm of this entry. Sir Thomas Gooch was not always acclaimed. See Mann and Cane, *Home and Abroad*, pp.25–6, for election riots, December 1832.

214 Diary: 28 June 1826. Sir Thomas later thanked him for his election-time exertions.

Longe continued active in matters political: in 1826, not only remaining resolutely opposed to Catholic Emancipation, he opposed alteration of the Corn Laws.[215] In 1831 he followed closely the stages of the Reform Bill, which he considered to be 'a most dangerous measure, ill-timed and pregnant with mischief to the constitution'.[216] He showed interest in the archbishop's Tithe Bill and the General Highway Bill.[217] Also in 1831, keen to replace the sitting county members, Longe canvassed unsuccessfully for signatures to support two other Tories.[218] Then, for the first post-reform election, Longe sent a large subscription to the Tory election fund of Henniker and Vere in the county's eastern constituency. He attended the Conservative dinner at the Great White Horse in Ipswich and a few days later Sir Charles Broke Vere (with Mr George Broke) called on him, doubtless to thank him for his support.[219]

Sometimes Longe's interests came satisfyingly together. Through his county MP, Mr Charles Tyrell, and probably on his own initiative, Longe obtained from the Commissioners of Public Records promise of a complete set of volumes of records. These were 'to be open to the perusal of literary and legal persons, inhabitants of the county of Suffolk'.[220] In summer 1832 two large packages arrived from London by water. The volumes were installed at Ipswich Moot Hall in the freshly fitted-out rooms of the new Literary Institution. Longe had that May been elected an honorary member in recognition of this success. Mr Tyrell too was thanked.[221]

Before secret ballots the support of a parson for the 'Blue' party was an important influence. Whilst most Anglican clergy were politically conservative in sympathy, few rivalled Longe in active involvement. Towards the end of his life party activism became viewed as unclerical, but Longe himself was undeterred in his sustained and public Tory support. His involvement in starting the county Pitt Club, however short-lived, and his enthusiastic involvement at election time illustrate the extent to which he was known as an activist in the 'Blue' interest. He had in any event long had a public profile in mid-Suffolk as a Justice of the Peace.

Magistrate (including houses of industry and turnpikes)

The duties of a magistrate were exercised in several different settings: in his own home, outdoors in the locality, at sittings often at local inns, as well as at Quarter Sessions (for Longe in Ipswich) and attending at assizes. Appointed in 1803 at the age of thirty-eight, Longe sat as a magistrate for thirty years, making his final appearance at Quarter Sessions only eight months before he died.[222]

Serious and substantial cases were heard by the king's travelling assize judges, in Longe's time sitting only at Bury despite the claim of Ipswich to alternate. Assize

215 Diary: 23 Oct. 1826. The meeting at Barham was probably for the Hundred.

216 1831 diary entries: 5 March (first Bill brought in), 24 March (just carried on second reading), 19 April (no division), 4 July (second reading of second Bill).

217 Diary: 16 Aug. 1831 and 8 March 1833.

218 Diary: 25, 26, 30 April, 10 May 1831.

219 Diary: 4 Jan., 6 May, 21, 26 Aug. 1833. The former was successful, the latter not, though both were successful in 1835. Half Longe's money was later returned to him.

220 This quotation, taken from Longe's papers, is printed in the twenty-five volumes held at SRO(I) fR 025.171. The Government Publications Sectional List 24 (1983 edn) lists them with others.

221 SRO(I) HA24/50/19/4.4(7): correspondence. Relevant diary entries: 31 Aug., 4 Sept., 28 Oct., 3 Nov., 6 Dec. 1831 and 3 March, 23 April 1833. See also SRO(I) K13/1/3.1 for the Institution minutes.

222 The context of Longe's service as a magistrate is given at Appendix H and summary of attendance at Quarter Sessions by both him and his colleagues at Appendix I.

judges were supported by a grand jury of gentlemen to examine each indictment before trial. Their names were customarily printed in local newspapers, thus emphasising their status, quite distinct from the petty jury. Longe frequently attended the assizes in that capacity and, whilst not sitting through every session, he did take careful note of proceedings, marking up his copy of the calendar.[223]

Much of the work was carried out at Quarter Sessions. It is characteristic of Longe that he had a good record of attendance for his part of the county. In two periods between 1803 and 1827, of the magistrates from time to time sitting at Ipswich (thirty-one and fifty-two) Longe ranked sixth most frequent in attendance.[224] His health and advancing years intervened, but he made a point of attending sessions on both days in January 1831 after the Swing disturbances.[225] From then until midsummer 1833 he sat eight times, when eighteen out of fifty justices did so only once or twice.

Longe's magisterial duties extended round the year. He sat with one or two others at fortnightly 'sittings' (petty sessions), held alternately at Needham Market and Coddenham, and was absent only when ill-health or holiday prevented. More serious cases would involve a warrant to commit to gaol pending trial, when he might act as prosecutor. Additional sessions were appointed for specific purposes and Longe also sat as tax commissioner to supervise assessors and to hear certain appeals. As an example of local administrative powers, he and a colleague ordered repairs at public expense to Claydon river-bridge.[226]

On the county stage he was present when magistrates resolved to purchase Melton house of industry (near Woodbridge) for a county lunatic asylum.[227] He visited the county gaol, both to examine a particular inmate and by rota, which might lead to further involvement, as in the Barlee case.[228] He was engaged on justice business in his own home, as needed.[229] When Coddenham's constable was ill Longe swore in a successor.[230] He addressed lawlessness in Crowfield.[231] In addition, he was involved in meetings, correspondence and travelling out of the parish. Sometimes an individual case made heavier demands on Longe's time, for example in 1827 when his neighbour Mrs Robinson suffered a nocturnal break-in. Although his efforts were unsuccessful, he attended Bury Assizes when one Coddenham suspect, convicted of another similar offence, was transported for life.[232] Such persistence was rarely required, but as exercised by Longe, his duties as a justice together

223 SRO(I) HA24/50/19/4.4(2): Longe preserved both his Assize and his Quarter Sessions Calendars from 1817 to 1832, and his notes on them confirm his presence.

224 Quarter Sessions attendance figures (Appendix I) have been compiled from Minute and Order Books (1803–33): SRO(I) B105/2/52 to /73.

225 Indictments were listed against rioters at Hoxne (of whom three were found guilty) and Bacton (where there was insufficient evidence for conviction).

226 Diary: 19 Dec. 1831.

227 The diary on and after 10 November 1826 suggests no hint of drama. Compare A.F. Watling, 'St Audry's Hospital' in C. Bentham (ed.), *Melton and its Churches* (Ipswich, 1981), p.55: the magistrates were subjected to a curt ultimatum and threat of public auction.

228 The Barlee case is discussed as a conflict above. Ipswich gaol was in Black Horse Lane, until new arrangements were made in St Helen's: Bishop, *Ipswich*, p.131.

229 Diary: 14 July 1826 ('engaged all the morning'); Diary: 30 Jan., 1 Feb. 1826 (Longe gave the clergyman complainant breakfast, although having little in common with his churchmanship).

230 Diary: 1 Aug. 1831.

231 Diary: 11 Aug. 1831: all in one day, when he was 'going through Crowfield'.

232 Diary: 1 June to 3 Aug. 1827. Later, Longe with others examined suspects in the gaol. Diary: 30 Aug., 8, 15 Sept. 1827.

formed a substantial work-load. In addition, he helped supervise the Hundred house of industry and neighbourhood turnpikes, as outlined below.

In the 1790s it was widely believed that the level of crime was rising and some feared that society would be engulfed.[233] With the advantage of hindsight we would associate most crime in the countryside with material poverty. In the absence of a police force, magistrates relied on informers to detect and private people to prosecute. Ipswich funded 'peace officers' who would attend court to give information.[234] Popular opinion did not always match the law in particular cases, of which notorious examples are the poaching of game, the smuggling of exciseable spirits and the nocturnal torching of hayricks. In such cases there was a greatly reduced prospect of information being laid.[235] Without higher detection rates heavy punishment was an ineffective deterrent. This led by the late 1820s to a tendency to reduce penalties and suspend enforcement of greater ones. Even the Game Laws were eased in 1831.[236]

The cost of prosecution led to the forming of voluntary associations.[237] As early as 1772, an advertisement had invited subscriptions from those 'determined to prosecute, with the utmost severity of the law, all offenders against the public peace, and personally to assist in quelling all riots and unlawful assemblies'.[238] Longe's diaries suggest that these associations were short-lived. The one Longe joined in his own hundred in 1826 was certainly not the first.[239] Another collapsed some years later, for magistrates were again planning to form a further association.[240]

From his lengthy and arduous work as a magistrate Longe no doubt derived a sense of usefulness to the community and a measure of prestige. He enjoyed membership of a network of like-minded colleagues of his degree, many of whom he also met socially.[241] His service did however have more negative social implications, visibly positioning him in a society much polarised in privilege and material wealth. His parishioners doubtless perceived him as a magistrate in judgment rather than a pastor in mercy. Being of the stricter school, Longe accepted that his service as a magistrate was one that men of his degree performed, despite the fact that it distanced him from most of his parishioners.

Many active magistrates had other public service responsibilities with colleagues from other parishes, in two areas that required a unit of administration larger than the parish. The first related to the poor. At Barham, in the house of industry serving the whole hundred, Longe shared legal responsibility with his fellow directors, supervising the resident managers. He served for nearly forty years, beginning before he

233 V.A.C. Gatrell, 'Crime, Authority and the Policeman State' in F.M.L. Thompson (ed.), *The Cambridge Social History of Britain 1750–1950*, 3 (Cambridge, 1990), pp.243–310, argues that not crime but the prosecution rate was rising. From 1801 to 1831 committals rose by 167 per cent. From 1806 to 1830, the death penalty rose by 316 per cent, but not all were executed.

234 For a case when Longe was sitting see diary: 29 Aug. 1827.

235 Alan Armstrong, *Farmworkers 1770–1980* (London, 1988), p.71; J. Gregory and John Stevenson, *Britain in the Eighteenth Century 1688–1820* (2000), p.226; J.M. Beattie, 'The Pattern of Crime in England 1660–1800', *P&P* 62 (1974), p.95.

236 Diary: 23 Oct., 13, 27 Nov. 1833. Longe nevertheless pursued to conviction two men for poaching on his land. Unable to pay his fine, one was committed to the county gaol for two months.

237 David Foster, *The Rural Constabulary Act 1839* (1982), p.4.

238 *IJ* 25, April 1772, quoted in A.F.J. Brown, *Prosperity and Poverty: Rural Essex 1700–1815* (Chelmsford, 1996), p.102.

239 Diary: 11 Jan., 3 Feb., 31 May 1826, 30 May 1827. Only fourteen dined at the first meeting.

240 Diary: 20 Nov. 1833.

241 Diary: *passim*.

became magistrate or indeed vicar of Coddenham.[242] His last few years at Barham were a time of particularly strained public resources. Relief was cut, at a time when the volume of medical need required a fourth surgeon.[243] The unemployed were put to work on the public roads and Longe himself proposed the renting of some land to provide horticultural work, in lieu of normal relief.[244]

Supervision was exercised at full quarterly meetings, preceded by small meetings to settle the agenda. Longe took his turn on the weekly committee that conducted detailed management, which might give him as many as ten meetings in a year. The desire to serve exceeded any sense of burdensome duty, for elections were needed.[245] As their Act was for a limited period, the Barham trustees applied to Parliament to renew their incorporation. A bill was enacted for this single hundred in 1833, shortly before the nationwide amendment of the Poor Law rendered it obsolete.[246]

Longe's other major administrative responsibility was for local turnpikes. On a national scale, the need for improved communications had led to larger units for administering the repair of main roads. In Suffolk lengths of road were transferred by degrees to turnpike trusts in the century from 1711. By 1838, 17 per cent of all roads nationally were turnpiked, largely funded by tolls from nearly 8,000 gates.[247] Longe saw the peak of stage-coach traffic on main routes, before its rapid decline with the spread of railways.[248] As for road surfaces in the county, the much-travelled Arthur Young, himself a Suffolk man, considered that they had improved greatly in the twenty years prior to 1797. Whilst accepting the better roads, travellers disliked turnpikes for expense, delays and over-officious gate-keepers. Regular users, such as farmers going to market, were particularly resentful. Travellers looked for alternative routes around gates, which caused trustees to respond by installing a second gate, often unauthorised.[249]

As a trustee, Longe shared this generalised hostility with his fellow trustees, all local gentlemen, aided by professional lawyers and surveyors. Parishes still had statutory responsibility, but most compounded it annually for a cash payment. This, with the net income from tolls, enabled each trust to maintain its road surfaces.[250] The capital for fixed plant was borrowed and the Helmingham trustees issued £50 bonds as security in 1812.[251] Since the 4 per cent interest fell heavily into arrears, loans were more a social service than an attractive investment.

Longe's main involvement was with the Helmingham trust, responsible from 1812 for two minor radial roads out of Ipswich to the north, totalling with a third

242 Diary: 7 Jan. 1796, when Longe was already undertaking duty. The context for Longe's service in Barham house of industry is given at Appendix J.

243 Diary: 19 July 1833.

244 Diary: 29 Dec. 1831. There is no record of the outcome, but a similar scheme in a parish nearby was abandoned as uneconomic. M.J. Stone, 'Poor in Tuddenham', unpublished, pp.28–29.

245 Diary: 29 June 1826, provides an example of a contest for a single director vacancy.

246 SRO(I) FB37/G2/1. Despite local opposition, the Act 3 and 4 William IV c.2 (38 pages), replaced the original one (4 Geo III c.57), granting Bosmere and Claydon Hundred, 'more effectual powers … for the better relief and employment of the poor'. Diary: 23 August, 29, 30 September 1831.

247 Alistair Robertson, 'Turnpikes and Stagecoaches' in Dymond and Martin, *Historical Atlas* (1999), pp.126, 127, 210.

248 E.W. Bovill, *English Country Life 1780–1830* (1962), p.51. The London–Ipswich–Bury line opened twelve years after Longe died.

249 The road joining Woodbridge Road (Ipswich) near the former toll-gate is still called Sidegate Lane.

250 Statute labour was abolished in 1835.

251 SRO(I)EN1/B3/11: bundles of redeemed securities.

road nearly forty miles. Carrying only local traffic, with correspondingly modest receipts, these roads nevertheless passed through seventeen parishes.[252] Normally between three and eleven Helmingham trustees met three times a year, although on one occasion seventeen attended.[253] Meetings were held at village inns, most frequently the Crown at Coddenham. Although he seldom travelled to another venue, Longe was among those most regular in attendance and often took the chair there.

Helmingham business was frequently routine although financial decisions did carry some commercial risk. Changes at Ashbocking crossroads involved the expense of a new toll-house and new gates. Elsewhere, based on surveyors' reports on physical matters, orders were made against encroachment and to protect the surface. One decision had to be defended in Woodbridge magistrates court.[254] The trustees also had human dealings, mostly with toll-gate keepers. All this public service Longe seems to have taken very much in his stride, as duties that a gentleman performed, enjoying the company of his fellow trustees over dinner.

Supposing it a mere formality, the Helmingham trustees applied for a renewal of their finite powers. 'The inhabitants of Ipswich', however, took advantage of their vulnerable position to demand the moving of a toll-gate by the Woolpack Inn near St Margaret's church, to free traffic forking onto another road. After their compromise response was rejected the Helmingham trustees conceded. They installed new toll-gates at Westerfield village some two miles north, rendered feasible by the enclosure of the green there. Armed with their new amended Act, they purchased a site, erected a new toll-house with gates and sold off the old.[255] To deal with this business the trustees needed six meetings between January and June 1833.[256] Longe was not to see the outcome, for nine months later he died.

Defence of the realm

Defence of the realm might be considered the first responsibility of government, yet Britons long resisted the adoption of both a standing army and compulsory conscription. Government policy in the eighteenth century envisaged a strong navy, plus a small regular army, backed for home defence by militia and volunteer units. Government then funded continental allies and their armies. During the French wars home defence was revealed as the weak link. Quality was sacrificed, both by substitution and by allowing exemption from militia service to recruits in untrained volunteer units. Thus militia were used for little more than policing the unruly at home. The discipline and even loyalty of volunteer units was so doubtful that at the first chance the government disbanded them. Equally seriously, recruiting to the regular army was also undermined by flawed concessions.

Much of the administrative burden within the county fell to gentlemen such as Longe representing the lord lieutenant. They worked with chief, high and petty constables through the structure of county divisions, hundreds and parishes. Eligibility lists were passed upwards and numerical quotas down. A balloted man might

252 SRO(I) B106/5A/1: before a statutory trust was established, a plan and list identifying the land were deposited with the clerk of the peace. Helmingham turnpike covered 128 parcels of land.

253 SRO(I) EN/B1/1: the only surviving Helmingham Minute Book starts at 1823.

254 After a small river was diverted and despite compensation being paid.

255 The siting of this gate became feasible because Westerfield common was by then enclosed, by an Act passed in 1808.

256 Minute Book as above: EN/B1/1.

arrange a substitute, having perhaps first insured against paying a bounty.[257] Such was the background to Longe's incumbency until 1815.

Whereas the ballot was unpopular there was much enthusiasm to don uniforms, at first for mere posturing but soon in fear of imminent invasion. Once Napoleon had command of estuaries in the Netherlands the Suffolk coast became a likely target. Martello towers were densely sited, but were completed too late to be militarily relevant. What were lacking were the military experience, discipline and arms necessary to combat veteran troops under proven commanders. Through the dominance of the navy that lack was never put to the test.

A troop of yeomanry might be raised by a single nobleman, but some volunteer units were raised by subscription, as when some forty Suffolk gentlemen funded four troops of fencibles to augment the militia on the coast.[258] With such activity Longe was familiar, introduced as a young man into the officers' mess of the East Norfolk Militia by his brother, at the newly erected cavalry barracks in St Matthew's parish (Ipswich). In 1797 Longe became liable to furnish a mounted trooper. After being personally sworn in, Longe then supplied his man with uniform and horse. He observed several parades.[259] The next year the archdeacon announced 'the bishop's approbation of the clergy taking up arms'. Longe immediately enrolled in the Ipswich Troop of Light Horse under Charles Maitland Barclay.[260] On sixteen occasions between June and November 1798, resplendent in his new uniform, he trained with the troop on local field-days. Winter training was to follow at the riding school in Ipswich.[261]

Colourful military preparation was not the only response to the threat of invasion. Under the leadership of the clergy and gentry, responsible to the lord lieutenant, the county was meanwhile preparing itself parish by parish for civilian evacuation westwards, with a rear-guard to harry the invaders. After a parish meeting in Coddenham church Longe had to list his parishioners by separate specified categories. Secondly, from the men of the parish he had to enrol pioneers and irregulars.[262] It was for Longe a busy time. The invasion never came but the county was in daily fear until late September 1801 when preliminaries to the extravagantly celebrated Peace of Amiens were signed.[263] As soon as the uneasy peace collapsed the need became urgent to re-arm and to re-form units unwisely disembodied. Swearing-in proceeded apace once more. Noblemen and gentlemen met to appoint and advise inspectors for hundreds, and superintendents in the parishes. Barracks were hastily built to replace winter billeting in inns. In Ipswich, maltings were converted and a

257 Vestries also paid bounties to substitutes, preferring to pay one lump-sum to a man with no family rather than also paying continuing allowances for the dependants of a family man.

258 Both joint promotions and individual sponsorship were noted by Oakes in 1794/5.

259 The Supplementary Militia levy: Diary, 11 Feb., 27 March, 22/23 May 1797, and 7 May 1798.

260 Diary: 23, 28 April 1798. Clergy had in Elizabeth's reign waived the privilege of exemption from military service granted in the ninth century: Robert Ryece, *The Breviary of Suffolk* [1618] (ed. Hervey 1902), p.97. John Blatchly, *The Topographers of Suffolk* (Ipswich, 1988), p.44.

261 Diary: 18 June to 19 Nov. 1798. Longe's kit purchases are listed at the foot of that year's diary.

262 SRO(I) HA24/50/19/4.5(20): the abstract of lists, from which is learnt both the required categories, and the figures for Coddenham: males between fifteen and sixty years of age (123), aged and infirm (23), men incapable of active service (2), women (156) and infants incapable of removing themselves (50).

263 Valerie Norrington, 'Peace at Last: Celebrations of Peace and Victory during and after the Napoleonic Wars', *SR* 40 (2003), pp.2–18.

hutted camp created to accommodate up to 8,000 troops. Half as many again took part in exercises on Rushmere Heath.[264]

In this context of crisis, Longe addressed a meeting of inhabitants in Coddenham church on 28 July 1803. He encouraged men to enrol again as volunteers under the 'alarm' of invasion by this 'fierce and powerful enemy'. That threats had come to nothing in 1798 should not reassure them since 'upwards of 200,000 men' were ready to embark against Britain.[265] Speaking of atrocities against women and children elsewhere at the hands of 'lustful and furious' French soldiers, he called for courage and resolution after the example of Agincourt and Crécy, as Britain stood alone in her liberty.[266] From the hundred a company of 300 volunteers was raised, under the command of William Middleton of Shrubland Park. Sharpshooters practised in makeshift butts in a narrow valley near Coddenham, reputedly used centuries before by archers destined for Agincourt.[267]

In 1803, Longe as superintendent received official detailed instructions. The sources of waggons, carts and horses were to be listed and a parish rendezvous appointed ready for mass evacuation of non-combatants. Longe would have at his disposal guides with knowledge of the area, some mounted. Other picked men were to execute the 'scorched earth' policy, destroying provisions and breaking upper millstones and communal ovens. Longe enrolled thirty-five Coddenham pioneers to assist defending forces by obstructing the invader, each man with a specified implement: axe, pick-axe, spade, shovel or bill-hook. Another dozen or so, the curate and farmers, were listed as ready to use fire-arms in defence of their own parish.[268]

For the three summers until autumn 1805 only the Royal Navy and the weather stood between Napoleon's massed forces and the people of south-east England. Traditionally, the credit has been given to Lord Nelson's resounding victory at Trafalgar for the lifting of the invasion threat. Napoleon had already abandoned his cross-Channel dream, but French power was demonstrated at Ulm and Austerlitz. As the threat receded and the regular army grew stronger, volunteer units were disbanded by the authorities. Longe's military role was at an end.

Rural disturbances

For sixty years after 1789 violent revolution sporadically engulfed many continental countries. Britain escaped. The numerous disturbances in England were local or at worst regional. For some years these had been most frequent in towns: violence from 'the mob' in London; bread riots; Luddite attacks in textile districts; conspiracy in Cato Street; the horror of 'Peterloo'. Although 'in the east of England every year was violent', during the wartime the desperation of impoverished labourers and lesser tradesmen did not erupt into widespread outbreaks.[269] Far from European peace bringing respite, the labouring classes fared worse than during the inflationary war years as agricultural prices collapsed, rural employment contracted and wages

264 Malster, *Ipswich*, p.118.

265 This number is likely to have been exaggerated, but it is what Longe believed.

266 SRO(I) HA24/50/19/4.4(6): this speech was neatly written on pages sewn together, suggesting that it was intended to be delivered to other audiences elsewhere by Longe or others. Victories against the French at Crécy (1346) and Agincourt (1415) were treasured corporate memories.

267 SRO(I) qs Cod 9: William Murrell Lummis, 'Material for History of Coddenham' (*c*.1933) (unpublished typescript), para. 70.

268 Lummis, 'Coddenham', para 70.01, 02, stated that John Longe had supplied these details.

269 Paul Muskett, 'The East Anglian Agrarian Riots of 1822, *Ag. Hist. Rev*. 32 (1984), p.1.

were cut. For the next twenty years, East Anglian landowners and large farmers feared that the fabric of society was close to disintegration. This was the background of Longe's life as potential target, as parish leader, and as magistrate.

Violence erupted first in Gosbeck, the parish immediately adjoining Coddenham and Crowfield to the east, when in February 1815 a group of men destroyed threshing machines. In ensuing angry scenes in Ipswich town centre the magistrate put in fear of his person was Longe's colleague on the bench, Sir William Middleton. Similar trouble followed in four nearby villages and by November deliberate fires were becoming a frightening form of protest.[270] For about six weeks in 1816 a combination of uprisings of farm labourers and continued arson troubled Suffolk. Petty and additional constables were sworn in, but neither their night patrols nor hired watchmen could protect all property.[271] County-wide that year, twenty-two serious fires were recorded and sporadic outbreaks continued despite nocturnal vigilance, notably at Stonham Aspal, near Coddenham.[272] If discontent among the working classes and the philosophy of radicals had been co-ordinated the outcome might well have been more serious. After 'Peterloo' in 1819, fearing that 'the spirit of insubordination' might widen into revolution, many gentlemen supported not demonstrations but strong measures against them.[273]

Those in Suffolk planning representations to George IV on his accession in 1820 agreed to despatch a separate address from each hundred. It fell to Longe to convene a confidential meeting at Coddenham Crown. The terms of his enthusiastic draft address show his mind-set. He accused 'a licentious press unexampled for its disloyalty, impiety and blasphemy' of aiming 'to poison the minds of the unwary and uninformed' and thereby 'to seduce them from their allegiance to their sovereign'. In the event, a shorter document was preferred and was exhibited at Coddenham's saving bank for general signature.[274]

In the whole period of agricultural depression, from 1815 to Longe's death in 1834, Norfolk and Suffolk suffered over five hundred fires of suspicious origin. In Suffolk the worst year was 1822.[275] Hungry men in their desperation blamed threshing machines for loss of winter work, in two months breaking 52 in forty Suffolk parishes. Longe with other magistrates met the Lord Lieutenant and a resulting poster was distributed.[276] County-wide, yeomanry detachments plus 250 special constables and numerous night-watchmen may not have prevented damage but they did bring 123 men to court.[277] The tension of the time is captured in a letter dated 1 March 1822 from a yeomanry colonel in north Suffolk writing to Longe's friend, Lieut.-Col. Edgar. He feared that the 'contagion' would spread if not immediately checked, and emphasised the threat of the firebrand, that 'most formidable of weapons'. He had orders to parade his troop ready to aid the civil power, but when

270 A.J. Peacock, *Bread or Blood* (1965); Paul Muskett, *Riotous Assemblies: Popular Disturbances in East Anglia 1740–1822* (Ely, 1984), pp.46–9.

271 SRO(I) HA24/50/19/4.4(6): John Longe listed two petty constables and fourteen additional constables.

272 John E. Archer, *By a Flash and a Scare: Incendiarism, Animal Maiming and Poaching in East Anglia 1815–70* (Oxford, 1990), p.67.

273 SRO(I) HA24/50/19/4.4(1): a paper, supporting the 'strong' measures taken, circulated from Norfolk in October. By keeping his copy Longe perhaps indicated sympathy with this view.

274 SRO(I) HA24/50/19/4.4(6). About thirty clergy and gentlemen had attended the meeting.

275 Archer, Flash and Scare, p. 67 *et passim*.

276 SRO(I) HA24/50/19/4.4(1): Longe kept his copy.

277 Paul Muskett, 'Agrarian Riots', pp.1–13, especially section VI; Archer, *Flash and Scare*, p.83.

requesting re-inforcement he was told that both Ipswich and Norwich were 'without troops'.[278] Longe and his fellow magistrates had no other effective defence. Such was agricultural distress in East Anglia that unpaid landowners knew they could gain nothing by taking rented farms back into possession.[279] The year 1823 was one of angry meetings and anxious watching. Cobbett, for example, addressed enormous audiences at Norwich and Bungay.[280]

Thereafter, East Anglia was briefly quieter but the poor harvest of 1829 led to resumed machine-breaking and further fires. The attention of historians has focussed on the regional Swing turmoil, but it was fully a year *before* then, at Michaelmas 1829, that twenty-eight defendants were convicted at Ipswich and Woodbridge Quarter Sessions for machine-breaking in four parishes around Coddenham.[281]

As Cobbett correctly prophesied, the uprising of 1830 was more general, affecting over twenty counties in the south and east of England.[282] Suffolk was neither the first to rise nor the worst affected. A county meeting of gentlemen convened at Ipswich in December 1830 led merely to the Lord Lieutenant reporting 'the state of the county'. Their printed posters referred to both aspects: the distress of the labouring population and the suppression of disturbances. Instructions were sent out to local leaders, and eighteen special constables were sworn in from Coddenham alone. Lord Melbourne, Whig Home Secretary, urged magistrates against making weak concessions, which would merely excite expectations and aggravate insubordination.[283]

It was relatively easy to apprehend and bring to justice the leaders of open and concerted disorder. To detect the individual operating under cover of darkness armed with the new lucifer was not. This difficulty was reflected in the scale of rewards offered by royal proclamation: £50 for the capture of rioters, but £500 for the conviction of incendiaries. Even so, any potential informer was dissuaded by the weight of popular opinion in his community. In 1816 and 1822 those convicted had received relatively mild sentences from local justices, responding to general opinion. By contrast, after assize judgments, two arsonists at Diss (just in Norfolk) were hanged. In continued belief that magistrates were too lenient the government appointed Special Commissions, though not in 1831 in Suffolk.

In the ninety courts in which a total of 1,976 Swing rioters were tried nationally, the sentences were diverse. On one analysis of seventy-one cases, a surprisingly high percentage (69 per cent) of accused were acquitted or merely bound over to keep the peace. Eleven per cent were transported. A further 20 per cent were imprisoned. One was sentenced to death.[284] Over a period of two months, sixteen Suffolk parishes had been troubled with demonstrations, rioting, anonymous letters and the insidious activities of the arsonist. The smoke of a burning rick or barn could be seen for many miles, provoking renewed fear of revolution. 'We are almost in the horrors of civil war', J. Barber Scott had written on 24 November 1830 from north Suffolk.[285]

---

278 SRO(I) HA247/5, but accessible in print in *SR* 5(1)(1980), 47–8.

279 SRO(I) HA24/50/19/4.2(1): letter dated 25 Oct. 1822 from Longe's wife, then at Salhouse.

280 John Barber Scott went to hear Cobbett: Mann and Cane, *Home and Abroad*, p.12.

281 Bury and Norwich Post, 29 Oct. 1829. Also Archer, *Flash and Scare*, p.87.

282 Cobbett was acquitted of seditious libel: George Spater, *William Cobbett: the Poor Man's Friend* (Cambridge, 1982), pp.2, 475.

283 SRO(I) HA24/50/19/4.4(1) and (6): 6 December 1830.

284 Hobsbawm and Rude, *Captain Swing*, pp. 308/9 and *passim*.

285 Mann and Cane, *Home and Abroad*, p.15.

Longe, a potential target for attack, grew increasingly anxious in his closing years. Concerted withdrawal of labour and riots at houses of industry continued, as did isolated outbreaks of incendiarism. In late 1831, after writing that fire had been seen late that night, Longe noted a second fire two days later: 'both by incendiaries'.[286] He recorded a farm fire a few yards outside his parish, although conceded that it might have been an accident. There were 'depredations in the night' close to the vicarage. Longe's rebellious young farm-tenant, in dismay at his conditions, was heard to have threatened in violent language 'taking up arms himself'.[287] Longe was in the front line.

Conclusion

If he is to be objective the historian must be aware of his own personal deep-seated beliefs and indeed prejudices, which on church matters are particularly sensitive. Moreover, he must resist attempts to assess the lives of past figures by standards other than those of their time. It is legitimate to compare centuries, but that is a different project. It is legitimate to examine abuses in the church, but the present purpose is to focus on a single parson, remembering that he had committed himself to the timeless core of the Christian gospel.

A rounded assessment of Longe will include some comparison of his style of life with that of his clerical contemporaries in Suffolk. Living in comfortable parsonage-houses in the villages of the county, a significant number of gentlemen-parsons, many sitting as magistrates, were financially secure on their tithes and glebe income. They were distinct from other groupings: the poorer majority of country clergy; the fashionable clerics at ease in cathedral closes; and the growing number of evangelical clerics. Of his particular social layer of rural clergy, Longe may be judged as typical.

To use a different measure, Longe may be compared with those clergymen who revealed much of themselves in published diaries or memoirs. He differed from Parson Woodforde of Norfolk in his higher standard of living, in his family, in his intellectual pursuits and in the extent of his public service. He may have shared antiquarian interests with two Somerset men, Holland and Skinner, but they did not equal his style and expansive outlook. Whereas the timid Jones of Hertfordshire was almost reclusive, Cobbold of Wortham knew and loved his humble villagers in a manner foreign to Longe. Longe had most in common, perhaps, with the Yorkshire clergyman-magistrate, Benjamin Newton. If a rigorous standard of comparison may be admitted from an earlier time, the life of George Herbert (1593–1633) would be an obvious choice. Most handbooks for parish clergy held him out as an ideal, referring to his book *The Country Parson*, re-printed in 1827. Longe would have known this simple guide on rural parochial duties, a model of loving pastoral care and prayer. The saintly early Jacobean observed high ideals indeed and the contrast with Longe is marked.

Parsons like Longe were not so much religious specialists as gentlemen who were additionally ordained to a function and status. The qualities required often related less to spirituality than to the social standards and manners of those educated lay gentlemen who lived upright lives, followed academic and antiquarian interests and were active in public service. Moreover, such rural lay gentlemen regularly

286 Diary: 10–12 Dec. 1831.
287 Diary: 19, 25 May 1833.

and visibly attended their village church, reinforcing their parson's moral teaching. For 'respectable' folk, religion was a bastion of public and community life. Longe ended one of his wartime sermons in words that summed up a shared ethic: 'Subjection to Governors, Peaceableness towards our equals, Gentleness towards Inferiors, Forgiveness of our Enemies, and Prayers to God for their Conversion'.[288]

Despite their church-going example gentry held values that by no means coincided with the gospel ideal. Worldly respectability substitutes for eternal judgment merely the opinion of respectable men. Whilst not forbidding material riches, the Gospel does challenge the prevalent attitude to them. Self-esteem and pedigree – seen in New Testament teaching as irrelevant, if not actual obstacles – were essential constituents of gentlemanly status. One does not expect of gentlemen the Christian virtue of meekness, the turning of the other cheek. The ideal of the English country squire was a tempting but deceptive model for a Georgian parson, for in offering for ordination a man was uniquely exposing himself to public judgment by the high standards of the Christian gospel. At Longe's ordination the bishop addressed questions to him. If put to him again forty years later, how in conscience would he have judged himself? He had not disobeyed his bishop and had consistently given a wholesome example to his flock, teaching from the pulpit, and instructing the young in the catechism. He alone would know how far his private prayer and bible study extended. Where he might feel challenged was in his attachment to the world and the flesh, however they were defined. If the reference to 'flesh' is extended to the traditional sin of gluttony, Longe is open to judgment in the extent of his cellar and hospitality, though specific evidence of consumption is lacking.

In the issue of involvement in 'the world' and indeed theology, Longe's position, held by the majority of clergy in the late 1820s, may be described as orthodox. To be orthodox was to be unsympathetic towards the growing evangelical tendency of concern for what an individual's actions in this world were doing to his immortal soul. Orthodox clergy thought communally of the church as the moral face of the state. In reducing the distinction between his church duties and his public service, Longe was in tune with the eighteenth-century identity of church and state. Then, in the last year of his life, a small group of university academics began to envisage a purer holier and more separated church, immune from 'interference' by politicians. Those subscribing to the Oxford Movement valued the mysterious and numinous. They elevated priestliness in lifestyle and dress and thus confined it within the church. They criticised clergy for sitting as magistrates, a view painful for Longe with his extended service.

In considering human relationship to the world, Christians have always held a range of interpretations between involvement and withdrawal, public and private. The very word 'world' has two meanings almost opposite, one positive and affirming, the other suspicious of all that draws people to value material things more highly than their creator. Over the centuries, only a few ascetic recluses have withdrawn from material things; the historical norm has been a whole community sharing in public worship. The moral behaviour that Longe preached was to be exercised by the whole community and within the world, not in a different ('godly') sphere over against it. For him the divine was to be found in ordinary things and ordinary people, which is why the church is to serve the world, rather than existing for the religious. He was not, of course, nostalgic for the peasant priest toiling among his people on

288 SRO(I) HA/24/50/19/4.5(3).

his glebe, as were both Oliver Goldsmith and William Cobbett. Nevertheless, in his different way, Longe too was bridging the gap between the everyday world and the timeless truths of the Christian gospel. His orthodox 'involvement' philosophy, no longer fashionable in his last years, was both honourable and sustainable. A simple visible example within the church building of Longe's theological outlook was the focal position of pulpit and lectern in the people's nave. By contrast, for those attracted by the Oxford Movement, the priestly sanctuary would be revered as the holiest place. But Longe was instituted not to a church sanctuary, nor to a gathering of the like-minded, but to the cure of *every* soul within the parish boundary, for their total welfare. This classical theory, however little observed by 1830, was a grand concept.

As magistrate and wealthy gentleman, a natural leader of paternalistic style, Longe believed that rights of property should be respected and that the law should be obeyed. Typical of his time, he exercised charitable help for the poor selectively in favour of the 'deserving'. He could share a particular occasion with his people (tithe-payers, farm-tenants with their wives, or those 'beating the bounds') but each knew his place and the hierarchical distance was undisturbed. The concept was shared that he should uphold the moral code by word and example, encourage stability within society, govern his household, and supervise his curates. Some would add that he should keenly defend his own rights, rents and tithes. Longe's substantial income gave him a high degree of independence. He was free of pressure from any patron (for he was his own), almost free of oversight by church authority and not financially beholden to his flock as was a dissenting minister. How he conducted himself was a matter for himself. Independence led some clergy to become eccentric but Longe was not one of them.

In matters of religious diversity Longe's attitude was clear. Confident that he and his colleagues were preaching the true gospel, he could make no meaningful relationships with critical evangelicals. To local Protestant Dissenters he seems to have conceded freedom to worship, so long as they were 'quiet', and to have disregarded any challenge to the established church that two dissenting chapels were presenting locally. In line with his eighteenth-century mind-set, his hostility to Roman Catholics had a strong constitutional element that he held to, but perceptions were changing around him.

One test of a parish clergyman relates to his performance of a specific function. It is a truism that at this time parishioners expected very little. It is doubly inappropriate to transfer to the Georgian age the Protestant work ethic that confined both earlier Puritans and later Victorians. Function was, all too often, reduced to the conduct of services, a duty easily delegated. Longe did at least take seriously his responsibility to choose and supervise his curates. When ready to retire, Longe appointed a second curate and prepared his own son Robert to succeed him. He fulfilled his function. Secondly, the parson may be judged by his personal qualities and leadership within the parish community. In Coddenham (if not in Crowfield) factors combined to ensure that Longe was accepted as head of the community. Whereas Squire Middleton was remote, Longe lived in the village for thirty-seven years. He involved himself in village affairs and his dominant style was as visible as his parsonage-house. No-one else rivalled this.

For Englishmen, one of the unifying factors between 1792 and 1815 was a sense of 'Englishness'. In Longe's early ordained years, this was embodied by the symbolic figure of John Bull. This universally recognised patriotic character was the construct of cartoonists and their literary counterparts. How far may Longe be justifiably identified with John Bull? In physical appearance, we may imagine Longe (like John Bull) as portly and solid of frame and of ruddy countenance, if only from his diet. Longe, like John Bull, was reliable and solemn rather than brilliant. The very name Bull denoted all that is tenacious and combative, qualities demonstrated by Longe in his conflicts. One would expect John Bull both to engage in public service and to enjoy the easy atmosphere of the gentlemen's club, preferring dining to dancing. Handel was his music. That was Longe precisely. Distrusting mystery and emotion, direct and uncomplicated, his was the Anglicanism of conservative temperament. Originally, when John Bull was used in patriotic mode in Government-sponsored newspapers, Longe readily identified with him. No one group, however, had a monopoly of this fictional character and the position was soon reversed. John Bull came to be portrayed as resentful of government and its taxes, by cartoonists who themselves were enthusiastically critical. Attractive as the comparison undoubtedly is prior to 1815, it ceases to enhance our understanding of Longe during the later part of his life. He was no longer the cartoonists' John Bull.

John Longe, far from being a gentleman of leisure, devoted much time and energy over some thirty-five years to leading roles in public service. He was known in his part of Suffolk as a staunch and reliable Tory, not shirking the lead in time of social crisis, keen on educating the poor and a genial dinner companion. The more cultured would know of his interest in antiquarian studies, reading and music. If he stood out from those who were active in public service, it was in the duration and intensity of his involvement, qualities characteristic of him. Within parish life, it was both by the accident of events and by his own temperament that Longe stood at a paternal remove from most of his parishioners. Though sharing his cure of souls with a succession of assistant curates, he retained oversight. By the standards of the age, as distinct from later more spiritual decades, Longe met his parishioners' modest expectations of their vicar. If that is to be the historian's measure, Longe did not fall short.

THE LONGE FAMILY

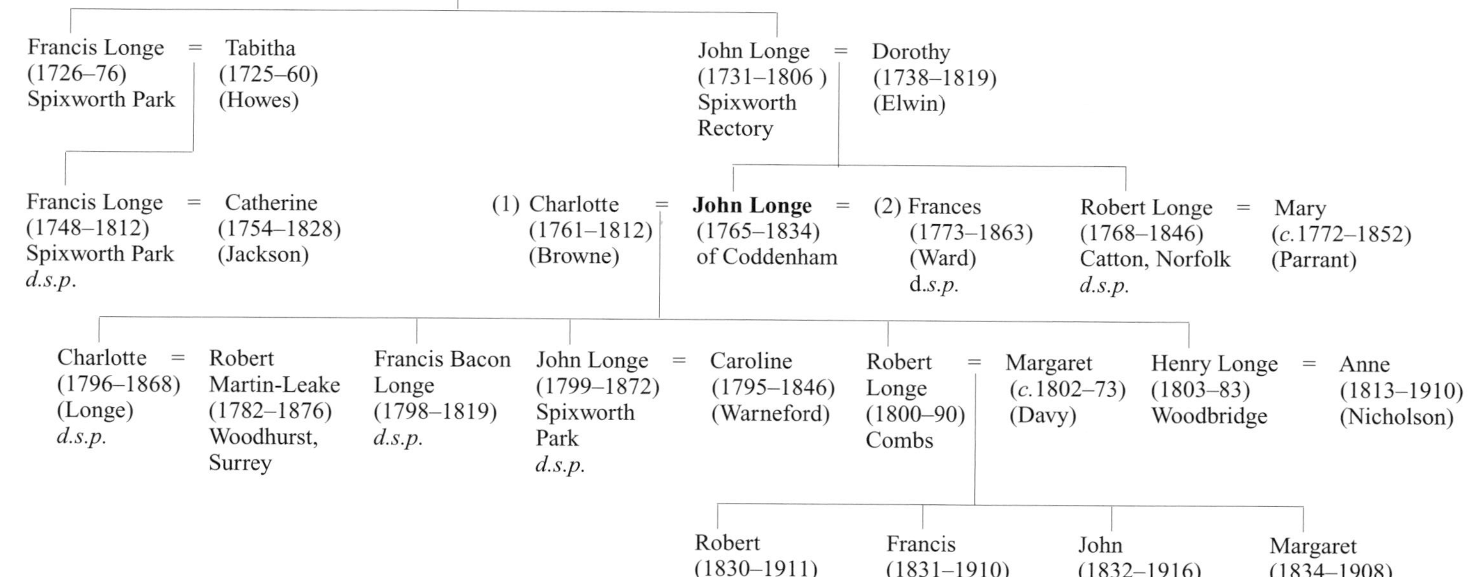

Notes

See also notes on people below.

Brackets indicate maiden surname.

The place indicated is the main connection during Longe's lifetime.

There was a distant connection of the Longes with the Norfolk Bacon family. Robert Longe, John Longe's great-great-grandfather, in 1656 married Elizabeth, the daughter of Sir Francis Bacon, kt (*c.*1587–1657), Judge of the Court of King's Bench.

Not shown are three of John Longe's children who died in infancy, 1792–4.

Only those grandchildren of John Longe born in his lifetime are included.

THE WARD FAMILY

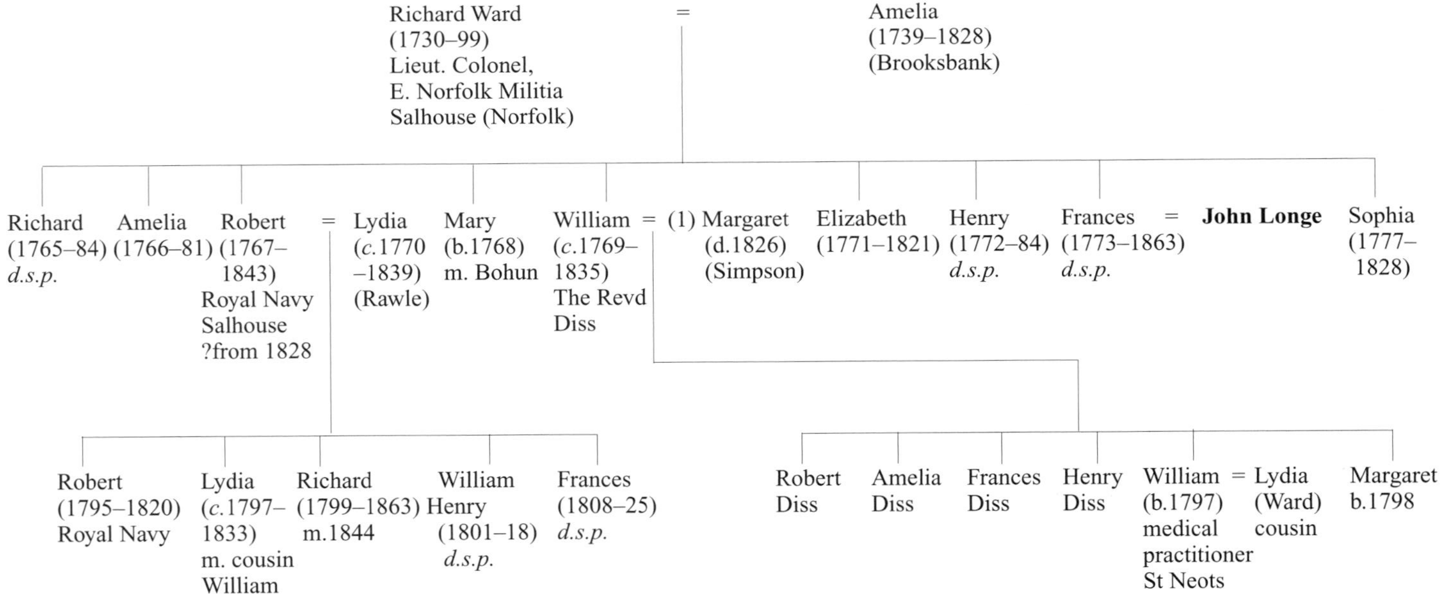

Unrelated: the Revd Dr James Ward DD of Coltishall, 1766–1842 (see following notes).

Notes to the Ward family tree, mostly from John Longe's Diaries

Salhouse Hall, the seat of Col. Richard Ward, was four miles from Spixworth rectory, the home of John Longe's father. They were contemporaries and intimate friends, as Longe was to state in his obituary note on Ward in the *Gentleman's Magazine*, 1799. The year 1798 was a time of deploying forces, in readiness to resist the French invasion that was realistically expected. The 68-year-old Richard Ward was stationed in the Ipswich area, in his capacity as a senior officer of the East Norfolk Militia. He was in contact with both the sons of his friend Longe. Robert, the younger, was an officer in the same unit. It is therefore not surprising that he dined several times that year with John Longe the diarist, newly installed in the vicarage at Coddenham. This is not the first mention of the Ward family in Longe's diary, for he had received a call from Richard's son William in January 1796, who was curate of three parishes in Norfolk.[1]

Some twenty years passed and Col. Ward's daughter Frances, then in her forties, in 1817 married John Longe (a widower), on his fifty-second birthday. She had until then continued to live at Salhouse with her widowed mother, Amelia, who herself is believed to have stayed on at Salhouse for nearly thirty years widowhood. Later, during the years 1826 and 1827, Mrs Ward's health caused considerable concern, and indeed she died aged eighty-eight in the following year.

Frances had no children of her own but had many nieces and nephews. Her older naval brother Robert (at Salhouse Hall until his death in 1843) had five children, of whom only two survived beyond 1825. Of these, her nephew Richard was not to marry until later but Lydia married her cousin (son of the curate William, also named William), a medical practitioner in St Neots. Frances' clerical brother William stayed in Norfolk. In addition to contact with him and his son the doctor, Frances received visits at Coddenham from five other Wards 'of Diss', four of whom were William's children, though the relationship of Robert is at present unproven. In the years 1826 to 1833 they would have been in their late twenties and thirties.

The references in the diary are:

2 June 1826	Miss Margaret Ward, the youngest (who is known from the Diss parish register to be the daughter of William and Margaret);
15 June 1826	Two of Mr William Ward's daughters, not named;
20 June 1827	Mr William Ward (recently a widower) with his two daughters Amelia and Frances;
22 April 1831	Miss Amelia Ward from Diss;
1 Dec. 1831	Two Miss Wards from Diss;
8 May 1833	Miss M. Ward with Mr Robert Ward;[2]
24–31 July 1833	Miss M. Ward and Miss F. Ward returned to Diss;
11, 16 Nov. 1833	Mr Henry Ward and his sister Amelia Ward of Diss.

The Revd Dr James Ward DD was unrelated to the Norfolk Wards, having origins in Hampshire. After serving as a senior chaplain with the Honourable East India Company in Bengal he settled in Coltishall, just north of Spixworth, with his wife and daughter. He is the 'Dr Ward' of the diary. See map of East Norfolk, on page 252.

1 William (*c*.1769–1835) was later in Diss. He served two parishes a few miles north of Diss: Bunwell and Carlton Lode nearby and also Swainsthorpe just south of Norwich.

2 Probably her brother. Her cousin had died in 1820.

TIME LINE, LOCAL AND NATIONAL

1765	15 April: birth of John Longe (JL) at Spixworth (Norfolk).
1775–	JL at school in Bungay, and then Norwich Grammar School.
1780	Nicholas Bacon (Shrubland Park) married Anne Marie Browne.
1783/87	JL undergraduate at Cambridge: Corpus Christi, then Trinity College.
1785	Anne Marie, wife of Nicholas Bacon, died.
1787	JL ordained deacon, curate to father at Spixworth.
1788	Nicholas Bacon inherited Shrubland on death of brother John, and sold part.
1789	Charlotte Browne's father died. JL ordained priest.
1790	1 January: JL became Bacon's curate at Coddenham-cum-Crowfield. 5 November: JL married Bacon's sister-in-law, Charlotte Browne.
1793	JL instituted as vicar of Henley, near Coddenham. Gipping Navigation opened (though incomplete). War with France began.
1794	JL's sermon at primary visitation (Ipswich), subsequently published. By this year, three children had died in infancy.
1796	**Pocket-book diary**. Daughter Charlotte born. The Revd Nicholas Bacon died, aged sixty-four.
1797	**Pocket-book diary** (extracts only). Institution of JL (+ induction and reading-in) to Coddenham-cum-Crowfield. Will of Nicholas Bacon upheld after Court case, and probate.
1798	**Pocket-book diary**. Alarm of invasion, preparations. Battle of Aboukir Bay (Nile). Son Francis born.
1798/99	Dispute between JL and Kilderbee over bond repayment.
1799	Son John born.
1799/1801	Dispute over glebe (from Bacon's time).
1800	Son Robert born.
1801	Start of dispute over roadside waste and right of way.
1802	Peace of Amiens.
1803	JL took oath as JP. Son Henry born. Napoleonic War resumed; invasion preparations renewed.
1805	Invasion threat lifted. Battle of Trafalgar.
1805–8	Improvements to interior of St Mary's church, Coddenham.
1806	Death of William Pitt and Charles James Fox. Primary Visitation (and ?Confirmation). JL's father died, aged eighty-one.
1810	School numbers raised from thirty to fifty.
1811	Start of Servants' Wages Book.

1811–12	Ipswich–Helmingham (etc.) Turnpike trust formed.
1812	Suffolk Society founded for education of poor (National Society).
	JL's cousin Francis died, aged sixty-four.
	JL's first wife Charlotte died, aged fifty-one.
1813	Primary Visitation and Confirmation.
	Naval engagement of Broke of the Shannon, Middleton's son-in-law.
	Charitable registration of school trust (1753 and 1791).
1815	Waterloo and peace.
	Riot at Gosbeck.
1816	East Anglian disturbances and riots.
	Stopping up of Pipps Way.
	School put into connection with National Society, and Madras system.
1816–23	JL researching Crowfield tithe on hay.
1817	JL installed church organ at St Mary's, Coddenham.
	Loan to Mrs C. Longe, by sale of trust investments.
	JL's second marriage, to Frances Ward of Salhouse (Norfolk).
1818	Founding of Coddenham Saving Bank.
1818–23	JL's opposition to the rating of his tithes.
1819	JL's mother died, aged eighty-one.
	JL's son Francis died, aged twenty.
1820	Primary Visitation and Confirmation.
1820–	Litigation with Birch concerning a bond.
1820–22	Arbitration between Middleton and JL over waste and right of way.
1820–23	Suffolk Pitt Club.
1821	Census Return.
1822	JL complaining of rating of tithes.
	Final judgment concerning Crowfield tithe on hay.
	Agrarian discontent, East Anglian disturbances.
	JL's daughter Charlotte married Robert Martin Leake.
1822–4	Roman finds at Coddenham (road, urn etc.).
1823	Croasdaile's conflict with JL, correspondence about Sleorgin's will trust.
	Dissenting Meeting House erected in Coddenham.
	Summons against JL for refusal to pay rates on tithes.
1824	Dissenting Meeting House erected in Crowfield.
1825	JL's contribution to *Gentleman's Magazine* on Roman finds.
	Longe's son Robert ordained priest.
1826	**Pocket-book diary**.
	Founding of Suffolk General Hospital, Bury St Edmunds.
	Barlee case, Chelmsford.
	Croasdaile (junior) to asylum in Norwich.
1826–7	Correspondence on unconsecrated status of Shrubland Chapel.
1826–	JL in dispute with son-in-law about future of family trust.
1827	**Pocket-book diary**.
	JL's son Henry ordained priest.
	Primary Visitation and Confirmation.
1828	JL's son Robert married Margaret Davy.
	JL's cousin's widow Catherine died, aged seventy-four.
1828–30	Legal negotiations for JL's son John to take Spixworth estate.
1829	JL's son John married Caroline Warneforde.

	Death of Sir William Middleton, 1st baronet.
	Catholic Emancipation Act.
1830	Swing Riots and counter-preparations.
	Correspondence with Major Leake.
	Repairs to chancel of St Mary's, Coddenham.
1830	Settlement of litigation with Birch.
1830/1834	Partition of trust assets planned, effective after death of JL.
1831	**Pocket-book diary**.
1831–2	'Public Records' obtained for Ipswich Town Hall.
1831–2	Coddenham church: glass with armorial bearings installed in east window.
1832	Formation of Ipswich Literary Institution.
	Parliamentary Reform Act.
1833	**Pocket-book diary**.
	Dispute over tithe status of demesne lands in Barham parish.
	Bosmere and Claydon House of Industry Act.
1834	Will of JL.
	Death of JL on 3 March.
	Arrangements between JL's children, and winding-up of his estate.
	Robert Longe instituted to benefice and moved into vicarage.

EDITORIAL NOTE

Longe's diary was not a literary or philosophical journal, but a daily record of events written by hand in printed pocket-books. Apart from a few reminders of future commitments, he was summarising the past: meetings with people, actions taken and business to be remembered. The core material comprises six annual pocket-books, here described as 'diaries', in which Longe jotted down such matters, often laconically.[1] Selected entries published some seventy-five years ago survive too from a seventh diary, believed to be since lost, and an exact copy of these entries as published has been added.[2]

The gaps between years are substantial. The first group dates from 1796, 1797 and 1798, when Longe was in his early thirties, whereas the second group (1826, 1827, 1831 and 1833) runs to within a few weeks of his death. This main gap between the groups has to some extent been bridged by including in this volume a transcription of Longe's 'Servants Wages Book' of 1811–23, which casts more light on his domestic life than is suggested by his title. Some other original material has also been transcribed to clarify particular aspects of his life and his home.

The main weakness presented by these sources relates to what is not here (the gaps), and the danger of drawing speculative conclusions to cover them. The silences are of different kinds. First, Longe chose to limit himself largely to facts and events, rather than confiding opinions and feelings. Then, as stated, primary material is known to be lacking for substantial periods. Thirdly, an unknown quantity of material has inevitably been lost to us by deliberate censorship or casual loss or destruction in the past. Of detectable destruction we know only of a single page cut from one pocket-book.[3]

Diary pocket-books (plate 8)

The six pocket-books are similar, though the early ones are not identical with those from 1826 to 1833. Each measures about 4 inches by 6 inches, and contains much printed information. All were printed in Ipswich. The one for 1796, from Shave and Jackson, is called 'Forster's Suffolk Gentleman's Memorandum Book or Pocket Ledger'. Those from the later years are entitled 'The Gentleman's Pocket Book' and are printed by R. Deck, priced 2s. 6d. and 4s. The later ones boast 'every local information connected with the four counties (Suffolk, Norfolk, Essex and Cambridgeshire) … accurately detailed'. The extent of the printed material in 1833 was forty-seven pages before the diary pages and twenty-one pages thereafter. There

1 SRO(I) HA24/50/19/4.3(1) to (6).

2 The printed primary source is *East Anglian Miscellany* 26, III and IV (1932), nos.8783, 8790, 8794 and 8799. The transcriptions of selected entries from the 1797 diary were originally contributed to the *East Anglian Daily Times*, but are now readily accessible in this bound re-print, a quarterly journal kept on the open shelves at SRO(I).

3 The missing page is the *recto* (25 June to 1 July 1827) and the *verso* of the following week. No evidence has survived of the material removed, who cut it out, when or why.

are a few blank pages for notes. In all the pocket-books the left page of each opening of the diary itself, for 'Appointments &c.', is ruled into the seven days of the week, with Monday first. The right page has a week number (1 to 53), and is ruled as a cash account with columns: left ('received') and right ('paid').

Longe wrote in ink, usually fairly legibly. He used the left page day by day as intended, for engagements, social events and often a short weather report. On the right, he wrote across the page, disregarding both the stated purpose and the cash columns. He dated or marked his entries on that page, the content being sometimes independent of the opposite page, occasionally in continuation, and sometimes in partial repetition or expansion. He tended to use the right page for substantial financial transactions, such as rent receipts, for notes of correspondence and memoranda on matters he expected to refer to again. As a simple example, a call from his medical adviser Mr Beck would be noted on the left page as an event, and might be repeated on the right page as an aid to checking his bill when received.

In this volume, the convention adopted in transcribing is to add any text from the right page for each day immediately after the text of the left page, neither attempting harmonisation nor omitting repetition, and without marking the transition. A fresh line has been used in the transcript where the sense seems to be improved for the modern reader, or to avoid an unhelpful run-over, especially of a short phrase or sentence. Most of the diarist's deletions, editorially marked, appear simply to relate to entries originally written in the wrong date. In transcribing, some underlining in the original text has been omitted as judged likely to have been made by a later hand.

The days of the week are not specifically named in this transcript, but are made obvious by a line break after each Sunday, which for the printer is the last day of the week. The week-number from the diary is inserted on the right side before the Monday transcript, but the repeated word 'week' has been omitted.

Upper-case initial letters, so much a feature of the period, have in the great majority of cases been reduced in the transcript to lower case. The convenience to the modern reader is thought to out-weigh the loss of period flavour. Original spellings have been retained, but modern punctuation introduced, except in the rare cases where questionable meaning might be imposed. Abbreviations have been extended without comment where obvious. Each pocket-book transcript has been introduced by an editorial note in italics.

Other documents than the diaries

A series of record items (pp.171–227) is transcribed to provide further information about Longe's life. Each is preceded by a brief explanatory note. On Longe's church life, a catalogue of sermons gives a flavour of the teaching he imparted; his report on Coddenham-cum-Crowfield follows. Then, turning to his home life, there is a transcript of the servants' wages book, mentioned above, accompanied by some additional material relating to domestic servants. A group of four items then sheds further light on physical aspects of Longe's household. These are followed by a summary of Longe's will and estate account. All these items have been selected from the substantial primary material listd in the bibliography below.

To free the text of the introduction, a number of appendices of different types have been added at pp.229–251 below. None is a transcript of Longe's writing, except that one is of mixed composition, placing a small amount of transcribed material on local dissenters alongside a summary of factual data with editorial commentary, the two being clearly distinguished from each other by the use of italics.

Cross-referencing

The style of the diary has dictated the number of footnotes. The number of people Longe names in his diary has led to a section of notes on people (pp.260–284) somewhat extended in total but individually brief. A glossary has been provided and a timeline, to give context and in response to the gaps between pocket-books. The introduction carries footnotes rather different in style, to provide cross-referencing to relevant entries in both the transcribed material and the appendices. It is however considered less helpful to refer so fully in the opposite direction, since any overview of a particular topic in the introduction is necessarily brief, and a relevant index is available below. In general, some repetition has been accepted as preferable to excessive cross-referencing. Only in rare cases have foot-notes been used to draw particular attention to explanation in the glossary, timeline, and notes on people. The ordered layout of those sections, supplemented where necessary by use of the indices, is thought to be sufficient for the reader.

General conventions

< >	deletions legible in the original
[*deleted*]	deletions rendered illegible
[*illeg.*]	illegible in the original
[*blank*]	empty space in the original
[*?*]	transcript reading of next word or number uncertain
[*sic*]	example of other editorial insertions

THE DIARY

DIARY OF 1796

To achieve prosperity and status in the late eighteenth-century Anglican church required family connection, a suitable marriage, or a personable character brought to the notice of a patron. This was an age when many a rich patron advanced the careers of young men, and there are scores of instances of preferment and of inheritance other than by blood descent. John Longe is an example of such a rise. He was born on 15 April 1765 in the parsonage at Spixworth, north of Norwich, where his father was resident rector, and his father's elder brother (Francis) held the substantial family estate. The Longe family can be traced back in Norfolk to at least 1485, and a Longe ancestor bought the estate at Spixworth about 1685. John's mother, Dorothy Elwin of Booton, was from Norfolk gentry too. His father held the consolidated livings of Reymerston and Hackford and also Horsham St Faith (all in Norwich diocese) and was from 1760 a royal chaplain, but he stated in the Visitation Return of 1794 that he 'served no other church besides Spixworth' (see map of East Norfolk, p.252).

After a period at Bungay Grammar School, Longe attended Norwich Grammar School (Mr Valpy's). He went up to Cambridge, first to Corpus Christi College (St Bene'ts) and then migrating to Trinity from where he graduated BA in 1787. He was admitted deacon in Norwich cathedral at Michaelmas that year and licensed to serve a curacy with his father at Spixworth, for £30 a year. His college confirmed in standard terms that he had diligently applied himself to good and useful learning, lived soberly and regularly amongst them and to the best of their knowledge never held or maintained any doctrine or tenet contrary to the Church of England. Either because he was not twenty-four until that year, or because he was not required for sacramental duties, John was not ordained priest until December 1789. He was then ready to seek another curacy.

He was recommended by the Revd Mr Reeve, his former schoolmaster at Bungay, to the Revd Nicholas Bacon, vicar of Coddenham-cum-Crowfield also in Suffolk. Longe entered upon the curacy in 1790, financially poor, but with prospects through his family and education. On his arrival in Coddenham, Longe was within seven years of enjoying, by a series of events and chances, one of the highest incomes among members of the Suffolk clergy, by obtaining one of the richest livings there and inheriting by marriage a substantial private income.

Back in 1775, the Bacon family, whose seat since about 1600 had been Shrubland Park near Coddenham, comprised three unmarried siblings. As estate owner, the Revd John Bacon, a bachelor, lived at the new Palladian mansion designed for him by James Paine. A mile north lived his younger brother, the Revd Nicholas Bacon, incumbent of the two family livings of Coddenham-cum-Crowfield and Barham, the latter served by his curate resident there. His Coddenham parsonage-house was a fine newly erected square red-brick house in an elevated position above the village and church. In May 1775, on a visit to the neighbourhood, the diarist Parson Woodforde took tea at Shrubland Hall, the home of John Bacon; in describing his host, Woodforde added that the 'great misfortune' was that 'the family of the Bacons have always been mad.' Next day, visiting Nicholas Bacon nearby, Woodforde described the 'lately built' vicarage as 'a very pretty house indeed'.

In his middle years, Nicholas Bacon married, but his wife Anna Marie Browne died in 1785 without children. Her sister Charlotte, thirty years younger than Nicholas, was a favourite of his, and when her father was dying, Nicholas assured Charlotte that he would always be a parent to her. He made a will, leaving to her his small estate, but when his brother John died shortly afterwards, all the family property devolved to Nicholas. He sold the Shrubland Hall and about a thousand acres to his neighbour, Mr William Middleton of Crowfield Hall, who moved to Shrubland. Nicholas did however retain a few farms and the advowsons of Coddenham-cum-Crowfield and Barham.

John Longe arrived in Coddenham as curate on New Year's Day 1790. Within ten months he and Charlotte were married at Coddenham church. The ceremony was conducted by Nicholas who placed a very substantial sum in trust for Charlotte. They took a house nearby at Bramford and continued to spend much time with Nicholas, who was not in good health. Through his influence with the dean and chapter in Norwich, Longe obtained the modest living of Henley, a parish of thirty-one houses adjacent to Coddenham. As there was no parsonage house he rented a property there. Although no longer involved in church duties at Coddenham, he and Charlotte continued in close social contact with Nicholas Bacon. In a fresh will Nicholas Bacon put a further substantial sum in trust for Charlotte and willed three farms and his residuary estate to Longe for life, entailed to Charlotte's children. He gave the advowson of Coddenham-cum-Crowfield absolutely to Longe and thus the right to present himself immediately to the living. It is unclear whether Mr Bacon made the beneficiaries aware of this great generosity in his lifetime.

In the first five years of marriage Charlotte Longe gave birth to three children, all of whom died in infancy. At the beginning of 1796, at the age of thirty, John Longe had a modest benefice, plus income from his wife's capital, but otherwise only expectations. The year 1796 was to fall into two dramatically different parts, the watershed being the 26 August 1796.

Diary

1

1 Jan. At Coddenham. I spent the forenoon in pruning the plantations, & in attending the replanting those parts which failed.[1]
We returned to Henley to dinner.

2 I took a ride to Needham.

3 m.[2] At home.

2

4 Jan. We spent the day at Coddenham, I in assisting to regulate the plantations.
We returned in the evening. Mr Bacon paid us £50.

5 I walked out a-shooting. Riches & son here 1 day, only the weather

---

[1] John Longe was working at the vicarage, being groomed to succeed (as did indeed happen).

[2] The abbreviations m. and a. stand for morning and afternoon prayer, though the latter was strictly 'evensong'. They were probably inserted by the diarist at the beginning of the year. Having only Henley to serve that year, Longe would normally alternate the two services on successive Sundays. He made no subsequent note.

becoming wet.[3] A letter from my brother informing us of a fire which happened at Purfleet, where he was quartered.[4] Letter from my father. Settled with Forsdike his last year's carpenter's bill £4 5s. 2d.
Expence of stalling stable was £5. 16s. 6d.
Memorandum. I paid half the expence, Mr Theobald the rest.[5]

6 A very wet morning.

7 I attended a meeting at the Barham House.[6]
Messrs Kirby, Theobald, Ripper, & Leeds dined here.

8 I rode to Coddenham. Savage & others employed by Mr Theobald in making a plantation by the stackyard, with plants from Bramford.
My brother left Purfleet.

9 Mr Bacon called. Riches & son here 1 day.

10 a. I preached at Coddenham for Mr Pettiward.[7]

3

11 Jan. At home. extremely mild weather, south wind. I wrote to my father & brother. Riches & son two days. My brother arrived at Spixworth.

12 We went to Ipswich & returned to dinner.
Mr Theobald spent the afternoon with us.

13 Wet day, at home. I wrote to Jos. Church.

14 I rode to Bramford, & called at Mr G. Capper's.

15 I walked out a shooting.

16 I rode to Needham. Mr Bacon drank tea with us.
A letter from my father & brother, & a turkey came by the mail.

17 m. I preached at Hemingstone.

4

18 Jan. We spent the day at Coddenham.

19 At home. Mr Goodwin put a pot upon the kitchen chimney.
Riches & son here 2 days.

20 I spent the morning at Coddenham in planting, & regulating the plantations.
Messrs Bacon & Pettiward dined here. I wrote to my father.

21 I attended a meeting at the House of Industry.
We sent a barrel of oysters to Spixworth.

22 Book Club. I dined there. Mr Bacon did not go.[8]
We slept at Coddenham tonight.

23 We returned home to dinner.

---

3 Riches was a gardener, probably Mr Bacon's, helping out at Henley. He and other family members are frequently mentioned in the diary: see index.

4 John Longe's brother Robert, at this time a bachelor aged twenty-seven, was an officer in the East Norfolk Militia, sometimes stationed in Ipswich as well as Purfleet, Essex, where fire was a constant concern at the huge gunpowder store. He lived in Norfolk, probably on the Spixworth family estate.

5 Mr Theobald of Henley Hall was Longe's landlord. On taking up the living of Henley in 1793, which did not include a parsonage-house, Longe had rented a property from him.

6 Before becoming vicar of Coddenham, Longe was already involved in the supervision of Barham house of industry. See Appendix J.

7 Longe took two services that day, deputising for the curate at Coddenham and returning the three or so miles to Henley (his own church) for 'evening' prayer.

8 Coddenham Book Club: Longe was an active member for the rest of his life. It met monthly at the Crown Inn in the centre of the village. Magistrates' petty sessions and turnpike trustees also met there.

24 a. At home. Extreme high wind.

5

25 Jan. A wet day, at home. Very stormy weather.

26 We went to Ipswich & returned to dinner. Very stormy & extreme high wind. Savage, lad, &c. employed this week in making the plantations at the approach to the house, by Mr Theobald.

27 I dined at Mr Pettiward's and met Mr Scott, Bacon, Mann, &c.

28 Mr William Ward called, & walked with me to Coddenham, where we dined, it being very stormy. A letter from my father.

29 Mr Bacon called here & I accompanyed him to Ipswich. He dined with us.
Memorandum. My brother went to London on account of his business with Mr Tryon this week.

30 I rode to Stowmarket, to speak to Nurse Abel at Mr Marriott's.[9]
Savage & lad at work today for me in levelling the vicarage fence.

31 At home. A great deal of very high wind, & heavy rains this week.

6

1 Feb. I went to Norwich by the mail & reached Spixworth by dinner & found my father, mother & brother well. I paid Forster's Bill £ 4 1s. 2d.
& Smith's ditto £ 2 5s. 0d.
3rd paid Beck's Bill £ 5 17s. 6d.
£12 3s. 8d.

2 Mr Jos. Church came to us to breakfast. We all walked out a-shooting.

3 Church, Robert & I went to Norwich, & returned to dinner.

4 All went a-shooting.

5 Wet morning.

6 Jos. Church left Spixworth. I left Spixworth & returned to Henley tonight by Forster's coach.

7 At home. A heavy rain tonight.

7

8 Feb. At home. Mr Bacon called here.
Paid Scott for 6 rodds of wand fence
against the Vicarage garden, at 4d½ per rodd: 2s. 3d. Memorandum. I owe him for 400 wands for which he is to have 1s. 6d per hundred. Paid June 5th.

9 Shrove Tuesday. I rode to Mr Bacon's, & returned to dinner.

10 Ash Wednesday. Prayers in the morning. We brewed a double brewing this week.[10]

11 I rode to Ipswich & returned, & called at Mr Kirby's.

12 At home. I wrote to my father & brother.

13 At home.

14 m. At home. Cold seasonable weather this week.

8

15 Feb. I took a ride to Needham.

16 <We went to Ipswich & returned to dinner.>

---

9 Longe was perhaps engaging Nurse Abel as midwife, since she attended for the baby Charlotte, born September 1796. Three of their children had earlier died in infancy.

10 Longe brewed normally twice a year. Double, probably, to produce a secondary 'small' beer.

I dined at Mr Pettiward's, met Mr Bacon, Kirby, &c.
Parker at work levelling the vicarage garden in front.

17 We went to Ipswich & returned to dinner.
Parker at work felling pollards in the churchyard.

18 I attended the House of Industry. We went to Coddenham.
Mr Pettiward dined there. Parker at work the rest of the week, riving billets. Paid him for this work, March 3rd.

19 Book Club. I dined there.

20 We returned to Henley in the evening.

21 a. At home.

9

22 Feb. I took a walk.

23 I took a ride to Bramford. Mr Kirby called. A letter from my father.

24 At home.

25 I dined at Mr Bacon's, met Messrs Kirby, Mann, Pettiward, & Leeds & Ripper.

26 At home.

27 At home. Stormy weather.
I received a parcel of cloaths from Forster's this week.

28 m. At home. Very cold , & frosty.

10

29 Feb. At home. Very cold wind with frost & sleet.
1½ chaldron of coals brought by Morgan.

1 March I walked to Mr Drury's. A parcel & letters from my father & brother.

2 At home. I wrote to my father.

3 At the House of Industry.

4 At home. Riches here 2 days.
A letter from Mr G. Smythe at Harleston, about his play.

5 I rode to Coddenham. I wrote to my brother.

6 a. At home.

11

7 March A very cold & snowy day. 1 chaldron of coals brought by Brook.

8 I walked to Coddenham and dined there. Mr Lynch there.
Mr Bedwell's people carting gravel today.
Forsdike & men putting up pales at the vicarage.

9 Fast Day. A very respectable congregation at church.[11]

10 Miss C. Acton & Miss Barry called. Messrs Bacon & Lynch dined here.
Forsdike & men putting up pales at the vicarage.

11 I caught a violent cold. We went to dinner at Coddenham, & slept there.
Met Messrs Lynch, Mann & Pettiward. Forsdike compleated the paling.

12 We returned home to dinner.

13 m. At home.

12

14 March At home busy in the garden, sowing annuals &c.
Riches & son here 3 days.

---

[11] Some fast days were in the liturgical calendar (notably Lent) and others decreed nationally, for example in times of war or epidemic.

15 At home, in the garden. Charlotte made a morning visit at Bramford. The[*?*]Suffolk [*?*]Pan sown with oats this week. A letter from my father.
I sent Maurice's Ind[*ustrial*] [*?*]An[*nua*]l to my father & we wrote to him.

16 At home in the garden. I got two pots of cucumber plants from Mr Brand's gardiner.

17 Messrs Pettiward & Marriott dined here. I answered Mr Smythe's letter.

18 Book Club. We went to Coddenham. I & Mr Bacon dined at the Club.
Memorandum. I paid Mr Trotman 8 shillings being my share of the expence of an haunch of venison last September.[12]

19 We returned to dinner home. A letter from my father.

20 a. [*no other entry*]

13

21 March We dined in Ipswich, & got the new steps put to the carriage.[13]
1 chaldron coals by Brook.
I received a pair of overalls from Farr, Norwich.

22 At home.

23 I attended the Association meeting at Needham.[14]

24 I attended the previous meeting at the Barham House.[15]
My brother got here to dinner, upon his new mare.
A letter from Jos. Church.

25 Good Friday. Prayers in the morning. My brother & I took a walk.

26 My brother left us. I accompanied him as far as Stratford, on his way to Braintree.[16]

27 Easter Sunday. m. Sacrament here.
A fall of snow last night. Very cold day.

14

28 March A fall of snow again last night, and very winterly weather today.

29 I dined at Mr Bacon's, & we attended the election of children into the Coddenham Charity School.[17]

30 I attended a general meeting at the House of Industry to determine the mode of relieving the poor. My mare shod.

31 I attended the quarterly meeting of the House of Industry, at Needham.

1 April I attended the meeting at the House of Industry for discharging the account of the last month for meal.[18]

2 At home. I wrote to Mr J. Church.

---

12 Venison was highly prized to place before dinner guests, suggesting that one had received a gift from a noble landowner, since it did not go on the market generally.

13 To keep a carriage, with associated costs of coach-horses, coachman and groom, was a visible sign of status, which many clergy felt unable to afford. For travel and transport, see Appendix E.

14 Local associations for prosecuting felonies were widely formed at this time, though often of short duration. Before the existence of professional police, they shared the cost of obtaining evidence from informers and bringing offenders to trial. See footnotes 241–4 in the introduction.

15 The 'previous': a small committee met to prepare for the general meeting that followed (30 March).

16 John Longe's brother was rejoining his Militia unit.

17 The school trustees selected children to fill vacancies. Numbers were limited to fifteen boys and fifteen girls.

18 It was unusual for Longe to attend business at the house of industry on three successive days.

3 a. At home.

15

4 April I rode to Ipswich. Turned the horses out for the first time today. I took out our hair powder certificate.[19] I wrote to my father.
5 I attended the House of Industry for Mr Theobald. Riches & son here.
6 I took a ride round Clopton & Grundisburgh. Charlotte took a ride to Crowfield, &c.
7 I walked to Coddenham. Returned to dinner. We began the last double brewing today.[20]
8 At home.
9 At home. The coach horses shod. A parcel and letter from Spixworth.
10 m. [*no other.entry*]

16

11 April I dined at Mr Marriott's, met Mr Pettiward, Mann & Mr J. Marriott.
12 I wrote to Mr F. Elwin & Mr F. Longe.
13 Mr Bacon & Mr S. Kilderbee called. We dined at Mr Kirby's.
14 Mrs L. Kilderbee & Miss Kilderbee called.
15 We dined at Mr Kilderbee's. Mr K. & I had some conversation, upon Miss K.'s connection.
16 A letter from Mr F. Elwin.
17 We spent the day at Mr Bacon's.

17

18 April Generals at Ipswich. I attended & dined at the White Horse.[21] Riches 2 days.
19 I spent the day in [*?*]trawling.[22] A letter from my brother.
20 I dined at Mr John Marriott's, met Messrs R. Marriott, Pettiward & Mann.
21 We dined at Mr Middleton's & met Messrs Bacon, Davy & Colonel Prince. A letter from my father.
22 I dined at the Club.
23 At home. Letter from my brother. I wrote to Mr F. Elwin.
24 m. At home.

18

25 April Mr Theobald dragged the river.[23] I afterwards dined with him. We brewed 4 coomb of malt this week. 15 lb. of hops of Bird.

---

19 Differential taxes were first raised to fund the War of American Independence, *c.*1780. They were assessed on the possession or use of comparative luxuries, visible signs of wealth normally limited to gentlemen or professional men: male servants, carriages, coats-of-arms, horses, dogs and (as here) hair-powder. Window tax was separate. The complex regulations and exemptions led to appeals, heard locally by commissioners, often JPs. Longe paid his taxes on 21 April, and see his note after 31 December.

20 The total quantities of home-brewed beer and ale consumed can be gauged from the amounts allowed to Longe's domestic servants, of whom he later had ten: men-servants three pints per day each, and maid servants one pint. In addition they were allowed 'small beer', the product of secondary brewing.

21 For the archdeacon's general visitation see glossary.

22 Ponds were dragged with nets, both to produce fish for the table, and to manage and clean them. See diary, 23 May to 2 June 1796, for more social occasions.

23 Which river? Henley stands high between the Fynn (a tributary of the Deben a mile east) and the Gipping with its Coddenham tributaries (two miles to the north and west).

26 I went to Tunstall & slept at Mr Ellis's. 1& ½ chaldron coals by Leathers.[24]

27 I returned home to dinner.

28 At the House of Industry. Mr Bacon called.
Letters from my father & Mr F. Elwin.

29 We drank tea at Mr Bacon's. Riches 2 days. I wrote to my brother.

30 At home.

1 May a. We went to Ipswich after church, drank tea at Mr Kilderbee's & I went in the mail to London.

19

2 May Got to town by 7 o'clock, called on Mr F. Longe & dined with him.
1½ chaldron coals brought by Morgan.

3 Transacted business with Mr F. Elwin at the bank, & dined with him at Mrs Tryon's. Went to Drury Lane Playhouse.
Memorandum. Mr F. Elwin undertakes to receive my dividends from this time gratis. I received dividends at the bank.[25]

½ year's dividend	3 per cent Consols	£ 20 5s. 0d.
do.	3 per cent Redemption.	202 16s. 0d.
do.	Vere's Legacy[26]	3 4s. 9d.
		£ 226. 5s. 9d.

4 Called on Mr Crespigny. Dined at the Coffee House. Called at Dr Bell's, & then drank tea at Mr Longe's, & supped at Sir G. Jackson's.

5 Breakfasted at Dr Bell's, & called on the bishop of Peterborough.[27] Saw the nobility, &c. go to the Queen's Drawing Room. Dined & supped with Mr & Mrs Longe at Sir G. Jackson's.[28] Sophy shod.[29]

6 Went to the Exhibition, packed up, dined at Dr Bell's, & set out for home in the mail.

7 Got home to Henley by 8 o'clock.

8 m. I preached for Mr Mann at Hemingstone.

20

9 May At home. Fine showery weather. I had a cold & cough.
Mr Bacon called & drank tea. I wrote to my brother.

10 At home. Riches here 2 days. Planted out melons into the hot bed, & also cucumbers.[30]

11 At home. We had 1 coomb of wheat of Mr Theobald which was ground at Baylham Mill.[31] Wrote to Mr F. Elwin.

---

[24] Local farmers, later including Longe's farm tenants, would collect coals by waggon from merchants.

[25] Along with the Tunstall rent, dividends were part of the Longes' private income at this time. This was probably the return on the sum of £10,000 that Nicholas Bacon had settled on Charlotte when she married John Longe in 1790. He was also to settle a similar amount on her by his will.

[26] Thomas Vere, of the long-established Henley family, gave an annual sum for the vicar, conditional on him teaching catechism, and delivering a sermon on St Thomas's day. See diary 21 December 1796.

[27] Could Longe have been looking for preferment in Peterborough diocese?

[28] Mr Francis Longe was John's cousin, owner of the Spixworth estate. He also lived in London. Sir George Jackson (otherwise Duckett) was his father-in-law.

[29] The care of his horses is considered in Appendix E.

[30] A melon bed or pit was a symbol of status, because of the cost of cultivation.

[31] The River Gipping formed the south-west boundary of Coddenham parish, with Baylham Mill more accessible from Coddenham and Henley than today.

12 We drank tea at Mr Bacon's. My mare shod. Wrote to my father.
13 At home.
14 We went to Ipswich, & returned to dinner. Mr Bacon drank tea here.
I took £100 out of the bank.
15 a. Whit Sunday.

21

16 May Mr Bacon & I went to Ipswich to attend Mr Middleton on his canvas.[32]
A letter from Jos. Church.
17 I walked to Mr Drury's.
18 At home. A letter from my brother.
19 Mr Bacon & I attended Mr Middleton on his canvas.
20 Coddenham Book Club. We went to Coddenham, & I & Mr Bacon dined at the club.
21 At home. I wrote to my brother, & sent his parcel of velvet & fishing tackle. My Mare Sophy was covered by Nimrod: 16 shillings & 1 shilling the servant.[33]
22 Trinity Sunday. m. Sacrament. A letter from my father.
Mr Drury's family & Messrs Bacon & Pettiward drank tea here.

22

23 May Went a-fishing with Messrs Davy, Lord Loraine, Marriott & Pettiward. Dined at Pettiward's.
24 We went to Ipswich.
25 Breakfasted at Mr Drury's. Fished with Messrs Pettiward & R. Drury & dined with them at Mr Kirby's.
26 At home. House of Industry meeting.
A letter from my brother. I wrote to my father.
27 I rode to Coddenham.
28 Ipswich Election. Candidates: Crickitt, Sir A. P. Hamond, & Middleton.
The latter lost his election. Mr Bacon & I were there.
Numbers upon Mr Middleton's leaving the hall:
Hamond: 371, Crickitt: 364, Middleton: 283. Majority 88.
29 a. preached for Mr Haynes at Swilland.

23

30 May An uncommon high wind & storm today which did much mischief to our garden. I dined at Coddenham.
31 Nomination Day at Stowmarket.[34] Mr Bacon, Mann & I were there, & a afterwards dined at Coddenham. Mann & I supped at Mr Brand's.
Called on Mr & Mrs Roberts, Creeting.
1 June We went to Ipswich & returned to dinner. Riches & son 2 days.
Memorandum. I received at Crickitt's Bank £5 3s. 0d. annual interest of Mrs Inglish's & her daughter's in money.[35]

---

32 William Middleton had been MP for Ipswich from 1784 to 1790. For his Parliamentary career see Appendix G.

33 Nimrod, a mighty hunter: Genesis 10.9. There is no evidence in the diary or other papers that Longe himself hunted on horseback.

34 On Nomination Day, Tories normally agreed two representatives for the county without formal contest.

35 Longe was a trustee in the small estate of Hannah Archer, an employee of Nicholas Bacon. Martha English, a beneficiary, was at one time paid by Longe through a bank in Chelmsford (Essex).

2 I had a fishing party: Lord Loraine, Mr Davy, Mann, Marriott & William Middleton.

3 County Election. Sir C. Bunbury & Lord Brome chosen.
We dined with a large party at Alderson's.

4 A rainy day. At home.

5 m. Preached at Hemingstone by exchange with Mr Mann.[36]

24

6 June Set out for Spixworth, in our own carriage to Scole, from there in post chaise to Norwich, & took an hack coach to Spixworth, got there by ½ past 5.[37]

7 Jos. Church dined with us.

8 My father & I rode to Norwich.
I paid Suffield the last year's bill for wine: £22 3s. 6d.

9 Spent the day with Jos. Church.

10 I drove Charlotte in my father's whiskey to Salhouse, & round by Coltishall, &c. 3 chaldron of coals brought by Morgan.

11 Jos. Church & I rode to Norwich, returned to dinner.

12 Mr Haynes preached for me at Henley. At home.[38]

25

13 June Jos. Church & Mr Church dined here, & Mr & Miss Carthew drank tea here. My Mare shod by Moniment.

14 I rode to Stratton & Horstead.

15 I rode to Norwich. In the afternoon took a ride with Charlotte in the whiskey. Memorandum. My father paid me 9 shillings which he received of Bacon for 9 copies of my sermon.[39]

16 I accompanied Messrs Churches & Gunn, to Booton to see Mr Elwin's pictures. Dined afterwards at Coltishall & returned in the evening.

17 Jos. Church dined here.

18 Left Spixworth, & returned to Henley. Our own chaise met us at Scole. Got home by ½ past 7.

19 m. At home. Wrote to my father.

26

20 June At home. Busy with Riches in the garden. Mr Bacon called.

21 At home. I wrote to my brother.

22 I spent the day with Mr Bacon & cleaned the pictures. Riches here 3 days.

23 I dined with a large party of Mr Middleton's friends at Alderson's: 105 persons. I received a quarter of a pipe of port from Mr Suffield: 20 bottles. Brewed 2 coomb of malt of Bird.

24 Midsummer. I dined at Coddenham Book Club.

25 We went to Ipswich & returned to dinner.
I paid Seaman 10s. 6d. admission into the Coddenham Association for

---

36 This occasion was not a service additional to his own.

37 The methods by which Longe and his family travelled to and from Norfolk, often recorded in the diary, are summarised at Appendix E.

38 The familiar 'at home' on this occasion refers to his parents' home in Spixworth.

39 Longe had been appointed to preach at the Ipswich visitation of Bishop Charles Manners Sutton (7 June 1794). This sermon when published was probably the one purchased by Parson Woodforde on 15 August 1794, as recorded in *his* diary.

prosecuting felonies.[40] A letter from my father. I settled accounts with Mr Theobald up to this day, & paid him £50 17s. 9d. balance.

26 a. At home.

27

27 June We began cutting hay; viz. the orchard, & M. Path Meadow.[41] Very fine hay weather.

28 John & Sam busy in the hayfield. I dined at Mr Bacon's & met Messrs. Middleton, Brand, Mann, Pettiward, Methold, Roberts & Lynch. A letter from my uncle, F. Elwin.

29 Mrs Acton, &c. called. Haymaking. Letter from Mr F. Howes.

30 Quarterly meeting, House of Industry at Coddenham. I attended. Mr F. & Miss Howes came here to dinner on their return from their tour. A letter from my brother.

1 July Mr & Miss Howes left us after breakfast. Riches & son here. We stacked the hay from the orchard & M. Path Meadow.

2 Mrs & Miss Turner drank tea here.

3 m. At home.

28

4 July We began cutting hay in the lawn, [&] vicarage pightle.[42]

5 Our coach horse received a wound in his off leg before. We cannot discover by what means. We called at Mr Roberts at Creeting. But little done in the hayfield, showery weather.

6 Busy in the hayfield, but a heavy shower at noon prevented our going on.

7 Busy in the hayfield all the day, but the weather still showery.

8 Busy in the hayfield, but rain came on at noon. I drank tea with Mr Bacon. I wrote to my father

9 Haymaking the greater part of the day. Mr Pettiward dined here.

10 a. I preached for Mr Mann at Hemingstone.

29

11 July We finished cocking the hay in the lawn. Mr Bacon & Mr Edmund Bacon called.[43]

12 John & Samuel & Molly engaged in throwing out cocks. I wrote to my father. 1 chaldron coals brought by Orford.

13 A good deal of rain last night. Strewing out haycocks. I rode to Mr Bacon's in the evening. I wrote to my brother. My mare shod.

14 We stacked the hay from the lawn & vicarage pightle.

15 John & Sam completing the stack. Riches & son 2 days.

16 At home. A letter from Mr Smythe of Harleston, & 8 copies of his play.[44]

17 m. Mr & Mrs Orford & Miss Thurland Broke drank tea here.

---

40 Presumably an association different from the one mentioned in the diary for 23 March 1796.

41 Is Longe implying that he was personally supervising this hay-making by his farm servants?

42 The Lawn (sometimes plural) is the sloping area to the south and east of the vicarage, still so called today. The name denotes not smooth cultivated turf, but a small park around this substantial residence, grown for hay and grazed by cattle after cutting. Vicarage Pightle had a frontage to the river nearby.

43 Mr Edmund Bacon was the son of the baronet of the same Christian name, whom he later succeeded.

44 Mr Smythe's play: see diary entries 4 and 17 March 1796.

A letter from my father.

30

18 July Charlotte & I went to Mr Bacon's. He & I dined at the Club, sale day. Mr Bacon inclined to high & unsettled spirits.
To books bought at the annual sale: £1 5s. 0d.[45]

19 I attended the House of Industry committee for Mr Bacon. Charlotte & Mr Bacon called at Crowfield. Mr & Mrs Roberts called.

20 Hay stack thatched. Mr Pettiward dined at Mr Bacon's. We returned home in the evening. Expence of moving & getting up hay from 9 acres, & thatching hay stacks: £3 5s. 2d.

21 I met Mr Ford's family & the Middletons at Mr Bacon's, & we all dined at Crowfield.[46]

22 I rode to Mr Acton's, & returned by Ipswich.
I took £50 out of the Ipswich bank. Coach horses shod.

23 At home.

24 a. At home.

31

25 July My father & mother arrived here by tea time: we sent our carriage for them to Stonham.[47]

26 Mr Bacon dined here. I wrote to Jos. Church & to my brother.

27 Mr & Mrs Davy called. We spent the morning at Coddenham.

28 My father returned to Spixworth by the mail.

29 We spent the day at Coddenham. Riches.

30 At home. Charlotte & my mother took an airing.
Letter from Jos. Church.

31 m. At home. The puppy sent home to Mr Lawton at Ash.

32

1 Aug. I dined at Mr Bacon's. Met the Fords, Maitlands, Middletons, Miss C. Acton & N. Colvile, & 2 officers of Warwickshire Fencibles.

2 I rode to Coddenham. Smart & a person with him there began the altar-piece. Tempest tonight.

3 At home. The Kirbys drank tea here. Sophy shod.

4 Fine harvest day. We went to Ipswich. I returned & dined with Mr Bacon & also a party of gentlemen. Mr Bacon very unsettled & wild.

5 At home. Riches & son 2 days.

6 At home. My mother & Charlotte called at Mrs Acton's.
Mr Bacon called.

7 a. My brother came to us this afternoon.
Mr Bacon very high this week.

33

8 Aug. At home. My father rejoined our party this evening. The oats cut today.

9 My brother & I rode to Mr Bacon's. Mr Bacon very unsettled & high.
Mr & Mrs & Miss Lynch came to Mr Bacon's.

---

45 The Book Club disposed of surplus books rather than accumulate a library, members having first choice. This generated funds each year towards the purchase of fresh books for lending.

46 Probably Crowfield Hall, where the younger Middleton lived for a time. The hall was later let and then demolished in 1829, the year Middleton succeeded his father at Shrubland Park.

47 Coaches from (and to) Norwich and Scole stopped at the Magpie Inn, Stonham Parva, where the inn-sign can still be seen over the middle of the main A140 road.

10 We all drank tea at Mr Kirby's, met Mr Bacon, &c.
11 We all dined at Mr Bacon's, met the Lynchs, Miss Pettiward, & Rodwell.
12 My brother & I rode to Ipswich to breakfast.
13 My father & mother left us this morning. My brother & I dined at Mr Bacon's, & met Earl Warwick, Captain Dilkes & Spooner, Admiral Reeve, Colonel & Mrs & Miss Reed, Mr Middleton, & Lynchs, & Mr & Mrs Coverdale. I wrote to Beatniffe to order Blair's Chronology.[48]
14 My brother left us early, & took a puppy of Mr Bacon's breed with him.
m. I preached at Claydon in the afternoon, & drank tea with Mrs Drury

34

15 Aug. I called at Mr Meek's, & afterwards dined at the Book Club.
I took my brother's bitch Fanny, liver colour & white to Coddenham, & left her there.
16 Mr Beck dined with us. A letter from my father.
17 I rode to Coddenham in the afternoon. We got up the oats this day.
A letter from my brother. I wrote to my father.
18 I rode to Ipswich. We drank tea at Mr Orford's, & met Mr P. Broke's family. I took the 2 first numbers of Martyn's edition of Miller's *Dietary*.
A letter from Frank Howes.
19 I took a ride to see the Warwickshire Cavalry.[49]
Messrs Bacon, Kirby, & Mr & Mrs Kilderbee dined here. Riches.
20 At home. I wrote to my brother.
21 a. Mr Bacon very high & unsettled. A letter from my father.

35

22 Aug. I dined at Mr Roberts's, met Dr & Mrs Sumner, Mr Bacon, Mr Pettiward, & R. Marriott. Mr Bacon very high.
23 Mrs & Miss Read drank tea here.
24 We went to Ipswich early. I afterwards dined at Mr Bacon's, & met a large party. Mr Bacon high & unsettled, symptoms of chilliness.
25 Mr Bacon was siezed in the garden with violent spasms. I went to Coddenham. Mr Bacon declined considerably.
26 Mr Bacon departed this life at 9 o'clock in the morning.[50]
At Coddenham. Returned home for a few hours.[51]
27 At Coddenham. Returned at night.
28 m. At Coddenham in the evening.

36

48 John Blair (1756–1826), *Chronological and Historical Tables, from the Creation to … 1753* (1754 and later editions).

49 As this regiment had been stationed at Ipswich for some months Longe had met some of the officers.

50 The Revd Nicholas Bacon, aged about sixty-four, lived a busy social life in his last fortnight. His death marked a transformation in the life of John Longe, both in the short term and for the next thirty-seven years.

51 Coddenham vicarage and farm were kept running by the staff. The parish was in the care of the curate, Mr Pettiward, under the first formal sequestration granted on the 30 August. See note: 17 September 1796.

29 Aug. Mr J. Kirby came over.[52] I came home after dinner.

30 Spent the day at home.

31 Went to Coddenham, & slept there.

1 Sept. I returned home. Sir E. Bacon came, & we went to Coddenham in the evening.

2 Poor Mr Bacon was buried this morning at 11 o'clock, & will opened. I returned to dinner with Sir Edmund Bacon. Mr John Bacon came this evening with his son & daughter. My father came to Henley this evening.

3 My father & I spent the day at Coddenham, met the executors. We returned again late at night.

4 a. Sir E. Bacon called in his way home. At home.

37

5 Sept. My father & I went to Ipswich to consult Mr Kilderbee on Mr Bacon's will.

6 My father & I met Mr Kirby at Coddenham. One of the coach horses there ill. Col. & Mrs Read called. I wrote to Mr S. Kilderbee.

7 I rode to Coddenham. Woods met me there, & bled the two new coach horses, & the mare. I wrote to Mr Alexander about the Coddenham coach horses. I wrote to Stephenson to come over.

8 We all went to Coddenham & returned to dinner.

9 My father left us this morning. I met Mr Stephenson at Coddenham, who examined the lame & ill horses there. I lent my father £10. Repaid December 2nd 1796. My mare shod.

10 At home busy in writing letters. I wrote to my cousin F. Longe, to Mr F. Elwin, to Mr Warburton.

11 m. At home. I wrote to my father.

38

12 Sept. I rode to Coddenham, & returned to dinner. Saw Mr Middleton. Mr William Lynch, Ipswich, an old friend of Mr Bacon's. I engaged to contribute, to pay £25 per annum towards the contribution for Mr Lynch, being the half of what Mr Bacon had intended to pay had he lived. To be paid half yearly, & first to commence at Michaelmas 1796.

13 I attended the House of Industry, & afterwards called at Col. Read's.

14 First day of shooting. I walked to Coddenham, where Col. Read & Mr Kirby met me, & we went a-shooting. Dined there & Charlotte & Miss Brome came to tea. A letter from my father & Mr F. Longe.

15 I walked a-shooting with Mr Theobald.

16 I carried Miss Brome home, & called on Mr Kirby, who told me that a caveat was entered against the probate of Mr Bacon's will.[53] I wrote to my father. Paid into Cornwell's Bank on Mr Middleton's account for Mr Lynch: £12 10s. 0d.

17 Mr J. Kirby came over, & Messrs W. Kirby & Ripper witnessed the

52 Mr J. Kirby (attorney) who managed the Shrubland estate, was an executor with Sir Edmund Bacon. The Revd W. Kirby, curate and later incumbent at Barham, was his son.

53 A will remains a private document until passed through the public process of proving or 'probate'. A caveat or warning suspends that process until the court, after hearing all relevant parties, gives judgment.

execution of Charlotte's deeds.[54] I slept at Coddenham tonight.
I wrote again to my father. I wrote to Baker & Moss to enter a caveat against institution to Coddenham & Barham livings.[55]

18 Returned to Henley after breakfast. I wrote again to my father.
a. Returned to Coddenham in the evening.

39

19 Sept. A fine rain from the north last night. I returned to Henley for breakfast. Afterwards went to Coddenham to meet Mr Kirby. Slept at Coddenham. Generals at Ipswich.[56] Book Club.

20 Returned home to breakfast, where Mr W. Kirby met me.
A letter from my father on the subject of the Coddenham & Barham livings. I wrote to Mr Pettiward at Harwich.

21 I set off early for Scole where I met my father & mother.
Dined there, & my mother returned with me to Henley.
My father went to Morningthorpe on his way home.[57]

22 I walked out a-shooting.

23 I spent the morning at Coddenham.
I wrote to the bishop requesting the sequestration of Coddenham.[58]

24 I walked out a-shooting.

25 m. At home.

40

26 Sept. I met Mr Kirby & Harris at Coddenham. I wrote to my father.

27 I attended the House of Industry, & then called on Col. Reed.
Charlotte was taken ill today about 2 o'clock. We sent for Mr Beck.

28 Charlotte was brought to bed of a fine girl at ¼ past 3 o'clock this morning. Blessed be God for it! Wrote to my friends 8 letters.
Mr Beck came at 4 o'clock & stayed till Charlotte was put to bed.[59]

29 Charlotte & daughter charmingly well.
House of Industry previous meeting. I rode to Coddenham in the afternoon. A letter from my father.
Mr Beck called. I paid him 5 guineas for his attendance.

30 I met Mr Kirby at Coddenham, & spent the morning there.
Mr Beck called.

1 Oct. Col. Read came to breakfast, & we beat the Witnesham Thicks.[60]
I shot a pheasant. I wrote to Sir Edmund Bacon.

2 a. I published the sequestration, & administered the sacrament at Coddenham. Mr Beck called.

41

54 In respect of assets in which she had life interests Mrs Longe had power to appoint who should benefit upon her own death. Here she deals with an earlier trust, not her legacy: see diary, 13 March 1798.

55 Longe was engaged simultaneously in two related issues: the caveat in the probate court, and right of presentation to the two church benefices, in the diocesan register: see notes to 23 Sept. and 22 Oct. 1796.

56 Longe perhaps considered himself too busy to attend the archdeacon's visitation.

57 Morningthorpe (Norfolk) was the home of the Howes family, related by marriage to the Longes.

58 The grant of sequestration to Longe in place of Pettiward did not prejudice the outstanding issues.

59 The baby, given the Christian name of her mother, the first to survive infancy, lived to the age of seventy-one. For a Longe family tree, see p.lix above.

60 Witnesham Thicks, an area of woodland still so called, a short distance south-east of Henley.

3 Oct. To dine at Col. Reed's, met Captains Dilke, Spooner, Clavering & Johnson of the Warwickshire Cavalry & Mr Richard Trotman.
I rode to Coddenham in the morning. A letter from Sir Edmund Bacon.

4 Mr Higgs breakfasted here. Mrs Sleorgin, & Mr & Mrs Cornwell came to look at the house. Mr Beck called.

5 I rode to Ipswich, saw the Warwick Fencibles reviewed, & called on Mr Kirby & dined at Mr Gee's. Letters from Mr Smyth & Mr Warburton.
I wrote to Sir E. Bacon.

6 I walked out a-shooting.
Wrote to my brother, Mr F. Elwin, Jos. Church & Mr Kilderbee.

7 To dine at Mr Drury's, met Col. & Miss Read. Mrs R. not well.
Wrote to my father, & Mr Warburton.

8 My mother & I took an airing to Coddenham.

9 m. Sacrament at Henley. Heavy rain this evening & very stormy.

42

10 Oct. Mrs Kilderbee & Miss Brome called. We gathered some of the apples.

11 I rode to Mr Davy's, & returned by Coddenham.
A letter from my father. My mare shod.

12 I breakfasted at Mr Brand's, & he & I shot at Coddenham.
Dined & supped with him, & returned home at night.

13 At home. We got the greenhouse plants in today.
A letter from my brother. Riches.

14 I rode to Mr Kirby's.

15 I expect Mr Ellis. Mr Ellis came & paid me his rent. Mr Davy called.
Ellis paid me balance of rent: £53 16s. 11¾d.

16 a. At home.

43

17 Oct. Book Club. I rode to Ipswich: saw Mr Kirby. Afterwards went to the Club, & slept at Coddenham. I wrote to my father & Sir Edmund Bacon.

18 St Luke. I drew the ponds at Coddenham & caught one large carp.
Got the greenhouse plants in there. Dined at the Crown with Henley parishioners, & received tythes. I received Simon's Lexicon from Elmsly.

19 At home. I wrote to Mr Freeling, General Post Office, respecting Jennings.

20 I rode to Coddenham to Sir E. Bacon & Mr Kirby; the latter did not come.
Sir Edmund & I stayed tonight at Coddenham, & Mr Pettiward dined with us.

21 Mr Kirby came to Coddenham & we examined writings.
Sir Edmund & Kirby went to Ipswich after dinner, & I returned home.
Letters from Mr Freeling & my father, & wrote to my father.

22 At home. Wrote to my uncle F. Elwin who sent me my Michaelmas dividend £202 16s. 0d.[61]
[*Wrote*] to Mr J Bacon about the grant of Coddenham advowson, &c.[62]

---

[61] Dividend: see note at 3 May 1796.

[62] John and Charlotte Longe needed both the validating of Nicholas Bacon's will and proof of title to the

23 m. I preached in the afternoon for Mr Lawton at Gosbeck.

44

24 Oct. Mr Howard to come. He came & paid me his rent. I went out a-shooting.
Howard paid me balance of rent: £51 17s. 11½d.

25 I rode to Coddenham. My father came hither per mail this evening.
Memorandum. I advanced £1 1s. 0d. this day to the old gardiner at Coddenham, he being ill.

26 At home all day. I wrote to Sir Edmund Bacon.

27 Goodwin & his men came to set out the necessary at the vicarage.
My father & mother left us this morning; our chaise took 'em to Stonham.

28 At home. Goodwin & men.

29 Nurse Abel left us. At home.
A letter from Sir Edmund Bacon, & from John Bacon.
Also from my father & brother. Paid the servants their ½ year's wages.[63]

30 a. I went to Ipswich after church, & met Sir Edmund Bacon.

45

31 Oct. Sir Edmund Bacon & I set out for London in post chaises. Dined with the East Norfolks at Chelmsford Barracks, & slept at the Black Boys.[64]

1 Nov. We proceeded on our journey, & got to town by 2 o'clock. Sir Edmund & I lodged at Webb's Hotel, King Street, Covent Garden.
The witnesses, &c. got to town today.

2 Dr Clubbe examined 8 hours at Doctor's Commons.[65]

3 Dr Clubbe again examined, & concluded.
Mr J. Bacon dined with us at the Piazza Coffee House.

4 Dr Clubbe & Kirby left town. Mr Davy's examination began.

5 Mr Davy's examination concluded. Our wedding day.[66]

6 Mr Davy & I set out for home in a post chaise, saw my brother at Chelmsford, & got home about 8 o'clock.

46

7 Nov. At home. Mrs Middleton & Miss Metcalf called. I wrote to my father.

8 At home.

9 We went to Ipswich. I settled accounts for the last year, & to this time with Mr Bedwell.

10 I rode to Coddenham. Mr & Mrs Edgar, Mrs [*?*]K. Edgar & Mr Brand dined here.

11 I walked to Ash, & called on Mr & Mrs Lawton.[67]
I settled accounts for the last year to this time with Mr Morgan.

---

advowson before they could receive both capital assets and the substantial income of the Coddenham living. On the second, Longe engaged in extended historical research.

63 Many domestic servants, receiving bed and board, were paid the cash portion of their remuneration only half-yearly. See Servants' Wages Book (p.178).

64 It was more convenient to lodge in the hotel where the coach made its brief early morning halt than in his brother's officers' mess. The Black Boy Inn survives in the town centre.

65 This preliminary court procedure followed the caveat against issue of grant of probate. See 16 Sept. 1796. The estate was frozen until the final outcome over a year later. See diary 5, 6, 13 Dec. 1797.

66 John and Charlotte's sixth wedding anniversary.

67 Ashbocking parish is to the east of Coddenham, but not adjoining.

Mr William Kirby breakfasted here. I went with him to Ipswich to see Mr J. Kirby, respecting the receiving the Coddenham Tythes, &c. A letter from my father.

13 a. Preached at Coddenham this morning. A letter from my father.

47

14 Nov. Book Club. I walked to Coddenham & dined at the Club & slept there.[68]

15 Mr Brand & I went a-shooting at Coddenham. I returned home in the evening.

16 We took up potatoes, carrots & parsnips. Riches.

17 At home. A flight of snow tonight.

18 At home. I wrote to my father, & brother.

19 Stormy day.

20 m. Our little girl not well, sent for Mr Beck, who came tonight.

48

21 Nov. Coddenham & Crowfield Tythe Audit. I attended & received the tythes with Mr Wenn, Mr Kirby's clerk.[69] Slept at Coddenham tonight. Memorandum. 2 guineas in addition to the 6 guineas for the audit dinner were allowed, for Coddenham & Crowfield. 1 & ½ chaldron coals brought by Mr Bedwell. Mr Beck came.

22 Barham Tythe Audit. Mr W. Uvedale received the packages for Sir William Johnstone.[70] I returned home to dinner. Mr Beck came. A letter from Spixworth which I answered.

23 I rode to Ipswich, & called on Mr Kirby. Called on General Tonyn.

24 Walked out a shooting. A letter from Sir Edmund Bacon which I answered.

25 Rode to Coddenham & returned by Barham. A letter from my brother. A letter from Jos. Church. I wrote to my father. 1 & ½ chaldrons coals by Bedwell.

26 At home. I wrote to Mr Carthew to authorise him to pay 2 guineas to Mrs Glover of Woodbridge.[71]

27 a. At home. Letters & parcel from Spixworth.

49

28 Nov. I set out in the mail for Norwich, walked to Spixworth, & found my father & mother well.

29 Sir Edmund Bacon came to dinner, we talked over matters respecting Mr Bacon's will. He slept at Spixworth tonight.

30 Sir E. Bacon left us. A very stormy & cold day. I rode to Mr Church's. A fall of snow tonight.

1 Dec. A deep snow. Jos. Church dined here, & slept here.

2 Jos. Church left us. I wrote to Mr Windus, &c.

---

68 Longe spent that night probably at Coddenham vicarage, not the Crown Inn.

69 Tithes were payable as usual, but the benefit had to be apportioned. Mr J. Kirby's clerk represented the estate of the deceased previous vicar. Longe represented the sequestration fund. See memorandum at end of the year and note at 7 February 1798.

70 As the estate itself was 'frozen' by caveat, this consignment for Lady Johnston, sister of the late Nicholas Bacon, must have been of Bacon family heirlooms. See note at 21 March 1798.

71 Mrs Glover was probably a beneficiary of a small legacy in trust, perhaps a retired servant. Carthew, of the prominent Woodbridge family, was either co-trustee with Longe or acted as trusted intermediary.

3 I left Spixworth, & returned in post chaises to Henley.
A pair of fustian breeches from Farr, unpaid for.
4 m. At home.

50

5 Dec. At home.
6 Dined early & set out for Ipswich after dinner. Drank tea with Mr Gee. Slept at the Golden Lion, to be ready for Shave's Coach.[72]
7 I set out for London, where I arrived about 8 o'clock.
8 Called on Mr Windus & went with him to the bank. Afterwards I called on Jenner. Dined with H. Elwin junior & supped with my uncle H. Elwin.
Memorandum. Paid to Mr Breckell in the Hay Market for Mrs Barker £5 5s. 0d.
9 Called in Brook Street. Afterwards dined at Mrs Tryon's, & supped with Mr H. Elwin. Purchased for my father at Burgesse's a pint of chili vinegar, & at Bayley's ditto lavender water.[73]
10 Day fixed for hearing the probate of the will. Sir Edmund Bacon came to town. He, Mr Windus & I attended in the court of Doctors Commons.
Memorandum. The adverse party not having sent in their answers, Sir William Wynne said that he should expect them the next court day: January 10th. In case this is not done, then excommunication.[74]
11 I left London & returned by the Telegraph.[75]
a. W. Kirby preached for me.

51

12 Dec. Charlotte met me at Ipswich. I called on Mr Kilderbee & Mr Kirby.
Expence of my London journey: £9 8s. 0d.
13 At home. A letter from Mrs Sleorgin, which I answered.
14 I rode to Coddenham.
15 I received Sir William Scott's Opinion about the lapse.[76] Wrote to my father. Letters from Jenner & Mr Caley. I wrote to my brother.
[*I wrote*] to Mr Windus with game, to Mr Jenner, [&] to Mr H. Elwin, & to my father with a basket, &c.
16 At home.
17 I rode to Mr W. Kirby's, & round by Coddenham. Wrote to Mr Church.
I received my petition from Doctors Commons – on a £6 stamp.[77]
18 m. At home.

52

---

72 See Appendix E.

73 Chilli, vinegar and lavender water were perhaps not obtainable locally. Or were goods from London thought superior, even if made from Norfolk lavender?

74 Another step in the legal saga. The printed extracts from the 1797 diary have nothing relevant on 10 January 1797. Note the harsh penalty for 'contempt' of this church court. Deliberate delay was suspected.

75 See Appendix E.

76 Probably Longe had requested the barrister's opinion in the probate case on whether there was any alternative to accepting the month's delay from 10 December (*q.v.*).

77 Stamp: the word here means the document liable for duty, duly stamped (either adhesive or impressed).

19 Dec. I met Mr J. Kirby at Coddenham & searched for the grant of the advowson.[78]

20 Staid at home. Mr Howes died this morning at ¼ past 6 o'clock.
A letter from Mr H. Elwin respecting his search for the grant of Coddenham for which fees, &c. I am indebted to him.
Letter from my father & Jos. Church.

21 St Thomas. Service at church, & I distributed Mr Vere's gift.[79]
A letter from [*?*]F. Howes.

22 I & Mr William Kirby went to Norwich, to petition the bishop for institution. Dined & supped at Mr Sutton's. Slept at the Maid's Head.[80]
A letter from Mr Windus.

23 I & Mr Kirby waited on the bishop. He declined instituting.[81]
I went in a post chaise to Spixworth. Heavy snow.

24 Left Spixworth after breakfast. Got home to Henley to tea.
Snow & sharp frost.

25 m. Christmas Day. Sacrament. Mr Kirby gave up his curacy of Coddenham.[82] Sharp frost, ground covered.

53

26 Dec. I walked to Coddenham. Hard frost & the ground covered with snow.

27 I walked to Mr Kirby's. I was taken ill with a violent sore throat, & Sam also. Letters from my father, brother & Mr H. Elwin.

28 Heavy rain & quick thaw. Sent for Mr Beck. Sam & I both very ill.
Mr Beck came. I wrote to my father & to Mr Windus.
Sam & I both very poorly. Mr Beck came, & ordered a blister on my throat.

30 The gout seized my feet & knees. Very ill all day. Mr Beck.

31 Very ill. We sent for Dr Clubbe, who came this morning.
Mr Beck stayed here all night.

Memorandum.[83] I received with Mr Wenn, Mr Kirby's clerk, the composition for tythes of Coddenham and Crowfield, amounting to £248 2s. 2d. which sum was paid to Mr J. Kirby by James Wenn his clerk. Mr William Kirby also paid Mr J. Kirby the sum of £5 15s. 6d. as composition for the tythe of land in Coddenham in the occupation of Robert Matthews.

Total money in Mr Kirby's hands Nov 23rd £248 2s. 2d.
5 15s. 6d.
£253 17s. 8d.

78 Longe's continued research into the history of the advowson. See note to diary entry, 22 October 1796.

79 For Mr Vere's gift see 3 May 1796.

80 The Maid's Head is an ancient Norwich inn near the west end of the cathedral.

81 Bacon's will enabled Longe to become vicar of Coddenham and his Barham curate William Kirby to take Barham living. The bishop was merely declining to proceed while the will was in dispute.

82 When in poor health, Bacon had engaged Kirby to take further duties as second curate at Coddenham-cum-Crowfield. Kirby knew that Longe would not require him to continue. He still had Barham.

83 See note to 21 November 1796.

<u>Hay Account</u>

Orchard	1	Load
M. Path Mead	3	ditto
Vic[*arage*] Pightle	1	ditto very large
Lawn	<u>5</u>	ditto ditto
	<u>10</u>	= 12 Common Loads.

Expences of cutting & getting up hay

To Mr T.'s men for mowing 9 acres of grass	£1 2s. 6d.
Paid women for making, & Keeble for assisting in getting up hay	1 12s. 8d.
Paid Gooch for thatching 2 stacks at 1sh. per square & allowance	<u>0 10s. 0d.</u>
	<u>£3 5s. 2d.</u>

Memorandum. Apr 21

I paid Mr B. Brook the taxes for the half year ending at Lady Day £14 5s. 0½d.

Hair Powder Tax 2 2s. 0d.

EXTRACTS FROM DIARY OF 1797

Since August 1796, John Longe had been busy working with Nicholas Bacon's executors: his relative Sir Edmund Bacon of Raveningham (Norfolk) and his attorney and estate manager Mr John Kirby. The immediate task was supervising the household and farm at Coddenham and for Longe also the parish. However, for sixteen months they were doing so in a legal vacuum. Although the provisions of Bacon's will were known there remained a major uncertainty, for Bacon's sister and heir-at-law, Lady Mary Johnston, challenged his mental capacity and thus the validity of that vital document. Not only was the estate frozen until a decision was made in the courts, but Longe did not himself know whether he and his wife would benefit at all. Nicholas Bacon's moods had certainly swung from low to elated, a condition that we might today describe as manic-depressive. The Court did eventually validate the will but not until December 1797

Uncertainty also hung over the Bacons' title to the advowsons. In the event, this had no comparable delaying effect but induced Longe to undertake historical researches which lasted for years. Despite the unresolved issue over the will, the bishop of Norwich surprisingly put in hand the legal requirements for Longe to become vicar of Coddenham-cum-Crowfield. It is unclear whether the diocesan officials had knowledge which did not appear in Longe's diary or papers, but he was formally instituted on his own presentation at the bishop's London residence on 27 February 1797 and shortly afterwards he was inducted by the archdeacon's representative at Coddenham. To secure the major part of the benefice income, Longe was soon busily engaged with his adviser in valuing the tithes and negotiating compositions into cash figures. It was however not until December 1797 that John and Charlotte Longe were secure in terms of both capital and income. At an unknown date that year, they moved into the large vicarage. Amidst all this Longe's daughter (also Charlotte) was born in September 1796.

Out in the world, meanwhile, the war against the French was having increasing impact.

As the original 1797 diary appears not to have survived, as have the other six that are transcribed here, the following are extracts taken from a printed version of 1932.[84]

84 The 1797 extracts were originally printed in the *East Anglian Daily Times*, in four parts numbered 8783, 8790, 8794 and 8799. The contributor was W.M. Lummis, the noted local historian on Coddenham. As was then the practice, they were later reprinted, under the same numbers, in the quarterly journal: *East Anglian Miscellany* 26, III and IV (1932): bound copy at SRO(I) on open shelves. The original pocket-book has not (seventy-five years later) been traced, but it was said in 1932 to have been in the possession of Mrs H. Martin of Coddenham, of the family who lived in Longe's time at Hemingstone Hall, later related by marriage.

6 Feb. We went to Ipswich and called on Mr Kilderbee and on Colonel Stisted about the cavalry.[85]

10 I rode to Ipswich in consequence of a note from Mr Kilderbee.

11 I rode to Ipswich, attended the meeting at the Shire House and was sworn in the provisional cavalry.

4 March I rode to Coddenham and was inducted into the church by Mr H. Lawton.[86]

5 I did duty both morning and evening at Coddenham and read the Declaration, Articles, &c.[87]

27 March James Mayhew was enrolled to serve as my substitute in the provisional cavalry.

22 March We went to prayers. I signified to Mr Pettiward my having engaged Mr Howes as my assistant curate.

15 April My birthday. 32 years.

19 April Sir William Rowley's hounds chased a fox through the home plantation.

26 April Mr Burton came and I rode with him about the parish to value the tything.[88]

27 I rode with Mr Burton, and examined the greater part of the land in Coddenham.

28 Mr Burton completed his examination of the land in Coddenham, leaving Crowfield till he comes again. He left us after breakfast.

29 We began carting gravel from John Bird's stony ground for the carriageway before the house, assisted by the parishioners.

9 May Mr G. Howes left us. I rode with him as far as Stonham.

22 May I rode to Ipswich. A muster of the provisional cavalry.

23 I paid for the uniform, etc. of James Mayhew junior my provisional cavalryman £2 10s. 6d.

5 June I went to London in the Blue Coach on account of the approaching tryal.

8 Prince William of Gloucester arrived at Shrubland New Hall, having hired it of Mr Middleton.

---

85 Each gentleman was required by law to provide a mounted trooper for a new corps: the Provisional Cavalry. See diary entries for 27 March, 22 and 23 May 1797, and 18 April and 7 May 1798. This was unrelated to Longe's own career in the Ipswich Troop of Light Horse: diary entry at 18 June 1798 etc.

86 The episcopally sealed document of institution was dated 27 February. It is unclear why the bishop did not await the court's decision on the will (December 1797). Induction into the *temporal* elements of the benefice was another part of the process, effected by the archdeacon's deputy.

87 This 'reading in' by public declarations was a further (but not final) part of the initiation; see 14 July.

88 Any new incumbent was much concerned in his first year to renegotiate levels of tithe, often the largest part of the benefice income. It is likely that Nicholas Bacon had let this aspect slip.

16 June Mr Burton settled with some of the parishioners a computation for tythe.
18 Mr Pettiward read himself in at Onehouse.

9 July I preached at Coddenham morning. Prince William of Gloucester came to church with his aid-de-camp. Mr G. Howes went to Crowfield for the first time.

13 July We all walked to see the Inniskilling Dragoons reviewed by Shrubland tower. I dined at Shrubland Hall by invitation from Prince William.
14 This day fixed for the tryal of our cause – since deferred. I and Mr Howes rode to Ipswich where I took the oath of allegiance for the living of Coddenham.[89]

4 Aug. I buried Mrs Brook this morning.

9 Sept. Robert Marsham esq. of Stratton, Norfolk died this day about 7 o'clock [*in the*] evening.

15 Sept. I received a letter from my father concerning Mr Seaton's preparing to dispute my institution to Coddenham living.

18 Sept. We set out for Spixworth at 8 o'clock; went to Scole in our own carriage. From thence in post chaise. Got to Spixworth at 4 o'clock.
22 King's Coronation. I am appointed to preach at the Cathedral. I preached, the Bishop, Dean and Dr Yates [*being*] present. Joseph Church returned with me to Spixworth.

2 Oct. This day fixed for Mr Burton to come over to settle Mr Middleton & tythe composition by arbitration. I and Mr Burton met Messrs Edwards and Josselyn at Shrubland to ascertain Mr Thomas Payne's and also Mr Uvedale's.
3 Mr Burton & I called on most of the occupiers in Crowfield. We did not come to any settlement of tythe composition with any one.
5 Mr Middleton took Scoggins' gun from him, on seeing him on Mr Kedington's farm.
6 I rode to Crowfield to remonstrate.

11 Oct. I married a couple at Henley, and [*in the*] afternoon called on several of the inhabitants concerning the dissenters' meeting lately set up there.
12 I rode to Mr Roberts' and called on Mr Bromley the dissenting minister at Needham.[90]
13 I attended a court at Barham Hall manor and was admitted to some copyhold land on the Hemingstone farm.[91]

---

89 The oath of allegiance, though belatedly taken, completed the legal requirements.

90 Mr Arthur Bromiley was minister of the Independent chapel at Needham Market. For dissenting congregations see Appendix B.

91 Copyhold, a relic of the medieval manorial lan-holding system, endured into the twentieth century.

17 Oct. I called on the occupiers in Crowfield to persuade [*them*] to compound for their vicarial tythes.
18 Henley tythe audit. I dined with my Henley parishioners at the Crown and received my tythe.
22 We began service at Coddenham church at 2 o'clock for the winter.
23 We brewed this week.
24 Riches here. He planted the beech masts.

1 Nov. Rev T. Warburton of Harleston died this day.
3 Mr Thomas Howes came to Coddenham.

7 Nov. I wrote to the bishop to excuse my preaching a charity sermon.

20 Nov. Miss Harriet Middleton was married this day to Capt. C. Armand Dashwood son of [*blank*] Dashwood esq. of Leicestershire.

5 Dec. Day fixed for the trial of our cause in Westminster Hall.[92] Our cause was tried before Lord Kenyon, and Mr Bacon's will fully established.[93] Our party dine at Richardson's. [*Attended a*] play in the evening.
6 I went to Mr Windus's where I heard that Sir William Johnston had stopped the proceedings in Doctor's Commons.[94]
7 Mr Gee recommended me and promised my admittance to the society for propagation C K.[95] Paid my benefaction on admittance: 1 guinea
9 We breakfasted with Major Gurdon. Attended parade, &c.

13 Dec. The cause heard this day in Doctor's Commons, & probate of the will decreed.
14 I gave an entertainment to those of my parishioners and neighbours who attended twice in London to give evidence if called upon. We course[*d*] in the morning and afterwards dined at the Crown.[96]

19 Dec. General thanksgiving for naval victorys.[97] I preach at Coddenham church and had a large and respectable congregation.

28 Dec. At home engaged in garden, making the new walk.

92 A number of higher courts were situated in the historic complex in this part of London. An official printed summary of the hearing is at SRO(I) HA24/50/19/4.6(4).
93 The successful outcome of the case enabled Longe to be confident of his position for the first time.
94 The decision made the previous day opened the way for probate to be granted.
95 The SPCK is correctly entitled the Society for *Promoting* Christian Knowledge.
96 The only mention of hare-coursing in the diaries; it was still considered an appropriate sport for a clergyman, and for celebratory entertainment.
97 Duncan against the Dutch at Camperdown, Jervis at Cape St Vincent, and perhaps others.

DIARY OF 1798

By the start of 1798 John Longe was taking control of his new position. By April he was receiving dividends, rents and earlier tithe income. It was to be a busy year. The fear of invasion led the bishop to permit clergy to serve in the armed forces in person, as distinct from proxy. Longe immediately enrolled in the Ipswich Troop of Light Horse and kitted himself out. Simultaneously, parishes were required to organise for duties both in support of defence and in evacuating non-combatants, and Longe became involved in administration and leadership. As Longe's very substantial income rendered pluralism unnecessary, he resigned the smaller living at Henley.

This was the year in which his son Francis was born. At home, Longe was caused anxiety by a delicate task. Nicholas Bacon had left a large well-furnished vicarage, most of the contents of which, having been his absolutely, passed to the Longes. Also in the house were family heirlooms over which Bacon had enjoyed no power of disposal. It fell to Longe to sort and dispatch objects both to Bacon's sister and to the family of Bacon's mother at Moor Park at Farnham (Surrey).

The second half of the year was marred for Longe by a dispute with his wife's relative, Mr Kilderbee, an attorney who made a bridging loan to him and his brother in their trust capacity. It suited Longe to buy a farm in Coddenham from Bacon's brother-in-law and to fund the purchase by selling another farm elsewhere which came into the marriage settlement from his father-in-law. There was a misunderstanding. No sooner was that resolved than an unrelated conflict arose over some glebe elsewhere in the parish.

1

1 Jan. A delightful fine day. Our tenants S. Fenn, R. Fenn, J. Brook & J. Bird, with their wives dined here.

2 Charlotte & Miss Brome called on Mrs Davy. Riches here 3 days, going on with the alteration in the garden.[98] A letter from Robert.

3 Charlotte & Miss Brome called on Mrs Brand.

4 Charlotte & Miss Brome called on Mrs Sleorgin. A letter from my mother.

5 Mr & Mrs Davy, Mr Roberts, Mr Waddington & Miss Brook dined here.
I wrote to my father.

6 Mr Howes returned from Thorpe.[99]

7 I preached at Crowfield.

---

[98] Riches was contracted for a certain number of days' gardening work. See also memorandum at the end of 1798. Payment of his annual wage of 20 guineas was shared equally between Longe and Sir Edmund Bacon, as surviving executor of Nicholas Bacon, who had perhaps neglected the vicarage garden.

[99] The Howes family of Morningthorpe: see note at 21 September 1796.

A letter from Mr Wenn about the copyhold land in Bird's farm which, with the house, Sir William Johnston is about to sell.[100]

2

8 Jan. I went to Ipswich, & called on Mr Kilderbee & Wenn concerning the copyhold in Malt House farm.
Riches here every day this week making a gravel walk in the garden.

9 At home. We laid the chalk in the new garden walk today.
A letter from my mother informing me of my brother's being appointed <Captain> Lieutenant.[101] I wrote to my brother & Mr Windus.

10 We dined with Mr Howes, & met the Miss Brokes & Miss M.A. Kirby.

11 At home. Engaged in attending to the alterations in the garden.
A letter from Mr Church informing me of the death of Molly's mother.

12 Mr Paske, &c. came to value the copyholds on Bird's farm. Mr Wenn met him & dined here. I wrote to my mother by Molly, who went over to her father's by the mail this morning.

13 Mr Howes dined here.

14 I received a copy of the late tryal in King's Bench, and a letter from Mr Windus.[102] Also a Stilton cheese from my brother.

3

15 Jan. Mr Howes spent the evening here. William Sheldrake paid me 1 year's rent of his cottage, £2 2s. 0d., due at Michaelmas 1796. Riches here.

16 I carried Miss Brome home, & Miss A. Broke went to Ipswich with us. My brother got to Spixworth tonight.

17 At home. Mr R. Marriott called. I wrote to Mr Windus & to Mr F. Elwin. Received a letter from my mother.

18 At home. I settled accounts with E. Brown & William Goodwin, & received their rents due at Michaelmas & Christmas 1797.

19 At home. I settled accounts with P. Scoggin for thatching done last year.[103] A letter from Sir Edmund Bacon.

20 At home. I wrote to Mr F. Elwin & Mr J. Bacon.

21 I preached at Crowfield in the forenoon.
J. Bird set out for London to attend Mr J. Bacon.[104]

4

22 Jan. A showery day. At home.

23 Mr Howes & I walked to Mr Roberts's & to Mr R. Marriott's.

24 At home engaged in replacing dead plants. Filling up vacancies in the home plantations.

25 We went to Ipswich, & returned to dinner. A letter from my brother.

26 At home. Mr Howes dined here.

---

100 Bird farmed at Malthouse Farm, across the valley from the vicarage. Nicholas Bacon's sister, Lady Johnston (and thus her husband) owned part of the land, inconveniently intermingled with Longe's part.

101 Promotion for militia officers normally required ownership of property. Robert Longe, the younger son of a younger son, owned none. John Barney, *The Defence of Norfolk 1793–1815* (2000), p. 29, suggests that family mattered more than property. As cousin to Francis Longe of Spixworth Park, Robert was from 'a most ancient and respectable county family'. He later rose to major's rank, after twelve years' service.

102 SRO(I)HA24/50/19/4.6(4): Longe's copy of the trial transcript. See also diary, 5 Dec. 1797.

103 This thatching may have been to hay-ricks or to cottages.

104 In undertaking such an errand Bird was probably acting as Longe's farm manager.

I wrote to Sir Edmund Bacon, to my father, [&] to Mr Windus & sent the discharges for Rushbrooke's & Barker's legacy.[105]

27 At home. J. Bird returned from town, & informed me that it was necessary for me to go to town on account of the legacies under Mr Bacon's will. I wrote to Sir Edmund & my father, Mr Windus & J. Bacon.

28 I preached both times at Coddenham.

5

29 Jan. I set out for town tonight, to settle the business of the legacies under Mr Bacon's will. Mr J. Edwards came over to show me papers concerning Mr Kedington's farm in Coddenham.

30 [*no entry*]

31 Mr Windus & I called on Mr J. Bacon & Mr Bicknell. Dined & supped with Windus. Mr John Bacon paid me the legacy under the late Mr Bacon's will to the poor of Coddenham, deducting 6 per cent duty:

legacy	£300 0s. 0d.
duty	£18 0s. 0d.
	£282 0s. 0d.
interest received at 4 per cent from 1 month after testator's death	£16 0s. 0d
Total received	£298 0s. 0d[106]

1 Feb I left town not having received my legacy.

2 Got home this morning.

3 At home.

4 I went to Ipswich tonight & slept at the Golden Lion.[107]

6

5 Feb. Went to town in the Blue Coach.

6 Mr Windus & I attended Mr John Bacon & then went to the bank, where he invested Charlotte's legacy under Mr Bacon's will in the 5 per cents of 1797.

cents of 1797.	Charlotte's legacy	£10,000.
	Duty at 6 per cent paid	£600.
	Balance received	£9,400.

The sum of £9,400 purchased this day in the 5 per cents 1797: £13,262 15s.8d. stock. Dividend due at Lady Day & Michaelmas.[108]
Received of Mr J. Bacon interest on £10,000 at 4 per cent for 5 months: £166 13s. 4d.[109]

7 Mr Windus & I settled accounts finally with Mr J. Bacon.
I called on Dr Bell in the evening, but did not see him.
Received of ditto [*Mr J. Bacon*] my portion of the tythes of Coddenham paid to Mr Kirby one of the executors in December 1796: £76 5s. 1d.[110]

8 I dined at Mr Longe's & spent the evening there.

---

105 Longe had earlier acted as intermediary in paying these Bacon legacies.

106 Even charitable legacies suffered duty. Interest on a legacy: executors were allowed one month from the death, and then interest was payable to compensate for delay, here caused by the court case.

107 The Blue Coach presumably went from the Golden Lion. See Appendix E.

108 Nicholas Bacon made two large gifts to Charlotte. This legacy was additional to one of similar amount settled on her at the time of her marriage.

109 Interest was due for a further year's delay in payment, at the standard rate of 4 per cent.

110 For the tithe earlier received by Mr J. Kirby, by his clerk Mr Wenn, see both diary for 21 November 1796, and memorandum at the end of that year.

9 I called on Mr H. Elwin & Messrs Tryon & Batchelor.
Left town this evening in the Telegraph.[111]
10 On return Charlotte met me at Ipswich, & we came home to dinner.
We brewed this & the following week, & filled 8 hogsheads of ale & the same of small beer.
11 m. [*no other entry*][112]

7

12 Feb. At home. I discharged the legacies under the late Mr Bacon's will to the servants, to the amount of £170 5s. 6d.
13 I called on Mr Davy, & communicated to him my intention of resigning Henley vicarage. Called on Mr Roberts. I this day paid into the Needham bank the sum of £40 the property of Samuel Riches senior for which I have Alexander's note, to be paid 3 per cent interest.[113]
14 At home. Mr Howes dined. I wrote to my father.
I received a piano forte from Broderip, Haymarket for 15 15s. 0d. His bill including package £16 8s. 0d. Undischarged.[114]
15 At home. Showery day.
16 We went to Ipswich. Miss Brokes drank tea here.
We sent Miss's puppy to the Revd J. Lewis at Sandon near Chelmsford, at my brother's desire. Wrote to Sir Edmund Bacon.
17 At home. A letter from Mr Windus.
18 a. I preached at Crowfield this morning.

8

19 Feb. We went to Spixworth & got there to tea. My brother at home, being engaged with the supplementary militia duty.[115]
20 Mr Jos. Church dined here & Mr Dan. Collyer.
21 Ash Wednesday – I read prayers for my father at Spixworth .
Afterwards called at Horstead.
22 My brother & I rode to Norwich. I deposited £30 in Kerrison's bank, the property of our cook Mary Kenny & her sister Elizabeth, which with £20 before in that bank makes £50, for which I received Kerrison's note this day; & also interest to this time on the £20. JL.[116]
23 My brother & I rode to Coltishall. Mr J. Church returned & dined with us.[117]
24 Mr J. Church, Robert & I rode to Norwich.
I paid Suffield's bill for port wine in 1796 £18 1s. 6d.
& Smith's ditto for 1797 £11 17s. 3d.
25 m. I preached for my father.

---

111 See Appendix E.

112 Longe again notes in the margin (m. or a.) to indicate the time of the main service, now at Coddenham.

113 Samuel Riches senior was to receive interest only. See note at 2 January 1798.

114 The firm of Broderip (also Longman & Broderip, and Broderip & Wilkinson) were internationally famous instrument-makers from *c.*1760. Their 'square' pianos were especially popular.

115 Supplementary Militia: the unpopular tripling in militia size effected in 1796. See also 23 May 1798.

116 Mary Kenny was in John and Charlotte Longe's service from the time of their marriage (1791). SRO(I) HA24/50/19/4.7(11): she retired as housekeeper in 1813 from 'age & infirmities'. Longe often added his initials 'JL' to indicate completion of an obligation or financial transaction.

117 Coltishall was the home of Joseph Church. See notes on people (p.264).

9

26 Feb. My brother & I dined at Coltishall.
I received a pair of striped fustian breeches from Forster.

27 Jos. Church & Monsieur Bernicoff dined here.

28 Robert & I went to Norwich. I met Sir Edmund Bacon on the business of settling the expenses of our late lawsuit.
I paid Beck's bill from last year: £5 4s.0d.
& Mrs Gillman's ditto: £5 7s.0d.

1 March My father taken ill this morning with an unusual pain in the stomach.
Col. Ward & family, & Jos. Church dined here.

2 My father very poorly, & sent for Dr. Donne who came in the afternoon.
Mr & Mrs Ficklin dined here.

3 My father's complaint appeared to be a jaundice. He again sent for Mr Donne. We left Spixworth today, & got to Coddenham to tea boil.
Memorandum. I bought a pound of snuff this week at Miss Gillman's, Norwich. Query – ? whether I do not hereafter wish I had never indulged my whim in this unnecessary fashion of taking snuff.

4 I preached at Crowfield this morning. a.

10

5 March I rode to Mr Davy's to talk with him concerning my resignation of Henley.[118] Messrs G. & Frank Howes dined here.
Paid Mr Seaman the poor's rate for the quarter ending January 20th at

8d. per pound.	Valuation	£129:	£4 6s. 0d.
	Cottage	£2	1s. 4d.
		£131:	£4 7s. 4d.

A letter from my brother. I wrote to my father.

6 Charlotte called on Mrs Roberts. I wrote to the dean of Norwich, Mr P. Wodehouse & Sir Edmund Bacon, concerning my intended resignation of Henley.[119] Received today by Telegraph coach a box containing a set of Shakespear 8 volumes, & of Hooker's works 3 volumes, from Elmsley – also bishop of Durham's charge.[120]

7 Fast Day. I preached at Coddenham morning, & Crowfield afternoon. Mr Howes at Henley morning. No afternoon service at Coddenham.[121] Riches here. A letter from my brother: my father better.

8 I rode to Ipswich, & dined on my return at Mr Kirby's ; met the Howeses.

9 At prayers. Messrs Howes dined here.

10 At home. Riches here.

11 m. I preached at Henley this morning. A letter from my father & brother.

---

118 Longe was safely installed in the rich benefice of Coddenham-cum-Crowfield. As on 13 February, it was with the Revd Charles Davy that Longe chose to discuss his resignation from Henley.

119 The patronage of the Henley living was vested in the Dean and Chapter of Norwich. Were Mr P. Wodehouse and Sir Edmund Bacon involved in that patronage?

120 Richard Hooker defended the Elizabethan Church of England from 1594 against Puritan influence.

121 Ash Wednesday, the first day of Lent. Prayers were read in Coddenham church every Wednesday and Friday throughout Lent. Longe contributed heavily to the Lent collection (12 March).

11

12 March I went round the parish to collect voluntary contributions to government, & the parish were as liberal as could be expected in these dear times.
I received an answer from the dean of Norwich. The collection in Coddenham & Crowfield amounted to £45 18s. 9d., of which I gave £20.

13 Charlotte & I went to Ipswich & we signed the declaration of trust for her legacy under Mr Bacon's will.[122]

14 At prayers. A letter from my father & brother. I wrote to my father.

15 I attended the meeting of commissioners for hearing appeals against the increased assessed tax; & appealed on income.[123]

16 At prayers. Mr Howes & I walked to Mr Roberts's.
We drank tea at Miss Broke's.

17 At home.

18 a. A letter from my father.

12

19 March Mr Howes & I rode to Ipswich. I paid into the bank the voluntary subscriptions of inhabitants in Coddenham.

20 At home writing letters. I wrote to Mr Windus, & sent up his & Wenn's accounts, & to Mr F. Elwin about Charlotte's legacy.

21 Mr Davy called. I wrote to Mr J. Bacon, & sent his picture according to his desire.[124] I wrote to my father.

22 Mr Howes & I rode to Woodbridge. Riches here.
Letters from my father, Mr Windus, Mr F. Elwin, Mr J. Bacon.

23 At home. I this day deposited £100 in Alexander's Bank, Needham, for my father's use, & sent him Alexander's receipt for the same.[125]
NB: this sum is part of the sum I received of J. Bacon in payment of the late Nicholas Bacon's legacy of £300 to the poor of Coddenham, which therefore I am to replace. JL.

24 At home.

25 m.

13

26 March At the Book Club.

27 At home. A letter from my father.

28 We made a morning visit to Crowfield, Mr & Mrs L. Acton & Miss C.A. & Miss Colvile being there.[126]

29 I planted the shrubs from Woodbridge.[127]
I & Mr Howes dined with Mr Roberts, met Messrs Davy, Mann, Marriott & Freeman junior. Memorandum. We determined to allow Mrs Glover of Woodbridge £10 0s. 0d. per annum to commence at Lady

122 By putting the capital of the legacy of £10,000 into trust, Mrs Longe ensured its future intact.

123 It was the expense of the war that led to increased taxation. See also note to diary: 4 April 1796.

124 Throughout the year, Longe was despatching items such as pictures and jewellery formerly enjoyed by Nicholas Bacon. See introduction (pp.xlii–iii), and notes at 22 Nov. 1796 and 30 March 1798.

125 This sum of £100 was probably a gift by the now wealthy Longe to his father, who had been frequently advising him. See also diary entry at 23 October 1798.

126 There was a social distinction between a morning visit and a call later in the day.

127 The two entries relating to shrubs (and perhaps other material at 29 and 30 March) had been accidentally transposed, as acknowledged by Longe writing '2' in the margin at 29 March.

Day 1798, & I sent this day by John a £5 0s. 0d to be placed in Mr J. Carthew's hands for her relief till Michaelmas. She has received from us before last month £5 3s. 0d. so that she has now had of us this year £10 3s. 0d. JL

30 I sent to Woodbridge for the shrubs. I was engaged in packing the busts & marbles to be sent to Moor Park.[128] A letter from my father.

31 Mr & Mrs Kirby, & Mr Howes dined here. Riches here 2 days.

1 April a. I preached at Crowfield this morning.

14

2 April Passion week – at prayers. We went to Ipswich & brought home Miss Turner. I paid Dr Hamilton my subscription to his book on hydrophobia, £1 1s. 0d. Wrote to Mr Windus about the sending off the busts, &c. to Moor Park.

3 I read prayers, Mr Howes being gone to Dedham.
Mrs & Miss Middleton, William Middleton & Mrs Brokes drank tea here.

4 Mr Wenn came over to meet Mr Paske, but he did not come, but fixed tomorrow. I gave Mr Wenn a draft on Crickitt's Bank for £20.
I wrote to my father & brother.

5 Messrs Wenn, Paske & Edwards here on the business of the copyholds. Bought this week of Mr Garrod of Blakenham 14 lb. of oats at 10s. – not paid for: £7

6 Good Friday. I preached at Coddenham.

7 Charlotte carried Miss Turner to Crowfield. A letter from my father.

8 m. Easter Sunday. I administered the sacrament at Coddenham, & Mr Howes at Henley. Preached at Crowfield chapel afternoon.

15

9 April Mr Howes went to London. Parish meeting. At home looking after the loading the packages on Hearne's waggon. I sent off the whole of the More Park heirlooms by Hearne's Stowmarket waggon, in all 62 packages.

10 I went over to Spixworth in the mail. My father but poorly. We got ½ a chest of oranges from Gidney's at Norwich for which I paid £1 15s. 0d.

11 I rode over to Mr Church's. Mr Jos. Church drank tea here.
Received from Forster's a grey cloth coat & pair of fustian breeches.

12 I returned home by the mail this evening. Left my father much recovered.

13 At home. My brother came with his division East Norfolk regiment to Stowmarket. A letter from my brother.

14 My brother spent the day with us.
Goodwin's men began the foundation of the new lean-to in the stable yard.

15 a. I administered the sacrament at Crowfield. I wrote to my father.

16

16 April At home. Miss Dennis drank tea here with the little Brands.

[128] Moor Park, Farnham (Surrey) was historically the seat of the Temple family, and by this time the residence of William Timson esq., from whom Longe had a letter on 18 April, having sent off the main consignment of heirlooms on 9 April.

Messrs S. Fenn paid me the year's rent	£86 0s. 0d.
R. Fenn	£26 5s. 0d.
J. Brook	£65 0s. 0d.
	£177 5s. 0d.

17 I rode to Ipswich & spent the day with my brother; dined with the East Norfolk mess. Paid Ipswich bills this day, of last year: £34 0s. 0d.

18 <At home> I rode to Ipswich. Provisional cavalry mustered today.[129] A letter from my father. [*Also from*] Mr Timson, & Mr Wenn concerning the payment of our dividends.

19 At home.

20 I rode to Ipswich. My brother & Captain Hale returned & dined with us.
Received a letter from Mr F. Elwin inclosing a receipt for our Lady [*Day*] dividend: £202 16s. 0d.[130]

21 At home. I wrote to Mr F. Elwin, to Mr Seton, to Mr Windus, & to Messrs Child.

22 Mr Howes not being returned, Mr Kirby preached at Henley, & Mr Tenant in the afternoon at Coddenham.

17

23 April Generals. I attended them; Mr Roberts preached a most excellent sermon on Jude vv. 17 & 18.[131] The archdeacon [was] signifying to us the bishop's approbation of the clergy's taking up arms.

24 Mr Wenn spent the day here when we settled with R. Fenn & James Brook concerning the leases of their respective farms. Mr Edwards attended.
Letter from Mr Seton.

25 Mr Marriott & I rode to Mr Methold's to confer with him as to enrolling ourselves. Mr & Mrs Dillingham & Miss Gurdon called.
A letter from my father, & Mr Windus about Bird's copyhold, &c.

26 Mr Sparrow came, & agreed with me for some furniture & various other articles which we had no use for. Sparrow's appraisement of furniture, &c. £46 10s. 6d., which sum he agreed to pay me in 3 months. JL.
I wrote to Jos. Church, & my father.

27 Sparrow's man here packing furniture. My brother & Lieut. Elwin dined here.
Cooper's man here to take down & put up beds in the attics, one day.

28 I attended a meeting at Ipswich to raise a troop of cavalry, to be commanded by Charles Maitland Barclay esq.[132] Mr Howes returned.
A letter & parcels from my father.

29 a. Mr Lodge held a meeting this evening to enroll men for a company of infantry, but did not succeed. The new lean-to in stable yard finished this week, except hanging doors & painting. Done by estimate.

---

129 For Provisional Cavalry see note at 7 May 1798 below.

130 Dividend. See also diary entries for 3 May and 22 October 1796. Longe signed the receipt.

131 The text refers to scoffers indulging their 'ungodly lusts'.

132 Additionally to his leadership duties in the parish in early May, Longe did enrol under Captain Maitland (entries for 18 June 1798 onwards). He also supported a provisional cavalryman (entry 27 March 1797).

18

30 April Book Club. Mr Thomas Howes came to his brother's. We dined at the Book Club, & afterwards I attended a general parish meeting at Henley.

1 May Nurse Abel came here today on account of my wife's approaching confinement. General parish meeting. Major Mapes called. We had a very fully [*sic*] meeting at church to fill up the schedules & to enroll pioneers, &c., &c.[133]

2 I drank tea with Mr Lawton.

3 Mr Ellis & Mr Howard came. Mr Howard paid me his ½ year's rent. I did not take it of Ellis, as he said he much wanted the money.[134]
I attended a hundred meeting at Needham this morning, & parish meetings at Coddenham & Crowfield in the afternoon.[135]
My mare Sophy foaled an horse foal last night: Poppet.
My brother left a note at the post office on his way to Norwich, having been appointed to the command of the detachment to bring up the remainder of the supplementary militia.

4 At home.

5 I went to Ipswich, & returned to dinner. We received from Mr Wenn a draft on Child for ½ year's dividend on 5 per cent stock, viz £331 11s. 4d.[136]

6 m. I preached at Henley in the morning. A letter from my father, who is now very much recovered from his late illness.

19

7 May I distributed great part of Mr Bacon's legacy of £100 this year amongst the poor belonging to this parish. A general muster of provisional cavalry at Stowmarket when they were embodied. I was obliged to buy an horse for the purpose, of Mr Keeble of Crowfield for £14.[137]

8 At home. Captains Hulton, Hale & Lieut. Bacon called. Wrote to Ellis respecting sale of Tunstall farm. Sent Mrs Longe's draft indorsed by her to Messrs Child for the sum of £331 11s. d.

9 Company. I rode out in the morning. Major Mapes, Captain Hale, Hulton, Lucy, Lieut. Bacon & Elwin dined here.

10 I attended a parish meeting at Henley.
We called on Miss Broke in the evening. Miss Jenney there.
Received Messrs Child's acknowledgment of having received the draft.

11 I went to Ipswich to speak to Mr Wenn, concerning the sale of Tunstall

---

133 Preparations for invasion: leaders such as Longe had to prepare an abstract of the lists of inhabitants in various stipulated categories. See introduction at footnote 266. The task was repeated in 1803. For the government's printed proposals for 'rendering the body of the people instrumental in the general defence', together with the duties of the guides and pioneers, see Lummis 70.01–2.

134 The fact that his tenant Ellis came perhaps elicited Longe's generous response.

135 At this time of crisis and preparation, the administration within the county headed by the Lord Lieutenant relied on passing instructions down to the hundreds, and by them to the parishes. Returns of information were passed upwards through the same structure. Gentlemen bearing authority as Deputy Lieutenants and Justices of the Peace were leaders (perhaps 'constables') within that structure.

136 The dividend was the first on the Bacon legacy to Mrs Charlotte Longe, invested on 6 February 1798. Whereas Longe's account at Childs' bank in London was in his name, the draft was drawn in his wife's.

137 Longe had been put under obligation in respect of the provisional cavalry the previous year. See entries for 11 Feb., 27 March, 22 and 23 May 1797, and 18 April 1798.

estate, & purchase of Sir William Johnston's copyholds.

12 At home.

13 a. I preached at Crowfield. Saw Mr Middleton & agreed with him that John Edwards should be employed to settle matters concerning vicarial tythe in Crowfield now depending between us.[138]
A letter from my father, brother & Jos. Church.

20

14 May A very fine rain today.
Miss Broke, Miss Jenney & Mr Howes drank tea here.

15 At home. We brewed this & the following week, & filled 8 hogsheads of ale & the same of small beer.

16 At home. Mr Howes dined here. Miss Jenney left Miss Broke's

17 At home. A fine showery day.
I received a letter from Wenn, informing me that Sir William Johnston had agreed to sell me Bird's house, & such land as devolved to him on Mr Bacon's death, for 1000 guineas, each of us bearing our own expences.[139]

18 I went with the parishioners the bounds of the parish of Coddenham with Crowfield. Some went the cross bound which divides the hamlet from Coddenham. We afterwards dined at the Crown.[140] I received this week a pair of boots from Brown Piccadilly. Unpaid for. Paid November 16th for entertainment to the parishioners £2 14s. 6d.
Memorandum.
Ackfield's bill was £5 9s. 0d., but I consented to pay myself half the expenses of the entertainment, the parish paying the other half. JL.

19 At home.

20 m. I preached at Crowfield in the afternoon.

21

21 May I called on Mr Kirby. Col. Ward dined with us. Mr Howes went over to Morning Thorpe. Mr Paske called about the sale of Bird's house & land.

22 I went with James & Phil Scoggan, & Henry Jay an old inhabitant, & ascertained as near as possible the bounds between the parish of Coddenham & the hamlet of Crowfield which was done with little difficulty. S. Riches here one day.

23 I rode to Ipswich & returned to dinner. My brother returned to Ipswich with a detachment of supplementary militia, which he marched from Norwich. A parcel & letter from Spixworth.

24 At home. Cope here & 2 men, painting the doors, &c. of the new lean-to.

25 Mrs & Miss Middleton drank tea here. Cope's apprentice here ½ a day. I settled farming & other accounts with Rushbrook up to the 5th of May.

---

138 For litigation over the tithe on hay, not concluded until 1822, see 1820 Visitation Return (p.175).

139 See note to diary 7 Jan. 1798. To fund the purchase of this nearby property the Longes decided to sell the farm at Tunstall tenanted by Ellis, left in trust to Mrs Charlotte Longe by her father.

140 The Rogationtide custom of perambulation or 'beating the bounds' included the internal boundary (the 'cross bound') and this year required of the new incumbent a supplementary visit (22 May).

I paid him a balance on farm account	£34 19s. 10½d.
For 1 & ½ chaldron coals bought of Alexander	2 15s. 6d.
14 [?]coomb of oats bought of W. Garrard	7 0s. 0d.
For an horse bought of John Keeble for the provisional cavalry to be paid for by the ballot	14 0s. 0d.
Given G. Rushbrook for his care of the farm	1 4s. 7½d.
Paid G. Rushbrook[141]	£60 0s. 0d.

26 At home. Mr Howes returned today.
a. I preached at Henley in the afternoon.

22

28 May I rode to Ipswich & returned to the Book Club. My brother & I called on Mr Kilderbee to consult with him on the sale of our Tunstall farm. I received a letter from Mr Windus, concerning Kirby's affairs & the chancery suit between Sir Edmund Bacon & his executors.[142]

29 At home. I wrote to my father.

30 Mr Howes & I rode to Ipswich; he dined here.

31 Charlotte had symtoms of her approaching labour this morning. Mr Beck came at 3 o'clock. Labour pains came on at 4 o'clock, & continued with very little intermission till ½ past 5 this morning, when she was delivered of a fine boy. Her labour was very severe, the worst she has yet had.[143]

1 June Birth of my son Francis. My brother dined here, & Mr G. Howes. I wrote to Mr Windus, to my father, Mr F. Longe & Jos. Church.

2 Charlotte was extremely feverish today. Mr Beck came at noon. Mr Beck.

3 Charlotte was worse this morning, & we therefore sent for Dr Clubbe who got here at 8 o'clock. I did not do any duty today. Charlotte in a very dangerous way today till evening, when the fever abated. Dr Clubbe. A letter from my father.

23

4 June Charlotte had a quiet night, & was considerably better this morning. Charlotte's fever abated a good deal. Mr Beck here all night. Dr Clubbe came this morning. Mr Beck called twice again in the course of the day.

5 She had a bad night but still no return of the fever, & Mr Beck thought the fever today much less, but she is now excessively weak. Mr Howes dined here. Mr Beck called this morning & evening. Riches here two days.

6 Mrs Longe continues to regain strength. My brother dined here. Dr Clubbe came today. Mr Beck called this morning. Memorandum. I gave them both £10 for their attendance on Mrs Longe.

7 At home. Mrs Longe is now out of danger & in a fair way of recovery.

141 As Rushbrook had made various disbursements on Longe's behalf, his status was probably more than tenant alone. The family had Lime Kiln Farm on the Needham road.

142 Mr J. Kirby, former attorney, estate manager and (jointly with Sir Edmund) Nicholas Bacon's executor. Longe was involved in the case after Kirby's death only as beneficiary in Bacon's estate.

143 Charlotte Longe had previously given birth to four children, but only one daughter (Charlotte) had survived beyond infancy. Francis was to die aged twenty. See p.lix above for a family tree.

I wrote to my father. A letter from Jos. Church.

8 I rode to Ipswich & returned to dinner. The Miss Brokes & Mr Howes supped here. Dr Clubbe made Mrs Longe a complimentary visit.
I gave Mr Wenn a draft for £10 on Crickitt's bank.

9 At home. Mrs Longe continues gaining strength.

10 I preached at Crowfield in the morning. Coddenham afternoon.
A letter from my father. I wrote to my father & Sir Edmund Bacon.

24

11 June I went to town in the mail this evening, to settle accounts with Mr Windus, & meet Sir Edmund Bacon.

12 Spent the morning at Mr Windus's with Sir Edmund Bacon.
Drank tea with Sir E. & Lady Bacon. Called on Mr Longe in the evening.[144]
Paid Mr Windus my share of his bill for lawsuit: £81 15s. d.

Paid him by draft on Child	£70 13s. 0d.

13 Went to the bank & spent the morning in shopping.

Received myself of Child	£30 0s. 0d.
	100 13s. 0d.

Sir Edmund & I dined at Mr Windus's.

In Child's bank *[previously]*	£331 11s. 4d.
Deduct	100 13s. 0d.
Remains in Child's bank	£230 18s. 4d.

14 I left town early this morning with Sir Edmund in his gig.
We dined with Mr Havers at Ingatestone, & slept at Witham.

15 Breakfasted at Colchester. I got to Ipswich by 4 o'clock.
We dined at East Norfolk mess.[145] I got home in the evening.

16 At home. Charlotte dined in the drawing room today for the first time.

17 m. Miss Brokes called to see Mrs Longe. A letter from my father.

25

18 June I married Miss Bedwell to Mr Knights at Henley.
Called on J. Edwards of Bramford, & afterwards spent the morning with the Ipswich troop of light horse with whom I am enrolled.[146]
Wrote to Bickner for a uniform, & to Hawkes for an helmet & belt.

19 My brother, Captain Aufrere, Mr Williams & Mr Howes dined here.
I wrote to my father. We began cutting grass in the lawn this week.[147]

20 I rode to Ipswich & returned to dinner. Paid Mr Wenn on account of expenses of the late law suit, by draft at Crickitt: £31 10s. 0d.

21 At home. Paid Mr Goymour the parish assessor this day 2 instalments on the contribution & aid. My reduced income £1045, a tenth of which is £104 10s. 0d. Each instalment being a 6th part is £17 8s. 4d.

---

144 John's cousin Francis, then aged fifty, son of John's father's elder brother, often lived in London although estate owner at Spixworth (Norfolk) since 1776.

145 The officers' mess of brother Robert's militia regiment, at the cavalry barracks, St Matthew's, Ipswich.

146 The Ipswich Troop of Light Horse was that formed by Captain Maitland: see diary entry for 28 April. The details of Longe's kit are given in a diary memorandum at the end of the year (below).

147 The lawn: see note at 4 July 1796.

	Paid 2 instalments due June 5th	£34 16s. 8d.
	Paid also Gabriel Parr's ditto	0 1s. 9d.
		£34 18s. 5d.

22 I attended on the troop at Bramford.
Mr Peter Elwin of Booton died this morning at 9 o'clock.
23 Captain & Mrs Dashwood, & Miss Middleton called.
24 I preached at Crowfield morning. a. Col. Ward came this evening.

26

25 June Col. Ward & I set out for Norwich in my chaise, which I left with Stodhart to be painted. I dined with Mr Baker in the Close. Got to Spixworth for tea. I resigned the living of Henley before Dr Colombine.[148]
26 Mr Jos. Church dined with us. I rode with him to see some Roman antiquities found at Buxton. I received this week a uniform jacket & waistcoat from Bickner in Soho Square Not paid for. Also a pair of leather breeches from Wild in Piccadilly Not paid for.
27 I rode to Norwich & returned to dinner. Mr H. Elwin came in the evening.
28 I returned with Col. Ward in the mail to Coddenham.
I received a cotton waistcoat from Forster's.
29 I rode to Robert Fenn's to give orders about his new barn floor.
S. Riches here 2 days.
30 The Miss Brokes & Mr Howes drank tea here.
1 July m. I preached at Crowfield in the afternoon.

27

2 July I was out with the troop. A tempest this morning.
Jos. Church came here this evening.
3 My brother came to breakfast, & spent the day with us.
4 Jos. Church, Mr Howes & I went to Ipswich, dined at Bamford's & rode to the raceground.[149]
5 We were prevented going to the Ipswich assembly by an heavy rain.
6 We drank tea at Mr Davy's. I wrote to my father.
7 Mr Church & I went to Ipswich, & returned to a late dinner.
I received a letter from Mr Williams. I received 2 pair of drawers from Forster & two pair of nankin breeches, nankin bought in town & paid for.
8 I preached my farewell sermon at Henley in the afternoon.[150]

28

9 July I was out with the troop. Church accompanied me, & my brother met us in the field.
10 A heavy rain this morning. Mr Church & I dined with my brother. Charlotte accompanied us, & we all went to the East Norfolk parade.

---

148 Many episcopal functions were delegated to senior clergy (surrogates) such as Dr Columbine.

149 Bamford's Coffee House was on the corner of Tavern Street and Tower Street. Ipswich racecourse with its covered stand was on heathland south-east of Ipswich, as shown on Hodskinson's map. It was not merely for cavalry officers, for large crowds were drawn and enjoyed other attractions: Robert Malster, *A History of Ipswich* (2000), pp.120–1. A ball or assembly followed the races.

150 Longe had been incumbent of Henley for nearly five years.

11 My brother, Messrs Howes, Mann & Pettiward dined here.

12 Mr Mr Church & I rode to Ipswich, & afterwards dined at Mr Brand's, & met Mann, Methold, & Johnson. A letter from my father. Rain.

13 I was out with the troop. Jos. Church rode on to Ipswich. Riches 2 days.

14 Jos. Church left us, & went per mail to Norwich. Heavy rain.
1 & ½ chaldron coals brought by J. Bird.[151]

15 Mr R. Marriott entered upon the curacy of Henley during the vacancy there.[152]

29

16 July I was out with the troop. A very refreshing rain. I sent off the picture of 'Roman Charity' to Moor Park. 1 & ½ chaldron coals brought by J. Bird.

17 I rode to Ipswich. Rain again.

18 Mr H. Lawton called. The Middletons & Actons dined here.
Mr H. Elwin came from Norfolk in [*the*] evening.

19 I went with Mr H. Elwin in the evening to Ipswich where he took the mail for London.

20 We went to the play with the Middletons, Miss A. Broke & Mr Howes: 'the Castle Spectre'.[153] I wrote to my father.

21 The Miss Brokes & Mrs Ray called. I sent this week my waggon for 3 chaldron of coals, which I took (at his desire) of J. Bird.

22 [*no entry*]

30

23 July I was out with the troop. Afterwards dined at the Book Club, when the books were sold.[154] Showery weather.

24 Mr Ellis came & paid me £40. My brother & Captain Waring, Mr Howes & his friend Mr Hibgame dined here
We began our harvest by cutting oats & peas.

25 To dine at Mrs Acton's. Met the Middletons & Miss Brokes.
An extreme heavy rain today.

26 I rode to Ipswich, & had much conversation with Mr Wenn, respecting Mr Kilderbee's conduct in settling the business of the sale of Tunstall farm.[155]
A letter from my father.

27 At home. I wrote to my father.

28 At home. Mr & Mrs Roberts called. I received from Mr Wenn an account of Mr Kilderbee's having paid 1000 guineas on my account at Child's for the purchase of Bird's house, &c., for which I gave him a bond. Paid Mr Wenn by draft on Crickitt & Co. £52 10s. 0d, to be paid

---

151 Coal was at its cheapest in the summer months.

152 When John Longe was instituted to Coddenham-cum-Crowfield, the care of Henley was ensured by the obligation upon him to employ an assistant curate. He was now put in temporary charge ('curacy').

153 To be rebuilt in 1803, the Playhouse, next to the Tankard Inn in Tacket Street, was the first permanent theatre in Ipswich. David Garrick (1717–79) began there. Malster, *Ipswich*, pp.119–20.

154 See note 45 above.

155 Details of the bridging loan dispute between Longe and Kilderbee are given in the introduction (p.lxii). The problem related to the terms of the bond (28 July), which was not redeemed until about Christmas.

by him to Sir William Johnston, on account of rent, &c. of Bird's house received by me, &c.

29 a. Mr Hibgame dined & supped here with Mr Howes.

31

30 July I was out with the troop. Mr Jos. Church came unexpectedly, dined & slept here. We drank tea at Mr Howes's. We began cutting our wheat.

31 Mr & Mrs Roberts, Miss Brokes, & Mr Brand dined here.

1 Aug. To dine at Crowfield. Met the Actons & Miss Brokes.
Goodwin & Cooper began altering the sashes in the new nursery.
Received a letter from Wenn, now in town completing the business with Sir William Johnston.

2 We went to Ipswich. I called at Col. Wodehouse's, but did not see them. We called at Mr Edgar's.
Bricklayers here. 2 Goodwins a day, man & boy.

3 We drank tea at Mrs Sleorgin's, & met Mr & Mrs Dillingham.
Goodwin & son, &c. here, finished the brickwork about the nursery windows.

4 At home.
Received of Mr F. Elwin my dividend due at Midsummer: £20 5s. 0d.[156]

5 I preached at Crowfield in the morning.

32

6 Aug. I was out with the troop.
Received an account of Wenn, of his agents having paid £29 13s. 9d into Crickitt's bank on my account. NB: dividend is trust property.

7 At home. Mr Howes dined here.
I received a letter from Mr Wenn informing me that he had completed the business with Sir William Johnston: the purchase of Bird's house, &c.

8 Col. & Mrs Wodehouse. We dined at Mr Kirby's.
A letter from my father.

9 My brother came to breakfast. Mr & Mrs Edgar & Mr E. Starkey dined here. Mr T. Havers also dined here on his way to the Red House.[157]
A letter from Jos. Church

10 Mr Jos. Church dined with us on his return from Polstead.
I wrote to my father, & to Mr Parkinson about the prescription which his tenant Pemberton alleges at Crowfield.[158]

11 At home. J. Riches & son 2 days.

12 Mr Howes went to Thorpe, after duty in the evening at Crowfield.

33

13 Aug. I attended with the troop in a field by Brooks Hall. Afterwards rode to Ipswich.[159]

---

156 Dividends from various investments came in regularly, after Lady Day and Michaelmas, notably on the two gifts by Nicholas Bacon to Charlotte Longe: see notes at 3 May 1796, 6 Feb. 1798.

157 The Red House, mansion of the Edgar family just north of Ipswich, was approached in Longe's time from near St Margaret's church (Ipswich) up the centre of Christchurch Park and further north via 'The Avenue'. The mansion was demolished in the 1940s and the estate broken up. The farmhouse remains.

158 HA24/50/19/4.5(16): the tithe dispute over hay. This clerical landlord was in Gunton (near Lowestoft).

159 Brooks Hall, less than a mile from the centre of Ipswich, was on the way there from Coddenham.

14 Mr Edgar's: we dined there and met Major Wyndham, Miss Broke & my brother. Goodwin here putting up the stove in the new nursery. Cope here painting new nursery.

15 At home. We finished our harvest this evening, getting up barley by the plantation. I sent for 2 cart colts, 1 rising 4 & the other rising 3, which I have purchased of Mr Edgar for 36 guineas.

16 At home. S. Riches & son 2 days.

17 Company. Col. & Mrs Wodehouse, Captain Aufrere, my brother, Mrs & Miss Middleton & Mr H Middleton dined here. A letter received from Mr Williams concerning the picture, which gives me great uneasiness.[160]

18 At home. Mr Kirby called. Mr Howes returned from Morning Thorpe. A letter from Mr Timson of Moor Park concerning the pictures, & from my father.

19 Answered Mr Timson's letter.

34

20 Aug. I attended with the troop, & we exercised in a field by Round Wood.[161]

21 Mr Howes & I dined at Mr Dillingham's, & met the Forsters, Cromptons, Captain Aufrere & Mr Higgs. Charlotte not quite well, & did not go.

22 Ipswich Lamb Fair.[162] I rode to Needham. Mrs Sleorgin & Mrs Crossdil & family, & Miss Brokes & Mr Howes drank tea here.
I received £130 at Needham Bank by draft on Messrs Child.
Paid Mr Edgar for 2 colts by draft on Crickitt & Co.: £37 10s. 0d.

23 I rode to Ipswich, & went to the lamb fair. A letter from Mr Davy desiring me to take his name out of the book society.

24 At home. Paid Mr Wenn by draft on Crickitt on account: £20.

25 At home. We were invited to dine at Mr Gee's, but excused ourselves. Mr Howes dined here.

26 Mr Howes preached for Mr Kirby at Barham.
I preached at Crowfield in afternoon.
I received my copy of picture 'Roman Charity' back again from Mr Paske.

35

27 Aug. Book Club. I dined there.

28 Went per mail to Norwich, & got to Spixworth by dinner.

29 I rode to Coltishall, & called at Mr Church's & Mr Ficklin's.

30 I returned home in the carriage, which has been painting & repairing at Stodhart's.

31 At home.

1 Sept. At home. Mr Howes dined here. A letter from Mr Windus.

---

160 The picture causing Longe unease was probably *Roman Charity.* See diary entries for 16 July, 26 Aug. 1798, for which the context in the diary is between 21 March and 9 April 1798, and between 17 Aug. and 26 Aug. 1798. See also Appendix F. For further developments, see 2 to 15 Nov. 1798.

161 Round Wood, about 1½ miles from the centre of Ipswich, is shown on Hodskinson's map.

162 Ipswich Lamb Fair was held annually for 3 days at the Corporation farm just west of Handford Bridge. In 1791 there were over 200,000 lambs for sale: G.R. Clarke, *The History & Description of the Town and Borough of Ipswich* (1830), p.184.

I wrote to Mr Windus, [&] to Mr Ellis for 5 lb. of seed wheat, [&] to Mr Wenn, [&] to my father.

2 I preached at Crowfield in the morning.

36

3 Sept. Exercise day. I attended with the troop.
Mr Wenn was here in the afternoon to correct an error in a trust deed.

4 I attended the committee at the House of Industry.
My brother & Mr Howes dined here. S. Riches.

5 At home.

6 At home.

7 A very refreshing rain this morning. J. Riches. Mr Windus, Mrs Windus & son came here late this evening.
Memorandum. Paid Mr Windus his bill, for attendance on me & on our legacy being paid us in February last £9 6s. 4d.
Paid also Murray's bill on same business which Mr Windus settled with him for me £5 8s. 6d.
£14 14s. 10d.

8 Mr Windus, his son & I rode to Mr Ray's at Hawleigh.[163]
Miss Brokes, Mr W. Middleton & Mr Howes dined here.

9 The Winduses left this evening on their rode [*sic*] to Sir Edmund Bacon's.

37

10 Sept. Very heavy rain. My brother & Captain Lucas dined here.

11 The review of the troop, Ipswich cavalry. I did not attend it, but went to the committee at the House of Industry.[164]
Goodwin (2 men & boy) began repairing the brickwork which had settled in the bow. A letter from my father.

12 Tunstall. Charlotte & I went to Tunstall to suffer recovery, &c. for copyhold land of Blaxhall manor which was done at Blaxhall Hall – my brother went with us. Goodwin, &c. here.

13 My brother came here this evening.
Goodwin, &c. here, pointing the window.

14 We walked out shooting. 4 brace killed. Mr Howes dined here.
Goodwin, &c. here. Riches & son.

15 My brother & I prevented from shooting by bad weather.
He left us in the evening. A letter from my father.

16 I preached this morning at Crowfield.

38

17 Sep. Generals. I rode to Ipswich.[165] My father & mother came here in the afternoon. A letter from Jos. Church which I answered.

18 I attended the House of Industry committee.
My brother here to dinner. Dr Bell came here this evening.

19 My brother went out a-shooting. We all walked round the plantations.
Mr Chevallier & Clement Chevallier, & Mr Kirby dined here.
Mr Sparrow paid me £20 in part for furniture which he took of me.

---

163 The turnpike ran through the parish of Haughley (the modern spelling) just beyond Stowmarket.

164 Here Longe made an interesting choice of priorities.

165 The archdeacon's visitation; see glossary.

20 We walked down to the church, & called on Miss Brokes.
Mr Smith of Scole Inn sent me 20 guineas for my post chaise.
21 My brother & I walked out a-shooting.
Miss Brokes dined here, & Col. Ward.
22 My brother out shooting. We all <walked> went to Shrubland.
23 a. I preached at Coddenham in the afternoon. A letter from Jos. Church.

39

24 Sept. We all went to Ipswich. I attended the cavalry field, & my father, mother & Dr Bell & Charlotte saw the East Norfolk regiment & heard their band.
25 I attended the House of Industry committee.
We drank tea at Miss Broke's.
26 At home. My brother came in the evening.
27 Dr Bell left us this morning. We went out a-shooting. I shot a bird.
28 A rainy day. Paid J. Bird for 2 score weathers [*sic*] at £14 per score: £28, bought at Bramford.
29 My father & mother left us this morning. My brother & I walked out a-shooting. He returned to Ipswich this evening.
Paid Benjamin Cooper on account, £20.
30 m. Mr Howes administered the sacrament at Crowfield.
Mr & Mrs Simpson arrived at Shrubland Hall.

40

1 Oct. My brother came to breakfast, & we went out shooting. I shot a partridge. A letter from my father.
2 At home. Coddenham Sessions.[166] Riches & son 2 days.
I bought 22 ewes of Mr Kersey for £19 16s. 0d.
3 I called on Mr Davy, & at Mr Roberts's.
The news of Admiral Nelson's having defeated the French fleet arrived.[167]
4 I attended a quarterly meeting of the House of Industry, at Claydon.[168]
A letter from my father.
5 Captain Lucas & my brother came here a-shooting unexpectedly, & dined here. We called at Shrubland, but did not find the family at home. Riches here.
6 At home.
7 I & Mr Howes administered the sacrament at Coddenham.
Mr & Mrs Sympson called.

41

8 Oct. I attended the field day with the troop. J. Hines paid me one year's rent of his cottage due from Michaelmas 1796: £2 2s. 0d.
9 I rode to Ipswich.
10 Mr Plestow breakfasted here. The Miss Brokes & Lloyds called.

---

166 Magistrates sat at the Crown Inn, Coddenham. Longe, not at this time a JP, may have attended to support the sitting magistrates at what was a public open court.

167 The two months for news to arrive of the naval victory at Aboukir Bay (the Nile) did not diminish the enthusiasm with which it was celebrated. See also diary at 16 Oct. and 29 Nov. 1798.

168 Claydon and Barham (the latter the site of the house of industry) are adjacent parishes, approached from Coddenham by the same lane. The meeting may have been held away from the premises.

11 I & Mr Howes rode to Mendlesham to see the school farm.[169]
Mr Howes dined here.

12 At home. Riches here. I wrote to Mr F. Elwin & sent him an hare.

13 At home. A letter from my father.

14 I preached at Crowfield in [*the*] morning. Mr & Mrs Sympson at church at Coddenham for the first time.

42

15 Oct. We went to Ipswich, & returned to dinner.
Received two hampers of apples from Spixworth.

16 We went to the ball & supper at Ipswich in honour of Lord Nelson's victory.
We began taking down the fir trees in the garden, & removing the sun dial.

17 At home. Mr Howes dined here. I received Child's acknowledgment of my draft for Michaelmas dividend: £331 11s. 4d.[170]

18 My brother came to breakfast – we went a-shooting.
Mrs S. Broke dined here.

19 My brother & I went a-shooting. I shot a partridge.
Col. Ward dined here, & my brother returned with him to Ipswich at night.

20 Charlotte & I walked to Shrubland, but [*did*] not see the family there.
I received a letter from Mr F. Elwin, with Esdaile's receipt for our Michaelmas dividend: £201 15s. 0d.[171]

21 a. I preached at Coddenham in the afternoon. A letter from my father.

43

22 Oct. I attended the field day. Coddenham Book Club – I dined there.[172]
The fir trees felled in the garden were removed to Cooper's yard to be sawed into planks.

23 Mr Plestow came & spent the day here, & we went out shooting.
Mr Howes dined here. I sent my father a draft on Child for £100, of which we begged his acceptance. Draft dated October 21 payable at 10 days' sight.[173]

24 At home. A heavy rain today.

25 We went to Ipswich, & brought home Miss Brome.
I drew on Child for £100 payable to Crickitt & Co. at 7 days' sight, & received the money at Crickitt's bank.[174]

26 Messrs H. Middleton, Methold, R. Marriott, Mann & Howes dined here.

27 A wet day. At home. Very heavy rain tonight.

28 I preached at Crowfield in the morning.

---

169 Rent from the farm at Mendlesham, the only endowment within the school charitable trust, comprised almost the whole of the school's income.

170 Dividend as a half-year earlier: see note at 5 May 1798.

171 Esdaile & Co. were London bankers (in 1826 at least) for the Ipswich bank of Crickitt & Co. and several other East Anglian banks. For another half-yearly dividend see note at 20 April 1798.

172 The field day was short enough for Longe to return to Coddenham to dine with his friends at the Crown.

173 For another gift to his father: see note at 23 March 1798.

174 The transfer between banks would cover the gift to his father despatched two days earlier with a deliberately delayed date of payment, to allow for the second transaction.

44

29 Oct. We dined at Mr Sympson's for the first time; met Mr & Mrs Mackay, & the Middletons & Mr Howes. I received a letter from Mr Kilderbee about his resigning my stewardship of vicarage manor, which I answered, & wrote also to Mr S. Kilderbee on Mrs Kilderbee's being brought to bed.[175]

30 I rode to Mr Roberts's.

31 Mr Sympson came & went a-shooting with me. Mr Howes dined here.

1 Nov. At home.

2 I went a-shooting with Mr Sympson at Shrubland. I shot an hare, & brace of partridge. I received a letter from Messrs Dobie & Thomas concerning my giving up the More Park trinkets, &c.[176]

3 At home. Riches here 4 days. Simon Fenn settled his rent account to Michaelmas last. I wrote to Mr Windus about Mr Dobie's letter. A letter from Mr Williams about the More Park pictures.

4 I preached at Coddenham in the afternoon.

45

5 Nov. At home, very wet weather. Mrs Howes came to Coddenham. I wrote to Burton, Ellis, & Howard.

6 We called on Mrs Howes. Mrs & Miss Acton called. Very heavy rain tonight. I married Mr James Brooke to the daughter of Mr Robert Groom of Crowfield.

7 Very wet morning. My brother to dinner, & slept here tonight on his way to Spixworth.

8 Company at home. Col. Ward called, & he & my brother proceeded on their journey. Mrs Sympson & Arbonin & Mr Robert Sympson, Brand, Howes & Miss Brokes dined here. A letter from Mr Windus about the More Park gems, &c.

9 At home. We drank tea at Mrs Broke's. I wrote to Mr Windus & to Mr Williams.

10 At home. Mr Beck called.

11 I preached in the morning at Crowfield. Mrs & G. Howes dined here. A letter from Mr Burton containing an acknowledgment of his drawing on me for £45 3s. 0d. in payment of his bill for valuing tythes, &c.[177]

46

12 Nov. At home. We drank tea at Mr Howes's. James Brook settled his rent account to Michaelmas last.

13 Mr Ellis & Howard. Mr Howard came & settled his rent. At home all day. Robert Fenn settled his rent account to Michaelmas last. 1¼ chaldron of coals by R. Fenn. R. Howard settled his rent account. J. Bird ditto, & he also paid me his tythe account, & I paid him his bill for malt, &c. to November 5th.[178]

---

175 Longe's court for his manor, one of five with lands in the parish, had been run by this attorney as steward. The resignation probably resulted from the dispute between the men over the unrelated bond. Longe's response to the son (Samuel) was intended to heal the rift.

176 The correspondence with Moor Park continued. By 8 November 'trinkets' had become 'gems'.

177 Mr Burton was acknowledging payment of his professional bill.

178 Farm tenants: a composite entry. Longe had noted in advance that he expected two tenants to call, to whom he had written earlier. Only one came, whose payment he noted on the left page. Since

14 We went to Ipswich & called on the Kilderbees.
Mr Ellis came. Mr Ellis settled his account to Michaelmas.[179]

15 Mr Kilderbee holds courts for Crowfield Hall & Aspall Stonham manors.[180]
At home. A letter from Mr Williams.

16 At home. I walked to Mr Brand's.

17 Mr & Mrs Roberts called. A letter from my father.

18 My little bitch Dido after a few days' gradual decline died early this morning. The most faithful & affectionate companion I ever knew.

47

19 Nov. Exercise day. I attended with the troop at Bramford. Book Club. I dined there. The meetings of the troop for the winter were settled today to be on foot at the riding school, Ipswich: every other Tuesday beginning December 4th. 2s. 6d forfeits for non-attendance.[181]

20 Mrs Kilderbee & Mrs Dupuis called. We dined at Mr Roberts's; met Mr & Mrs Studd, Mr Brand & Mr Howes.
Received a parcel of acacias & other shrubs from Spixworth.

21 We carried Miss Brome home. Our little boy showed signs of inflammation on the penis, for which we sent for Mr Beck, who ordered a cold poultice. Received a basket of Cottenham cheeses, a present from Mr Church.[182] Mr Beck came to see the little boy this evening late.

22 At home. Rainy weather. Mr Beck called; Francis much better.

23 I rode to Mr Kirby's to consult with him on the purchase of the land tax belonging to the House of Industry, but did not see him.[183]
Mr Beck dined here.

24 At home. I wrote to my father & to Mr Jos. Church.

25 I preached at Coddenham in the morning.

48

26 Nov. Mr Kirby breakfasted here, & we went to consult Mr Brand on the redemption of [*the*] House of Industry land tax. J. Edwards brought [*the*] valuation of Mendlesham farm & other tythe valuations.

27 To dine at Mr Brand's; met Messrs Middleton, Sympson, Davy, Waddington, Howes & Mann.

28 At home. A letter from Jos. Church.

29 Thanksgiving Day. I preached at Coddenham, Mr Howes at Crowfield, to good congregations.[184] The Miss Brokes, & Mr & Mrs Howes dined here.

30 At home.

1 Dec. I went to Ipswich with Mr Kirby on the sale of the land tax business.

---

money was involved, Longe made a note on the right page too. A third tenant brought both coal and rent. Longe had a triple transaction with a fourth.

179 The second (Tunstall) tenant came to settle a day late.

180 Longe was noting that his recently resigned manorial steward had retained other posts.

181 The riding school was part of the cavalry barracks in St Matthew's parish, Ipswich (closed 1929).

182 This Cambridgeshire village was only twenty miles from Stilton, where better-known cheese was sold.

183 By the 1790s land tax produced little revenue and the burden could be redeemed ('purchased').

184 The government appointed thanksgiving days centred on a church service. See diary at 3 Oct. 1798.

I received a letter from Mr Kilderbee and Mr Wenn, concerning the payment of his bond; requiring it to be discharged from my private pocket, not from the purchase money of Tunstall now due, as at first settled, in which I think he has used us very ill.

2 I wrote to Kilderbee in answer to his letter.
Preached here in the afternoon. A letter from my father.

49

3 Dec. Coddenham tythe audit. I met the parishioners at the Crown at 11 o'clock, & dined with them there.[185]

4 Crowfield tythe audit. I met the parishioners at the Crown as usual, & dined there. Drank tea at Mr Howes's.

5 A very wet day. At home.

6 We called on Mrs Symson & Mrs Arbonin. Drank tea at Miss Broke's. I received a letter from Mr Windus, informing me of his having received the costs of the late suit from Sir William Johnston, viz. £241, of which my moiety (after deducting Mr Windus's account which is £20 7s. 9d) is £110 6s. 1½ d.[186]

7 I rode to Ipswich to consult with Wenn on Kilderbee's conduct.

8 A letter from my father concerning Mr Kilderbee's ill conduct to us.[187]
At home. Mr Marriott & Norford called concerning his institution to Henley.

9 I preached at Crowfield in [*the*] morning. A letter from Kilderbee.
I wrote to my father tonight, & sent him a copy of Kilderbee's letter.

50

10 Dec. We went to Ipswich, & talked with Mr Wenn about our dispute with Kilderbee. I wrote to my brother from Ipswich.

11 Mr Norford called to settle with me his demands for dilapidations at Henley. I dined at Mr Robert Marriott's & met a party of gentlemen.
Paid Revd. Mr Norford for dilapidations at Henley [?]allowing my proportion of tythes, &c.: £10 0s. 0d.[188]

12 At home.
Sent per post a draft on Child, payable to J.I. Meyer Taylor for £4 18s. 0d.

13 At home. A letter from my father.

14 At home. Frost broke up today. A letter from my father.
I paid Benjamin Cooper £25 on account.

15 At home. Mild drizzly weather. A letter from my father, inclosing one from my brother to Mr Kilderbee. Wrote to Mr Wenn.

16 Preached here in the afternoon. My brother sent us some snipes.[189]

51

---

185 Parson Woodforde held his annual tithe 'frolic' in his parsonage but Longe used the local inn each year: a significant distinction.

186 Although not a primary party, it appears that John Longe funded half the executors' legal costs, because he and his wife were substantial beneficiaries much affected by the result.

187 The dispute with Kilderbee over the non-payment of the bond came to a head during December. See introduction (p.xlii) and notes at 17 May, 26 July, and (nearing completion) 24 Dec. 1798.

188 Dilapidations were negotiated between the incoming clergyman and the outgoing man (as here, but often in practice his widow). Compensation was payable to a successor who took over outstanding obligations to the landlord with apportioned income set-off. See note to diary at 5 Jan. 1796.

189 The snipe is still sometimes served at table.

17 Dec. We dined at Mr Theobald's, & met Mr & Mrs Kirby, Mr Rodwell, Mr William Leeds, Mr Pearson & Mr Howes.
Carted gravel & chalk this week for the garden.

18 At home. I expected Mr Middleton, who did not come, to compound with me for Crowfield tythes, &c.
Mr F. Howes was married to Miss Franklin of Attleborough. I received a letter from Wenn, informing me that Kilderbee was inclined to alter his sentiments respecting the trust money.

19 Mr Middleton called, & promised to fix a day with Edwards to meet me here.

20 To dine at Mr Gee's. Mrs Longe being unwell did not go. Mr Howes & I went, & met the Middletons, John Edgars & Miss Acton. I wrote to my father. Nat. Keeble here felling firs, & cutting out stuff for railing.

21 Mr Francis & G. Howes dined here.
I wrote to Mr Elwin, & sent a turkey. Nat. Keeble [*here*] ditto.

22 At home. Sent my father some game.
2 Barkers, felling the apple trees in the lawn.

23 I preached at Crowfield [*in the*] morning, & here afternoon. I distributed 30 shillingsworth [*of*] bread among the poor inhabitants of Crowfield.

52

24 Dec. Book Club. We went to Ipswich & executed the conveyances of Tunstall farm to Mr Thellusson.[190] Dined at the club.
Weather very cold, & a flight of snow tonight.

25 Christmas Day. Sermon & sacrament at Coddenham. Afternoon service at Crowfield. Very coarse & snowy day. Received a box of presents from Spixworth, & letters. Letter from Mr F. Elwin.

26 To dine at Mr Howes's. We met the Miss Brokes.
More snow & severe frost. Wind north-east.
J. Edwards called, & promised to settle the composition which Mr Middleton is to pay me for Crowfield tythes in the course of next month.

27 To dine at Miss Broke's. Met Mrs & G. Howes. I was much indisposed with a cold. Deep snow now & severe frost. Wind north.

28 I did not go out today, being very unwell with my cold & cough.
A letter from my father. I answered it. Very severe frost.
The thermometer in the vestibule stood at 22.[191] Wind north-west.

29 I stayed within, nursing for my cold.
Wind changed to the south & the frost relaxed.

30 I dropped the morning service here, on account of my indisposition.
Milder air, & a gentle thaw. Wind south.

31 I did not go out today, my cold better. Mr Pearson of Framlingham called to speak about my demand of glebe land in Mrs Towel's farm.[192]

---

190 The documents of sale. The transaction could now be completed and the Kilderbee bond redeemed.

191 22 degrees Fahrenheit = 10 degrees of frost.

192 A dispute over land boundaries complicated by a road diversion in 1791. See introduction (p.xliii).

The following note appears on a blank page at the beginning of the book:

Game killed 1798

September	14	4 brace of partridge
	19	2 & ½ ditto, lease of hares
	3 ditto	
	1 & ½ ditto	
	26	2 & ½ ditto, & hare
	27	1 brace
	29	1 & ½ [*ditto*], & hare
October		1 2 ditto, & a brace of hares, & 1 pheasant
	5	a lease of partridge
	11	an hare
	13	a pheasant
	18/19	a brace of partridge, & ditto hares
	25	brace of pheasant, ditto partridge
November	1	an hare, & partridge
	16	a pheasant, & brace of partridge
	a couple of wood-cocks	
December	4	brace of hares, & ditto partridge
	8	an hare, & leash of partridge
	13	a brace of pheasants
	20	a brace of hares, & ditto pheasants
	21	an hare, & brace of partridge
	30	a brace of pheasants
1799 January	7	a lease of hares, & lease of pheasants

[*Total*] Partridge 26½ Brace Pheasants 7 Brace Hares 10 Brace

The following note appears just before week 1:

S Riches Apr 20th 10 Guineas per annum

Paid him one quarter's salary due at Lady Day, on my own account £2 12s. 6d.

June 23rd paid S. Riches, on account of Mr E. Bacon, for ½ year ending at Midsummer £5 5s. 0d.

(NB Sir Edmund Bacon does not owe me this)

November 3rd paid Riches 2 quarters' salary due at Michaelmas, on my account £5 5s. 0d.

Paid him 1 quarter ditto due at Michaelmas, on account of Sir Edmund Bacon £2 12s. 6d.

January 12 1799 paid S Riches 1 quarter's salary due at Christmas 1798, on my account, & the same on Sir Edmund's £5 5s. 0d.

£21 0s. 0d.

From this account, Sir Edmund owes me £5 5s. 0d.

The following note appears after week 52:

Expences of various accoutrements, &c. on my enrolling in Captain Maitland's Troop of Cavalry

Pair of doeskin uniform breeches	–
Uniform jacket & waistcoat	–
Helmet	–
Boots	–
Velvet cravat	£0 2s. 6d.
Blue cloak	3 3s. 0d.
Saddle & holsters & pad	6 1s. 6d.
Bridle	0 19s. 0d.
A white feather	0 7s. 6d.
Oct 25 – paid to Treasurer for cartrich box, &c.	1 10s. 0d.
Spurs	0 9s. 6d.

DIARY OF 1826

In January 1826, John Longe was aged sixty, living at Coddenham Vicarage with his second wife Frances, about eight years younger than he. His daughter Charlotte had left home when she married three years earlier. All three boys had graduated from Cambridge and Robert had been ordained priest six months before. Henry was planning to be ordained deacon during 1826. All three sons were based at Coddenham, although John was visiting friends in Norfolk for about three months early in the year and again for two months before joining his father on his Norfolk holiday.

During the year both Robert and Henry were to take curacies and a match was made for John with a young lady from Wiltshire. Longe himself has a busy year but makes visits to Bungay and for over three weeks to Norfolk. There was the first sign of conflict with his son-in-law. For the last three months of the year ill-health incapacitated him severely, as he noted in his diary.

1 Jan. I preached here, morning. Sacrament at Crowfield, 24 Communicants.
Wet day. Thaw set in. Mrs Longe ill with cold & did not go out.
My little spaniel bitch Frisky produced 4 puppies.
She shall bring up one, a dog.

2

2 Jan. Fine bright day. Our tenants & families dined here; with my own family, 20 at dinner.[193] Frost at night.
Settled accounts with Thomas Diggens to Michaelmas, & received of him on account of Michaelmas last: rent - £45. The arrears of balance still due is £108 18s. 4d. which he engages to pay in a month.

3 All at home. Fine bright day. North-east wind & very cold.
Wrote to my daughter Charlotte Leake now at Woodhurst, Surrey.[194]

4 Sittings at Needham. I did not attend.[195] Dry cold day.
Mr George Turner came here to dinner on a visit.
The children who sing at church had their treat here, & 6d each.[196]

5 Dry very sharp air. Mr Roberts dined here. Henry dined at Mr James's.
Wrote to Bickners for a suit of cloaths.

6 Very cold showery day.
Messrs William Leeds, Crowe, & Roberts dined here.

7 Mr George Turner left us after breakfast.
Received from Marshall, Cambridge, 4 soft Cottenham cheeses.

---

193 Longe invited his farm tenants with their families to dinner each New Year. Thomas Diggens, who leased Longe's Valley Farm, was later a churchwarden: see memorial window in St Mary's, Coddenham.

194 Charlotte and her husband Major Leake were visiting his father at 'Woodhurst', Oxted, Sevenoaks.

195 In addition to other duties, Longe and his fellow magistrates sat in twos or threes on appointed dates in 'Petty Sessions' or 'sittings', at Needham Market and in the Crown Inn at Coddenham. For the work of the magistrates, and their attendance at Quarter Sessions, see Appendices H and I.

196 Longe was ahead of his time, since few village churches then had a children's choir.

8 I preached here, afternoon. My sermon lately composed on the New Year.[197]

3

9 Jan. Very sharp frost. Mr Betham came here to dinner & slept here. John went to visit his friend Mr Jolly. Received from Otto Bickner a black superfine cloth coat, a black kerseymere waistcoat & breeches.

10 Mr Betham left us after breakfast. Mrs Selvin called. North-east wind. Thermometer [*with*] north aspect: 5 degrees below freezing point. Paid Mrs Longe in discharge of balance of house accounts to the end of 1825: £51.[198]

11 I attended a meeting of the hundred to consider of a plan for a general association for conviction of offenders of the hundred, which was agreed on.[199] I called at Shrubland Sir Philip Broke, &c. there. Sir Charles Vere called when I was out.

12 At home. Miss M.A. Davy came here on a visit.[200] Thermometer [*with*] north aspect at 9 o'clock a.m.: 7 degrees below freezing point. Felled the hazel & ozier underwood in the plantation before the house, & got two small waggon loads of faggots from it. Planted in spring of 1818.

13 Mrs Longe, I & Miss Davy went to Ipswich. I attended the Quarter Sessions. Returned to a late dinner. Sir Philip Broke called. To Mrs Longe on her private account £10. I sent a certificate of my life to Messrs Child for the Irish Tontine.[201] Thermometer the 3 last days at 9 o'clock a.m. out of my study window at 25 degrees, i.e. 7 degrees below freezing point. North wind.

14 At home. Robert & Henry dined at Mr Martin's. Mrs Longe & Miss Davy called at Shrubland. Sir Philip & Lady Broke, &c. there.[202]

15 I preached here, morning. At 11 o'clock p.m. thermometer [*with*] north aspect at 19 degrees fahrenheit, 13 below freezing point.

4

16 Jan. Mr & Mrs Brown dined & slept here. Wind changed to south-west. Air milder. Thermometer at 9 o'clock [*with*] north aspect: 16 degrees fahrenheit; out of my study window: 20 degrees.

17 Wind south, air much milder. At home. Mrs Longe & Miss M.A. Davy called on Mr Heath. James Brook settled accounts for rent, &c. due at Michaelmas last. Balance received £58 12s. 3d.[203]

---

197 By this time Longe did not compose many new sermons, but this was a favourite season for one.

198 It was Longe's practice to keep close control over all domestic matters.

199 The twenty-one hundreds in Suffolk were ancient units of administration. Bosmere and Claydon (originally two units but then one) had been incorporated earlier for poor-law purposes.

200 Miss Margaret Davy from nearby Barking was to marry Longe's son Robert in October 1828.

201 Longe's father had left him a share in an Irish tontine. This annuity, on survivorship of the 705 lives, had been issued in 1774 from Treasury Chambers, Dublin, to raise £265,000. Longe had periodically to confirm through Childs (his London bankers) that he was alive.

202 Sir William Middleton, then of Crowfield Hall, had in 1788 purchased Shrubland Park (the seat of the Bacon family for nearly two hundred years). Sir Philip Broke (Broke of the Shannon) was his son-in-law.

203 Brook was another of Longe's farm tenants. Longe had land in trust from three sources: modest glebe, plus the benefit of a trust from the mid-eighteenth century set up by the Revd B. Gardemau, who had married a Bacon heiress; thirdly, through his first wife, by wills of both Nicholas Bacon, and her father.

18 I attended the sittings at the Crown, and a vestry meeting to make a subscription for coals for the poor.[204]

19 I attended a meeting at the Crown (Helmingham Turnpike) to apportion statute duty.[205] Letter from my daughter Charlotte Leake from Woodhurst. [*She*] expects to come to see us about the 4th of February.

20 Miss M.A. Davy left us, & we walked with her to Mrs Brown's where she stays. Messrs John Methold & Benjamin Heath dined here.
John Fox settled accounts for rent, &c. for Widow Rushbrooke, due at Michaelmas last. Balance received: £41 14s. 5d. Young Henry Brown divided a drawer in my secretary into two, & put a lock on. Not paid for.
To Mrs Longe for her own use £5.

21 At home.

22 I preached here, afternoon.
At a Vestry meeting held January 18 it was agreed to let the poor have 2 bushels each of coals at 6d per bushel. My subscription [*is to be*]£5 which Diggens pays for me, being the sum due to me for my apprentice girl Mary Ann Goldsmith.[206] 1 bushel was distributed on January 19. I also contribute £3 towards coals for the poor of Crowfield. John Banyard provides them for parish & hamlet.

5

23 Jan. I & Robert dined at the Book Club.[207]

24 Mrs Longe, Robert & Henry went to the Ipswich County Ball. Examined accounts with Mrs Longe when it appears that, deducting £15 advanced to her January 13 & 20, there is a balance due to her from me of £58 11s. 1d.

25 I attended an appeal meeting [*on*] assessed taxes at Barham Sorrel Horse.[208] My sons Robert & Henry dined with Mr John Methold. My poor fawn Phyllis, which was given by Diggens to my dear son Frank in 1818, was worried by a stray greyhound & so much injured that I was obliged to kill her, now 8 years old.[209]

26 Mr Hamilton came here to dinner on a visit to my sons.

27 Mr Hamilton left us. Robert went to Barking, & Henry dined at Mrs Uvedale's. My old pointer bitch Phyllis after a gradual decline died, now about 9 years old.[210]

28 Dr & Mrs Sutton called.

29 I preached here, morning.
Fine dry weather with slight frosts all this week.

---

204 The Crown Inn: see note at 22 January 1796.

205 In Longe's time, parishes were statutorily responsible for the maintenance of roads, even after they were turnpiked. This responsibility was often discharged by a negotiated money payment to the trust.

206 Children in the house of industry were taken by rate-payers into apprenticeship as farm or domestic servants on a rota basis. A contribution was made from parish accounts, here still due.

207 Longe was in this monthly book club for over thirty years. See, for example, diary 22 Jan. 1796.

208 For assessed taxes see note at 4 April 1796. The Sorrel Horse public house stands on the old turnpike.

209 Francis (Frank) Bacon Longe, eldest of Longe's sons to survive infancy, died aged twenty in 1819.

210 Calling two animals by the same name may indicate a slip by the diarist. See also 25 Jan. 1826.

6

30 Jan. Revd Mr Wilcox breakfasted here. [*His*] complaint against Mr Blomfield of Little Stonham [*is*] to be heard on Wednesday.
Mrs Longe called at Barking.
Thomas Diggens paid arrears of rent due at Michaelmas last, left unsettled [*on*] January 2. Deducting some bills, &c., balance received £87 8s. 2d.

31 At home.

1 Feb. Attended the sittings. Mr Wilcox's complaint against Mr Blomfield was compromised.
Letter from my brother to Robert. John is still with him, & very well.

2 Mrs Longe & I went to Ipswich. Mr Cooke came to dinner. Robert dined at Mr Phear's. I arranged means with Mr Bacon for discharging last year's bills, &c. – deposited in [*his*] hands checks, &c. for £152 3s. 3d.
Sent an order to Child to pay £650 to my account with Ipswich bank for payment of bills, &c. of 1825.[211]

3 I & Mr Cooke attended a meeting at Barham, when we established the Association of Bosmere & Claydon Hundred. The Association rules are remodelled & improved today, & by the returns from the parishes, it appears that 45 persons have become members of it.

4 Mr Cooke left us after breakfast.
Letter from Charlotte now with Mr J. Leake at Thorp Hall, Essex.
She & Major Leake will be here to dinner on Monday next.

5 I preached here, afternoon. Robert at Henley & Creeting for Mr Heath.
Letter from John still at Blofield.[212]

7

6 Feb. At home. Major & Mrs Leake arrived here from Thorp Hall to dinner, both quite well. Sent Mr Brown 12 ilexes, raised here.

7 At home. Robert at Barking.[213] Wrote to John, my brother & Mr Church.
Wrote to Sir Thomas Cullum, & sent him a plant raised from an acorn of the old oak at Winfarthing in 1821.[214]

8 Ash Wednesday. Prayers here morning, & at Crowfield afternoon.
Mr Roberts dined here. Major Leake, Charlotte & I called at Mr Selvin's.
Prior's Grove today cleared of the wood faggots, poles, &c., &c.
I have been assisted by Brook's & Diggens's waggons.[215]

9 Confined within by a severe lumbago.

10 I am better today & walked out.
The Davys, & Mrs & Miss M. Martin called.

---

211 Edward Bacon, Ipswich Tory and banker, is not to be confused with the earlier Shrubland family.

212 Blofield (Norfolk) was then the home of Longe's younger brother.

213 Robert was doubtless at the parsonage there, home of Margaret Davy, his future wife.

214 Winfarthing (Norfolk): an ancient forest, but in Longe's time one giant tree was especially famous.

215 Prior's Grove is a small wood near the vicarage. The benefice owned half, divided lengthways. The priory of Austin canons at Royston (Herts.) had owned Coddenham church from the thirteenth century.

11 The severe pain in my back & loins returned, which quite disabled me from going out today. Henry went to Mr Bennet's, Finborough. Mrs Jane Fenn sent me the bills for my Malt House Farm for 1825, & an account of half year's rent due at Michaelmas 1825: £40. I was not well enough to settle these accounts with Mr Robert Fenn senior who brought me the money. Fine mild spring day. I heard the ring dove in the cedar this morning, first time this year.

12 I rose this morning free from pain, but remained at home. Robert officiated for me, morning.

8

13 Feb. A very fine mild day. I am now nearly free from any remains of lumbago. John returned from Norfolk. A letter from Sir Thomas G. Cullum. Note from my brother by John.

14 <I & Major Leake & Mrs Leake went to Ipswich, & I discharged my Ipswich tradesmen's bills for 1825.> Wet day – all at home.

15 At prayers.[216] Company to dinner <We dined at Mr Davy's, met Messrs Phear & J. Methold.> – the Martins & Davys & John Methold.[217]

16 I & Major Leake & Charlotte went to Ipswich, & I discharged all my Ipswich tradesmen's bills. In consequence of a letter from Dr Colvile to Robert offering him his curacy of Brome by Bungay, Robert went immediately by coach to Bury to see Dr Colvile on the subject.[218] Total Ipswich bills discharged today by checks on Ipswich bank: £237 15s. 11d. I ordered my name to be taken off from the dinner party at Gooding's Bear & Crown, Ipswich, as the forfeits are now made high.[219] I also intend to subscribe no longer than this year to the Ipswich Charity School, as they charge me for forfeits.[220] Wrote to Mrs Mackie for garden seeds, [&] to Freeman for a frame for my drawing of Andrea del Sarto.[221] [*Wrote*] to Mr Church & my brother, by my son John.

17 At prayers. We dined at Mr Davy's, & met Messrs Phear & J. Methold. Robert having seen Dr Colvile, returned today. Dr Colvile received him very kindly & gave him time to consider about taking the curacy of Brome.

18 Robert & Henry dined at Mr [*?*]Brown's.

19 Very wet morning. I did no [*sic*] go to church [*in the*] morning, but preached [*in the*] afternoon.

9

20 Feb. Mrs Longe & Charlotte called at the Red House.[222] Mr Edgar confined by the gout. John went to Norwich on a visit to Mr Church, & Robert

---

216 Prayers (public worship in the church at set times) were customary during Lent on Wednesdays and Fridays, then each day in Holy Week and shortly after Easter. See also 7 March 1798.

217 The deletions at 14 and 15 February result from Longe having begun an entry on the wrong date.

218 The modern spelling is Broome (Norfolk). There is also a Brome near Eye (Suffolk).

219 The Bear and Crown was on the south side of Westgate Street, Ipswich. Since the landlord would cater for the number of a club expected to dine, a forfeit payable by an absentee was reasonable.

220 There were several charity schools in Ipswich at that time. In view of Longe's commitment to the National Society (see 2 March 1826 and the introduction) this is probably their two central schools.

221 Andrea del Sarto of the Florentine School (1486–1530). This drawing was of St John the Baptist.

222 The Red House, mansion of the Edgar family, just north of Ipswich.

[*went*] to Bungay to look at Broome curacy, &c. I dined at the Book Club.

I sent by John, Frisky's puppy now 7 weeks old, a present to Mr Gostling my brother's friend at Plumstead. A very handsome red & white dog puppy, & a very engaging one.

21 Company to dinner – Drurys, Kirbys, Browns, Mr Parker, & Edwin P. & Mrs Edwin Paske, & Mrs & Miss Robinson.

Wrote to Mr Chevallier to come here March 6.[223]

22 Mr & Mrs Brown left us, after prayers. Fanny & Charlotte called on Mrs James & at Bosmere. Robert returned from Bungay much pleased with what he saw & heard of Broome curacy. Received ½ lb snuff from Churchman.[224] Letter from Mr William Blake: half year's interest paid to Gurney's on Saturday 18th, £125.

23 Wet morning. We dined at Mr Bellman's, met the Grooms, Mr Jackson & Mr Bellman of Soham. Engaged yesterday & today, in settling accounts & paying bills of 1825 in Coddenham.

24 All at prayers, & all dined at Mr Martin's; met Mr Methold who returned to Stonham yesterday, & his son John Methold.

25 We called at Mr Heath's, Mr Beck's, & on Major Broke at Mr Selvin's, Bosmere.[225] Robert went to his friend Mr Westhorp at Sibton, to officiate at Blighborough & Walberswick, which he engaged to do, tomorrow.

26 I preached here, morning.

10

27 Feb. Mr Lacey, a connection of the Leake's, came here to dinner on a visit. Robert returned from Sibton.

28 Major & Mrs George Broke, &c. called. Mr Roberts dined here. Robert at Barking. All the family went to the Ipswich Ball except myself.

Wrote to John at Mr Church's in a parcel by Star Coach.[226]

Mr Murray junior served me with a subpoena to attend at Chelmsford Assizes, March 6, to give evidence in Mrs Barlee's indictment of the Barlees. Received £5 for travelling expenses.[227]

Paid Mrs Longe on her own account £5, to send to Mrs Garrod.

1 March At prayers. Afterwards attended the sittings.

2 I & Major Leake went to Ipswich, took Mr Lacey with us on his return home. I attended the National School.[228] Settled with Mr Bacon to go with him to Chelmsford on Wednesday. Went over the County Gaol with Major Leake.[229]

---

223 Mr Chevallier, involved later in the Croasdaile saga, did call on John Longe, a fortnight later.

224 This family had a tobacco business near the West Gate in Ipswich, and later a cigarette factory in Portman Road. One Churchman (Lord Woodbridge, d.1949) gave two large Ipswich parks to the town.

225 Bosmere House stands by the River Gipping and the mere which gave its name to the hundred.

226 For the Morning Star coach, plying daily between London and Yarmouth, see Appendix E.

227 The Barlee case (7 to 11 March below) attracted great attention. See introduction (p.xliii).

228 This was probably the pair of 'central schools' in Ipswich, conducted by Suffolk's affiliated 'National' society formed in 1812. Longe had been involved ever since. See introduction (pp.xxxiii–iv).

229 Opposite the first four lines of 2 March is a figure 3, suggesting that the entry should be transferred to the next day. Longe often attended as JP at the County Gaol, near Ipswich West Gate. The new gaol in St Helen's parish was not commissioned until after his death.

A letter from Mr Murray with a copy as stated of my affidavit, but I query whether a correct one? Requires me to be at Chelmsford on Wednesday next, March 8. On conversing with Mr Sparrow [*at*] Ipswich today, I have reason to believe it is correct.

3 At home.

4 At home. Showery. Robert went to Sibton for his duty tomorrow. Much rain at night. Wrote to Mr Blake, & inclosed a receipt for Mrs Longe's half year's interest due last month.[230]
[*Wrote*] to Mrs Mackie for garden seeds, &c. concluding as I have not yet [*received*] what I sent for, that my order by John did not reach her.

5 I preached here, afternoon.

11

6 March At home.

7 Went to Ipswich. Breakfasted with Mr Bacon, & proceeded to Chelmsford in the Shannon.[231] Arrived there at 3 o'clock, where I found several other witnesses at the White Hart Inn, where I dined & slept.

8 The trial of indictment against the Barlees postponed till tomorrow 9 o'clock. In court this morning. I bought at Guy's, bookseller, Chelmsford, a good copy of Phodra's *Variorum a Leasontio* & of Seneca's *Tragedies Variorum Elgeoir*, both very clean copies in vellum, for £1. 1s.[232]

9 The trial commenced at ½ past 9 o'clock before Baron Graham & a special jury. He sat till 5 o'clock p.m.

10 In court again at 9 o'clock. I was examined by Mr Price & cross-examined by Mr Broderick. We left the court as yesterday at 5 o'clock. I dined with Mr Methold at Mr Bartlet's.

11 In court again at 9 o'clock. After Mr Methold's examination we left the court at 12 o'clock & he & [*I*] returned in a post-chaise.
Mrs Longe met me at Ipswich & we got home about 6 o'clock.
The trial Barlee v. Barlee, &c. terminated today at 1 o' clock.
Verdict for the defendants. <This week, Thomas Diggens paid Mrs Longe for my 2 fillies: £29. To Mrs Longe on her own account; £29.>

12 I preached here, morning. Mr Bellman dined here.
Fine dry March weather since Tuesday.

12

13 March At home. Attended the Saving Bank.[233] Robert returned from Sibton.
Letter to Robert from John – still at Mr Church's & quite well.

14 At home. Mrs Longe went to Ipswich. Wrote to Mr Guy, Chelmsford, to send me a very valuable copy of *Diadorus Siculus*, 2 volume folio in vellum, which I saw there last week, price £6 6s. 0d.

15 Mr Methold & his son John dined here.

---

230 John Longe had made a loan to Mrs Catherine Longe of Spixworth Park, the impecunious widow of his cousin Francis: see introduction (p.xliii).

231 The Shannon left Ipswich every morning for London. See Appendix E.

232 *Variorum* editions contain scholarly notes. Having studied the classics as a young man, Longe may have valued these writers for their material, rather than as a collector. Seneca the Younger (3 BC – AD 65) wrote nine tragedies, adapted from the Greek. Little is known of Phodra or this work. See also 14 and 16 March for Diodorus Siculus (90 – 21 BC), a Sicilian Greek historian.

233 Coddenham Saving Bank had been founded in 1818 and was flourishing enough to have a branch at Stowmarket, at least by 1844 (White's *Directory*).

Robert & Henry went to Mr James's to stay 2 nights.

16 At home. I received from Mr Guy the above copy of *Diadorus Siculus*, & on Friday 17 by his desire paid the price charged (£6 6s.0d.) to Mr Postle Jackson, Ipswich, for which I have his receipt.

17 I & Charlotte carried Miss Croasdaile to Ipswich.[234] I attended the National School weekly committee. We called on Mr Edgar now recovering from a severe illness, gout, &c. Robert has received from Dr Colvile his nomination to the curacy of Broome-by-Bungay. In consequence, I wrote to Mr Kitson on the 18th respecting license, &c.

18 At home. Mr Davy called. Robert went to his churches at Blighborough & Walberswick. My young cart mare Diamond, now very forward in foal, was taken ill. I had her bled by Smith, 4 quarts, & gave her an ounce of oil of turpentine in gruel. She is better this evening.
Mr Diggens paid me for my 2 young fillies by Brunette: £29.
To Mrs Longe on her own account: £29.[235]

19 I preached here, afternoon.

13

20 March Passion Week. At prayers. Attended the Saving Bank. Mr & Mrs Chevallier called on their way to Bildeston. Book Club: I did not dine there. Letter from my brother. I received last week from Freeman, Norwich, a black & gold beaded frame for my black chalk drawing of St John Baptist by Andrea del Sarto – no glass sent with it.

21 At prayers – afterwards attended a Commissioners meeting at the Crown to swear in assessors.[236] Mr Charles Brook of Ufford & Captain Allen with him called. Wrote a few lines to John in a letter of Henry's to him.
Letter from Mr Kitson in answer to one from me respecting Robert's nomination to the curacy of Broome.

22 At Prayers. The Leakes & my sons dined at Mr Phear's.
Letter from John with a present of fish.

23 At prayers. Robert went by coach to Yoxford to attend his churches tomorrow, & from there goes to Bungay. Robert will enter on Dr Colvile's curacy of Broome next (Easter) Sunday, & will go to Norwich on Monday to give his nomination to Mr Kitson & get his license. He intends looking out for lodgings at Bungay on Saturday. I gave him a note of introduction to Dr Camell, who will I hope assist him in the enquiry.[237]

24 Good Friday. I preached here morning.
Mr Roberts officiated at Crowfield, afternoon.

25 At home.

26 Easter Sunday. Sacrament here: 86 communicants.
Mr John Methold assisted me, Mr Roberts being requested by Mr Heath to officiate at Creeting, himself being too ill to attend.

---

234 Miss Croasdaile features more extensively later in the year: see diary between 7 Nov. and 22 Dec. 1826.

235 Longe deleted his entry at 11 March 1826. The replacement entry at 18 March was subtly different.

236 For assessed taxes see note to 4 April 1796.

237 An example of Longe's paternalism. Robert was aged twenty-five.

Very cold north-east wind all this week, with storms of snow & sleet.

14

27 March Easter Monday. At prayers, & vestry meeting afterwards.[238] At Saving Bank. Severely cold north-east wind & snow. My Brunette mare slipped her foal.

28 Easter Tuesday. At prayers. Robert returned from Bungay by the Star. The wind changed to south-west & a very pleasant mild day. We dined at Mr Brown's. Robert has engaged lodgings at Bungay at 10s. 6d per week, at Mr Sporle's. Wrote to Spratt to say that I would take the landaulet away, & leave my present one with him about the 13th of next month, when I intend going into Norfolk for a few days.

29 I attended the sittings at Needham. Overseers appointed.[239]

30 I attended the quarterly meeting, House of Industry. Mr Cooke returned with me.

31 Mr & Mrs Wenn spent the day [*with us*], Mr Wenn by my desire, to consult with me on the steps necessary to be taken for the disposition of the property here.[240]

1 April Mr Cooke left us. Robert went to Bungay to take possession of his lodgings there & his curacy of Broome. I lent Robert my bay horse Captain for the present.

2 Sacrament at Crowfield, 18 communicants. I preached here, morning.

15

3 April Trustees' meeting, Charity School. Sir William Middleton & Mr Kirby present.[241] I, Major Leake & Charlotte, & Henry dined at Mr Kirby's, met Mr & Mr Rogers, &c. Mrs Longe received intelligence of the death of poor Mrs William Ward of Diss.[242]

4 I attended a meeting of [*the*] General Committee [*of the*] National School Society at Stowmarket.[243] Saw Dr Colvile there. Letter from John, which I answered same day.

5 I with Major Leake & Charlotte went to Framlingham to shew him the castle, &c. – returned to dinner.

6 At home.

7 I attended the Quarter Sessions. Very little business. Dined at the White Horse. Left my banking book with Ipswich bank with Mr Smith the clerk, & desired him to pay £450 of my money now in this bank, in

---

238 This annual meeting of parishioners was traditionally on Easter Monday. Churchwardens were then chosen. As in Lent, prayers were read during the week after Easter.

239 Overseers of the poor were nominated in parish vestry but their formal appointment lay with the JPs. For responses to poverty, see Appendix C.

240 Longe was considering the position on his death. Although he owned no land outright he could crucially decline to join in adjusting the terms of family trusts created long before his second marriage, to fit the unequal position in life of his four children. Note too that his second wife was unprotected upon his death, with neither a share in Bacon's earlier generosity nor the right to occupy the parsonage house.

241 The number of trustees was down to 3 by 1826. For the village school see introduction (p.xxxii).

242 Longe's wife Frances was the daughter of Col. Richard Ward of Salhouse Hall (Norfolk). Other relatives lived at Diss and St Neots. For the Ward family tree, see pp.lx–lxi above.

243 Longe was still serving on the main committee fourteen years after this county charity had been formed for educating the poorer sections of the community. Stowmarket was a central county venue.

part of payment of my last year's overdrawn account due to Messrs Bacon & Co.

8 Very warm spring day. Wind south-west.
Major Leake & Charlotte left us to go on a visit to Mr Edgar's.
From Churchman ½ lb black rappee – due.

9 I preached here, afternoon.
Mild spring day. Slight mild showers this evening.

16

10 April John returned home by the Star. Robert came home to dinner.
Began to brew, spring brewing.

11 I & Mrs Longe went to Salhouse, saw my new landaulet at Spratt's which is now completed. Called on Mr Valpy, & reached Salhouse at 6 o'clock. [*We*]found Mrs Ward better than expected. Showers today.
My wife designs to stay with her mother & brother & sister at Salhouse this and next week, to go to Diss early in the following one, & to return home on Friday fortnight, April 28.

12 Fine rains in the night, & showery day.
I & Mr Ward walked to my brother's & saw him & my sister.[244]
He now quite recovered from his late gouty indisposition.

13 Mr Ward & I went down to the Broad to take up [*?*]bev. nets, &c. but caught only a few eel.[245] Sir Edward & Mr Jonas Stracey called.

14 I left Salhouse after breakfast, left my old carriage at Spratt's, for which he is to allow me £25, & proceeded home in my new one.
Arrived home at 5 o'clock dinner.

Price of the new landaulet complete	£180
Spratt allows me for my old one	25
Balance due to Spratt	£155

15 All at home. Robert left us for Bungay on the grey mare, which I lent him.
I had a long conversation with my sons & Charlotte & Major Leake about the disposition of our property after my death. She & the Major are anxious that we should cut off the entail. I told them that after mature consideration, & after consulting with my sons, I am determined not to take this step hastily. There does not appear to be any propriety in doing this immediately.[246]

16 I preached here, morning.

17

17 April I & John went to Ipswich, & consulted with Mr Wenn as to the future disposition of Coddenham property. I dined at the Book Club, & drank tea with Mrs A. Broke, where Major & Mrs Leake & my sons dined.
Desired Mr Wenn to draw up queries as to several points of Mr Bacon's

---

244 Longe always referred to his brother's wife Mary as his sister.

245 Salhouse Broad lies downstream from Wroxham.

246 An entail in a trust is inalienable, except by advance agreement ratified by court order. Only with Longe's active agreement could the entail be barred. If unamended, the wording of Nicholas Bacon's will would, on the death of both Longe and one of his four children, ultimately favour only the diarist's male grandchildren. In 1826, none of his four children had issue.

will, particularly as to my powers as to the livings of Coddenham & Barham.[247]

18 All at home. The Bellmans & Miss Hervey called. Mild day – south wind. I heard nightingales this evening. Henry had heard them the latter end of last week.

19 All at home. Dry cool day. Frost.
I examined today my pass-book with Ipswich bank & find it correctly balanced. My debt to Bacon & Co. this day is £101 1s. 3d.

20 All at home. Dry east wind. Sent an order to Messrs Child for payment of £146 13s. 6d. to Mr B. Woodd, & £10 7s. 0d. to Messrs Bradell.[248]

21 My daughter & Major Leake left us this morning for London by Bury. I attended the archdeacon's visitation at Ipswich & dined with him, and drank tea at Mr Cooke's. Wrote to my wife in Charlotte's letter to her. I heard the cuckow first this spring.
Mr Parker of Ringshall preached at St Mary Tower from 1 Cor 9.16; 'Woe is me if I preach not the Gospel'. He very properly repelled the charge of those both in & out of the church who accuse us of not preaching the Gospel. A very good discourse.[249] I brought home Ryece's manuscript 'Suffolk Antiquities' lent me by Mr James Conder of Ipswich.[250]

22 Fine mild warm day. Wind south. All at home.

23 I preached here, afternoon. Finished brewing.

18

24 April John attended his troop in Shrubland Park & dined with them at Needham. Henry also dined there. I attended the Saving Bank for Mr Bellman.[251]
I have felt gouty tenderness in my left hand some days. Today my 4th finger is swelled & inflamed, having had some pain in it in the night.

25 Showers today. Wind south. I walked to view a piece of ground taken in from the highway by James Durrant by the new cottages, Crowfield Road.[252] Letter from Mrs Longe, to send the carriage to Diss for her on Friday. My son John went by the Star Coach to visit Robert at Bungay.

26 Attended the sittings.
The sewers, &c. all cleaned by Scrutton & Hobart this week.

27 At home. <Helmingham Turnpike trustees annual meeting at the Crown Coddenham. Dinner 3 o'clock.> Letter from Robert. Henry went to Bury by coach on a visit to Mr Rogers at Lackford. Wrote to the bishop

247 Two advowsons were assets within the Bacon will trusts, of monetary value to a layman only if sold. For Longe's ordained sons the right to present would be the key to a lifelong enjoyment of a benefice, giving both status and income. The advowson to Coddenham-cum-Crowfield was exercisable on Longe's death; that to Barham on Kirby's death. Kirby, six years older than Longe, outlived him by sixteen years.

248 Note the enormous bill to one of Longe's wine merchants (B. Woodd) and see 31 May.

249 This entry shows not only the prevailing criticism but also clerical awareness of it.

250 Other versions of the manuscript of Robert Reyce (otherwise Ryece) (1555–1638) existed. In 1902, Lord Francis Hervey published a transcription: *Suffolk in the XVIIth Century: the Breviary of Suffolk*.

251 The trustees of the Saving Bank exercised supervision of the bank on a rota basis.

252 Physical encroachment was the concern of the vestry, of which Longe was *ex officio* chairman.

of Norwich, to request him to dispense with the requisite of a title in my son Henry's case, who applys for deacon's orders next ordination.[253]

28 Mrs Longe returned home to dinner. Helmingham Trustees Turnpike meeting [*at the*] Crown, Coddenham. Dined with them. 6 only in company.[254] Mr E. Edwards drank tea here.

Wind north-east & the ground covered with snow early in the morning, & snow & hail storms in the course of the day.

29 Sharp frost last night. At home.

30 Sharp frost. I preached here, morning. Cold day, wind north.

Engaged closely this week in making extracts from Mr Conder's Suffolk manuscript. Answer from the bishop: he very kindly will admit my son Henry without a title. Engaged all this week in making extracts from Mr Conder's manuscript.

19

1 May Cold showery day. Wind north. Robert came home from Bungay on his new mare. My son Robert has lately purchased a very promising bay mare 4 years old, of a farmer at Thorington, for 40 Guineas.

I set on Meek & my day men, & cut & cleared the approach to the house, which was completed in the day. It is set out full 8 feet width.[255]

2 Fine mild day. All at home. Robert went to Barking.

3 At home.

4 Messrs Parker & Crowe dined here accidentally, on some tench, &c., a present sent this morning by Mr Theobald.[256]

5 I & my son Robert met the parishioners at ½ past 8 o'clock, & went with them the bounds of the parish of Coddenham with Crowfield. Returned for ½ past 5 o'clock. I rode good part of the way. Robert by choice walked the whole round.

Perambulation of the parish. We had a very favourable day for our perambulation. Had an excellent breakfast at Crowfield Rose. I walked with them nearly to Mr Edwards at Crowfield, & then mounted my mare & rode the rest of the round by the roads. On our return at ½ past 5 we had a very nice cold dinner at the Crown. 30 at dinner. The inferior people had bread & cheese & beer in the room below, & we sent them a cold round of beef from our table, about 40 young men & boys.[257]

6 Robert left us at noon on his return to Bungay.

John & Henry returned from Cambridge to dinner. Mr Diggens & Thomas Edwards, Church & Chapel Wardens, arranged everything as to the provisions & the perambulation extremely well.

---

253 As the Church of England ordained only to a specific training post (the 'title'), a candidate to the diaconate needed to have been conditionally accepted. Longe was asking the bishop to trust him to take interim responsibility for his son. This the ever-compliant Bishop Bathurst did.

254 The Helmingham trustees had responsibility for two lengths of turnpike running northwards out of Ipswich, and an east–west stretch joining them. The chairman chose the venue, between three local inns. For Longe as a trustee see the introduction (pp.xlix–l).

255 The carriageway through the park (the 'lawn') to the vicarage was over a quarter mile long.

256 'Accidentally' means 'without prior arrangement'.

257 In the Visitation Return of 1820 (p.175 below), Longe said that the circumference was about twenty miles. The Rose public house is over three miles from the centre of Coddenham. Seventy parishioners took part.

7 I preached here, afternoon. Very cold stormy weather this latter end of the week. Wind north & north-east. Engaged closely all this week in making extracts from Mr Conder's Suffolk manuscript.
Letter from Charlotte.

20

8 May Mr & Miss Caroline Davy called. Sent [*to*]my son Robert to Bungay an hamper with 2 & ½ dozen of port wine & an ham, by Betts's waggon to Norwich, to be forwarded from Schole by the Harleston carrier.[258]

9 Col. Stewart of Melton, a friend of my son John's, came & spent the day here.

10 At the sittings. Mr & Miss Margaret Davy called.

11 At home.

12 At home. Henry dined at Mr Davy's.

13 At home. Letter from my brother, which I answered by return of post, saying that I thought we could receive them here, the beginning of next month.

14 Whit Sunday. I preached here, morning.
Mr Roberts administered the sacrament at Crowfield: 21 communicants.
Letter from Robert at Bungay.

21

15 May Mr Cooke came here to dinner.

16 Mr Betham spent the day here.

17 At home. Mr Cooke left us. Sent an order to James Brook to pay Robert Proctor the assessor his charge viz: Land Tax 2 quarters

	£15 9s. 0d.
½ year's assessed taxes	35 5s. 6½d.
	£50 14s. 6½d.[259]

I sent my son Henry's testimonials, &c. for orders to Mr Kitson, for tomorrow morning's mail.

18 Very warm day. Mrs Longe called at Mr James, & at Mr Davy's.
Wrote to my son Robert. Sheep washed today.

19 At home. Mrs Longe & John went to Ipswich. Lady Middleton & Miss Leveson Gower called. A letter from Major Leake to Henry, in which he treats the subject of an arrangement of the reversion of the property here to my children in a very uncandid & indelicate manner.[260]

20 All at home. Blighting fog from the east this morning, but warm sunny day after it. I wrote to Charlotte in answer to her letter received the 7th of this month, and told [*her*] my sentiments on Major Leake's very unhandsome conduct. Letter from Robert who comes on Monday.
Sheep clipped today. Mr De Carle sent home the new brass mounted harness for the coach horses.

21 Trinity Sunday. Sacrament here, 74 communicants.

22

22 May My son John set out on a tour to Cheltenham with Major Turner of Ipswich. Robert arrived here from Bungay soon after breakfast.

---

258 Betts's waggon went to Norwich weekly. See Appendix E.

259 Longe's farm tenant James Brook of Choppins Hill was indebted to him.

260 The reversion in these trusts established earlier would take effect upon John Longe's death.

I & he dined at the Book Club. James Brook carted home my top-wood from Prior's Grove: 5 loads & the large battling. He has taken himself 4 load, & [*?*]compost 1 ditto for which he owe me 12 shillings per load.

23 I attended a Commissioner's meeting at Claydon.[261]
Henry dined at Mr Bellman's, & Robert at Mr Brown's.

23 & 24 Francis Mayhew of Baylham brought my timber from Prior's Grove to my saw-pit, with his drag & 4 horses. I paid him for the 2 days' work at 25 shillings per day £2 10s.

24 At the sittings. Mr Crowe dined here. A most acceptable rain came on about 2 o'clock from the north & continued with little intermission till 12 o'clock at night. Edward Edwards paid me £4: 1 year's interest on £100 bond, Helmingham Turnpike Trust, due July 2nd 1819, at 4 per cent only.[262]
We have had no rain for nearly a month, & the cold north & north-east winds & frosty nights have kept back the grass & clover which is now very short. The corn crops however look very promising. This most acceptable rain will be of great service to everything.

25 At home. Robert at Mr Davy's. Fine mild showers almost all day.

26 Mr Davy came with Robert by my desire, when I informed him of the whole of Major Leake's very unhandsome conduct respecting the reversion of Coddenham property.[263]
John Goldsmith, Fenn's malster, broke his thigh, being beat down by his horse running away with the cart. It is said that he was in liquor, which he is very apt to be. A sad drunken fellow.

27 Robert left us for Bungay. Mrs Longe & I went to Ipswich, where I saw Mr Wenn. A fine ground rain this morning.

28 I preached here, morning. Dry day.

23

29 May Showery day. Wind north. Engaged all the morning in justices' business.
My son John reached Cheltenham, after going to Oxford in his way. A letter reached me from him, June 1. He had seen Miss Flower who was well, & received him very kindly.[264]

30 Showers from north & north-east. We dined at Mrs Collier's, Ipswich – met Mr John Collier & Lieut. Col. Collier lately returned from India. James Brook paid me on account of Lady day rent: £45.

31 Lady Middleton & Mr Acton called. I dined at the Crown, 1st meeting of the Bosmere & Claydon Association against felons, &c. 14 present. Bill 5s. 6d each, besides the 2 guineas allowed from the funds.[265]
I began reading the ordination service for deacons with my son Henry,

---

261 Local tax commissioners (magistrates and others) supervised national tax assessment on the individual and would hear appeals against the decisions of officials. They sat in more than one place during the year.

262 Longe had invested in the turnpike trust, formed in 1812. Note the delay in payment.

263 Under the will of Nicholas Bacon, the four Longe children received substantial assets for life, upon John Longe's death. Mr Davy's concern was as father of Robert's future wife Margaret.

264 The reception of Longe's son by this maiden lady led to his engagement to her neice, Caroline.

265 This Association was presumably the one formed after the diary entry of 11 Jan. 1826.

with Bishop Mant's notes, &c.[266] Received from Basil Woodd an hogshead of sherry, & some claret & chablis all got home safe.

1 June Mrs & Miss Collyer, Colonel Collyer & Mr John Collyer & his two daughters, Mrs A. Broke, Mr & Mrs Brown & Mr Roberts dined here, & Mr Treadway. Heavy rain at night. Letter from Dr Ward of Coltishall about the cask of Lachryma Christi wine.
I wrote to Robert saying that finding Henry very deficient in his preparation for the ordination examination, I could not satisfactorily leave him next week, in hopes of rendering him some assistance.

2 Dry day. Mrs Longe went to Ipswich & carried Miss Margaret Ward to Miss Burwell's there. We called on Sir Philip & Lady Broke, &c. at Shrubland, from where I walked home.

3 Fine mild day. All at home. Mrs Longe received a very extraordinary letter from her brother Robert Ward saying that Mrs Ward had resolved to make a new will, & a different disposition of her property. This will be his will & not Mrs Ward's; his conduct is very mean and dirty. He ought to have informed his sister earlier.

4 Mild warm day. I preached here, afternoon.

24

5 June Dry warm day. Engaged all the forenoon in the garden, clearing the flower beds in the shrubbery. Mr Phear & Mrs Fonnereau, &c. called.

6 All at home. Wrote to John at Cheltenham.

7 Showers this morning from the north. At the sittings. Mr Davy called.

8 I & Mrs Longe went to breakfast at Mr Bellman's, & we all went to Easton, & spent the morning in seeing Lord Rochford's house & pleasure ground, & then dined at Mr Bellman's.[267]

9 At home. Very hot day. I wrote to Robert announcing our intention of going to Bungay for a night or two on Monday.

10 Very hot day. At home.
Thomas Diggens paid me on account of Lady Day rent: £100.
Paid Mrs Longe £80 on h[*ousehold*] account & her private account.

11 I preached here, morning. My son Henry left us to go to Mr Methold's this evening, & to proceed with Mr John Methold to Norwich tomorrow in his gig. Letter from John at Cheltenham. I wrote by Henry to my brother, & to the bishop to thank him for his kindness in dispensing with a title for orders in Henry's case.

25

12 June Mrs Longe & I went to Bungay to spend a few days with my son Robert.
Breakfasted at Scole where we found Henry & Mr John Methold. Called on Mr Sandby at Denton, & reached Bungay by ½ past 2 o'clock. At the Tuns. Very hot day. Ipswich Borough Election began.

---

266 George D'Oyly and Richard Mant, *The Holy Bible … with Notes Explanatory and Practical* (1817, 1823, 1845) was a manual popular among ordinands. Mant was bishop of Down and Connor.

267 The mansion at Easton (Suffolk) of the earls of Rochford and dukes of Hamilton no longer stands but much of the 'crinkle-crankle' wall does. It was said to be, of its kind, the longest in the world.

Candidates: 'Blues' MacKinnon & Dundas. 'Yellow' Haldimand & Torrens.[268] In the evening made a sketch of Bungay Castle.[269]

13 Made a sketch of St Mary's Church, Bungay.[270] Called on Dr Camel & Mr Bewicke. The Bohuns came to breakfast & spent the day with us. In the evening all went to Brome. Went over Brome Hall, & church, & saw the Queen Oak felled there last year by Sir William Middleton, said to contain, branches & all, 15 loads & 38 [*?*]feet of timber.[271] At Coddenham in the evening a very heavy rain fell with violent thunder, lasted about an hour. We had little of it at Bungay.

14 We went to Mettingham Castle of which I made 2 sketches.[272] Mr Sandby called on me. Drank tea at Mr Bewicke's. Very hot day. Wind south-west.

15 Left Bungay at 6 o'clock, got to Scole by breakfast, & home by ½ past 2 o'clock. Fine warm day but a brisk wind. At Scole, 2 of Mr William Ward's daughters met us, who told us that Mrs Ward of Salhouse had been taken dangerously ill last week, & continued so ill that Mr William Ward went to Salhouse yesterday. Bill at the Tunns [*at*] Bungay including servants & horses £7, of which Mrs Longe paid me £2.[273]

16 MP nomination [*at*] Stowmarket. I went there in the gig. Sir Thomas Sherlock Gooch & Sir William Rowley nominated. No opposition, no-one else proposed; a very peaceable meeting.[274] The new turnpike road from Coombs [*sic*] to the bridge, altered by my first suggestion to the trustees, is now completed, & open to the publick, & a great improvement.[275]

17 We went to Ipswich, & brought home Miss Lucy Preston on a visit. Ipswich Election. Poll Books closed about 3 o'clock, & return made in the evening for the 'Yellows' Haldimand & Dundas. The 'Blues' say it is a false return, & that they have a majority of 5.

18 I preached here, afternoon. My son Henry was ordained by the bishop of Norwich in Norwich cathedral.

26

19 June Robert came home to breakfast. Mr Phear called. I dined at the Book Club.

20 Suffolk County Election, Ipswich. We all set off from hence at ½ past 8. Met Sir Thomas Gooch at the Roundwood toll gate.[276] A very numerous & a most respectable cavalcade. I dined with the 'Blues' at

268 The two 'Yellow' candidates were returned but the result was later reversed on petition. See 17 June 1826, note at 18 April 1827 and Appendix G.

269 The ruins of Bungay Castle, a few yards from the centre of the town, date from the twelfth-century baronial power of the Bigod family.

270 St Mary's, the larger and grander of the two town churches, is now redundant.

271 How Sir William Middleton came to fell 'the queen oak' has not yet been traced.

272 The ruined Mettingham Castle is fourteenth-century in date.

273 The passage from 'At Scole' is dated 14 June but this must be in error as the meeting at Scole Inn must have occurred on Longe's return journey home on 15 June.

274 Elections for two Suffolk MPs ('knights of the shire') were rarely contested at this time. See Appendix G and the note at 16 May 1796.

275 Approaching Stowmarket from the south-east, the turnpike crossed a tributary of the Gipping in the parish of Combs, originally at a ford. A sharp deviation today takes the road to the bridge.

276 Longe made a shorter entry on the left page and a longer one on the right. The Roundwood toll-gate, on high ground on the Woodbridge road, was over 1½ miles east of Ipswich town centre.

the old Assembly Room.[277] Mrs Longe, Robert & Miss Preston dined at Mrs Collier's. I gave a breakfast here as usual to the freeholders of Coddenham & the neighbouring ones whom I know. Total at breakfast at 7 o'clock [*blank*]. I got a new blue calico flag with tassels, &c. this time, & we all set off at ½ past 8 o'clock to meet Sir Thomas Gooch at the Roundwood toll gate at ½ past 10. Mr Theobald & his friends joined us at Claydon. [*We*]went through Ipswich. The attendance for Sir Thomas Gooch was more numerous than ever. That for Sir William Rowley very small. All went off in a very harmonious manner. Nothing said about the Catholic question, but on Sir Thomas Gooch after dinner giving the toast of "the Protestant Ascendancy" the cheering was general & long continued, & the feeling of the 'Blues' on this subject clearly manifested itself.[278]

21 At the sittings. Robert went to Barking, & took my mare.
A little rain in the evening.

22 Mr Ball tuned the pianoforte. Mrs Longe & Miss Preston called at Barking. Letter from Henry. Wrote to John at Cheltenham.

23 All busy in the hay field. Robert returned from Barking to dinner.
Half year's rents received today: Richard Fenn, Hemingstone, balance £56 16s. Mary Fenn, Malt House Farm, balance £22 4s. 3d.
Widow Rushbrooke by check on Alexanders for £85.
Nat Keeble & William Barker here some days this week, repairing the forcing pump. The floor over the well, where decayed by the dripping of the water, repaired with oak plank, [*?*]churled, & the whole floor pitched inside & out.

24 Robert left us in the afternoon to return to Bungay, where Henry is to come to him from Blofield.

25 I preached here morning. In the afternoon Miss Preston played the organ.
My son Henry officiated for his first time at Broome church, Robert's curacy. Very hot weather all this week with bright sun.

27

26 June Very hot day. Mr Phear & the Baileys, &c. called.
We drank tea & spent the evening with Mr & Mrs Crowe.

27 We all went to Stowmarket, I to attend a General Committee meeting [*of the*] National School Society, & Mrs Longe & Miss Preston called on Mrs Pettiward at Finborough.[279] I got some beds of the white single & double moss roses from Mr Crabb's, Stowmarket.

28 Very hot day. All at home. Miss Robinson dined here. Letter from Mr Gooch to thank me for my exertions, &c. on his election last week.[280]

---

277 The old Assembly Room in Tavern Street retained its popularity after new rooms were opened in Northgate Street in 1821. Both buildings still stand.

278 Churchmen feared that to give Catholics full rights of citizenship would mean the end of establishment. They questioned the loyalty of Catholics to the Crown. 'The Catholic question' had been a burning issue for decades, but emancipation followed controversially in 1829.

279 Finborough is near Stowmarket. To make full use of the wheeled transport, Mrs Longe often arranged social calls to coincide with her husband's business journeys.

280 Longe omits the title of Sir Thomas Gooch.

A present from Mr Fox, taken from his pond next the road: 7 fine tench & carp. [*I*] put 4 into the pond in front of the Vicarage, [*and*] cooked the rest.[281]

29 June I attended a quarterly meeting [*at*] Barham House. Henry returned from Bungay, where he has been on a visit to Robert. Barham House. Election of a director. Benjamin Morgan of Baylham elected by a majority of 3 against Mr Brown, Hemingstone. I withdrew Mr Phear's name whom I had nominated with his consent.[282] Ordered 2 & ½ rates for this quarter.

James Brook paid me arrears of Lady Day rent: £39 10s. 5½ d.

A long letter from Major Leake.

30 Mr Buck, Luxmoore, Roberts, & Mrs & Miss Robinson dined here.

1 July We went to Ipswich, saw Mr Wenn about the Chancery suit with Mrs Longe, &c.[283] A fine shower of rain, with distant thunder at night.

2 Henry read the morning service & preached, & read evening service here. We all thought that [*he*] went through the whole very respectably. Mr & Mrs Brown drank tea here. I paid Mr Brown, Mr Arbonin's bill for Teneriffe wine £24 14s. 2d. I wrote to Major Leake by Henry.

28

3 July My son Henry left us on his way to London, on a tour in Scotland.[284] All at home. Very hot day.

4 The haymakers had their plum pudding & beef dinner. Very hot all day.

5 All at home. Very hot day. Mr Davy called.

Letter from Mr Church, & Mr Smith of Oakley.

6 Very hot day. In the evening Mrs Longe, & Misses Preston & M. Davy, went to Ipswich to hear the Infant Lyra.[285]

7 Very hot day. All at home. A gentle shower at 4 o'clock.

8 Very hot day again. A slight shower in the evening.

Letter from Robert – John did not receive my letter duly, has had a return of his disorder, & on account of the excessive heat of the weather is gone to Malvern.[286] Letter from Major Leake.

9 Early in the morning a fine steady shower for 3 hours. Showers also till noon. I preached here, morning.

29

10 July Robert came over to breakfast. We dragged the ponds but with little success. Mrs A. Broke & Mrs Bailey to tea. Robert has lately had a letter from John by which it seems mine of 22nd June had not reached him.

He has suffered much from the heat of the weather, and had a return of his disorder, & is gone to Malvern Abbey.

---

281 There are still ponds at Ivy Farm, Coddenham, one each side of the road.

282 A contested election for a directorship of the house of industry may suggest party politics.

283 Mrs Catherine Longe (aged seventy-two), John Longe's cousin-by-marriage, lived at Spixworth, the Longe family seat. Widowed in 1812, to raise funds she took various steps damaging to the estate. The diarist acted to protect the reversionary interest of his eldest son, also John, including litigation.

284 Henry was able to take a three-week holiday just after his ordination, because he had no post.

285 Lyra, an infant prodigy who performed on the harp, outshone the slightly older Franz Liszt (born 1811).

286 John's disorder is further mentioned in the diary on and after 27 March 1827 and in 1831.

11 I attended the House of Industry for Mr Methold.[287] The Edgars & Davys to dinner, & Mr Roberts. Miss Margaret Davy left us.

12 I attended Quarter Sessions at Ipswich, & returned to tea.
Robert went to Barking. Wrote to my brother by Mrs Longe, & to Hart the organ builder to come & put in the 2 bass open diapason pipes ordered some time ago, & to tune the organ.[288]

13 Mrs Longe & Miss L. Preston left me for Norwich, Mrs Longe to visit Mrs Ward at Salhouse. Robert returned here to dinner, and Mr Roberts dined with me.
A fine rain came on at about 5 o'clock which last[*ed*] about an hour.

14 Engaged all the morning in justice business with Cattermoul, Ling's apprentice of Crowfield. I & Robert dine at Mr Davy's. Letter from my brother. Letter from John now at Clifton. He writes in good spirits, & desires me to write to him at Cheltenham, where he intends to be on Tuesday on his return home. I wrote to him an answer this evening.

15 Robert left me to return to Bungay. I called on Mr & Mrs Gaunt, who are now at Mrs A. Broke's. A fine shower of rain this forenoon.
Robert left his dog Rover here who has had the distemper, to be nursed.

16 I preached here, afternoon. Shower in the morning.

30

17 July Revd Thomas Singleton called. I dined at the Book Club, annual sale. Drank tea with Mr Pettiward at Mr Roberts. Hot day. Wrote to my daughter Charlotte by Mrs Bayley. Began mowing peas this morning. I procured for the Club an haunch of venison from Mr Fonnereau & a turbot & lobsters from Townsend pr[*ice*]d 1s. 3d.: both excellent.

18 I dined at Mr Roberts's, met Messrs Pettiward & Gaunt.
A letter from Mrs Longe.

19 Wrote to her. [*I*] shall send the carriage for her to Diss next Tuesday. The lumbago, which I have had something of these 2 days, is now very painful & almost disables me from walking. Messrs Singleton, Pettiward, Brown & Roberts dined here. Mr Singleton slept here.

20 Mr Singleton left me after breakfast. Very full of pain in my loins & back all day. Obliged to give up going to the annual Suffolk Clergy Charity meeting at Ipswich.[289] A letter from Henry, dated Portobello, Edinburgh, July 16. [*He said that he*] had an attack of cholera morbus last week, & leaves Edinburgh by a Leith packet as this day.[290]

21 Fine shower early this morning. A great deal of pain all day.

22 Fine mild showers this morning from the north-west. My pain is abated today. In the evening a settled mild rain which continued more or less all night. Samuel Smith of Mendlesham having expectedly disappointed

[287] Directors supervised the workhouse weekly in rotation. Absence from committee required a deputy.

[288] Mr Hart from London had in 1817 supplied and fitted the church organ at Coddenham.

[289] Clergy provided for their own old age by staying in post and paying deputies as necessary. The greater problem was provision for their widows and any orphans. The clergy charity helped in this.

[290] Morbus simply means disease. Cholera was known and named earlier than the pandemic some five years later. Here a false alarm.

me of his last half year's rent, I sent a note to him by John Gowers. His answer is that he will pay it in three weeks.[291]
Engaged in preparing information respecting the Booths of Shrybland Hall, [*their*] armorial bearings, &c., for Mr Robert Blake by his request.[292]

23 Rain continues mild but plentiful. So wet that I am obliged to drop my morning duty here. With about 2 hours' intermission at noon the rain continued till about 7 o'clock [*in the*] evening. It was much wanted and must be very serviceable to all the crops.

31

24 July Fine sunny day. Henry returned, having got on shore at Harwich; quite well. Henry's disorder appears to have been a severe diarrhoa, for he was not confined above a day, & has not felt any other symtoms of cholera.
I therefore apprehend it to have been a salutary effort of nature. Sent my packet of memorandum of the Booths of Shrybland to Mr Robert Blake.

25 Fine harvest day. Mrs Longe returned home to dinner from Diss. Began reaping wheat.

26 Fine harvest day. Henry dined at Mr Drury's.

27 At home. Letter from John.

28 I attended a Crowfield Hall manor court, at Crowfield Hall. My son John returned home, very well.

29 We went to Ipswich, called at Christ Church.[293] Went to Mr Pearson's & saw a portrait of him done by Bennet who is now staying with him.

30 Very hot day. Henry read prayers here, afternoon. I preached.

32

31 July Robert came here to breakfast. Mr Pettiward called. We dined at Mr Drury's, John with us, met the Theobalds & Col. Burton, Bacons, &c. Very hot day. Revd Henry Hill of Buxhall died.
Began carrying in wheat. My spaniel Miss puppied; 4 pups.

1 Aug. Mr Pettiward called. We dined at Mr Theobald's, John with us.

2 Magdalen Fair, Sprowston [*was*] discontinued by order of the lord of the manor this year.[294] I attended the sittings. Mr Cooke came to dinner. Fine harvest weather. James Barker 3 days putting up the brewing copper, which has been new bottomed, & whitewashing the brew house. [He] finished this evening. Letter from my daughter Charlotte Leake, now with Major Leake at Cheltenham.

3 Robert went to Barking. I, my sons John & Henry, & Mr Cooke dined at Mr Daniel Pettiward's, met Mr Pettiward, &c.
John Chaplin my tenant in Choppyngs Hill Cottage died aged 64. At his widow's request, I permit her to continue in the cottage.

---

291 Longe sent his coachman to be sure of an immediate commitment, even if not cash, and perhaps impress upon the tenant the importance of prompt payment of rent.

292 The Booth (Bothe) family held Shrubland in the fifteenth and sixteenth centuries, before the Bacons.

293 The Fonnereau family had Christchurch (mansion with park) from 1735 until it came to the borough of Ipswich in the 1890s.

294 Longe has added this note to the printed words 'Magdalen Fair'.

4 A shower in the night. Mr Cooke & I called on Mrs A. Broke, Mr Martin & Mr Brown. Company to dinner; the Drurys, Theobalds, & Col. Barton & Bacons, Messrs Buck & Jackson.

5 Mr Cooke left us. All at home.
My pointer bitch Juno who is nursing 2 puppies, when Miss was absent got to her puppies & killed them both. Those puppies were by a red & white spaniel lent me by Mr James of Barking Hall.

6 I preached here, morning. Henry [*officiated*] for Mr John Methold at Henley.

33

7 Aug. Mr James & Mr Davy called. All at home. John went on a visit to Mr Drury's. Very hot day. I began my sermon for "After Harvest".

8 We all dined at Mr Davy's, & met the Turners of Kettleborough.
The wheat field (Ladycroft) cleared: all got up without a drop of rain.[295]
We received the annual present of half a buck from Countess Dysart.[296]

9 Henry dined at Mr Drury's.
At home. A fine mild rain in the afternoon & evening.

10 Fine harvest day. At home. Henry rode to speak to Mr Mumford about the curacy of Bricet, Wattisham &c.[297]

11 Gentle showers this forenoon. Company to dinner: Sir William Middleton, the Martins, Bellmans & Browns, & Mr Roberts. Helmingham venison, dinner very excellent [*illeg.*]. Rain in the evening.

12 We went to Ipswich. I saw Mr Wenn, & settled with him to take steps to get a valuation of my property here.[298] Fine dry day. I received £200 at Ipswich bank, & by Sunday's post sent an order to Child to pay the above sum to Sir James Esdaile, to my account with Ipswich bank. Brought home an old Shrubland picture which Smart has cleaned & repaired, & which proves a very fine portrait (unknown) by Sir Peter Lely: a person in armour.[299]

13 I preached here, afternoon. Henry assisted Mr M. Edgar at St Nicholas's Ipswich & dined with him.

34

14 Aug. John returned from Mr Drury's. I dined at the Book Club.
A fine shower fell in the evening. Thomas Diggens paid me on account of rent due at Lady Day last: £55 11s.0d. & deductions allowed £33 9s. 0d – total £89. Arrears still due of Lady Day rent: £21.

15 Fine harvest day. All at home.
Finished getting up barley from [*?*]Cabbage Hill. The corn now all up in excellent order. Wrote to Charlotte, & sent Mr Bell's Opinion.[300]

16 Showery morning. [*To*]Mr Edgar's. We & John dined there, met Dr &

---

295 Ladycroft is the large field to the north-west of Vicarage Farm.

296 In Helmingham Park deer still abound.

297 Nothing came of his enquiry at these parishes.

298 Longe was again considering how to dispose affairs in the event of his death.

299 This may be one listed in 1890 as of Edward, 1st Lord Sandwich, and only 'after' Peter Lely (1618–80) the Dutch-born portrait painter. See Appendix F.

300 On behalf of Longe, Mr Wenn often took the written opinion of appropriate counsel on matters of law. This one related to Longe's disposition of the family wealth after his death.

Mrs Beck. My son Henry having been informed that Mr Carthew will be without an assistant curate shortly, went to Woodbridge & spoke to him on the subject. From all he saw & heard about the curacy, he is inclined to engage in it. Stipend £90 per annum.

17 At home. We drank tea at Mrs Robinson's.

18 At home. John & Henry dined at Mr Roberts's.
Wrote to Robert to say that we intend being at Bungay on Tuesday evening. I finished my Sermon for "After Harvest".

19 At home. Very hot day.
Paid Mrs Longe weekly house account from April 1 to Aug 5th:£92.
Letter from Charlotte. She has received my letter with Mr Bell's Opinion.

20 Henry officiated here for me, morning.
I preached my sermon for "After Harvest", afternoon.

35

21 Aug. At home packing up for our excursion. Mr Beck called.
Letter from Mr William Blake informing me that he had paid £125, Mrs C. Longe's interest money, to Gurney for Sir James Esdaile, &c.

22 Mrs Longe, I & John set out at 8 o'clock morning, breakfasted at Scole & reached Bungay by 3 o'clock. Robert came to us at the Tuns. He has had a second attack of bilious complaint.

23 We went to Beccles, Robert rode with us, & dined & slept at Mr Bohun's.
Robert returned to Bungay in the evening.

24 Robert came again to breakfast, & he & the Bohuns accompanied us to Lowestoft.[301] The Bohuns left us in the evening. We slept at the Queen's Head. Concert in the evening.

25 We called on Mr Acton, the Wests, Lady & Col Durrant, Mrs & Miss Morse, Mr Downes & Mr Crowe. Robert left us to return to Bungay.

26 Left Lowestoft, & went to Yarmouth. [*We*] took up our abode at the Nelson Hotel, where we found my brother & sister.
Walked to the jetty in the evening.

27 At church, morning & evening. Called on Mr Dawson Turner & on Revd Richard Turner. We drank tea with Mr Dawson Turner.
Saw the Humfreys, who are staying here.

36

28 Aug. Bathed. [*I*] went to Mr Dawson Turner's, & spent some hours in his library. At the play in the evening.

29 Called on the Humfreys & Miss S. Fellowes. We all dined at Mr D. Turner's. Letter from Henry [*that our*] garden [*has been*] robbed of filberts. Meek has behaved very ill, & is negligent. Wrote to him by return of post.[302]

30 Drove to the Nelson Column, then took a boat to Burgh Castle, made some sketches, & returned by water to a late dinner.[303]

---

301 Lowestoft and Yarmouth were fashionable summer resorts as well as fishing ports.

302 Meek, the gardener, left Longe's service six weeks later: see diary entry at 11 October.

303 Burgh Castle is a 5-acre Roman fort with massive walls surviving on three sides.

31 We went with the Humfreys, Miss Susan Fellowes, Mrs Hulton & family & Miss Begge [*on*] a sea excursion. At the play in the evening.

1 Sept. Called on Mr Dawson Turner & Mr Richard Turner.
Drank tea with Mr Dawson Turner. Rain at night.
Letter from Robert now at Coddenham, & wrote to him & Henry.

2 Heavy rain in the forenoon, Spent some hours in Mr Dawson Turner's library. He shewed me Mr Colby's two Rembrant portraits.
We all went to Miss Cramer's benefit play in the evening.

3 Mr Greene breakfasted & spent the day with us.
At church, morning & evening. I called on Miss Emily Aufrere, &c.

37

4 Sept. Left Yarmouth, stopped & made a sketch of Caister Castle, got to Salhouse to dinner, & found Mrs Ward much recovered.[304]
At a Trustees' meeting held this month, the tolls at the several gates on the Bosmere & Claydon turnpikes were [*let*] to Gnott, the surveyor, for 1 year ending November 1827, at £1805. It was resolved to remove the gate at Stonham back to Brockford, where it lately was placed. Next year the tolls to be reduced.

5 At Salhouse. Mrs Longe went with Mrs Ward to Rackheath. Sir Edward & Mrs Edward Stracey called on us. My brother & sister dined here.

6 At Salhouse. A thorough rainy day detained us here.

7 Left Salhouse. [*We*] rested at North Walsham, & reached Cromer by ½ past 2 o' clock. Found accommodations at Tucker's New Inn. Very comfortable.
Letter from Robert to John - Mr Davy dangerously ill with strangury. Wrote <*to them*> by return of post [*?*]to Robert & Henry.

8 Showery morning. At noon we walked to the lighthouse, &c.
Made a sketch of Cromer.

9 Bathed in a very bad shower bath. Took a drive to Sheringham & Beeston. Made sketches of Beeston Priory.[305] Dr & Mrs Maltby drank tea with us.

10 At Cromer church, morning & evening.
Drank tea with Mrs Clitherow & the John Straceys.

38

11 Sept. Left Cromer, rested at Aylsham. Stopped at Mr Church's Frettenham a few hours, & got to Norwich in the evening. Slept at the Norfolk Hotel.
Letter from Henry. Mr Davy better.

12 I & John called on Mr Valpy & the bishop, & saw them both.[306]
We went to Mr Preston's, Stanfield Hall to dinner. Mr Anguish, Sir Windsor Sandys, &c. there.[307] I called on Mr J.S. Cottman, & desired him to send me copies of his *Norfolk & Suffolk Brasses*, & *Norfolk Antiquities*.[308] Ordered at Ling's a silk MA gown, the silk from Eaton's. Paid William Spratt, coachmaker, Norwich for a new landaulet the price

304 Caister Castle, north of Yarmouth.
305 Beeston Regis has considerable remains of this Augustinian priory.
306 Bishop Bathurst's career is briefly considered in the introduction (pp.xxxiv–v).
307 Stanfield Hall is to the east of Wymondham.
308 J.S. Cotman (1782–1842) was an architectural draughtsman and etcher, not merely a water-colourist.

of which is £180. He allowed me £25 for my old carriage, & I paid him by a draft on Child dated Sept 12, £155.

13 Made a sketch of Stanfield Hall. Walked with Mr Preston about his grounds & home farm.

14 Mr Geo. Preston, I & John drove to Kimberly, & called on Lord Wodehouse, who received us very kindly & appeared in very good health. Afterwards to Hingham, saw the church, & east painted glass window lately presented by Lord Wodehouse, ancient glass which cost him £1500. Saw the tombstone of one of my ancestors Johan Longe & Margaret his wife. In the centre of the nave west end. The brass nearly gone, but the name is still legible.[309] Returned by Wymondham, & viewed the church, &c.

15 Breakfasted at 7 o'clock, rested at Scole Inn, & reached home by ½ past 4 o'clock. Found Henry remarkably well. We have had a very agreeable excursion.

16 At home.

17 I preached here, morning.
Henry [*preached*] afternoon for Mr Davy at Darmsden Chapel.

39

18 Sept. Very wet day. Went in the evening with Mrs Longe & Henry to Bury by invitation from Mr Hasted, for the oratorio [*to mark the*] opening of the new organ at St Mary's. The new organ at St Mary's is built by Gray London (from whom I bought our church organ). It is a very good instrument.

19 We all attended the oratorio, which was well performed. A large party at dinner at Mr Hasted's. Concert at the theatre in the evening. Miss Paton (Lady William Lenox) & Sapio & [*?*]Atkyns from London. The performances gave much satisfaction, & the church & theatre were very full. All the chief families in the neighbourhood were at the oratorio.[310]

20 Made some morning visits to Mrs Wayth, Sir Thomas Cullum, &c., & returned home in the evening.

21 At home, engaged in justice business.
Wrote to my brother to come next week – & to Robert.

22 Mrs Longe & I left our cards at Shrubland for Mr & Mrs Middleton, now there. Mr Middleton called here in my absence.[311]
Mrs Longe brought Mrs William Ward of St Neots here on a visit.
Began to gather apples. Letter from my brother, which I answered in my letter not yet sent. He & my sister come on Thursday the 28th September.

23 At home.

24 I preached here, afternoon.
Henry [*preached*] in the morning for Mr Davy at Barking.

40

309 Hingham church is still noted for the Flemish glass in its east window. Longe's ancestors were living there from the reign of Henry VIII, and nearby in 1485.

310 Two events in Bury's elegant social calendar. Built in 1819, the Theatre Royal is a rare example of a late Georgian playhouse. The diarist James Oakes also refers to this oratorio: Fiske, *Oakes*, p.315.

311 Mr William Middleton the son, soon to succeed his father, seems to have moved from the dilapidated Crowfield Hall into the parental home: see note at 21 July 1796.

25 Sept. Showers. Attended a parish meeting for nominating surveyors.[312]
Mrs Longe & Mrs W. Ward went to Ipswich.
Received by Mr Pritty my bank book with Messrs Child, balanced to Sept 20 – balance then due to me £177 15s. 8d., but my draft to Spratt not yet paid which will reduce my balance with Messrs Child to £22 15s. 8d.

26 Mr Barstow came here to shoot. Mr Kirby called. Showers.
Wrote to Mr Ling [*at*] Norwich for a bombazine AB gown for my son Henry.[313]

27 At the sittings. John & Henry dined at Shrubland.
Received from Gall, Chymist, Bury, six boxes of his dentifrice, for which I owe him 6 shillings.

28 Farming. My brother & sister came on a visit to us. [*They*] left home this morning at 8 o'clock & reached us by ½ past 4 o'clock.

29 Mrs A. Broke, the Gaunts & Mr Roberts dined here.

30 At home. I wrote to my daughter Charlotte Leake.

1 Oct. I preached here, morning.

41

2 Oct. I felt symtoms of gout in my left hand, which at night became very painful. Robert came home this morning.
Began taking up midsummer potatoes in the orchard.
James Barker began making a new sewer at the back of the house, as I intend removing the old one. Andrew Gowers assists him in the digging.

3 My sons [*went*] shooting pheasants with Mr Middleton, &c. Mr Brown dined here. The gout in my left hand is now very violent [*with*] great swelling & inflammation. A letter from Mr Robert Blake.

4 Felt very feverish & ill & constant pain. My left hand quite disabled, & my right hand also attacked.
The new cooler put up in the brewing office. The other repaired.

5 Very unwell all day.
Acfield here altering & repairing the pipes in the brewery office, &c.

6 I had a better night , & freer from pain. I am freer from fever today, but feel symtoms of gout in my left elbow, & ancle.
Mrs William Ward left us for St Neots.

7 I am now so lame as to be obliged to confine myself to my chamber, & removed into the front bedchamber.

8 The gout in my feet & legs increased.
Robert officiated for me at church. Sacrament here, 72 communicants.

42

9/10 Oct. The disorder increases, & I am now very feverish, with severe pain, my limbs much swelled. I am confined to my chamber all this week, but with assistance got into my armchair in the day-time.

11 Mrs Longe settled accounts with Alexander Meek, my gardiner to this day, when he quitted my service, & gave him an order to go with his family into the Barham House. I purchased of Alexander Meek the

312 Merely 'nominated', since the actual appointment was by the magistrates.

313 Henry would need a Bachelor of Arts gown for preaching.

fixtures in the gardiner's house for the use of the new gardiner. I sent Crack with my waggon to Holbrook for Robert Cowles's (my new gardiner's) furniture. He returned with them, & entered into my service this day.[314]

12 [*no entry*]

13 My son Robert left us to return to Bungay. He intends to remove into the parsonage house at Broome next week.

14 James Barker has now completed the new sewer, & Andrew Gowers, &c. are proceeding with taking up the bricks of the old one, & filling it up as they go on.

15 My son Henry officiated for me here, morning, & for Mr Paske at West Creeting, afternoon. Fine mild weather all this week.

43

16 Oct. I had a slight return of gout in my left hand. I sent Crack to Broome with a cart & 2 horses, to carry a load of furniture for my son Robert.

17 Crack returned by 2 o'clock, with a letter from Robert.
He took the furniture, &c. quite safe.

18 I got on my crutches for the first time & with difficulty walked into the drawing room. The old sewer bricks are now all removed & cleaned, [*and*] the cavity completely filled up. Began brewing October beer. Received from Ling, Norwich, an [*?*]armozoen MA gown for myself, & a bombazian BA ditto for my son Henry.

19 My son Robert, with his housekeeper & man servant, got into his parsonage house at Broome.[315]

20 [*no entry*]

21 I have been recovering my strength though slowly, and today walked with more ease on my crutches than I have yet done. Mrs Longe, my brother & sister, & John went to Ipswich, the latter to stay at Mr Edgar's.

22 Henry officiated for me at church, afternoon.
I got into the drawing room to dinner.

44

23 Oct. Meeting at Barham House, to petition both houses of Parliament against any alteration of the Corn Laws.[316]

24 Mr Jackson, Mr & Mrs Gaunt & Mrs A. Broke called, & Mr Edgar, &c.

25 Mr & Mrs Davy & Miss Margaret Davy called.
Mr Brown shot with Henry & dined here. Heavy rain today, which is much wanted, to enable us to break up land for wheat.

26 Mr & Mrs Robert Norris & 2 daughters called on their way to Bury.
Mrs Longe & my sister went to Ipswich & brought home John.

27 Rainy day. All at home. I got downstairs with difficulty to dinner.

---

314 For Meek's departure see 29 August. His admission to the Barham house of industry, not necessarily for life, ensured vacancy of the cottage for his successor, quickly recruited.

315 Many absent incumbents let the parsonage house at good rent, leaving a curate in cheaper lodgings.

316 Corn Laws, of 1815 and later, were designed to protect farmers and landowners. Consumers reacted strongly and the laws remained a bitter political issue until repeal in 1846.

A letter from Robert, which I answered by return of post.

28 I got downstairs with difficulty to breakfast. A letter from my daughter Charlotte Leake. They leave Cheltenham about the 16th of next month. I caught cold today, & at night was seized with a severe pain & oppression on my chest which was lessened by peppermint water, but in the night a violent sickness came on with vomiting which relieved me. My stomach was loaded with acidity.

29 Mr Henry Beck called accidentally.[317]
My son Henry preached here, morning.

45

30 Oct. Having had a bad night & the pain in my stomach & bowels continuing, I sent for Mr Beck, who gave me an injection which relieved me much. There was a very obstinate obstruction in the small intestine which was not removed without some powerful aperients.
Towards evening I felt much more easy.

31 I am very feverish today with gouty pains in each of my limbs. In the evening the gout returned into my left elbow & hand, & I had a very painful night. Mr Beck.

1 Nov. The paroxysm in my left hand abates, but my hand & arm totally helpless.
Gouty stiffness in both knees. Mr Beck. My brother & sister left us this day. My son Henry went to Woodbridge to his lodgings there. My son John went on a visit to Barking. Mr Henry Beck. Finished brewing.

2 My fever is now abated, & I got into the drawing room.

3 I am better today, but a constant diarrhoa is very troublesome. Mr Beck.
Very heavy rain last night & this morning.

4 Considerably better today in all respects. John returned from Mr Davy's.

5 Mr Roberts officiated today, morning & afternoon, here. By my direction the service for November 5 was used.[318] Mr Betham at Crowfield, whom I have engaged to assist me at [*the*] chapel, till I am well enough to take my part in the church duty. Letter from my brother; they got through on Wednesday, but had a very wet journey.
Mrs Longe received an alarming account of Mrs Ward, who has lately had some new symtoms of internal decay, from her sister Sophia, who I did not know until today has been some time at Salhouse.[319]

46

6 Nov. I am considerably better today & got into my study & dined below. Mr Roberts dined here. Inclosed a note to my brother in an hamper of swans egg, French & [*?*]Chanmontella pears.

7 My son Robert came over unexpectedly. [*He is*] quite well. Mr Parker & Crowe called. A letter from Henry expressing himself well pleased with his situation.[320] Sent John G[*owers*] with a letter to Dr Chevallier

---

317 As before (4 May 1826), 'accidentally' means 'without prior arrangement'.

318 By directing use of the official prayers of celebration, Longe showed his own anti-Catholic views.

319 Mrs Ward was the mother of Mrs Longe. See the Ward family tree, pp.lx–lxi above.

320 Henry had settled into his curacy duties at Woodbridge.

at Aspal respecting Mr Henry Croasdaile now under his care, & in a deranged state.[321]

8 John left us for Cambridge, &c.
Mrs Longe went to Ipswich. Sir William Middleton called.

9 All at home.

10 Miss Croasdaile met Dr Chevallier here, & the day being wet stayed all night. Robert dined at Barking. Lunatic Assylum. Meeting of magistrates at Stowmarket when it was resolved that the Melton House of Industry shall be purchased for a Lunatic Assylum. Brown, County Surveyor, ordered to survey, & report its value.[322]

11 Robert left us to return to Broom.
Mrs Longe carried Miss Croasdaile home. Letter from Joseph Church.

12 Mr Betham officiated at Crowfield for me, morning. Mr Roberts today told me that he wished, when convenient to me, to quit my curacy. [*He*] pleaded as usual want of nerves, &c. I told him for his own sake, I recommended not to quit his employment here, till he met with some move to his mind. He will look out, & give me ½ year's notice.[323]

47

13 Nov. Mr Beck called. Mr Cooke came to dinner. Heavy rain at night.

14 Very wet day. All within doors. A letter from John at Cambridge. Received from Raw, 2 copies of Carey's Abstract of Schleusner's *Lexicon* for Robert & Henry. Wrote to my sons Robert & Henry, & packed up for Robert an hamper of apples, pears, &c. & a turkey, & for Henry one containing 2 dozen port & 1 dozen sherry a present to him, & some pears, apples, &c.[324] Note from Henry, quite well.

15 Mr Cooke left us. Mr & Miss C. Davy called.

16 Very fine dry day. I was out a considerable time.
Mr & Mrs Brown called.

17 Mr & Mrs Brown & Mr Roberts dined here.
Wrote to Mr Church, & to my son John at Cambridge.

18 I & Mrs Longe went to Ipswich. Mr Wenn pressing me much to sign my answer to the Bill in Chancery without delay.[325]
I with difficulty got in & out of the carriage. Letter from Henry.

19 Mr Roberts officiated here, morning [&] afternoon.
Mr Betham at Crowfield.

48

---

321 This was an important meeting, of Miss Croasdaile with Dr Chevallier (10 Nov.), for the future care of her brother. For her brother's mental illness, see the introduction (pp.xliii–iv) and the diary up to 22 Dec. 1826.

322 The house of industry at Melton, built in 1765, was sold by virtue of an Act of Parliament in 1826. After this meeting, the magistrates were subjected to a curt ultimatum and threat of public auction by the Melton trustees. See A.F. Watling, 'Hospital', in Cecil Bentham (ed.), *Melton and its Churches* (Ipswich, 1981), p.57. The site is now residential. Some original documents and artefacts may be seen in the St Audry's room (the name much later adopted for the asylum) at the Felixstowe Museum.

323 Mr Roberts left, apparently with no employment, in October 1827.

324 Carey, John (1756–1826), *Lexicon Graeco-latinum in Novum Testamentum* (1826) was based on J.F. Schleusner's *Lexicon* (1808). Note the attractive contrast with the hampers.

325 This was one of the cases relating to Catherine Longe, the Spixworth widow: see introduction (p.xliii).

20 Nov. I & Cowles set out the line of the intended fosse next the terrace, preparatory to removing the present thorn fence.
The barometer up to settled fair. Wind north-east.

21 Engaged in writing letters. Walked & called on Mr Crowe.
Letter from Robert, & one from Mr Church to whom Major Leake has applied for documents relative to the disposition of trust moneys, &c. By this I find that Major Leake has also applied to Mr Edgar, who has sent him copies, as I conclude, of certain clauses in our marriage settlement. Of this Mr Edgar has not informed me, but has employed Pearson to copy them.[326] Answered by return of post.
Andrew Gowers, Richard Kerridge & William Rainbird began cutting up the whitethorn fence against the terrace.

22 I attended the sittings.

23 I walked down to the farm. Engaged in preparing a letter of remonstrance to Mr H. Croasdaile on his conduct in his son's affliction.

24 We called on Mr Edgar, when I had a long conversation with him about Miss Croasdaile's & her brother's affairs, & also again with [*regard to*] Major Leake, & afterwards [*we called*] on Miss Croasdaile.[327]
Wrote by Miss Croasdaile's desire to her father at Stanstead to press him to take some measures for the safety of his son now in an insane state of mind, & pressing him for an immediate answer.
[*Wrote*] to Mr Betham to decline his further assistance at Crowfield. He has officiated there for me 3 Sundays, for which I am to pay him.[328]

25 Fine dry but cold day. Wind south-west.

26 Very bright fine day. I walked to church & went through the whole duty this morning. In the evening a heavy flight of snow. Ground covered at 8 o'clock. Wind north-west.

49

27 Nov. Very sharp frost. North wind. Snow fell again in the forenoon.
Mr Pettit called. Sent for Henry to Woodbridge in the gig, & Robert also came to us from Broom.
Mr Pettit paid me arrears of tithe due Michaelmas 1825, £3 9s. [329]

27 & 28 Note from Mr Wenn, & sent him by Wells on Tuesday my marriage settlement & my late dear wife's appointment, from which he is to send Major Leake [*an*] extract & copy by his desire. Wind south-west & thaw. Mrs Longe & Robert went to Barking, & brought back Miss Margaret Davy on a visit. Mild evening. Snow all gone. Letter from my brother.

29 Mrs Brown dined & slept here.
Engaged in preparing papers for my tithe audit.
Eclipse of the sun. The day so cloudy that we could not observe it.

30 All at home. Dry day. Letter from Mr Church. <Henry shooting.>
<Mr & Mrs & Miss Caroline Davy dined here. Heavy rain evening.>

---

326 Entitled to request copies of legal documents for his wife, Major Leake lacked tact.

327 Longe was confiding in his old friend Mr Edgar about the two confrontational situations he faced.

328 It was perhaps Mr Betham's age (seventy-seven) that made his ministry 'unsatisfactory' at Crowfield.

329 These tithe arrears were thus fourteen months overdue.

1 Dec. Henry shooting. Mr, Mrs & Miss Caroline Davy dined here.
A letter from Mr Lawrence containing a copy of one from Mr Croasdaile senior in answer to mine of the 25th, sent by his desire.

2 I sent the gig with Henry to Woodbridge, & Robert also left us after breakfast to return to Broom. Dry day. Towards night my right instep very uneasy. Wrote to Miss Croasdaile this evening.

3 Not so well today, but officiated here, afternoon. I think I caught cold yesterday, & do not feel so well as I have been lately.

50

4 Dec. Tithe audit, Coddenham. The gout returned in my right foot, [*so I was*] unable to dine at the Crown with my parishioners.
Sent my son John an hare & brace of pheasants to Cambridge.

4 & 5 I informed my parishioners that in consequence of the present uncertain state of the Corn Bill question, I consent to accept the present composition, the period of which expired last Michaelmas, for the current year.[330]

5 Tithe audit, Crowfield. I had a bad night & with difficulty got downstairs.
Mr Edgar called about Miss Croasdaile's affairs.
Mrs Longe went to Ipswich.

6 Very feverish & ill today, & so lame that I cannot get downstairs.
Miss Margaret Davy left us.
Wrote to Dr Wright for the forms necessary for young Croasdaile's being placed in his asylum, Miss Croasdaile having resolved on this measure.

7 Still very lame & gouty pains in various limbs. The workmen completed the new fosse by the terrace, filling up the old ditch as they went on.
Letter from Mr Dawson Turner. Wrote to my son John.

8 A severe attack of gout in my left hand, very feverish & ill.
Miss Croasdaile met Dr Chevallier here & determined on her brother's being placed under Dr Wright's care at Norwich.

9 The gout now now [*sic*] in my left elbow & hand & my left foot. [*I am*] in a very helpless state. Received an hogshead of Lachryma Christi from Bingham & Richards, London. Wine forwarded from Naples by Mr Cotterell. Dr Ward's recommendation.

10 Mr Bellman preached for me at Crowfield, morning. Not better today.

51

11 Dec. I had a severe attack of gout in my left foot & leg with a good deal of fever. Book Club. Annual audit of Saving Bank accounts.
Mr Phear called & kindly offered to assist me in my church duty next Sunday.

12 My fever less, but unable to get off my chair.
Wrote a few lines to Henry, & sent him a joint of pork by James Brook.

13 Had a good night & feel better today.
I was dragged in my chair into the drawing room.

---

330 For medical matters, see Appendix D. Longe was avoiding confrontation with the tithe-payers.

14 No fresh attack of gout, but the swelling of my feet is so great that I cannot bear on them, nor can I use my crutches.

15 Better today. Mr Benjamin Heath called, & Mrs Robinson's son John, now a midshipman in the Tyne [*under*] Captain White.
Letter from John by Mr B. Heath.

16 I got into the drawing room on my crutches.
Henry rode over unexpectedly on a chestnut mare which he has on trial from Shortens, Ipswich. We all think [*her*] a very clever one.
The chestnut mare which Henry has on trial is £20 price.
Now rising 6 yrs. She is a little [*?*]sickle-toed & cuts a little behind, warranted sound & Henry says very gentle & free from vice.
Letter from Robert which I answered, & sent the letter by Henry.

17 Mr Phear officiated for me here this afternoon.
Mr Roberts at Crowfield afternoon.

52

18 Dec. I trust I am now regaining my strength daily. Mr Crowe called.
Wrote to my daughter Charlotte in Harpur Street.[331]
Major Leake has taken lodgings in Princes Street, Hanover Square.

19 Mrs A. Broke & Mr Brown called.

20 Mr Cooper Brook & his son called.

21 I got downstairs to dinner, & am much recovered within the last 2 days.
I wrote to my brother, to say that we shall send him a turkey by Saturday's mail coach.

22 Mrs Longe went to Ipswich. A letter from Miss Croasdaile saying that she has heard from Dr Wright, & that her brother Mr Henry Croasdaile settles at the asylum better than could be expected.

23 I am now considerably better, but my feet still much swelled & very weak.
Sent turkeys to Charlotte, Robert & Henry.

24 Morning service here dropped.
Mr Roberts officiated Crowfield, morning – here, afternoon.
Wrote a few lines in Mrs Longe's letters to John & Robert.

53

25 Dec. Christmas Day. I not able to attend my church. Sacrament here.
Mr Roberts dined here, & the workmen, &c. [*dined here*] as usual.[332]

26 Mrs Longe left me at 9 o'clock on a visit to Mrs Ward at Salhouse. She went in the carriage to Scole. Mr Barlee called.[333] Letter from my daughter. The barometer has now been for several days as high as 'settled fair'. Wind north-east, but little.
Wrote to Henry by Mrs Proctor. Letters from John & Henry.

27 My son John returned from Cambridge to dinner, remarkably well.
Mr Crowe drank tea here.
Scogging took my valuable pointer [*?*]Perry into Gosbeck Wood, where he was caught in a snare, & had strangled himself before he could find him. As good a pointer as ever was.

331 Harpur Street is east of Southampton Row (London), and Princes Street is off Regent Street.

332 It was a widespread custom for clergy to give Christmas dinner to workmen, the parish clerk and some poor parishioners, with perhaps a cash gift for wives and a meal sent to housebound poor.

333 Probably William Barlee, curate at Ashbocking.

28 Mr Josselyn came to look at my farms, & plans of the estate, in order to make a valuation of it.[334] Mr Pettiward called.
Letter from Mrs Longe. [*She*] found Mrs Ward much as usual.

29 Fine weather. [*I*]walked in the garden. Smith [*from*] Mendlesham came, & settled accounts for rent to Michaelmas last.[335] My Bitch Juno goes to heat, shut up with Jingo, both pointers. I wrote to Mrs Longe.

30 Mr Martin & Mr Davy called. A letter from Mrs Longe.

31 I walked down to church with much difficulty, & read prayers only, morning. Fine & uncommonly calm weather all this week.

Game Account

January 1 to December 11			
	Pheasants 12 Brace	Partridges 44 Brace	Hares 1 Brace.
	Henry		
December 19	Leash Pheasants	1 Hare	

Coal Account 1826

There are 22 entries, dated, for a stated number of chaldrons, usually 1½ , each entry against the name of one of John Longe's farm tenants. The year's total is 33½ chaldron. A chaldron was 25½ cwt. The price per chaldron varies from 42 shillings (winter) to 37 shillings (summer). The names of the tenants are: Diggens (13½), Brook (9), Richard Fenn (4½), Rushbrooke (4), Widow Fenn (1½) & Crack (1).

334 Longe had discussed this valuation with his solicitor on 12 August 1826.
335 Smith was tenant of the school's farm.

DIARY OF 1827

Mr Beck the medical practitioner was frequently consulted during the year, both for Longe himself and for his son John, the latter for facial pain of a nervous origin. Longe was however able to enjoy his leisure activities, prepare young people for confirmation and (when fit) to fulfil his public duties which included trying to establish a case against burglars. His conflict with his son-in-law increased, but Robert's courtship prospered. Health reports were also received on Mrs Longe's mother, Mrs Ward, and on Longe's cousin, Mrs C. Longe (whose death would give his son John possession of the Spixworth estate). Longe took a holiday in Norfolk in September, but for less than a fortnight. Robert returned to Coddenham to act as his father's curate, but Longe became anxious about his son's forthcoming marriage and indeed ended the year in a state of depression.

1

1 Jan Fine dry clear day. Wind north-west. My sons Robert & Henry came here to dinner. Mr Kirby called to consult me about a petition against the Roman Catholics.[336]

2 Robert went to Barking.[337] Frost very sharp at night.
Wrote to Dr Colvile about [*the*] archbishop's petition proposing a junction of the two archdeaconries, & a meeting at Stowmarket.[338]

3 Mrs Longe returned from Salhouse & brought Miss Morse with her. She left Mrs Ward as well as usual. Mr Orbel, Veterinary Surgeon, Ipswich, came to examine Henry's mare which brushes with her hind legs. He advises him to keep her, & thinks that by a peculiar mode of shoeing, she may go well, & that it proceeds from weakness having been rode hard when very young. She is now only rising 5 years.

4 We had my tenants & families here to dinner.[339] Frost.

5 Mr Roberts dined here. Frost but not sharp.
Prince Frederick duke of York, after a long illness which ended in mortification, died this evening in the 64th year of his age.[340]

6 Henry left us to return to Woodbridge. Thaw set in this evening.
Answer from Dr Colvile: we are too late for a junction, [*under*] the

---

336 Catholic Emancipation was finally settled by Parliament in 1829. Together with the associated repeal of the Test Act in 1828, it changed concepts of the church. See notes at 20 June 1826 and 5 March 1827.

337 Barking, near Needham Market, was the home of Robert's fiancée, Margaret Davy.

338 Part of Norwich diocese, almost all Suffolk was in two archdeaconries, east and west. The change proposed in 1827 (but never carried out) was to make Suffolk a single archdeaconry. Ten years later, a change did take place: the eastern archdeaconry was enlarged by two deaneries north-west of Coddenham and the reduced western one was added to the diocese of Ely. That was broadly unchanged until 1914.

339 The customary annual entertaining of farm-tenants in early January.

340 Frederick, brother of George IV, was his ally in their younger days, pressing for a regency.

Sudbury archdeaconry petition drawn up by Dr Colvile, [*which*] I conclude has been a fortnight in circulation and is numerously signed. I sent this answer today to Mr Kirby.

7 Thaw continues. Robert officiated for me here, afternoon. It being wet underfoot, I did not [*go*] to church.

2

8 Jan. At home engaged in making an extract from deeds of conveyances of my property for Mr Josselyn for valuation.[341] Robert rode to Woodbridge on a visit to Henry. At General Grant's auction [*at*] Bredfield, he bought for me 1 dozen Old Jamaica Rum, per [*blank*]. John dined at the Book Club.

9 Ditto [*ie engaged in making extract from deeds*] Mrs & Miss Robinson, Mr Benjamin Heath, Beck & Roberts dined here.

10 Mrs Longe, Miss Morse & John went to Ipswich. It proved a very wet stormy day.

11 Mrs Longe, Miss Morse & my sons John & Robert dined at Mr Davy's. Sent by William a packet with note & documents respecting the property here to Mr Josselyn.[342]

12 At home. Robert returned from Barking in the evening. Letter from my brother with a piece of cheese.

13 Robert left us for Broom.[343]

14 I walked to church & performed the whole of the duty this morning. Fine dry day.

3

15 Jan. Very fine clear day. I walked & continued so long on my feet that I suffered much from pain and tenderness in them afterwards.

16 John dined at Mr Davy's. James Brook settled accounts with me to Michaelmas. Balance of rent received £30 9s.0d.

17 I attended the sittings. Mr Beck called.

18 Mr Marriott & Roberts dined here.

19 Attended a meeting [*of*] trustees [*of*] Helmingham Turnpike at the Crown. Mr Wenn dined here. Mr Wenn (after the turnpike business) came & we had a long conversation respecting Major Leake's objections, &c. & his letters to Mr Wenn, respecting my late wife's appointment and our marriage settlement. His objections appear to be frivolous & absurd. Mr Wenn will be in town next month, & will then see Major Leake & endeavour to bring him to a right understanding, & in the meantime I shall write to my daughter on the subject but decline any correspondence with Major Leake.

20 All at home. Flight of snow in evening. Late duke of York's funeral at Windsor.

21 I preached here, afternoon. A good deal of snow fell in the evening.

---

341 Longe was still considering some re-arrangement effective upon his death. See 31 March 1826.

342 William was one of Longe's servants.

343 Robert was resident curate in charge at Broome (near Bungay) for over eighteen months.

Ground covered. Fine dry open weather all this week till Saturday, when frost and snow set in.

4

22 Jan. Heavy fall of snow this morning, and sharp frost. Mr & Mrs Davy & 3 daughters, & Messrs Roberts & Crowe dined here. Miss Caroline & Margaret Davy stay. Richard Fenn settled accounts with me for rent due at Michaelmas last. Balance received £51 11s. 0d. Letter from Henry.

23 Deep snow and much drifted, & sharp frost.
I had a return of gout in my right foot at night.
Robert Fenn for his daughter-in-law came, & I arranged the accounts with her for the Malt Office farm. He brought no money, and I told him I should expect her to pay the half year's rent due last Michaelmas [*in*] the 1st week in next month. (Balance received February 19: £56 18s. 5d.)

24 Henry rode over to breakfast & returned to Woodbridge, being engagd to dinner. Mr & Mrs Brown dined & slept here.

25 I have caught cold in my right foot, very much swelled & so tender that I with difficulty got downstairs. John dined at Mr Leeds's.

26 The gout is confined to my right foot & ancle: unable to get downstairs. John dined at Mr Brown's. Received some draughts from Mr Beck, my bowels being not in a proper state, and stools extremely black.

27 In the drawing room.

28 Morning service dropped. These draughts not having any effect, I sent for Mr Beck, who ordered me some other medicines.

5

29 Jan. Miss Davy left us. Very faint & weak today, sent for Mr Blomfield who came, & gave me a colocynth pill. No relief from my bowels till the evening. Mr Beck. Letter from Robert: [*he*] will come here next Monday.

30 I feel better today. Mr Beck. I have passed a great deal of extravasated blood, which is caused by the breaking of a small blood vessel, & weakened me extremely.

31 My bowels now in a better state. John shooting at Shrubland and dined there. Thaw set in today. The bloody stools have ceased.

1 Feb. Miss Morse left us to return to Norwich. Mr Beck.

2 A slight gouty tenderness in my left heel. Mr Kirby called, looks ill. John went to dine & sleep at Mr Beck's. I dined below today. Fall of snow again. Mr Beck. Mr John Fox settled accounts for rent, &c. of the Lime Kiln farm due from Widow Rushbrooke to Michaelmas last. Balance received in notes £79 4s. 7½d.[344]

3 Mr Martin & the Phears called.
Mr Beck. My digestion obstructed: took 2 colocynth pills.

4 Mr John Methold officiated for me at Crowfield.
I trust I am recovering my strength and feel better in all respects today.

6

5 Feb. My sons Robert & Henry came to dinner. Book Club. John dined there.

344 Lime Kiln Farm and Malt Office Farm (23 Jan.): both near the Coddenham road to Needham Market.

Mr & Mrs Middleton, &c. called. Mr Beck. I am now somewhat recovered in strength, and hope I am regaining my health.
6 All at home. Mr Brown called. Very indifferently this evening.
7 Mr Edgar called. Robert & Henry dined at Mr Brown's.
Fine dry weather. Mr Beck.
8 Sharp rhime frost. Robert & Henry dined at Mr Davy's.
Wrote to Messrs Child, sent a certificate of my life for the Irish Tontine.
Ordered payment of wine merchants', &c. bills in London, viz. total £130 3s. 9d., & desired a statement of my balance & ditto of Irish Tontine to Christmas last.
9 I am better this morning, & walked some time in the garden without feeling so much fatigue.
Settled accounts for rent, &c. with Thomas Diggens to Michaelmas last. Received on account of balance due £100 6s. 4½d. £50 still remaining in arrear, which Thomas Diggens engages to pay within a month.
10 My sons Robert & Henry left us this morning. Mr Beck.
11 Mr John Method officiated here for me, afternoon, & dined with us.

7

12 Feb. Stormy day. John went to dinner & to sleep at Mr Phear's.
13 Flight of snow last night & today. Mr Martin made me a long visit.
14 John went to Ipswich, to dine & sleep at Major Turner's. Mr Beck.
15 John returned to dinner. Very snowy day.
Wrote to my daughter to remonstrate with her & her husband's unhandsome conduct towards me respecting our family affairs.
16 Mrs Longe went to Ipswich. Mr Crowe & Dr Thomas dined here.
Mrs Longe deposited for me in Ipswich bank £266 3s. 0d in notes and checks, to answer payment of Ipswich tradesmen's bills of 1826.
17 Very sharp frost. John went in the gig to Woodbridge on a visit to Henry.[345]
I have, by God's blessing, regained strength considerably this week.
18 Mr John Methold officiated for me here.
Extremely cold day. East wind and intense frost. The weather has been more severe this week than at any time this winter.

8

19 Feb. Very sharp frost & north-east wind, drying wind. The weather is now severer than any time this winter. Mr Beck.
Old Robert Fenn paid me the balance due to me from Mrs Jane Fenn for Malt House farm for rent to Michaelmas last. Received £56 18s. 5d.
20 Sharp frost & very cold north-east wind. Mr Martin called.
John returned from Woodbridge, & left Henry well. Wrote to Mr Church, & to Mr Dawson Turner in answer to a letter from him received yesterday. [*He*] will come here on Monday next. Letter from Robert.
21 John went to Mr Parker's & slept there. Snow at night.
22 Mrs Longe went to Ipswich.
Milder air today. Wind north-west. Snow at night.

345 In the winter an open gig was a conveyance suitable only for a younger gentleman.

23 John went to dine & sleep at Mr J. Methold's. Weather milder today.

24 John returned this morning. Mild day.

25 Very cold day. I officiated this afternoon at church, but suffered much from fatigue and cold afterwards.

9

26 Feb. Very stormy day but milder. Mr Jackson called.
Mr Dawson Turner of Yarmouth & Miss Turner came to dinner by appointment. The gouty tenderness in my right foot & ancle returned, but without any fit of pain or inflammation.

27 Very stormy night. Mr & Miss D. Turner left us after breakfast for Bury.
Mr D. Turner took my copper plate of Sir William Temple to town, & will get me 25 plates taken from it, to be left for me on his return from London.[346]

28 Ash Wednesday: unable to attend my church, or sittings. Rain from the south but cold. Mr Roberts dined here. No congregation at Crowfield. Wrote to my son Robert.

1 March Very high wind all day. Mr Cooke came here to dinner. Heavy rain at night from south-west. Mr Beck – made an alteration in my draughts.

2 Very rainy day till 2 o'clock when weather became fine & mild. A high flood. My meadows completely covered with water.
Wrote to Robert Blake, fishmonger, Yarmouth for a small cask of kipling or sounds, & 200 yards of mended netting for garden.

3 Fine dry day. Mr Cooke left us.

4 I went to church in the carriage & officiated morning. I went through the whole service, without much fatigue. Henry Beck.
Mrs Longe received a letter from my daughter Leake, who has been seriously ill from cold, her legs affected. [*She*] is now better, and if well enough, intends to go to Brighton for change of air[347]

10

5 March Dry day. My son Robert came hither from Broome, quite well, & brought his pointer bitch Belle with him.
Catholic claims. Sir Francis Burdett's motion, 'That the House deeply felt impressed with the necessity of taking into consideration the present laws inflicting penalties & disabilities upon their Roman Catholic fellow subjects with a view to removing them'. The motion was rejected by a majority of 4 after 2 nights' debate in the fullest house ever assembled. 548 Members present: viz 420 English, 91 Irish, 37 Scotch.

Of the	Irish	57	for the Motion,	34	against it
	English	193	…………	227	…….
	Scotch	22	…………	15	……

leaving a majority of 34 English members against the motion.[348]

6 Very stormy last night, and today wind south-west.
Robert went to Barking.

---

346 For the Temple family see notes at 30 March 1798 and 24 July 1831.

347 The Prince Regent had made Brighton a fashionable seaside resort.

348 For Catholic Emancipation see notes at 20 June 1826 and 1 Jan. 1827. Sir Francis Burdett was by this time a veteran radical politician. A similar bill did pass to law in 1829.

7 Fine dry morning, but much rain in the afternoon.
John dined at Barking, & he & Robert returned at night.

8 Robert rode to Woodbridge to call on Henry, & Henry returned with him to dinner. [*He is*] quite well. Letter from Henry [*that he*] has engaged the curacy of Ufford [*with*] Mr Charles Brook's.[349]

9 At prayers. Henry left us to go to Ipswich in his way back to Woodbridge. I & Mrs Longe made a visit to Mr Phear. John dined at Shrubland. Henry to look at a riding horse at Shorten's, as he must part with his mare being unsafe. Wrote to my daughter Charlotte, who has been ill, to propose her coming to us for change of air with Major Leake.[350]

10 Robert left us to return to Broome. Mrs Longe & John dined at Shrubland, met Mr Acton, &c. I excused myself [*as*] not well enough.

11 I officiated here, afternoon. [*I*] walked to church & home.
John had a return of pain in his face, I think from cold.
Robert Cowles, gardiner & lad, and Kerridge, Charles Gowers & Harold at work all this week on the foss, & alterations by the terrace.

11

12 March I attended Saving Bank. My son John went in the gig to Woodbridge. Volunteer Cavalry [*?*]play.[351] Book Club. I did not dine there. Mr Phear dined there & called here in his way.

13 I returned calls after my illness, at Shrubland, Mr Kirby's, Mr Drury's, Mr Theobald's, Mr Montgomery & Kedington, Mr Brown's & Mr Martin's. James Barker began the stone wall agst the terrace fosse.

14 I read prayers at church, Mr Roberts being at Woodbridge.
John returned home to dinner. Answer from Mr Blake. Money will probably be paid to Gurney's on Saturday.
John complains of having had much pain in his face.

15 At home busy about the new shrubberies on terrace.
Letter from my daughter now at Brighton, where she & Major Leake went [*on*] Wednesday 7th. She is much better. They intend remaining there till May. Letter from my brother.

16 At prayers, but Mr Brown coming, & I having a cold and cough he read for me. Heavy rain at night from north-west. Received from John Woods, Woodbridge, a collection of shrubs, &c. for the new shrubberies.

17 Very stormy day. All within.
Wrote by Sir William & Lady Middleton's desire to Mr Kitson, to enquire whether he can find any documents in the registry to shew whether or not the chapel of Shrubland was ever consecrated.

18 I preached here, morning, & attended service, afternoon. Dry cold day.

12

19 March Attended Saving Bank. Engaged all day in planting the shrubs from Woods's in the new terrace shrubberies, &c. Fine dry day, but cold.

349 Henry was still curate at St Mary's Woodbridge but undertook occasional services also at Ufford.

350 The context of this invitation was the fragile relationship between Longe and his son-in-law.

351 The performance of a theatre company was often sponsored, not commercially but socially, the sponsor underwriting a block of seats. The theatre flourished when Woodbridge was a garrison town.

My pointer bitch Juno produced 3 puppies. Saved 2, a dog & bitch (by Jingo). Stock in Saving Bank to 19 March: £14,092 2s. 10d.

20 Warm showers this morning. Mrs Longe went to Ipswich. Harold & Kerridge cutting a drain from the melon pit through the north slip.

21 Mild day. At prayers. Called on Miss Leveson Gower at Mrs A. Broke's. Wrote to Mr Woods, Woodbridge, for 350 hollies. 2 dozen of varieties, the remainder common hollies for fences.

22 Very fine dry day. Busy in the garden.

23 At prayers. Mrs Longe went to Ipswich. Mr Roberts & Mr W. Lynn dined here, & Miss Edgar came on a visit for a few days. James Barker finished the stone wall by the terrace, & also the brick drain from the melon pit. Received from Mackie a cargo of thorns and scotch roses. *Received*] from Mr Dawson Turner a letter with my copper plate of Sir William Temple and 25 impressions for which I owe him 7s. 6d.

24 At home, busy about the new shrubberies.
Letter from Mr Kitson in answer to my enquiries about the consecration of the chapel at Old Shrubland, of which he tells me he can find no traces in the books of the bishop's registry. Paid Mrs Longe for weekly household accounts from January 5 to March 10: £55 10s. 7½d.

25 I preached here afternoon. Mr Beck came to see my son John, who has suffered much pain this week, & is now in a very weak state.

13

26 March I carried Messrs Wall Lynn & Roberts to Ipswich, and attended the adjourned sessions. Miss Leveson Gower came to dinner on a visit. Began brewing ale & beer.

27 Mrs Longe & Miss Leveson [*Gower*] called at Barking.
Mrs A. Broke dined & slept here. Mr Beck to John, who is now very much afflicted with pain in his face, a nervous disability.[352]

28 At prayers. Miss Leveson [*Gower*] left us. Mrs A. Broke stayed & slept here. I transmitted Mr Kitson's letter respecting the Shrubland chapel with a note, to Lady Middleton. This she returned to me through Mrs A. Broke on 30th, desiring me to read it to Sir William F. Middleton.

29 Mrs A. Broke left us after breakfast.
Charity School trustees' meeting. Sir William Middleton & Mr Kirby attended.[353] Mr Beck to see John, who I hope is a little freer from pain.

30 At home. Busy completing the foss and shrubberies, which are now finished. Wrote to Mr Dawson Turner, & to Samuel Smith, Mendlesham, inclosing trustees' notice to quit or enter into a new agreement at Michaelmas. Paid Robert Cowles, gardiner, wages 12 weeks to Lady Day £10 16s.[354]

31 At home. John rather better.
By Lady Middleton's desire I sent Kitson's letter, with one containing some hints as to the chapel, to Sir William Middleton.

---

352 Longe notes at this early stage that his son's facial pain was of nervous origin.

353 For school trustees see 3 April 1826.

354 Wages of 18s. a week indicate that the gardener took his meals 'out', in his own home, a cottage supplied by Longe as employer. Most domestic servants were single, and lived 'in' with bed and board, plus a lower cash wage: see M.J. Stone, 'Below Stairs, or the Servant Problem', *SR* 39 (2002), pp.2–8.

1 April I preached here, morning. Mild showers in the evening. Wind west. Letter & fruit basket with apple seyons from Mr Church.

14

2 April First warm spring day with drizzling rain from the south-west. Robert & Henry arrived here to dinner, quite well.
<Began brewing ale and beer.> Grafting apple trees in the garden & orchard. Mr Beck to John, who has had a severe attack of pain today.

3 At home, busy in the garden, &c. Robert & Henry at Barking & Onehouse. I grafted 7 seyons of scarlet & double blossom thorns on the fence of plantation opposite the vicarage.
Harold clearing suckers & rubbish from plantation by the stables.

4 At prayers, Henry read. Sir William Middleton called to thank me for my note about Shrubland chapel. <Finished brewing.>

5 At home, busy in the garden. Robert & Henry dined at Barking.

6 At prayers. Had some conversation with Lady Middleton about the Shrubland chapel. Mrs Collyer & daughter with Miss Lucy Preston called. The latter [*they*] left here on a visit.[355] I had a slight return of gout in the toe of my right foot last night. Mr Beck to John.

7 Robert and Henry left us.
Mr Brook & Mrs Brook called on their return from Bury Assizes.

8 Being very lame in my right foot, I did not [*go*]to church till afternoon, when I preached, and gave public notice of the confirmation.[356]

15

9 April At prayers. I dined at the Book Club. Mrs Bellman, Robinson & daughter dined here. Wrote to the bishop of Norwich to invite his friend the bishop of Chichester, who visits for him, to come here on his progress, & [*wrote*] to Mr Dutton to decline taking his *Suffolk Herald*[357]
Mr Henry Beck to John who still suffers severe pain in the face.
Nightingale: first this spring, heard by Mr Crowe by Dunstan's.[358]

10 At prayers. Messrs Pettiward, Roberts, Crowe & Brown dined here.

11 At prayers, afterwards at sittings. The Davys & Mr Barlee called. Finished brewing.

12 At prayers. Mrs Longe and Miss Preston went to Ipswich.
Heavy rain at noon from south. Mrs Longe received a letter from Mr Kidd to announce the death of his wife last night. Mr Beck to John.
Diamond mare produced an horse foal.
I heard nightingales in the Lawn late this evening.

13 Good Friday. I preached here to a good congregation, & Mr Roberts at Crowfield where was also a good attendance. Mr Roberts dined here.

14 At home. Mrs Longe ill with a severe cold.
Received an answer from the bishop now at Cheltenham. He

---

355 Miss Preston from Stanfield Hall (Norfolk), who had no means of transport, was visiting the Longes within her visit to the Collyers. See diary entry at 18 May 1827.

356 Longe had been notified by the bishop's secretary of the dates of the confirmation and visitation. The bishop's progress included Stowmarket as the centre in mid-Suffolk. See diary, 10 and 11 May 1827.

357 The mid-week *Suffolk Herald* (also known as the *Bury Gazette* and later as the *Bury & Suffolk Herald*) championed the land-owning élite and Protestantism.

358 Dunstons is the name still given to the junction of Sandy Lane (Coddenham to Claydon) with Rectory Road, Hemingstone, although re-positioned in the time of Longe's son.

acknowledges in very handsome terms my letter, & says that I can make the offer to the bishop of Chichester when I meet him at Stowmarket.

15 Easter Sunday. I & Mr Roberts administered sacrament to 79 communicants. I preached here, afternoon, & afterwards received the applications of young persons for confirmation, in the vestry.[359] Mr Beck to John. John has been extremely troubled with pain in the face, & also cold in his head and limbs all this week.

16

16 April Easter Monday. I at prayers, & afterwards attended the vestry meeting.[360] Vestry meeting: having paid a moiety of the expence of the perambulation of the parish last year viz £8 9s. 1½d., I told the church-wardens that I would not pay to the rate for the other moiety. Wrote to Mr Gaunt by Mrs A. Broke, who goes to London tomorrow, to request him to pay our subscription to Society [*for the*] Propagation [*of the*] Gospel £2 2s., & sent the money.[361] [*I*] sent my bank book with Child to be balanced & returned by Mrs A. Broke, and [*I also asked him*] to get me 2lbs [*?*]Mayenne snuff from Beynon's for which I am to repay Mrs A. Broke on her return home.

17 At prayers. Miss Preston left us to spend the week at Mr Edgar's. <I had a return of gout in my left foot.>

18 <Very lame today which> At home. Mrs Longe better and got down to dinner. I had a return of gout in my left foot tonight. Messrs Mackinnon & Dundas the MPs for Ipswich chaired – a public dinner, &c. at Ipswich.[362] Wrote to Mr Blake, & sent him a receipt for Mrs C. Longe's interest money due 10th February last, and [*wrote*] to my son Robert.[363]

19 Very lame today which prevented my attending the quarterly meeting.[364]

20 Took physic. Mr Kirby called. My left foot & instep very painful tonight. Sent a present to Mr J.W. Methold of the last edition of Valpy's Greek Testament in return for his assistance in my church duty last winter.[365]

21 Henry came here to breakfast. Sent the carriage for Miss Preston to Mr Edgar's, who returned here to dinner. My left foot worse towards night. Mr Waller, farmer of this parish, returning from Ipswich with Mr Richard Keeble, farmer of Creeting, who it is said was not sober, in Mr Waller's gig, was shot at by a person unknown, on the turnpike road between Mrs Kerridge's house & Brook's Hall. The ball grazed his

---

359 This eighteenth-century vestry, shown in an etching by Henry Davy (plate 2), was demolished some 70 years later when the present vestry and organ chamber were constructed on the north side.

360 Probably the annual meeting of all inhabitants, traditionally held on Easter Monday.

361 The SPG, under royal charter worked in the colonies. The significance of this subscription is that it confirms Longe's orthodox churchmanship, rudely called 'high-and-dry'.

362 The 'Blues' successfully petitioned after the Ipswich borough election of 1826. See Appendix G.

363 Longe had made a loan to his Spixworth cousin-by-marriage Catherine, hoping to save intact the estate to which his eldest son John was heir. See introduction (p.xliii) and note at 26 May 1827.

364 A meeting at Barham house of industry.

365 The Revd Edward Valpy (1764–1832) was High Master of Longe's old school: Norwich.

collar bone, and his great coat [*was*] set on fire by the wadding. The night was very dark, so that the person was unseen.[366]

22 Unable to get to church. Morning service dropped.
Sacrament at Crowfield chapel. 22 communicants.

17

23 April Engaged in examining young men for confirmation.

24 Engaged in examining young women for confirmation.
The gout is now abated, and my foot recovering, though still very lame.

25 I attended the sittings. Messrs Davy & Parker called.
Mrs Longe went to Ipswich, & brought back Miss Preston.
John is now, thank God, much better.

26 Engaged in examining young persons for confirmation.
Mr H. Beck to John.

27 Engaged in examining young persons for confirmation. Attended the Helmingham annual turnpike meeting, and dined with Mr Edgar, &c. at the Crown. Letter from Robert. John came downstairs and dined below.

28 At home. Mrs Longe, Miss Preston & John called at Barking.
Mr Beck to John.

29 I preached here a sermon on confirmation, afternoon, & instructed some young persons afterwards in the vestry.

18

30 April Henry came over to breakfast, & returned in the evening.
The Colliers & Browns called. Robert came here to dinner.
Mr Bellman called. Very warm mild day.

1 May Very warm day. At home.
<Mr Davy called & brought Miss Margaret Davy on a visit.>

2 At home. Mr Davy called & brought Miss Margaret Davy on a visit.
From Churchman's ½ lb Hardham's snuff. Due.
I saw Mr Clarke of St Helen's, Ipswich, tuner of instruments. He will undertake to keep the church organ in tune at £2 2s. per annum.

3 I attended a vestry meeting to examine & sign the new terrier.[367]
Mrs Longe, Miss Preston & John went to Ipswich. Dr & Mrs Sutton, & Mrs Kirby called. Mrs Longe brought me from Mr Wenn a very unhandsome letter dated April 30 from Major Leake to him, for my perusal.[368]

4 At home. Mr Roberts dined here. Mrs Dupuis, wife of Colonel Dupuis, & only daughter of Mr Kilderbee late of Ipswich, my dear late wife's cousin, died of inflammation on the lungs.

5 Dr Sutton breakfasted here. Fine mild rain came on at noon.
Mr Beck to John. Wrote to my daughter to acquaint her with Mrs Dupuis's death. Letter from Dr Kilderbee [*concerning*] death of Mrs Dupuis. Wrote to him in answer, & to Mr Cooke requesting him to see Col. Dupuis, & assure him of my wish to do anything which may tend

366 For Brooks Hall see note at 13 Aug. 1798.

367 The terrier was produced at the bishop's visitation (11 May). The professionally engrossed duplicate copy was retained in the parish chest: SRO(I) FB37/C5/1–6 (1794–1834).

368 The diarist originally made entries for Wednesday 2 May and Thursday 3 May in the reverse order on the left-hand page. He then corrected them by writing the correct days of the week opposite them.

to console him, & to offer to receive him here for a few days, if he wishes to quit his house and does not chuse to go so far as Glemham.

6 Gentle showers all day. Robert officiated for me, morning.

19

7 May I dined at the Book Club. Mrs Bellman & Mr Treadway, Miss[*e*]s Brown, & Robinsons dined here.
I returned Major Leake's letter to Mr Wenn to him, by my son Robert.

8 Robert rode to Woodbridge, and spent the day with Henry.
Mrs Longe & Misses Margaret Davy & Preston dined at Mr Phear's. I did not feel well enough to go. On Robert's return in the evening his horse started & threw him, but fortunately he got no hurt. I advised him to sell the horse immediately to Shorting.

9 At the sittings. Afterwards Mr Heath & Mr Davy & Mrs James called.

10 Bishop's confirmation, Stowmarket. I took Mr Robertson's 2 daughters Henrietta & Ellen with me, and returned by ½ past 2 o'clock.
Mr Beck to John. I sent Crack with my waggon to carry the young women to Stowmarket for confirmation, and the farmers provided a waggon for the young men[369]

11 Bishop's visitation, Stowmarket. I went there early. Mr Parker preached, and Mr Yonge the chancellor's son read the bishop of Norwich's charge. I dined there.

12 Robert left us afternoon to return to Broome.
By John's desire, Mr Lynn of Woodbridge met Mr Beck here to consult on his case. Robert left his horse here, which I think is unsafe for him, & turned it out at home for the present, & I lent him the bay Captain horse.[370]

13 Very cold north-east wind, with frost at night, all this week.
I preached here, afternoon. I sent by post Henry's testimonial (signed by Messrs Davy, Brown & Kirby) to him at Woodbridge.

20

14 May Showers from north and north-west all day. Mrs Longe & I, & Miss Preston, dined at Mr James's, met the Davys & Mr Heath. Mr James taken ill. Mr Beck to John who is still very much afflicted with pain.

15 Showery day & milder air. We dined, Miss Preston with us, at Barking, met Mrs James & Mrs Justin, the Phears, &c.
Mrs Longe received a letter from Mr Henry Brooksbank informing her of the death of her aunt Mrs Stracey in town. She has left the bulk of her property to Messrs Robert & William Ward & their children. [*She left*] to Mrs Longe a legacy of £100. Wrote to my brother.

16 At home. A fine ground rain at night.

17 Mr Parker's [*for*] 5 o'clock dinner. We met Mr & Mrs Johnson of Bilderston [*sic*] & Mr Jackson. Showers and again at night. Letter from Henry: Mr Carthew has given him a title for priest's orders, and Henry delivered all his papers to Mr Kitson at the visitation on Monday.[371]

---

369 Longe's confirmation candidates: in 1813, he had 71: 22 boys and 49 girls Seven years having lapsed since the previous confirmation, the age range was thirteen to twenty-five. In 1820 there were 107 candidates.

370 Having named the horse 'Captain', was it family drollery to call him 'Captain Horse'?

371 There was a sense in which in his year as deacon a man was on probation.

John had a letter from Mr Church, containing an account of Mrs C. Longe's health, who is now thought to be in a rapidly declining state.

18 We took Miss Preston to Ipswich, & left her at Mrs Collier's. I called on, & saw, Colonel Dupuis & Mr Cooke. Showers in the night again. Mr Wenn being out of town, I left a statement of money accounts with my daughter, in order to satisfy her & Major Leake that they cannot charge me with any unfairness in her business.

19 At home. I wrote to Mr Church. Mr Beck to see John. John has been freer from pain for the last 3 days.

20 I preached here morning. Fine warm growing weather all this week.

21

21 May Fine mild day. Mrs Longe called at Shrubland & Mr Martin's, &c. At home.

22 Showery day. Wind south-west. Mr Bellman called. James Brook settled accounts for rent, &c. due at Lady Day last. Deducting taxes, &c. paid for me, balance received £65 6s. 5½d.[372] S. Smith of Mendlesham came and discharged the rent due at Lady Day last.

23 I attended the sittings. John took an airing with Mrs Longe.

24 Henry came to breakfast, & Robert from Earl Soham afterwards. Mr Lynn met Mr Beck here to consult on John's illness. My son John: I find now that Mr Lynn's decided opinion is that the whole of John's nervous complaints originate in a seminal weakness, which has caused all the debility & nervous complaints he has so long suffered from. [*He therefore states*] that the pain in the face is one effect of this, & that his sole object is to restore strength to his constitution in general, without attending to the pain in the face in particular. I am happy to find that Mr Lynn & Mr Beck think John is as much better as can be expected, from the small doses of the preparation of iron & bark which he has been taking and the mode of diet, &c. now adopted.

25 John out in the carriage with Mrs Longe. Showery day.

26 Robert left us after breakfast for Broome. Robert, not quite well from indigestion and pain in the bowels, consulted Mr Blomfield. Mr Gaunt, in answer to a letter of enquiry to Mrs A. Broke, now in town, tells us that he learns from Dr Hawkins, who sees Mrs Longe often, that he thinks her constitution breaking up, but does not see immediate danger. She has been rather better this week.[373]

27 Heavy shower in afternoon. I preached here, afternoon. Mr Beck to John.

22

28 May All at home. Fine warm grey day. The Davys & Mr Brown called.

29 All at home.

30 Mrs Longe went to Ipswich. Messrs Davy, Davy & Barlee called. Mr Cooke came & dined with me at the annual Bosmere & Claydon Association dinner. Mr D. Davy called to examine the church and

---

372 James Brook, one of his farm tenants, paid Longe's taxes to reduce indebtedness.

373 Mrs Catherine Longe died on 25 June 1828 aged seventy-four. John, aged twenty-eight, took possession of the estate only after complex legal negotiations. See introduction (p.xliii).

registers. [*He*] is engaged next week & the following one, after which he will write to propose a time to come here, & spend a day or two in examining into Suffolk antiquities.[374] Mr Edward Edwards paid me 1 year's interest on £100, due July 2 1820, Helmingham turnpike trust: £4.

31 At home. Mr Roberts dined here.

1 June Mr Cooke left us this evening. Between 11 o'clock at night [&] 1o'clock [*in the*] morning of 2nd [*June*], Mrs Robinson's house was broken into by 3 men, and sundry small articles taken away. Mrs Robinson gave the alarm, which Mr Crowe fortunately heard, & went to her as soon as possible. The thieves made off on hearing Mrs Robinson call for help, & the night was so dark that no one was seen.[375]

2 Very showery day. Engaged in the morning with Mrs Robinson & Mr Crowe about the burglary.

3 Whitsunday. Sacrament at Crowfield, 22 communicants. I preached here, morning.
Rainbird laid by with a severe cold which affects his lungs.

23

4 June Mr Brown, Madam Dulevic, Mrs Beck & Lady Middleton called.
J. Fox settled accounts with me for his sister Widow Rushbrook's rent due at Lady Day last. Balance received by check on Alexander's £72 5s. 2d[376]

5 Mrs Longe & John made a visit at Mr Edgar's. Very showery day. Crack lame with a strain in the knee.

6 At the sittings. Showery day. Engaged these 3 days in writing notices to various people, & taking every possible measure to discover the persons who broke into Mr Robinson's house on Friday last.

7 At home. Showers.

8 I & Mrs Longe walked, & called on the Martins & Browns. Mr Kirby called here. A letter from my daughter now in London, where she & Major Leake returned from Brighton last Saturday. Wrote to Robert to tell him that, in consequence of Rainbird & Crack being disabled, I cannot send my waggon for his furniture next week as intended.

9 At home. Sheep washed.

10 Trinity Sunday. I preached here, afternoon. Ordination at Norwich. My son Henry was ordained priest by the bishop of Norwich, at Norwich cathedral. 31 deacons and 27 priests: total 58.

24

11 June Engaged morning in Justice business. Mr Betham came and dined here. I dined at the Book Club. Acfield began to paint the portico, &c.

---

374 This brief visit to Longe by David Elisha Davy is not mentioned in Davy's journal, but he was in Crowfield church the day before. For relevant church visits, see John Blatchly (ed.), *A Journal of Excursions through the County of Suffolk 1823–44*, SRS xxiv (1982), pp.46–8 (May 1824), pp.89–90 (May 1827). For Davy's stay at Coddenham vicarage, see diary below: 6–9 Aug. 1827.

375 Mrs Robinson lived near Coddenham church. Longe's involvement shows the scope of a magistrate's duties prior to an effective police force, though perhaps not many acted with his zeal and persistence. Enquiries continued until at least 8 September, after the Assize hearing on 3 August (below), when a likely culprit was sentenced for a similar offence elsewhere.

376 The Rushbrooke family of Lime Kiln Farm had large pits near the farmhouse. When the widow died her son advertised the continuance of the 'lime trade': *IJ*, 1 Dec. 1832.

Letter from Robert who is in doubt whether he shall see Dr Colvile, who is ill, in time to settle his affairs at Brome quite so soon as he intended.

12 Mrs Longe and I went to Ipswich. Had a long interview with Mr Wenn who has lately seen Charlotte and Major Leake in London.
Called on our return on Mr Kirby, to see Mr Hasted now there.
Ordered Mr Raw to procure for me Arrowsmith's *New General Atlas*, on liking, & also Bryants' map of Suffolk which he will bind in folio, as he did Mr Deane's.[377] Sheep clipped.

13 At home. Mrs Longe & John took Mrs A. Broke to call at Barking, & Mrs A. Broke dined here. Wrote to my son Robert at Broome, & enclosed him a check on Ipswich bank for £20, a loan at his request, see his letter of the 11th. He repaid me August 28. JL.
I brought home from Robert Deck's Ipswich on Tuesday, a cargo of writing paper, viz. ½ ream copy, in part cut into quarto. Ditto foolscap, ditto thick plain post. 2 quires blotting paper.

14 At home engaged in justice business, endeavouring to detect several persons concerned in the late burglaries in the neighbourhood.

15 Mr Betham and his son Sir William Betham, Ulster King at Arms, dined here.

16 Mrs Longe and John went to Ipswich. I at home.
Letter from Robert, [*that he*] will be here on Tuesday.

17 I preached here, morning. Mr Betham came to church afternoon, & dined & slept here. A very acceptable refreshing shower in the evening. 25

18 June Henry came from Woodbridge to dinner.

19 Oratorio at Ipswich, St. Mary Tower Church. Mrs Longe, I, John & Henry went there: a very good performance. Robert arrived here from Brome to dinner, and also his furniture by a Bungay waggon. The principal female singer was Miss Goward, an Ipswich woman, now a very superior singer.

20 At the sittings. Mr William Ward, & his 2 daughters Amelia & Frances, came to dinner.

21 Henry left us to return to Woodbridge. The Crowes & Mr Roberts dined here. Miss Robinsons to tea. Robert indisposed with a bilious complaint, which we think tending to jaundice. He has been taking medicines for it some time, but the complaint is not removed.

22 All at home. Gentle shower in afternoon.
Began to cock clover, &c. in vicarage pightle.

23 Mr W. Ward & daughters left us early.
I went to Ipswich, & took Mrs Robinson, to meet Mr Edgar at the gaol, to examine Samuel Clow charged with 2 burglaries. Mr Edgar & I examined Samuel Clow at the county gaol, & fully committed him for trial at next Bury Assizes, for a burglary at Richard Grayston's, & another at Revd J. Young's, both at Clopton. He is strongly suspected

377 Arrowsmith, Aaron, *A New General Atlas* (Edinburgh, 1817, 1823, 1829). Longe expected to take it on approval. Bryant had published his map of Suffolk in 1825–6 on a scale of 1 inch to 1 mile.

of being concerned in the late burglary at Mrs Robinson's, but we have not yet got sufficient evidence to charge him with it.

24 I preached here, afternoon.

26

A page has been cut from the original: right-hand page of week 26, & left-hand page of week 27.

25 June Fine mild day. All busy in the clover, cocking.

26 Mr Wenn came here for the day to consult with us about the division of our property, & the propriety of cutting off the entail.

27 John went to Barking to stay a few days. Busy in the hay fields.

28 A fine mild ground rain.
I attended the quarterly meeting, House of Industry.
Mrs Longe went to Ipswich. Robert went to Barking to dinner.

29 Robert returned, but went again to Barking, and dined and slept there. I and Mrs Longe dined at Shrubland, met the Jameses & Bellmans & Mr Pearson. Dry day.

30 Fine hay day – cocking hay & stacking clover. A short but heavy shower about 4 o'clock. John and Robert returned from Barking in the evening.

1 July I preached here, morning.

27

(2) Mr Bellman informed me that Dr Kilderbee of Glemham, having very much embarrassed himself, by building & extravagant mode of living, & [*having*] involved himself in debts to a great amount, quitted Glemham privately last Tuesday.

(3) Mr Edgar called to inform me of some disclosures made by Samuel Clow, now committed for trial at the assizes for burglary, concerning his accomplices.

(4) Wrote to Mrs Wayth to inform her of the unfortunate affairs at Glemham.

5 Early this morning 4 persons committed for felony escaped from the county gaol, amongst them Samuel Clow.

6 Settled accounts with Mr Robert Fenn for his daughter Widow Margaret Fenn, for rent due at Lady Day last, deducting bill for malting barley and grass purchased of her, £60 5s. 5d. Balance received in cash £7 4s. 7d.
Letter from my daughter now in town.

7 Thomas Diggens paid me on account of rent due at Lady Day [*?*]£60. Letter from John at Aldborough.

8 [*no entry*]

28

9 July I attended the Saving Bank on the Friendly Society business.
Benjamin & Miss Heath, the Robinsons & Mr Brown dined here.
Received of Richard Fenn on account of rent due at Lady Day last, £40.
Received of Thomas Diggens on account of ditto after deducting some bills, £86. A letter from Mrs Wayth about Glemham affairs.

10 I attended the weekly committee [*at*] Barham House [*of Industry*].
Mr Parker dined here unexpectedly. Wrote to John & Henry.
Letters from John and Robert with a basket of soles from Aldboro.

Robert desires to give up taking my curacy at Michaelmas.

11 Mrs Longe & I, with Messrs Brown and Benjamin Heath and Miss Caroline Davy, breakfasted with Mr Cooke, and all went to Felixstow in Brooke's barouche, returned home by 11 o'clock.

12 I went to Ipswich in the gig, & returned to a late dinner. My Peacock coach-horse's lameness increasing, I desired Shorting to procure me a coach-horse.

13 Mrs Longe & I went to Ipswich. She dined at Mr Bacon's, & I at the sessions dinner [*at the*] White Horse. Mr Berners sent a buck.[378] Saw Henry at the Shire House, quite well, & lately left John & Robert both better.[379]

14 At home. Wrote to Mr Hasted to accept his offer of a bed at the assizes.

15 I preached here, morning.

29

16 July I attended the Savings Bank. Very hot day. I paid Mrs Longe £110 on house account to July 7th. Received at Savings Bank, Messrs Jackson & E. Paske, managers, present: £2. 12. 6 for J. Blomfield of Ash Bocking under an order of magistrates directed to me & Robert Hayward, trustees of the Coddenham Friendly Society. I proposed to Mr Buck taking my curacy, as Robert declines it. Mr Buck declines –19th [*July*].

17 Company to dinner: Mr & Mrs James, Mr & Miss M.A. Davy, Mr & Mrs Parker, Mr Heath & son, Messrs Roberts & Buck, & Mr & Mrs Crowe. Engaged in examining Major Leake's late letter to Mr Wenn respecting the cutting off the entail, & division of property here.

18 I attended the sittings. Began cutting up peas in Ladycroft.

19 Suffolk Charity annual meeting, Ipswich. I & Mrs Longe took Mr Roberts to Ipswich, heard Mr Cooke's sermon. Dined at White Horse, & drank tea at Mr Cooke's. Mr Cooke's sermon at St Mary Tower, Suffolk Charity anniversary, an excellent one on Luke chapter 10, verse 29.[380] Fine showers in the course of the day, & heavy at night. Wrote to my daughter Charlotte Longe with a box of linen, &c. for which she has lately written to Mrs Longe, & [*wrote*] to my son John at Aldboro'.

20 At home. Called on Mrs A. Broke, who returned home yesterday. Mrs A. Broke tells me that she hears from Mrs Bayley that Mrs Longe had a severe attack of the asthmatic complaint lately, which it was feared would have been fatal, but that she is since better again, & much in the same state as before.[381]

21 At home. Some fine mild showers. Wrote to Henry at Woodbridge to propose spending a day or two with him next week.

22 I preached here, afternoon. Showers in the evening.

30

23 July Mrs Longe & I went to Woodbridge on a visit to my son Henry.

---

378 For the keeping of deer see notes at 18 March 1796, 26 Aug. 1826 and 1 Aug. 1827.

379 The Shire House in Ipswich, hired by the county for Quarter Sessions for that rural quarter of the county, was dilapidated and soon replaced at St Helens. Only the name of the yard survives.

380 Luke 10.29: 'Who is my neighbour?' Jesus answered with the story of the Good Samaritan.

381 For Catherine Longe see note at 26 May 1827.

He dined with us at the Crown Inn.[382]
In the evening saw Mr Thomas's gardens.

24 Went to Ufford, saw the church [*with its*] curious gilded font, & Mr Charles Brook's grounds. Called on Mr Davy E. Davy, then to Rendlesham, saw the church & late Lady Rendlesham's monument by Flaxman.[383] Mr Davy E. Davy will come to me for a few days on Monday sennight August 6.

25 Took post-horses, my Peacock coach-horse being very lame, & spent the day at Aldborough with John & Robert.
John very poorly. John is still very weak, has neither bathed, nor pursued Mr Lynn's directions as to medicines & management of himself, & is certainly not the better for Aldborough. Robert now determines to take my curacy when Mr Roberts leaves it at Michaelmas next.

26 Called on Mr Wall Lynn, & saw his collection of coins. After a luncheon with Henry, we returned home by 6 o'clock. Fine rain this evening.

27 Mrs Ann, & Mr & Mrs Cooper Brook called. We dined at Mr Heath's, & met the Bellmans & Parkers. My Peacock coach-horse being now very lame from a contraction of the foot, I must turn him off for a time. And this day I purchased, from Mr William Woodgate of Raydon, a brown bay gelding now rising 5 years old. Price 50 guineas, for which sum I paid Mr Woodgate a check on Ipswich bank.

28 We went to Ipswich to see Mr Wenn on the Spixworth affairs, & to look at some French silks belonging to Lady Dysart now on sale, but no one attended the auction. Had there been an auction, I intended to have bought some silks for curtains, &c. for John against he goes to Spixworth.[384]

29 I preached here, morning.
Extremely hot day. Thermometer at 2 o'clock in the sun 99 degrees.

31

30 July Tempest 7 o'clock am. Thunder very loud, but the cloud very high, & no mischief near us. Fine shower of rain. Henry came to breakfast.
I sent an answer to the enquiries of the Commissioners of Charities, respecting the charitable foundation here.[385] Letter from my brother.

31 Company to dinner: the Kirbys, Theobalds, Meeks & Madame du Riviere, & Mr & Miss Gear, Mr Kirby's nephew, dined here.
Wrote to my brother, & to Mr Dawson Turner, Yarmouth, to decline visiting him next month.

1 Aug. Henry spent the day at Mr Simpson's, Mickfield. Very hot day. At the

---

382 The Crown Inn, Woodbridge, stands on the corner of the Thoroughfare and Quay Street.

383 At Ufford, it is the wonderful font-cover that is gilded. At Rendlesham, Arthur Mee in flowery language described the monument figure as attended by 'an angel bearing her heavenwards, and two sorrowful figures below': *Suffolk* (1941), p.327.

384 Longe is anticipating by a year the inheritance of his son; see note at 26 May 1827.

385 An illustration of the growth of central control over local affairs.

sittings. The Browns & Miss C. Davy called. Wrote to Mr Wenn for the Helmingham venison to be sent the latter end of next week.[386]

2 Bury Assises. I went to Bury by the coach. Mr Hasted from home, but gave me a bed. Dined at Sir Thomas Cullum's, met Messrs Pettiward & Palmer Cullum. Judges of Assise: Sir William Alexander, Chief Baron of Exchequer, & Sir William Garrow, [*Baron of the*] Exchequer, who opened the commission on Thursday afternoon & immediately after went to church, so that the assise business was begun at 9 o'clock Friday morning in the Nisi Prius Court, & in the Crown Court at 12.[387]

3 In court all the morning after breakfasting at Mr Cocksedge's. dined with the judges, & drank tea at Sir Thomas Cullum's. Samuel Clowes, one of the 4 who broke into Mrs Robinson's house [*on*] June 1, tried & convicted for breaking into Grayston's house at Clopton, & sentence of death recorded. Transported for life.

4 Breakfasted at the Angel. Did not go into court, but spent the morning in calling on Miss [*sic*] Wayth, &c. & errands. [*I*] returned by the coach, & reached home by late dinner.

5 I preached here, afternoon.
A fine mild rain in the afternoon, which is very much wanted.
Mrs A. Broke informed me that she heard from Mrs Bayley yesterday, that Mrs Longe has had last week another severe attack of her disorder. 32

6 Aug. Mr D.E. Davy of Ufford came here to dinner, & dined with me at the Book Club.[388]

7 Mr Davy & I walked to Shrubland. Sir William Middleton showed us his Mausoleum.[389] Messrs Jackson & Roberts dined here.
Note from Henry by Wells, who carried his minerals & press to Woodbridge today. Henry says his mare is not well. Rt Hon. George Canning, Prime Minister, died of inflammation in the bowels.

8 Mr Davy & I engaged all the morning examining papers & antiquarian documents. Mr Barlee dined here.
Note from John by James Brook. He & Robert will be here on Friday.

9 Mr D.E. Davy left me at noon. I lent him several documents. At home.

10 Showers this morning. John & Robert returned home to dinner. John much better in health. Thunderstorm & rain. The thunderstorm which was trifling here was very severe at Wolverston, & at Edwardstone. The lightning struck a farmhouse which with the barn was burnt down. We should be thankful for the providential mercy shown us here. The cloud divided to the north & south.

11 I & Mrs Longe went to Ipswich. I visited the gaol with Mr Mills. Saw Henry at Ipswich.

---

386 Helmingham Park deer: knowing earlier of an intended gift of venison, Longe arranged his dinner party for 15 August and then took up the gift, with the attorney acting as intermediary.

387 As a JP, Longe was interested in the arrangements. For the Robinson break-in, see the diary: 1 June.

388 For Mr Davy's account of this visit, see his journal: Blatchly (ed.), *Journal*, pp. 95–6.

389 Was Sir William persisting in planning burial in his 'chapel', formerly part of Old Hall? See the introduction (pp.xli–ii). The word 'mausoleum' hardly suits the vault in Barham church, where Sir William was in fact buried in 1829. See also M.J. Stone, 'Where to be Buried? A Sequel', *SR* 41 (2003), p.2.

12 I preached here, morning. My son Robert read prayers.
Letter from Mr Blake. Has directed Messrs Gurney to pay the ½ yr's interest now due, into Ipswich bank.

33

13 Aug. At home. Fine harvest day. Considerable showers at night.

14 Showery. Robert at Barking, returned at night. Wrote to Mr Robert Blake in answer to a letter of his dated October last enquiring into the arms, &c. of the Hopton family of Yoxford.[390] [*Wrote to*] Revd Mr Leathes [*of*] Herringfleet & sent him particulars respecting the Lachryma Christi wine I had from Naples. [*Wrote*] to Mr Brown, Marlesford, concerning an infirm man now in Ipswich county gaol, whom he committed for vagrancy.

15 Showers with thunder from south-west.
Company to dinner (Helmingham venison). Sir William & Lady Middleton, Mr & Mrs Drury, Mr Heath & son, Mrs Phear (only), Miss Ibbetson, Messrs Cooke & Roberts.

16 Showers at noon, but fine weather afterwards.
Robert went on his business to Mr Norris's at Broome on Captain horse.[391]

17 Mr Cooke left us after breakfast. Fine dry day.

18 Showery day. Some steady ground rain till 2 o'clock. Rest of the day fine. Robert returned from Broome to dinner.

19 I preached here, afternoon. This evening my son Henry with his friend Mr Walford, set out for London on a fortnight's tour to Portsmouth, & the Isle of Wight, &c. Wrote to Mr Preston, Stanfield, to invite him & Mrs & Miss Preston here, next week or the week after.

34

20 Aug. At home. Finished getting in wheat today which concludes my harvesting crops. A letter from my brother.

21 At home. Mrs Longe & John called at Mr Davy's & Heath's.
Wrote to Mr William Blake, & sent him a receipt for Mrs Longe's half year's interest.

22 Mrs Longe took John to Mr Drury's on a visit.

23 We & Robert dined at Mr Pettiward's [*at*] Finborough, met Sir Philip & Lady Broke, Miss Broke & Miss Leveson [*Gower*], the Miss Lloyds, Miss Ibbetson, & Colonel & Mrs Camac.

24 We dined at Mr Bellman's, met Sir William & Lady Middleton, Mr & Mrs & Miss Davy, Mr & Mrs Groom & Mr [*blank*] Bellman. Venison. Rain at night.

25 Showery day. Robert went in the evening to Woodbridge, to officiate at Bucklesham & Newbourn tomorrow for Mr Walford.

26 I preached here, morning. Robert returned here in the evening.

35

27 Aug. Mr & Mrs Phear, & his pupils Messrs Carlyon & Dennis, & Mr Roberts dined here. Benjamin Heath here in the morning. Archery in the lawn.

---

390 A good example of Longe's heraldic expertise, but note the delay of 10 months.

391 Longe had lent this horse to his son.

28 I attended the annual meeting [*of the*] Suffolk Charity & National School Societies at Stowmarket.[392] We dined at Shrubland, met the Drurys & my son John, Robinsons, &c. Turtle dinner.[393]

29 Attended the sittings. We dined at Mrs Uvedale's, met the Davys & Parkers, &c. Sparkes & Smith of Ipswich, Peace Officers, attended sittings to give information respecting Thomas Rassels & others concerned in stealing Mr Theobald's clover seed, &c.[394] My son John went to town tonight on his way to Woodhurst, intended to go with Major Leake & Charlotte to Tunbridge.[395].

30 We went to Ipswich, I to attend a meeting of some magistrates to examine some of the gang of thieves now in custody.

Robert dined at Mr Bellman's. Heavy rains.

Received from Robert Deck, Bromley's *Catalogue of English Portraits*, procured by my order from his brother at Bury, where I lately saw this book, but had not opportunity to go & buy it. I owe Deck for it.

31 Mrs James called, with Mr Horton James. Mrs & Miss Collyer & her grandson Revd Robert Collyer, with Mr H. James & the Robinsons dined here.

Received from Mr Wenn his bills for law business from 1814 to 1827.[396]

1 Sept. At home. Robert & Mr Brown shooting all day. I wrote to Mr Church, having heard from Mrs Collyer that Mrs Church has been very ill.

My son Henry returned from his tour with his friend Walford, to Southampton, Isle of Wight, &c., & back to Canterbury & Rochester. They had a delightful tour, saw a vast deal in the time, a fortnight.

2 I preached here, afternoon. Mr Mortlock with Mr Roberts dined here.

36

3 Sept. My son Henry & Mr Walford came to breakfast for a few days' shooting.

I dined at the Book Club.

4 At home engaged in justice business.

5 Justice business. [*I*] committed James Stammers of Stonham Parva for an assault on his wife to Ipswich county gaol for sessions. Letter from John at Woodhurst: my daughter Charlotte now very well but thin.

6 Mrs Longe went to Ipswich. Mr Jackson called to ask me to meet Dr French, Master of Jesus College at dinner on Thursday next.

James Barker began the brickwork for a strong staith by the ford at my home farm.[397]

---

392 The two AGMs were held at the same venue on the same day, as so many gentlemen attended both.

393 Turtle, like venison, was a delicacy for offering to one's guests.

394 Peace Officers were employed by prosecuting associations before the days of professional police.

395 Woodhurst (Surrey): Major Leake had moved with Charlotte to the property left by his late father.

396 Mr Wenn's billing arrangements may surprise us. Was this a professional man's way of hinting that he was not reliant on fees, in other words was a gentleman?

397 Two streams from Crowfield and Hemingstone having joined above the track leading to Vicarage Farm, the little river flows into the River Gipping. It is hard to suppose that the staithe was anything other than an aid to recreation but, in general, small commercial barges did use very narrow waterways.

7 At home, arranging my new leases of farms, & looking after James Barker, &c.

8 We went to Ipswich. [*I*] attended the magistrates at the gaol.
Several persons lately taken into custody belonging to the gang of housebreakers [*were*] committed for further examination.

9 I preached here morning, & my son Robert afternoon for Mr Roberts, now absent in search of a curacy. Wrote a joint letter with Robert to my son John now at his friend Mr Farley's at Woking, Surrey.

37

10 Sept. Trustees turnpike meeting at Claydon to let the tolls. I attended.[398]
Fine rain good part of the day. Messrs Gnott & Copsey hired the tolls of the four gates for 1 year from November next at £1805. There being no bidders, they took by tender.
S. Kerridge my butler having been very rude to me, I this day gave him warning to leave me at old Michaelmas next.

11 At home. James Brook here all the morning. Making arrangements with him for new leases of Choppyngs Hill & Malt House farms.

12 Attended sittings at Needham, licenses day for ale-houses.
We dined at Shrubland, & met Sir Philip & Lady Broke, Major George Broke, Miss L. Broke, Miss Leveson Gower, Mr Muir & the Bellmans.

13 At home. Showers.
I paid Mrs Longe £53 4s. 1d. for house accounts to September 8th.[399]

14 At home. Dry day. Packing up for Norfolk. I had the shoes taken off the Peacock coach-horse, & turn[*ed*] him off in the Lawn, in hopes of his recovering his lameness. The hoofs are in very good state.

15 I & Robert went to Ipswich. I engaged all the morning at the gaol, examining several of the gang of housebreakers all re-committed for examination next Saturday. N. Keeble every day this week preparing oak & larch timber for the new staith at the farm.

16 I preached here, afternoon. John Gowers went forward with the coach-horses to Scole Inn.[400] Robert received letters from Charlotte & John, now at Mr Edwin Parker's near Reading.

38

17 Sept. Mrs Longe & I set out for Salhouse. [*We*] went post to Scole, [*then*] called on Mr Kidd at Norwich, & reached Salhouse by 6 o'clock [*in the*] evening. Mrs Ward much declined, & very poorly.
William Hales, Mr Reeve's of Lowestoft butler, met me by appointment at Gurney's Inn, when liking his appearance, & having a very satisfactory character of him from Mr Reeve, I engaged him as butler at £35 per annum, & tea & sugar. [*He is*] to come to me Saturday October 20.

18 Norwich Musical Festival. <We went to the oratorio [*at*] St Andrews Hall [*in the*] morning, & returned to Salhouse to dinner.> At Salhouse

---

398 The main roads out of Ipswich to Bury St Edmunds and Norwich used to follow the turnpike routes, forking in Claydon village. This trust administered the main turnpike from near Ipswich towards Norwich.

399 John Longe was precise in all financial matters.

400 For travel arrangements to Spixworth (near Norwich), see Appendix E.

all day. My sister called on us. My pointer bitch Juno produced 7 puppies by an excellent dog of Mr Phear's: a dog & bitch saved.

19 We went to the oratorio [*at*] St Andrews Hall [*in the*] morning, & returned to Salhouse to dinner.

20 We made morning visits to Sir Edward, & Mr John Stracey.

21 We went to the oratorio [*in the*] morning. [*We*] dined with my brother & sister & Henry at the Maids' Head. [*We went*] to the ball at night, & slept at the Maid's Head.

22 Making calls & shopping in the morning. Henry left Norwich to return to Woodbridge, & we returned to Salhouse to dinner.

23 At Salhouse church in the afternoon.
My spaniel bitch Frisky produced 5 puppies, liver colour & white by a small spaniel of Mr George Goodwin's: a dog & bitch saved.

39

24 Sept. I went to Norwich in the morning, & we dined at Sir Edward Stracey's, a family party. Dr Ward called at Salhouse on us.
I ordered at Freeman's, Norwich, a pair of Sinumbra table lamps [*the*] pair £7 7s., & a cast of Lord Verulam from the bust in Trinity College library for £2 2s. [*These are*] to be sent me by the Norwich wagon.[401]

25 We called on Mr George Howes at Spixworth in our way to Mr Church's where we spent the day.

26 We spent the day with my brother at Blofield.

27 We called at Dr Ward's, Coltishall, & at Mr Humfrey's. Miss Warberton there. Saw both families. My son John returned home from a visit to Charlotte, & other friends in Surrey. Very finely in health.

28 Left Salhouse at noon & slept tonight at Scole.
We left Mrs Ward better than we found her last week.

29 Reached Coddenham about 1 o'clock & found all well, & John who returned home on Thursday. I brought home 2 wool packing cloths from Mr William Everett's, wool stapler in Magdalen Street who will buy my wool. Mr Shrimpling will see it weighed & settle the price for it, & also receive the money for me. I am to send the wool <next week> [*on*] September 8 by Norwich wagon.[402]

30 Robert officiated for Mr Welford at Bucklesham & Newbourn.
I preached here, afternoon.

40

1 Oct. I dined at the Book Club. My spaniel bitch Miss produced 6 puppies, but mongrels. 2 [*were*] saved, but one was taken away by Juno the pointer bitch after a few days, & the other died.

2 At home. John Gowers took Robert in the gig to Woodbridge to shoot by invitation at Mr Sheppard's, Ash, tomorrow.[403]
Mr Roberts dined here. I paid Mr Roberts 1 quarter's salary to this time, when he quits my curacy, by check on Messrs Bacon & Co. for £25.

---

401 Lord Verulam (d.1626) was a Bacon, and Trinity was Longe's college. See Appendix F.

402 Longe's farm was not purely arable, despite the rush to plough farmland earlier under war conditions.

403 Not Ashbocking, but Campsea Ashe near Wickham Market.

3 We dined at Mr Phear's, met the Middletons, Sir Frank & Henry Watson & Lady, Sir George Dennys, &c.
Mr Roberts left Coddenham for his old lodgings at Needham.[404]

4 Quarterly meeting at Barham House. I attended it.
Wrote to Mr Hasted in answer to his enquiries about Mr Roberts, for Mr Waddington of Northwold, who wants a curate. [*Wrote*] to Mr S. Smith [*of*] Mendlesham to order him to attend here on Monday next to settle terms of rent.[405] I received at Ipswich bank £100 placed to my account.

5 Robert returned with Henry to dinner.

6 Henry left us after breakfast. Mrs Longe, I & John went to Ipswich. I met Mr Methold at the gaol.

7 I preached here, morning. Robert at Crowfield, morning (sacrament 21 communicants), & here afternoon. I consider that my son Robert enters on my curacy this day, at stipend of £150 per annum.

41

8 Oct. A meeting of trustees [*of the*] Charity School held at my house, to arrange matters of rent with [*the*] tenant [*of*] Mendlesham Farm. Mr Kirby only attended. It is agreed that S. Smith shall hold the Mendlesham Farm for one year from Michaelmas 1827 at the present rent: £75.

9 Showers from south-east. Sir William Middleton called.
My brother & sister came to us on a visit.

10 I attended sittings at Needham [*for*] appointment of surveyors.
Heavy rain began at noon.

11 At home. Benjamin Heath here shooting, & dined here.

12 We went to Ipswich, & saw Mr Green ascend in his air balloon near the gas-works. He descended at Hollesley: no accident. Henry went to Bury for the ball. I consulted Mr Wenn about the disputes between the executors of [*the*] late Robert Fenn & the incoming tenants (James Broke & his son Robert), about the fixtures on the Malt Office farm.

13 At home. Sent a present of game to Mrs Wayth: brace of pheasants & hare. Mr Freeman Abbott, appraiser for James Brook, after much difficulty settled the affair of fixtures at Malt Office with the Fenns.

14 Sacrament [*at*] Coddenham. 72 Communicants.
I preached afternoon, & Robert at Crowfield.

42

15 Oct. I went in the gig to call on Mr Methold, but did not see him.

16 Mrs & Mrs R. Longe made a morning visit at Barking. Robert went to Admiral Carthew's auction at Woodbridge. Mr Sandby came to dinner on a visit.

17 Mrs Longe called on Miss Ibbetson.
Mr Sandby went to view his farms at Otley & Swilland. All at home.

18 Mr Sandby left us after breakfast on his return home. I paid Samuel Kerridge my butler his wages due, & discharged him from my service.

19 I & Mrs Longe went to Ipswich, I to attend the sessions. Mr Methold

---

404 Mr Roberts had not found a regular curacy, in what had become an over-crowded profession.

405 Longe's peremptory tone perhaps indicates anxiety about the school's reliance on this income.

resumed the chair, after 2 years absence.[406] At sessions all day & returned late in the evening, but did not dine at White Horse. I attended the commissioners for enquiring into charitable trusts, &c., Dr Burnaby, [*illeg.*] Adams & [*blank*], and exhibited the Charity School (Mendlesham farm) trust deeds & account book. All settled without any difficulty.

20 At home. William Hales, my new butler entered on my service.

21 I preached here, morning & afternoon, in order to admit of my son Robert officiating at Claydon in the afternoon for Mr Drury who is at Aldborough.

43

22 Oct. Showery day. Engaged in justice business. John & Robert dined at Mr James's. Sent a copy of the clause in Church Farm trustee deed, [*of the*] £5 for cloathing the poor inhabitants of Coddenham, to the Commissioners of Charities at Ipswich by their request by post.

23 Heavy shower early in the morning. I walked to & from the House of Industry, first Tuesday of my attending the weekly committee.[407]

24 At sittings. The Davys called. Fine dry day.
Robert Fenn settled accounts for half year's rent of Malt House farm for Margaret Fenn the tenant to Michaelmas, October 11 1827, when she quitted my farm. Balance received £47 18s. 7d.

25 I attended a vestry meeting. Mr Parker & Crowe called. Heavy rain in the evening. A puppy of Frisky's saved for Miss Ibbetson, missed from the stable. [*We*] supposed that Juno the pointer bitch, who had puppies, took it away as she has done before.

26 At home. John Methold shooting, & dined here.

27 At home. Mr Longe & my sister went to Ipswich.

28 I preached here, afternoon.

44

29 Oct. Miss Sandby came to dinner for the ball tomorrow night.
I dined at the Book Club.

30 I attended [*the*] House of Industry committee.
Mrs Longe, Robert Longe & Miss Sandby in my carriage, & John & Robert in a post-chaise, went to the fancy [*dress*] ball at Ipswich. Mrs Longe dressed in the old point lace, John in his Voluntary Cavalry uniform.

31 Mr Crowe dined here. Richard Fenn of Hemingstone settled accounts for half year's rent due at Michaelmas last, & also Thomas Taylor's rent 1 year to ditto for the cottage. Total received £52 4s. Remaining on account of rent: £4 19s. 11d.

1 Nov. Mr Cooke came to dinner.
S. Smith, Mendlesham, paid me £14 on account of Michaelmas rent, & engaged to settle all accounts of arrears, &c. [*on*] December 10th.

2 Miss Sandby left us after breakfast, & also Mr Cooke.
Miss Ibbotson & the Davys dined here.

---

406 Canon Methold, chairman of the Ipswich division of the county Quarter Sessions from 1811, had periodic duties at Norwich Cathedral.

407 At the house of industry a small number of directors and guardians in weekly committee attended to matters of detail, serving in rotation.

3 At home. My son John received a friendly letter from Miss Flower, respecting her niece Miss Caroline Warnford, & proposes that John should go to Cheltenham next month, when Miss Flower will be at home, & expects Miss C. Warnford on a visit to her.[408]

4 I preached here, morning.

45

5 Nov. Mr & Mrs Bellman called. Mrs Longe, John & my sister called at Mr Edward Paske's. Mr Roberts drank tea here.
Finished setting wheat in Carborough Hill.

6 I attended the committee [*of the*] House of Industry.
My brother & sister left us on their return home, to sleep at Scole.

7 I attended the sittings. Mr Methold & Heath called afterwards.

8 We dined at Miss Ibbetson's, Bramford Hall. [*We*] met Mr Heath, Mr Campbell, Mrs Johnson & her son Captain Johnson, & Mrs Smith wife of MP for Norwich.[409]
Paid Mrs Longe for house accounts for 9 weeks to November 3rd, £55 7s.

9 Called on Mrs A. Broke & Mrs Seaman. We dined at Mr James's, [*and*] met Sir William & Lady Middleton, Sir Henry & Lady Watson, Mr & Mrs Penrice & Revd. Mr Vernon. Philip Reynolds came & had a bed here. I paid him my gift for 2 quarters to Michaelmas last: £2.

10 Mrs Longe & John went to Ipswich.
Intelligence received of a most bloody action between the allied squadrons under Sir Edward Codrington, & the Turco-Egyptian fleet in Navarin Bay in Greece on October 20 last. The latter completely destroyed. In this action Sir Philip Broke's 2 sons Philip & George were on board the Genoa & Glasgow, and escaped without wounds.[410]

11 I preached here, afternoon.

46

12 Nov. Mr & Mrs Phear called. We began brewing, with malt from James Brook.

13 I walked to Barham House & attended the committee, the last time of my month.

14 We went to Ipswich. I & John consulted Mr Wenn about an arrangement for discharging his bills, &c. Afterwards called on Mr & Mrs Edgar, Red House. I left with Mr Wenn instructions for short leases of Choppyng's Hill & the Malt Office farms, to James Brook & his son Robert Brook.

15 Wet day. At home. Letter from Mr Joseph Church.

16 At home. Wet.
Received from my brother a present of Gloucester & Cheshire cheese.

17 At home.

18 I preached here, morning.

---

408 Miss Caroline Warneford, daughter of Col. Warneford of Wiltshire, married John in June 1829, after he inherited the Spixworth estate.

409 William Smith of Harlow (Essex) and in London, but he would also attend his Norwich constituency.

410 The Allies (Britain, France and Russia) whose joint fleets were engaged in the action, were attempting to give Greece at least partial independence within the Turkish empire.

Henry rode here unexpectedly by 2 o'clock, & slept here.

47

19 Nov. I & John dined with Robert, met Messrs Bellman & Treadway & Brown.

20 We all dined at Mr Martin's, met Davys & Browns.

21 At sittings. Letter from my brother.

22 At home. Mr Kirby called. Mr Kirby being to go to London next week, he undertook to pay mine & Mrs Longe's annual subscription to *[the]* Society for [*the*] Propagation of [*the*] Gospel, due for year ending at Christmas next: £2 2s., which money I paid him.
Wrote to Sir Edmund Bacon, to apply for his nomination to a scholarship at Corpus Christi College, Cambridge, at the request of Mr Philip Meadows of Bealings, for his son admitted at that college.[411]

23 Mrs Longe & I called on Mr & Mrs Middleton, lately come to Shrubland.
Sharp frost, & flight of snow last night. Wrote to Mr Church.

24 At home. Very cold day. Finished brewing this evening.

25 I preached here, afternoon. Mr Middleton called.

48

26 Nov. Henry came here to breakfast. Mrs Longe, Robert & Henry dined at Mr Collier's, & went to the Assembly Room to see Mr Matthews's Imitations, &c. Wrote to my brother.

27 I, John & Henry walked up to Gosbeck Wood to look at the felling [*of*] underwood. Mrs Longe & Henry drank tea at Mrs Broke's.

28 At home. Mr Beck called from Shrubland. Heavy rain in the night. Answer from Sir Edmund Bacon, [*that he*] will send a nomination to Corpus Christi College, of Mr Meadows' son to the scholarship in Sir Nicholas Bacon's foundation. Communicated this to Mr Meadows by tonight's post. Sir William Middleton taken alarmingly ill last night: inflammation on the chest.

29 Showery all day.
John & Robert dined at Mr Davy's. [*They*] had Haggar's post-chaise.

30 Very damp foggy weather. I & Mrs Longe went to Ipswich. I called on Mr Cooke & had some conversation with him about my son Robert's affairs.

1 Dec. Mr Davy called & we had a long conversation, at which Robert was present, about his intended marriage. Mr Crowe called. Mr Crowe called, to say that he was going to apply for the Paymastership of the East Norfolk Regiment Militia, now vacant by the death of Mr F. Hope, and requested me to write him a letter of introduction to Col. Wodehouse.

2 I preached here, morning. I am much distressed in mind about my son Robert's affairs, & think he had much better not think of marrying & settling in the curacy of Coombs, which Mr Davy would give him.

49

3 At home. I am very far from well, & labour under great uneasiness of

411 A good example of the working of patronage. An intermediary gave access to a titled patron.

mind. Mr Beck dined here. I began to take camphor julep by Mr Beck's advice, my spirits being very low.

4 At home, engaged preparing lists of the poor for Christmas gift. Mrs Longe called at Barking.

5 I attended the sittings. My dear son John left us for London, & to proceed to Cheltenham. My spirits very low.

6 Tithe Audit, Coddenham. No alteration in my composition & all went off without any altercation.[412] I & my son Robert dined with the parish. Received from Ringrose, Ipswich, a grey bath coating dressing-gown [*made from*] cloth from Shewell's, Ipswich.

7 Tithe Audit, Crowfield. All attended. No difficulties occurred. I & Robert dined at the Crown, but my spirits are so low that I stayed but a short time after dinner, both days.

8 At home. Crack got home a cow & calf bought of Mr Simpson of Ufford, now 5 years old, per £16, which Crack paid to Mr Simpson's servant who met him at Otley Bottom with the cow & calf.[413] Mr Beck called to see me. My dejection of spirits distresses me much.

9 I preached here afternoon, but under great uneasiness of spirits.

50

10 Dec. Showery day, but mild. Annual meeting of trustees, &c. of Bosmere & Claydon Bank for savings. I attended.[414] Mrs Longe called at Mr James's & Davy's.

11 We called on Mr & Mrs Methold. Letter from my son John at Oxford.

12 Mr Cooke came here to dinner. Mr Beck came to see me.

13 We with Mr Cooke called on Mr Kirby, & at Shrubland. Very fine bright day. Assessed taxes: William Leggett the surveyor called, & left a notice with me that £2 5s. 6d per annum is added to my composition, being the 2nd [*half of*] 5 per cent per annum, one moiety of which had been omitted from the last ½ year's assessed tax bill.[415]

14 Very wet day. All within. Letter from my son John, now at Cheltenham. [*He*] has received every civility & encouragement from Miss Flower & Miss Caroline Warneford: a very comfortable letter.

15 Mr Cooke left us after breakfast. Dr, Mrs & Miss Ward of Coltishall came to dinner, from Sir Robert Harland's on a visit. Mr Beck.

16 I preached here, morning, & Dr Ward [*gave*] an excellent Advent sermon in [*the*] afternoon.

51

17 Dec. Fine dry day. Dr & Mrs & Miss Ward made a morning visit to the Edgars. We at home.

18 The Wards left us after breakfast. Very wet day. Mr Beck here to see me in the evening.

19 Showery day. I attended the sittings. Robert had a very comfortable letter from John.

---

412 Retaining the old tithe calculation defused active discontent.

413 Otley Bottom is still the name of the junction to which the Coddenham–Woodbridge road descends.

414 The hundred had a Savings Bank as well as the substantial Coddenham one.

415 For assessed taxes see footnote at 4 April 1796.

20 Fine dry day. At home. Crack began to cart faggot wood home from Gosbeck Wood. Wrote to my brother.
Paid Mrs Longe for house accounts to December 15th: £32.

21 We went to Ipswich, called on Mr Cooke. Paid to Mr Dunningham, Ipswich bank, £130 15s., to be placed to my account.

22 At home. Mr Beck. He made some alteration in my medicines.

23 I preached here, afternoon.

52

24 Dec. < Fine dry day. Dr & Mrs & Miss Ward made a morning visit to the Edgars. We at home.> At home. Very wet day.
Mr Crowe called & told me that the money in the Saving Bank belonging to the Society [*of*] Brotherly Love in Coddenham was this day paid to their stewards, & their receipt given for the same.

25 Christmas Day. I & Robert officiated. I preached. Sacrament here: 79 communicants. Robert officiated at Crowfield at 2 o'clock.
My son Henry came here to dinner. He has now parted with his mare which he says was too low for him, & bought another which is warranted sound & quiet. I am very sorry that he parted with the other: it was so safe an one. Letters from my son John & Mr Church.

26 At home. Robert & Henry rode to Ipswich. Mr Beck.

27 All at home.

28 My son Henry left us & Robert accompanied him, to go to Mr Thomas's ball tonight at Woodbridge. Mr Beck.

29 All at home.

30 I preached here, morning.
My spirits very low, & much agitated all this week.

53

31 I & Mrs Longe called at Mr Brown's. Mrs Edgar & Miss Sandby called.
I labour under great lowness of spirits.
Wrote a few lines to John, & sent him some game, & an hamper of doe venison received today. Parcel sent January 1, 1828. Mr Beck.

A loose sheet at week 39

Coal account – J Byles & Co.

Jan. 15	1& ½ chaldron (Crack had 9 bushels = ¼ ch.)			Diggens
Jan. 22	1 & ½ chaldron			Diggens
Feb. 12	1 & ½ chaldron at 37sh.			Diggens
[?]	1 & ½ ditto			Diggens
[?]	1 & ½ ditto			Richard Fenn
[?]	1 & ½ ditto			Brook
[?]	1 & ½ ditto			Brook
[?]	1 & ½ ditto	37sh.		? [*sic*]
- - 19	1 & ½ ditto		(above covenant) –	Diggens
- - 24	1 & ½ ditto	37sh.		Widow Fenn
- - 25	1 & ½ ditto			Widow Fenn
- - 5	1 & ½ ditto	37sh.		Diggens
- - 21	2 chaldron			Widow Rushbrooke

- - 26	1 & ½ ditto	Diggens
- - 1	2 chaldron	Widow Rushbrooke
- - 8	1 & ½ ditto	Diggens
Dec. 1	1 & ½ ditto 40 sh.	Brook
3	1 & ½ ditto	Diggens
5	1 & ½ ditto	Diggens
26	1 & ½ ditto	Brook

31 Chaldron at from 37sh. to 40 sh. per chaldron.

DIARY OF 1831

The years 1828 to 1830 saw several domestic changes. Longe's son John married after inheriting the Spixworth estate, though this inheritance was only achieved after extended legal negotiations. The diarist's next son Robert also married and was employed by his father-in-law as resident curate of Combs near Stowmarket, where his first son was born. Longe himself employed two curates full-time to serve Coddenham and Crowfield. Henry was still lodging in Woodbridge, but was no longer curate at St Mary's church. He had become chaplain to the Bridewell, with occasional duties at Ufford. At Shrubland, Sir William, the second baronet, succeeded his father who died in 1829. Longe's old friends, Colonel Edgar of the Red House Ipswich and Joseph Church of Norfolk, had also died.

In January 1831 Longe attended the Quarter Sessions which dealt with some 'Swing' rioters. He later had a frightening collapse, but was soon fit to attend church. He expressed his views against the Reform Bill, as he had previously against Catholic Emancipation. A visit to Norfolk had to be extended to eight weeks before Longe was well enough to travel home, but his two curates took services and Robert supervised the household servants. He resumed normal life in Suffolk, a mixture of public duties and leisure interests. He engaged in a successful attempt to obtain a copy of public records to be housed in Ipswich Town Hall. He arranged the rebuilding of the east window of Coddenham chancel. His second grandson, Robert's child, was christened, but he was troubled when his son Henry disregarded his advice and entered into an engagement.

1

1 Jan. Very fine mild day. Henry walked here from Dedham after the ball on Friday.
He came unexpectedly about 8 o'clock [*in the*] evening, & slept here.

2 Henry went in the gig part of the way to Woodbridge.
At church, morning & afternoon.[416] Mr Treadway dined here.[417]

2

3 Jan. At home. Thaw continues. Sent a turkey to my daughter Charlotte Leake in London. Received a parcel of cheeses & letters from John.
A letter from John respecting his intended gift to the poor of Coddenham & Crowfield.

4 We went to Ipswich & called on Mr Cooke who has been long ill with

416 In the diary, abbreviations 'm.' and 'a.' form part of a regular Sunday entry, but are here extended. Morning Prayer and Evening Prayer (the latter in the afternoon, except perhaps in the summer) were the basic services from the Book of Common Prayer. Other elements were added.

417 The curates customarily dined with the Longes on Sundays, perhaps regarded as a perquisite of the post. It was certainly an opportunity for supervision.

a spasmodic disorder. Lady Middleton called about the distribution of Sir William Middleton's bequests.[418]
I took my bank book to Bacon's bank & had it balanced to the end of the year. My balance is £123 0s. 10d. I deposited today £200 in Ipswich bank. My poor old spaniel Bustle died of old age, now 12 years old. Ordered at Ipswich bank my subscription to National School Society due January 1, 1831 to be paid: £2. 2.[419]

5 Very cold damp air. At home engaged in preparing for a distribution of coals part of late Sir William Middleton's bequest to the poor of Coddenham.

6 I attended to the distribution of coals [*from*] Sir William Middleton's bequest at Diggens's. Robert & Henry came here, & tenants & families dined here.[420] Letter from Charlotte.

7 Ipswich Quarter Sessions. I attended the sessions. Robert accompanied me & returned here to dinner, & he left us in the evening.
I made a point of attending the sessions, it being desirable that all magistrates should attend, on account of indictments against rioters at Hoxne & Bacton. Three of those at Hoxne were found guilty. The charge against those at Bacton was not supported by evidence & they were acquitted.[421] Letter from my brother.

8 I again attended the sessions. Mr Brown went with me.

9 Taylor officiated here morning for Mr Treadway, absent on account of his mother's affair. Mr Nunn here afternoon.

3

10 Jan. Stormy day. Sent the carriage for Robert & Margaret & the child, who came here to dinner on a visit.[422] Wrote to John.

11 Robert shooting.[423] Robert & Margaret dined at Sir William Middleton's.

12 At sittings. The Browns, Mrs A. Broke & Mr Crowe dined here.

13 Robert went to Woodbridge & brought Henry back with him.
Paid Mrs Longe for weekly house accounts to December 31 1830: £247 9s. 8½d in notes & cash.

14 I attended a parish meeting. Henry walked to Mr Methold's, &c.

15 Robert took Henry to Ipswich in his way home to Woodbridge. Margaret went in our carriage to Barking & stayed there, the family being all ill.

16 At church, morning & afternoon. Mr Treadway dined here.

---

418 Sir William Middleton, the first baronet, had died in 1829.

419 The National School Society: Longe had been a committee member of the Suffolk affiliated charity from its formation in 1812. The subscription may have been to this, rather than the national body.

420 Hospitality to his farmer tenants was an annual occasion, as on 2 January 1826.

421 The Epiphany Quarter Sessions, named from the church festival after Christmas. The Swing Riots affected thirty-eight counties in south and east England in 1830–31, but Suffolk was by no means the worst affected.

422 Robert kept a carriage, but it was more convenient that his father sent his own coachman and carriage at the outset, which were also readily available for the return journey. Nonetheless, there is a touch of the authoritarian father in the arrangement.

423 By 1831 Longe himself seems to have given up shooting.

I sent a certificate of my life to Messrs Child for the Irish tontine agent, & desired a statement of my balance in their hands to be sent.[424]
Paid Mr Treadway for duty here for 13 weeks to January 2nd: £13.
Uncommonly gloomy weather all this week: heavy days & no wind.

4

17 Jan. I & Nunn attended with Sir William & Lady Middleton at Pretty's to distribute blankets to the poor of Coddenham & Crowfield [*bought with the*] late Sir William Middleton's bequest. We all dined at Mr Brown's.

18 At home. Mrs Martin called. Robert shooting.
Richard Fenn settled accounts for rent, &c. to Michaelmas last. Balance received: £18 5s. 4d. Wrote to my brother.

19 I attended a meeting [*of*] Helmingham turnpike business at the Crown. Mr Wenn there.

20 Engaged in examining bills, &c. Very rainy day.
Sent my brother a cheese, & John a cheese: a present from Diggens.

21 Very wet day. The Martins & Mrs Bellman, & Mr Treadway dined here.
Robert Brook settled accounts with me for rent & tithe due at Michaelmas last. Balance received: £22 17s. 6d.

22 Showery day. Coals, part of our subscription, distributed by Diggens to the poor of Coddenham at 6d. per bushel. Coals distributed at Crowfield by Thomas Edwards 1 & ½ chaldron, part of Sir William Middleton's bequest.

23 Very wet day. At church, morning & afternoon. <Robert>
Mr Nunn dined here.
Received of Sir William Middleton a check on Alexander's for £30 on account of old Sir William Middleton's bequest to the poor of Coddenham.

5

24 Jan. I & my son Robert went to Ipswich. Snow at night. Ground covered.
I paid the bill of Lines & Fisher, Ipswich: for coals distributed to the poor of Coddenham: £10 9s. 0d.

25 Henry came here, & went on with Robert & Margaret to Combs, who left us this morning. Snowy day.
I gave Robert £5, & shall pay £5 which he owes John, as John's subscription for coals for the poor of Coddenham. My present therefore to my son Robert is £10.

26 I attended sittings at Needham. J. Fox settled accounts for rent of Lime Kiln Farm: half year to Michaelmas last. Balance received: £66 6s. 9d.[425]

27 Very snowy day. Engaged in settling accounts all day. Sharp frost.
James Brook settled accounts for half year's rent due at Michaelmas last.
Balance received on account £120. Arrears due £29 18s. 0d.

28 Henry came from Combs, & my gig took him on to Woodbridge.
Engaged settling accounts, &c. After walking pretty fast, I found my breath much oppressed, & great faintness came on. My strength failed

424 For the Irish tontine see note at 13 January 1826.

425 Local farmer John Fox of Ivy Farm assisted his sister Widow Rushbrooke: see note at 4 June 1827.

me in walking up the hill to my house, & I was obliged to lean on the rails by the terrace, but soon fainted. When I revived, I found myself lying on the grass, but I had not lain long. I sent to Mr Beck to come to me.[426]

29 At home. Very sharp frost. Mr Beck came, & thinks my attack yesterday happened from my stomach being disordered, & weakness of the muscles of the stomach.

30 Sharp frost. At church, morning & afternoon. Messrs Nunn & Treadway dined here. Mr Beck sent me the [*?*]drams which I began to take today.

6

31 Jan. Snow showers all day. I dined at the Book Club. Mr Colvile slept here.[427] Settled accounts for rent, &c. with Edward Brown & James Barker.

1 Feb. Very heavy fall of snow. Mr Colvile left us after breakfast.

2 Thawed moderately. Robert called here. Snow showers. Sharp frost at night. Mr Beck. My medicines continued. Ordered him to let me have my bill.

3 Henry came here to dinner. Thaw set in rapidly this evening.
All the workmen employed in removing the snow from the stables & round the house, &c. & clearing the drift ways.

4 Ditto [*removing snow*] Henry left us after breakfast on foot for Ipswich on his return to Woodbridge. Rain & rapid thaw: very high flood.
Letter from John with a pike, & some pamphlets.

5 Snow storms from the north-west & very cold. Frost at night.

6 At church, morning & afternoon. Mr Nunn dined here. Dry day.

7

7 Feb. At home, settling accounts. Very mild day. Settled accounts with Thomas Diggens for rent due at Michaelmas last. Balance received £119 11s. 9d. Paid Thomas Diggens my subscription for coals for the poor of Coddenham: £5, Mrs Longe's £3, & my son John's £2.
Mrs Longe paid me her subscription for coals to Coddenham £3, to Crowfield £2: total £5.

8 Very mild air. We went to Ipswich, & I discharged all my Ipswich tradesmen's bills of 1830. Showery in the afternoon. Total checks on Ipswich bank dated February 7/8 & paid this day in Ipswich: £114 9s. 6d.

9 I attended the sittings. Robert came to dinner, to stay with us, Margaret & [*their*] infant being on a visit at <Combs> Barking.

10 Mr Beck came, & from the oppression in my breath in walking not being relieved, thought it better to bleed me. Mr Beck. I sent my waggon for coals, for the subscription [*gift, for the*] poor of Coddenham.

11 We went to Ipswich, & Robert also. Very fine mild day. Henry came to

[426] Oppression on the chest, rather than gout, caused most concern to Longe in the next three years.
[427] The overnight hospitality for Mr Colvile was probably brought about by the snowy weather.

dinner. Received an iron roll for the garden from Ransom, Ipswich: for £2. 15s. Due.[428]

12 Robert & Henry left us this morning. Fine weather. Mr Beck. From the state of my blood, he thinks it was highly proper to bleed me. I think I feel more comfortable, & my breath in walking less oppressed.

13 Showers. At church, morning & afternoon. Messrs Nunn & Treadway dined here.

8

14 Feb. I attended a commissioners' tax meeting at Needham.[429]

15 At home. We called on Mrs A. Broke. The Browns called here. Mrs Longe received intelligence of the death of Mr Paulet, her relation by marriage. Wrote to John.

16 Ash Wednesday. At church. Mr Nunn officiated, here & at Crowfield at 2 o'clock. The wall against the garden at the church-gate house fell down into the barn-yard. The foundation was very defective, & too much earth had been removed on the barn-yard side.

17 We went to Ipswich & called on Mr Cooke, who is far from well. Paid for my son John, a bill of Seaman's, Ipswich, for stuffing birds, &c. in 1830: £3 3s. 0d.

18 At prayers. Letter from John.

19 At home. Stormy day.

20 At church, morning & afternoon.

9

21 Feb. At home. Henry went to Spixworth on a visit to John.

22 We dined at Mr Kirby's & met Mr Hasted.

23 At prayers, & afterwards I attended the sittings at Needham. I sent Robert a waggon-load of faggot-wood & battens.

24 We dined with my son Robert. My son John gave a fancy [*dress*] ball at Spixworth. Henry was there.

25 At prayers. Rain in the evening. My wife has reason to think that Margaret is again in the family way.[430]

26 At home. Henry returned by mail from Spixworth & slept here. [*He*] left John suffering much from his pain in the face.[431] He went to Woodbridge in the gig next morning

27 Very wet morning. At church, afternoon. Messrs Nunn & Treadway dined here.

28 Feb. Book Club morning. Mrs Longe called on Lady Middleton at Bramford. Stormy day.

1 March We went to Ipswich, & brought home Miss Croasdaile on a visit. Showers at night. I consulted Mr Wenn respecting the necessity of appointing one or two new trustees under our marriage settlement, by Mr Edgar's death my brother being now the sole surviving trustee. The appointment rests with me, & I must consult my children upon it. I wrote to John on the subject.

2 At prayers. Robert came to dinner. Mr Beck.

---

428 Ransomes of Ipswich were already famous for iron-work.

429 See note to diary: 23 May 1826.

430 This euphemism for pregnancy is not modern.

431 Longe's son John had for years suffered from this 'pain in the face': see note at 27 March 1827.

3 I went with Robert in his carriage, & called on the Bellmans.
Henry came here to dinner. Letter from my brother.
Received from Mr Addison a statement of my balance in Child's bank to February 28: viz. £1165 7s. 2d.

4 At prayers. Henry read them. Robert & Henry left us this morning.
Ipswich adjourned sessions. Mr Brown qualified as a magistrate.
Mr Nunn received an account of the death of his relative Mr Leeds.

5 At home. Bill for reform of Parliament brought in by government on Tuesday, March 1.

6 At church, morning. Heavy rain at noon.
Received a note from Henry to say that he has bought a saddle mare of Mr Sharp, Woodbridge, for £30, which is likely to suit him.

11

7 March I attended the Saving Bank committee.
Fanny & Miss Croasdaile made a morning visit at Combs.

8 Mr Crowe dined here. James Barker finished rebuilding the wall against the garden of Church Gate House.[432] Wrote to my brother.

9 At prayers. Attended the sittings. Mr Beck called when I was absent.

10 Mr & Mrs Parker called. Henry came at noon on his new mare. We dined at Mr Davy's, [&] met Robert & the [?] Kirbys & Richards. [*We*] left Miss Croasdaile there on a visit. Received from Dawes & Co., 15 King Street, Covent Garden, London: 12 dozen/ 1 gross crest buttons for livery coats. Bill £2 2s. 8d. Due.[433]
Henry's mare appears to be a very useful safe creature.

11 Very wet day. Within all day.
Ackfield here, repairing the underbench in the brew-house, & lining it with sheet lead, which he says will cost about £5.

12 Henry left us at noon. Rain in the afternoon, & very heavy storms of wind at night. I paid Mrs Longe [*her*] house account from January 18 to March 5th inclusive, 9 weeks: £42 3s. 7½d.

13 Showery day. At church, morning & afternoon. Mr Treadway dined here.

12

14 March I attended a trustee meeting [*of the*] Claydon turnpike at Claydon.
Robert came to dinner and left us in the evening. Norfolk Assizes at Thetford. My son John is on the grand jury for the first time.[434]

15 Very wet day. Mr Beck. The tonic medicine which I have lately taken being too heating, I am now to take decoction of bark.

16 At prayers. Mrs Longe called at Shrubland.
I employed Lincoln to plant oaks & ashes in Gosbeck Wood, where the underwood was felled last & this year.

17 Robert & Henry came here to dinner. Henry slept here.
My son Henry's birth day. [*He*] now enters his 28th year.

18 At prayers. Henry officiated, Mr Nunn being absent.

---

432 For the fallen wall see diary entry for 16 February.

433 Crested buttons for the livery of Longe's servants were not available locally.

434 The grand jury of magistrates and other gentlemen judged whether cases were appropriate for trial by judge with (petty) jury. Criminal justice affected the whole community, especially after the Swing Riots.

19 At home. I wrote to John, & [*also*] to Major Leake & sent him a copy of the clause in my marriage settlement relative to the appointment of new trustees.[435]

20 At church, morning & afternoon. Mr Nunn & his brother dined here.

13

21 March I attended the Savings Bank.

22 We went to Ipswich.

23 At prayers. I attended the sittings at Needham.
Robert called on his return from a visit to Henry.
Letter from Major Leake. Robert brought me a bitch puppy of Henry's spaniel bitch bred from Robert's dog Rover, brown & white.

24 Trustee meeting [*for the*] Charity School. Mr Kirby attended & dined here with Mrs Kirby, Miss Gear & Mr Crowe. Very cold with snow storms. The second reading of Lord John Russell's Reform Bill carried in the House of Commons by a majority of one. A most dangerous measure.
Most ill-timed & pregnant with mischief to the constitution of the country.[436] Assizes at Norwich by special commission for trial of some incendiaries & some murderers. My son John was on the grand jury.[437]

25 At prayers. Very cold day. North-east wind.

26 Showery day. At home.

27 At church, morning & afternoon. Messrs Treadway & Nunn dined here.

14

28 March At prayers. Saving Bank & Book Club. Passion Week. Letter from John.
At prayers. Very cold day.
We went over to Combs, and stayed [*to*] dinner there.

30 At prayers. Henry came to dinner & left us in the evening.
My little grandson Robert's birthday: 1 year old this day. He can now walk alone pretty well.

31 I attended the previous meeting at the House of Industry.[438]
Mrs Longe called at the Red House & saw Miss Croasdaile.[439]

1 April Good Friday. At church. Mr Nunn officiated here, & at Crowfield at 3 o'clock. He & his brother dined here.

2 Mrs Theobald & Miss Drury called. Mr Beck dined here. Mr Beck.
The first brick of Sir William Middleton's additions to Shrubland Hall was laid this day.[440]

3 Easter Day. Sacrament here. I & Mr Treadway officiated: 85

---

435 Longe was concerned for the future of the family trusts for much of the rest of his life.

436 This first Reform Bill was introduced to the House of Commons on 1 March 1831 and immediately aroused much interest on both sides. It passed this second reading at 3a.m. in the largest house of living memory on Irish votes. The following month, the Tories won at the committee stage, and in some haste the king dissolved Parliament. In June, after the general election, the second bill was substantially unchanged.

437 Norwich Assizes were dealing with Swing rioters. See note at 7 January 1831.

438 For a previous meeting see note at 24 March 1796.

439 For the Red House see note at 9 August 1796.

440 The new Shrubland Hall: built on a new site ¾ mile from the Old Hall by John Bacon to designs by James Paine (1770s). The Middletons made substantial changes: in 1808, then with architect J.P. Gandy-Deering (1831–32), and with Charles Barry (1850s).

communicants. Mr Nunn administered the sacrament at Crowfield: 28 communicants.

15

4 April Easter Monday. At prayers, & I attended the parish meeting at vestry.[441] Henry A. Croasdaile, esq. of Hargrave Place, Stanstead died: Miss Croasdaile's father.[442]

5 At prayers. My son John came in his gig on a visit, and Henry spent an hour with him, but returned home to dinner.[443]

6 I attended the sittings at Needham. Robert & Margaret came to dinner, to stay with us.

7 I attended the quarterly meeting [*at the*] House of Industry.
Henry came to dinner. At the quarterly meeting, the allowance to children of persons who have above 3 children [*was*] discontinued.
On Mr Davy's motion, it was resolved that is adviseable to apply to Parliament for a new act, for management of the poor.

8 Quarter Sessions, Ipswich. Heavy rain.
Henry left us at noon for Dedham ball.

9 We went to Ipswich, & Robert & Margaret. John did not go with us, but drove to Mr Davy's. Heavy showers in the evening.

10 At church, morning & afternoon. Messrs Treadway, Nunn & John Nunn dined here.

16

11 April At home. Mrs Davy, &c. called. Mr Brown & Mr Beck dined here. Warm spring day. I paid Mr Beck by check on Ipswich bank his bill from January 27 to December 9: £91 5s. 0d. Ditto for servants £4 18s. 6d; a bill due from my brother to June 8 1830: £3 8s. 0d. Amount of checks dated Apr 11: £99 11s. 6d.

12 Robert & Margaret left us to visit Mr Gibson, Earl Soham.
We & John called at Mr Martin's. Very warm day.

13 We went to Woodbridge on a visit to Henry, & John also in his gig. [*We*] slept at the Crown Inn.[444] My son John paid me money advanced by me for him, his subscription for coals to the poor of Coddenham £5, & Seaman's bill £3 3s. 0d: [*total*] £8 3s. 0d. John's subscription to the poor of Crowfield through Robert, who owed him £5, but which I remitted to my son Robert. (see January 25). Nightingales heard today.

14 We with Henry called on Major Moor, & saw Great Bealings church, [*and*] returned home to a late dinner.

15 My birthday & our wedding day.[445] John, Robert & Margaret, & Henry, Mr & Mrs Brown, & Mr Taylor here to dinner.
I heard a nightingale in the garden, for the first time this spring.

16 Robert & Margaret, & Henry left us. We went to Ipswich, & I attended the archdeacon's visitation. <I lent Henry £ [?]> Paid.

17 At church, morning & afternoon. Mr Nunn dined here.

---

441 For the annual parish meeting see note at 27 March 1826.

442 Conflict between John Longe and Mr Croasdaile of Stanstead is summarised in the introduction (pp.xliii–iv).

443 It was unusual for Henry to travel back to his Woodbridge lodgings mid-week.

444 For the Crown Inn, Woodbridge, see note at 23 July 1827.

445 Longe's sixty-sixth birthday and fourteenth wedding anniversary.

17

18 April Henry breakfasted here in his way to Bury. Mr Betham called. John left us on his return to Spixworth. I wrote to Mr Parker to request him to become one of the new trustees with Mr Taylor & my brother (the only surviving one), under my marriage settlement.[446]

19 We dined at Mr Kirby's, met the Davys, Mr Brown, & Mr William Rodwell. Lord John Russell's Reform Bill debated in committee: no division, but adjourned to tomorrow night.

20 Henry called here on his return from Bury. We dined at Mr Bellman's & met Mr & Mrs Only, Mr Chafy, Mr Brown, & Mr Gross.

21 We walked to the Row to examine the premises held of the vicarage manor, lately bought by Cuthbert.[447]

22 Miss Amelia Ward came here from Diss. We dined with Robert. Began Spring brewing with my own barley of last year, & hops from Pritty's. Finished brewing April 28.

23 At home.

24 At church, morning & afternoon. Mr Treadway dined here. I received a very kind answer from Mr Parker who accepts the trust. Mr George Taylor also to whom I applied last week, very kindly accepts the trust. They therefore will be the new trustees together with my brother under my marriage settlement.[448]

18

25 April We walked up to Shrubland with Mr Bellman, to see the gardens, &c. I dined at the Book Club. Repairs to the brook road in Crowfield began today. Letter from John who is now better. Circular from Mr William Rodwell with a proposal of nominating Sir Thomas Gooch & Sir Charles Broke Vere as <repres> members for Suffolk, & desiring me to canvas for signatures to the request, & then to present the nomination.

26 I canvassed the freeholders in Coddenham, but got 6 names only.

27 Dr & Mrs Sutton called. I attended the annual trustee meeting [*of the*] Helmingham turnpike, and dined there at the Crown. I wrote to my daughter Charlotte to inform her of our having our having [*sic*] engaged Messrs Taylor & Parker as trustees under my marriage settlement. Mr Wenn delivered to me the trust deed of church property with the addition of Messrs Edward Paske, Thomas Brown & John Phear as new trustees. The pointer bitch Belle produced 10 puppies.

28 At home. Paid servants wages, ½ year to Lady Day: total £62 10s. 6d. Paid Mrs Longe house account, 7 weeks to April 23: £43 5s. 6½d, & servants wages to Lady Day ½: £62 10s. 6d.[449]

---

446 For trustees of the marriage settlement see note at 24 April 1831.

447 Coddenham Row was a remotely sited line of farm-workers' cottages, long since demolished. From its reputation it was known later as 'Cuckold's Row'. Its position is marked by a copse.

448 Longe had earlier invited Mr Taylor to act as trustee of this trust.

449 For the wages of his servants, see Servants' Wages Book (pp.178–209).

29 I walked to view the brook road in Crowfield, now under repair.[450]
Fanny called on Miss Ibbetson.[451]
Robert & Margaret, & Henry came to dinner. Wrote to John.

30 Robert & Margaret & Henry left us. We went to Ipswich to enquire whether any new candidates are to be nominated for this county. I saw Mr Capper & others, & am sorry to find that there is no encouragement to hope that any attempt can be made with a prospect of success to dislodge the late members for Suffolk.

1 May At church, morning & afternoon. Mr Nunn dined here. Some showers at noon. Letter from my daughter. She & Major Leake approve of the new trustees.

19

2 May At home. Ipswich Borough Election.[452]

3 Showery morning. We called at Mr Methold's. Mr Siely dined here. Mr Siely promised to procure for me from Lisbon an hogshead of genuine wine, either Bucellas or Lisbon. I bespoke one of Bucellas about £16 the hogshead which he says will cost me about 2 shillings per bottle all charges included.[453]

4 I attended the sittings. Showers.

5 Showers. I & Mrs Longe called at Mr Kirby's, & I on Mr Wood, Claydon, to endeavour to settle a charge of assault committed by his son & a pupil on Mr Turner's, the tailor's son, but without success. I therefore issued the summons, that the charge may be heard next sittings. Charles Wood & Henry Payne are the boys charged. The assault is a shameful one.[454]

6 At home. I feel symtoms of gout in my left instep & ancle.
Letters from John at Cambridge, & from my brother who has engaged an house at Catton.

7 Robert came over to breakfast, and left us at noon.
I wrote to John to say that I hoped, if my gouty complaint does not prevent me, to go to him at Spixworth on Wednesday next.

8 I was so lame that I could not get to church.
Messrs Nunn & Treadway dined here.

20

9 May I continue very lame but without any severe pain. My right heel now affected. Mr Brown here on justice business. Robert dined here.

10 My gout is less troublesome today. Packing up for Spixworth.
Henry came to dinner. Suffolk County election. Sir Henry Bunbury & Charles Tyrell, esq. Elected. No opposition.[455]

11 Mrs Longe & I set out for Spixworth. [*We*] left John [*Gowers*] & our horses at Scole & proceeded on with posters. [*We*] reached Spixworth

---

450 Longe was inspecting this parish road in his capacity as *ex officio* chairman of vestry.

451 Longe usually referred to his second wife in his diary as 'Mrs L.' which is expanded in this transcript to 'Mrs Longe'. Less often he used her christian name, Frances or Fanny.

452 When younger, Longe attended the Ipswich Borough election with Bacon. Diary 19 and 28 May 1796.

453 For Mr Siely's connections with Lisbon see notes on people (p.273).

454 This involvement is an example of a magistrate attempting informal mediation.

455 The two unopposed candidates were the sitting members for the county, against whom Longe was earlier canvassing. For parliamentary representation see Appendix G.

by 5 o'clock, & found John & Caroline well. My brother & sister at Spixworth.

12 Dragging the ponds in the park, but lame with gout in my left foot & hand.

13 Messrs Francis Howes & Shirley to dinner.

14 Quite confined to the house by the gout.
Lincoln & Scott have been 3 days cutting out & clearing the sides of the coach road to the vicarage, from the gate by the church to the end of the stables, for which he was paid 13s. 6d, at 2s. 3d per day each.[456]

15 Not able to get to church. Mr George Howes to dinner.

21

16 The gout better. John & Caroline & Mrs Longe went to the play at Norwich.

17 [*deleted*] We dined at Salhouse.[457] John did not think himself well enough to go. Letter from Robert.

18 My brother & sister left us. We went to Norwich & brought back Miss Morse on a visit.

19 John went with the parishioners the bounds of Spixworth.
Wrote to Robert.

20 Mr George Norris, Mr Mann & other company to dinner.
The sewers & privies were cleansed this week by Hobart & Scrutton, for which I paid them 10s. They were about 1 & ½ day about them. Paid them 5s. each: 10s.

21 I dined with John at the Norfolk Club. My left hand very painful at night.

22 At church, afternoon. Very ill at night.
Whit Sunday. Sacrament at Coddenham church.

22

23 May At home all day, my left hand quite disabled.

24 Mrs Longe & I called on Sir Edward & Lady Stracey at Rackheath. Company to dinner.

25 We went to the Horticultural Exhibition at Norwich.
John stayed & dined there.

26 We dined at <the Blofields'> my brother's, & met Mr George Norris, &c.
Letters from Robert & Henry.

27 We dined at Mrs Burroughs' at Hoveton, & met the Blofields, &c.

28 We called on Mrs Church, & Mrs Ives, &c. at Catton, & returned by Horsford & called on Mrs Day. Miss Bohun there. Mr Batchelor to dinner.

29 <At> Trinity Sunday. At church & received the sacrament.[458]
Mr George Howes to dinner. Sacrament at Crowfield chapel.

23

30 May We called on Dr Ward at Coltishall, & dined at Mr Blofield's.
A fishing party, but no sport.

---

456 Maintenance work on the ¼-mile carriage road to the vicarage continued in Longe's absence.

457 Salhouse Hall (Norfolk): the family home of Longe's wife Frances, née Ward.

458 Longe himself received communion in Norfolk at this customary season, while recording the arrangements made earlier to cover his absence from his churches.

John caught cold returning at night in his gig. Wrote to Henry.
31 Mrs Church came to dinner.
1 June We went to Norwich, & I called on the bishop & on the Metholds.[459]
John had an archery party & cold collation.
Mr Marsham Elwin died after a long & painful illness.
2 The Metholds called. We dined with Mr Humfrey at Wroxham. John not well enough to go.
3 We went to Costessey to see Lord Stafford's new house.[460]
John ill with the pain in his face.
4 Mr Wegeman from Norwich here all day, taking our portraits in black lead pencil. Letter from Robert.
5 At church, afternoon. Mr George Howes to dinner.

24

6 June Mrs Longe & Caroline went to Norwich.
I walked & called on Mr Shirley, who was from home.
7 The Blofields, Humfreys, & Mrs Ives, &c. to dinner.
8 Mrs Longe & Caroline went to Norwich.
We left the Hall, & removed to Mr George Howes's on a visit.
9 The Humfreys, Wards & Mrs Day & Miss Bohun to dinner.
10 We dined at Mr John Stracey's, & met Sir Edward & Lady Stracey.
11 We went to Norwich, Mr George Howes with us, & dined at Mr Methold's.
12 At church.
John & Caroline dined with Mr Howes, & also Mr Herring of Norwich.

25

13 June I called on Mr & Mrs Marsham at Stratton. We dined at the Hall, & met Mr Herring, who has given John a prescription for his disorder.
14 Went to Costessey. Letter from Robert.
Mr Willins & his son came to dinner, & slept at Mr Howes's.
John went to Yarmouth to attend the East Norfolk Militia training.
15 Caroline dined at Mr Howes's. Rain in the evening.
16 Mr Wegeman here finishing our portraits.
Left Spixworth for Salhouse. Mr Howes went with us. To dinner there, met the Humfreys, & my brother & sister to dinner [*sic*].
17 Mrs Longe called on the Humfreys.
I was attacked by a return of gout in my right foot.
18 Confined to the house.
19 Quite disabled from getting out of the house. Showers today.
Letter from John.

26

20 June Mrs Longe called on my brother, & saw Caroline there on her way to join John at Yarmouth.
I was now so disabled as to be confined to the chamber.

---

459 Calling, being without appointment, does not imply meeting the named person. A visiting card marked the attempt. Elderly Bishop Henry Bathurst was rarely in Norwich. Longe's neighbour, Canon Methold, residing in the cathedral close at Norwich for his tour of duty, on 11 June hosted a dinner party there.

460 The 3rd Lord Stafford, whose family had owned Costessey manor and park from the fifteenth century, built a 'gothic fantasy' designed by J.C. Buckler, which dwarfed the old manor-house.

21 Very ill with much pain & fever.
Guild day: John was there & slept at Mr Herring's.[461]
22 Horticultural meeting. John was there.
23 My brother & sister called upon us. Very fine day.
We saw Mr Green's balloon which passed in front of Mr Ward's house.[462]
24 Confined to the chamber. <Mrs Lydia Ward came>
The fever & pain still continues.
25 Ditto. Mrs Lydia Ward came to Salhouse.
26 A little better today but confined above stairs. Showers.

27

27 June Still confined to my chamber. The gout now in my right foot & left knee & hand. Ordered payment at Ipswich bank to Mr Richard Porter, Premium & Protector Fire Office, due at midsummer for the year ending midsummer 1832: £21 11s. 0d.[463]
28 Ditto [*still confined, &c.*] Borrowed a pair of crutches of Mr Barber of Salhouse. Letters from Robert & Charlotte to announce the death of Mrs Leake, Major Leake's mother.
29 I am something better today. Norfolk Sessions at Norwich. Mr Ward qualified as an acting justice.[464] Wrote to my daughter.
30 My brother & sister called.
1 July Ipswich Quarter Sessions. I have no return of gout but feel very much debilitated. I wrote to John at Yarmouth.
2 I with much difficulty got downstairs to dinner.
Our haysele at Coddenham finished. A pretty good crop, & all excellent hay & clover, & well got up. Mrs Longe paid for me to Messrs Gurney Norwich bank my annual subscription to [*the*] Society for [*the*] Propagation of [*the*]Gospel for the current year, due at Christmas 1830: £1 1s. 0d. She paid her own subscription [*at the*] same time.
3 Got down stairs, [*but*] not able to go to church.
Thunderstorm & very heavy showers.

28

4 July Finding myself well enough to travel, we left Salhouse, & got to Scole in the evening, where we slept. Second reading of the Reform Bill: the debate began in the House of Commons.
5 We reached home by 2 o'clock, & found Robert here, all well. Robert dined with us. Mr Crowe called.
I find that much more rain has fallen in Norfolk than hereabouts. The ground is very dry, but the crops look well.
6 Engaged in my study. Robert came at 2 o'clock, dined here, & went on my mare to the races, & returned in the evening.[465] Mrs A. Broke drank

461 Guilds normally celebrated annually the patronal festival of the saint to whom they were dedicated. Perhaps they were marking (three days early) St John the Baptist's day.

462 The first manned flight by balloon, of 9 kilometres over Paris, had been in 1783.

463 Longe took a period of free credit before settling most bills. He was however punctilious in paying his fire insurance premium, encouraged no doubt by the spate of grudge arson attacks.

464 An 'acting' justice was one who had taken the oath (*dedimus potestatem*) empowering him to sit in judgment. Others never sat at all but took the appointment simply as a mark of social degree.

465 For horse-racing see note at 4 July 1798.

tea here. On Wednesday morning the youngest coach-horse seems to have got cold & fever & soreness in the throat. Sent for Fenn, who by my order bled him, & gave him a dose of mild physic.

7 Mr Martin called, & Mr Brown.

8 Mrs Longe called on the Martins & Browns. I wrote to John at Yarmouth.

9 Mr Betham called. I have had no return of pain yesterday, & I hope am recovering.

10 Unable to go to church. Mr Treadway here afternoon. He & Mr Nunn dined here. A very mild continued rain, afternoon & evening.
I have not been able to go out of the house since my return home, but I hope the gout is now leaving me, & my right foot is recovering its strength though slowly.

29

11 July I feel much better today. Robert & his wife & child, & the Browns came to dinner, the former to stay.

12 Robert went early, to spend a day & night with Mr Bellman at Aldborough.[466] Henry came to breakfast, & left us at noon.
Misses Martin & Arabella Martin dined here.
Letters from Charlotte & Mr William Smith of Oakley.

13 Heavy showers. Robert returned from Aldborough in the evening.

14 Mr Catt of Ipswich came over with a phaeton & poneys on sale, but they are too small & slight for my use. Mr & Mrs Brown called. Wrote to my brother.

15 St Swithin. Heavy showers. Henry came here to dinner. James Brook paid me on account of half year's rent due at Lady Day last: £106. Arrears due, £44. Wrote to Charlotte.
Paid Mrs Longe house accounts for 11 weeks (of which we were in Norfolk, 9) to July 9: £38 17s. 11d. Letter from John at Yarmouth.

16 Showers. Henry left us at noon.
Wrote to Mr Crosswell, not having received an hogshead of Bucellas ordered for me from Lisbon by Mr Siely.

17 I walked to church, morning & afternoon. Mr Nunn dined here.
My foot is now considerably recovered.

30

18 July Henry came to dinner. The Martins & Messrs Treadway & Brown to dinner. Mr Godbold of Combs brought a chestnut cob gelding for me to look at, rising 4 years old, which promises to suit me: price £25. He will send it over here for a few days' trial, on Monday next.
Received a present of a fine turbot from John at Yarmouth.

19 Robert & Margaret, & Henry, left us at noon. John & Caroline left Yarmouth.
Letters from my brother, & from Crosswell about the Bucellas wine.

20 We went, Robert with us, to the oratorio at Woodbridge church, which was a very respectable performance. Dined with Henry & returned in

---

[466] The small coastal town of Aldeburgh had become fashionable from about 1790, following the example of sea-bathing set elsewhere by the Hanoverian court.

the evening. My coach horses being ill, I had a pair of posters from Haggar, for the day.

21 Bury Assizes. Suffolk Clergy Charity meeting. Showery day.
Robert, Fanny & I went to Ipswich with post horses, dined at [*the*] White Horse, & drank tea with Mr Cook[*e*].
Sent a certificate [*for the*] Irish Tontine to Messrs Child.
Mr White of Stradbrooke, preacher, [*gave*] a very superior discourse from Micah chapter 6, verse 8, 1st part.[467] Hagger: pair of posters for the day.

22 At home. Wrote to my son John, & to Mr Gray about chiffonier, &c.

23 Norfolk & Norwich Assizes. At home.
Henry called in the evening on his return from Bury Assizes.

24 At church, morning & afternoon. Mr Treadway only dined here.
The Miss Martins called. Letter from Sir William Betham, relative to the Temple manuscripts. His friend Mr T.P. Percival is writing a life of Sir William Temple, & applies for the use of the manuscripts.[468]

31

25 July Began harvest, cutting oats in the lays.
Mrs Longe called at Combs, & drank tea at Mrs Uvedale's.
Book Club sale day. Venison: I dined there. Richard Fenn paid me an half year's rent, due at Lady Day last: £47 16s. 0d.

26 At home. Mr & Mrs Nunn called. Wrote to Mr Willins to come after August 7. Mr Godbold left his chestnut cob gelding here on trial.

27 I attended the sittings at the Crown. Company to dinner: the Bellmans, George Taylors, Nunns, Crowes, Messrs Cooke, Brown, & Robert & Henry, & D. Pettiward.
I received the hogshead of Bucellas procured by Mr Siely from Lisbon, from Mr Crosswell, London agent. Began reaping wheat.

28 We all went up to Shrubland, & saw the new buildings, house, &c., & to Barham Church to see the alterations inside. Called on Mr & Mrs Kirby. Henry left us at noon. We all agreed that the alterations of the pews, pulpit, &c. in Barham church are injudicious; & the wainscot altar rails with half-naked caryatides, grapes, &c. & cupids are improper.
They were originally in some gentleman's hall, date 1670.[469]

29 Mr Pettiward left us, & Mr Cooke in the evening. Very hot day.

30 We went to Ipswich. I saw Mr Wenn, & consulted him about my tenants who are backward in paying rents, & [*also saw*] Mr Rodwell & gave him directions in the Croasdaile trust business.[470]

---

467 The first half of the verse in Micah 'He hath shewed thee, O man, what is good', is followed by the challenge, immediately recognised by the preacher's audience: 'and what doth the Lord require of thee, but to do justly, and to love mercy, and to walk humbly with thy God?' Longe valued this ethical dimension.

468 Longe received the Temple manuscripts from his benefactor the Revd Nicholas Bacon: see notes at 30 March 1798, 27 Feb. 1827 and 5 Oct. 1831.

469 Shrubland Hall: see note to diary entry for 2 April 1831. These altar rails (still in place in Barham church) may not offend all visitors. To H. Munro Cautley, for example, they are simply 'richly carved' (*Suffolk Churches* (1937), p.221). Others share the earlier opinion.

470 For the Croasdaile trust see the introduction (p.xliv).

I saw Mr Catt at Ipswich & ordered a low phaeton, very nearly similar to that which he built for Mr Squire. Price about £50.

31 At church, morning & evening. Mr Nunn dined here. Very hot day. Paid Mr Treadway for assistance, 12 Sundays to June 26th inclusive: £12.
Letter from Mr Willins, who cannot visit us at present. Sent an order to Messrs Child inclosed with my banking book, for payment of £35 5s. 0d to Mr Crosswell for the hogshead of Bucellas.

32

1 Aug. Engaged in settling accounts with tenants. In the evening, we went to Bury, taking posters at Stowmarket, by invitation from Mr Hasted. My object was to ascertain the state of Mrs Wayth's health, Henry having been told of Mrs Hyde that she was not so well as usual.
Sent my banking book with Child to Mr Wenn who takes it to town this evening. Paid Mr Godbold, Combs, for his chestnut cob: £25.
Letter from my brother, who will be here next Monday.
James Scoggin being ill, I this day swore in John Acfield [*as*] constable of Coddenham. Thomas Diggens & Robert Brook on account of half year's rent to Lady Day last, paid me £99 5s. 5d. cash, besides bills allowed.

2 I called at Mrs Wayth's & had a long conversation with Mrs Hyde, who said Mrs Wayth had for the last fortnight been very poorly, & that her strength was declining. The Cocksedges, Dr & Mrs Probert & Dr Baines to dinner. Hyde, [*in a note*] delivered by the page to Mrs Wayth, said she [*Mrs Wayth*] was sorry not to be well enough to see us. Hyde said she saw no one, & had refused admitting Mr Sp[*encer*] Kilderbee who called there in the spring. On my enquiring of Hyde whether Mrs Wayth had given any directions as to her funeral, &c., should she be taken away, Mrs Hyde told me that about 3 or 4 years ago she had sent for Mr Holmes, attorney of Bury, & had settled all her affairs, when the decease should happen, with him, & that Mrs Wayth desired her to tell me she was much obliged to me for my solicitude on her account.

3 Went with Mr Hasted to see the improvements & alterations in the two Churches.[471] Mrs Longe called at Mrs Wayth's & saw Mrs Hyde. She is satisfied with Mrs Hyde's conduct. Left Mr Hasted's in the evening, & reached home by ½ past 9 o'clock. I paid Mr Hasted a donation to the Bury County Hospital: £5, & told him I should in future become a subscriber to it of £2.2s. annually, which should be paid in January next.[472]

4 Very hot day. Mr Kirby called. Miss Ibbetson called & dined here. Distant thunder storm in the evening.

5 We spent the morning with Mr D. Pettiward at Onehouse, & returned to dinner. Note: *Quarterly Review* received from John, by Mrs Martin who returned from Spixworth today.

---

471 Mr Hasted had connections with both medieval churches in Bury St Edmunds: St James' (now the cathedral) and parallel to it across the churchyard, St Mary's.

472 Until the subscription hospital in Anglesea Road (Ipswich) was opened in 1836 the hospital in Bury was the only one in the county. For a doctor's view a few years later see E.E. Cockayne and N.J. Stow (eds), *Stutter's Casebook*, SRS xlviii (2005).

6 At home. Henry came to dinner, & Miss Martins drank tea here.

7 I preached here, afternoon, on the crime of murder [*since there was a*] dreadful one lately at Ipswich, Mr Treadway being in Norfolk.[473]
Received my & Mrs Longe's portraits in pencil from Freeman's, who framed them.

33

8 Aug. Extremely hot day. Mrs Longe called on Lady Middleton at Bramford. Sir William & Lady Middleton are now with her.
My brother & sister came to dinner. I despatched by Beart's Norwich waggon my pair of magnificent globes to Spixworth, a present to my son John. Wrote to John to advise him of it. Letter from John, who will come to us on a short visit next Saturday.

9 Very hot day. All at home. Robert came to dinner, & left us in the evening.
Wrote to Charlotte to inform her of Mrs Wayth's weak state of health.

10 I attended sittings at Needham, & called on Mr Beck.
Fanny & my brother & sister made a visit at Mr Pettiward's [*at*] Finborough, & at Combs.

11 We all went to Debenham, called at Mr Chafy's & Mr Jacob Norris's. [*We*] saw the church & copied some inscriptions, &c. Mr Brown dined here. In going through Crowfield, I saw & discharged James Brooke from his office of constable of Crowfield for continued drunkenness & misconduct. [*I also*] reprimanded Ling & Mrs Chittock for keeping their beer-houses ill, & finding there is not a pair of stocks in Crowfield, sent for Gibbons to make one. I swore in Robert Grechard [*as*] constable of Crowfield.[474]

12 Henry came here to breakfast. We all drank tea with the Browns.

13 We all went to Ipswich. John came to us at noon, & Robert to dinner, who with Henry left us in the evening. John informs me the celestial globe sent by Beart on Monday was much injured, the frame broken, & of course the globe defaced. How the accident happened we have not learned. The other globe reached Spixworth safe.

14 All at church, morning & afternoon. The congregation not being so large as usual last Sunday afternoon, I today repeated my sermon on murder & drunkenness. Mr Nunn dined here.

34

15 Aug. My brother & sister & John called at Combs.

16 Company to dinner: Mr & Mrs Henry Methold, Mr & Mrs Bellman, Mr & Mrs Parker, Miss Ibbetson, Messrs Treadway, Chafy, Captain Stracey, Brown, John & Robert, & my brother & sister.
Helmingham venison, extremely good. Received from Mr Smith of Oakley, a copy of the archbishop's Tithe Bill, through Lord Bayning.[475]

17 Wrote to thank them for it. John left us at noon for Mr Martin's.

---

473 I have not been able to trace details of this murder in Ipswich.

474 An excellent example of Longe's supervision in Crowfield, as magistrate and chairman of vestry.

475 This Tithe Bill (five years before the final Act) was Archbishop Howley's tentative proposal for reform, designed to defuse the radical threat.

At home. Letter from Charlotte who leaves Woodhurst this week for their lodgings in Bulstrode Street.[476]

18 We dragged the pond on Chapman's farm in Splashes, & the home farm pond. Robert came this morning, & dined at the Martins'. Mrs Ann Broke dined here. In Splashes pond we caught about half a dozen very fine tench, at least ¾ lb. each, & several pike which we now put into Denny's pond, meaning to keep Splashes pond for tench & carp only. In my farm pond, we caught 2 brace of good table pike, the largest 7 lb. weight, & a great many large roach. These & the small pike we put in again.

19 John called to take leave us. He slept at Scole tonight on his return home.

Mr Beck dined here. My brother & sister left us about 5 o'clock p.m. to sleep also at Scole, & get home tomorrow.

20 Heavy storm of wind & rain early this morning. We went to Ipswich. Received from Ablet a ring: green onyx antique, having sent my seal to be altered, & the stone set in gold as a ring, & left two rings, an amethist, [&] a cornelian antique cameo, to be new set. These rings & seal were Mr Bacon's.

21 Showery day. At church, morning & afternoon. I preached a sermon on harvest. Messrs Treadway & Nunn dined here.

35

22 Aug. Book Club. Mr & Mrs Taylor & her sister called. Mr Richard Ward came on a visit. Robert came to dinner with his child, [*having*] left Margaret at Mr Brown's.

Received 3 hampers of wines from Mr Basil Woodd, [*sent*] to Ipswich by sea, [*& conveyed*] from there by Wells, carrier.

23 Robert left us early on a visit to John at Spixworth. Margaret came in the evening. I attended a meeting at the House of Industry, when it is determined to call a general meeting about a new act of incorporation. A general meeting of owners & occupiers ordered to be called on Friday September 23 at 11 o'clock.

24 I attended the sittings at the Crown. Mrs Longe, Margaret & Mr Richard Ward went to Ipswich. The Warnefords are now at Spixworth, (their first visit). John had an archery party, dinner & ball, rustic sports & fireworks. About 130 dined at the Hall.

25 Mrs Longe, I & Mr Ward went to Helmingham, & spent the morning there, [*having*] left Margaret at Mr Brown's.

26 At home, arranging portfolios, &c. Mr Brown dined here.

27 At home. Margaret left us , & returned to Combs in our carriage.

28 At church, morning & afternoon. Mr Nunn did not dine here.

Letter from Caroline, to ask us to go to Spixworth on Monday, September 5th, to meet the Warnefords.

36

29 Aug. I attended a commissioners' tax meeting at Needham, & we all dined at Combs.

---

476 Woodhurst, Oxted, Surrey. Bulstrode Street lies between Oxford Street and Regents Park (London).

30 I attended the annual meeting of the Suffolk Clergy Charity, & [*then of the*] Suffolk National Society for Education at [*the*] Kings Head, Stowmarket, & dined there. Mrs Longe, Robert & Mr Ward dined at Miss Ibbetson's. At the annual meeting at Stowmarket, I was elected a vice-president & auditor of the Suffolk Clergy Charity.[477] Mrs Longe had a pair of posters from Hagger. Letters from my brother & John.

31 We dined at Mr James's, met Sir William & Lady Middleton, Miss Ibbetson, Mr William Colvile, & Robert. I wrote to Mr Tyrrell MP about a copy of the public records for this county.[478]

1 Sept. Henry came to breakfast. He & Robert shooting, but returned at noon, heavy rain coming on. My sons saw a great many partridges & shot 4 brace.

2 Showery morning. My sons shooting. Mr Richard Ward left us for Huntingdon. Mrs Longe & I went to Ipswich at noon.

3 Robert & Henry shooting. Both left us in the afternoon.
Packing up for Spixworth.

4 At church, morning & afternoon. Messrs Treadway & Nunn dined here. Letter from Mr Tyrell. [*He*] will make application to the Chancellor, & inform me of the result.

37

5 Sept. We went to Spixworth, with our own horses to Scole, & forward with posters to our own carriage. Reached Spixworth. [*We*] found John & Caroline well, & Colonel & Mrs & Miss Warneford with them.

6 Mrs Longe & Mrs Warneford & Caroline went to Norwich.
I called on Mr George Howes. Showers.

7 We with Mrs Warneford called on Mr J. Stracey, Salhouse, & Mr Blofeild's. Showers. We find Col. Warneford & family most agreeable friendly people. I am very sorry to observe that John does not treat them with the civility & attention which he should do, nor is he so kind to Caroline as I wish to see him. The Warnefords were much pleased at our going to pay our compliments & be introduced to them, & will come to us for a few days on their return to Wiltshire next Wednesday.[479]

8 Coronation Day [*of*] William 4th & Queen Adelaide. We had post horses & took Mrs Warneford to Stratton, [*where we*] saw Mrs Marsham, [*& to*] Aylsham & Westwick. Mr George Howes to dinner.

9 Very wet day. All within doors.

10 We, with Mrs Warneford, went to Norwich.
I called on the bishop & Dr Sutton.
From Freeman, Norwich, unpaid for, I bought an engraving framed portrait of the bishop of Norwich, Dr Bathurst, 2 bronze candelabras for chimney pieces, [*&*] an ormolu cieling lamp for the drawing room.[480]

---

477 For Stowmarket as venue see note at 28 August 1827. Longe was respected by county clergy.

478 See diary 4 Sept., 28 Oct., 3 Nov., 6 Dec. 1831. This public records project did come to fruition: see summary in the introduction (p.xlvi). Diary: 3 March, 23 April 1833.

479 Longe accurately discerned a rift between his son John and Caroline, for they separated permanently eighteen months later. See diary entries between 26 March and 17 April 1833.

480 Bishop Bathurst was not popular among many of his clergy but Longe expressed no criticism.

11 At Spixworth Church, afternoon. Mr George Howes to dinner.

38

12 Sept. Left Spixworth at 12 o'clock, & reached home by 6 o'clock [*in the*] evening. Our own horses met us at Scole. Found Robert here, who had fine dry day, & shot us some partridges.
We weighed at Spixworth. My weight is now 13 stone 8 lbs.[481]
Mrs Longe's: 9.11½ .

13 At home. Received of James Brook, Choppyngs Hill, arrears of half year's rent due at Lady Day last: £44.

14 Colonel & Mrs & Miss Warneford came from Spixworth to dinner on a visit to us, on their return to Wiltshire.
Wrote to my brother, & sent him two powers of attorney for his signature as my sole trustee, for stocks in 3 per cent Consols, received this morning from Wenn.
Having received a 3rd power of attorney from Wenn this morning for the church property stock to be transferred to the new trustees, I wrote a 2nd letter to my brother, & enclosed this to him today.[482]

15 Henry came to breakfast.
Company to dinner: Dowager Lady Middleton, Mrs A. Broke, Mr, Mrs & Miss C. Davy, Capt Stracey & Mr Brown, & Robert & Henry dined here.

16 We all called on Robert, & at Finborough Hall. Henry shooting.
Company to dinner: the Bellmans, Messrs Treadway, Nunn & Cooke.

17 We all went to Ipswich. Col. Warneford & I called on Col. Dupuis.
I brought home 5 volumes of Britton's *Cathedral Antiquities* bound by Shalders.[483]

18 The Warnefords went to church with us, morning & afternoon. Messrs Treadway & Nunn dined here. Received a letter from my brother, with the 3 powers of attorney executed by him.

39

19 Sept. The Warnefords left us after an early breakfast. At Book Club.
The Metholds & Bellmans called here. Mr Nunn went to London on business. Disturbances at night here. The direction post, &c. broken by the bridge, &c.[484]

20 We called on Miss Ibbetson, Messrs Tiley, Kirby, & at Shrubland.
We dragged Rushbrooke's pond, & got 4 brace of good sized pike, a quantity of roach & some [*illeg.*].
Mr Kirby executed a power of attorney for transfer of church stock: 3 per cent Consols £1,475 15s. 10d., to the new trustees.

21 Very wet day. Mr William Smith came to dinner.
I attended the sittings at Needham, & afterwards a private meeting of Directors [*of the*] House of Industry at Shrubland to consult about the general meeting called next week. Robert & Henry came.

22 Engaged in justice business. The Metholds & Miss Ibbetson dined here.

---

481 Despite his enjoyment of the dinner table Longe was not unduly portly.

482 Longe derived benefit from a number of trusts and quasi-trusts, with legal requirements.

483 John Britton (1771–1857) antiquary and topographer, was a prolific compiler of illustrated books on British historic architecture.

484 Nocturnal damage was not necessarily social protest, but the Swing Riots were recent in memory.

Robert & Mr Smith shooting.

23 I expect Mr Yarrington about [*the*] painted glass for the chancel window.
Mr Smith left us after breakfast. Mr Yarrington came & examined my old painted glass, & took measures of the east window of the chancel in which I shall place it. I am to arrange the glass as far as may be, & Mr Yarrington will then come over, & take it home with him, so as to complete the window next spring.[485]

24 Mrs Longe went to Ipswich. I engaged at home, putting up the lamp in the drawing room, &c. Mr Nunn returned. Received from J. Freeman, Norwich, an ormolu cieling lamp for the drawing room, per 6 guineas, but bill not sent.

25 At church, morning & evening. Mr Nunn dined here.
Note from Robert to inform us that his wife was delivered of a fine boy this morning ½ past 8, after a short & favourable labour.
Thank God both mother & child are doing well.[486]

40

26 Sept. Mrs Longe went to Ipswich. I called on Mr Brown & the Martins. Wrote to my brother, to engage his two stoves at half price, viz. £4 8s. 0d., & to my son John.

27 I attended a [*sitting of*] Denny's Man[*orial*] Court.[487] We dined at Mr Methold's, met the Phears, 2 Miss Martins, &c., & went to the Debenham ball, a very good one. Mr Burrows, plumber, Ipswich, repaired the forcing pump, which had been some time out of order. Himself & man here all day. Margaret indisposed with the [*?*]birth fever.

28 Dinner at Miss Ibbetson's, met the Metholds, Stewards, Seagraves & my son Henry.

29 Previous meeting [*at the*] House of Industry. I attended.

30 General meeting [*at the*] House of Industry. We dined at Mr Brown's, & met Mr & Misses Gamble, & Mrs A. Broke & Mr Crowe.
Fine rain at night. Hales went to Norwich, &c. to see his friends.
I wrote to John by him, & also to Mr Willins to fix the time of his visit here. Sir William Middleton's resolution to apply to Parliament for an amended act for Bosmere & Claydon Hundred was rejected by a large majority of farmers, &c.[488]

1 Oct. Robert & Henry came to breakfast to shoot. [*They*] dined here & left us in the evening.
Major & Mrs Leake, & Miss Flower are now staying at Spixworth.

2 Sacrament [*at*] Coddenham. I & Mr Nunn administered.
75 communicants. Mr Nunn & Treadway dined here.

---

485 Longe had sole right to change glass in the chancel. The design of his re-made window is summarised in the introduction (p.xxvii). For further preparations see also diary 12 Oct., 31 Dec. 1831. For S.C. Yarrington, the well-known Norwich glazier, see B. Haward, *Nineteenth Century Norfolk Stained Glass* (Norwich, 1984), pp.217–22.

486 Longe's second grandson (Francis) was baptised on 14 November 1831.

487 The name 'Denny's', survives today in a pond: see diary at 18 August 1831.

488 Despite this rejection a new statute for the house of industry followed. See diary at 4 April 1833.

I sent the gig for Henry in the afternoon, who comes here to take the mail to Morning Thorp tomorrow on a visit to Mr Howes.

Wrote by Henry to Mr Howes, to invite them here on a visit this month.[489]

41

3 Oct. Major Moor, his son & Mr Wood <company here>spent the morning here.

Taking up midsummer potatoes in the orchard. Showers at night.

4 Mr Bellman's to dinner. [*We*] met Mr & Mrs Kerrison Harvey, Dr & Mrs & 2 Miss Chevalliers, Messrs Pattison & Barlee.

5 Attended the sittings at the Crown. Dined at Mr Methold's, & met 2 Miss Fishers, Mr & Mrs Kirby, & Mr Brown & Miss Gear.

Letter from the bishop of Norwich, applying for the loan of the Temple manuscripts for his relative & friend, Mr Thomas Peregrine Courtnay.[490]

6 Attended the quarterly meeting [*at the*] House of Industry.

7 At home. Received from Gray, Norwich, furniture: a chiffonier, sideboard, 2 arm-chairs & 1 ditto for myself with an high back & foot board.

8 We went to Ipswich. I ordered at Abletts an amethyst seal to be engraved with my crest.

9 Mr Treadway here, morning. At church, morning & afternoon. Mr Nunn dined here. Sacrament at Crowfield. Showers during the night every day this week. Mr Treadway told me that he thinks he must shortly give up assisting me in the church duty, as he has now Ottley.

42

10 Oct. Robert & Henry here at breakfast to shoot.

Mr & Miss Willins & Miss H. Bohun came on a visit. Mr & Mrs Phear and Mr Budd to dinner.

11 Robert & Mr Willins went to Ipswich, & Mrs Longe, &c. to Combs.

I at home. Mr Beck drank tea here. Showers in the evening.

Answered the bishop's letter, declining in as civil a manner as I could to part with the Temple papers out of my own possession.

12 A great deal of rain today. All at home.

Arranged the painted glass for the chancel window.

13 Heavy showers. I & Mr Willins drove to Barham Church to see the repairs, &c. which are now completed. It looks well, & much improved.[491]

Mrs Longe rode the little poney for the first time. Miss Willins & Bohun also rode it.

14 Showery in the forenoon. Capt. Stracey shot with Robert, & dined here.

Mr & Miss Willins left us on their return home at 3 o'clock.

15 At home. Robert left us this morning.

Paid Mrs Longe house accounts to October 1 for 12 weeks: £ 66 13s. 3½d.

16 At church, morning & afternoon. Messrs Treadway & Nunn dined here.

489 Morningthorpe (Norfolk): the home of the Howes family, connected by marriage with the Longes.

490 For the Temple manuscripts see footnotes to diary at 30 March 1798, 27 February 1827, 24 July 1831, and footnote 167 in the introduction. These entries underline their importance.

491 For critical comment on Barham church see diary entry for 28 July 1831.

43

17 Oct. Mrs Longe & Miss Bohun went to Ipswich. Wrote to my brother, & sent him by Mr Treadway a power of attorney for his signature.
James Barker repairing the brick work at the foot-bridge in the Lawn leading to Malt Office.[492]
Received an [*sic*] gold amethyst seal with crest & cypher from Ablett's.

18 We dined at Mr Pettiward's, Finborough. Met Mr & Mrs Oxendon, &c.

19 I attended sittings at Needham. Appointment of surveyors, &c.
We dined at Mr Brown's, & met his brother & sister.
Charles Berners, esq. of Wolverston Park died of apoplexy, aged [*blank*].[493]

20 Henry breakfasted here on his way to Mr Phear's.

21 We went to Ipswich, & I attended the Quarter Sessions, & returned to a late dinner. Robert left us at noon.
Letter from my brother, inclosing the power of attorney executed by himself, for receipt of dividends in 3 per cent reduced annuities.

22 At home. Showers at noon. Mr Treadway slept here tonight having returned from Norwich by the mail.

23 At church, morning & evening. Showery all day.
Mr Crowe's brother Philip died in London of mortification from his leg, where it had been amputated.

44

24 Oct. I attended a trustees meeting [*of the*] Claydon turnpike at Claydon.[494]
Dined at the Book Club, Robert with me. Mrs Bellman dined here.
Wrote to my brother to say we had sent him a brace of pheasants, & to Mr Willins to inform him of the particulars of poor Mr Berners's death.
Read, my gardiner, taken ill with cold & fever.

25 I attended [*the*] weekly committee [*of the*] House of Industry for Mr Methold.[495] Robert left us, & took Miss Bohun with him on a visit.

26 At home. Called on Mr Crowe & Mr Proctor. Showery day.

27 Heavy showers. Company to dinner: the Pettiwards, Martins, Messrs Stracey, Chafy, Marriott, Treadway, Robert & Miss Bohun.

28 Dry day. We held a special sittings for sale of game licenses, but no one applied.[496] Mrs Wayth died this morning about 5 o'clock. She has left legacies to the Rabetts of Carlton, & to her [*illeg.*] servants, & all the rest of her property to Mr Spencer Kilderbee.
Letter from Mr Tyrrel inclosing a note to him from Lord Brougham respecting the application for copies of the public records for this county.[497]

29 At home, engaged in writing to my sons respecting Mrs Wayth's death.
Letter to Mrs Longe from Mr Hasted announcing Mrs Wayth's death.

---

492 There is still a footbridge across the stream at this point for a public footpath.

493 Woolverstone Hall (1776) with its park is now occupied by an independent day-school.

494 Claydon turnpike: diary note for 10 September 1827.

495 Deputising for colleagues at the weekly committee was quite common.

496 The landowner alone enjoyed the right to take game, until it was extended to tenants in the current year: 1831.

497 The progress with these volumes may be traced in outline in the diary: from 31 August 1831 through to 3 March and 23 April 1833, with further information in the introduction (p.xlvi).

He & Mr Orbell Oakes are executors. Wrote to John, Robert & Henry to inform them of it. Wrote to Mr Dawson Turner about public records.

30 At church, morning & afternoon. Messrs Nunn & Treadway dined here. Letter from Mr Willins.

45

31 Oct. We made a morning visit at Combs & found all well. I saw Robert's infant for the first time.[498]
Letter to John in answer to mine announcing Mrs Wayth's death. Wrote to Mr Hasted on Mrs Wayth's death, he being one of her executors.

1 Nov. I attended the weekly committee [*of the*] House of Industry. We dined at Mr Martin's. [*We*] met Miss Ibbetson, Capt. Stracey, Ainsly & Mr Brown.

2 I attended the sittings at the Crown.
Robert & Mr Treadway here, shooting.

3 Henry came here to breakfast. Showery day. At home.
I sent the power of attorney to Messrs Child for them to receive my dividend on 3 per cent stock (3 per cent reduced annuity).
Wrote to Mr Tyrell & Dawson Turner about the copy of public records for the county. To Mr Crosswell, London, payment of £2 0s.10d ordered to be paid him by Messrs Child for additional duty on cask of Bucellas.

4 I attended a house committee [*at*] Barham House.
Henry left us this morning. Very cold day.

5 At home. Mrs Longe called at Combs. Stormy with thunder.

6 At church, morning & afternoon. Showery day.
Paid Messrs Nunn & Treadway their quarter's stipends to Michaelmas.

46

7 Nov. Mrs Longe with Lady Middleton, &c. distributed cloathing amongst the poor at Crowfield, from the cloathing club fund. I wrote to John.

8 I attended the committee [*of the*] House of Industry.
Henry came here, & dined at Mr Martin's.
Miss Eliza Martin was married to the Revd. Charles Townley, vicar of Abington, Cambridge.

9 Henry left us at noon. Mrs Longe called at Mr Martin's, Mr Briggs's, &c.
Sharp frost.

10 Robert came to breakfast, & [*to*] shoot. I called on the Martins & Mrs A. Broke. Mrs Longe & Robert dined at Shrubland. I sent Robert a present of 3 dozen of Bucellas wine, & some faggot wood. I was prevented dining at Shrubland by a bilious complaint which affects my bowels.

11 <Robert left us after breakfast to shoot>.
Robert left us after breakfast. At home, having taken physic.
County meeting at Stowmarket to petition for the Reform Bill.[499]

12 Mrs Longe went to Ipswich. At home.

13 At church, morning & afternoon. Messrs Nunn & Treadway dined here. Frost at night. The king's letter to [the] archbishop of Canterbury

---

498 For the child's birth see diary at 25 September 1831.

499 Longe was himself strongly opposed to the Reform Bill. See diary at 24 March 1831.

was read in this church after evening prayer, & a collection made at the church doors: received £1 10s. 2½ d. Mr Nunn with Diggens, my churchwarden, will collect from house to house tomorrow. This collection is in aid of the Society for the Propagation of the Gospel.[500]

47

14 Nov. Very cold day. Henry came to breakfast, & we all went to Combs at noon to the christening [*of*] Robert's infant, & dined there. Met Mr Parker.
Robert's infant (his 2nd) was named Francis Davy. Henry & Mr Smith my former curate, now rector of Honingham, Norfolk [*were*] godfathers, & my wife godmother. I stood as Mr Smith's proxy.

15 I attended weekly committee at Barham House. Very cold day.

16 Snow storms. I attended the sittings at Needham.
Robert brought Henry back on his return to Woodbridge.

17 Sharp frost. We dined at Mr Briggs's, Creeting, for the first time.
Met the Metholds, & John Methold, & Mr & Mrs Richards.

18 Mr Roberts came to dinner, & slept here.

19 Mr Roberts left us. At home.

20 At church, morning & afternoon. Very cold day [*with*] sharp frost.

48

21 Nov. Showery day. Mild. Book Club. I & Mrs Longe, & Sir William & Lady Middleton, Mrs A. Broke & Mr Nunn attended at Pritty's & distributed cloathing to the members of the cloathing Club.
Mr Parker came to dinner, & slept here.
We began to brew autumn beer with malt of my own barley.

22 Mr Parker left us. I attended the weekly committee [*of the*] House of Industry. Very mild damp day.
Henry went by mail on a visit to John at Spixworth.

23 Engaged in business all the morning with Mr Morgan about tithe compositions. Hobart & Smith began to fell trees & clear away plum suckers, &c. to thin the plantation by the stables.

24 Robert came to breakfast & to shoot.
We went to Mr Girling's nursery, Stowmarket, & bought some chrysanthemums, &c. Robert returned in the afternoon.

25 We went to Ipswich. A warm drizzly day.
I paid for the Society [*for the*] Propagation of [*the*] Gospel the collection in Coddenham & Crowfield made in consequence of the king's letter, £5. Inclosed in the printed form to Mr Markland, London, & sent by post.
My subscription, to make up the sum of £5, is £2 3s. 3½d.[501]

26 At home. Very cold damp day.

27 At church, morning & afternoon. Messrs Nunn & Treadway dined here.

49

28 Nov. At home.

29 I attended the weekly committee [*at*] Barham House. Very cold day.

---

500 The king's letter was an annual national appeal for one of three charities ancillary to the established church. For the SPG see note at 16 April 1827.

501 Longe personally again paid nearly half of the amount sent from his two churches.

30 Very wet day. I attended the sittings at the Crown.
Mr & Mrs Crowe dined here. We finished brewing autumn beer. Brewed 2 hogsheads of strong ale to be reserved.

1 Dec. We went to Ipswich. 2 Miss Wards from Diss came on a visit.
A fire broke out in Mr Whiting's premises at Ipswich early this morning. The workmen lost their chests of carpenters tools, for whom a subscription was made. I gave £1.
Henry returned this evening from Spixworth by Halesworth.[502]

2 I attended a committee [*at*] Barham House. Robert made a morning visit here.

3 At home.

4 At church, morning & afternoon.

50

5 Dec. I have a slight gouty tenderness in my right ancle. Fanny & the Miss Wards went to Combs, & brought Robert back to dinner. Henry came to dinner. Mr Kirby called. I lent Mr Kirby my map of Barham parish, to settle a dispute about the bounds with Hemingston parish.[503]

6 Henry, Robert & Miss Wards left us. Mr Morgan here about the tithe composition. Wrote to Mr Tyrell to tell him that the Ipswich bailiffs will provide a depositary for a copy of the public records, if he succeeds in his application for them, in the corporation library.

7 Very wet day. At home preparing papers for my tithe audit. Very warm air; wind south & south-west. Letters from John & my brother by Henry.

8 Very wet day & remarkably warm. At home engaged in my tithe audit business, &c. Heavy rain from the south at night.

9 At home. Ditto [*tithe audit business*]. Wet day.
James Brook paid me on account of rent due at Michaelmas:
£57 15s. 0d
[+] tithe composition £42 5s. 0d: £100.

10 At home. Dry day. Fire seen late this night which proved to be Mr Parsons's, farmer at Tendring.

11 At church morning & afternoon. Messrs Nunn & Treadaway dined here.
Fine day.

12 [*sic*] Another fire seen in nearly the same direction tonight: both by Incendiaries.[504]

51

12 Dec. Tithe Audit Day for Coddenham. Mr Morgan attended, on account of alterations in late Sir William Middleton's occupation. I & Robert dined with my parishioners at the Crown.
Sent the carriage for Robert & Margaret & their infants to stay.

---

502 For coach routes see Appendix E.

503 The implications of the exact position of parish boundaries included rates and entitlement to tithe.

504 Frequent at this time was the venting of rural distress by arson of farm buildings and stacks. Tendring Hall at Stoke-by-Nayland was thirteen miles south-west and Tendring village (Essex) nearly twenty miles south.

13 Tithe Audit for Crowfield. Mr Morgan here again, & we dined with my parishioners. All went off satisfactory, & farmers chearful.
I sent John Gowers for my new low phaeton built by Catt, Ipswich, who got it home safe.
I sent Thomas Cornish to Handford Hall cattle shew, who bought for me of Mr Nunn of Whitton, cattle dealer, 3 Galloway Scots for £27 15s. 0d.[505]

14 I attended the sittings at Needham. Mr Richard Martin came to shoot with my sons, & dined here. Henry here.

15 At home looking over my tithe receipts. Henry left us.
Mrs Longe & Margaret went to Ipswich. Robert & I called at Shrubland.
Henry informed me of an attachment he had formed with Miss Amelia Pogson, daughter of Colonel Pogson of Little Bealings. I recommended caution to him.[506] I wrote to John & mentioned with much grief the strange & unhandsome conduct lately of the Leakes to my brother & sister, Robert & Margaret, & to me & Fanny.

16 The Davys, Phears, Messrs Crowe, Nunn, & Brown dined here.

17 At home. Henry came unexpectedly, & dined here. Much rain at night.

18 At church, morning & afternoon. Notwithstanding my advice to Henry not to make a rash engagement with Miss Pogson, he told us today that she had an independence (but which is only in reversion), [*and that he*] had made her an offer [*which*] was immediately accepted.
He also informed us of his having bought 3 shares for £9 in a copper mine speculation in the parish of Constantine, Cornwall, which promised to be very advantageous to him.[507]

52

19 I attended a trustee meeting [*of the*] Claydon Turnpike at Claydon. Tolls not let. Mr Brown & I ordered repairs to the railing, &c. of Claydon bridge to be done at the expence of the county. Letter from John.

20 Mrs Longe has got a bad cold , but we went to the ball at Ipswich, Mr Treadway & Miss Briggs with us, who returned & slept here. Henry & the Pogsons at the ball, to whom he introduced us.
With Sir William Middleon's permission, I set out with Mr Cornish a small piece of land, part of May Down, [*the*] field against the road to Hemingston by Dunstan's, to be thrown into the highway, in order to take off the angle & thus make more commodious the curve of the road, on which to employ the labourers now without work.[508] Sent a turkey to John, & another on Wednesday to my brother by the mail coach.

21 I & Robert took old James Mayhew with us to Foxborrow Hill, &c. to

---

505 Cattle and lamb fairs had been held just south of Ipswich for centuries. See note at 22 August 1798.

506 Henry Longe did not marry Miss Amelia (otherwise Emily) Pogson (1807–34). She (and seven of her ten siblings, children of Col. Pogson) died under the age of thirty-five: see the memorial in All Saints, Kesgrave.

507 Speculation in Cornish copper mining companies was frequent. Several of the Longes held shares.

508 For Dunstans see note at 9 April 1827. The higher land nearby is still known as May Down.

examine my glebe lands, the situation of the meres of which he pointed out to us.[509]

22 I attended the previous meeting at Barham House.

23 Robert & Margaret & children left us. Messrs Parker & Crowe dined here.

24 At home. Henry came to breakfast. [*He*] now has the curacy of Framlingham in view. I wrote to Mr Kitson to request his interest with the bishop in promoting Henry's view to the curacy of Framlingham.

25 Christmas day. Sacrament here. I & Mr Nunn administered [*to*] 85 communicants. Messrs Nunn & Treadway at dinner.

53

26 Dec. Henry, Mr Nunn, Treadway & Mrs A. Broke dined here.
In consequence of Mr Kitson's recommendation, I wrote to the bishop of Norwich, now in town, to solicit the curacy of Framlingham for my son.

27 Engaging [*sic*] within. Afterwards, called on Mr Brown, & he & Mrs Brown called here. Wrote a long letter to John, & mentioned particularly my desire to see all family differences removed.

28 I attended sittings at the Crown, at which we had a discussion about the choice of a clerk, in the place of Mr Edward Abbott lately deceased. Candidates: Pownall & Marriott. The election of a clerk to the magistrates of this hundred is fixed for Wednesday January 11 at Needham. For Pownall: myself, Brown & Paske. For Marriott: Methold, Davy & Phear.

29 I attended the quarterly meeting at Barham House. I proposed & carried a resolution to discontinue the money payment to unemployed & [*illeg.*], & to employ them on land to be hired.[510]

30 We dined at Mr Martin's, met the Halls of Bosmere, Browns, Mrs A. Broke, & [*?*]Mrs I.R. Edgar. A very handsome letter from the bishop.

31 We went to Ipswich. Saw Henry late in the day at Mr Cooke's.
I carried the picture of Nathaniel Bacon, & left it with Smart to clean & varnish, to gild the frame, & add a tablet with inscription thereon. This portrait I have promised to present to the Corporation of Ipswich, for which borough Nathaniel Bacon had been a very useful & able Member of Parliament.[511]
Henry told me he had this week been up to London, called on & was admitted to the bishop who is hurt by a fall, in the eye & knee. He received him very kindly, & told him that, as the parish of Framlingham is a very large one, & the charge an important one, he wished to appoint to the curacy an older & more experienced person.[512]
I spoke to Mr Hare about a wire screen for the east window of the

---

509 Foxburrow Hill was situated to the south of Limekiln Farm towards the turnpike, but away from the parish boundary. The meres may have indicated ownership boundaries.

510 The use of land by a public authority to provide work for those otherwise unemployed had a poor record of success. A similar experiment a few miles away was discontinued when losses were sustained in two successive years: M.J Stone 'The Poor in Tuddenham prior to 1834' (1994), SRO(I) qs Codd 362.5.

511 The portrait of Nathaniel Bacon, ancestor of Longe's benefactor, hangs in the Mayor's Parlour of the Town Hall. He compiled *The Annals of Ipswich* (1654), serving as recorder, town clerk and MP.

512 Bishop Bathurst resided more in London and Cheltenham than in Norwich.

church, to be filled with painted glass. He will come over on Tuesday & bring Mr Lake the plaisterer with him.[513]

Coal Account

Jan.	4	2	chaldron	at 37 shillings	(all to Cornish)	My own Waggon
	12	1 & ½	do		Rd Fenn	
Mar.	18	1 & ½	chaldron	at 30 shillings	Js. Brook	
Apr.	12	2	chaldron		Rushbrooke	
	21	1 & ½	chaldron		Diggens	
June	14	1 & ½	do	at 32 shillings	Js. Brook	
	17	1 ½	do		ditto	
July	15	1 & ½	do		Diggens	
	27	1 & ½	do	at 30 shillings	ditto	
Aug.	1	1 & ½	do		ditto	
Sept.	22	1 & ½	do	30 shillings	Brook	
Nov.	16	1 & ½	do		R. Brook	
	26	1 & ½	do		Diggens	
		2	do	33 shillings	for Cornish	My Waggon
Dec.	1	1 & ½	do		Robt Brook	
	17	1 & ½	do	33 shillings	Diggens	

Game Account

Sept.	1	Robert & Henry	5	brace partridge
	2	ditto	3	ditto
	3	ditto	8	ditto
			16	
Sept.	3	Sent a Leash of Partridges to Mrs Wayth		
Sept.	8	?		
	12	Robert	5 & ½	brace partridge
	15	Henry	3	ditto
Oct.	1	Robert & Henry	1 & ½	Br Pheasants
			4 & ½	ditto hares
			1 & ½	ditto partridges
			3	brace rabbits
Oct	2	Sent Mrs Wayth	an hare & pheasant	
		Mr William Ward, Diss	an hare	

513 For the chancel window see note at 23 September 1831.

DIARY OF 1833

In 1832 Longe suffered a diminution in his powers and he was ill that October. It was six months before he could preside at a Communion service and in May 1833 he was consulting a further doctor in Bury St Edmunds. Indeed he was never again to enjoy full health. Although Longe proudly stood as godfather for Robert's third son, the family were distressed to learn of the breakdown in the marriage of Robert's brother John.

In the wider church, Longe witnessed the beginning of the Oxford Movement. In his parishes, the Sunday services were kept going by his son Henry as second curate, who travelled from Woodbridge, where he was chaplain of the Bridewell. In September Longe and his wife managed to pay their customary fortnight's visit to Norfolk. It was to be his last and the diary shows how his world was closing in. He was to die at Coddenham on 3 March 1834, just short of his sixty-ninth birthday.

1

– I am now, thank God, well in health, but my limbs [*are*] still very weak. I however gain some strength daily.

1 Jan. Henry came to us from Combs at noon, & Mrs Longe & he dined at Shrubland, met the Dowager Lady Middleton, the Davys & Messrs Campbell & James. Letter from my brother.

2 Henry left us for Woodbridge this morning, being sessions there.[514]
A very affectionate letter from Charlotte. Wrote to her the same day.

3 Mr Martin called.
Wrote to John & sent him & Charlotte a turkey each by tonight's mail. Wrote to Mr Capper respecting I. Woolner & James Southgate now in Ipswich gaol for trial for stealing William Barker's tools.

4 Ipswich Quarter Sessions. Mr Beck called, & Robert & Mr Pettiward. Sent an order to Messrs Bacon & Co. to pay to the election fund for Henniker de Vere £50 my subscription, & to send me £100 which they did by John Gowers.[515]

5 Very fine frosty morning. I got into the garden, first time since my relapse. Letter from John.

6 Mr Nunn dined here.
Letter from John, & another from Charlotte to thank us for the turkeys.

2

7 Jan. Book Club Dinner. Mrs Longe <made some visits> went to Ipswich. Mr George Taylor called. Letter from John to thank us for the turkey.

8 Henry & Mr Carthew came to breakfast & for shooting, & dined here.

514 Henry was still in lodgings in Woodbridge in church ministry. Woodbridge was one of four venues in the (non-borough) county for Quarter Sessions, and thus with Epiphany sittings.

515 His constituency for the 1833 General Election was the new eastern division. See Appendix G.

Henry slept here, & left us [&] went [*to*] Ipswich.

9 Tithe Audit Day, Coddenham. Mr Wenn came here to breakfast. Robert came & dined at the Crown, & slept here. I wrote to Col. Warneford, & sent him a present of 2 rings of 8 bells For.his sheep flocks, & also an hen turkey.

10 Tithe Audit Day, Crowfield. Robert dined with the parishioners, & left us at night. Mr Morgan attended by my desire both days.[516]

11 Mrs Longe called on the Davys, James's & Briggses. Paid Mrs Longe for house accounts: 11 weeks from October 1 to December 29 1832: £74 0s. 1½d.

12 Sharp frost for several nights past. A severe cold & great tenderness in my left foot has prevented my getting out this week.

13 Weather changed. Showers from the south. Mr Nunn dined here. Mr Beck called. I had a return of gout in my left foot this evening, & slept in the nursery.

3

14 Jan. Very lame today.

15 Rather better. I had a return of gout in my left wrist & hand at night. Mr Beck.

16 I am very poorly today, & my left hand full of pain. Henry came to dinner.

17 Feverish & occasionally returning of pain. Mr & Mrs Paske & Edwin Paske called. Henry left us to dine at Mr Taylor's. Mr Beck.

18 I have less fever today, but still very helpless. Robert & Mr Brown called. Letter from Col. Warneford, thanking us for the turkey & sheep bells.

19 Mr Treadway called on his way home from Norfolk. Mr Treadway brought me a letter from John, enclosing £10 for coals for Coddenham & Crowfield, & a present of oysters & sounds.

20 Remarkably fine weather all this week. Mr Nunn dined here. The king's letter for a general collection for the National Society [*for the*] Education of the Poor was read at church, & collected at the church doors: 15s. 7d.

4

21 Jan. Fine bright cold day. No return of gout. Sharp frost at night [&] east wind. I sent Robert a load of faggot wood, & the presents from John.

22 I took a blue pill last night & an aperient draught this morning, by Mr Beck's direction. I added my own contribution under the king's letter read last Sunday, viz. £1 4s. 5d., to make up the sum of £2 which I enclosed in the printed letter, sent to the Secretary of State, Whitehall, according to the directions, by post this day from Needham.[517] Mr Beck.

23 I am stronger on my feet today, & got into the library on my crutches. Mrs Longe went to Ipswich. Fine sharp frost.

24 Robert, Mr Cooper Brook, & Mrs Davy & Margaret called.

---

516 Robert, deputising for his father on both occasions, would soon be receiving tithes in his own right.

517 Again Longe contributed well over half the donation in response to the king's letter.

Frost. Bright day. Received from Mr Watson, treasurer to National Society [*for*] Education, a receipt for £2 sent.

I wrote to John, & asked him to send me some plants for the rockery, which I am about to remove to the terrace.

25 Mr Brown & Mrs Uvedale called. Sharp frost. I continue free from any return of gout. Fountain Elwin esq., my uncle, my mother's second brother, died at Dulwich, aged 96 years.

26 Mild air & rapid thaw. Frost again at night. Read & 2 day men began removing the rockery from the west slip in the garden, to the terrace.

27 Mr Nunn dined here. Fine bright day.

25 [*sic*][518] Lincoln & Scott began planting oak, ash & beech in Gosbeck Wood & the chalk pit. Also hazels for underwood.[519]

5

28 Jan. Mild grey day. I continue mending daily.

Cornish has fetched some rockstones & flints from Choppyngs Hill for the rockery. Read & 2 men engaged about it.[520]

Read & son & 2 labourers engaged in the new rockery on the terrace.

29 I took an aperient from Mr Beck. Robert came to breakfast to shoot.

I paid Mr Byles £10, for 8 & ¾ chaldron of coals, the amount of my son John's annual gift. I shall pay the porterage & carriage.

30 Robert assisted in distributing coals, £5 in value, to the poor inhabitants of Coddenham. Fine bright cold day.

31 I attended an Helmingham turnpike meeting at the Crown. At this turnpike meeting it was resolved unanimously that the toll gate in St Margaret's Ipswich shall be removed.[521]

Robert left us at noon. Coals distributed to the poor of Crowfield. Mr Nunn attended to it. Letter from Henry, now at Spixworth.

1 Feb. Dry fine day. A flight of snow at night.

2 The snow soon disappeared, but a heavy rain from [*the*] south continued [*a*] great part of the day, which occasioned a flood in the meadows.

3 Dry day. Mr Nunn did not dine here.

6

4 Feb. Showery. Sent the carriage for Robert & Margaret & their 3 children, who with 2 nursemaids came to us to dinner. Robert exchanged his horse, which is too spirited for his carriage, with Mr Feaveryear of Helmingham, for a brown mare 9 years old which promises to suit.

5 I attended a general committee meeting [*of the*] Suffolk Society [*for*] Education at Stowmarket.[522] Very bright mild day.

I received a letter from Caroline which distressed me much. She complains of a continuance of ill treatment from John, & is resolved to consult a lawyer. [*She*] proposes Sewell & Blake, Norwich, & asks

518 This entry, clearly dated 25, was written out of its order.

519 Longe owned part of this ancient wood: Tithe Apportionment (1837) SRO(I) FDA66/A1/1a.

520 Choppyngs Hill Farm was owned in trust by John Longe.

521 This toll-gate stood by a fork in the Ipswich roads leading to the villages of Westerfield (the turnpike) and Tuddenham (not turnpiked). To attain a new Act unopposed the Helmingham turnpike trustees conceded under pressure from Ipswich: SRO(I) EN1/B1/1 (19 Oct. 1832 and 18 Jan. 1833).

522 The Suffolk Society, a separate charity, was affiliated to the National Society.

my advice. She says she can go on as she has now done so long, no longer.[523]

6 Mrs Longe & Margaret made some morning calls. The Bellmans called here. Mr Brown to dinner. Fine warm day.

7 Fine bright day. Henry came.
Our tenants & their families, & Messrs Pettiward, Nunn, & Robert & Margaret attending at dinner. The rockery on the terrace finished.

8 We all went to Ipswich. I attended a trustee meeting [*of the*] Helmingham turnpike at the White Horse.[524] Henry left us early.
I wrote to Caroline to urge her not to take the step she proposes yet, and told her I would write to Col. Warneford to beg of him to come over here, asking she shall then meet him, with or without John as they prefer.

9 Mr Pettiward left us. All at home.
Wrote to Col. Warneford, sent by Sunday night's post.

10 Heavy rain in the morning. Mr Nunn dined here.
Robert attended his duty at Combs, & returned to dinner.

7

11 Feb. Very bright mild day. I walked down to the bottom of The Lawn for the first time, & find my insteps stronger. Lincoln finished planting in the chalk pit. Paid him his bill for 11 days work [*of*] 2 men at 4s. 6d: £2 9s. 6d. Smith began planting the old whitethorn, removed from plantation fences now thrown down, against the river.[525]

12 We called on the Bellmans, & left Margaret at Mr Brown's for a night. Dry day. Letter from Charlotte to announce the death of Mr Leake, Major Leake's father, on Friday last, aged 85. Settled accounts for rent, &c. with Robert Brook. Balance received: £16 16s. 7¼d.

13 Rain early this morning. Showers greater part of the day.
Mrs Longe called at the Martins, & brought home Margaret.

14 At home. I paid the servants' wages: ½ year to Michaelmas last: £63 6s. 6d. Wrote to my daughter Charlotte Leake, [&] Messrs Baldwin & [*?*]Gedoch, & [*also*] Messrs Child an order to pay £400 to Ipswich bank, & £26 12s. to Thomas Dunston on Anna Maria mine account.[526]

15 Company to dinner: the Kirbys & Miss Gear & Bellmans & Mr Treadway & Mrs A. Broke.

16 Mrs Longe & I went to Ipswich, called on Lady Berry now in Leverets' lodgings. Saw Mr Wenn & Mr Cooke. I ordered at Ipswich bank my subscription of £5 to the relief of the Irish clergy.[527]

17 Dry cold day. Mr Nunn dined here.

8

---

523 Longe's concern about his son John's domestic relations goes back eighteen months. See diary 7 Sept. 1831.

524 Within eight days it was agreed to erect a substitute toll-gate with house at Westerfield.

525 The word 'fence' was used for a living hedge as well as for an inert structure.

526 For the Cornish mine see note at 18 December 1831.

527 In this time of agricultural depression the largely Catholic rural population withheld (Anglican) tithes.

18 Feb. Very heavy rain at noon. High floods. I attended an appeal meeting [*on*] assessed taxes at Needham.
Robert went to Henry's [*at*] Woodbridge to dinner.

19 Mrs Longe & Margaret called on Mr Kirby. Mr Wenn gone to London. Paid my subscription to [*the*] Society [*for the*] Propagation [*of the*] Gospel due at Christmas last, to Mr Kirby, who is going to London next week & will pay it to the treasurer.
A letter from John, complaining of his wife's behaviour.

20 Ash Wednesday. Mr Drake officiated here & Mr Betham at Crowfield for Mr Nunn. I attended the sittings here. Cold stormy day.

21 Showery. Company to dinner: the Metholds, Davys, Martins, Mr Drake, Robert & Henry.[528] Letter from Col. Warneford. Sent Mr Betham, at his desire, by his servant £15 for assistance at Crowfield chapel.

22 Showery. Robert read prayers. Mrs Longe, Margaret, Robert & Henry dined at Mr Martin's. I was too much fatigued & unwell to go.

23 [*no entry*]

24 Stormy day. Mr Nunn dined here.

9

25 Feb. Dry day. The Miss Martins & Mr Crowe called.
I gave John Rushbrooke verbal notice to quit the Limekiln farm at Michaelmas next.[529] Settled accounts for rent of farm & cottage with Richard Fenn, Hemingstone. Balance received: £40 14s. 5d.
The channel across the road by the churchyard gate, to convey the water into the ditch of my Bridge Meadow, begun by the parish surveyors.[530]

26 Showery. All at home. I wrote to John about his domestic quarrels.

27 Showery. Robert & Margaret & children left us. He went round by Ipswich, & his family to Combs in our carriage.

28 Being a bright morning, we went to Ipswich, but an heavy rain came on at 2 o'clock. I paid almost all my Ipswich tradesmens' bills of 1832.

1 March Very stormy day. Being very far from well myself, & Mrs Longe having a cold, we declined dining at Mr Methold's today as we had engaged to do. A letter from Charlotte informing me that the late Mr Leake had made a very satisfactory disposition of his property. [*He*] has left Major Leake Woodhurst, and his personal estate in equal shares between his son & daughter.[531] Having felt more than usual oppression on my chest, I sent for Mr Beck who came today, & will give me some medicine for it.[532]

2 Dry day. Henry dined here, & returned in the evening to Woodbridge.

3 Fine day. Mr Nunn dined here. Letter from John, & from Mr L.P. Cooper, Secretary to the Public Record Commission, about the copies of public records procured at my request by Mr Tyrell.[533]

10

---

528 Note that this dinner party was during Lent.

529 For Limekiln Farm see notes at 25 May 1798, 4 June 1827 and 26 January 1831.

530 The lower churchyard gate is near the road bridge over the river.

531 Woodhurst (Surrey) was soon to become the home of Longe's daughter and her husband.

532 'Oppression on the chest': breathing troubled Longe for the rest of his life. See Appendix D.

533 For earlier progress on the public records see introduction (p.xlvi) and diary from 31 Aug. 1831.

4 March I attended the Saving Bank. Book Club, morning meeting. Mr Parker unexpectedly dined here. Dry. Settled accounts with J. Fox, Widow Rushbroke's executor, for half year rent for Lime Kilns farm due at Michaelmas last. Balance received: £76 10s. 5d.

5 Robert called. Dry day. Ditto. [*Settled accounts*] with James Brook [*of*]Choppyngs Hill for ditto [*half year rent due at Michaelmas last*]. Received on account of balance: £40.

6 I attended the sittings at Needham. Very wet day. Mr Beck.

7 Dry cold day. North-east wind. Snow showers at night.

8 I & Mrs Longe went to Ipswich, & returned to a late dinner. I attended an adjourned sessions. I wrote to Mr Portman MP, to submit some additional clauses in the new general Highway Act under his care. I see by the paper, that at this very time he has just resigned his seat in Parliament for Mary le Bone in disgust.[534]

9 Snow showers. Henry came to dinner, & left us in the evening. Very cold day.

10 Very sharp north-east wind. Mr Nunn dined here. John Read my gardner laid by all this week with cold & fever.

11

11 March Mr Brown called & Mr Treadway. Mr Brown informs me that the new Act for Bosmere & Claydon Hundred will soon pass both houses, without any material opposition.[535] Settled accounts with Thomas Diggens for rent, &c. to Michaelmas last. Balance received by check, £146 18s.

12 Robert called on his way to Mr Bellman's. Mr Beck. My poor old dog Dash, who so long had been so good a guard at my home farm died, nature being exhausted & dropsy coming on.

13 Robert breakfasted here on his way to Combs, & returned to a late dinner with Henry. I attended prayers, the first time I have been in the church since my illness.

14 Snow storms. North-east wind & very cold.

15 Bury Assizes. At prayers. Robert called on his way home from Woodbridge. Mr Nunn & his brother dined here. Fine dry day. North-east wind. Sir William & Lady Middleton returned to Shrubland.

16 Very sharp [*?*]east wind.

17 Cold dry day. I had intended going to church, but have got cold, & am not well enough to do so. My son Henry's birthday, who is now 30 years of age.

12

18 March Very cold day. Henry & Robert came to dinner. Mr & Mrs I.R. Edgar & Mr Nunn dined with us. Robert left us at night, & Mr & Mrs I.R. Edgar slept here. I wrote to my brother.

19 Very cold day. Henry, & Mr & Mrs Edgar, left us at noon. Mrs James called. Mr Beck.

---

534 Longe's interest in highway legislation illustrates his active concern in public matters. Soon after his death the Highway Act of 1835 was an important step in the developing law.

535 The local incorporation needed legislation to renew and extend its powers. The new Act was soon overtaken by the national amendment of the Poor Law, also shortly after Longe's death.

20 At church, & afterwards attended the sittings. Cold stormy day.
Very lame today, & my feet & insteps much swelled.
Sir William Middleton called when I was at sittings.

21 I with difficulty got down stairs. Very feverish, with pain & swellings in the parts lately attacked by gout.

22 Very ill & continued in bed all day. Lady Berry called.
Sent for Mr Beck, who changed my medicines.

23 I am unable to get out of bed, but have no fresh attacks of pain.
Mr Beck.

24 Still very feverish, but sat up in my chamber. Very stormy day.

13

25 March Snowstorms all day. I am something better, & was wheeled into the dressing room to breakfast. Book Club dinner: I should have presided.
Robert & Henry came, & dined here. Robert returned at night.
Mr Beck.

26 Henry here. Showery, but wind changed to south & air milder.
In the drawing room. Frisky shut up by herself, as I [*do*] not intend to let her breed at this time. Letter from John, a most distressing one, says that a separation between him & his wife is agreed on. After mature consultation we all agreed it would be a serious step to both, & Henry very kindly proposed to go immediately by coach to Spixworth to dissuade John from adopting this plan. Wrote a few lines to John by him.

27 Showery day but milder air. Mr Bellman & Mr Davy called.
Henry returned at night from Spixworth by mail. Mr Beck. My fever is now removed. Henry was unsuccessful in his endeavour to dissuade John; any further attempt is useless.

28 Henry left us this morning, & Robert called soon after he was gone.
Fine mild weather.

29 I was able to walk into the drawing room on crutches. Mrs Martin called. I continue recovering.
John Riches, 'Dumby', died this night. He lay dozing for some hours, & had a very quiet departure. Nature quite exhausted, in his 80th year.[536]

30 Very fine day.
Letter from my daughter Charlotte Leake, which I answered this day.

31 Fine dry day. Sir William & Lady Middleton called.
Mr Nunn dined here. I owe Mr Betham for assistance at Crowfield to this day inclusive. Next Sunday Mr George Taylor will take one part of the duty here, & Mr Nunn will officiate at Crowfield.

14

1 April Stormy day. Mr Betham being very infirm, I have dismissed him, and engaged Mr George Taylor to assist me here for a few Sundays, till I am able to resume my duty.[537] Mr Beck. I wrote to John.

---

536 Longe described John Riches, when dismissing him as gardener in 1811, not only as dumb but also as lame and ill. See Servants' Wages Book (p.179). Nevertheless, he survived twenty-two years after that.

537 Longe was being optimistic in expecting to resume his duty. Although he did take the Holy Communion service on 21 April, that was an isolated occasion.

2 Mrs Longe went to Ipswich. Mild day. I got a malt mill from Ransome's, price £4, who will allow me for the old one, which is worn out.

3 Dry day. Robert dined here. The carriage left at Catt's for a thorough repair. Mr Morgan called to speak to me about the allowance to be made to Rushbrooke for rent & muck laid on the Riding Field, which I have taken to let in allotments to the poor.[538]

4 Thorough wet day. A meeting of directors & acting guardians at the House of Industry, in consequence of the new act of incorporation, which was passed & received the Royal Assent last week, being now in force.

5 Good Friday Mrs Longe at church.
My feet are better, & I got downstairs.

6 Dry day. Mrs Longe went to Combs. Henry dined here.
Letter from John. Mr Beck called.

7 Easter Sunday. I unable to attend at church. Mr George Taylor officiated for me, afternoon [*for the*] 1st time. Mr Nunn at Crowfield, afternoon. Coddenham: 84 communicants.

8 April [*no entry*]

9 Mrs Longe called at Barking on Mr James & Davy. Mr Kirby called. Showers but mild.

10 Messrs Wenn & Morgan here by my appointment, to confer in respect of the Crowfield tithes & other business. Showery but mild.
A special sittings at Needham to examine into settlement of poor in consequence of the new incorporation act now in force.

11 Mild showers. Henry came to dinner & slept here. Adjourned meeting at the House of Industry, for the usual quarterly meeting business.

12 Showers. Robert came to dinner, & left us in the evening.
Messrs B. Colchester, Land Surveyor, &c. of Ipswich & Woodbridge, & his friend Mr Gower came over to view the Lime Kiln which Mr Gower is inclined to have. He likes it & will hire it, if we can agree on the rent. I am to send him my forms, as soon as I can fix them.[539]

13 Fine day. Mrs Longe called at Mr Kirby's, Bramford & Shrubland. Showers at night. Mr Beck.

14 Thanksgiving for preservation from the late epidemic disease.[540]
Sacrament at Crowfield: 30 communicants. Mr Taylor here, morning. 2nd Sunday. I gave a silver-plated flaggon, which holds 1 quart, to the chapel at Crowfield for the communion. Bought of Cole, Ipswich, for £5 exclusive of a wainscoat box to keep it in.

16

15 April I went in the carriage (for the first time since my relapse) to the Barham House special sessions, to determine settlement cases on account of the new incorporation act. Rain all the afternoon.

---

538 The movement to provide allotments for the poor was in its early days nationally.

539 The farm at Limekiln (83 acres) was in 1837 still occupied by John Rushbrooke but under the new ownership of Sir W.F.F. Middleton: Tithe Apportionment, SRO(I) FDA66/A1/1a.

540 The cholera epidemic had reached London from abroad by January 1832 and then spread.

I sent a letter to my brother. My birthday.[541]

16 Heavy rain & high flood last night. At home. Dry day.
Received a note from my brother, with piece of Gloucester cheese, by which I find that poor Caroline left Spixworth for London on Friday last, the 12th instant, to reside in a clergyman's family there.

17 Sittings [*at the*] Crown Inn. Engaged till 5 o'clock in determining settlements of the poor. Showers afternoon. Received a short letter from John, informing me that poor Caroline left Spixworth on Friday.

18 Showers. We called at Dr Elough's [*in*] Claydon, & Shrubland (neither family at home), & at Mr Kirby's & Mr Martin's, whom we saw. Note from Robert, who has heard from John about his separation from his wife.

19 Very fine mild day. I walked in the garden, & called on Mr Crowe.
Mrs Longe took Mrs A. Broke & the Martins to call on Miss Ibbetson.
Henry came to dinner. I wrote to John.

20 Archdeacon's visitation [*at*] Ipswich. Showery. Henry went with us to Ipswich to attend the archdeacon's visitation. I & he dined at the White Horse, & met Mrs Longe at Mr Bacon's at tea, where she dined.

21 Very fine mild day. I went to church, & read the Communion service [*for the*] first time since my illness in October last.
Mr Taylor here, afternoon, and dined here. 3rd Sunday.

17

22 April Bright warm spring weather. Mr Crowe & Mrs Philip Crowe called.
Mr William Colvile, & Robert & Margaret & Robin spent the forenoon here. Began to brew spring beer this evening. James Barker & man here, cleaning & whitewashing the walls of the cellars.

23 We went to Ipswich. I spent some hours at the Literary Institution rooms, and examined some of the volumes of the public records.[542]
Brought Mr Cooke home with us on a visit.
I executed at Mr Rodwell's a deed of trust for Mrs Croasdaile's property, by which two Messrs Barnets, bankers [*in*] London, are appointed co- trustees with myself, I having become on Mr Theobald's death sole trustee.
Messrs Barnet were appointed by Mrs Croasdaile's desire.

24 The Charity School trustee meeting. Sir William Middleton & Mr Kirby attended at my house, I having got a bad cold which confined me within doors.[543] Mr Beck.

25 All at home. Fine dry day. Henry called on his way to Robert's.
I have still a good deal of fever, & a vast discharge from the head & lungs.
I heard a nightingale in the plantation before the house; first this spring.

26 Still very ill with constant cough & great discharge from the head & throat, & much fever. Mrs Longe carried Mr Cooke home. She has now

541 Longe's last birthday (sixty-eight). The timing of the gift on the previous day may have related to this.

542 The availability of these records, the printed volumes obtained from the Commissioners in London, was the culmination of Longe's efforts. See the introduction (p.xlvi) and diary from 31 August 1831.

543 For the school trustees see note at 3 April 1826.

caught the same complaint. Mr Beck. I sent Mr Betham [*the*] balance due to him for assistance at Crowfield chapel to March 31st inclusive, 9 Sundays at £1: paid £9. Then I dismissed him.

27 Robert & Henry came to dinner. Robert's infant a day or two ago Broke its right arm above the elbow, but not known how or when.
He is however doing well. Letter from John. Wrote to him & my brother by Robert, who is going to Spixworth on Monday. Mr Beck thinks my fever less.

28 I am unable to venture to church from my cold & cough.
Mr Taylor here, morning. Mr Nunn dined here. Mrs Longe has caught the influenza as well as I. It is now very prevalent around us.

18

29 April Fine dry day, but cool. We are both much indisposed with the influenza & obliged to keep indoors. Mr Beck here.

30 I am better today. Mrs Longe very poorly.
Severe thunderstorm passed over us. Much rain & hail.

1 May Cold & stormy. I attended a special sitting at Needham for swearing in constables. I have now a great hoarseness, so that I can scarcely speak.
I wrote to my daughter Charlotte. Mr Beck to see Mrs Longe.

2 Mrs Longe still very poorly. Heavy showers all the forenoon.

3 I attended meeting of house committee at Barham House.
Robert returned in the evening from Spixworth. [*He*] left John well.[544]
Finished brewing spring beer.
Note. A packet of annuals from John, & note from my brother.

4 At home. Very mild summer day. I sent Robert home in the gig.

5 Mr Taylor officiated here, afternoon, & dined with us.
My hoarseness continues very troublesome.

19

6 May I attended a meeting of trustees [*of the*] Helmingham turnpike at the Crown, & dined there. Mrs Bellman dined with Mrs Longe. Book Club.
At this meeting, Mr Wenn presented his bill for total expenses of the new act of Parliament (Helmingham turnpike) which amounts to £176 3s. 10d., which was thought a very moderate bill.
Letter from my daughter Charlotte Leake.
James Barker here cleaning [*&*] [*?*]washing brick flues to the melon pit.[545] Mr Wenn informed me that he had to return me (from my subscription for Sir Philip Broke Vere's election [*fund*] of £50) £25, which I desired him to pay to my account at Ipswich bank.[546]
Sir William Middleton got a serious fall from his horse, & broke the bone of his elbow. His horse fell with him.

7 We called at Ringshall, then Mr Parker executed a power of attorney for 3 per cent Consols - & at Mr Davy's.[547]
<Mr Robert Ward & Miss Mary Ward, Diss, came to dinner on a visit.>
<Henry came late last night.>

---

544 Longe's son John was by this time at Spixworth alone. He lived to the age of seventy-three.
545 For melon pit see note at 10 May 1796.
546 For the election fund see diary 4 January 1833.
547 Executing a legal document: see also diary entry at 13 May 1833.

8 I attended the sittings at Needham. Mr Ward & Miss M. Ward came to dinner. Henry came here in the evening.

9 Mr & Mrs I.R. Edgar & Mr Brett came to dinner, & slept here.

10 Mr Brett & Henry left us. We all went to see Barham church, & called at Shrubland on our return. The Edgars left us in the evening.[548]

11 Mrs Longe, & Mr & Miss Ward made a visit at Combs.
I at home. Very hot day.

12 I walked to church, morning & afternoon. Mr Taylor here morning Mr Nunn dined here.

20

13 May Mr & Miss Ward left us after breakfast.
We called on Mr & Mrs Methold.
Returned 2 powers of attorney for 3 per cent Consols annual dividends, after being executed by my trustees, to Messrs Child, by Mr Pritty.

14 Henry came to dinner, & Mrs Longe & he dined at Barking Hall.
Mr Beck.

15 I attended the sittings at the Crown. Henry dined here, [*& then*] left us for a concert at Ipswich in the evening. Extreme hot day. The weather is so unusually hot, [*with the*] thermometer [*at*] 76, that I feel extremely weak & relaxed.

16 The hottest day this season. Thermometer here, north side, 84.
At home. Very weak & faint. Mr Beck.

17 We went to Ipswich. I saw Mr Wenn, & consulted with him about the Crowfield modus, & saw Mr Cooke.[549] Catt will complete the repairs to the chariot in a month. Mr Wenn will pay by my order into Ipswich bank £31 2s., the amount of 2 fines paid by Sir William F.F. Middleton on admission to copyhold land on vicarage manor.[550]

18 Mr Errington, Mr Methold's curate, called. Robert & Margaret dined here on their return home from a visit at Mr Brown's.

19 A fine ground rain today, which was much wanted.
Mr Taylor here, afternoon. He & Mr Nunn dined here.
Mr Nunn informed me that a day or two ago he heard my tenant, Robert Brook, use some very improper expressions before some workmen, & that Diggens was present, & [*that*] he & Mr Nunn remonstrated with him. Robert Brook said that things went on badly, & that he should not mind taking up arms himself, & help to right themselves.[551]

21

20 May Fine mild day. The Miss Martins drank tea here. Mr Beck.

21 My son Henry came to dinner and slept here.

22 Henry left us after breakfast. He goes for a few days to Cambridge

---

548 The entries for 8, 9 and 10 May, wrongly inserted, were then corrected: 'Thursd.', 'Frid.', 'Wedn.'

549 Modus: a combination of improved yields, inflation and legal doubts encouraged tithe recipients to try to renegotiate earlier fixed arrangements. By establishing a time limit for litigation Lord Tenterden's Act of 1832 caused a rush of court applications.

550 Longe was *ex officio* lord of this manor, one of five with land in Coddenham parish. Here, the second baronet, whose father had died in 1829, was probably routinely registering his succession.

551 Further violence in France in 1830 had been a reminder of 1789. Suffolk too had seen disturbances in 1815–16, 1822 and 1830. Longe felt threatened by the radical views of this young farm tenant.

this afternoon with his friend Mr Carthew. Mrs L. drove in her poney gig to Combs. Received from Joseph Phelps, stationer at No 44 Paternoster Row, London, a complete set of Langley's county maps: 53 maps coloured, for £1 17s., for which I owe him. Wrote to Dr Probert, proposing to consult him for the oppression on my breathing, on Monday or Tuesday next at Bury. Mr Beck will accompany me.

23 Company to dinner: the Metholds, Mr John & Mrs Methold, Mr & Mrs James & Mrs Lawson, Messrs Colvile & Errington, Miss Arabella Martin.
And Robert & his wife dined here & slept. Mr Kirby called, & left with me Mr Rodwell's statement & Mr Rolfe's opinion, on Sir W. Middleton's new claim of certain lands at Shrubland being exempt from tithe.[552]

24 Robert & his wife left us after breakfast. We dined at Mr Brown's: met Mr & Mrs I. Robert Edgar.

25 Very hot day. We washed the sheep. Letter from Dr Probert.
Ditto from my brother, who & my sister have been ill with influenza.
Mr Beck & his son Henry. Answered my brother's letter about his Irish Tontine by return of post.[553]
Depredations in the night in Mr Nunn's & Read's gardens.[554]

26 Mr Taylor here, morning. Sacrament at Crowfield: 26 communicants.
I went to church, afternoon. Mr Nunn dined here.

22

27 May We went to Bury, I to consult Dr Probert for the oppression on my breath, under which I have for these 2 years at least suffered.
We dined and slept at Mr Hasted's. I saw Dr Probert. He pronounced my complaint to be owing to too much action of the heart.
Sheep clipped.

28 Mr Beck by appointment met us at Dr Probert's, when after a consultation he gave Mr Beck his prescriptions, &c.
In the evening we returned home, & conveyed Mr Beck back to Needham.
We went with Dr Beck to Dr Probert's. Dr Probert directs me to be cautious in my diet, to avoid repletion & any great exertion. Paid Dr Probert £2 fee. Paid Mr Hasted my subscription to the Suffolk General Hospital due January last £2 2s. (He did not give me a receipt).[555]
Mrs Longe had a letter from John in answer to one of hers to him.
He is very well, & goes to London to visit Charlotte, &c.[*on*] the 29th.

29 I attended the sittings at Needham, & Mrs Longe went on to Combs, & found the infant's arm fast recovering. We went in the phaeton with the Smiler cob.

30 At home. Mr Beck put a blister on my left breast, & I began taking Dr Probert's prescribed medicine, viz. draughts & an aperient bolus at night.

552 Mr Kirby, as incumbent of Barham, was directly affected by any loss of tithe income there.
553 For a tontine see glossary. The two brothers had inherited their father's shares.
554 This attack on these nearby gardens was probably an expression of social protest.
555 For the county hospital see note at 3 August 1831.

31 We called on Dowager Lady Middleton at Bramford, & at Shrubland where we saw Sir William & Lady Middleton.[556]
Henry came in the evening.

1 June At home. Mr Errington called, & Robert came to dinner. He & Henry left us in the evening. I am very weak & poorly today, from the effects of the blister, which has operated very powerfully.

2 Trinity Sunday. Too weak & inconvenienced by the blister to go to church. Sacrament here: 75 communicants. Mr Taylor officiated here afternoon, & he & Mr Nunn dined here. Mr Beck.
I not well enough to attend the church.

23

3 June I attended a trustee meeting [*of the*] Claydon turnpike, at Claydon.
A very acceptable shower of rain fell early this morning. Everything requires rain very much. Mr Beck.

4 Archdeacon Berners visited Crowfield chapel & Coddenham church. Mr Nunn met him at Crowfield. The archdeacon & Mr Steward took a cold collation here, & Mr Nunn dined here.[557]

5 Mrs Longe called at Shrubland. Lady Brownlow & daughters there.
I paid the servants wages for the half year ending at Lady Day last: £75 8s. 6d.

6 At home. Mr. Beck.

7 Mrs Longe went early to Diss, her niece Lydia being now with Mrs William Ward. <Henry> I attended a superintendent committee at Barham House. Henry came to dinner. A letter from John to Mrs Longe. He is now in London on a visit to his sister, & stays till Friday next.

8 Mr Pickering called. Robert came to dinner. Mrs Longe returned in the evening, & Robert & Henry left us.
Mr Taylor here, morning. Mr Nunn dined here. The weather very dry & hot since Monday. Everything much parched.

24

10 June I attended an Helmingham turnpike meeting at the Crown.
Henry called here on his way to Combs. Sir William & Lady Middleton called. I was absent at the meeting. Mr Beck. James Brook, Choppyngs Hill, paid me arrears of rent due last Michaelmas:
£19 13s. 7½d.

11 We attended the christening of my son Robert's infant, for whom I Stood godfather, named John. Afterwards, dined with the Daveys & Parkers at Combs. Began mowing clover & ray grass in the valley.
An uncommon hurricane which did some damage in the neighbourhood.

12 I attended sittings at the Crown, from whence I did not return till 7 o'clock [*in the*] evening.[558] A few showers at noon.
I made Robert a present of £30 by check on Ipswich bank.

---

556 Harriet, widow of the first baronet, retained her title with the prefix 'dowager'.

557 The archdeacon's periodic inspection of the church's buildings included the parsonage house. Edward Steward, a practising Norwich attorney, was his deputy registrar.

558 Reference to sitting into the evening may indicate that it was rare, but it is still surprising.

13 A fine ground rain at 7 o'clock this morning. Lady Middleton (Bramford), & Mr Pettiward, & Mr Ward of Trinity College called.

14 We called at Shrubland, & went on to Ipswich, in order to see Mr Wenn about the Crowfield modus. I spoke to Sir William Middleton about the Crowfield alleged modus, in hopes of making an arrangement without an Exchequer suit.[559]

15 At home. Much indisposed with a cold & cough.

16 Unable to go to church. Kept my bed till the afternoon, having taken some James's powders. Mr Taylor, afternoon [&] dined here. I am now very ill with a severe oppression on my chest, & great defluxion from the head.
It seems a return of influenza.

25

17 June Very ill with oppression on my chest, which occasions extreme difficulty of breathing. Mr Cooke came to dinner. Took more James's powder at night. Mr Beck & his son Henry.

18 I lay in bed all day. Mr Henry Beck bled me plentifully, 24oz., which gave me immediate relief. Mr Cooke attended a National Society [*for*] Education general committee meeting at Stowmarket. Mr Henry Beck. Robert & Margaret & family went to Aldborough for a month's sea air. [*They*] called here on their way there.[560]

19 Mr Cooke left us after breakfast. I am now better, & came downstairs. Mr Beck & his son Henry.
Mr Wm Rodwell called, & brought 2 powers of attorney for Transferring the late Mrs Sleorgin's stock in the 3 per cent Consols & 3½ per cents into the names of myself, only surviving trustee, & Messrs James & George Henry Barnett, the 2 new trustees, which I this day executed.[561]

20 A fine rain of 4 or 5 hours. I feel myself now recovering, [&] my cough is much abated. Thunderstorm. Mr Henry Beck.

21 I feel not so well today. In the evening I had a gouty tenderness in both my hands. I sent a liver colour & white pointer puppy of Belle's to my son John at Spixworth.

22 Very poorly. Robert dined here on his way from Aldborough to Combs.[562] Letter from my daughter Charlotte. Mr Beck.

23 Gout in my right elbow, & so lame that I could not get downstairs. Mr Taylor here, morning. Mr Nunn dined here. Mr Henry Beck.

26

24 June Very languid & uncomfortable. Henry came, & went on to dine with Mr Errington. Robert called on his return to Aldborough.
Dr, Mrs & Miss Elough, and Mr Roberts called.
Mr Beck. Letter from John, who will come over next week.

---

559 For modus see diary entry for 17 May 1833 and note. The Exchequer was the appropriate court.

560 For Aldeburgh see note at 12 July 1831.

561 Longe was retiring as trustee in Mrs Sleorgin's trust at the request of her daughter, the widowed Mrs Croasdaile. See introduction (p.xliv).

562 Robert returned from his family seaside holiday (18 June to 20 July) to take Sunday service at Combs, rather than arrange a deputy. Conveniently for him, Coddenham lay on his route.

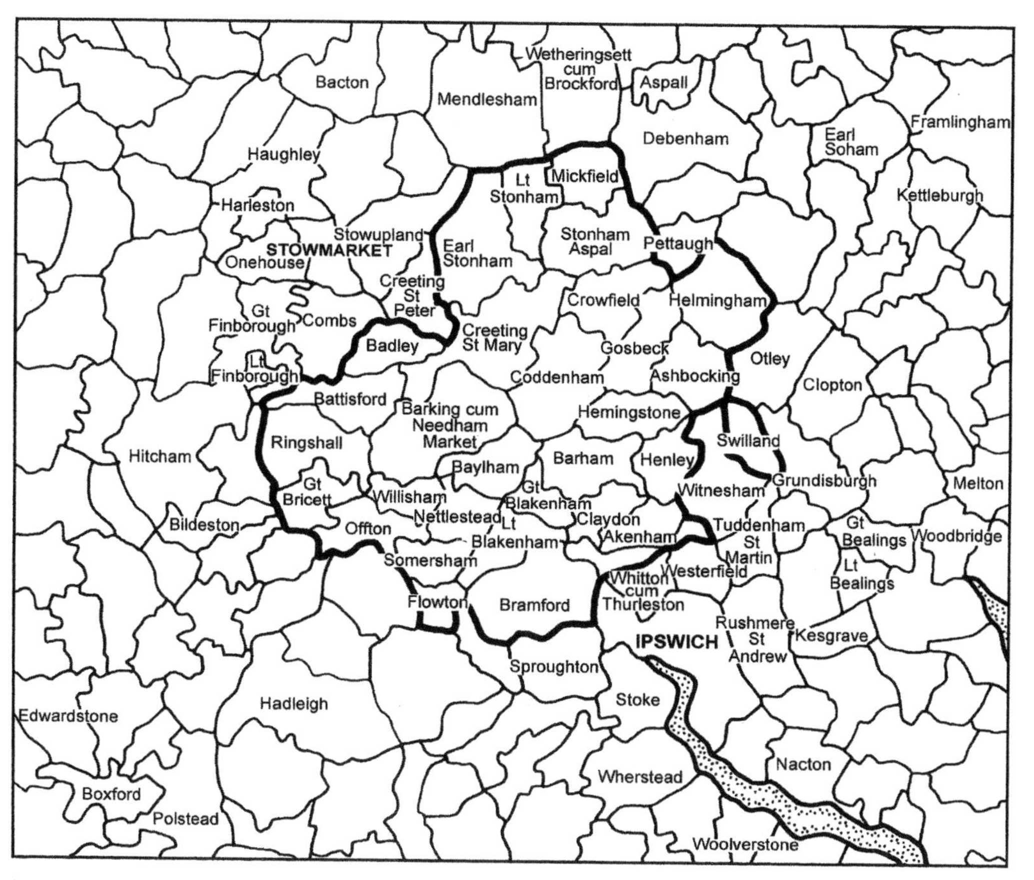

1. Bosmere and Claydon hundred, its boundary in heavier print, with some of the towns and parishes mentioned in the text. Bury St Edmunds lies twelve miles west of Stowmarket on one turnpike, and the posting inn at Scole village twelve miles north of Little Stonham on another.

2. St Mary's church, Coddenham, from the south, drawn etched and published by Henry Davy, Ipswich, 1841. Note the length of the chancel. This south aspect is unfamiliar, as the entrance porch is on the north side by the tower.

3. All Saints church at Crowfield (Longe's 'chapel') early in the twentieth century. From the lane it is obscured now from view by trees growing on the moated site of the first hall, long since gone. William Middleton's hall (itself demolished in 1829) was to the south-west. Reproduced by permission of the National Monuments Record.

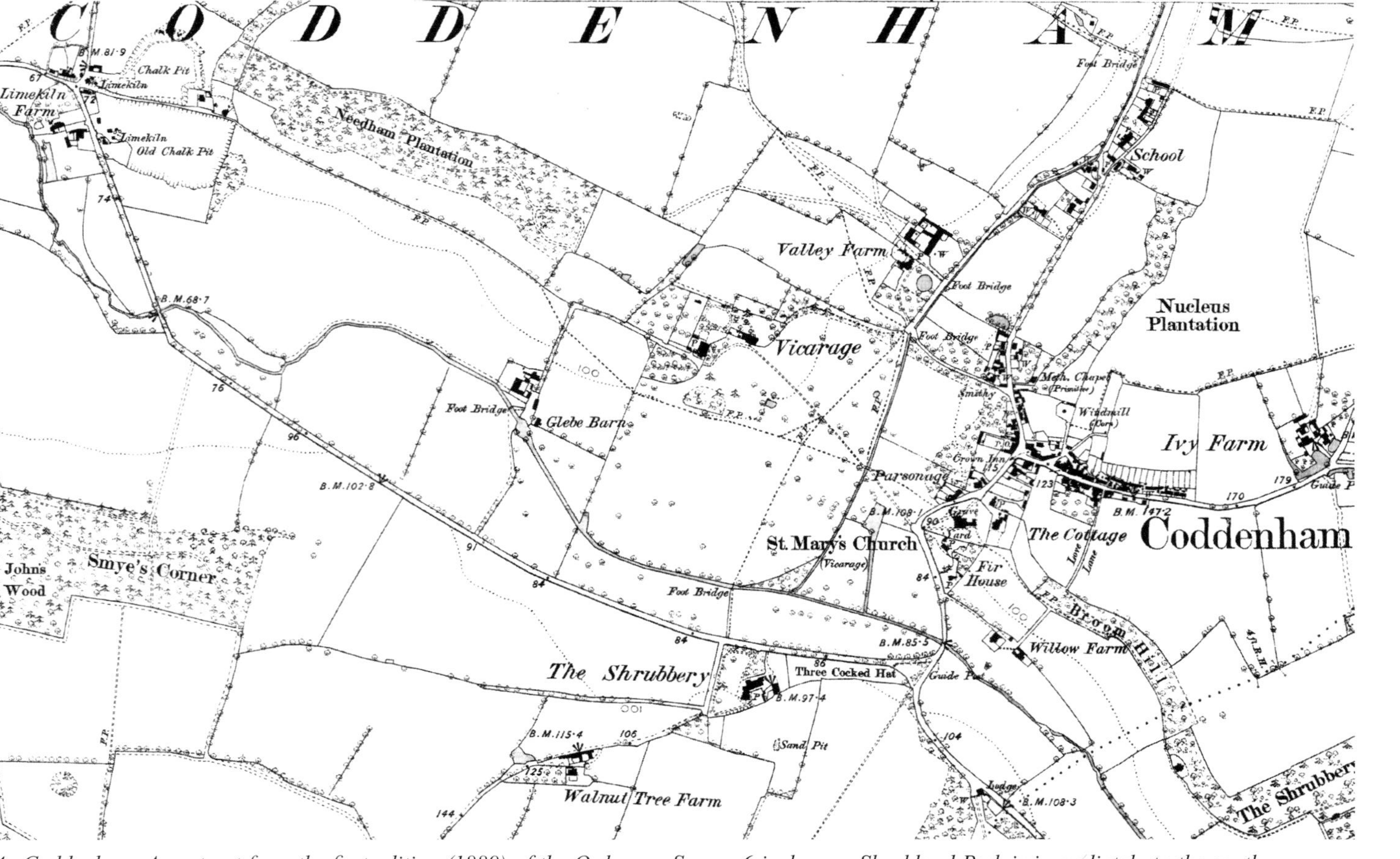

4. Coddenham. An extract from the first edition (1889) of the Ordnance Survey 6-inch map. Shrubland Park is immediately to the south. The un-named buildings by 'Glebe Barn' were Longe's Vicarage farm. Two streams meet, one from the north and one from Hemingstone. Copyright Ordnance Survey.

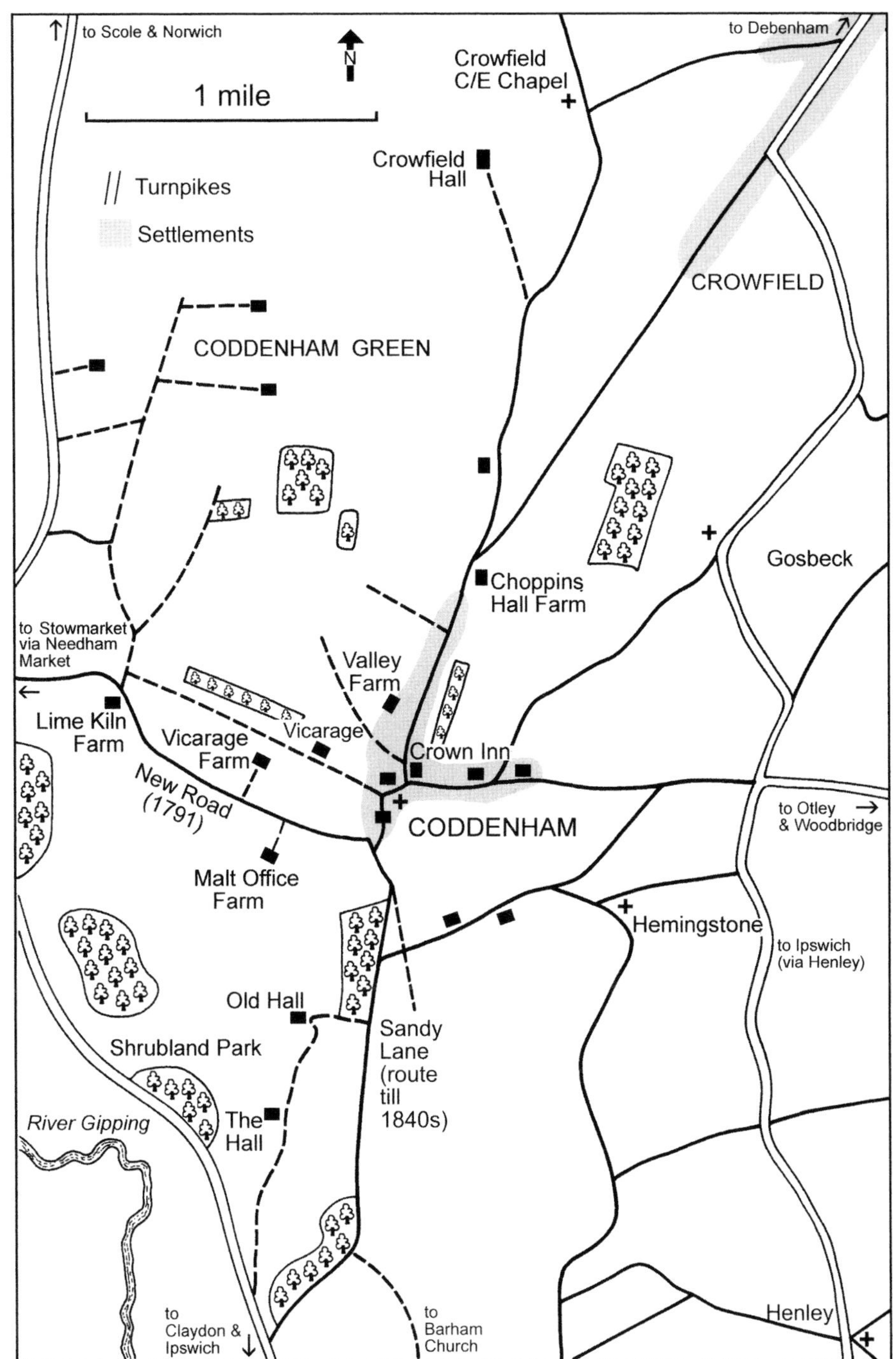

5. The roads of central Suffolk. To the west of Coddenham village runs the Ipswich–Scole–Norwich turnpike. Parts of the Helmingham turnpike lie to the east. Two lanes were diverted, one away from the vicarage (1791) and one from Shrubland Hall (1844–45).

6. Coddenham vicarage (and stable block) from the south-east in the early nineteenth century, from a watercolour by an unknown artist, now in private hands. In 1836 the further end of the annexe, the roof-parapet and the attic floor were removed.

7. Coddenham House (the old vicarage) from the south-west today. Compare with the previous plate for the changes effected in 1836. The house stands up its carriage-drive on higher ground a quarter of a mile from the church. From a photograph by Chris Rawlings.

APRIL—MAY, 1831.

APPOINTMENTS, &c.

25 Monday — Duchess of Gloucester born, 1776.

26 Tuesday

27 Wednesday

28 Thursday

29 Friday

30 Saturday

1 Sunday — MAY. Mayor of Norwich elected.

APRIL HAS XXX DAYS. [Week 18

Received.	CASH ACCOUNT.	Paid.

MAY.

8. From Longe's pocket-book for 1831. The double spread shows the week number (18, top right), his daily entries on the left, and the cash-account layout on the right which Longe usually ignored. Courtesy: Suffolk Record Office.

25 Mrs Longe & Henry called at Mr Davy's & Mr Briggs's. Henry left us this evening.

26 I attended sittings at Needham.
Thunderstorm & heavy showers in the afternoon.

27 I attended the quarterly meeting [*at*] Barham House.
Mrs Longe went on to Ipswich. Revd Stephen Jackson was elected a director [*of the*] Bosmere & Claydon incorporation.

28 I attended a tax meeting at Needham, & afterwards called on Mr Briggs. Showers in the evening.

29 At home. I walked down to the farm. Robert dined here on his way to Combs from Aldborough for his duty tomorrow. The hay got up from the bridge meadow, & stacked. Clover in Coppyngs cooped.[563]

30 At church, morning. Mr Taylor officiated here afternoon, & he & Mr Nunn dined here. Mr & Mrs Martin called in the evening. Mr Beck.

27

1 July Showery day. Book Club, morning meeting.
Robert called on his return to Aldborough. Henry came to dinner, & Mr Betham dined here. The Parkers, &c. called.
Letter from John, who now says he will be here on Saturday next.
Eclipse of the moon. The evening being clear was seen beautifully, but I did not recollect it, & so did not observe it. Finished stacking clover.

2 Henry & Mr Betham left us after breakfast. At home.

3 At home. Robert to us unexpectedly to dinner. He is tired of Aldborough, & goes to London tomorrow for amusement. Wrote to John, & to my daughter Charlotte Leake, to be sent with some music by Henry, who goes to London on his western tour on Sunday evening.

4 Robert left us, & went by the Star coach to London.[564] At home.

5 Ipswich Sessions. I attended & dined at [*the*] Great White Horse on Mr Berners's venison.[565]

6 I went to Ipswich again early, & remained in court till 3 o'clock.
My son John came here to dinner. John brought me a letter from Mr George Howes, whom I had invited to come with John, but he declines.

7 At church, morning. Mr Taylor here. Mr Nunn dined here.
Fine mild rain at night. Severe thunderstorm at Norwich.

28

8 July I attended Sessions. [*The*] Ipswich prisoners [*were*] tried, which concludes the business. John went to Ipswich. My brother & sister arrived here at 7 o'clock. Fine mild rain [*in the*] morning from the north.

9 Mr Kirby called. Company to dinner: Mr & Mrs Martin, Mr & Mrs Davy, Miss Ibbetson, Mr George Taylor & Mr Brown.
Paid Mrs Longe on house accounts, from April 6 to June 29 inclusive: £73 1s. 0d. Mr Beck. Mr Kirby says that he can make no progress with Sir William Middleton, about his claim of exemption from tithes of the

---

563 Bridge Meadow lay opposite the churchyard. Choppyngs was by the stream on the Crowfield road.

564 For the Morning Star coach see note at 28 February 1826 and Appendix E.

565 Longe's last attendance at Quarter Sessions (Ipswich) on the Friday, Saturday and Monday. Woolverstone Hall had a deer-park.

demesne land of Shrubland Hall, & asked me what assistance I would give him, as I am interested in this question as patron of Barham. I advised him to file a bill in the Exchequer, & promised to go halves with him in the expences, for I have every reason to think Sir William Middleton has been put up to this claim by Pownall, & there is no foundation for it.[566]

10 Sittings at the Crown. I did not attend.
Mrs Longe, my sister & John went to the play at Ipswich.[567]

11 All at home.

12 Robert returned from London. Company to dinner: Dr & Mrs & Miss Elough, Mr & Mrs Kirby & Miss Gear, Messrs Drake & Errington.
Robert Brook settled accounts for rent due at Lady Day last. Received £20, deducted malt bill £21 6s. 8d.: total £41 6s. 8d. Arrears still due: £22 11s. 4d.[568]

13 At home. Robert left us in the evening for Combs.

14 At church, morning & afternoon. Messrs Taylor & Nunn dined here.

29

15 July Robert breakfasted here on his way to Aldborough. John also went there for the week. My brother drove in his gig to Ipswich, & Mrs Longe & my sister to Helmingham. Richard Fenn paid me on account of rent due on Lady Day last: £35. Arrears due: £12.
Thomas Diggens ditto by check: £137 10s. Arrears due: £50.

16 I measured the cedars & other trees with my brother's assistance.
We dined at Mr Davy's, met Dr & Mrs Elough, Mrs H. E. & Miss Elough. Letter from my son Henry from Falmouth.

17 We all went to shew my brother & sister Barham church & Shrubland.
Extremely hot day. Eclipse of the sun: began at about 5 o'clock, ended 6.49. Digits eclipsed: 8 degrees 49minutes 1½seconds. The morning was bright, & I had a good view of it with my reflector.[569]
Went to the play, to see Marie Celeste. I drank tea with Mr Cooke.

18 We all went to Ipswich. [*At the*] Suffolk Clergy Charity Anniversary [*meeting*], Mr Rose of Hadleigh preached a very superior discourse.
I & my brother dined at [*the*] White Horse. 61 at dinner.[570]
Mrs Longe, my sister & brother [*sic*].

19 I attended a meeting of [the] superintending committee [at] Barham House, to regulate the division of parishes amongst the surgeons, as there is now to be fourth surgeon, which is most wanted.[571]
Fine mild showers today with distant thunder.

20 At home. Robert & his family left Aldborough.
John returned to us in the evening. Showery.

21 Mr Taylor here, morning. I attended at church. Mr Nunn dined here.

---

566 For the tithe dispute at Barham see diary entry for 23 May 1833.

567 For Ipswich Theatre see note at 20 July 1798.

568 Malting was still a small-scale operation but some farmers would take in barley for malting on contract.

569 A reflector, suitably dimmed, protected the eyes from direct view of the sun.

570 Significantly, this occasion lay midway between two famous events at the outset of the Oxford Movement and Tractarianism: Keble's Assize sermon at Oxford (14 July 1833) and the Hadleigh Conference hosted by H.J. Rose (25–29 July 1833).

571 The incorporation supplied medical attention for the poor out in the parishes.

30

22 July All at home. Showery all the forenoon.

23 We all went to Ipswich, & saw the Ipswich Literary Institution rooms & museum. We called on Col. & Mrs Stisted. Very heavy showers.
Letter from Henry, dated Gloucester. He returns on Friday next.

24 John left us this morning for Spixworth. Mrs Longe & my brother & sister spent the morning at Combs, & set me down at Needham for [*the*] sittings. 2 Miss Wards came to dinner. Fine dry day.

25 At home very poorly, the oppression on my breath very distressing. Mrs Longe, my brother & sister & Miss M. Ward dined at Miss Ibbetson's. Miss F. Ward [*dined*] at Mrs A. Broke's.

26 Very hot day. I am very poorly, & did not stir out. Robert & Margaret & little Robert came here to dinner. Shower at night.
My spaniel bitch Dido produced six puppies. [*I*] reserved 2, a dog & bitch, [*but*] both died in a month.

27 Very hot day. Robert & Margaret left us before dinner.
My son Henry returned safe & well, after a very agreeable tour to the Lands End, Cornish mines, &c. [*He came*] home by Leamington, Cheltenham, &c.

28 Very hot day. I went to church, afternoon. Mr Taylor preached, & dined here.

31

29 July Very hot day. Henry came to dinner. Mr Errington called.
John Lincoln & Scott began to cut & regulate the approach road to the house. Letter from John.

30 Company to dinner, [*with*] Helmingham venison: the Bacons & Mr L. Bacon, the Parkers, Mr Jackson, Robert & Henry, Mr Roope.
Venison fat & good.[572]

31 The Miss Wards left us on their return to Diss. All at home. Shower in the night from [*the*] north-west. Roger Pettiward, esq. of Finborough Hall died, while on a visit to Mr Trafford in Cheshire, aged 79 years.

1 Aug. My brother & sister left us on their return home, after an early dinner. Henry left us this evening. I wrote to John, & sent him by his desire a copy of Balls's hymns, & some new scarlet melon seed.
Wrote to Mr George Howes.
Began to reap wheat in Vicarage Pightle, & to mow oats in Barn Field.

2 I went to Barham House [*for a*] superintendent committee, but nobody attended.

3 Henry returned here to dinner. Mr Beck.
John Lincoln completed regulating the approach tonight, for which I paid him at 4s. 6d per day himself & Scott: £1 0s. 3d.

4 Henry officiated here for me this morning for the first time.
Fine harvest weather all week. As I am unable to officiate at church myself, from the severe oppression on my breath, Henry will take the duty here one part of the day for me.

32

5 Aug. Book Society, sale of books. I dined there.

572 For Helmingham deer see note at 8 August 1826.

I paid Mr Taylor for assistance at Coddenham church from Easter Sunday to July 28 inclusive. 17 Sundays: £17 17s.

6 We called on the Metholds, who returned to Stonham after his residence on Saturday. Mr Methold very well.

7 I attended the sittings at the Crown, & called on Mrs Bailey at Mrs A. Broke's. Robert came to dinner with me. Mrs Longe dined at Mr Martin's. I excused myself. Sir William & Lady Middleton returned to Shrubland this evening. His arm very much recovered.

8 At home.

9 We went to Ipswich. I saw & consulted Mr Wenn on various matters of business. Henry came to dinner. Letter from Charlotte.
Got up wheat & oats into the barns.[573]

10 We made a morning call on Sir William & Lady Middleton.
Henry left us in the evening. My little red & white spaniel Miss produced 3 puppies by Ranger. They are both now 14 months old each. 1 red & white one [?]brought up for Mr Jackson. The other two red, exactly like Ranger, I destroyed.

11 Henry officiated here for me, afternoon. 2.[574] Mr Nunn dined here.

33

12 Aug. We called for the first time on Mr & Mrs Pleas, the new vicar of Ashbocking. Mr Beck.

13 At home. I have a gouty tenderness in my right heel, & do not feel well. Letter from John.
Wheat all got into the barn, in the best possible order.

14 Very poorly today. [*I*] did not go out. Very cold air [*&*] wind north.

15 I am better. Robert & Margaret & 2 children dined here unexpectedly. Fine mild harvest day.

16 We spent the day with Henry at Woodbridge, & called on Mr George Taylor in our way. Paid John Woods, Woodbridge nursery, his bills for fruit trees, &c. & seeds to March 21st last: £3 14s.

17 Miss Ibbetson called. Henry came here to dinner.
The peas all stacked in the best order.

18 Henry officiated here, this morning. 3. I went to church. A fine rain at 1 o'clock, which continued some hours. Fine harvest weather all this week, but rain much wanted for turnips & clover.

34

19 Aug. Mrs Longe took Mrs A. Broke & Mrs Bailey to Combs.
Sir William & Lady Middleton called. Mr Beck.

20 Mrs Elough & Mrs Henry Elough, Mrs A. Broke & Mrs Bailey, Lady Berry, & Mr & Mrs Pleas & family called. Mrs Longe went to Crowfield.

21 I attended the sittings at Needham, & went from thence, taking Mr Brown with me, to the Conservative dinner at the White Horse Ipswich. Brought Mr Nunn home at night. The Conservative dinner was most numerously & respectably attended. Sir William Middleton in the

573 The entries for 8 and 9 August were transposed and then corrected.

574 Longe inserted a numeral in the margin of the pocket-book to mark Henry's taking of services, for payment purposes. In transcribing, these numerals have been placed into the text.

chair. Lord Henniker, Sir Charles Vere, & Sir Edward Kerrison present. Robert & Henry met me there.

22 At home. Robert called. Began mowing barley in the lays.
Letter from my daughter Charlotte Leake, [*her*] first letter from Woodhurst, which house they took possession of last week.[575]

23 Mr & Mrs Crowe called, & stayed to dinner. I wrote to John.

24 We went to Ipswich. I consulted Mr Wenn about the Crowfield tithe modus [*&*] Lord Tenterden's Act.[576] Received notes & cash at Ipswich bank, for a draft of Thomas Diggens, dated July 15: £137 10s.[577]

25 At church, morning & afternoon. Henry officiated, morning & slept here. 4. Fine harvest weather, except a shower on Wednesday night & Saturday night [that] were very acceptable. Grass burning up by drought.

35

26 Aug. Book Club. Sir Charles B. Vere & Mr George Broke called. Carrying barley.

27 We went to Stowmarket. I dined at the annual Suffolk Clergy Society dinner with Robert. Mrs Longe to Combs, where we drank tea.
I see on examining the Suffolk Clergy Charity court book, that I was elected a vice-president & auditor at a general court [*held on*] August 30 1831, on the decease of the Revd. Thomas Cobbold of Ipswich.[578]

28 Messrs William Ward of Diss, his son William & Mr Richard Ward came to dinner & slept here. Mr Beck. Wrote to my daughter Charlotte.

29 They left us after breakfast. Mr R. Ward stays. Mrs A. Broke & Mrs Bayley, & Mr & Mrs Nunn dined here.
Mr Henry Beck came by Mrs Longe's desire to meet Mr William Ward, & consult on my complaint of shortness of breath, &c., which Mr William Ward tells me is a slight affection of the vessels of the heart, which cannot be removed, but may be palliated by attention to my diet, & digestion.

30 I attended an assessed taxes appeal meeting at Needham.
William & Mr R. Ward dined at Mr Briggs's, met the Metholds, Phears & Messrs Colvile & Nunn. Heavy storm of rain in the evening, which is much wanted. Finished stacking barley this day, just before the rain fell.

31 Showery day. Henry came to dinner.

1 Sept. Showery morning. Henry here, morning. 5. I went to church, afternoon.

36

2 Sept. Robert & Henry came to breakfast to shoot, & had good sport.
Robert returned home at night, & took Henry with him.

3 Showery day. Mrs Longe & Mr Richard Ward went to a dejeune at Mr Edgar's, [*at*] Red House. I excused myself, not feeling equal to the fatigue & late hour.[579]

575 Longe's son-in-law had inherited the house from his father. See entry 1 March 1833.
576 For Lord Tenterden's Act see note at 17 May 1833.
577 It took Longe nearly six weeks to cash this cheque: a sign of old age?
578 Longe is forgetting what he recorded in his diary on 30 August 1831.
579 For the Red House see note at 9 August 1798.

4 I attended the sittings. Robert & Margaret & her family came here to dinner.

5 Company to dinner: Lady Berry, Sir William & Lady, & Dowager Lady Middleton, the Metholds & Miss Hales, the Bellmans & Mr Treadway & Mr William Colvile, & our own family. We sent Mrs Colby to Bury for admission into the Suffolk General Hospital, for cataract in her eyes. She is quite blind: a Coddenham labourer's wife, aged 32.[580]

6 I attended a superintending committee [*at*] Barham House.
Mrs Longe & the rest of the family went to Ipswich. Letter from John.

7 All at home. Answered John's latter, saying that we would be with him (God willing) on the 16th.

8 At church, morning & evening. Henry officiated here afternoon (1), & slept here. September 9: I paid my son Henry for 5 Sunday's assistance at Coddenham church to September 1 inclusive: £5 5s.

37

9 Sept. Robert shooting. Mr Richard Ward left us. We dined at Shrubland, met Col. & 2 Miss Rushbrookes, Miss Ibbetson, Mr & Mrs Colvile of Livermere, Messrs Capper, Crofts, Penn, & George Broke, & Dowager Lady Middleton. Henry left us in the evening.
I attended a Claydon Turnpike meeting. Lord Henniker & Sir Charles Vere qualified, & some others. Mr Pownall mentioned an intended dissolution of partnership with Mr Hunt, which will cause a new appointment of clerk to the trustees.

10 Dr Elough & ladies called. Robert & children left us. Robert's children have all slight symtoms of scarletina which is prevalent around us.

11 At home.

12 Mrs Longe & I went to Ipswich. I had a long consultation with Mr Wenn on various business. Called on Mr Cooke. I paid Mrs Longe on account of house bills from July 6 to September 7 inclusive:
£50 12s. 6d. Bought of Cole, Ipswich, a small diamond pin £1 14s. for Mrs Longe, a single turquoise ditto 7s. 6d. for myself [*and*] a silver pen case 6s. 0d. [*for myself*]. Not paid for: £2 7s. 6d.

13 Robert & Henry came to breakfast to shoot. Robert left us in the evening. Henry stayed. Our servants Bennet & Ann Brown both ill with scarlet fever. Mr Beck.

14 Henry shooting at Hemingston. Mr Parker dined here unexpectedly, on his road home from Aldborough.[581]
Sent for Mr Beck to see the maid servants.

15 At church, morning. Henry officiated, & left us after duty. 2.

38

16 Sept. Showery morning, but fine at 10 o'clock. On account of Bennet's & Ann's illness, we deferred leaving home till tomorrow. Mr Beck thinks Mr Bennet convalescent, Ann Brown recovered.

17 We set out for Spixworth, left our horses at Scole, where we took posters & reached Spixworth by 5 o'clock. Found Messrs St John & George Turner with my son. Norwich Musical Festival.

---

580 A subscriber was entitled to nominate for admission to the hospital. See diary at 3 August 1831.

581 Unexpected calling just before a mealtime seems to have been accepted.

18 Mrs Longe went to the concert in St Andrew's Hall in the evening. My breath very much affected.

19 Mrs Longe & my sister went to Norwich, & I spent the morning with my brother, who has got the gout.

20 I am so ill that I sent for Mr Crosse, who bled me, & sends me medicine. Mrs Longe went to the fancy [*dress*] ball at St. Andrew's Hall. Mr Crosse.

21 We called on my brother. Mr George Turner left Spixworth.
Mr Crosse. By his direction, an ammonia blister was put on this morning, to the pit of my stomach.

22 Not well enough to go to church. 3.
The Howeses, & Dr & Mrs Robert Blake dined at Spixworth.

39

23 Sept. We went to Salhouse on a visit to Mr Ward, his son Richard there. Mr Crosse.

24 At Salhouse. I am still very much distressed by the oppression on my breath.

25 Horticultural Meeting at Norwich. We went there, returned to dinner with my brother, & to Spixworth in the evening. Saw Mr Crosse at Norwich.

26 John had company to dinner: the Humfreys & Miss Warburton, Mr & Mrs Henry Evans & Mrs Cubit, Messrs St John & Matchett.

27 Mr Willins & the Howeses to dinner. Miss Henrietta Howes staid. Mr Crosse.

28 Mr Willins left us.

29 I attended morning service, & received the sacrament at Spixworth church. Sacrament at Crowfield: 22 communicants. Mr Crosse. 4.

40

30 Sept. We left Spixworth to make my brother a short visit. He had Dr & Mrs Wright, & Mr Smith & John to dinner. Mr Crosse.
I consulted Dr Wright on my oppression on the lungs, & arranged with him to meet Mr Crosse, at my brother's on Wednesday.

1 Oct. We called at Sir Edward Stracey's, & Mr John Stracey's, but did not see any of the families.

2 After a consultation with Dr Wright & Mr Crosse, we went to Norwich & made a visit to the bishop, &c. Dr Wright left a prescription for me with Mr Crosse. Mr Crosse.

3 John breakfasted with us, & then we left my brother & sister, & reached home by half past 6 o'clock. Found Robert here who left us in the evening. I have now had for some days a constant cough, but more towards night, with great expectoration.

4 Henry came to dinner. Engaged all day at home. I began to take Dr Wright's prescription: draughts & pills.

5 Henry left us after breakfast. Mr Parker called.

6 Sacrament [*at*] Coddenham: 72 communicants. Henry officiated, afternoon. 5. I not well enough to attend the church. Paid Henry for 5 Sunday's assistance to this day inclusive, [on] October 18: £5 5s.

41

7 Oct. Henry left us at noon. Mr & Mrs Brown called. Mr Beck.
Wheal Anna Maria mine. Wrote an order to Messrs Child to pay

to Messrs Williams, London, to the account of Thomas Dunston, Cornwall: £24 2s. [*This is*] the amount due to him on a call for May & June last. Of this sum, £2 10s. only is my payment. The remaining £21 12s. is Mrs Longe's & Henry's, which sum they have repaid me.[582]

8 Very fine mild day. We walked down to the farm.
I wrote to my son John.

9 At home. <Dr & Mrs Henry Elough called.> Mr Beck.

10 At home. Robert came to breakfast. Dr & Mrs Henry Elough called. Robert left us in the evening.
John Read, my gardiner, quitted my service after having been with me 5 years. I discharged him, because he was become indolent & very slow in the garden & advanced in years, but an honest quiet man.

11 At home. Mr Beck. James Hynard from Mr Charles Rowley's came to me as gardiner on the same terms as John Read did, & entered on my service, October 12.[583]

12 Henry came to breakfast, & shot here.
Poor Mrs William Ward died at Huntingdon, after a long & afflicting illness, dropsy in the womb, aged about 35.

13 Henry officiated here, morning. 1.

42

14 Oct. Showers at noon. Robert & Margaret came to dinner. Mr Beck.
I wrote to Charlotte to inform her of the death of poor Mrs William Ward.

15 Robert & Margaret left us at noon. Showers at night. Letter from my brother, which I answered by a few lines in one from Robert to him.
We brewed 4 Coombs of malt (remaining of last year's barley) & 1lb.10[*oz.*] of hops.[584]

16 Mrs Longe went to Ipswich. Fine dry day. Letter from Charlotte to me, enquiring after my health. Our letters have crossed. Mr Beck.

17 Henry came to breakfast, & afterwards went to Combs, & found Robert better. Heavy showers. Robert ill with a severe cold & sore throat.

18 Fine dry day. At home. Letter from John, at Bishop Stortford.

19 We called at Combs, & found Robert considerably better.

20 I attended church this morning. Henry officiated here afternoon & slept here. 2.

43

21 Oct. At home. Henry spent the day with Mr Errington, & dined with him at Mr Methold's. Showers in the evening. Mr Beck.

22 At home. Fine dry day. Henry <left us> shooting this day at noon. Engaged with Mr Brown in justice business.

23 At home. Very fine day. Engaged in justice business.
Henry left us at noon. Got Mr Brown to execute summonses for John Abel & William Wright, for coming upon my land in pursuit of game on Wednesday October 16. This day John Abel & another person

---

582 Cornish mineral-mining enterprises were popular, if speculative, investments.

583 Longe had clearly made advance arrangements for this change of staff (on old quarter day, 11 October). He paid Hynard the cost of conveying his goods to Coddenham: see p.209.

584 The brewing entry is written at the foot of the page, but dated.

with him were seen by Scoggin & William Cornish in my Needham plantation again, where Abel shot an hen pheasant.[585]
Sent my son Robert a load of firing wood & sack of potatoes, &c.

24 At home. I have now a considerable gouty tenderness in both my feet. Sent the Leakes a brace of pheasants [&] an hare.

25 Robert called. Now much recovered. The Briggses called. Mr Beck.

26 Very fine mild day. At home. My cough which has been extremely troublesome for the last 5 weeks is now abated, & the gouty affection of my feet going off. My ancles & insteps however are much swelled.

27 I attended morning service at church. Henry officiated, & left us at noon. 3. Fine mild day. Letter from Charlotte: the game arrived safe.

44

28 Oct. Book Club dinner meeting. I not well enough to go. Messrs Methold, George Taylor, Daniel Pettiward, & Edward Paske called. Fine day.

29 We called on the Briggses, & at Mr Beck's, where I saw him. Very fine day.

30 Engaged all the morning at the sittings. Robert & Margaret came to dinner & slept.

31 Robert & Margaret left us on their way to Mr Groom's, Earl Stonham. Very foggy day, but cleared up.

1 Nov. We went to Ipswich, called on Wenn, but he was from home. Called on Mr Cooke. Very fine bright day.
I took at Ipswich bank £30, intending to take the money lately paid in through Wenn received of Edward Field (the Mendlesham farm tenant) on account of rent, but I since find that he paid Wenn £27 only. £3 therefore must be placed to my private account.

2 Robert called on his way home.

3 Henry officiated, afternoon. 4. I was not well enough to go to church today. Henry slept here.

45

4 Nov. Henry left us by mail coach on a visit to Mr Walford at Long Stratton. Robert & Margaret called. Sir William Middleton called.

5 At home. Very wet day.

6 We called at Mr Methold's. Family not at home.

7 Mrs Methold called here. We began to brew autumn ale & beer, with malt last week, made by Robert Brook from my barley of this year's harvest.

8 Mrs Longe called at Shrubland. Family not at home. Henry returned this evening from Long Stratton.[586] Mr Beck.

9 Mr Crowe called. Henry shooting.

10 Henry officiated here, morning. 5. Mr Nunn afternoon, & dined here. I not well enough to go to church. Very cold damp day. Paid Henry, November 19, for assistance at church: 5 Sundays to October 10 [*sic*] inclusive £5 5s.

46

[585] Scoggin was Longe's gamekeeper and Cornish his farm manager. As landowner, Longe had strong possessive instincts against even small-scale poaching 'for the pot'. The game laws had been eased.

[586] This mail-coach worked daily between Norwich and the Great White Horse, Ipswich.

11 Nov. Showery day. Mr Henry & Amelia Ward of Diss came to dinner.

12 Robert came to breakfast to shoot.

13 I attended the sittings at Needham. William Wright of Needham was convicted of being in pursuit of game in company with John Abel of Creeting St Mary, in my plantation by Coppyngs, on Wednesday October 16 & Wednesday October 23, & also offering game for sale on October 16. Mitigated penalty for the 3 offences: £4 15s. including costs. Not being able to pay, Mr Davy committed him for 2 months to the county gaol, Ipswich. Summons directed to be served on John Abel for the above offences.

14 Henry & Robert came here to shoot. Very fine day. [*They*] had a very successful day. They both left us in the evening. Letter from John, who will be here on Saturday. Finished brewing autumn beer. My old friend Revd Daniel Pettiward, rector of Onehouse, after a few days illness, died at the Angel Inn, Bury, of inflammation in the trachea from colds.[587]

15 At home.

16 Mr Henry Ward drove his sister to Combs on a visit to Margaret. My son John came here from London.

17 Henry officiated here afternoon. 1.

47

18 Nov. My sons all shooting.

19 I attended the weekly committee [*of the*] House of Industry, [*the*] lst week of my month. Mr Cooke came to dinner. Henry & Robert left us.

20 I & Mr Cooke attended a meeting of magistrates, & Sir William Middleton, at Needham, to form a plan for an association to prosecute felonies, &c. John left us to spend a few days with his brothers at Woodbridge. Mrs Nunn confined with a son. Received a present of 2 Wiltshire cheeses from Warneford Place, & a letter from Mrs Warneford, who says Caroline is now staying there, & well.

21 At home. I am now very weak, & my breath greatly oppressed. Henry sent his horse here with my desire, to turn it for the winter into my straw-yard, his hoofs being in a contracted state.

22 Mrs Longe went to Ipswich, & took Mr Cooke home.

23 Robert brought Henry with him here, & went on to Combs, having spent some days with Henry at Woodbridge.

24 Henry officiated here, morning. 2. Showery day. Mr Beck. I am now very much distressed for breath, & my legs are greatly swelled. He proposed my consulting his son Dr Beck, to which I agreed, & Mr Beck will meet him here tomorrow.

48

25 Nov. Book Club. Mr Beck & his son Dr Beck here. They agreed on changing my medicines. Dr Beck, 1st visit. He thinks he can remove my present distressed breathing. Not knowing his physician's terms, I did not give him any fee.

26 Mr Wenn breakfasted here on his way to Debenham. Sir William Middleton kindly attended at Barham House for me. Robert called.

---

587 The two Pettiward brothers died in quick succession. See diary entry for 31 July 1833.

Mr Morgan called, & I engaged him to attend my tithe audit days, which I fixed for Monday & Tuesday, December 9 & 10. I engaged Mr Wenn to come over on Wednesday, December 4, to take instructions for my will.

27 I was not well enough to attend the sittings at the Crown.
Robert & Margaret called. Sir William Middleton called.
John Abel was convicted, in penalty 40 shillings & costs, for poaching here October 16 last, which sum was paid.

28 Mr & Mrs Ward of Salhouse came unexpectedly for a few days.
I am very poorly today. Very stormy night. Dr Beck, 2nd visit.

29 Very showery day. All within doors. I feel my breathing oppressed today. Mr Henry Beck. Mr Beck confined with a bad cold.

30 Mr & Mrs Ward left us after breakfast. Mr Henry Beck.

1 Dec. Henry officiated here, afternoon. 3. Mr Nunn dined here.
My son Henry has been with us all this week.

49

2 Dec. Robert shot here, & left us to return to his own dinner, [*as he was*] expecting the Browns.
Dr Beck, 3rd visit. Mr Beck met him here. An alteration made in my medicines. I have found some benefit from them. Thank God, my breath is easier, & my legs less swelled. Letter from John.

3 Mrs Longe ill with cold & sore throat. Mr Methold made me a long visit.

4 Mr Wenn to breakfast. I sent Henry in the gig home to Woodbridge. His horse [*he*] left here. Mr Wenn came here by appointment, to assist me in preparing a disposition of my personal property.[588]

5 Robert came to shoot, & slept here. Mrs Longe went to Ipswich.
Mr Henry Beck.

6 Robert left us at noon. Mr Beck.
I wrote a few lines to John in a letter to him from Robert. I wrote to Mr Rolfe Hempnall, & inclosed an half sovereign at his request towards a memorial of Revd J.S. Parris, late curate of Shelton.

7 All at home. Very wet day. Sent the gig for Henry, who came to dinner.

8 Henry officiated here morning, & I sent him home in the gig afterwards. 4. John came unexpectedly by [*the*] mail, kindly to see me.
Dr Beck, 4th visit, & Mr Beck.
Wrote to Mrs Warneford this week, & sent a turkey & some sausages.

50

9 Dec. Tithe Audit day, Coddenham. Mr Benjamin Morgan attended. John & Robert dined with the parish at the Crown. Very stormy day.

10 Tithe Audit day, Crowfield. Mr B. Morgan attended. Robert dined with the parishioners at the Crown. All in good humour both days.
John left us by Star coach.[589] Mr Beck & his son Henry.
Mr & Mrs Kirby, & Miss Ibbetson called. Very stormy night.

11 I not well enough to attend the sittings at Needham. Robert shooting, & left us to dine at Mr Colvile's on his return to Combs. Fine sharp air.

588 SRO(I) HA24/50/19/4.1(3): copy will. See below, pp.224–5.

589 For the Morning Star coach see diary and note for 28 February 1826 and Appendix E.

12 At home. Flight of snow this morning. Letter from Mrs Warneford. Turkey reached them in good order. Caroline still there. Mr Beck.

13 At home. Very sharp frost.
Sent my son Robert a load of firing wood this week.

14 At home. Very mild air. Mr & Mrs Briggs called. Mr Beck.

15 Sent for Henry to Woodbridge, who officiated here, afternoon. 5.
Paid my son Henry (December 21) for assistance: 5 Sundays to December 15, inclusive: £5 5s.

51

16 Dec. I & Mrs Longe went to Ipswich. I attended a meeting of the clergy convened by archdeacon Berners to adopt an address to the archbishop of Canterbury.[590] Henry went to Combs in the poney gig on a visit to Robert.
I had an interview with Dr Beck at his own house, & paid him £9 fees for attendance to this day inclusive. His fee is 2 guineas a visit to me at the vicarage.

17 At home. Sir William & Lady Middleton called.

18 At home. Remarkably fine mild day. Miss Caroline Davy called.

19 Sent for Henry to Combs, who came to dinner. Mr Beck.

20 Robert called from Barking, where he & Margaret are on a visit.
I wrote to Charlotte to say that we will send a Christmas turkey & ham, by Sunday night mail coach.

21 Showery day. All at home. I wrote to my brother, & sent him a turkey [*on*] December 22.

22 Henry officiated here, morning. 1. He went to Hasketon for afternoon service in my gig. Mr Nunn dined here.
Wrote a few lines to John by my brother's parcel.[591]

52

23 Dec. Henry walked here, & dined at Mr Martin's. Heavy rain at night.
Dr Beck at 11 o'clock, he came, & Mr Beck & his son Henry met him. Finding myself very much weakened by the powerful aperients, they are now to give me tonics.
Paid Mrs Longe, on account of weekly house bills to December 14: £50.

24 Heavy showers [*in the*] morning. Henry went in my gig to Woodbridge & returned to dinner, in order to assist Mr Nunn in the church duty tomorrow.[592] Sent my son Robert 2 sacks of goldfinder potatoes.

25 Christmas Day. Wet morning, but cleared up. Mr Nunn & Henry officiated here. Henry preached. Sacrament: 79 communicants.
The usual party dined below, &c.

26 Robert came & shot here, & dined with us.

27 Fine dry day. Mrs & Miss Martin called. Thomas Cornish [&] the gardiner, &c. dined here. Letter from Charlotte, [*that she*] received turkey & ham safe. Total eclipse of the moon this evening, but the atmosphere was so cloudy that it was invisible here.

---

590 Details of this address to the archbishop have not as yet been traced.

591 Longe's brother lived not far from his son John of Spixworth Hall.

592 Henry retained his lodgings and his chaplaincy post in Woodbridge whilst serving at Coddenham.

28 At home.

29 Henry officiated here, morning. 2. Sacrament at Crowfield: 21 communicants. Henry returned to Woodbridge after church in my gig.

53

30 Dec. Showery day. Dr Beck, a visit. Paid him 2 guineas. [*He*] has changed my medicines for diuretics, the dropsical swelling in my legs & thighs having increased within the last week.
A kind letter from Mr Batchelor, who has been very ill.

31 Showery till noon-time. I feel very ill all day, & the oppression in my breath very severe. Mr Beck here.[593]

Coal Account 1833[594] Byles & King, Ipswich

January	4	1 ½	chaldron	(at 28s.)	James Brook
	14	1 ½	"		Diggens
	19	1 ½	"		Robert Brook
February	7	1 ½	"		James Brook
March	7	1 ½	"		Richard Fenn
	19	1 ½	"		Diggens
	17	2	"		Rushbrooke
May	3	1 ½	"		James Brook
June	6	1 ½	"	(24s.)	Richard Fenn
	6	1 ½	"		Diggens
August	5	2	"	(25s.)	Diggens
September	28	2	"		–
October	2	1 ½	"		James Brook
	4	1 ½	"		Robert Brook
	15	1 ½	"		James Brook
	23	1 ½	"		Diggens
November	9	1 ½	"		Diggens
	29	1 ½	"	(at 26s.)	James Brook
December	4	1 ½	"		Diggens
	9	1 ½	"		Diggens
	13	1 ½	"		Robert Brook
	21	1 ½	"		Diggens

593 Longe died nine weeks later.

594 All those named were farm tenants of Longe and had carts suitable for conveying coal the eight miles or so from Ipswich (or Stowmarket). No use seems to have been made of the Gipping Navigation for this.

OTHER DOCUMENTS

CATALOGUE OF SERMONS

HA24/50/19/4.5(2)

John Longe was ordained deacon in September 1787. Early in the next month he noted the first sermon that he composed, as his father's curate at Spixworth. He had listed thirty-seven by the end of 1789. He then moved to Suffolk and in the next seven years as a parish priest there, he listed only twenty-two sermons. After becoming vicar of Coddenham-cum-Crowfield early in 1797 he catalogued only twenty-seven sermons in twenty-eight years, with none after 1825. However, there was a well-established custom that earlier sermons from published collections were read from the pulpit and Longe undoubtedly followed this practice, perhaps even on all the occasions not listed below. He had an extensive library including collections of sermons.[1] *He may also have read his father's sermons to his congregations, left to him in manuscript form in 1806. It is unlikely that Longe ever preached without a script.*

The source is an exercise book and although it is only one–quarter full we cannot even assume that it is a complete record of all his compositions. Once he left his father's supervision he may possibly have listed only those sermons on which he took particular pains. A further complication is that the exercise book is so regularly written, with identical appearance of ink, that he may have compiled it at a single sitting after 1825 as a retrospective record, either from rough notes or listing the sermon manuscripts that he had retained. If so this too reduces the likelihood that it contains all his compositions.

Of the listed texts, 40 per cent are from the Old Testament: mostly from the book of Psalms, with a majority from the New Testament, especially the gospels according to Luke and John. Longe noted his sources for these composed sermons.

No. & Date	*Text*	*Author made use of*[2]	*Subject and occasion*
Nov.13 1787			
1.	Eccles. 6.12	Blair vol.1, ser.8	Ignorance of good & evil in this life
2.	Eccles. 12.8	Blair vol.2, ser.7	On the proper estimate of human life
3.	Prov. 16.6	Mr Tapps	The fear of God
4.	Acts 16.30–31	T	The fear of God
6.	Titus 2.10	T	Honour due to the Christian religion

1 No list of Longe's books survives. Circumstantial evidence comes over fifty years after his death, shortly after the death of his son Robert in 1890. The two-day auction then held included some 2,500 books. Few were listed but among these were Blair's sermons (8 vols), those of Tillotson, '&c.' (20 vols), Hewlett's Bible (4 vols), Leland on Revelation (2 vols). These were surely John's that Robert had inherited. See Appendix F.

2 Brief notes on these 'authors made use of' are given in notes on people (pp.283–4).

7.	Matt. 5.29	T	Government of the passions
8.	Ephes. 5.6,7	T	The excellency of the scripture doctrines
9.	Ps. 66.18	T	Purity of heart
10.	Matt. 5.20	T	Righteousness of the scribes & pharisees
			[*2*]
11.	1 Cor. 6.20	Mr Tapps	Duty of glorifying God in our bodies
1788			
12.	Ps. 119.59	T	Lent: the duty of self-examination
13.	Acts 23.1	T	Conscience
14.	Isaiah 55.6	T	Lent: imprudence of deferring repentance
15.	Romans 6.1	T	Lent: repentance
16.	Proverbs 18.14	T, Atterbury vol.4, ser.8	Conscience
17.	Deut. 29.29	T	Trinity Sunday – mysteries.
18.	Eccles. 12.1	Joslin vol.7,ser.8	The duty of serving God in our youth
19.	Matt. 11.30	part 1st T	Superiority of Christianity to paganism, Judaism, & Mahomadenism [*sic*]
20.	Matt. 11.30	part 2nd T	Nothing exceptionable in the Christian doctrines
21.	Phil. 4.11	part 1st T	The nature of contentment
22.	Phil. 4.11	part 2nd T	The advantage & means of contentment
23.	2 Cor. 5.10	Hewlet	On the Resurrection – Easter Day
24.	Gen. 45.5	–	The history of Joseph
25.	Matt. 26.22	Hewlet	The frailty of human virtue &c.
26.	Luke 10.33	Hewlet	The parable of the good Samaritan
			[*3*]
27.	Matt. 25.13	Hewlet	On death
28.	Prov. 16.32	Hewlet	On the government of the temper
29.	Luke 2.14	Hewlet	On the birth of Christ – Christmas Day
30.	2 Cor. 5.7	Hewlet	On faith as the rule of conduct
31.	Matt. 12.13	Hewlet	The charity & forbearance of Christ &c.
32.	Acts 4.32	Hewlet	Unanimity in religion
33.	John 4.24	Hewlet	On devotion
34.	1 Cor. 15.35,36	Hewlet	On the immortality of the soul
35.	2 Sam. 23.3,4	partly from Sherlock and the rest my father's[3]	April 23rd 1789. Thanksgiving for the king's recovery[4]
36.	Deut. 4.9	Hewlet	On the benefits of experience & reflection
37.	Ps. 103.14	Hewlet	On the goodness & mercy of God &c.
1790			
38.	Luke 10.37	My father	Charity Sermon
1791			
39.	Gal. 6.14	Atterbury	Of glorying in the cross of Christ – Good Friday
1793			
40.	1 Cor. 13.13	Ibbotson	The true notion of Christian charity
41.	1 Tim. 2.1,2,3	[*?*]Black, Moss, Tillotson	Fast Day, April 19th 1793
42.	Luke 22.19	Dr Adams	Lord's Supper
			[*4*]
1794			
43.	Luke 22.19	Dr Adams	Lord's Supper
44.		Dr Adams –	Lord's Supper

3 Still at Spixworth, Longe did not commence the curacy at Coddenham until 1 January 1790.

4 After some months of illness George III was sufficiently recovered for the *London Gazette* to announce on 27 February 1789 that no further bulletins would be issued.

45.		Dr Adams –	Lord's Supper
46.	1 Pet. 2.16	my father	Fast Day, February 28th 1794
47.	Gal. 4.4,5	Leigh	Christmas Day
48.	Luke 6.5	myself assisted by my father.	On the institution of the Lord's day. preached at the bishop's visitation, Ipswich, June 17th 1794 and afterwards published
49.	Ps. 36.7	myself	Goodness of God in creation & redemption
1795			
50.	Isaiah 29.6	Moss, bishop of London's charge, 1794	Fast Day, Feb. 25 1795
51.	Luke 16.31	Archbishop Sharpe	Superior evidence of a standing revelation
52.	Prov. 22.2	Bishop Coneybeare	Relative situations of rich & poor considered
1796			
53.	2 Chron. 30.8	myself	Fast Day, March 9th 1796
54.	Matt. 16.26	Moss	Of gaining the whole world, & losing one's own soul
55.	Luke 11.13	Moss	Sunday – efficacy of prayer for obtaining the Holy Spirit
56.	Luke 15.32	Bishop Horne	Parable of the prodigal son
57.	John 9.4 (1)	T. Pyle	Christ's work on earth
58.	John 9.4 (2)	*idem*	The work of a Christian
			[5]
59.	Num. 23.10	T. Pyle	Balaam's wish
1797			
60.	Ps. 68.18	*idem*	Ascension Day or Whitsunday
1798			
61.	Ps. 105.1,2	partly from Fothergill	General Thanksgiving, Nov. 29 1798
62.	Heb. 11.3	T. Pyle	The gospel salvation & the danger of neglect
1799			
63.	Prov. 13.44	partly Fothergill	The different consequences of righteousness & sin to nations: General Fast, 27 Feb. 1799
1800			
64.	Ps. 57.1	*idem*	Trust in God: General Fast, March 12 1800
64[*sic*]	Phil. 2.8,9	altered from Mr Gardemau's }	Humiliation of our saviour
65.	Phil. 2.9	MSS Sermons. }	Exaltation of our saviour
1801			
66.	John 5.28	Gilpin vol.1	The hour cometh
67.	Ephes. 5.16	Rogers	The duty of redeemimg time: Lent
68.	Heb. 1.1	Gilpin vol.1	The gradual progress of verbal prophecy
69.	John 3.14	Gilpin vol.1	On typical prophecy
70.	Isaiah 63.10	Pyle vol.1	Sin of vexing the Holy Spirit
71.	John 1.14	Leland's *Necessity of Revelation* & Tillotson	Christmas Day
1802			
72.	Ps. 29.10	T.L. Fothergill & Bennet	Thanksgiving Day for General Peace 1802

1803			
73.	John 13.34,35	principally compiled from various sermons preached at the annual meeting church schools in St Paul's	Charity Schools
			[*6*]
74.	Ps. 83.4	JL[5]	General Fast, October 19th 1803
75.	Rom. 13.11	Skelton	1st Sunday in Advent
76.	Ps. 90.12	Riddock, Clapham's Collection.	New Year, text and introduction new
1804			
77.	John 14.15	Riddock	Sacrament Lord's Supper, text & introduction new
1805			
78.	Isaiah 53.5	Rogers vol.2,s.7	The death & sufferings of Christ foretold & described – Good Friday
79.	Ps. 97.1,2,3	principally compiled from Clark, Bishop Smallridge, Fothergill & a sermon of my father's.	Thanksgiving for Naval Victory off Trafalgar, 5 Dec. [*sic*].1805
1808			
80.	Heb. 13.1	My father	Suffolk Charity Clergy Widows & Orphans
1823			
79[*sic*]	Prov. 11.29.	Pott	The fate of the troubler
1824			
80[*sic*]	1 Cor. 4.1	Berens	Christian priesthood against dissenters &c.
1825			
81.	Matt. 28.19	Gilpin s.27, vol.2 & notes to Munt's Bible	Trinity Sunday
82.	Ps. 31.17	in part from Blair, the rest my own	A New Year
83.	Gen. 8.22	JL	After Harvest

5 Inserting his own initials seems to imply the repeating, in amended form to fit the different text, of an earlier sermon of his own, such as no. 63 or 64 above.

VISITATION RETURN, 1820

NRO, DN/VIS/ 55/7

The queries addressed to the incumbent on behalf of Bishop Bathurst before his visitation were theoretically searching, but there is no evidence in Longe's surviving papers that the responses were ever followed up and they may have simply been filed away without action. The questions are clear from John Longe's answers.

Coddenham

1. Extent The parish of Coddenham, exclusive of the hamlet of Crowfield, contains about 2430 acres. 94 houses. There are no families of note in it, but that of the vicar.[1] The circumference of the parish of Coddenham is about 20 miles; exclusive of the hamlet of Crowfield about 12 miles.

2. Papists We have no Papists in the parish.

3. Dissenters There are a few Dissenters in the parish of low condition who attend the Independent meeting house in Needham, and there is a cottage licensed for Independents here at which teachers of different persuasions occasionally attend, but their congregations consist chiefly of people from neighbouring parishes. We have no meeting house in the parish.

4. Quakers We have no Quakers in the parish.

5. Absentees To the best of my knowledge there are no persons who commonly absent themselves from public worship in either parish. Our congregations are usually large, particularly in the afternoon.

6. Non-residence/Pluralism I constantly reside in my parsonage and am not often absent. I have no other benefice, nor do I serve any other church.

7. Curate I have an Assistant Curate, the Revd Thomas Greene, who resides in a house of mine in Coddenham. I pay him a salary of £100 per annum, and allow him a dwelling house free of rent. He serves no other cure.

8. Services Divine Service is performed and sermons preached twice on each Lord's Day, and prayers read on Wednesdays & Fridays during Lent.

9. Services To the best of my knowledge, divine service was not omitted on any Lord's Day last year.

10. Catechism I & my assistant curate catechise every Sunday. We make use of the National Society's school books, & Lewis's exposition of the Catechism.[2]

---

1 Old Hall in Shrubland Park stood just within Coddenham parish but the exact date of the demolition (of all except the chapel) is uncertain. If standing in 1820 it was probably occupied by the manager of Middleton's Home Farm, who would not have ranked with Longe as 'of note'.

2 See introduction, p.xxvi and footnote 57.

11. Sacrament Four times in the year, viz. At Easter, Whitsunday, Michaelmas & Christmas – about 100 usually attend.

12. Schools There is a Charity School in this parish, in which 50 children of poor families are educated. This school is in connection with the National Society for the Education of the Poor. There is no other free school, hospital or almshouse.

13. Sunday Schools There is a Sunday School supported by the voluntary subscription of the inhabitants, which at present contains 14 children. They are taught to read only, and are usually removed into the charity school as vacancies occur.[3] This school is also in connection with the National Society for the Education of the Poor.

14. Endowments (the church or the poor) Nothing has been left to the best of my knowledge for these purposes.[4]

15. Offertory money It is distributed in part to the poor present, after the Communion, & the remainder given to those most in need subsequently.

16. Other —

Crowfield

1. Extent Contains about 1527 acres. It is 8½ miles in circumference. There are 48 inhabited houses, 66 families. There is no family of note at present, Crowfield Hall being now unoccupied.[5]

2. Papists There are no Papists.

3. Dissenters There are no Dissenters to the best of my knowledge.[6]

4. Quakers There are no Quakers.

5. Absentees None. The chapel [*of the established church*] is usually well attended.

6. Non-residence/Pluralism I reside in my parsonage house in Coddenham, of which Crowfield is an hamlet possessing *jura parochialia*.

7. Parsonage House Crowfield has none. I have an Assistant Curate, the Revd Thomas Greene, who resides in a house of mine in Coddenham.

8. Services Divine Service is held once on each Lord's Day in Crowfield chapel.

---

3 For the Sunday School to act as a preparation for the 'full-time' school runs counter to the practice understood to obtain in the towns. Taught to read, some respectable adults, whilst favouring this, believed it was unnecessary and even dangerous for village children to learn to write.

4 This appears to be incorrect, since an eighteenth-century predecessor as vicar, the Revd Balshazar Gardemau, and his wife Lady Catherine (formerly Bacon) set up Coddenham charities for the vicar, for the poor and for a charity school, plus a small clothing charity. The first and third of these were endowed with land, the first substantially. These charities still exist, and this editor was formerly a trustee.

5 Crowfield Hall, owned by the Middletons, was probably in a dilapidated condition in 1820 as it was sold for demolition in 1829.

6 Appendix B (below) compares this and other returns with factual Conventicle records, to assess the strength of dissent in both Coddenham and Crowfield.

9. Services To the best of my knowledge, divine service was not omitted on any Lord's Day last year.

10. Catechism My assistant curate catechises the children every Sunday. Lewis's exposition is used with those who are sufficiently qualified to profit by it.

11. Sacrament Four times in the year.

12. Schools, &c. There is no free school, hospital or almshouse.

13. Sunday Schools There is a Sunday School supported by the voluntary subscription of the inhabitants, which at present contains 20 children. They are taught to read only, and are usually removed into the charity school as vacancies occur. This school is also in connection with the National Society for the Education of the Poor.

14. Endowments (the church or the poor) Nothing has been left to the best of my knowledge for these purposes.

15. Offertory money It is distributed in part to the poor present, after the communion, & the remainder given to those most in need subsequently.

16. Other Sir William Middleton, proprietor of the great tythes within the hamlet of Crowfield, in the year 1814 advanced a claim to the tythe of hay there, which from time immemorial have been paid to or compounded for to the vicar of Coddenham with Crowfield as by the custom of the parish a vicarial or small tythe, although he himself had soon after my institution in 1807 entered into an agreement to pay me that with the other vicarial tythes for our joint lives or during my incumbency. This unexpected claim I have resisted, and filed a bill in chancery against him and Charles Woodward his principal tenant in the hamlet of Crowfield. The suit was heard before the Vice-Chancellor on April 27 last and an issue ordered at the next Suffolk Assizes. Neither Sir William Middleton nor any of his predecessors, [*as*] proprietor of the great tythes of Crowfield, have ever demanded or received the tythes of hay in kind or any composition in lieu thereof, but merely the corn tythes within the said hamlet. Sir William Middleton rests his claim solely upon the presumption of hay being by law a great tythe. I shall therefore abide the issue.[7]

7 Nationally, the distinction between great tithes (corn, wood and often hay) and small tithes (of all other produce) already dated back centuries. Ownership of the great tithes in some parishes came into lay hands after the dissolution in the reign of Henry VIII of religious houses, which had acquired by earlier gift the valuable right of collection. In Coddenham, the distinction had become of no practical relevance because of the generosity of Balshazar Gardemau in the eighteenth century. In Crowfield the Middletons owned the great tithes, which rendered the distinction vital, whether collection was in kind or by cash in lieu. The custom of the place frequently prevailed. The outcome after 1820 is summarised in the introduction (p.xli).

SERVANTS' WAGES BOOK, 1811–23
with Additional Material

SRO(I) HA24/50/19/4.7(11)

At the beginning of 1811 John Longe was firmly established not only in the county magistracy, his parishes and his home farm, but also in his own household at Coddenham vicarage. By then aged forty-five, he had been married twenty years. There had been no more infant death; his daughter was aged fourteen and there were four schoolboys aged from twelve to seven. He started a note-book to record dealings with the domestic staff (as distinct from the farm staff) in which diary entries were to continue to 1823. Our knowledge of the staff is extended by occasional references in the diaries, and additional archival material, set out after the transcript of the Servants' Wages Book (see pp.206–207 below).

Three dramatic domestic events occurred during the period covered by this book. John's wife Charlotte died at the age of fifty-one (20 May 1812). The provision of mourning wear for the servants is transcribed at p.209 below. Five years later, in 1817 on his fifty-second birthday, Longe re-married. His second wife was Frances Ward of Salhouse, Norfolk. Longe also suffered the loss of his eldest son in 1819 at the age of twenty.

The Servants' Wages Book is an unlined exercise book (7.8 x 6.4 inches) with a blue paper cover, written in black ink. Longe normally kept apart the accounts of monetary transactions (nearly always recto) from notes and memoranda (nearly always verso). The entries did not always correspond on opposite pages, or relate to neat periods. A sectional arrangement is therefore offered, with accounts and memoranda covering the same period, whether short or long. Whereas in the original the pages are unnumbered, in the transcript each spread is given a number (in italics), for example: 14.1 for verso page, 14.2 for recto page.

The transcript is divided into sections as indicated in the following tabulation, which uses the page numbering that is inserted in italics into the transcript. With a single exception on page 22, indicated below, each section of the transcript comprises whole pages in the original document.

2.1, 2.2	2 January – 9 December 1811
3.1, 3.2, 4.1	27 December 1811 – 10 October 1812
4.2, 5.1, 5.2, 6.1	22 November 1812 – 23 February 1813
6.2, 7.1, 7.2, 7.3	6 March – 9 December 1813
8.1, 8.2	15 January – 24 February 1814
9.1, 9.2, 10.1	6 April – 25 November 1814
10.2, 11.1, 11.2	25 November 1814 – 17 November 1815
12.1, 12.2, 13.2, 14.1	2 December 1815 – 2 December 1816
14.2	2 December 1816 – 18 February 1817
15.1, 15.2	12 March – 12 October 1817
16.1, 16.2, 17.1, 17.2, 18.1	16 October 1817 – 12 November 1818
18.2	30 November 1818 – 29 March 1819
19.1, 19.2, 20.1	28 May – 17 December 1819

20.2, 21.1, 21.2, 22.1, 22.2 (part), 23.1, 23.2	23 January 1820 – 29 July 1821
(p.22.2: the dates 18 Jan. and 10 May 1822 are out of chronological order in Longe's text)	
24.1, 24.2, 22.2 (part), 25.1, 25.2	3 December 1821 – 31 December 1823

[*p.1.1*] *Inside front cover is blank*

[*p.1.2*] Allowance of ale to the servants
Men servants, 3 pints per day each. Maid servants, 1 pint per day each.
Gardiner, when here, 3 pints per day. Small beer a reasonable quantity.
Nov 24 1812 I allow Crickmay, the gardiner, 1 pint of ale per day.
Riches & son, when here, 3 pints per day each of ale.
The same quantity of small beer.

2 January – 9 December 1811

[*p.2.1*]
January 2nd 1811 Servants now in the family & wages per annum[1]

Samuel Barrell, butler, at wages	£40 0s.0d.
John Gower, coachman (livery & frock & waistcoat &c.)	£20 0s.0d.
William Lambert, footman & groom(ditto)	£14 14s.0d.
James Scoggin, gamekeeper, at 7s. per week & his board	[*£18 4s.0d.*]
John Brunwin, servant boy, no wages as I cloath him.[2]	– –
Quitted me & entered Mr Acton's service as 2nd postillion	
James Keeble, came here in his place	– –
Mary Kenney, housekeeper	£ 7 7s. 0d.
Elisabeth Hammond, cook	£ 9 9s. 0d.
Elisabeth Garnham, nursery maid	£ 8 8s. 0d.
Amy Mayhew, housemaid	£ 8 8s. 0d.
<Elisabeth> Mary Davy, kitchen girl	£ 3 0s. 0d.
from this Lady Day, Elisabeth Davy is to be paid £3 3s. 0d per annum	

John Riches, the dumb Gardiner having been for some time so lame, & otherwise ill, as to be confined to his house, I engaged at Lady Day Edward Edwards, single man aged 25, as Gardiner, to board & sleep in the house at £25 per annum, and if he suits me and continues another year here, £26 per annum.[3] I received a very favourable character of him from Mr A. Steward of Stoke Hall where he had worked as gardiner for 1 year under his father, who is a gardiner, and lives in St Matthews, Ipswich.[4] April 15 1811: Samuel Barrell, having conducted himself improperly while I was

1 Domestic servants named in the book are listed by post with their dates of service at section III of notes on people below (pp.281–2). Other servants named in the diary are also listed.

2 'Cloath' and 'Cloaths' is Longe's invariable spelling.

3 'Gardiner' is Longe's invariable spelling.

4 Stoke: part of Ipswich south of the river. St Matthew's parish was the western edge of Ipswich in 1811.

absent in Norfolk, and taken a bottle of wine (at least) without informing me of it, and I having good reason to believe that he is not deserving of confidence, I paid him his wages to this day & discharged him.
April 28 1811: John Allen, late butler of Mr Frere of Roydon came as butler out of livery, on trial till Midsummer, at £40 per annum wages.

[*p.2.2*]
1811 Servants' wages for the half year ending at Lady Day

January 2nd	paid Samuel Barrell, 1 quarter's wages due Christmas last	£10 0s. 0d.
April 15	paid Samuel Barrell, wages to Lady Day £10 & ditto for 3 weeks to this day, £2 3s. 6d.	£12 3s. 6d.
June	Servants' wages for the half year ending at Lady Day last, paid in June – total paid	£36 3s. 0d.
Memorandum	June 28th 1811 at William Lambert's request, he having been in all respects a good servant to us, I consented to raise his wages to 16 guineas per annum from Lady Day last.	
July 25	paid John Allen, 1 quarter's wages due at old Midsummer last	£10 0s. 0d.
September 28	given John Brunwin on leaving me, as a reward for his good behaviour	£ 1 0s. 0d.
October 15	paid Elisabeth Davey an half year's wages due at Michaelmas, when she left us	£ 1 11s. 6d.
	<Elisabeth>Mary Gooch succeeded her at £3 per annum wages	

Servants' wages due at Michaelmas for an half year

October 30	paid J. Allen, 1 quarter year's wages to Michaelmas	£10 0s. 0d.
December 9[5]	paid John Gowers, an half year's wages	£10 0s. 0d.
	paid William Lambert, ditto	£ 8 8s. 0d.
	paid James Scoggin, wages for 27 weeks to September 29 @ 7sh.	£ 9 9s. 0d.
	paid Edward Edwards, gardiner, an half year's wages to Michaelmas at £25 per annum, deducting 10sh. for the fortnight he was absent with the Militia	£12 0s. 0d.
	Mary Kenney	£ 3 13s. 6d.
	Elisabeth Hammond	£ 4 14s. 6d.
	Elisabeth Garnham	£ 4 4s. 0d.
	Amy Mayhew	£ 4 4s. 0d.
		£137 11s. 0d.

[5] Already a pattern is set of late payment of wages. 8 servants were paid wages due over 2 months earlier.

27 December 1811 – 10 October 1812

[*p. 3.1*]
Memorandum April 20 1812
John Allen, my butler, being this day arrested for a debt of of [*sic*] £13 10s. 0d. at the suit of a Mr Porter of East Lopham, and the charges of Attorney & Sheriff's Officer amounting to £8 18s. 0d., I to save him from prison advanced him the sum of £8 18s. 0d., which is to be deducted from his wages for the present quarter.

Edward Edwards' wages from Lady Day 1812 are at the rate of £26 per annum.

Memorandum We this year altered our livery to that of Mr Longe of Spixworth, viz. brown cloth, with orange cuffs, capes & waistcoats, and a silk lace.[6] Black velveteen breeches. Frocks of the same cloth, but no lace, & waistcoats ditto. Lace used 3 & ½ yards. No great coats this year, as they were new last year.
May 19: received through Porter 30 yards of livery lace, in two parcels, made by Mersey, No.71 Long Acre, Mr Longe's laceman, at 3sh. per yard: £4 10s.0d.[7]

August 8 Having discovered this morning that Elisabeth Hammond, the cook, is with child by Edward Edwards, the gardiner, I paid him his wages to Midsummer, £6, & discharged him, intending to pay him what may be due to him for service from Midsummer to this day, 6 weeks & 3 days, when I know what debts he may owe in the family.[8]
Paid him in full wages due August 8 when I discharged him — £3 5s. 0d. September 13.

October 3 Discharged Elisabeth Hammond, the cook.

Mary Gooch quits my service thinking herself equal to a superior place. She behaved extremely well while here. After she had left me, I was told by Kenney that she would have been glad to have continued here. She let herself on leaving me to George Goodwin at Ipswich. Had I known her wishes, I would willingly have increased her wages.

[*p.3.2*]
1812 [*sic*] Servants' wages

December 27	paid Mary Gooch, kitchen maid, 1 quarter's wages to	
1812	Xtmas	0 15s. 0d.
February 3	paid John Allen, butler, 1 quarter's wages to Xtmas	£10 0s. 0d.
April 20	paid John Allen, 1 quarter's wages to Lady Day	£10 0s. 0d.
	advanced towards wages for the present quarter	£ 8 18s. 0d.
21	paid John Gowers, wages for half year due at Lady Day	£10 0s. 0d.
	paid William Lambert ditto	£ 8 8s. 0d.

6 The colours of brown and orange, near to the red and gold of the Longe family, as adopted by his cousin.
7 Longe's wife Charlotte died 20 May 1812. For the servants' mourning wear see below, p.209.
8 Longe often used the word 'family' to mean the whole household, including resident servants.

	paid Edward Edwards, gardiner ditto	£12 10s. 0d.
	paid James Scoggin, wages for 26 weeks to March 29 at 7s.	£ 9 2s. 0d.
23	paid Mary Kenney, an half year's wages to Lady Day	£ 3 13s. 6d.
	paid Elisabeth Hammond ditto	£ 4 14s. 6d.
	paid Elisabeth Garnham ditto	£ 4 4s. 0d.
	paid Amy Mayhew ditto	£ 4 4s. 0d.
	paid Mary Gooch, kitchen maid, 1 quarter to ditto	0 15s. 0d.
	[*sub-total*] £87 4s. 6d.[9]	
September 13	paid Edward Edwards, gardiner, wages due August 8, when I discharged him	£ 9 5s. 0d.
October 3	paid Elisabeth Hammond, wages to new Michaelmas last for an half year £4 14s.6d., and further for staying 5 days beyond the quarter day 5s.6d.	£ 5 0s. 0d.
10	paid Mary Gooch, an half year's wages to Michaelmas when she leaves us, and 4s. as a present	£ 1 14s. 0d.
	[*sub-total*] £15 19s.0d.	
	[*carry forward*]	£103 3s. 6d.

[*p.4.1*]
1812 Servants discharged & hired

August 21 I engaged Ann Tomlinson, late ladies' maid to Mrs Marsham – from whom I received a very satisfactory character for honesty & sobriety, with whom she had lived 12 years as lady's maid – as housekeeper, aged 48, at 16 guineas per annum wages. She entered my family September 28.
(April 29 1813, I consented to allow her in addition to her wages £1 1s. per annum for tea & sugar.)[10]

<August> September 7 I engaged Charles Crickmay, late in the service of Mr Steward of Norwich, from whom I had a very satisfactory character, as gardiner, at 1 guinea a week wages, & I am to furnish him with a dwelling to board himself. No engagement made as to beer or any other allowance. A married man, but has no family – aged 30. He entered my service October 1, & will continue to lodge & board in my house till the dwelling now building in addition to Parr's house is ready for him.[11] For this board & lodging a proportional deduction must be made from his wages. Crickmay took possession of his house Friday October 23, with his wife.

September 11 I engaged Phoebe Davey (who now lives with Mr Morgan of Henley, from whose housekeeper I had a very good character of

9 The total given is in error by 6d., one of several minor discrepancies in arithmetic.

10 Tea and sugar were, because of their high cost, often kept under lock and key. If the housekeeper held the key ways had to be found to reinforce her trustworthiness. To allow the key-holder a supply in kind as part of her remuneration was an attempt to protect the interest of the employer. Cash in lieu was a survival.

11 Gabriel Parr and his wife had been farm servants on Vicarage Farm since at least 1797.

her) as kitchen girl at £3 per annum wages, aged [*blank*] – entered my service October 13th.

September 22 I engaged Ann Leggatt as cook at 10 guineas per annum wages. Came to us October 11th, aged 24. Lived last for a short time with Mrs Clarke, East Bergholt from whom I had a satisfactory character. Before this she lived some time with Mr Kilderbee, & Mrs Dupuis gave me a very good character of her as to her behaviour while there.

22 November 1812 – 23 February 1813

[*p.4.2*]

1812	Servants' wages to Michaelmas brought over	£103 3s. 6d.
November 22	paid J. Allen, butler, balance of wages due at Michaelmas last	£11 2s. 0d.
November 23	paid John Gowers, ½ year's wages due at ditto	£10 0s. 0d.
	paid William Lambert, ditto	£ 8 8s. 0d.
	paid James Scoggin, wages for 27 weeks to October 3	£ 9 9s. 0d.
	paid Mary Kenney, ½ year's wages to Michaelmas last	£ 3 13s. 6d.
	paid Elisabeth Garnham, nursery maid ditto	£ 4 4s. 0d.
	paid Amy Mayhew, house maid ditto	£ 4 4s. 0d.
December 28	paid Phoebe Davy, kitchen girl 1 quarter's wages	0 15s. 0d.
1813		
January 7	paid Charles Crickmay, gardiner, wages from October 1 to December 26 (for 3 weeks while he boarded & lodged in the house at 10sh. per week & 9 weeks at £1 1s.)	£10 19s. 0d.
11	paid Mary Kenney wages, 1 quarter to Xtmas 1812, & as she staid till this day, I paid her	£ 2 2s. 0d.
	Total wages 1812	£168 0s. 0d.
1813 January 11	given Mary Kenney on leaving us	£ 5 0s. 0d.
		£173 0s. 0d.

January 14 Mary Kenney, who left us this day, lived with us ever since we married, now 22 years. Her age & infirmities obliged her to quit us. She has ever been a most faithful honest servant. As a reward for her services, I allow her £5 per annum as long as she lives, and gave her £5 on leaving the family.[12]

[*p.5.1*]

1813

February 15 The maid servants have for some weeks shewed an unwillingness to be under controul of my housekeeper Tomlinson, and have all at different times behaved very ill to her. Elisabeth Garnham was the first who became dissatisfied, & before Tomlinson came talked of leaving the family. Finding I had no prospect of reconciling

[12] Mary Kenney seems to have been underpaid as housekeeper by comparison with other servants.

them, I enquired after a servant in her place while in Norfolk on our way home. February 12 gave her warning to leave me at Lady Day.

February 13 The next day, Amy Mayhew (housemaid) & Ann Leggatt (cook) gave me warning.

February 15 Finding that they had set the kitchen maid against Tomlinson, & that she had also been extremely rude, I gave her warning to leave me at Lady Day.
The above four maid servants refused to stay until Lady Day but left me at a month's warning.

February 15 William Lambert, groom & footman, applied for an increase of wages.
As he is a good servant, I consented to pay him from Lady Day next 18 guineas per annum wages, & also he is to have a pair of cord breeches to wear with his morning frock.

New Maid Servants

February 17 I hired Sarah Girling as kitchen girl, at £3 per annum wages. To come at Lady Day, or before if wanted. Aged 16 next June. Entered my service March 14th.

February 20 I hired Lucy Taylor as cook, at wages £8 per annum. Having had a good character of her from Mr Stimson, whom she left last Michaelmas, & from Mrs Kerridge, China Shop, Ipswich, where she has lived since. As she does not understand cooking further than plain roasting & boiling, I am to get Kenney to instruct her.[13] Aged 21 years. Entered my service March 14th.
I yesterday received a letter from Elisabeth Christopher (sister of Mr Church's butler) whom I spoke with while in Norfolk last week, by which she engages …

[*p.5.2*]

… herself to come to us as Charlotte's maid, & to attend to the children when at home, their linen &c.[14] Wages 12 guineas per annum, & to have my daughter's & sons' cloaths.
She lived last as lady's maid to Mrs Gooch & her daughters at Saxlingham, Norfolk, from whom I had a good character of her. Before this she lived several years at Mrs Rolfe of Heacham, Norfolk. Came here by mail [*coach*] March 18th.

February 23 I hired Charlotte Warren as housemaid, at 8 guineas per annum. She lived last with Mrs Henry Berners, from whom I had a very satisfactory character of her. Aged 21 years.
Entered my service March 14th.

[*p.6.1*]
John had a box coat this year, & William a great coat

13 Mary Kenney had left Longe's service two months earlier. No further payment is recorded.

14 Charlotte was aged sixteen and a half, and her four younger brothers were all away at boarding school.

6 March – 9 December 1813

[*p.6.2*]

1813	Servants' wages	
March 6	paid John Allen, butler, 1 quarter's wages to Xtmas last	£10 0s. 0d.
March 13	paid Elisabeth Garnham, an half year's wages which would be due at Lady Day next	£ 4 4s. 0d.
	paid Amy Mayhew, an half year's wages which would be due at Lady Day next	£ 4 4s. 0d.
	paid Phoebe Davy, a quarter's wages which would be due at Lady Day next	0 15s. 0d.
	As it is so near Lady Day, I made no deduction from their wages.	
	paid Ann Leggatt <an half year's> wages due this day from October 10 1812 at £10 10s. per annum £4 13s.	£ 4 13s. 0d.
	Given her above her wages	0 2s. 0d.
April 27	paid John Allen 1 quarter's wages to 28th April	£10 0s. 0d.
	paid John Gowers an half year's wages due at Lady Day last	£10 0s. 0d.
	paid William Lambert ditto	£ 8 8s. 0d.
	paid Charles Crickmay, gardiner, wages for 13 weeks to March 27 at £1 1s.0d. per week	£13 13s. 0d.
	paid James Scoggin wages for 25 weeks to March 27	£ 8 15s. 0d.
	paid Ann Tomlinson an half year's wages due at Lady Day last at 16 guineas per annum	£ 8 8s. 0d.
	paid her for tea & sugar at £1 1s.0d. per annum	0 10s. 6d.
	given her half the expense of getting her boxes & drawers here	10s. 6d.
	Total wages to Lady Day 1813 [*carry forward*]	£84 3s. 0d.

[*p.7.1*]

1813 Memorandums

June 19 — Sarah Girling left me, her health not admitting of her continuing in a place of so much work, as scullery maid. She behaved in every respect well while she was in my service.

Elisabeth Wasp of Westerfield came in her place June 26. Wages £3 per annum.

July 9 — Ann Tomlinson, my housekeeper, told me that she had decided on accepting an advantageous offer from a female friend of living with her at Norwich, & therefore wishes to leave me as soon as I can meet with a person to supply her place.[15] She quitted my family September 29.

August 14 — I engaged Phoebe Caldwell who lives separate from husband, aged 39.

She lived 2½ years with Baroness Montesquieu in London, 2½ years at Mr Fonnereau's, Christchurch, Ipswich, & last 1 & ¾ years

[15] Four months earlier four maid-servants had left Longe's service blaming Tomlinson, and Longe seems to have stood by her then. Her wish to leave was ironically soon.

at Mrs Cath. Collett's at Kelsal.[16] Wages 20 guineas per annum. No allowance for tea, but I told her if she suited me, and conducted herself well, I would make her a present of a pound of tea occasionally. I received a very satisfactory character of her from Mrs Collett..

September 27 Phoebe Caldwell entered my service September 27th

December 9 Phoebe Caldwell gave me notice that she should be glad to give up her place as soon as I can meet with a person in her place. She says she finds the place too much for her. She is of an hasty discontented temper.

[*p.7.2*]

1813	Servants' wages	brought over	£84 3s. 0d.
June 21	paid Sarah Girling for 1 quarter & given her 5s. 0d. as she stayed a short time beyond it		£ 1 0s. 0d.
July 31	paid J. Allen 1 quarter's wages due at Midsummer last		£10 0s. 0d.
	paid Charles Crickmay, gardiner, wages from March 27 to June 27 inclusive, 13 weeks at £1 1s.0d. per week		£13 13s. 0d.
September 28	paid Ann Tomlinson, my housekeeper, on her quitting my service, an half year's wages due this day at 16 guineas per annum		£ 8 8s. 0d.
	given her for tea at £1 1s.0d. per annum		0 10s. 6d.
October 16	paid Charlotte Warren, housemaid, an half year's wages due at new Michaelmas last at £8 8s. 0d. per annum, & 6s. 0d. for the few days she was here previous to Lady Day		£ 4 10s. 0d.
November 16	paid Lucy Taylor, cook, an half year's wages as due new Michaelmas, & 6s. 0d. for the few days she was here previous to Lady Day		£ 4 6s. 0d.
November 22	paid Charles Crickmay, gardiner, wages from June 27 to October 3 inclusive 14 weeks at £1 1s. 0d. per week		£14 14s. 0d.
	paid Elisabeth Christopher, (Charlotte's maid) an half year's wages due at Michaelmas last at 12 guineas per annum		£ 6 6s. 0d.
	paid ditto part of expense of her journey here when she first entered my family		0 10s. 6d.
November 24	paid John Allen, 1 quarter's wages to Michaelmas		£10 0s. 0d.
	paid John Gower, an half year's wages to ditto		£10 0s. 0d.
	paid William Lambert, ditto at £18 18s. 0d. per annum		£ 9 9s. 0d.
25	[*paid*] Elisabeth Waspe, 1 quarter to new Michaelmas at £3 per annum		0 15s. 0d.
27	paid James Scoggin, wages for 27 weeks to October 3		£ 9 9s. 0d.
	Total to Michaelmas 1813	[*carry forward*]	£187 14s. 0d.

16 Christchurch mansion with park was previously in the private occupation of the Fonnereau family.

[*p.7.3, loose sheet*]
Increase of servants' wages 1813

Total wages 1812	men servants	£121 0s. 0d.
	maidservants	£ 36 12s. 0d.
		£157 12s. 0d.
Total wages from Lady Day 1813	men servants	£151 14s. 0d.
	maidservants	£ 48 16s. 0d.
	Total 1813	£200 0s. 0d.
	Total 1812	£157 12s. 0d.
	Increase in 1813	£ 42 18s. 0d.

viz. gardiner's wages increased	£ 28 12s. 0d.
William Lambert	£ 2 2s. 0d.
difference between Tomlinson's & Kenney's wages	£ 9 9s. 0d.
ditto between Christopher's & Garnham's ditto	£ 4 4s. 0d.
	£ 44 7s. 0d.
cook's wages diminished from the late cook's, deduct	£ 1 9s. 0d.
	£ 42 18s. 0d.

N.B. against this increase of wages, I must set off the gardiner's board as Edwards boarded here & lodged, & Crickmay does not – this at 4s.0d. per day would amount to £73.[17]

15 January – 24 February 1814

[*p.8.1*]
1814

January 21 Phoebe Caldwell, housekeeper, quitted my service.
Amy Alldis, widow, aged 52, of Harwich, entered my service as housekeeper – January 21, at wages 20 guineas per annum, no perquisites & no allowance for tea. She kept Mr Robertson's house at Harwich, but has been some months out of service.
Clothing from Pritty for servants

J. Gowers & William Lambert:	Haverhill Institution stable jacket Fustian overalls
Boy James Keeble	Blue great coat at 7 sh. per yard & Haverhill Institution jacket & waistcoat
J. Gowers & William Lambert:	no great coats this year

[*p.8.2*]

1813	Servants' wages continued	brought over	£187 14s. 0d.
1814			
January 15	paid J. Allen, wages 1 quarter to Xtmas last		£ 10 0s. 0d.
	paid Charles Crickmay, gardiner, wages for 12 weeks to December 25th 1813, at £1.1s. per week		£ 12 12s. 0d.

17 Longe valued board and lodging at 4s. a day (£73 a year) each servant. This both puts into perspective the modest cash wages and indicates the substantial extent of his expenditure.

January 20	paid Phoebe Caldwell, housekeeper, wages for 1 quarter & 1 month, at 20 guineas per annum due to this time, when she quitted my service	£ 7 0s. 0d.
February 24	paid A.Alldiss the expense of a post chaise from Mistley to Ipswich January 21 when she entered my service	£ 1 1s. 0d.
	Total wages 1813	£218 7s. 0d.

6 April – 25 November 1814

[*p.9.1*]

Agreed with Elisabeth's Waspe's mother that she shall be paid from Midsummer 1814 to Christmas next at the rate of £4 per annum. James Keeble, servant lad, left us, to live with Mr Fitch, Ipswich. He was here 3 years, in every respect a very good servant. His brother William Keeble came here in his place – aged 15 years.

[*p.9.2*]

1814		
April 6	2 pairs worsted stockings @ 2s.6d. & 1 [*illeg.*] of twilled cotton for 2 neck handkerchiefs for James Keeble – bought of Pritty	0 7s. 9d.
April 16	Servants' wages to Lady Day last	
	J. Allen, 1 quarter at £40 per annum	£ 10 0s. 0d.
	J. Gowers, ½ year at £20 per annum	£ 10 0s. 0d.
	William Lambert, ditto at 18 guineas per annum	£ 9 9s. 0d.
	James Scoggin, 25 weeks to March 27 at 7sh. per week	£ 8 15s. 0d.
	Charles Crickmay, 13 weeks to March 27 at 1 guinea per wk.	£ 13 13s. 0d.
	Amy Alldiss, 9 weeks to Lady Day at 20 guineas per annum	£ 3 12s. 0d.
	Charlotte Warren, housemaid, ½ year at 8 guineas per annum	£ 4 4s. 0d.
	Lucy Taylor, cook, ½ year at £8 per annum	£ 4 0s. 0d.
	Elisabeth Christopher, Charlotte's maid, ½ year at 12 guineas per annum	£ 6 6s. 0d.
	Elisabeth Waspe, scullery girl, ½ year at £3 per annum	£ 1 10s. 0d.
July 12	Elisabeth Waspe, 1 quarter at £3 per annum	0 15s. 0d.
September 28	paid J. Allen, 1 quarter's wages due at Midsummer last	£10 0s. 0d.
	paid Charles Crickmay, ditto 13 weeks to June 26th	£ 13 13s. 0d.
November 15	gave James Keeble, servant lad, when he left us	£ 1 0s. 0d.
	Wages to Michaelmas	
November 25	J. Allen, 1 quarter	£ 10 0s. 0d.
	J. Gowers, ½ year	£ 10 0s. 0d.
	William Lambert, ditto	£ 9 9s. 0d.
	[*carry forward*]	£126 13s. 0d.[18]

[18] The page total should be £126 13s. 9d.

[*p.10.1*]
Buttons & lace for servants' liveries &c.

	<livery coats – large buttons – 2 dozen>	1 & ½ dozen each coat	
	waistcoats – small ditto	– 2 dozen – 10 each waistcoat	
	brown frocks & waistcoats	ditto	
	stable jackets & waistcoats	2 & ½ dozen small size	
	<livery lace 4 yards>		
1814	total servants' wages 1814		£198 1s. 0d.
	total clothing for ditto		£ 43 18s. 5d.
			£241 19s. 5d.

25 November 1814 – 17 November 1815

[*p.10.2*]

1814	Servants' wages to Michaelmas (continued)	
	brought over	£126 13s. 0d.
November 25	Charles Crickmay, gardiner, 14 weeks to October 2nd	£ 14 14s. 0d.
	James Scoggin, 27 weeks to October 2nd	£ 9 9s. 0d.
	Amy Alldiss, housekeeper, half year to new Michaelmas	£ 10 10s. 0d.
	Elisabeth Christopher, ditto	£ 6 6s. 0d.
	Charlotte Warren, ditto £ 4 4s. 0d.	
	Lucy Taylor, ditto	£ 4 0s. 0d.
	Elisabeth Waspe, 1 quarter to ditto	£ 1 0s. 0d.
	paid Cockrell for shoes & mending for James Keeble for servant lad	£ 1 12s. 9d.
1815		
February 14	J. Allen, 1 quarter's wages to Christmas last	£ 10 0s. 0d.
	Charles Crickmay, 12 weeks to Christmas Day 1814	£ 12 12s. 0d.
18	Cockrel's bills for shoes & mending for James Keeble from July 9 to November 12	£ 2 0s. 1d.
	(Miller's bill for making cloaths for servants in 1814	£ 5 18s. 6d.
	(Pritty's bill for cloathing for servants in 1814	£ 6 5s. 3d.
	[*both*] entered also in my account book	
	Porter's drapers bill for cloathing for ditto 1814	£ 22 19s. 6½d.
	Cook's bill for hats for ditto 1814	£ 2 15s. 6d.
August 4	shirting for servant lad 16s.9½ d. & making 3s.0d. (entered in my book)	0 19s. 9½d.
	Total paid 1814/15	£241 19s. 5d.

[*p.11.1*]
May 18 Elisabeth Waspe, kitchen maid, gave me warning to leave me at new-midsummer, having got a nursery maid's place at General Wilder's of Westerfield. I paid E. Waspe wages for the full quarter to Midsummer although I have released her from Wednesday 14th June, having behaved extremely well in her service.

June12 Mary Farrow, aged 15, came in the place of Elisabeth Waspe at wages £3 per annum.

October 16 William Lambert, having formed an improper connection with Ann Cornish my farming man's daughter who is with child by him, I thought it right, he being a married man, to part with him, though he has been a very good servant, & has lived here 5½ years.
And James Keeble, who lived here as servant lad, & who left me <at Michaelmas 1814> November 1814 came here again in William Lambert's place at wages £12 12s. per annum, and the same clothes as usual – aged 18.
J. Gowers & William Lambert had great coats this year.

[*p. 11.2*]

1815		
February 22	6 yards cotton twist for shirts for servant lad, William Keeble at 1s.6d.: 9s. 2 pairs stockings worsted at 2s.7d. 1 coloured handkerchief for 2 neckcloths: 2s.4d. Buttons & thread: 6d.	0 17s. 0d.
March 16	paid Mrs Keeble for making the above for her son	0 2s. 4d.
	Servants' wages due at Lady Day	
May 26	paid J. Allen, <a half> 1 quarter year's wages due at Lady Day last	£10 0s. 0d.
	paid John Gowers, an half year's ditto	£10 0s. 0d.
	paid William Lambert, ditto	£ 9 9s. 0d.
	paid James Scoggin, wages 25 weeks to March 25 at 7sh. per week	£ 8 15s. 0d.
	paid Charles Crickmay, ditto 13 weeks to ditto at £1 1s.0d	£13 13s. 0d.
	paid Amy Alldiss, ½ year's wages to Lady Day last	£10 10s. 0d.
	paid Charlotte Warren, ditto	£ 4 4s. 0d.
	paid Lucy Taylor, ditto £ 4 0s. 0d.	
	paid Elisabeth Waspe, ditto	£ 2 0s. 0d.
	paid Elisabeth Christopher, ditto	£ 6 6s. 0d.
June 7	paid Elisabeth Waspe, 1 quarter's wages to Midsummer	£ 1 0s. 0d.
July 24	paid J. Allen, 1 quarter's wages to Midsummer	£10 0s. 0d.
	paid Charles Crickmay, ditto 13 weeks to June 25th	£13 13s. 0d.
October 16	paid William Lambert, an half year's wages due at Michaelmas when he left my service	£ 9 9s. 0d.
	Given him because I kept all the cloaths he had this year, for James Keeble who succeeded him in the place	£ 1 11s. 0d.
November 17	A Duffeld great coat from Wells for servant lad	0 16s. 6d.
	[*carry forward*]	£116 6s.10d.[19]

[19] This total should be £116 5s. 10d.

2 December 1815 – 2 December 1816

[*p. 12.1*]

December 2 Amy Alldiss, after a month's illness which began with an inflammation on the lungs, died.

7 I paid the amount of her wages due to October 29th, when she was taken ill, to her daughter Mary Alldiss, viz. £11 15s. 0d.
I also paid the expense of her illness & funeral.

6 Charlotte Warren, housemaid, gave me warning. Her brother has just lost his wife, & is desirous that his sister should go to live with him.

29 Charlotte Warren left my service. Her conduct has been uniformly good.
She is a complete housemaid, & I am very sorry to be obliged to part with her.

28 Martha Frost entered my service. She has lived 4 months at Mr Wythe's at Eye Park, since that a year & ½ at <Mr Woods> Revd. Mr Woods Needham as nursemaid, but we had a good character of her from Mrs Wood, saying that she was equal to an housemaid's place. Age 23. Wages £9 9s. per annum.

The servants had great coats this year

Total servants' expenses	£231 3s. 0¾d.
Porter's bill for liveries	£ 26 17s. 1¾d.
	£258 0s. 2½d.
deduct cloathing	£ 46 14s. 2½d.
wages 1815	£212 6s. 0½d.

Of this account, linen & shoes &c. for the servant lad amounts to £5 18s. 1d.

December 18 Ann Tomlinson, who lived here as housekeeper in 1813, entered my service again as housekeeper. Wages 20 guineas per annum.

[*p. 12.2*]

1815	Servants' wages to Michaelmas (continued) brought over	£116 6s.10d.
December 7	John Allen, 1 quarter to Michaelmas	£ 10 0s. 0d.
	John Gowers, ½ year to ditto	£ 10 0s. 0d.
	James Scoggin, 27 weeks to October 1 at 7sh. per week	£ 9 9s. 0d.
	Charles Crickmay, 14 weeks to ditto at £1 1s. 0d. per week	£ 14 14s. 0d.
	paid Mary Alldiss, her mother's wages due at her death	£ 11 15s. 0d.
	Elisabeth Christopher, ½ year to Michaelmas	£ 6 6s. 0d.
	Charlotte Warren, ditto	£ 4 4s. 0d.
	Lucy Taylor, ditto	£ 4 0s. 0d.
	Mary Farrow, 1 quarter to ditto	0 15s. 0d.
14	Cockrill's bill for shoes &c. for William Keeble to June 18	£ 1 5s. 2d.

29	paid Charlotte Warren, wages 1 quarter to Christmas: £2 2s. + 18s.0d. because, if she had continued with us, her wages were to have been increased	£ 3 0s. 0d.
	paid Mrs Keeble for making 2 shirts for servant lad	0 2s. 0d.
1816		
January 25	paid J. Allen, 1 quarter's wages due at Christmas last	£ 10 0s. 0d.
	paid Charles Crickmay, wages for 12 weeks to December 24th 1815 at £1 1s. per week	£ 12 12s. 0d.
February 20	Cockrill's bill for shoes William Keeble to December 20	£ 1 10s. 7d.
	Miller's bill for making servants' clothes	£ 5 5s. 0d.
	Spurling's bill for gaiters &c. servant lad	£ 1 4s. 6d.
22	Pritty's bill for cloathing had in 1815	£ 5 11s. 5¾d.
26	Cook's bill for livery & plain hats 1815	£ 3 2s. 6d.
		£231 3s. 0¾d.

[*p.13.1, blank*]

[*p.13.2*]

1816	Servants' wages to Lady Day	
April 13	J. Allen, 1 quarter to Lady Day	£ 10 0s. 0d.
	J. Gowers, ½ year to ditto	£ 10 0s. 0d.
	James Keeble, ½ year to ditto (14 days short)	£ 6 0s. 0d.
	James Scoggin, 26 weeks to march 31 at 7 sh.	£ 9 2s. 0d.
	Charles Crickmay, 14 weeks to ditto at £1 1s.0d.	£ 14 14s. 0d.
	Ann Tomlinson, 1 quarter to Lady Day at 20 guineas per annum	£ 5 5s. 0d.
	Elisabeth Christopher, ½ year to ditto	£ 6 6s. 0d.
	Martha Frost, 1 quarter to ditto at <9 guineas per annum>	£ 2 7s. 3d.
	Lucy Taylor, ½ year to ditto	£ 4 0s. 0d.
	Mary Farrow, ½ year to ditto	£ 1 10s. 0d.
	wages paid April 13: £69 4s. 3d.	
July 11	Charles Crickmay, 12 weeks to June 22nd	£ 12 12s. 0d.
	J. Allen, 1 quarter to Midsummer	£ 10 0s. 0d.
August 2	Martha Frost, in payment of wages due at Michaelmas	£ 3 0s. 0d.
September 2	Cockrill's bill for shoes & mending for William Keeble from January 7 to June 27	0 16s. 2½d.
4	paid Pritty's bill for fustian (Haverhill), for stable jackets, 2 pairs overalls, & jacket & waistcoat for boy	£ 4 1s.10½d.
December 2	Servants' wages to Michaelmas	
	J. Allen, 1 quarter to Michaelmas	£ 10 0s. 0d.
	J. Gowers, ½ year to ditto	£ 10 0s. 0d.
	James Keeble, ½ year to ditto	£ 6 6s. 0d.
	[*carry forward*]	£126 0s. 4d.

[*p.14.1*]

total servants	£233 8s. 7d.
[*less*] clothing	£ 40 16s. 8d.
wages 1816	£192 11s.11d.

2 December 1816 – 18 February 1817

[*p.14.2*]

1816	Servants' wages to Michaelmas		
	brought over		£126 0s. 4d.
December 2	James Scoggin, wages 26 weeks to September 29 at 7 sh.		£ 9 2s. 0d.
	to ditto expense of a Fustian jacket & waistcoat		£ 1 6s. 8d.
	Charles Crickmay, 14 weeks to September 29 at £1 1s.		£ 14 14s. 0d.
	Ann Tomlinson, ½ year to Michaelmas		£ 10 10s. 0d.
	Elisabeth Christopher, ditto		£ 6 6s. 0d.
	Martha Frost, balance due having been paid £3, August 2nd		£ 1 14s. 6d.
	Lucy Taylor, ½ year		£ 4 0s. 0d.
	Mary Farrow, ditto		£ 1 10s. 0d.
	paid 2 December wages £74 2s. 6d.		
1817			
January 31	Cook (Ipswich) hatter		£ 3 2s. 0d.
February 4	Porter draper		£ 23 0s. 2d.
7	Cockrill boy William Keeble		£ 1 6s. 9d.
	Spurling ditto		£ 1 3s. 0d.
8	Henry Miller making liveries &c.		£ 4 13s. 6d.
11	Pritty articles for William Keeble		
September 9	1[*illeg.*] cambric 2s. 3d.		
	2 pairs cotton stockings	5s. 0d.	
December 20	6 yards twist cotton for shirts at 1s.4d.	8s. 0d.	
	1 handkerchief	2s. 2d.	
	thread & buttons	3½d.	
	2 pairs worsted stockings at 2s.6d.	5s. 0d.	
	1 & ½ yards fustian & thread	3s.11½d.	£ 1 6s. 8d.
February18	J. Allen, 1 quarter's wages to Christmas last		£ 10 0s. 0d.
	Charles Crickmay, ditto 13 weeks to December 29		£ 13 13s. 0d.
			£233 8s. 7d.

12 March – 12 October 1817

[*p.15.1*]
1817

March 25 William Keeble, servant lad, left my service, being sufficiently qualified for a superior place. Mr Pearson of Ipswich hired him. He behaved well while here.
John Crooks came here as servant lad. I pay him no wages, but find

him with cloaths & linen. On Crooks coming here from the farm, I took Jonathan Scott as farming boy in his place.[20]

September 29 Mary Farrow, servant girl, left us, being equal to a superior service. Always conducted herself well.
Amy Bent came here in her place, aged 19 years, at wages £3 per annum, no perquisites. Amy Bent proved 7 months gone with child, & was discharged, October 12th.

October 6 James Keeble, footman & groom, left my service to live with Revd. J. Deere, Bures. He was a quiet sober man, but dull & sometimes very thoughtless. The immediate cause of my parting with him was his leading my mare & directing the boy to lead the pony (which had got into the garden) down the steps into the store yard, & on my taking him to task for it, he behaved extremely rudely. I gave him however as good a character as I fairly could to Mr Deere, who hired him.

October 6 James Brown, who lived last 14 months with Mr Vernon as groom, entered my service as footman & groom today, at wages 14 guineas per annum & the usual cloaths. His father has long been bailiff to Mr Collinson at the Chantry, & this young man was brought up in the family, as servant of all work, till he let himself to Mr Vernon <whom he left> who discharged him for not taking good care of his horses, but I had a good character of him upon the whole.[21]

[*p.15.2*]

1817	<u>Servants' wages, &c.</u>		
March 12	paid Mrs Keeble for making shirts & handkerchiefs for her son William Keeble in December last		0 2s. 2d.
April 11	J. Allen, 1 quarter to Lady Day		£10 0s. 0d.
	J. Gowers, half year to ditto		£10 0s. 0d.
	James Keeble, ditto £ 6 6s. 0d.		
	James Scoggin, 26 weeks to Mar 30 (2sh.deducted for lost time)		£ 9 0s. 0d.
	Charles Crickmay, ditto 13 weeks to ditto at £1 1s.		£13 13s. 0d.
	Ann Tomlinson, ½ year		£10 10s. 0d.
	Elisabeth Christopher, ditto		£ 6 6s. 0d.
	Martha Frost, ditto		£ 4 14s. 6d.
	Lucy Taylor, ditto		£ 4 0s. 0d.
	Mary Farrow, ditto		<u>£ 1 10s. 0d.</u>
	Wages to Lady Day		<u>£75 19s. 6d.</u>
12	from Pritty [*for*] Crooks		
	6 yards twist shirting at 1s.4d	8s.0d.	
	1 handkerchief <2s.0d.>	2s.0d.	
	2 pairs worsted stockings at 2s.3d. <4s.6d.>	4s.6d.	
	cotton & buttons	<u>3d.</u>	0 14s. 9d.

[20] Longe married Frances Ward on 15 April 1817.
[21] The Chantry is the substantial house standing in what is now a public park between the roads out of Ipswich to London and Hadleigh.

	October 21 paid Mrs Crooks for making ditto	0 2s. 3d.
July 21	J. Allen, 1 quarter to Midsummer last	£ 10 0s. 0d.
	Charles Crickmay, 13 weeks to June 29	£ 13 13s. 0d.
September 29	Mary Farrow, ½ year to Michaelmas when she quitted	£ 1 10s. 0d.
	given ditto as a present for good behaviour	0 2s. 6d.
October 6	James Keeble an half year's wages to Michaelmas when he left my service	£ 6 6s. 0d.
	given him as a present	0 3s. 0d.
	September 30 paid Cockril bill for shoes for servant lads from January 1 to May 21	£ 1 14s. 6d.
12	Given Amy Bent for the short time she was here as servant girl	0 3s. 0d.
	[*carry forward*]	[22] £111 10s. 8d.

16 October 1817 – 12 November 1818

[*p.16.1*]

1817

October 16 Elisabeth Scrutton, aged 19, entered our service of kitchen girl, from Mrs George Goodwin's, Stowmarket at wages £3 per annum.

1818 Memorandum

April I this year ordered the pocket flaps of the liveries to be altered – to slips with orange cloth & lace, & 3 buttons. The livery coats now therefore require each 1 & ½ dozen large buttons, & 3 & ¼ yards of lace each.

The cloaths were this year made by Ringrose.

No great coats. John Gowers & Charles Sporle: a pair of fustian breeches each, & also a pair of Haverhill Institution overalls.

1817	total servants'	wages	£201 2s. 6d.
	ditto	clothing	£ 48 12s.10d.
			£249 15s. 4d.

[*p.16.2*]

1817	brought over	£111 10s. 8d.
October 27	paid J. Allen, 1 quarter's wages to last Michaelmas	£ 10 0s. 0d.
	paid Martha Frost, in part of wages due at ditto	£ 3 0s. 0d.
December 15	J. Gowers, ½ year's wages to ditto	£ 10 0s. 0d.
	Charles Crickmay, 14 weeks to October 5	£ 14 14s. 0d.
	James Scoggin, 27 weeks to October 5	£ 9 9s. 0d.
	Ann Tomlinson, ½ year to Michaelmas	£ 10 10s. 0d.
	Elisabeth Christopher, ditto	£ 6 6s. 0d.
	Martha Frost, remainder of wages due at ditto	£ 1 14s. 6d.
	Lucy Taylor, ½ year to ditto	£ 4 0s. 0d.

22 The total should be £110 10s. 8d.

1818			
January 10	J. Allen, 1 quarter to Christmas		£ 10 0s. 0d.
	Charles Crickmay, 12 weeks to December 28		£ 12 12s. 0d.
February 26	paid Pritty bill for fustian cloathing &c. for servants 1817		£ 5 4s. 0d.
	paid ditto for stockings &c. for servant boy, October 20 1817		0 5s. 6d.
March 3	H. Miller	tailor's bill	£ 5 15s. 0d.
	J. Cockrill	bill for shoes &c. servant lad	£ 1 7s. 9d.
	William Spurling	bill, servant lad, glover	£ 1 8s. 0d.
6	Porter's	bill for cloathing	£ 29 5s.11d.
	Cook's	ditto for hats	£ 2 13s. 0d.
			£249 15s. 4d.

[*p 17.1*]

February 29 I engaged Reuben Lord (who has lived some time with Mr Joseph Smith of Ipswich, & since a short time with Mr Davy of Wickham Market), as butler at wages £35 per annum. Entered my service March 25th.

February Mrs Longe engaged Frances Underwood as cook, at £10 10s. per annum wages. Lived last at Mr Joseph Smith's Ipswich – no perquisites.
Entered my service March 12th.

March 11 I engaged Charles Sporle, of Debenham, who has lived last at Mr George Cobbold's of Trimley, & before at Mr Wade's Debenham, as footman & groom, at £10 per annum wages & the usual cloaths – aged 17. To come for a month on trial at Lady Day – entered my service March 25th.

March 11 Lucy Taylor, who has lived with me 4 years as cook, left us to go to Lady Broke as cook & housekeeper. She behaved here very well, but was inattentive, and not a good cook.

March 25 I parted with Allen, because he became very indolent & slovenly, & being now advanced in years, his eyesight began to fail. In many respects a good servant. Lived here near 7 years.
I discharged James Brown, finding him very awkward at indoor business, & not inclined to improve himself by the butler's instruction. He was a good groom, & a sober steady young man.

October 12 Elisabeth Scrutton left the family, having behaved well, & got a superior service.
Ann Hill came in her place, at wages £3 per annum.

[*p.17.2*]

1818 Servants' wages

March 11	Lucy Taylor, wages to this day, when she left us. I made no deduction, but paid her for the half year to next Lady Day	£ 4 0s. 0d.
25	John Allen, wages for one quarter to this day, when he left my service	£ 10 0s. 0d.

	Given him as a present	£ 1 0s. 0d.
	James Brown, wages for 1 quarter to this day, when he left my service	£ 7 7s. 0d.
April 23rd	John Gowers, half year's wages due at Lady Day	£ 10 0s. 0d.
	James Scoggin, wages for 25 weeks to March 29	£ 8 15s. 0d.
	Charles Crickmay, ditto for 13 weeks to ditto	£ 13 13s. 0d
	Ann Tomlinson, ditto for half year to Lady Day	£ 10 10s. 0d.
	Elisabeth Christopher, ditto	£ 6 6s. 0d.
	Martha Frost, ditto	£ 4 14s. 6d.
	Elisabeth Scrutton, ditto	£ 1 10s. 0d.
June 27	Reuben Lord, 1 quarter to new Midsummer	£ 8 15s. 0d.
	paid Mrs Crook, for making 2 shirts 2sh., & for a small piece of cloth in addition 1s.3d.	
	Ditto making 4 neck handkerchiefs 4d., for her son	0 3s. 7d.
July 2	Charles Crickmay, wages for 13 weeks to June 28	£ 13 13s. 0d.
October 12	Elisabeth Scrutton, ½ year's wages to Michaelmas October 11, when she quitted my service	£ 1 10s. 0d.
November 12	Reuben Lord, 1 quarter to new Michaelmas	£ 8 15s. 0d.
		£110 12s. 1d.

[*p.18.1*]

Memorandum

Livery crest buttons

I had this year from Mr Porter ½ a gross coat buttons at 48 sh. per gross	£ 1 4s. 0d.
& ½ gross of waistcoat ditto at 24 sh. per gross	12s. 0d.
	£ 1 16s. 0d.

48 sh per gross large buttons is 4sh. per dozen
24 sh. per ditto small ditto is 2sh. per dozen

Servants' wages for the year 1818	£198 0s. 0d.
ditto Liveries, cloathing &c.	£ 42 14s. 8½d.
Total	£240 14s. 8½d.

30 November 1818 – 29 March 1819

[*p.18.2*]

1818	brought over	£110 12s. 1d.
November 30	Charles Pritty bill for 6½ yards Aberdeen [*?*]dowlas at 1s.6d. for 2 shirts, 1 square cambric muslin [*at*] 1s.6d., 2 pairs br. cotton stockings at 1s.6d., buttons & cotton for servant lad John Crook – sent May 1	0 14s. 6½d.
	Half year to Michaelmas	
December 11	John Gowers, ½ year's wages to Michaelmas last	£ 10 0s. 0d.
	Charles Sporle, ditto	£ 5 0s. 0d.
	James Scoggin, ditto 26 weeks to October 4	£ 9 2s. 0d.
	Charles Crickmay, 14 weeks to ditto	£ 14 14s. 0d.
	Ann Tomlinson, ½ year's wages to Michaelmas last	£ 10 10s. 0d.
	Elisabeth Christopher, ditto	£ 6 6s. 0d.

	Martha Frost, ditto	£ 4 14s. 6d.
	Frances Underwood, cook, ditto, & about a fortnight before Lady Day 8sh.	£ 5 13s. 0d.
	Given John Crook, servant lad	0 5s. 0d.
	James Scoggin, for a shooting jacket	£ 1 0s. 0d.
1819, belonging to 1818		
March 15	Cockrill's bills for shoes for Crooks in 1818	£ 2 4s. 1d.
	Spurling's bill for ditto	£ 1 2s. 6d.
March 11	Porter's draper's bill for liveries	£ 24 5s.10½d.
	Ringrose, taylor's ditto for ditto	£ 4 4s. 0d.
	Miller's, ditto Coddenham for ditto	£ 1 9s. 3d.
19	A. Cook's, Ipswich, hatter	£ 3 4s. 6d.
27	Charles Pritty, bill for fustian, jackets &c.	£ 4 6s. 4½d.
29	paid Reuben Lord, 1 quarter's wages to Christmas	£ 8 15s. 0d.
	paid Charles Crickmay, wages, 12 weeks to December 27 last	£ 12 12s. 0d.
		£240 14s. 8½d.

28 May to 17 December 1819

[*p.19.1*]

1819 John Crook, servant lad, left us about old Lady Day, having got a better service, & I took Charles Offord, aged 15 & ½ years.

May 28 Reuben Lord applyed for £5 per annum additional wages. I do not consent to give it, he not being a compleat butler. His present wages £35 per annum.

Charles Sporle having conducted himself to my satisfaction during the year he has served me, I told him I would increase his wages to £12 per annum from Lady Day 1819.

Martha Frost applyed for an increase of wages. She has now £9 9s. per annum – has now lived here 3 & ½ years.

August 24 Reuben Lord renewed his application for an increase of wages. On consideration of his being in many respects a good servant, though not a complete butler, & rather than part with him, I consented to pay him from Midsummer last at the rate of £40 per annum.

[*p.19.2*][23]

1819	Servants' wages (& quarterly payment)	
May 28	Reuben Lord, 1 quarter to Lady Day	£ 8 15s. 0d.
	J. Gowers, ½ year to ditto	£ 10 0s. 0d.
	Charles Sporle, ½ year to ditto	£ 5 0s. 0d.
	James Scoggin, 25 weeks to March 28 at 7sh. Gardiner entered in Garden Account Book	£ 8 15s. 0d.
	Ann Tomlinson, ½ year to Lady Day	£ 10 10s. 0d.
	Elizabeth Christopher, ditto	£ 6 6s. 0d.

23 Some words clearly added in a different hand have been omitted from this transcript.

	Martha Frost, ditto	£ 4 14s. 6d.
	Frances Underwood, ditto	£ 5 5s. 0d.
	Ann Hill, ditto	£ 1 10s. 0d.
August 24	Reuben Lord, 1 quarter to Midsummer	£ 8 15s. 0d.
	< Charles Crickmay, 12 weeks to June 27 (he having been absent 1 week) >	<£ 12 12s. 0d.>
December 10	Cockrill's bill for shoes for Crooks & Charles Offord to June 22nd	£ 2 3s.10d.
16	Reuben Lord, 1 quarter to Michaelmas at £40 per annum	£ 10 0s. 0d.
	J. Gowers, < 1 qur> to ditto ½ year's wages	£ 10 0s. 0d.
	Charles Sporle, ½ [*year*] to ditto at £12 per annum	£ 6 0s. 0d.
	James Scoggin, 27 weeks to October 3rd	£ 9 9s. 0d.
17	Ann Tomlinson, ½ year wages to Michaelmas	£ 10 10s. 0d.
	Elizabeth Christopher, ditto	£ 6 6s. 0d.
	Martha Frost, ditto	£ 4 14s. 6d.
	Frances Underwood, ditto	£ 5 5s. 0d.
	Ann Hill, ditto	£ 1 10s. 0d.
	[*carry forward*]	£135 8s.10d.

[*p.20.1*][24]
Memorandum The servants i.e. coachman & groom had Haverhill fustian overalls this year.

23 January 1820 – 29 July 1821

[*p.20.2*]

1819	Servants' wages, &c.	
1820	brought over	£135 8s.10d.
January 23	Martha Frost, wages to this time when she quitted our service	3 3s. 0d.
27	H Miller, taylor – bill for 1819	£ 1 15s. 0d.
March 2	Spurling, mending breeches, servant lad	0 3s. 0d.
9	Mrs Lord, making 2 suits of mourning for R. Lord, butler at 15 sh.	£ 1 10s. 0d.
23	R. Lord, 1quarter's wages to Christmas last	£ 10 0s. 0d.
27	Charles Pritty, bill for fustian jackets & other cloathing for servants	£ 9 5s. 4½d.
<April> 7	James Cooper, 1 pair worsted stockings for Charles Offord, made in the Charity School (September 23rd)[25]	0 2s. 6d.
paid March 9	1821 Porter, draper, bill for mourning & liveries in 1819	£ 39 11s.7½d.
	Ringrose, Taylor, &c. for making	£ 5 10s. 0d.
April 5	Butcher, Ipswich, bill for hats	£ 2 19s. 0d.
due	Cockerill – shoes for servant lad	£ 1 5s. 0d.

24 Longe's son Francis died on 17 January 1819 aged twenty.

25 The girls in Coddenham Charity School had three sessions in the week for sewing and knitting.

	[26] £210 12s. 4d.
Liveries & cloathing	£ 64 4s. 4d.
Wages	£146 8s. 0d.

[*p.21.1*]
1820

January 23 Martha Frost, housemaid, having lived in my service about 4 years, during which time she conducted herself uniformly well – married John Turner, taylor of Great Blakenham, & quitted us.
Ann Fair succeeded her as housemaid - wages 9 guineas per annum, aged <23> 27. Her friends live at Hadleigh. She came to us from Mrs Rodwell's of Ipswich, with whom she lived, nursemaid, about 2 years, who gave her a satisfactory character. She entered our service January 25.

August 4 Ann Hill, scullery girl, left us, being qualified for superior service, & let herself to Mrs Edgar, Red House.
The same day, Mary Jessup from George Rushbrooke's took her place here at £3 per annum wages.

October 6 Ann Tomlinson quitted our service, having lived here as housekeeper the second time of her coming, 4 years & 3 quarters. In every respect a worthy, good servant. We part with her now as Mrs Longe wishes to make an alteration, & keep a person as cook & housekeeper.
Mrs Longe hired Elisabeth Scholding, aged 32 as her own maid, & to have care of everything but the … [*continued on p.22.1*]

[*p.21.2*]

1820	Servants' wages, &c.	
May 21	Reuben Lord, on account of wages due at Lady Day	£ 5 0s. 0d.
August 4	Ann Hill, wages for 10 months due at this day when she left us	£ 2 10s. 0d.
September 28	Reuben Lord, balance of wages due at Lady Day	£ 5 0s. 0d.
	J. Gowers, ½ year wages to lady Day last	£10 0s. 0d.
	Charles Sporle, ditto	£ 6 0s. 0d.
	James Scoggin, 26 weeks to April 2nd at 7sh.	£ 9 2s. 0d.
	Ann Tomlinson, ½ year to Lady Day last	£10 10s. 0d.
	Elizabeth Christopher, ditto	£ 6 6s. 0d.
	Ann Fair, 9 weeks to ditto	£ 1 15s. 3d.
	Frances Underwood, ½ year to ditto	£ 5 5s. 0d.
October 5	Ann Tomlinson, ½ year wages to Michaelmas when she quitted our service	£10 10s. 0d.
11	paid Henry Miller, taylor, for making servants' stable jackets &c. & mending lad's cloaths, to Michaelmas	£ 2 5s. 6d.
16	Mrs Offord making 2 shirts, 4 neck handkerchiefs & 2 pocket ditto for [*sic*] J. Offord, servant lad	0 2s. 6d.
	[*carry forward*]	£74 6s. 3d.

[26] This sub-total should be £210 13s. 4d.

[*p.22.1*]

[*continued from p.21.1*] … the kitchen, at wages £12 12s. per annum. She entered our service October 6.

Frances Underwood, not being a good cook, Mrs Longe discharged her at Michaelmas, & hired Lydia Cobb as cook & to make pastry, preserves &c., at wages £14 14s. per annum. She entered our service November 3rd.

1821

26 March — Charles Spall quitted my service, having let himself to Revd. Thomas Reeve at Ipswich.[27] He behaved on the whole well during 3 years he was in my service, but having had some disagreement with Lord, my butler, he gave me warning.

Elizabeth Scolding quitted my service. She conducted herself well during the half year she lived here.

I placed Charles Offord, who has lived here 2 years as boy, into the footman's place on trial, & Henry Fenton succeeded him as servant boy, aged [*blank*]. (Charles Offord, wages £10 per annum.)

January 31 — Ann Fairs, housemaid, quitted our service on account of her not being comfortable with her fellow-servants. She alludes to Christopher, who is a bad temper.

Elizabeth Wade, daughter of the late Mark Wade of Gosbeck, succeeded her as housemaid, & entered our service <this day> February 2nd at wages 8 guineas per annum.

[*p.22.2*]

1820	<u>Wages to Michaelmas</u>	
	brought over	£ 74 6s. 3d.
December 26	Reuben Lord, ½ year to Michaelmas	£ 20 0s. 0d.
	J. Gowers, ditto	£ 10 0s. 0d.
	Charles Sporle, ditto	£ 6 0s. 0d.
	James Scoggin, 27 weeks at 7sh. to October 8	£ 9 9s. 0d.
	Elizabeth Christopher, ½ year to Michaelmas	£ 6 6s. 0d.
	Ann Fair, ditto	£ 4 14s. 6d.
	Mary Jessup, scullery girl, 9 weeks to Michaelmas at £3 per annum	£ 0 11s.10d.
<March 26	Charles Spall, wages for ½ year to Lady Day when he quitted my service £6 0s. 0d.> See 1821	
1821		
March 9	Ringrose, taylor, bill for 1820	£ 4 4s. 0d.
April 5	Butcher, Ipswich, bill for hats	£ 2 19s. 0d.
May 19	Reuben Lord wages, 1 quarter to Xtmas 1820	£ 10 0s. 0d.
1822 [*sic*]		
January 18	Richard Porter, draper, Ipswich, livery cloth	£ 19 17s. 6½d.
May 10	Charles Pritty, bill for fustian &c. & cloth for servant lad &c. in 1820	<u>£ 7 15s. 9½d.</u>
	Total 1820	<u>£176 3s. 11d.</u>
	deduct servants' liveries &c. £ 37 4s. 4d.	
	wages £138 19s. 7d.	

[27] Sporle now appears as the more usual spelling: Spall.

[*p.23.1*]

1821	Memorandums
Liveries –	coat buttons 1 & ½ dozen each coat waistcoats 10 small ditto each waistcoat 3 & ¼ yards of lace each coat
June18	Lydia Cobb, cook & housekeeper, quitted our service. A good cook, & honest servant, but not a good temper. She engaged herself as cook & housekeeper to Mrs Thomas Cocksedge, Bury.
June 24	Robert Taylor entered my service as butler, having been hired April 7th 1821 at £30 per annum wages, no perquisites. Aged 25 years. Lived first at Mr Skiller's, Golden Lion, Ipswich, next at Hon. Miss Morgan's, Roehampton as footman, then at Thomas Smith's esq. Berkley Street, Portman Square 1 year, which service he quitted on account of ill health. Mr Bellman satisfied me as to character & I resolved to make trial of him, although a younger man than I could have wished. Servants had great coats this year.
April 23	I had from Porter, ½ gross coat livery buttons at 48sh. per gross, & ½ gross ditto waistcoat at 24 sh. gross Reuben Lord, on my having some altercation with him, gave me warning twice – afterwards would have willingly continued, but being of a very irritable temper, and not so cleanly as he should be, although a very honest good servant in other respects, I discharged him, June 25.
June 18	Mary Feaveryear entered our service as cook & housekeeper (in place of Lydia Cobb). Wages 16 guineas per annum, no perquisites. Aged 32. We had a good character of her from Mr Borton's, Bury, where she lived last. Her friends live at Blighborough.

[*p.23.2*]

1821	Servants' wages	
February 1	Ann Fairs, housemaid, wages 3 months & 6 weeks wages to February 1 when she quitted our service	£ 3 11s. 0d.
March 26	Charles Spall, an half year's wages to Lady Day, when he quitted my service	£ 6 0s. 0d.
	Elizabeth Scolding, ditto to this day when she quitted	£ 6 6s. 0d.
June 25	Reuben Lord, an half year's wages due June 24th 1821, paid this day on his quitting my service. By cheque on Ipswich bank	£20 0s. 0d.
18	Lydia Cobb, wages for 3 quarters of a year to June 26, when she quitted our service	£11 0s. 0d.
November 5	John Gowers, ½ year to Lady Day last	£10 0s. 0d.
	Robert Taylor, butler, 1 quarter to Michaelmas	£ 7 10s. 0d.
	Charles Offord, ½ year to ditto at £10 per annum	£ 5 0s. 0d.
6	Elizabeth Christopher, ½ year to Lady Day	£ 6 6s. 0d.
	Elizabeth Wade, 7 weeks & 1 day to ditto	£ 1 1s.10¾d.
	Mary Jessup, ½ year to ditto	£ 1 10s. 0d.

	James Scoggin, 24 weeks to March 25 1821 at 7sh. per week		£ 8 8s. 0d.
(14 March 1823)	Porter, draper, bill for cloathing		£ 26 17s. 1½d.
	Ringrose, taylor, ditto	£ 5 8s. 0d.	
	Butcher, hatter, ditto	£ 2 19s. 0d.	
	Livery, lace & buttons	£ 2 10s.10½d	
May 7	Cockerill, shoes for servant lad		£ 2 1s. 0d.
July 29	Pritty, Cloathing for servants & apprentice girl		£ 7 19s. 5d.
	[*carry forward*]		£134 8s. 3¾d.

3 December 1821 – 31 December 1823

[*p.24.1*]
1821

December 3 Sarah Durrant entered our service as housekeeper & cook, at wages 16 guineas per annum, no perquisites. Lived last at Mrs J. Farr's, Beccles – 3 months – before at Mrs George Preston's Stanfield, from whom Mrs Longe had a good character.

Mrs Longe takes Mary Feaveryear, our late cook, as her own maid, and to have the care of the linen, at reduced wages 12 guineas per annum.

1822 January 16 She [*Sarah Durrant*] continued with us only 6 weeks, as we soon found her in every respect unequal to the place – a strange & half crazy woman – & discharged her.

May 20 Elizabeth Parish entered our service as cook, from Mr Page's Woodbridge. A quiet civil servant, but soon found the family too large and quitted us, 17 July – her wages were at 16 guineas per annum.

Mary Jessup quitted us to live with Mrs Robinson – a quiet good servant girl.

Mary Gaskin, a pauper from the House of Industry, who was allotted to me at Michaelmas last (1821), & whom we had put to Mrs Crickmay for board & instruction from that time, entered our service in January last <in Mary Jessup's place> & now supplies Mary Jessup's place.[28]

July 17 Ruth Margery, a widow aged 38 years, entered our service as cook and housekeeper, at wages 16 guineas per annum, no perquisites. Lived last 1 month at Revd. Mr Tweed's at Capel, [&] before this at Mrs Paul Smith's Ipswich, 3 months, from whom we had a good character.

---

[28] The child allotted to Longe from the house of industry. He boarded her with the gardener's wife before taking her into his household as scullery girl. See diary at 22 January 1826 for another example. About 1819 Longe transferred Crickmay's wages entry to Garden Accounts Book.

[*p.24.2*]

1821	Servants' wages to Michaelmas brought over	£134 8s. 3¾d.
December 3	Coach hire from Norwich for Sarah Durrant	0 9s. 0d.
1822		
January 16	Sarah Durrant, wages from December 3 1821 to January 16 1822, when she quitted	£ 3 6s. 0d.
	John Gowers, ½ year to Michaelmas 1821	£ 10 0s. 0d.
	James Scoggin, 27 weeks to September 29	£ 9 9s. 0d.
17	Mary Feaveryear, 1 quarter to Michaelmas & 1 week before Midsummer	£ 4 10s. 0d.
	Elizabeth Christopher, ½ year to ditto	£ 6 6s. 0d.
	Elizabeth Wade, ½ year to ditto	£ 4 4s. 0d.
	Mary Jessup, scullery girl to ditto	£ 1 10s. 0d.
		[29] £164 2s. 3¾d.

Cloathing	£ 47 15s. 5d.
Wages	£116 6s. 10d.

Wages to Lady Day &c. 1822

March 4	paid Robert Taylor, butler on account	£ 5 0s. 0d.
	Mary Feaveryear, 1 quarter at 16 guineas	£ 4 4s.
	& 1 quarter to Lady Day at 12 guineas per annum £3 3s.	£ 7 7s. 0d.
	<Sarah Durrant, cook & housekeeper about 6 weeks £2 2s.> (entered before: January 16)	
May 20	Mary Jessup, from Michaelmas 1821 to this day	£ 2 5s. 0d.
	Mrs Crickmay for her board & to [*illeg.*]	£ 2 2s. 0d.
July 17	Elizabeth Parish, cook, 2 months	£ 2 13s. 6d.
August 1	Robert Taylor, ½ year to Lady Day, balance due	£ 10 0s. 0d.
	John Gowers, ½ year to ditto	£ 10 0s. 0d.
	Charles Offord, ½ year to ditto	£ 5 0s. 0d.
	James Scoggin, 26 weeks to March 31 1822 at 7sh per week	£ 9 2s. 0d.
	[*carry forward*]	£ 53 9s. 6d.

[*p.25.1*]

1822	Servants' wages to Michaelmas, &c.	
	brought over	£ 53 9s. 6d.
Wages to Lady Day continued		
August 1	Elizabeth Christopher, ½ year to lady Day	£ 6 6s. 0d.
	Elizabeth Wade, ditto	£ 4 4s. 0d.
Wages to Michaelmas &c.		
December 2	Ruth Margery, 6 months to this day, when she quitted us	£ 8 8s. 0d.
4	Elizabeth Christopher, ditto, when she left us	£ 6 6s. 0d.
1823	Wages to Michaelmas 1822	
March 15	Robert Taylor, half year	£ 15 0s. 0d.

[29] This total should be £174 2s. 3¾d.

	John Gowers, ditto	£ 10 0s. 0d.
	Charles Offord, ditto	£ 5 0s. 0d.
	James Scoggin, 26 weeks to September 29 at 7sh.	£ 9 2s. 0d.
	Mary Feaveryear, half year	£ 6 6s. 0d.
	Elizabeth Wade, ditto	£ 4 4s. 0d.
March 14	Ringrose, Ipswich, taylor's bill for cloathing 1822	£ 4 4s. 0d.
	Butcher, Ipswich, hatter, ditto	£ 2 19s. 0d.
26	given Henry Fenton, servant lad, on quitting my service	£ 1 0s. 0d.
May 7	paid Cockerill, shoes for servant lad & 2 apprentice girls, bill for 1822	£ 4 18s.11d.
July 29	Pritty, bill for cloathing for servants in 1822	£ 7 0s.11d.
	ditto for ditto, my two apprentice girls, ditto	£ 2 9s. 9d.
December 27	Porter, Ipswich, livery cloth &c. in 1822	£ 18 19s. 9d.
	ditto, livery lace (March 27): 1 piece of 36 yards figured silk & worsted at 2s.4d. per yard	£ 4 4s. 0d.
31	[?] John James Scoggins' cooper's bill, pattens for 2 apprentice girls	0 2s. 8d.
	[30] £174 3s. 9d.	<£171 13s. 9d.>

[*p.25.2 – inside of back cover*]
1822

Elisabeth Shilcot, a pauper in the House of Industry, being allotted to me at Michaelmas, we took her into our service, October 12th, as a servant girl of all works.

December 5 Elizabeth Christopher, who has lived with us as my daughter Charlotte's maid, ever since March 18th 1813, quitted us [*deleted*] on my daughter's marriage, December 5th, to live with her in the same capacity. We always thought her an honest, respectable servant, but of a quick unpleasant temper.[31]

December 2 Mrs Longe discharged Ruth Margery, cook & housekeeper, at a minute's warning, having conducted herself extremely ill in many instances.

A woman of very violent temper.

December 3 Sarah Barrel, aged 31 years, whose friends live at North Lopham, came to us as cook. She lived last with Lady Charl. Cameron at Wortham.

Wages 14 guineas per annum, no perquisites, & a promise was given her by Mrs Longe of advancing her wages next year if she suited us.

Mrs Longe now considers Mary Feaveryear as housekeeper & lady's maid at 12 guineas per annum.[32]

30 This total should be £174 4s. 6d.

31 Within two months of her marriage Charlotte wrote to her father that this lady's maid had behaved badly towards her, once free of the paternal discipline.

32 This servant accepted, on transfer of duties, a reduction in wages from 16 to 12 guineas.

REFERENCES TO SERVANTS IN THE DIARIES

Paraphrased and with comment,
mostly excluding farm staff and contracted men.

1796

John and Sam completed stacking hay at Coddenham. (15 July)
Longe lent a guinea to the old gardener at Coddenham, who was ill. (25 Oct.)
Longe paid the servants (at Coddenham?) their half-year's wages. (29 Oct.)
Sam was ill at the same time as Longe, who sent for Mr Beck for both. (27 Dec.)

1798

On the death of her mother, Longe gave his maid-servant Molly leave to go to her father, probably in Norfolk. (11/12 Jan.)
Longe paid the legacies left by Nicholas Bacon to the servants: £170 5s. 6d. (12 Feb.)
Longe deposited in a bank money due to his cook/housekeeper Mary Kenny. (22 Feb.)

1826

Longe received £5, for taking into his household as scullery maid an apprentice girl, Mary Ann Goldsmith. The parish vestry paid this 'bounty' since the rates were relieved of maintenance for the child. She stayed until early 1830. (22 Jan.)
Alexander Meek and others worked on the approach to the house, 8 ft wide. (1 May)
Longe sent John Gowers, his coachman, to try to collect some rent. (22 July)
While Longe was away, he learnt from his son Henry that Meek, his gardener, had been negligent. (29 August) Longe discharged him, with a letter admitting him with his family into the house of industry. Longe purchased the fixtures in the gardener's cottage for the use of his successor, Robert Cowles, who started immediately. Longe sent his farm waggon for the new man's furniture. (11 Oct.)
Longe sent his coachman, John Gowers, with a letter to Dr Chevallier at Aspal. (7 Nov.)
Longe's pointer was killed in a snare in a local wood. There is no record of Scogging the gamekeeper being blamed. (27 Dec.)

1827

Longe sent his man-servant William with a packet of documents to Mr Josselyn, his land surveyor, (at Sproughton?). This may have been the groom/footman. (11 Jan.)
Robert Cowles, gardener (+ three men & a lad), worked on garden alterations. (11 March) Longe paid Robert Cowles 12 weeks wages to Lady Day: £10 16s. (30 March)
Kerridge, butler, given notice expiring at old Michaelmas for rudeness. (10 Sept.)
To assist Longe and his wife going to Norfolk by post-chaise, John Gowers was sent ahead with the coach-horses to Scole Inn. Longe would have hired horses for the first leg of the journey. (16 Sept.)
While in Norfolk, Longe met by appointment and engaged William Hales, butler, at £35 per annum, to start on 20 October. (17 Sept.)
John Gowers took Longe's son Robert in the gig to Woodbridge for shooting. (2 Oct.)

Longe discharged his butler Samuel Kerridge. His successor seems to have been still in post at Longe's death in 1834. (18 Oct.)

1831

Longe paid Mr Beck's apothecary bill (servants): £4 18s. 6d. (below). (11 April)
Longe paid servants wages for the half-year to Lady Day: £62 10s. 6d. (28 April)
Scoggins, the gamekeeper, needed replacement as parish constable when ill. (1 Aug.)
Longe's butler, Hales, was given leave to go to Norwich to see friends. (30 Sept.)
Longe's gardener was taken ill with cold and fever. (24 Oct.)
Longe sent John Gowers for his new low phaeton, built by Catt of Ipswich. (13 Dec.)

1833

John Read, the gardener (plus two day men), began moving the existing rockery to the vicarage terrace, also using some stones and flints fetched from Choppyngs Hill by William Cornish, Longe's farm bailiff. (26, 28 Jan.)
Longe paid the servants wages for the half year to Michaelmas: £63 6s. 6d. (14 Feb.)
Read, gardener, was laid up all week with cold and fever. (10 March)
Read suffered nocturnal damage in his cottage garden, owned by Longe. (25 May)
Longe paid the servants wages for the half year to Lady Day: £75 8s. 6d. (5 June)
Longe's servants Bennet (perhaps the housekeeper's husband) and Ann Brown were ill with scarlet fever. Longe postponed leaving on his holiday. (13 Sept.)
Longe discharged John Read, his gardener of five years, honest and quiet, but through old age indolent and slow. Next day James Hynard came to succeed him. (10 Oct.)
Two men were seen on Longe's land after game. Both were later convicted. (23 Oct.)

THE BILL OF MR E.B. BECK, APOTHECARY OF NEEDHAM MARKET, FOR TREATING LONGE'S SERVANTS, 1827–1830

[*Submitted to John Longe for his servants, 1827–30*]

HA24/50/19/4.8(2)

1827		
February 8	Servant lad pint mixture	5s. 0d.
10	Pint mixture repeated	5s. 0d.
	Six powders	2s. 6d.
	Draught	1s. 6d.
13	Pint mixture	5s. 0d.
	8 quinine powders	4s. 0d.

14	ditto	4s. 0d.
	Pint mixture repeated	5s. 0d.
	Fever mixture	2s. 6d.
16	ditto	2s. 6d.
17	Journey	3s. 6d.
	Mixture repeated	2s. 6d.
	Pint mixture repeated	5s. 0d.
12	quinine powders repeated	6s. 0d.
24	ditto	6s. 0d.
March 1	Six leeches	4s. 0d.
April 11	Kitchen maid- journey	3s. 6d.
	Examining the shoulder, &c.	2s. 6d.
12	Bathing liniment	1s. 6d.
1828		
February 23	Box of pills	2s. 6d.
	Pint mixture	5s. 0d.
28	Box of pills	2s. 6d.
March 6	Six leeches	4s. 0d.
13	Large box of pills	2s. 6d.
18	ditto	2s. 6d.
July 4	Housekeeper bolus	0s. 6d.
	Draught	1s. 6d.
	Box of pills	2s. 6d.
1830		
May 31	Housekeeper, paper of powder	1s. 6d.
		£4 18s. 6d.[33]

SERVANTS' WAGES, 1830–34

1830 [*½ years to Lady Day and to Michaelmas*]

HA24/50/19/4.5(21), loose note

William Hales	½ year	£18 10s. 0d.		£18 10s. 0d.
John Gowers	½ year	£10 0s. 0d.		£10 0s. 0d.
William Suttle	½ year	£ 7 0s. 0d.		£ 7 0s. 0d.
James Scoggins	25 weeks @ 7sh.	£ 8 5s. 0d.	27 weeks	£ 8 5s. 0d.
John Read	12 weeks @ 8sh.	£10 16s. 0d.		–
E. Bennett	½ year	£ 7 7s. 0d.		£ 7 7s. 0d.
Sarah Smith	½ year	£ 3 3s. 0d.		£ 3 3s. 0d.
Matilda Cornish	½ year	£ 1 11s. 6d.		£ 1 11s. 6d.
given May Ann Goldsmith		5s. 0d.		–
Ann Brown		–		£ 4 14s. 6d.
		(paid 26 April)		(paid 22 November)

[33] Mr Beck's other bill for the four years 1827–30 for John Longe and his family was £99 16s. 6d.

1833 ½ year to Michaelmas 1833

A24/50/19/4.8(2) loose note

William Hales, butler	£18 10s. 0d.	
William Suttle, footman & groom	£ 7 0s. 0d.	
John Gowers, coachman	£10 0s. 0d.	
James Scoggin 27 weeks @ 7sh.	£ 9 9s. 0d.	
E. Bennett, housekeeper	£ 7 17s. 6d.	
Ann Brown, housemaid	£ 4 4s. 0d.	
Sarah Smith, cook	£ 4 14s. 6d.	(paid 7 January 1834)

1834 Receipt 12 weeks wages to 6 January 1834 @ 18sh. per week	£10 16s. 0d.
& for carriage of his goods here 11 October 1833	£ 1 1s. 0d.

signed James Hynard *X his mark*

MOURNING WEAR

[*on the death of Mrs Charlotte Longe in 1812*]

HA24/50/19/4.8(2)

[*List of items certainly or probably for the servants, extracted from the bill of Mrs J. Smart, tailoress & dressmaker.*][34]

7 pairs of stockings for servants		£1 10s. 0d.
7 muslin caps	@ 9s. 6d.	£3 6s. 6d.
7 bonnets	15s. 0d.	£5 5s. 0d.
7 sarsnit handkerchiefs	14s. 6d.	£5 1s. 6d.
7 black muslin handkerchiefs	6s. 6d.	£2 5s. 6d.
58 yards fine bombazett	3s. 0d.	£8 14s. 0d.
making 7 gowns	4s. 6d.	£1 11s. 6d.
4 yards brown calico	2s. 0d.	8s. 0d.
11 yards ribbon	10d.	9s. 2d.
6½ yards lining	2s. 0d.	13s. 0d.
[*?*] galloon		5s. 6d.
tape, buttons, &c.	1s. 4d.	
37½ yards bombazett for coats	2s. 8d.	£5 0s. 0d.
making 7 coats	2s. 0d.	14s. 0d.

34 Mrs Smart's total bill to Longe including for family and friends was £105 9s. 3¾d.

INVENTORY OF CODDENHAM VICARAGE, *c.*1797

SRO(I) HA24/50/19/4.7(2)

The inventory, in John Longe's handwriting, relates only to the living quarters of the vicarage and is undated. One possible time for him to have made such an inventory was between the death of Nicholas Bacon (August 1796) and his own move into the vicarage in the following year. If that was so, the inventory covers mostly what Bacon bequeathed to the Longes, but also items to which others were entitled as heirlooms. Although he was not an executor, Longe was certainly in and out of the vicarage, which was looked after by some at least of Bacon's servants. Before moving in he would not perhaps have had access to the whole property, which might explain why the service quarters and servants' rooms were not listed. Bacon was a bachelor, and rooms later used for Longe's children may in 1796–7 have even been unfurnished. On the other hand, the bold heading 'My own bedchamber' suggests that Longe had already taken possession and moved in with his previously owned belongings. Somewhat later in 1797 seems the more likely date.

Longe's inventory was made in a small exercise-booklet in marbled covers, giving twenty sides of paper (each 16 x 10 centimetres). The pages are not numbered, but the booklet already in 1797 contained (on pages 6 to 10) in Nicholas Bacon's hand inventories of the plate and the contents of the stable (transcribed on p.221 below). Page 5 being blank, Longe's inventory is on pages 1 to 4, and 11 to 20. Longe seems to have started his listing on page 11, since he numbered the first three sections. In this transcript his likely order has been followed, with the page numbers of the booklet added on the right.

Three interesting comparisons are possible, though not here pursued. In an identical exercise-book in 1774, Nicholas Bacon also made an inventory, but only of the humbler contents of his newly completed vicarage: SRO(I) HA24/50/19/4.7(1). On Longe's death in 1834 there was a transaction between his son Robert and his widow Frances, referred to at Appendix F below (p.242 at note 1). Then, on the death of Longe's son Robert in 1890, a sale catalogue was compiled of the contents of the vicarage, and some of the items are clearly those which his father had acquired under his benefactor's will in 1796: SRO(I) HA24/50/19/4.7(4). (Also Appendix F.)

In 1993, under the title 'Raphael's Seven, Bings of Port Five', a transcript of Longe's exercise-book was made by a palaeography group from Suffolk College (under UEA) led by John Ridgard. There is a copy at SRO(I) under reference qs 92 LON. This has been used as a resource for doubtful readings and was valuable in view of the cramped nature of the original writing.

The present transcribing convention has been to itemise, although the original runs consecutively, to eliminate capital letters except at the start of each line, to use no full-stops, and not to italicise the names of pictures. The initials NB, where the context admits, indicate Nicholas Bacon. The word 'No' was probably a later insertion, for example to indicate that an item was missing on a later inspection. One may guess, though less confidently, that the initials 'NP' indicate absence on a further inspection. Such absent items probably include heirlooms despatched to Bacon's maternal relatives at Moor Park, Farnham.

Unfamiliar words have been noted in the Glossary, and other information given in footnotes.

No.1 Entrance Vestibule [*p.11*]

One shoe mat, one ditto, hairbrush scraper screwed down to the floor
One globe lanthorn <*over*> hanging from the arch
One square lanthorn over the door leading to the back stairs
One barometer, thermometer & hygrometer in one frame, [*by*] Moore Ipswich
One shoe <*scraper*> mat, and one hair brush scraper at the back door of the vestibule leading to the garden. One copper coal scuttle
A pair of very large mahogany dining tables. One ditto smaller corners cut off
One ditto, 2 leaved, 2 drawers in front
A painted floor cloth. Two pieces of ditto
15 thick painted floor cloth step covers. 1 piece on the landing

Staircase

One hexagon glass lanthorn, gilt brass frame, with a lamp of 3 lights on a treble chain within it, the whole hanging from the ceiling by a large gilt brass chain.

Upper Vestibule

One painted floor cloth
One mahogany settee, with 3 cushions & 2 pillows
3 large armed chairs stuffed with horse-hair covered with green Norwich damask
One mahogany pembroke table

No.2 Library Stucco painted light green [*p.12*]

1 bright bath stove & fender, poker, shovel & tongs to ditto, moveable iron cheeks, hearth-brush
2 (very large) mahogany book-cases with glass doors at top & whole mahogany doors at bottom, one on each side of the chimney
One smaller ditto, [*with*] glass doors at top & whole mahogany doors at bottom, divided into three parts
One large mahogany escritoire & book-case, [*with*] glass doors to the latter
One mahogany library [*blank*] covered with green cloth with drawers etc. for papers.
One mahogany library stool with steps, covered with black Spanish leather & gilt nails
6 mahogany chairs covered with the same leather etc. & nails
Mahogany close-stool chair, black stove bottom, [*&*] pan to ditto
One high mahogany desk table, with escritoire
Drawers. One high pear-tree desk
One round mahogany eating-table
One square mahogany pembroke table, with 2 leaves
One mahogany dressing-stand with drawer for shaving things

Library (continued) [*p.13*]

1 pair high mahogany steps
one small oak reading desk
1 case of bottles, painted deal
a large camera obscura
one wainscot tool-box
One mahogany tea-chest. Walnut-tree cannisters
one horse, for airing linnen

(over the smaller mahogany book-case)
One pair of globes
1 wedgwood bust of Lord Bacon
2 bronze figures of centaurs and women
(over the escrutoire) [*sic*]
Dr Priestly's apparatus for making miniral [*sic*] waters
Three green Norwich damask window curtains
Three green sun-blinds, with tops & strings to ditto
Pictures (over the chimney)
Mr. Gardemau by Old Richardson
2 pieces of wild beasts in marble, inlaid. N.P.
2 copper plates & Roman Sacrifice N.P.
Spanish Armada in water colours N.P.
Woman & boy with globe etc. in ditto N.P.
Holy Family in ditto N.P.
<*late*> George 2nd, late Prince & Princess of Wales, a Cleopatra, and Ann of Austria & her son Louis 14 in wax N.P.
A head painted by Elmer of Farnham N.P.
(over the high mahogany desk-table)
Lady Catherine Gardemau
(over the door)
A drawing in black & white by [*blank*] Kent
(over the smaller book case)
A ditto
One 8-day clock in a black case with brass ornaments, [*by*] More of Ipswich, on a black-stained brackett
2 mahogany clothes brushes. Hat ditto with a plush cushion
Brass mortice lock on the door, with key

[*p.14*]

No.3 Comon [*sic*] Parlour paper'd & painted blue in water colours
One bright stove & fender, poker, shovel & tongs to ditto, moveable iron cheeks, hearth-brush
2 blue moreen window curtains
two green sun-blinds
2 large fixed mahogany cupboards, one of them fitted as a beuffet, the other a book-case
One black & gold high polished marble sideboard, and a mahogany carved frame. One printed leather cover to ditto
One pair of mahogany card-tables
One pillar tea table with a raised border of open work, gothick pattern
2 armed chairs & 6 chairs virginia walnut, one with black horse-hair bottoms
One pair of back-gamon tables
(between the windows)
an oval looking glass in a burnished silk frame
(chimney piece)
One old Delft pepper box. No.
Ivory Madonna N.P. No.
One pair of blue & white old china small jars & covers No.
1 pair of ditto beakers & covers with brass gilt edges; Welsh taylor & wife No.
French horn & lutenists No.

1 pair of Derby china girandoles No.
Two small ivory busts N.P.
Brass & marble clock & key
Pictures. Drawings, Prints etc.
(over the chimney)
A portrait supposed [to be] of Henrietta Maria of France, in a black ebony frame
Drawing of the Resurrection by [*?*]Passagnano in a black & gilt frame
Lord Sandwich & his lady in water colours by Singleton
Oliver Cromwell in ditto by Turner
A goldfinch in tambour-work by Mrs Edgar, a present from her
Cornerwise, cut in vellum, by Miss Rivett (now Mrs Shepherd) a present from her

[*p.15*]

Print of Sir Nicholas Bacon, Lord Keeper, in gilt frame
Two ovals of Wedgwood's composition: viz. Marriage procession of Cupid & Psyche, & Oedipus doing penance at the temple of the Furies, in black frames, one each side of the chimney
A lanscape in copper gilt frames
Over the black and gold marble side-board table
The *Royal James* in which Edward, Earl of Sandwich, was blown up in 1672, a copy from a very fine picture of Vandervelde in the possession of Anthony Deane Esquire at Whittington in Staffordshire, [in] gilt frame
2 landscapes in copper & gilt frames
A drawing in pencil by Miss Isted of [*?*]Eaton Northam, a present from her
Ditto in water colour by Miss Susan Edgar, a present from her.
All these in gilt burnished frames
a head of our Saviour in Wedgwood composition black frame
(on the opposite side of the room)
2 landscapes in copper gilt frames
(over the door)
a landscape, copy from an Italian [*illeg.*] in a burnished gilt frame
(next the door)
a picture of our Saviour in copper black frame
(on the tea table)
6 finest nanken cups & saucers, a tea-pot, sugar basin, saucer & cover, slop basin, one larger slop basin, 6 blue & white coffee cups, a brown china cream pot
a sea piece by P. Monamy bought of Warden, price 18 guineas

[*p.16*]

Housekeeper's Room
1 Bath stove with unpolished bars, 1 open work fender, poker, shovel & tongs to ditto, 1 pair of bellows
1 brass plate lock to the entrance door, key to ditto
1 Iron plate lock to the bathroom door, key to ditto
1 wainscot bureau, 3 keys to ditto
1 walnut-tree looking-glass, with one drawer
1 mahogany press
Bed, red & white check furniture
1 feather bed, 1 bolster, 1 pillow, 3 blankets, 1 painted cotton quilt

1 chestnut-tree china & linnen cupboard. 1 large Indian chest
1 round chestnut-tree dining table
1 mahogany close stool chair, pan to ditto
1 large oval mahogany brass hooped tea tray, 1 smaller long square worked bordered ditto, 1 large plain round ditto, 1 smaller round ditto, 1 small ditto for the dutch tea kettle
1 old needlework octagon fire screen
3 glass chamber lamps

[*p.17*]

Great Eating Parlour with a Bow Window stucco painted yellow
3 large yellow Macer dish window curtains
One bright moveable iron grate, open work fender, poker, shovel & tongs to ditto, hearth brush
One painted floor cloth covers the whole floor
One large mahogany side-board table with a drawer, one each side & drawer under
One fan-shaped cellar lined with lead for liquors and for a chamber pot (placed in the corner of the entrance)
18 Virginia walnut-tree chairs, [*with*] horse-hair bottoms, covered with yellow & white striped check.
One carpet for the marble slab
(on the chimney piece)
One large covered jar of the lava of Visuvius
1 pair of ditto screwed covers
1 pair of coffee cups
1 round cup NP No
2 yellow-ware flower potts & pans, scallop'd edge. 1 pair of ditto beakers
(on the sideboard table)
A pair of mahogany knife cases, silver rings & scutcheons each containing 12 green handled knives & forks
2 French [*illeg.*]
picture brushers

Pictures
2 mahogany brackets with gilt wire flower baskets one each side of the great picture of the death of Abel
A japannned iron bottled cistern
Brass mortice lock & key

[*p.18*]

Great Eating Parlour (continued) Pictures
(over the chimney piece)
A Landscape by Gainsborough
(right-hand of chimney)
The Virgin by Sassafirrata
Holy Family by Stella, on black marble
(on left-hand of the chimney)
The city of Lyons paying divine honors to Harry 4th of France & his queen, by Rubens
Angel appearing to the shepherds, by Jac. Bassan, on black marble

(opposite the windows)
The Transfiguration, of Raphael, copy'd by Carlo Maratti
On the right hand side of this, Edward, first earl of Sandwich, [*a*] copy from an original of Sir Peter Lely in the possession of the Revd. John Bacon of Shrubland Park by [*?*]W.Withrorli.
On the left hand of it, Lord Bacon from a very fine original of
Cornelius Jansen also in the possession of the Revd. J. Bacon by [*?*]W.Withrorli
(over the door)
A fruit piece with a jay, by Jones of Bath
(opposite the chimney)
The death of Abel by Francis Floris

[*p.19*]

Drawing Room Indian paper, gilt paper-mache border
A Biddy patent stove, fender, poker, shovel & tongs
3 striped silk curtains
Settee
10 chairs and 3 windows stools painted green & white, catherine-wheel pattern, horse-hair bottoms covered with the same silk as the curtains, and over that a Manchester green & white striped stuff
A pair of looking girandoles [with] gilt burnished frames (opposite the chimney)
An India paper screen, mahogany pillar & frame
A Wilton carpet over the whole room. Green bays cover to ditto
2 flowers stands between the window[*s*]
2 flower gilt-wire baskets painted tin, insides painted as the settee, chairs & stools
A pair Worcester china blue & gold small jars
(on the right side of the chimney)
A long square open-work mahogany tea table, with 12 coloured china teacups,
10 saucers, 9 coffee cups & 10 saucers, slop basin, sugar dish No.
Large <brown> <deleted> coloured china tea pot, with red pattern No.
1 mahogany tea kettle stand
(on the left hand of the chimney)
A fine old japanned card table, with printed leather cover
A pair of old japan Indian fire screens
(on the chimney piece)
1 pair of very large blue & white china bowls No.
1 pair of blue & white china basins No.
1 pair of coloured finest old china figures of [*?*]Bongees No.
A castle in bones made by the French prisoners at Porchester Castle
Brass mortice lock & key to the door

[*p.20*]

Bed Chamber over the Comon Parlor [*Blue*] & white paper
One bright stove, whole fender, poker, shovel & tongs to ditto
One mortice lock & key to the door
One walnut bureau & escrutoire with looking glass doors –
A mahogany chest of drawers (between the windows)
(upon it) an oval dressing table looking glass with painted frame
(over it) a large looking glass, with gilt corners

A mahogany night table & pan
A mahogany washing stand with china bottle & basin,
2 green painted sun-blinds
2 large window curtains, same cotton as the bed
1 large mahogany bedstead with <*mahogany*> posts <*& frame*>
Blue & white check cotton furniture, with peacocks, &c.
In the <*furniture*> pattern a red carpet
1 Manchester cotton counterpane, 3 blankets, 1 hair mattress, 1 down ditto, 1 feather bed, 1 bolster, 2 pillows
1 large armed easy chair, green damask covered with green & white check
1 armed chair, & 4 small painted wood [*chairs*], with cushions covered with the same cotton as the bed

(over the chimney piece)
1 Delft coffee pot
1 pair of fine blue & white china bottles. 1 pair of finest ditto coffee cups
1 pair of English china jars

(over the chimney)
A drawing by J. Baldry

[*p.1*]

My own Bedchamber Red & white check paper
One bright stove & fender, 1 brass plate lock, key to ditto
One mahogany bedstead with plain <*pillars*> posts
Red & white check furniture
1 painted cotton quilt, 1 feather bed, 1 bolster, 2 pillows
1 pair of red check window curtains
1 mahogany table
A small red carpet
1 large mahogany plate cupboard, with the Bacon arms on one door & the Mountague & Gardemau on the other, [&] Bacon crest in the pediments
1 washing-stand with china basin to ditto
1 pear-tree dressing table
1 uncut glass dish and beaker, [&] (over it) a glass in a white painted frame
1 small stand looking-glass (on the side of the chimney)
One large easy armed chair stuffed with a cushion to ditto, & covered with the same check as the bed
One large armed chair, mahogany frame, stuffed & covered with a green & white check

(over the chimney)
1 gun, S. Bacon maker
2 brass mounted blunder busses, Jover maker
2 pair of horse pistols, brass mounted, with the Bacon crest on the stock plate, same maker
2 pair of very neat pocket pistols, with cypher NB & Bacon crest in silver, same maker
Powder flask & bullet <*shot*> bag, on a blue string to the horse pistols
1 small ditto covered with red morocco leather for the pocket pistols
1 shot belt, 1 cleaning rod in a leather case, 1 dog whip

My own bedchamber (over the chimney) (continued) [*p.2*]
2 very neat polished steel hilted swords
1 pair of green ivory & carved silver hilted hangers

Prints, Drawings etc.
(over the chimney)
A large print of St Cecilia in a black & gilt frame & glazed
The new building of Emmanuel College, Cambridge, plain mahogany frame & glazed
(round the room)
8 prints of the life, death, &c. of King Charles 1st, black frames & glazed
(left side of the bed)
King William 3rd
(right-hand side of ditto)
Queen Mary
(under these) 7 of Raphael's cartoons, black frames not glazed
(next the window)
Sir William Temple, black frame & glazed
Lord Bacon, black and glazed
Pierre Fr. le [?]Courayer, black & gilt frame & glazed NP
(left side of the bed)
A flower piece in water colours, black gilt frame & glazed NP
(on the right of ditto)
A Farm-yard in water colours, black & gilt frame & glazed NP
(left side of the chimney)
Pedigree genealogical table of the Royal Family of Great Britain, black & gilt framed & glazed
(on the chimney piece)
A glass small hand lanthorn, a shagreen case, a pair of money scales & weights
A pillar money scale

[p.3]

Bedchamber over Library Papered with colored running-pattern paper
1 bright bath stove & fender, poker, shovel & tongs. 1 pair bellows
1 brass mortice lock to the entrance door, key to ditto
1 brass mortice spring to the dressing-room door
1 mahogany dressing-table with drawer
1 mahogany night table & close-stool pan
1 mahogany escrutoire & book-case
1 dark brown vase with red pattern on the pediment of ditto
1 model of a house in mahogany frame, glazed.
NB. This was the work of Miss Catherine Bacon
1 large mahogany bedstead with fluted posts, coloured cotton furniture
1 hair mattress, 1 down ditto, 1 feather bed, 1 bolster, 2 pillows
1 quilt, same cotton as the bed
1 bed carpet
1 pair of window curtains, same cotton as the bed
1 gilt looking-glass frame, glass broke
1 washing stand
(over the chimney)
Picture of a lady (gift of Mr Bolton)
1 large easy chair green damask, and with green & white check cover
1 armed chair and 4 small ditto, painted wood with cushion covered with the same cotton as the bed

(on the chimney piece) [*p.4*]

1 fine old china salver without a foot, much green in the pattern
4 green fine old china scalloped small plates
1 pair of coloured ditto, 1 pair of ditto
1 very fine belly'd colored china basin, 1 finest ditto
1 finest colored [*?*]Birrnit in pint ditto
1 pair of fine old colored china small basins & covers. A single ditto
1 pair of enamelled candlesticks
1 Derby china figure of Sir J. Falstaff

Pink Dressing Room yellow ground

1 Wilton carpet over the whole floor. 1 green bays cover to ditto
1 chintz window curtain lined with a Devonshire brown Indian sarsinet lining
1 deal <dressing> side-table
1 Indian painted gause toilette furniture. 1 flowered muslin laced ditto
1 oval looking glass, painted frame
1 large Indian japan cabinet on black & gold frame
1 inlaid table with a drawer
1 set of japan dressing boxes
1 finest Delft bowl & cover
2 Wedgwood small busts: of Anthony & Cleopatra

INVENTORY OF PLATE

SRO(I) HA 24/50/19/4.7(1)

It is likely that this 1774 inventory of plate was taken by Nicholas Bacon (then aged forty-two) when setting himself up in the newly erected Coddenham vicarage which Parson Woodforde described when visiting him there in May 1775 as 'lately built'. The fact that Longe kept the inventory suggests that it remained a reliable record when he succeeded Nicholas Bacon some twenty-two years later. It is neatly written at pages 7 to 10 of the exercise-booklet described in the introductory note to Longe's inventory (p.210 above).

May 19th 1774

2 hand waiters	18oz. 8dw. at 7s.5d. per oz., engraving 7s.6d.	£7 3s. 6d.
Turenne ladle	9oz. at 8s.8d. per oz., engraving 6d.	£3 18s. 6d.
2 black shagreen cases with 12 white china-handled knives & forks with silver ferrils & 12 table spoons in each		
1 pair of large silver candle- sticks with nozzles NB: These were a present from my Aunt Mrs Temple of More Park in Surry	54oz. 15dw.	
1 pair ditto, the same pattern		
A pair of steel snuffers with silver bows		18s. 0d.
A black fish-skin case with 12 silver knives & forks & spoons		
A pair of sauce ladles & a pair of marrow scoops		£1 0s. 0d.
A chased coffee pot		£7 0s. 0d.
A waiter <*& milk ewer*>	21oz. 5dw. at 5s.6d. per oz.	£5 16s. 4½d.
A chased bread basket	46oz. 10dw. at 7s.6d. per oz.	£17 07s. 9d.
4 ragout spoons	12oz. 2 dw. at 5s.7d., making engraving 16s.2d.	£4 05s. 0d.
pillar candlestick	6oz. 10dw. at 5s.7d., making engraving £1 9s.6d.	£3 05s. 0d.
12 coffee spoons	8oz. 1dw. at 5s.7d. making engraving 18s.	£3 02s.11d.
3 labels:	madeira, port and white wine	
2 ditto	sherry and calcaveela	
A black shagreen case with 12 tea spoons, tea tongs and strainer NB. these were a present from my sister Catherine Bacon, September 3rd 1764		£4 02s. 9d.
A very large silver waiter NB. This was the piece of plate that is given annually by Emmanuel College in Cambridge to the best proficient that takes his Batchelor of Arts degree in that college. 6 pound is allowed by the college and I added £12		£18 00s. 0d.
A punch ladle with a whale-bone handle		

4 salt spoons
A silver funnel £1 11s. 6d.
2 silver cork tops marked port and white wine

July the 3rd 1774

A pair of hand candlesticks with silver nozzles and extinguishers and steel snuffers, each engraved with the letters NB in French cipher
weight of one [*blank*]
of the other [*blank*]
of both [*blank*] £ 8 14s. 0d.

1 Fish trowel
1 French plate cross, for the middle dish
1 lignum vitae cruet frame with glass cruets & silver furniture
2 large mahogany knife cases with 18 knives & forks in each: green ivory handles
1 black shagreen case with 12 dozen small knives and forks
4 silver bottle stands
A neat plain beaded silver urn 93oz. 15dw. at 8s. per oz £37 10s.0d.
Heater and wainscot case 1 6s. 0d.
Arms engrav'd 6s. 6d. £39 2s. 6d.
4 silver salt spoons NB engr. in French cypher 0 18s. 0d.
1 silver argyle with the crest a boar passant ermined
weight 6oz. 17dw.
1 small plain silver coffee pot with a cypher WEG, and the inscription
G. Cadby Nicholas Bacon amicitiae ergo
weight [*blank*][1]
1 openwork silver sugar vase, with a blue glass to it
1 ditto cream vase with a ladle & blue glass to it

October 19th 1780

A large tea table waiter	118 oz. 102dw. at 7s: 7½d. per oz.		£45 0s. 0d.
	engraving ditto		– 18s. 0d.
A silver snuffer stand	3 oz 14 dw.	£2 2s. 0d.	
	engraving crest & cypher	0 3s. 6d.	
			£2 5s. 6d.

[1] Disappointingly, there is no 'G. Cadby' entry in Venn, *Alumni Cantabridgienses*.

INVENTORY OF CONTENTS OF THE STABLE

SRO(I) HA24/50/19/4.7(2)

It is likely that this 1775 inventory of the contents of the stable was taken by Nicholas Bacon (then aged forty-two) soon after setting himself up in the newly erected Coddenham vicarage. The fact that Longe kept it suggests that it remained a reliable record when he succeeded Nicholas Bacon there some twenty-two years later. It is neatly written at page 6 of the exercise-booklet described in the introductory note to Longe's inventory (p.210 above).

November the 7th 1775

1 pair of post-chaise harness. 1 saddle & saddle-cloth to ditto
1 pair of bridles
3 false collars
1 set of single chaise harness. 1 saddle, saddle-cloth & bridle to ditto
3 riding saddles
2 pony saddles
saddle cloth
Surcingle & 2 Bridles
1 bit & [*?*]bradson bridle, black leather furniture
1 best London bit ditto, same furniture
1 best snaffle ditto, same furniture
1 [*?*]curb double reined ditto
1 first bitting ditto
1 second ditto
2 chaise-horse watering ditto
3 chaise-horse clothes, 2 rowlers, 1 old rowler
1 leather saddle-cover surcingle
2 chaise-horse surcingles
2 pair of blinders
4 Whitney horse-clothes
1 tin oil-kettle & brush
1 cloathes brush. 1 hard ditto
1 male pillion
6 padlocks & keys
2 stable pails
6 halters
1 corn-sieve. 2 ditto baskets
3 stable forks
Sacks

CELLAR RECORDS, 1800, 1811

SRO(I) HA24/50/19/4.7(3)

The original material comprises a few sheets in John Longe's handwriting. In 1800, Longe had become settled into his new way of life. It may be significant that 1811 was the year that Longe began his Servants' Wages Book.

In 1993, under the title 'Raphael's Seven, Bings of Port Five', a transcript was made by a palaeography group from Suffolk College (under UEA) led by John Ridgard. SRO(I)qs 92 LON.

State of the Cellar in 1800

BINGS	No.1	8 dozen sherrey from London bottled 1797
	No.3	Port Bottled in April 1795, 3 dozen
	No.4	Old Madeira 4 dozen <& Port, April 1795>
	No.6	Sherrey bottled 1789, 2 bottles
	No.10	Sherrey bottled May 1797, 10 dozen
	Nos. 11,12,13 <14>	Port bottled December 1797, full
	No 14	Port ditto, 1797, in use, about 8 dozen remain
in letter	A	Gineava
	B	Old Hock 1 dozen and 8 bottles
	C	White Brandy, 8 bottles
	D	Calcavala 1 dozen & 9 bottles
	E	Cowslip
	F is	Cowslip
	L	Tenerife, 8 bottles
	M	Cyder
	N is	Cyder
	O	Brandy & odd bottles of spirit
	Right Hand Shelf	Rum & Madeira from Mr Hollands.
	Left Hand Shelf	Perry & sherrey from Norwich
	Middle Shelf	Dry Cyder, Mr Bird's, & 2 bottles orange

1811

May 3 Received from Messrs Page an hogshead of sherry procured by him from Mr Thomas Morgan:

	67 gallons	£64 8s. 6d.
	cash, &c., &c.	3 10s. 0d.
Total expence		£67 18s. 6d.

Memorandum: this wine was procured by William Higgins from Mr Thomas Morgan & Co., no. 13 Savage Geardens, Tower Hill, with whom Higgins tells me he has made an arrangement to be permitted to have the choice of his stock for his own customers. See his letter dated 16 Apr.1811.

May 15 I bottled the above sherry, which filled 26 dozen bottles, & 2 ditto rather thick. Placed it on the platform over cells A, B, C & D on the left, & on the platform over cells H, I, K & L on the right, & the remainder in cell C.

Given Allen & John Gowers a bottle each for bottling.

Sept. 2 dozen of Studd's porter bottled.

Oct. 4 dozen old beer brewed in Oct. 1810, ditto.

Consumption 1811 Port: 13 dozen & 8 bottles Sherry: 7 dozen & 9 ditto.[1]

---

1 There is also, in tabulated form, a detailed wine-consumed record for 1811 with dated entries from 1 Jan. to 28 Dec. at approximately fortnightly intervals, showing how the above totals of consumption of port (164 bottles) and sherry (93) were made up. Nine bottles of the port are (on four occasions) noted as 'of 1790'. There are three additional columns: Madeira (7), [?]Chamus (2), Teneriffe (2), and notes of [?]Consta. (1) and Malmocy (1). Longe also occasionally gave his butler a bottle, a total of nine in the year. Until 31 March this was Barrell, and from 4 May, Allen.

WILL AND ESTATE ACCOUNT

Summary of 1834 documents: John Longe's will, residuary estate account and Bacon Trust assets

SRO(I) HA24/50/19/4.1(3) & 4.1(4)

On 4 December 1833 John Longe invited his friend and attorney James Wenn to breakfast at Coddenham vicarage to assist him in preparing a final disposition of his property by will. That will, summarised below, is brief and clear. In addition to the obvious issues and the property Longe owned absolutely, they considered the financial implications of his death. Longe had been beneficiary for life of substantial trust property, which would pass according to the original terms. By contrast with what he had enjoyed in his lifetime, the property within his power to dispose was surprisingly little, as appears from the account transcribed below. The land and church property alone of the Bacon trust was valued at over five times the net personal estate disposed by Longe's own will. In addition there were cash investments in that and other smaller trusts.

One might suppose that Longe's prime concern was his wife Frances, aged sixty, since she had no right to remain at the vicarage on his death, and no part in any of the earlier trusts, for they all pre-dated his second marriage. Although they had been married for sixteen years, it was intended that she should make her home back in Norfolk among her kinsfolk, from where she had come as a spinster in 1817. In the event, she was to live to the age of ninety. One must admit to an inability to understand the thinking that lay behind the seemingly modest provision Longe made for her. The largest asset in Longe's 'free' estate was a holding in securities which passed to him under his father's will. This he regarded himself as duty bound to leave to his younger brother for life. In the event, Longe's widow Frances was not to draw the income from this holding for another twelve years. The net residual estate passing to his widow and the two younger sons comprised goods valued at a mere £1,742 2s. 3d., and no cash.

SUMMARY (not a transcript) of John Longe's Will

Attached to the sealed Probate, the original will in professional script fills one side of a parchment measuring about 75cm x 60cm. It was proved on 17 April 1834 in the Prerogative Court of Canterbury.

Executors: his 3 sons
£2,850 17s. 2d. in 3½ per cent annuities to his brother Robert for life and then to his wife Frances and then to his sons Robert and Henry equally.
A choice of his household goods to his wife Frances.
The residue of his household goods except plate to his son Robert.
The residue of his plate to his sons Robert and Henry equally.

Two shares in Wheal Anna Maria Copper Mine (Cornwall): one to his son Robert and one to Robert's son John at age 21.
£100, one-half for the resident poor of Coddenham, one-half for the resident poor of Crowfield.
To each servant one year's wages.
All farming live and deadstock to his son Robert.
All the residue of his personal property to his wife Frances.

Signed John Longe, *in the presence of* Charles Crowe *and* James Wenn

ESTATE ACCOUNT

The figures below are the manuscript figures inserted in a duplicate form, as issued by the Stamp Office at the time the will was proved (Register RM. No.1 1834 f.120). *It is a Residuary Account, which is endorsed as bearing nil duty, but the figures exclude the legacies in the will to the poor and to the servants, which were potentially liable for Legacy Duty.*

The words given below are part of the printed form (except a manuscript entry for the mining shares). One column on the form is for Money received and Property converted into Money*; another is for* Value of Property not converted into Money *(the latter items here marked 'v').*

Cash in the house		£ 905 5s. 11d.	
Cash at the bankers		2,193 13s. 4d.	
Furniture, Plate, Linen, China, Books, Pictures, Wearing Apparel, Jewels and Ornaments	[*v*]	1,407 2s. 0d.	
Wine and Liquors	[*v*]	191 5s. 0d.	
Horses and carriages, and other farming stock and Instruments of Husbandry	[*v*]	652 11s. 0d.	
Rents due at the death of the Deceased		179 16s. 1½d.	
New 3½ per cent stock	[*v*]	2,850 17s. 2d.	
Value of two shares in the Wheal Anna Maria Copper Mine	[*v*]	6 0s. 0d.	
[*Gross assets other than legacies liable for duty*]			£8,386 10s. 6½d.
Payments			
Probate or Administration		£180 8s. 0d.	
Funeral Expenses		272 4s. 5½d.	
Expenses attending Executorship		20 0s. 0d.	
Debts on simple Contract, Rent and Taxes, Wages, &c. due at the death of the Deceased per Schedule annexed [*none*]		1,128 10s. 6d.	
Pecuniary legacies per Account annexed [*none survives*]		1,470 18s. 2d.	
Delapidations of Vicarage House & Premises in Coddenham		721 10s. 0d.	
Total payments			£3,793 11s. 1½d.
Net amount of property [*gross less payments*]			4,592 19s. 5d.
Payment on Account of annuities (*stock*)			2,850 17s. 2d.
Net residue			1,742 2s. 3d.

The Bacon Trust

The assets were considerable. By professional valuation, excluding liquid investments ('money in the funds'), approximately 60 per cent of the Bacon trust comprised some 460 acres of farms in and around Coddenham. A further 28 per cent was represented by the access to income implicit in the Coddenham advowson and (more speculatively) 12 per cent by the Barham advowson.

All the trust assets would pass on Longe's death to the four children of his first marriage, who were thus well provided for in addition to their existing circumstances. Longe had grandchildren only through Robert at that stage. The father-in-law of Charlotte (aged thirty-seven), wife of army officer Martin Leake, had on his death set the couple up at Woodhurst, Oxted, Surrey. For his second surviving child, also named John (aged thirty-three), the diarist had earlier taken strenuous action to preserve ownership of the family estate at Spixworth, Norfolk, although it had been much reduced by the family predecessors. John was separated from his wife. The next son, Robert (aged thirty-two), was being groomed to succeed to the vicarage at Coddenham, to which he would move with his wife and four young children. In 1826 the annual net income there (after property maintenance, tithe-collecting expense and a curate's stipend) was £558 5s. It was planned that Longe's youngest son Henry (aged twenty-nine), as yet unmarried, should follow the Revd William Kirby as incumbent at neighbouring Barham. In the event that intention was frustrated by Kirby's survival until 1850.

As appears from the diary, Longe did not, or was not allowed to, ignore the financial implications of his own death. Knowing that it was inappropriate for the four children to hold these assets jointly *on his death, as they would by operation of law, he began to consider partition as early as 1826. Through Mr Wenn, he instructed counsel (one Mr William Morgan) to value the advowsons. By 1828 he was planning a possible partition between the four of the next generation, the interests of Charlotte being represented by her husband. That was also the neatest way of securing succession to the Coddenham vicarage for Robert, and the prospect of the smaller living for Henry. As well as dividing the cash in the trusts, this was the course they themselves later took, with cash equalising payments.*

There are at least six surviving documents over the period 1826 to 1836. Unfortunately, the final outcome is unclear, since the acreages, values and disposals all vary, but the likeliest result is as follows.

	Acreage	Professional Valuation	
Bolton's or Chapman's farm	250 3 32	£10,212	Major Leake
Fenn's farm	141 1 22	5,325	Robert
Malthouse & other	8 1 24	665	John
Hemingstone farm	67 2 32	2,660	Henry
Total land for partition	468a 1r 30p	£18,862	
Add Advowsons (Mr Morgan's Valuation)			
Coddenham		£8,330	Robert
Barham		3,696	Henry
Total for partition		£30,888	

This total value, plus both money 'in the funds', and the proceeds of minor property sold, was to be divided by four, with timber to be paid for in addition, and equalising cash payments made. Robert had a substantial equalising balance to pay, and may well have been looking to make that investment since his future was assured at the vicarage. John may well have been in need of a substantial equaliser in cash. The other two men were involved in smaller balancing figures.

John Longe signed the will six weeks later, on 14 January 1834, in the presence of Mr Wenn and his Coddenham neighbour. He died some seven weeks after that.

APPENDIX A

Extract from the 1851 Census of Religious Worship[1]

Before 1851 the only official figures of attendance numbers at church services and the taking of Holy Communion ('the sacrament') were in the returns made prior to the episcopal visitations, theoretically every three years. John Longe's diary notes are useful to supplement those for Coddenham and Crowfield.

Although seventeen years elapsed between the death of Longe and the 1851 census of religious worship in the time of his son Robert, the census figures are of value for present purposes, showing for example the extensive progress of Dissent in John Longe's parishes after his time. An editorial summary is here given rather than a full transcript.

St Mary's Coddenham
Seating claimed: 900
Numbers present on census day: 137 + 70 scholars (morning)
234 + 72 scholars (afternoon)
Holy communion (six times a year), average: 90 communicants.

All Saints, Crowfield
Seating claimed: 200
Sunday service, alternate weeks morning and afternoon.
Numbers present on census day: 96 + 21 scholars (afternoon)
Attendance (averaged): 65 + 25 scholars (morning)
120 + 25 scholars (afternoon)
Holy Communion (six times a year), average: 20 communicants.

Coddenham Chapel – Independent
Erected as a Wesleyan chapel 1823 and later sold.
Seating claimed: 165
Numbers present on census day: 53 (afternoon)
120 (evening)
Attendance (averaged): 60 (afternoon)
120 (evening)
(Preaching at afternoon service was introduced only about six months previously.)

Crowfield Chapel – Particular Baptist
Erected about 1830.
Seating claimed: free 80, others 160
Numbers present on census day: 140 + 7 scholars (morning)
202 + 7 scholars (afternoon)
(Sunday school said to be small by reason of several charitable schools nearby.)

[1] Extracted from T.C.B. Timmins, ed., *Suffolk Returns from the Census of Religious Worship, 1851*, SRS xxxix (1997), pp.89–90.

APPENDIX B

Local Dissenters

The formal reports to the bishop (Visitation Returns) on Coddenham-cum-Crowfield signed by Longe survive for the years 1801, 1806, 1813, and 1820 as does the pair for 1838 by his son Robert.[1] *In the matter of Dissent these returns should be treated with caution as written for a particular reason. (The return in 1820 is given in full as a transcript at p.175 above.)*

Another primary source is the Conventicle Register. Every building used for public worship other than the established church, whether a dwelling or a chapel built for the purpose, was required by law to be licensed as a conventicle. The diocesan records accurately show the granting of licences but their value as evidence is reduced by their recording no cessation of use and often no details of the persuasion of Dissent.[2]

The dated passages below preceded by a year in brackets are extracts transcribed from the visitation returns made by Longe and his son. The italicised passages are not transcripts but editorial summaries of the licences with some comment.

In 1799, two private houses in Coddenham were licensed on the application of two men, of whom one was Arthur Bromiley, the Independent minister at Needham Market. Longe reported:

[*1801*] There are no professed Dissenters but there are a few who sometimes attend the meeting houses in the adjoining parishes. The two houses which were a few years since licensed in this parish have not been used for dissenting meetings of late.

[*1806*] At present no Dissenters, except William Lines who attends the Independent meeting house at Needham and is a quiet well-disposed husbandman. The Dissenters in this parish are fewer than formerly.

In 1811, Bromiley was granted licence for a house in the street adjoining the premises of a barber. In 1813 the barber was applying for one for his own house. Six months later a man from Ipswich applied for a third Coddenham property, suggesting another congregation. Longe reported:

[*1813*] There are a few of the lower order of people who occasionally attend the Independent meeting at Needham and also meet at a cottage licensed a few years since in this parish, most of whom, if not all, attend also their parish church.

Arthur Bromley [*sic*], residing at Needham Market, is the Independent teacher. Within a few months some Baptists of very low education and condition have held meetings in the same licensed cottage, which sect appears to be increasing in this

1 NRO, DN/VIS/38/8, 43/6, 49/3 and 60/6 (John Longe); 65/11 (Robert Longe). No visitation return survives between 1820 and 1838. There was a visitation on 10 and 11 May 1827 and the next on 17 and 18 April 1834 (about six weeks after Longe died but before his son was instituted).

2 Register of Dissenting Meeting Houses, otherwise called Conventicles: NRO, DN/DIS/4/1 and 2.

neighbourhood …[3] Those who attend these meetings are (to the best of my knowledge) quiet and orderly.
[*1820*] There are a few Dissenters in the parish of low condition who attend the Independent meeting house in Needham and there is a cottage licensed for Independents here, at which teachers of different persuasions occasionally attend, but their congregations consist chiefly of people from neighbouring parishes.

Considerable activity soon followed. In 1822 a house and, in 1823, Coddenham Methodist chapel 'recently erected' were both licensed.[4] *The relationship between different persuasions is shown in the main text. In Suffolk, Independents (or Congregationalists) and Baptists were more numerous than Methodists. Since a private house was licensed in 1833 clearly two congregations persisted in Coddenham. Robert Longe succeeded his father. He stated in his first visitation return:*
[*1838*] A very few Dissenters only, certainly not increasing.

For the hamlet of Crowfield, Longe's Visitation returns, were brief:
[*1813*] There is one family – Chittock – who are Independents and attend the meeting at Needham. Dissenters in this hamlet are not increased. Some few who attend the Chapel [*Church of England*] sometimes also go to the meetings in the neighbourhood.
[*1820*] No Dissenters to the best of my knowledge.

In fact, in Crowfield, three applications were made for conventicles shortly afterwards, in 1823–4. First, for established premises, one was made in the name Chittock and one by John Gibbons for his carpenter's shop. Next year, William Chittock and another man jointly applied for the licensing of 'a meeting house now erected on the premises of William Chittock junior'.[5] *Fourteen years later, John Longe's son Robert reported:*
[*1838*] A few Dissenters (Baptists). Diminishing.

The queries from the bishop also sought information on inhabitants who habitually absented themselves from all *places of worship. Among the few were named two farmers in Crowfield: one called himself a Quaker 'but never attended their meetings' and, unlike convinced Quakers, paid his dues to the vicar without compulsion. A third man in 1813 was the tenant of Crowfield Hall, the only sizeable property in the village, let to him by the Middleton family, doubtless a disappointing example.*

3 Longe gives the names of four preachers from Ipswich and Needham Market.
4 This building lies back some yards from the road leading to Crowfield and was until about five years ago in weekly use by the small Methodist congregation. It is now in light industrial use.
5 This Baptist chapel is today in regular use, near the premises of the Gibbons family, builders.

APPENDIX C

Responses to Poverty

In this period poverty was under constant debate among both politicians and churchmen. Many gentlemen concluded that since some poverty was inevitable, nothing could be done beyond modest parish relief and local charity. Others distinguished the widespread condition (to be relieved only in acute temporary periods) from chronic individual indigence which, being adjudged blameworthy, merited stern correction. They urged that prolonged 'broadcast' charity should be discouraged as undermining individual 'improvement'. The issue was regarded as a local one. To suggest that the appalling rural poverty, creating 'two nations', could or should be addressed as a national issue was to be labelled radical or even revolutionary.[1] There was a tendency to look to the church, accepting that its response would be limited to individuals.

The slight improvement in the early 1820s resulted not from the timid legislation but from economic causes. Then in 1834 sustained intervention by the state, though generally unacceptable, was pushed through by a small but influential group converted to a new secular ideology. Most parish clergy accepted the principle of reform but wanted relief kept local. Longe's own social ethics, as so often, were derived from his place in society and his time, and by those standards he is to be judged.[2] He did not live to see the Poor Law Amendment enacted.

Local provision for poor families came in several forms. Historically, giving had been charitable and voluntary, channelled through the church. When freewill giving by 1600 proved inadequate, funding became compulsory through parish rates, and that had by Longe's time become the basic source. Although *ex officio* chairman of vestry, Longe distanced himself from the actual allocation of rate relief.[3] He channelled his energies through his poition as a director of the house of industry at Barham serving the incorporated hundred, as explored in the introduction.

The period just before and after 1795, the year of the Speenhamland decision, had been particularly bad for farm labourers. Despite wartime conditions favouring farming until 1813, this acute distress continued, primarily because of the high price of basic food. Further deterioration followed the war, since wages and day-rates were cut as farm incomes fell, and home-work in the textile industry had already collapsed. On behalf of powerless agricultural labourers, William Cobbett attacked the more comfortable clergy for their politics, their decisions as magistrates, and their tithe-gathering. Nostalgic for a mythical time when the parson lived humbly

---

1 Benjamin Disraeli's novel *Sybil or the Two Nations*, though set at this time, was published in 1845.

2 E.R. Norman, *Church and Society in England 1770–1970* (Oxford, 1976), pp.1–5.

3 This aspect is therefore not dealt with in this volume.

among his flock, Cobbett blamed the distancing of the clergy of his time from poor parishioners, a characteristic of Longe's ministry.[4]

Longe's involvement in distributing alms, and also coal, blankets and other comforts purchased from other voluntary giving, is touched on in the diary, as is his encouragement of thrift and self-help.

4 Dyck, *Cobbett*, pp.95, 128.

APPENDIX D

Medical Matters

The only evidence that Longe suffered ill-health as a young man was an episode of gout in his legs just after Christmas, possibly linked with a violent sore throat for which blistering was administered.[1] Dr Clubbe was called in for a second opinion.

At least by the time he was in his sixties, Longe's diaries show how frequently his medical advisers attended, as well as some of the treatments offered. One form of recurrent suffering was his gout.[2] In 1826, when he was aged sixty-one, after a brief episode in the spring, he was substantially disabled throughout the last quarter of the year, as shown by his diary, when his afflictions included lumbago and bowel problems.[3] Most significantly of all, he suffered painful 'oppression on his chest' for which he was prescribed only peppermint water.[4] Modern diagnosis might well connect some of these difficulties.

Longe's gout continued into 1827, when his treatment included draughts and purgative colocynth pills.[5] Towards the end of that year Longe was very aware of low spirits, although the camphor julip prescribed may suggest that Mr Beck was addressing Longe's chest as well. Longe's sadness continued to the year's end but was not necessarily clinical depression.[6]

A worrying development in 1831 was a fainting fit after physical exertion, probably relating to the oppression on the chest.[7] Mr Beck's name appears in the diary nine times in the next seven weeks. Mr Beck saw his stomach as the seat of the problem and also bled him. Tonic bark was tried, perhaps to reduce fever.[8] Later in the year, Longe experienced an attack of gout prolonged for over two months and again briefly in mid-December.[9]

Longe's involvement with the medical profession continued to be substantial in 1833 as he neared the end of his life. His gout was troublesome for much of January. A blue (mercury) pill was administered as an aperient.[10] During his prolonged attack of gout in late March/April 1833, exacerbated by influenza, we can follow Longe's progress about the house on crutches, having difficulty in getting downstairs, resting in bed all day, sitting up in his chamber, being wheeled into the dressing-room for

1 Diary 27–31 Dec. 1796, when he was aged thirty-one.
2 Diary 24 April 1826.
3 Diary 9–13 Feb. and 18–22 July 1826.
4 Diary 28, 30 Oct. 1826.
5 Diary 15 Jan. – 26 Feb. and again 6–24 April 1827.
6 Diary 3–9, 22, 30, 31 Dec. 1827.
7 Diary 28 Jan. to 12 Feb. 1831.
8 Diary 14 March 1831.
9 Diary 6 May to 17 July 1831, 5 Dec. 1831.
10 Diary 12–22, 29 Jan. 1833.

breakfast and finally downstairs.[11] He was fit enough to lead a Communion service after Easter but it was the first service he had taken for six months.[12]

Longe's most threatening condition related to his breathing, for which he consulted Dr Probert of Bury St Edmunds.[13] Perhaps for the first time, this problem was linked with the action of his heart and his diet. A blister was tried and James's powders, probably to reduce the fever and perhaps inflammation, and then he was treated by bleeding[14] Longe complained of oppression on the chest in each of the next three months. When on a visit to Norfolk, needing the professional care of Mr Crosse and later Dr Wright, he was both bled and blistered.[15] Thereafter medical attendance was almost continuous, with a succession of treatments up to the end of the year and a new description of 'dropsical swelling'.[16] John Longe lived only nine weeks into the new year.

Thus, in the diaries of the 1820s and 30s Mr Beck's name appears on many occasions, latterly with his two sons who were also medical practitioners. Sometimes a second opinion was appropriate, including that of local practitioner Barrington Blomfield.[17] With the benefit of modern knowledge on dietary matters, and with hindsight, we may well attribute most of John Longe's ill-health to excesses and imbalances at the table. Both his pattern of eating and drinking and the medical advice and treatment he received must, however, be judged by the standards of his day.

Mrs Charlotte Longe. Having lost three children in infancy by the end of 1794, the level of anxiety for John Longe and his wife was high at the time of her subsequent confinements but healthy children were born to them: a daughter in September 1796, and sons in 1798, 1799, 1800, and 1803. Her sudden death came after an asthma attack.

Longe recorded medical problems experienced by his surviving three sons when adult. His son John, in his late twenties, suffered pain in his face.[18] When it recurred he was regularly attended by Mr Beck and his son Henry Beck. Small doses of a preparation of iron and bark and a particular diet were recommended. Mr Lynn of Woodbridge was also involved and advised that the pain was of nervous origin, linked with an underlying constitutional weakness.[19] Though quite ill, young John did not help himself when despatched for his health to Aldeburgh by neglecting to follow medical advice including sea-bathing.[20] One is left to speculate that the breakdown of his marriage a few years later may have been linked with this ill-health.

Longe's son Robert features in the diary with illness only when in 1827 he suffered persistent bilious problems.[21]

---

11 Diary 20 March – 5 April 1833. He suffered again from gout from 21 June, 13 August and 24 November, but this was not presumably a life-threatening condition.

12 Diary 21 April 1833.

13 Diary 22 May – 19 June 1833.

14 Diary 16–18 June 1833.

15 Diary 25 July, 29 August, 20 Sept. – 2 Oct.1833.

16 Diary 2, 26 Oct. 1833 (cough); 21 Nov. – 2 Dec. 1833 (breathing); 24, 26 Oct. (gout); 24 Nov., 2, 30 Dec. 1833 (swelling of the legs).

17 Diary 29 Jan. 1827. See notes on people (pp.260–76) for all the practitioners named.

18 Diary 11, 14, 25 March 1827.

19 Diary 29 March – 27 May 1827.

20 Diary 25 July 1827.

21 Diary 26 May, 3 August 1827.

Longe's son Henry also seems to have enjoyed good health, apart from an exaggerated fear when on holiday in Scotland that he had had a cholera attack.[22]

Mental illness features in Longe's experience in several ways, though not in his own family. For example, he was involved in having Miss Croasdaile's brother admitted to Dr Wright's Asylum in Norwich.[23]

John Longe became a subscriber to the County Hospital at Bury St Edmunds which entitled him to nominate for admission. A Coddenham labourer's wife with cataracts was a later beneficiary of this entitlement.[24]

---

22 Diary 20–24 July 1826.

23 Diary Nov.–Dec. 1826.

24 Diary 3 Aug. 1831, 5 Sept. 1833.

APPENDIX E

Travel and Transport

The chief impression gained from the diaries is the great reliance placed by man upon the trusty horse by all those who could afford to ride rather than walk. Saddle horses, coach horses working as a team and ponies drawing lighter conveyances all feature in the diaries. Longer journeys were made by various forms of horse-drawn wheeled transport, or in a man's younger days on horseback. To keep a carriage was a public declaration of a certain status, for it took both care and expense to maintain stables, conveyances and staff.

It is not that Longe was a great traveller outside Suffolk. As far as we have record for holidays he travelled only into his native Norfolk, to stay with family or to visit Yarmouth and Cromer. His brief London visits, although including social meetings, were primarily for legal and financial business.

Part I: from 1796 to 1798

As a young man, Longe would use horseback for the frequent local journeys that he made. A journey of thirty miles or so was not considered too great to undertake in a day.[1] He also rode on horseback when on exercise with his troop, including the journey there and back.[2] By contrast, men would walk a great distance on occasion, as when a militia contingent was marched from Norwich to Ipswich, although John's brother and his fellow-officers were doubtless mounted.[3]

There were other journeys for which riding was inappropriate. When going to Norwich on his own, Longe would use either the mail-coach, which left Ipswich every morning from the Great White Horse, or a commercial stage-coach such as Forster's.[4] He would on occasion walk on from Norwich to Spixworth.[5] At other times he might hire post-chaises for the whole journey, or even in poor weather for the few miles between Norwich and Spixworth.[6] However his usual mode of transport for the journey from Suffolk to Norwich was a mail-coach which he called 'the mail'.[7] Once, when his own chaise needed painting and he chose to use a Norwich coach-builder, he travelled back home by the mail and later used the same means to collect it.[8] On those occasions when Longe is silent as to method on longer journeys he probably used the mail.[9]

As Coddenham vicarage was not far from the turnpike it was not essential to

1 Diary 26 March 1796. All dates in the footnotes to this appendix relate to the diaries but the source of the coach timetables is the printed material in the pocket-books: SRO(I) HA24/50/19/4.3(1–6).

2 Diary: weekly from June 1798.

3 23 May 1798. Ipswich to Norwich was over forty miles, and Ipswich to London about double that.

4 1, 6 Feb. 1796. The mail coach left the Great White Horse for Norwich at 4.30a.m., but that time he took a different service back. The mail coach for London arrived back in Ipswich at 10.30p.m.

5 28 Nov. 1796.

6 3, 23 Dec. 1796.

7 10, 12 April, 28 June and 28 August, all 1798.

8 25 June and 30 August 1798.

9 22, 24 Dec. 1796, 29 Jan., 1 Feb., and 19 Feb. and 3 March 1798.

board or alight in Ipswich. When his parents visited from Norfolk, travelling south by public coach, Longe sent his carriage to meet them at the Magpie, the coaching inn at Little Stonham.[10]

When travelling to Spixworth with his wife for a visit a more complicated method was used with the aid of their coachman. In June 1796, when Charlotte was six months pregnant, they set out in their own carriage to Scole with its well-known coaching inn, near the boundary of Norfolk and Suffolk. They transferred there to a post-chaise to Norwich and again to another for the last four or five miles of their journey. Meanwhile, their coachman took their carriage back to Coddenham. On their return a few days later they arranged for their own conveyance to meet them at Scole.[11] They made similar arrangements the following year when (as Longe recorded) the journey took eight hours.[12] In 1798, it was doubtless the birth of their second child that prevented Charlotte from joining her husband in a visit to Norfolk.

When going to London, which John Longe needed to do both for court hearings and financial business, the disadvantage of the mail-coach was that it involved travelling through the night both ways.[13] It was probably to avoid that night journey that Longe used Shave's coach, which left the Golden Lion Ipswich early in the morning, and the Telegraph, which travelled daily via Ipswich between London and Yarmouth.[14] In the next two years, Longe travelled by both the Telegraph and 'the Blue Coach'.[15] The Blue Coach went from the Golden Lion, which faces the Cornhill, the central square in Ipswich.[16] In the 1790s, Longe's journeys were quite frequent. He was once obliged to return to London only four days after coming home from there, having also been there in the previous month.

Longe made other journeys to London by different means. When involved in a court case with colleagues, he travelled up with Sir Edmund Bacon of Raveningham in post-chaises, breaking the journey at Chelmsford overnight to dine with his brother's militia fellow-officers. He returned on the Sunday following, again by post chaises, that time with his clerical friend Charles Davy.[17] When on other business one summer Longe went up to London by mail-coach, but returned in a colleague's two-seater gig, taking two days on the journey.[18]

Whilst staying with relatives in Norfolk Longe would presumably rely for social visits upon the loan of a saddle-horse. There is however also mention of his father's whisky.[19]

The other use of horse-drawn vehicles was for transporting goods. Coaches were used, for example when sending a perishable gift, or by a book-seller filling an

10 25 July 1796.

11 6, 18 June 1796.

12 18 Sept. 1797. See also notes below.

13 1, 6 May 1796, 11 June 1798. The Great White Horse was the Ipswich stop.

14 6, 7, 11 Dec. 1796. Again the Great White Horse in Ipswich.

15 5 June 1797; 5, 9 Feb. 1798.

16 Later records show that there were two Blue coaches daily out of Ipswich: Haxell's from his premises in Brook Street to Charing Cross, and Wright's from the King's Head via Bishopsgate to Piccadilly. The printed material in Longe's pocket-books gives information on coaches and wagons.

17 31 Oct., 6 Nov. 1796.

18 11, 14, 15 June 1798. The colleague happened to be Sir Edmund Bacon again.

19 10, 15 June 1796.

order.[20] When Longe needed to despatch a substantial number of family heirlooms to Surrey however, because of the bulk he chose Hearne's wagon.[21]

The trouble and expense for those maintaining their own forms of transport included the care of their horses. In the single year 1796, Longe records nine occasions of having horses shod, probably at the Coddenham blacksmith.[22] There might be foaling, illness or accident. Keeping any sort of stable and coach-house suggests the need for staff (a coachman and/or groom) though records are lacking of Longe's household in the 1790s. Even the use of coaches on the turnpikes involved some form of 'feeder' transport with a servant to avoid the expense and even risk of stabling a horse at the inn of departure. Longe's account of journeys with his wife into the Norwich area give an indication of the need for advance planning and for staff. The convenience of keeping a carriage was considerable but so was the expense and thus it was a public indication of status.

Part II: from 1826 to 1833

By the time Longe was in his sixties his travel was more restricted. He seldom went further than Ipswich, Stowmarket and Woodbridge, some eight or ten miles from his vicarage. When obliged to attend a trial in Chelmsford, some forty miles away, he travelled there by the daily Shannon coach. He returned to Suffolk by post-chaise with a fellow witness.[23] The other stage-coach he mentioned in his diary was the Morning Star, to which he consigned a parcel and which his sons John and Robert used too.[24] There was an alternative route between Ipswich and Norwich via Woodbridge, by changing at Halesworth, a method which suited Henry.[25] For other parcels Longe used either the mail coach (as for turkeys at Christmas-time) or the commercial waggons for non-perishable items.[26] Betts' waggons plied three times a week through Ipswich.[27] Beart's went weekly between St Margaret's Street (Ipswich) and Norwich via Stowmarket and Scole.[28]

In the four years of the later set of diaries, Longe was able to continue his visits into Norfolk. In 1826, after a brief visit in April (and another by Mrs Longe alone), they had a more extended holiday together. They went first to Bungay to visit his son Robert, having breakfasted at Scole. Then, for over three weeks they travelled around Norfolk visiting friends and relatives, a 'very agreeable excursion'.[29] The following autumn they 'went post' to Scole for the first stage of their journey. They did not need their own carriage because they were staying throughout at Mrs

20 16 Jan. 1796, 6 March 1798.

21 9 April 1798. Not unlike the farm waggons used to fetch coal, this conveyance trundled off to London once a week from the Griffin Inn, Ipswich.

22 These premises still stand, in School Road.

23 7, 11 March 1826. The Shannon left Ipswich at 10a.m. for London, alternately from the Crown & Anchor and Haxell's.

24 28 Feb., 28 March, 10, 25 April 1826 and 4 July 1833. The Star travelled daily between London and Yarmouth via Ipswich, Scole and Bungay.

25 1 Dec. 1831.

26 21 Dec. 1826, 3 Jan. and 20 Dec. 1833.

27 8 May 1826. Betts served London and Norfolk.

28 8, 13 Aug. 1831. This is the service called by Longe 'the Norwich waggon': diary 29 Sept. 1827. Longe's own waggons had other uses, such as moving furniture and taking the young people to and from their confirmation in Stowmarket: diary 11, 16, 17 Oct. 1826; 10 May 1827; 19 June 1827.

29 22 Aug. to 15 Sept. 1826.

Longe's parental home at Salhouse. On the return journey to Suffolk they stopped overnight at the Scole Inn.[30]

In 1831, to visit John then living on the family estate at Spixworth, his father and step-mother made the journey in their own carriage, drawn for the first part by their own horses and for the second stage by hired post-horses ('posters'). Staying at Spixworth over a month they visited many Norfolk friends before moving on to Salhouse. They would rely on others for means of transport. On their homeward journey, postponed because of Longe's prolonged attack of gout, they again stopped overnight at Scole Inn on their way home.[31] Both Longe's brother and his son John took this overnight stop.[32] That September, John Longe and Frances were invited to Spixworth again for a week, and for a day-outing he hired post-horses to draw his own carriage.[33]

For an autumn visit to Norfolk in 1833 they left their carriage-horses at Scole Inn, completing the journey to Spixworth with hired post-horses. Longe's health again proved a problem but they did stay with his brother for a few days before returning to Coddenham.[34] This was John Longe's last visit to his native county.

The carriage was sometimes used for shorter journeys, for example to fetch a lady coming for a visit or, when Longe was recovering from illness, for the short distance to the house of industry at Barham.[35] When Robert had young children Longe would facilitate visits to the vicarage by sending his carriage for the family or for their return home to Combs.[36]

In none of these four diary years did Longe travel to London, but he did undertake journeys to Bury St Edmunds. These visits were to enjoy this social and cultural centre or for the annual assizes (when it was usual to mix judicial and social life), and once later for medical advice.[37]

Other conveyances than coaches, post-chaises and carriages are mentioned in the diaries. Longe bought a new landaulet from Spratt of Norwich (on part exchange), travelling in his old model to Norfolk and home in his new one. As this was combined with his wife staying at Salhouse where her mother was ill, Longe sent the carriage to enable her to return to the vicarage.[38] When Mrs Longe paid a further visit to Salhouse, travelling by public conveyance with a lady friend, Longe again sent the carriage for her return.[39]

Longe's gig features frequently in the diaries, sometimes for his own journeys into Ipswich or Stowmarket or nearer.[40] More often, he made it available to his sons, sometimes to drive themselves and sometimes with a servant. As young men they did not always have a horse available and only later did Longe's son John have his

30 16, 17, 28 Sept. 1827.
31 11 May to 4–5 July 1831.
32 6 Nov. 1827, 19 Aug. 1831.
33 5 to 12 Sept. 1831.
34 17 Sept. to 3 Oct. 1833.
35 23 Oct. 1827 (when he had walked), 15 April 1833. For lady visitor: 21 April 1827.
36 10 and 15 Jan., 27 Aug. 1831, 4 Feb. 1833.
37 18–20 Sept. 1826, 2–4 Aug. 1827, 1–3 Aug. 1831, and 27/28 May 1833. Ipswich to Bury was about twenty-five miles.
38 28 March, 11, 14, 25, 28 April 1826. His wife also visited other relatives, at Diss.
39 13, 19, 25 July 1826; 26 Dec. 1826 – 3 Jan. 1827.
40 16 June 1826, 12 July and 15 Oct. 1827.

own gig, at his new home at Spixworth.[41] Journeys by gig had their hazards.[42] Mrs Longe is only once mentioned as riding, but she also used a lighter pony-gig. Henry borrowed this when travelling frequently to and from Woodbridge.[43]

Another conveyance was a phaeton. Longe declined to buy one offered by Catt of Ipswich but then ordered one to be built for him.[44] Longe also employed Catt to undertake repairs and painting of his carriage, which was presumably the vehicle Longe called the 'chariot'.[45] On one occasion, a barouche was hired for a party of six to have a summer excursion to Felixstowe.[46] Apart from post-chaises for specific journeys hiring also related to coach-horses, when Longe's own were ill or lame or otherwise unavailable, to draw his own carriage. For this he turned to Haggar, for example on four occasions between July and September 1831. His sons also hired a post-chaise from Haggar for a winter dinner engagement.[47] In older age Longe did not abandon completely his riding, for example in undertaking part of the traditional perambulation of the parish boundary.[48]

The condition of their horses was of constant concern for Longe and his sons, particularly when a mare was in foal or a coach-horse went lame or was ill.[49] Horses needed resting.[50] To make this possible for his sons or to help them when for other reasons they lacked means of transport, Longe would lend a suitable horse or make his gig available.[51]

Although riding accidents are more associated with the hunting field than a simple journey mishaps could occur at any time.[52] The condition or behaviour of a horse might well lead to a decision to sell and to buy another and such transactions are recorded by Longe.[53] Robert on one occasion exchanged a horse found unsuitable for carriage work.[54] Henry seemed to have particular disappointment, either because he was at the modest end of the market or because his judgment was not sound.[55] He was, however, ready to walk substantial distances when lacking a mount.[56] At other times Longe's sons made extensive tours. Henry, for example, went to Scotland in July 1826, toured in the south of England with a friend the following year and in 1833 he was away in the west country for three weeks.[57] Leisure travel within this country was possible for young gentlemen even if the aristocrat's foreign tour was not.

41 5, 13, 18 April 1831.
42 30 May 1831.
43 13 Oct. 1831, 22 May, 16 Dec. 1833.
44 14, 30 July, 13 Dec. 1831. Longe had to wait several months. See also 29 May 1833.
45 3 April, 17 May 1833.
46 11 July 1827.
47 29 Nov. 1827.
48 5 May 1826.
49 18 March 1826, and three entries in a single month 12, 25, 27 July 1827.
50 12 May, 14 Sept. 1827, 21 Nov. 1833.
51 1 April, 1 May 1826, 12 May, 16 Aug. 1827, 6 July 1831, 4 May 1833.
52 8 May 1827, 6 May 1833.
53 14, 18, 26 July 1831. Longe might, for example, decline an offer and it was not unusual to take a horse on approval.
54 4 Feb. 1833.
55 16 Dec. 1826, 3 Jan., 9 March, 25 Dec. 1827, 6 and 10 March 1831, 21 Nov. 1833.
56 1 Jan., 4 Feb. 1831.
57 3–24 July 1826; 19 Aug. – 1 Sept. 1827; 3, 7–27 July 1833.

APPENDIX F

Continuity within Clergy Families (as evidenced from schedules of contents)

In Longe's time it was by no means unusual for one family to supply several generations of clergy to a region. The Longe family is but an example after the diarist's clerical father held livings in Norfolk. During his forty-three years as a clergyman in and around Coddenham, the diarist himself had two ordained sons. Robert (1800–90), the elder of these, followed his father as vicar of Coddenham-cum-Crowfield. Robert's own son John (1832–1916) was to hold a succession of clerical posts in Suffolk in his turn. The continuity of those times may be illustrated in other ways. For over fifty-five years Robert Longe lived as vicar in the same Coddenham parsonage house as had his father, namely from 1834 until his death at the age of eighty-nine in January 1890. It was precisely one hundred years earlier, in January 1790, that his father had entered into the assistant curacy there. Moreover, it is likely that Robert retained most of the contents of the vicarage.[1]

This continuity at the vicarage was to be sharply broken in 1890 for Robert's family had by then dispersed, his wife Margaret having predeceased him. Robert's three sons and one daughter had homes of their own. Within a few weeks of Robert's death a two-day auction was held at Coddenham vicarage. The sale catalogue of thirty-seven pages itemises nearly 800 lots, many of which were multiple.[2]

Of 2,500 books offered, almost all that are separately listed bear dates prior to Robert's adulthood, suggesting that the grandchildren disposed of what by then were antiquarian books. Although no schedule of John Longe's books survives it is reasonable to suppose that the 1890 list comprised part at least of the diarist's library, and its retention by his son underlines continuity. The 1890 catalogue, in addition to listing sermons and works on theology, ranges widely to cover history, geography and travel and literature, and earlier periodicals.

In 1797, before moving from Henley into Coddenham vicarage, Longe had probably acquired relatively few possessions, even if they were included in the inventory. What he listed was largely if not entirely what had been left to him by Nicholas Bacon.[3] The paintings listed in 1890 were few, but some can be identified with those in the earlier Inventory.

Unknown, after Lely	Portrait of Edward, first Lord Sandwich[4]

1 SRO(I) HA24/50/19/4.1(3). Household goods: by his will Longe gave his widow her choice of these with the residue to Robert (except half the plate which Henry was to have). It is believed that Frances Longe (then aged sixty)) returned to her brother's home at Salhouse Hall. Her step-son Robert did pay her £199 4s. 6d. in June 1834 for a miscellaneous list of items of no great distinction: SRO(I) HA24/50/19/4.7(3).

2 SRO(I) HA24/50/19/4.7(4).

3 For inventory of vicarage contents *c*.1797, see pp.210–18 above.

4 See diary 12 Aug. 1826 and note. The Sandwich/Montague connection with the Bacons was through Lady Catherine, daughter of this Edward Montague, 1st earl of Sandwich. She married one Nicholas

Unknown	Blowing up the *Royal James* in the battle of Southwold, in which ship the Earl of Sandwich perished[5]
	A pair of portraits: Sir Wm. and Lady Temple[6]
	Pair of portraits: William and Mary
Stella	Holy Family (on marble)
Carlo Marratti, after Raphael	Transfiguration
Stone, after van Dyck	Henrietta Maria, Queen of Charles I
Mrs Wetherall	Portrait of Lord Sandwich
Monamy	Ship on fire

One picture listed in 1890 is mentioned in John Longe's diary, but not in his inventory: Roman Charity by Smart, after Domenichino.[7] Other pictures listed in 1890 are not readily identified with those of the 1797 inventory: some by Elmer (of Farnham) for example.[8] The sale also included four pairs of landscapes and a single one, all of the Dutch School.[9]

Items other than books and paintings offered in 1890 are harder positively to identify from the 1797 listing, but some do reinforce the thesis that, amid all the many changes in the long reign of Queen Victoria, some things did not change:

A handsome large mahogany secretary cabinet, inlaid with coloured woods, and with interior fittings, the panels inlaid with the arms of Bacon, Montague and Gardemau
Antique walnut bureau bookcase with plate-glass
Two brass blunderbusses by Jover, London
Two pairs of brass-mounted flintlock horse pistols, by Jover
Two pairs of flintlock pocket pistols by Henshaw
Two dress swords
A fine black Jasper Wedgwood bust[10]
Model in bone of a castle, made by the prisoners in Porchester Castle
Antique bracket clock by T. Moore, Ipswich, engraved back, ormolu and brass face in mahogany case, mounted in brass and ormolu
Pair of elegant antique carved pedestal girandoles, with urn-shaped vases &c.
A pair of bronze figures of centaurs, 9 inches
A pair of mahogany knife cases, each containing 12 knives and 12 forks
A number of items of mahogany furniture[11]

Bacon and they became the grandparents of Longe's benefactor, also Nicholas Bacon. Catherine's second marriage was to the Coddenham vicar, the Revd Balshazar Gardemau.

5 The terrible naval battle against the Dutch in Sole Bay, off Southwold, 28 May 1672.

6 Temple family. Nicholas Bacon's mother, Dorothy, was grand-daughter of the statesman Sir William Temple of Sheen, 1st baronet.

7 Smart was an Ipswich painter. Diary 16 July, 26 Aug. 1798. The context of those two entries appears in the diary between 21 March and 9 April 1798, and between 17 Aug. and 26 Aug. 1798.

8 One speculates that Elmer was patronised by the local Temple family whose seat was Moor Park, Farnham (Surrey), and that these works are among those listed in 1797 with imprecise descriptions.

9 Longe lists a number of landscapes.

10 Said to be of Shakespeare, but corrected in pencil to Lord Bacon, this is presumably the one Longe bought in 1827 (diary 24 Sept. 1827).

11 Both lists contain a substantial number of items of furniture in mahogany, with the likelihood of identity not here pursued.

APPENDIX G

Parliamentary Representation, Suffolk and Ipswich 1796 to 1834[1]

The general scene prior to 1832

Before 1832 the House of Commons was elected by a traditional process, both complicated and to modern eyes unfair. In 1831, the right to vote (the 'franchise') was enjoyed by only about one in thirty-five of the population, averaged across England and Wales. In the county, a man uniformly qualified by possessing freehold property worth 40 shillings a year, but in the seven boroughs there was great variety of franchise. The whole of Suffolk had about 6,200 electors in 1830, a number artificially inflated by Ipswich having created burgesses for political reasons. Additionally, varied and changing numbers in the population of constituencies resulted in huge discrepancies in the number of adults represented by one member. Moreover many borough voters were non-resident, and probably had a vote in more than one constituency, easily exercisable when polling lasted for fifteen days.

Because voting was 'open' influence and even pressure was general, despite legislation against buying or selling parliamentary seats. Close results were almost routinely challenged by petition to the House of Commons, usually on technical grounds, readily proved, rather than by bribery, which was more easily concealed.

Three types of constituency returned members to the Commons: disputed larger boroughs, 'pocket' boroughs and the rest of the shire. Before 1832 seven Suffolk boroughs had their own members: three were large towns (Ipswich, Bury and Sudbury), Eye in north Suffolk, and three historic but small coastal settlements, of the type that were 'in the pocket' of aristocratic patrons. It did not follow that a large town had a large electorate, for the franchise in Bury St Edmunds was limited to thirty-seven 'members of the corporation'. The anomalies resulted largely from ancient privileges zealously guarded. Two knights of the shire in the county constituency had been returned since the late thirteenth century. The right of each of the boroughs to return two members had also been granted long before, at various dates from then until Charles I's reign.

Political parties in the modern sense had not developed by this time and loyalties were often personal. However, active loyalists in the 'Country interest' (the 'Blues'), were gradually coalescing into the Tory party, keenly defending the economic interests of the landowning gentry and the established position of the church along with the ancient prerogatives of the Crown. Although the violence of partisan politics ebbed and flowed, nationally the 'Blues' had held office continuously in the time of Pitt the Younger and from 1812 to 1830.

[1] This appendix has been compiled from: Clarke, *History of Ipswich, passim*; Gwyn Thomas, 'Parliamentary Constituencies' in Dymond and Martin (eds), *Historical Atlas*, pp.30–1, and Warnes and Blatchly, *Bribery Warehouse*.

The county prior to 1832

In the shire constituency (the whole county of Suffolk apart from boroughs) the Tories were so dominant that their nominated candidates could proceed unopposed if limited to two. Any sense of contest was thus transferred to the Tories' nomination meeting held at Stowmarket, a preliminary used to dissuade any third candidate from standing at the election itself. The absence of a contest in the county elections prevented neither excited celebration by the 'Blues' nor attempts by the 'Yellows' to upset the triumphant chairing of successful candidates.

The two knights of the shire from 1796 were Sir Thomas Charles Bunbury and Lord Brome who were both also returned in the next election. When Lord Brome died his place was taken by Sir Thomas Sherlock Gooch. Bunbury and Gooch were also successful in 1806 and 1807. From 1812, the county was represented by T.S. Gooch and Sir William Rowley and this pairing was re-elected in 1818, 1820, and 1826. In 1830 and again in 1831 the two nominees duly elected were Sir Henry Edward Bunbury (nephew and successor to the baronetcy of the above) and Charles Tyrell.

Ipswich prior to 1832

The contrast between the county and Ipswich is marked. As in many larger boroughs at election-time the voters were wildly partisan and contests were violent. Street fights were common and for some days bands of dockers and other brawny men would terrorise the town, which the authorities lacked resources to prevent. A close result would be followed by a legal challenge by petition. The elected members for Ipswich (all 'Blue') between 1796 and 1818 were:

1796 C.A. Crickett, Sir Andrew S. Hamond
1802 the same, but when Crickett died, then William Middleton
1806 Hon. Robert Stopford, Richard Wilson
1807 Sir Home Popham, Robert Alexander Crickett
1812 R.A. Crickett, J. Round (jnr)
1818 R.A. Crickett, William Newton

Thereafter, close results led to challenges.

1820 the votes cast were: R.A. Crickitt (Blue) 430, William Haldiman (Yellow) 428, Thomas Barrett Lennard (Y) 427, Round (B) 324. However, four of Crickett's votes were cancelled on petition, and the two Yellows were thus declared and chaired.

1826 R.A. Crickitt was by then bankrupt. The results announced were: Haldiman (Y) 496, Col. Torrens (Y) 495, Charles Mackinnon (B) 488, Robert Adam Dundas (B) (488). However, in a reversal of the previous election, the two Yellow candidates each had sixteen votes disallowed as having been illegally cast by voters holding jobs, so the petition succeeded.

1830 Mackinnon (B) and Dundas (B) were returned again, unopposed, but in the House of Commons they found themselves in opposition, since Earl Grey formed an administration, with a cabinet almost exclusively of titled Whig lords.

1831 the national swing in expectation of Parliamentary Reform was reflected in Ipswich, where the two Yellows (James Morrison and Rigby Wason) were returned, by a margin of 468 to 327 over the Blues (Mackinnon and Capt. Fitzroy.) Incidentally, only 39 per cent under the 'old' franchise were Ipswich residents, and more than half the rest came from London.

William Middleton of Shrubland Park
Middleton had a chequered career. He was MP for the borough of Ipswich twice, once by election from 1784 to 1790 and then (1802–6) to replace C.A. Crickitt who had died. When newly a baronet he offered himself in 1806 in the *county* as one of three candidates, disturbing the usual cosy arrangement. His reluctance to withdraw despite lack of support led to him being publicly criticised. He also failed at the nomination stage in three following county elections. Accepting his lot by 1820, he never obtained a county seat and died in 1829.

The reform of 1832
This reform was preceded by a massive survey of the British Isles. The 1832 Acts may have been seen later as a turning point but in truth the reforms introduced were modest. The franchise was extended in the county and made uniform in the boroughs, raising the Suffolk electorate to 10,394. The timidity of the change was shown in Ipswich, for example, where the registered electorate was still only about one in seventeen of the population.

The three coastal boroughs were disenfranchised, but Eye (enlarged by a further ten parishes) retained one member. The three bigger towns retained their two members. The county was split into two divisions, each returning two members. A new system of electoral registration was inadequate to end corruption; nor did the Act introduce the secret ballot, a change supported only by the most radical.

Post-reform elections 1832 (county)
In the eastern division of the county, those returned were: Lord Henniker (Thornham) and Robert Newton Shawe (Kesgrave) (Sir Charles Vere Broke, the disappointed contestant, would however oust Shawe three years later.) For the western division: Charles Tyrell and Sir Hyde Parker bt (Melford Hall) were returned.

In the eastern division, the custom of the 'cavalcade' continued. Processions into the town centre of Ipswich included the carriages of gentlemen with younger gentry and tenantry on horseback. Two of the favourite routes were the Woodbridge Road from the east (1½ miles) and Norwich Road from the north-west. Because there was no contest the climax was the chairing on the Cornhill of unopposed and therefore successful candidates. This was often the focus for disruptive behaviour by the frustrated 'Yellows'.

Post-reform elections 1832 and 1835 (Ipswich)
In 1832 the tide of reform gave the two Yellows a considerably increased majority, enhanced by lack of agreement within the Blue ranks which resulted in their fielding a third candidate. The two Yellows (James Morrison and Rigby Wason) polled 594 and 593 votes, whereas the result for the three Blues was 308, 265 and 94.

In 1835, after Longe's death, a reaction led to initial success for the two Blues: Robert Adam Dundas and Fitzroy Kelly. The election was, on petition, declared void and since two further Blue candidates failed in the fresh election that quickly followed the above the two 'Yellows' resumed their seats.

The atmosphere of these elections was captured by Charles Dickens who, as journalist for the *Morning Chronicle*, reported elections at both Ipswich and Sudbury in January 1835. *Pickwick Papers*, published in weekly instalments shortly after, gave a lively account generally supposed to be based on Sudbury.

APPENDIX H

Magistrates and Quarter Sessions

In most matters affecting rural society real and effective power in Georgian times was wielded not by central government, but by magistrates. They cherished their independence in the face of directives from Whitehall and their influence often reached Westminster through their colleagues elected to the Commons. In Suffolk, outside the borough of Ipswich, the traditional networks of gentry remained intact as yet undiluted by the growing power of others.[1]

Appointment to the county bench was by the Crown, in practice upon the recommendation of the Lord Lieutenant, a major county landowner appointed for life.[2] Some noblemen and prominent gentry, accepting appointment as one of status, chose never to sit or, having taken the oath, felt free to sit very infrequently. Further down county society membership of the bench was extended to those not engaged in anything classed as work, a leisured criterion met by the increasing number of clergy who ranked as gentlemen. Seen solely from the viewpoint of justice, willing clergy enhanced the bench, raising standards both of mind and impartiality, and were moreover conveniently dispersed geographically. The effect on their parochial work and pastoral relationships is another matter.

From about the time of George III's accession the clergy came to form a significant proportion of the magistracy. This situation lasted about seventy-five years until numbers fell sharply, partly under the influence of the Oxford Movement.[3] In the list of active Suffolk JPs (1796–1833) between 34 per cent and 40 per cent of the total were clergy.[4] Magistrates frequently acted alone or in twos and threes, but the greater powers were wielded when they sat as a bench for a few days in Quarter Sessions at four venues in the county. The Ipswich division covered about a quarter of the county, extending through mid-Suffolk from the Waveney to the Stour but excluding Ipswich and Eye boroughs. The court sat at Ipswich Shire Hall.[5]

Quarter Sessions were the county power base, with jurisdiction extending beyond criminal cases to administration of matters that are in our time regarded as executive and specialist functions. Their remit ran to highways and bridges, navigable rivers and harbours, waterworks and sewers, lighting and power, lunacy, gaols and prisoners, charities and friendly societies, the poor law, Dissenters, weights and meas-

---

1 David Eastwood, *Government and Community in the English Provinces, 1700–1870* (1997), pp.96–101.

2 For boroughs, it was their ancient charters that governed choice of magistrates.

3 Eric J. Evans, 'Some Reasons for the Growth of English Rural Anti-Clericalism c.1750–c.1830', *P&P* 66 (1975), pp.100–4; Alan D. Gilbert, *Religion and Society in Industrial England 1740–1914* (1976), pp.76, 133; Peter Virgin, *The Church in an Age of Negligence: Ecclesiastical Structure and Problems of Church Reform 1700–1840* (Cambridge, 1989), pp.13–125.

4 See the printed section of Longe's pocket-books: of 1796, 1826, 1827, 1831 and 1833.

5 Despite being praised as commodious by Clarke, *History of Ipswich*, p.293, this hired venue was by Longe's time so dilapidated that it was demolished when courts were built at St Helen's in 1837. The name of the yard survives, some 600 yards south-east of the Cornhill.

ures, and all licensing and registration. Their substantial budget from parish rates covered the county gaols, houses of correction and after 1826 the county lunatic asylum. Moreover, in a typically English pragmatic way, magistrates made unchallenged changes in the law, as at Speenhamland. The importance of the contribution made by JPs should not be underestimated.

APPENDIX I

Attendance of Magistrates at Quarter Sessions, Ipswich Division, July 1803 – July 1833

Although Magistrates had other duties besides sitting at Quarter Sessions (Appendix H), their record of attendance there, being measurable, is a useful guide to their individual contribution. The Ipswich division covered about a quarter of the county, extending through mid-Suffolk from the Waveney to the Stour but excluding Ipswich and Eye boroughs.

These attendances are taken from Quarter Sessions Minute and Order Books for the years 1803 to 1833 (SRO(I) B105–506). The records have gaps from April 1809 until January 1811, and also within the period 1813–15. It is likely that those shown below as sitting from 1803 would have had attendances before that year and those shown as sitting in 1833 would have continued after that year. Both are here unrecorded. Note that many other magistrates in the division sat on *fewer* than sixteen occasions in these thirty years.

Name	*Address*	*Dates*	*Number of attendances*
Gibson, John, esq.	Ipswich, St. Helens	1803–30	96
Methold, Thomas, Revd	Stonham Aspal	1803–33	89
Capper, George, Revd	Wherstead	1803–31	86
Berners, Charles, esq.	Woolverstone	1803–31	83
Middleton, Wm, esq.	Shrubland Park	1803–28	68
Longe, John, Revd	**Coddenham**	**1803–33**	**65**
Chevallier, John, Revd, MD	Aspall	1816–33	64
Ward, John, Revd	Stoke Ash	1816–33	53
Davy, Charles, Revd	Barking	1803–33	52
Rust, John E., esq.	Stowmarket	1816–33	52
Edgar, Mileson, esq.	Ipswich, Red House	1804–25	43
Godfrey, Peter, esq.	East Bergholt	?1811–29	40
Berners, H.D., Revd	Woolverstone	1809–33	37
Steward, A.H., esq.	Ipswich, Stoke Park	1823–33	35
Pettiward, Roger, esq.	Finborough	1804–32	34
Harland, Sir R. bt	Nacton	1803–31	33
Hotham, Fredk, the hon. Revd	Dennington	?1811–32	31
Heath, B.G., Revd	Creeting	1812–29	29
Theobald, J.M., esq.	Claydon	1804–28	25
Western, Thomas, esq.	Tattingstone	?1811–30	24
Hill, Henry, Revd	Buxhall	1803–25	22
Barlee, Edward, Revd	Worlingworth	1817–33	20
Paske, George, esq.	Needham Market	1821–31	16
Betts, Thos D., Revd	Wortham	1826–33	16

APPENDIX J

Houses of Industry

In rural east Suffolk, under a pioneering system anticipating both Gilbert's Act (1782) and the 1834 Poor Law unions, many of the obligations towards the poor were met at the level of the hundred, legally incorporated for this purpose. A hundred might comprise two dozen parishes. Within a decade after 1756 seven large houses of industry were established in Suffolk, each to serve one or a pair of the hundreds.[1] These replaced individual parish workhouses. Under powers given by a specific Act of Parliament, Bosmere and Claydon (by then a single hundred) erected an establishment in 1766 at Barham, some two miles from Coddenham.

The motive was cost efficiency, proof of which from Suffolk encouraged the Poor Law Commissioners in the 1830s to follow that model nationally.[2] Through the 1820s, notwithstanding that cost efficiency, poor rates in Suffolk generally were rising alarmingly. This resulted partly from difficult agricultural conditions and partly from the Speenhamland concession, well-meant but in the long-term seriously demoralising.[3] Rising costs hardened attitudes towards pauperism, which led to efficiency being given high priority.

Longe and his colleagues may well have considered that conditions were no more uncomfortable at Barham house of industry than in the humble cottages from which its inmates had come. Indeed, an influential Ipswich committee alleged in a pamphlet of 1822 that conditions were too soft.[4] Surviving primary sources for Barham are disappointingly few but a recent study on Samford (south-east Suffolk) house of industry from 1766 to 1834 concluded that the treatment of inmates was by the standards of the day reasonable and humane.[5] There is however little indication that individuals welcomed admission, even prior to the 1834 Act.

An analysis of admissions to another house of industry (at Nacton, serving Carlford and Colneis hundreds in south-east Suffolk) showed that between 1793 and 1835 most inmates stayed only a short time, many adults discharging themselves. The largest category of admissions (26 per cent) was youngsters aged between eleven and sixteen, sent there briefly as an essential condition to being placed in parish apprenticeships. The perception that the elderly were admitted only to die is not borne out, for in the over forty years of this survey, only two aged over sixty on admittance remained until they died. Of only seven other recorded deaths, five were

---

1 Two more followed in 1780. Broadly, six of these covered the south-eastern and south-central quarter of the county, Woodbridge being a notable exception, and three partly covered the north-east.

2 For a summary of this largely East Anglian trend see: David Dymond, 'Parish and Hundred Workhouses before 1834' in Dymond and Martin, *Historical Atlas*, pp.120, 121, 209.

3 Nationally, the total expenditure doubled between 1785 and 1803 and further between 1819 and 1823: Eric J. Evans, *The Forging of the Modern State 1783–1870* (2001 edn), p.511.

4 Bishop, *History of Ipswich*, p.125.

5 Sheila Hardy, *The House on the Hill – Samford House of Industry* (Tattingstone, 2001), p.157.

infants of mothers admitted when pregnant. One extended family provided twenty entries, some for repeated short stays, often pregnant or with a young child.[6]

Situations like these were doubtless experienced at Barham, and familiar to Longe, for he acted in a supervisory position there for well over thirty years.

6 SRO(I) qs Nacton 362.5: M.J. Stone, 'Nacton House of Industry' unpublished (1994), SRO(I) qs Nacton 362.5. Nacton is north of the Orwell estuary. The 171 admissions traced were from a single parish but there were no indications that the sample was untypical.

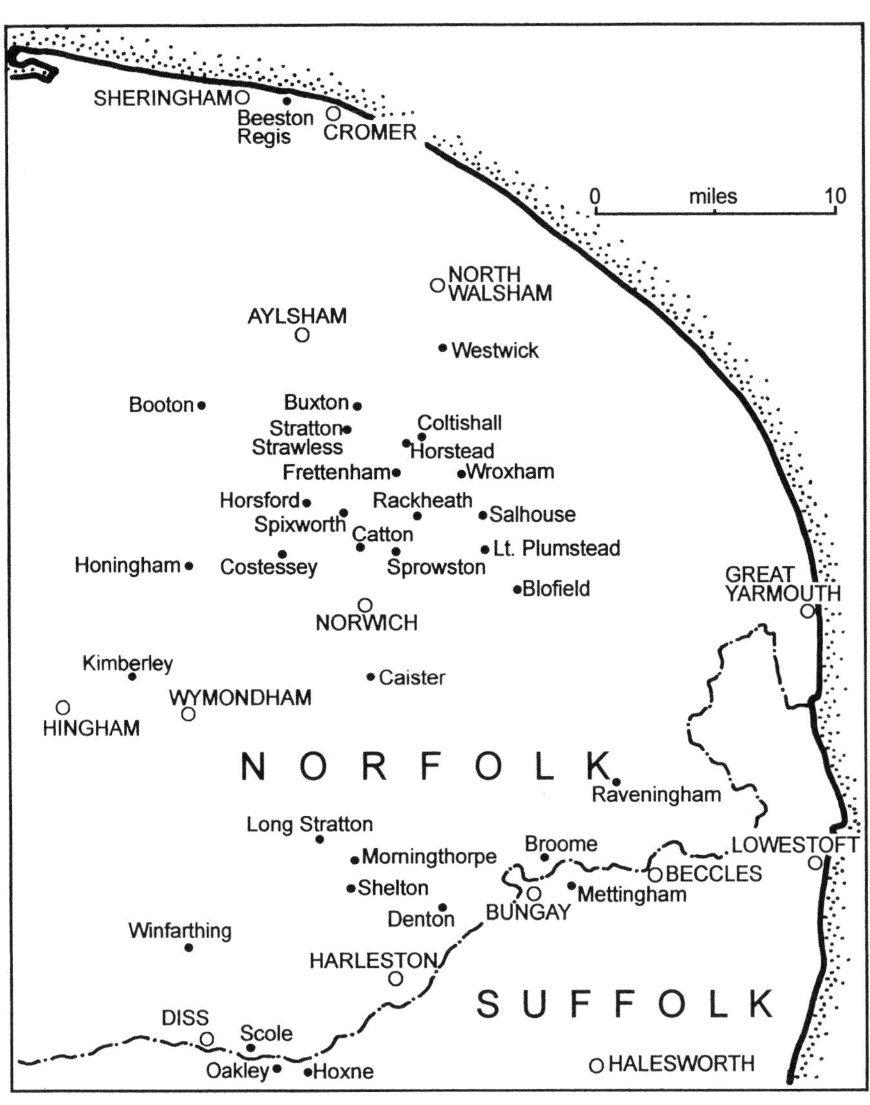

9. East Norfolk, Longe's ancestral area. Until the end of 1789 Longe himself was based on the family estate at Spixworth. He viewed early family memorials at Hingham; his mother's family lived at Booton, and his second wife came from Salhouse.

GLOSSARY

advowson: or patronage, the right to present a clergyman to a particular benefice, for formal institution by the bishop. The advowson was in English law a right to property, and could thus be bought and sold, as well as left by will.
airing: a walk or ride for the benefit of health.
ale: strictly differs from beer, in containing no hops, but also used loosely for beer.
altarpiece: a picture or sculptured panel on the wall immediately above the holy table.
aperient: laxative medicine.
apoplexy: loss of consciousness similar to a stroke. The term was more widely used for sudden death from natural causes.
apprentice: (1) a child in the house of industry put out to work by the parish, mostly as a farm or domestic servant, the employer often being chosen by rota. Children were often sent there briefly for that purpose. (2) More generally, any child taken by an employer, to learn a trade.
argyle: a small metal vessel, usually of silver, for serving gravy hot.
armazoan: stout plain silk fabric favoured for black clerical gowns.
assessor: a local tax official dealing with assessed taxes.
association: formed locally (before professional police) to share the cost of obtaining evidence from informers and to bring offenders to trial, thus discouraging crime. Some had a constitution based on principles of mutual insurance.
audit: (1) independent examination to verify accounts; (2) the occasion of payment of sums of tithe previously agreed, or by a previously agreed formula.
barouche: four-wheel open carriage with a hood, raised to afford protection over half.
battlings: medium-sized branches, either lopped from the growing timber tree, or removed from a felled tree, to enable the trunk to be transported.
bequest: a gift by will, either of a specified sum of money or of an identified article.
bing or **bin**: a large receptacle for storing wine in bottles or other containers (as 'bin end').
blinders: a pair of blinkers, to restrict horse's peripheral view.
blister: result of applying any medical substance, such as ammonia, believed to give relief, for example to inflamed membranes. Also used as verb.
blunderbuss: an early gun with short barrel of large bore, firing a ball or solid slug.
bolus: a large pill.
bombazine: twilled or corded stuff, for lower-status clerical gowns and for mourning.
bounds: parish boundary. To go (or beat) the bounds was the customary and ritualised perambulation, by a party of parishioners in May, to note its exact position. Youngsters would be encouraged to remember salient features.
bradoon: snaffle and rein of a military bridle.

breviary: although often meaning a book of daily prayer, it also meant all abridged work (such as Ryece's history in the early seventeenth century).
Bridewell: a prison aiming at reforming the inmates.
bucellas: Portuguese wine from that region just north of Lisbon.
buffet: a recessed cupboard (or sideboard) for the display of china, &c.
calcavella: a sweet white wine from the Lisbon area.
calico: a cotton cloth, especially unbleached or plain white.
cambric: a fine white fabric, cotton or linen.
camphor julep: sweet drink to mask the bitter taste of the medicinal camphor.
cargo: consignment, bundle.
caveat: court process to suspend a legal step, pending a fuller hearing.
chaldron: measure of coal by volume; had some regional variation but usually 36 bushels, 25½ hundredweight, about 1¼ tons.
[*?*]**chamus**: possibly champagne is intended, as Longe's manuscript is nearly illegible.
chariot: a four-wheeled carriage with forward facing seats only.
chased: (of metal) engraved with pattern.
cheeks: pair of side-pieces to contain the hearth-fire.
chestnut-tree: wood for furniture manufacture.
chiffonier: a small sideboard with drawers.
chili vinegar: the base of a curry sauce.
cholera morbus: an infectious intestinal disease of bacterial origin, often fatal.
Christmas: 25 December, the fourth quarter-day.
close-stool: a commode, chair concealing a chamber-pot or pan.
cob gelding: a sturdy male horse, short of leg, impliedly steady rather than high-spirited.
cocking: standing smaller bundles of hay together to form a conical hay-cock to dry it.
colocynth: a purgative drug obtained from this pulpy gourd.
composition: (1) an agreed cash settlement, by a figure or formula, often for tithe (as agreed alternative to payment in kind) or parish's obligation to maintain the turnpike; (2) of a picture-frame, an artificial substance to imitate wood or metal or pottery.
cooped: harvested crop placed in a suitable container or cage.
croft: in Suffolk not a small farm, but used for any small enclosure.
cypher: a monogram with interlaced initials.
damask: a woven fabric (often linen) with pattern visible on both sides.
decoction: a liquid extracted by boiling.
dedimus: more fully *dedimus potestatem*: the authority for a magistrate to sit in judgment, joining the list of those who were acting in the courts.
defluxion: discharge, for example of bodily fluids.
dejeune: (French) a social gathering, usually evening, with light meal.
dilapidations: cash compensation for any lack of maintenance of tenanted property or parsonage house at the end of a tenure.
demesne: an area of land around a manor-house. One significance of its boundaries lay in its being free of tithe, as a garden of a cottage would be.
dentifrice: a paste or powder for cleaning teeth.
diapason: in a pipe organ, a main stop affecting the whole compass of the instrument.
diuretics: medicines to increase the passing of water. See also *dropsy*.

Doctors' Commons: the familiar name for the College of Advocates, the professional body of civil lawyers enjoying a monopoly of practice in that code, distinct from common law. The expression covered the building and its court sittings. All matters of probate, for example, were conducted by this system until 1857.
dowlas: a coarse linen or strong calico fabric.
draft: cheque or similar, often further defined by adding the name of the bank.
dram: measure of weight, one-sixteenth of an ounce.
draught: dose of liquid medicine.
dropsy: excess of watery fluid in the body.
duffeld: more usually duffel, a thick woollen cloth.
entail: (1) (noun) a trust, basically inalienable, with particular reference to the future after the first tenant-for-life. The succession was controlled, as for example down the line of the first-born male child only. An entail could be barred under some circumstances, but the approval of the court as well as the agreement of all concerned was needed. (2) Associated verb, to impose such control.
ermine: (in heraldry) white fur marked with black spots.
escritoire: writing-desk with drawers (also spelt by Longe escrutoire).
expectoration: spitting out of phlegm from the chest.
extravasated: the forcing of fluid from its normal course.
faggot: bundle of sticks for fire-lighting.
fence: used of living hedge, as of thorn-bush, as well as for an inert structure.
fencibles: unit of soldiers enlisted for service limited to defending the home country.
ferrule: a band strengthening a joint in metal vessel, or the end of a stick or tube.
flagon (flaggon): (1) a lidded jug, normally of metal with base wider than top, with single handle opposite the pouring spout. The lid has a projecting flange for opening and holding open with the thumb. In some cultures, beer is drunk straight from the flagon. (2) The same used as Holy Communion vessel to supply the chalice.
fosse: in gardening terms, the trench below a retaining wall, together making the feature known as a 'ha-ha', a barrier to livestock between park and garden.
frock: a man's long-skirted coat, as well as a woman's dress.
fustian: a thick twilled cotton cloth.
galloon: narrow close-woven braid, for binding other fabrics.
generals: the gathering of clergy at a local centre, sometimes with churchwardens, for the archdeacon's visitation. Dues were collected by the archdeacon's registrar. Dinner was a normal part of the occasion, with fines for non-attendance.
gig: a light two-wheeled one-horse open carriage.
girandole: branched candle-holder, usually mounted as wall-bracket.
hack-coach: hired conveyance, implying shorter journey with lower-grade horse.
hair-powder 'tax': imposed from 1795 as a stamp duty of £1 1s. 0d on a certificate, which those using hair-powder were obliged to purchase annually, subject to a penalty of £20. Exempt were clergy with average annual income under £100.
haysel: haymaking time, the season of cutting and drying the grass.
Haverhill Institution: low quality working jacket, probably made in the Haverhill house of industry.
heirloom: an item of personal property with trust status passed down within a family.
high fever: abnormally raised body temperature, with associated symptoms.

hogshead: a liquid measure with regional variation; usually 50–54 gallons, or 216 quarts, or 320 smaller bottles.
hundred: an ancient unit of administration, comprising typically about two dozen parishes. By the nineteenth century there were twenty-one hundreds in Suffolk plus the three largest boroughs. From 1894, hundreds were succeeded by rural and urban districts.
hygrometer: instrument for measuring humidity, for forecasting weather.
ilex: both the common holly, and (here less likely) the evergreen holm-oak.
incorporation: the process of being given legal status as a unit by Act of Parliament; in eighteenth and early nineteenth-century Suffolk. Often used as a noun, synonymous with the hundred, which needed the status for its house of industry.
indictment: formal accusation leading to criminal court proceedings.
James's Powders: a prescription to reduce fever. Marketed originally by Dr Robert James (died 1776) and remained popular fifty years after his death.
japan: a hard glossy varnish, usually black, as used originally in that country.
jura parochiala: a parish in law (as Crowfield, although its church was merely a chapel)
kerseymere: a twilled woollen cloth, allegedly named from the Suffolk village, and thus trousers made of such cloth.
kipling: small smoked herring, diminutive of kipper.
Lachryma Christi: an Italian wine from the Naples region: literally 'tears of Christ'.
ladle: large long-handled spoon with deep bowl for serving soup or gravy.
Lady Day: 25 March, quarter-day, the Annunciation to the Blessed Virgin Mary.
landaulet: small four-wheeled carriage, part-enclosed by removable cover and folding hood.
lanthorn: lantern, a source of light such as candle, in glass case, portable or hanging.
lay or **ley**: a field temporarily under grass, but the term (in several spellings) is used as a more permanent area name, regardless of crop.
leash or **lease**: a set of three, linked or strung together, especially a string of game.
lexicon: dictionary, frequently Greek (either classical or New Testament).
lignum vitae: a hard, dark wood.
liking: on approval, to be accepted back if not liked.
livery: uniform clothing of a servant, distinctive of the family, particularly of men-servants seen by the public, such as coachmen and footmen.
lumbago: rheumatic pain in the muscles of the lower back, the lumbar region.
macer-dish: a container for soaking to soften. Of curtains, a design.
malt mill: apparatus for grinding malted barley ready for the fermenting process.
malmocy: malmsey: a strong sweet wine from Greece, or later mostly from Madeira.
mere: a lake or pond, often associated with parish or other boundary.
mess: a group of men taking meals together, especially in the armed forces, and by extension the shared building.
Michaelmas: quarter-day, St Michael and All Angels, 29 September (or 11 October).
Midsummer: quarter-day, 24 June, also St John the Baptist.
modus: a past agreement or established custom for calculating cash payment for tithe, often rendered favourable to the payer by virtue of improved yield and/or inflation.

morbus: disease.
moreen: a strong ribbed fabric used particularly for curtains.
morocco: a fine flexible leather used especially in book-binding; originally goatskin from that country, but later elsewhere of calf.
mortice: here, the recess in a door-frame receiving the tongue of the lock.
mortification: gangrene.
muslin: woven lightweight cloth.
nankeen or **nankin**: (1) a yellowish cotton cloth, and thus trousers of that cloth; (2) oriental porcelain. Both were originally made in Nanking, China.
necessary: one euphemism (among many in English) for the toilet.
office: (1) non-residential premises, typically a shop or workshop; (2) domestic kitchen or minor service area such as a brew-house.
ormolu: a gold-coloured or gilded alloy metal, used to make fittings and ornaments.
packet-boat: a mail-boat taking passengers, usually coastal or cross-channel.
pales: wooden fencing, with the verticals often cut to a point.
passant: (of an animal in heraldry) side view with three paws on ground, one raised.
pear-tree: wood for quality furniture manufacture.
pembroke: smallish drop-leaf table popular since the eighteenth century.
perpetual curate: parish incumbent where the greater part of the income of the living was held by another, and thus usually with the lowest stipend (distinguished from curate employed by an incumbent as his assistant).
phaeton: a light open four-wheeled carriage, usually drawn by a pair of horses, named after the sun-god of Greek mythology.
physic: a dose of any form of medicine, or the medicine itself.
pightle: a small enclosure, often triangular in shape.
pillion: cushion or light saddle for seating a second rider behind.
plush: luxury cloth with long soft nap.
pointer: a dog trained to stand still on scenting game, to mark its position for shooting.
pollard: to cut the head of a tree, to encourage the growth of multiple branches. Also a noun.
post-chaise: a hired carriage with horses, together with a ‘post-boy’ to return it.
posters: post-horses hired to draw travellers’ own chaise, with ‘post-boy’ to return them.
postillion: when no coachman, the servant riding one coach-horse of a team.
poultice: a soft usually heated mass applied to the body (e.g. to relieve swelling).
press: (1) cupboard, often over drawers; (2) display cabinet for specimens.
previous: committee meeting to establish the agenda and conduct prior to full meeting.
quart: 2 pints, and thus just over a litre.
ragout: (French) seasoned stew of meat and vegetables.
rappee: coarse snuff, the tobacco having been rasped.
ray-grass: rye-grass.
recovery (to suffer): to be obliged to give up possession, under operation of law.
reversion: an interest in capital funds or landed property effective upon the death of the life-tenant. Both the date of vesting and the value at that time were uncertain. The life-tenant could make unilateral dispositions effective on his death, only if given express power of appointment.

riving billets: chopping wood (e.g. for firewood) by splitting with the grain.
rowler or **rowel**: (1) circular disc of spur; (2) leather disc with hole, inserted under horse's skin for medical reasons.
sarsnit or sarsinet, sarcenet: a fine silk lining material.
saw-pit: a hole enabling two men to use a two-handled saw vertically, one below.
scalloped: ornamental edging in imitation of a scallop shell.
scarlatina: scarlet fever, an infectious bacterial fever with rash, mostly of children.
scutcheon: a plate, often brass, usually inscribed with a name. A debasing of the earlier word escutcheon, a shield or emblem bearing heraldic arms.
secretary: secretaire, writing-desk.
sennight: shortened form of 'seven-night', that is a week: as: 'Thursday sennight'.
sequestration: the legal power temporarily to manage the financial affairs of a vacant benefice, pending a permanent appointment. The bishop normally delegated it.
seyons (or scions): grafts for apple and other trees.
shagreen: untanned rough leather dyed green, or its imitation.
sickle-toed: deformed horse's hoof of that curved shape.
sittings: an informal version of the word 'sessions'; the operation of a law-court.
slip: an incline, often artificial, giving access to a main path or road.
small beer: weak or table beer, from the second or third mashing of the malt.
snaffle: a simple bridle-bit without curb, usually with single rein.
sound: part of a fish also known as swim-bladder.
spasmodic: sudden involuntary muscular contraction, part of a medical condition.
SPCK: Society for Promoting Christian Knowledge, founded in 1698 to work both abroad and at home. Membership implied orthodoxy within the established church.
SPG: Society for the Propagation of the Gospel, founded in 1701 to encourage the spread of Christianity in foreign colonies and plantations among both Europeans and native peoples. Membership implied orthodoxy within the established church.
staithe: small landing stage or wharf.
stamp duty: a government duty, payment being evidenced at point of issue by stamping a document, either by affixing an adhesive stamp or impressing. An unstamped document could not be received in court evidence, and was thus unenforceable.
strangury: a painful condition with urinary retention.
stucco: plaster (or externally cement) coating wall surface, or to create mouldings.
surcingle: girth band for horse, to keep a pack or weight in place.
surrogate: a substitute for the bishop with specific duties.
tambour: circular drumlike frame for holding fabric taut for embroidery.
Teneriffe: in the Canary Islands, and thus the wine produced there.
terrier: a church's record, originally of the extent of land belonging to a benefice (latin: *terra*), but also listing goods and ornaments entrusted to the incumbent.
testimonial: an essential character reference before ordination.
thick(s): thicket, the dense vegetation of a small wood.
tontine: a form of insurance (and perhaps annuity investment) with a large element of chance, based on the principle of survivorship among the lives of participants. The relevant one was issued from Treasury Chambers in Dublin in 1774.
tureen: deep lidded dish for serving soup.

turnpike: during the eighteenth and early nineteenth century, a stretch of main road entrusted to a legal body to maintain. This shared the cost of maintenance between the parish (previously responsible) and the users (through payment of tolls at toll-gates, where passage was controlled, by a bar or 'pike').
turpentine: an oil distilled from fir-tree resin, used in mixing paint and varnish. Earlier, medically, both to make liniment, and as a strong medicine taken internally.
underwood: all woody growth of small diameter, distinguished from timber trees.
variorum: an edition of a classic work containing scholarly notes.
vellum: fine parchment, originally calf-skin, including imitations.
visitation: periodic supervisory meeting of the bishop or archdeacon with parish clergy (and others). The visitor would be supported by a legal/secretarial official. In a 'primary' visitation, typically every third year after Easter, the bishop would progress round a number of centres, confirming candidates one day, and meeting his clergy the next. For the archdeacon's general visitation, clergy gathered at a series of centres, usually twice a year. Churchwardens were sworn in. On a parish visitation the archdeacon would inspect parsonages and the fabric, goods and ornaments of churches.
wainscot: wooden panelling on internal walls, but also on small items such as chests.
waiter: salver or metal serving-tray.
walnut-tree: wood for quality furniture manufacture.
wand fence: a live hedge planted with young shrubs, each a single sprig.
wether: castrated ram.
whiskey: light two-wheeled one-horse carriage.
wilton: a type of woven carpet, originally made near Salisbury (Wiltshire).

NOTES ON PEOPLE

I Social contacts, professional people, farmers etc. Many single or sparse entries in the diaries are omitted, where their infrequency suggests that they had little influence upon John Longe, who must remain central. For those with the same surname entries are in order of dates of birth. Original spellings are usually retained.

II Trade and Commerce, including local people Longe employed on a contract basis: p.276.

III Longe's farm and domestic staff: p.281.

IV Authors from the catalogue of sermons (p.171) and artists and others named in the inventories (pp.210–20): p.283.

I

ACTON, Nathaniel Lee (d.1836 *s.p.*) of Bramford Hall and Livermere estates, brother of Lady Middleton (*q.v.*) of Shrubland Park. High sheriff of Suffolk, 1789.

ACTON, Caroline (d.1838), 'Miss C.' Unmarried sister of N.L. Acton (*q.v.*). She died in Southwold, her regular holiday home, and was buried at Baylham.

ANGUISH, the Revd George (1764–1843), prebendary of Norwich, from 1790 to 1820, rector of Gislingham from 1797 to 1833, with four other livings. He inherited Somerleyton in 1810.

ARCEDECKNE, Andrew of Glevering Hall, Hacheston. High sheriff of Suffolk, 1819.

AUFRERE, the Revd Philip D. (1776–1848), rector and vicar of Scarning (1808–48), rector of Bawdeswell (1810–48) (both Norfolk).

AUFRERE, Capt. –, member of the family of Hoveton Hall (Norfolk).

BACON, Nathaniel (1593–1660), ancestor of Nicholas Bacon (*q.v.*). Son of Edward Bacon of Shrubland Park. Parliamentarian, MP and Recorder for Ipswich, editor of *Annals of Ipswich*. Longe gave his portrait to Ipswich Corporation.

BACON, Nicholas the Revd (*c*.1732–96), vicar of Coddenham-cum-Crowfield (1768–96). Married to Anna Marie Browne (1753–85) but childless. Inherited Shrubland Park estate at Coddenham and Barham after his brother John in 1788, most of which he then sold. Generous benefactor to Longe's wife his sister-in-law Charlotte Longe (*q.v.*) and to John Longe who succeeded him as vicar.

BACON, John, FSA (1738–1816). Lifetime career in the Office of First Fruits (Queen Anne's Bounty). Lived north of London. Published an improved edition of Ecton's *Compilation of Ecclesiastical Valuations* (1786) and undertook historical enquiries for Longe on Coddenham advowson. *ODNB*.

BACON, Sir Edmund, bt (1749–1820), of Raveningham (Norfolk). Seventh baronet of Redgrave and 8th baronet of Mildenhall. Relative and executor of the childless Revd Nicholas Bacon (*q.v.*), the winding up of whose affairs led to friendship with Longe. His sister-in-law Mrs Custance was wife of Parson Woodforde's squire.

BACON, Edward, banker. See section II.

BAYNE, William J. (in the diary called BAINES), medical practitioner in Bury St Edmunds in 1830s.

BAKER, –, secretary to the bishop of Norwich, living in the cathedral close in 1787.

BARCLAY. See Maitland Barclay.

BARKER, Mrs Hannah. Housekeeper from 1794 to the Revd Nicholas Bacon and legatee in his will.

BARLEE, a Suffolk clerical family. C.W. Barlee esq. and the Revd Edward Barlee were involved in the celebrated case (1826) in which Longe was a witness.

BARLEE, the Revd Charles (1756–1831), rector of Fritton (1788–1831), rector of Worlingworth (1780–1831). He changed his name from Buckle in 1811, as a condition of an inheritance.

BARLEE, the Revd William (1761–1830), younger brother of Charles also changed his name (1811). Resident curate at Ashbocking in the 1820s, and when curate of Gosbeck (1824–30), took services for Longe. Also rector of Wrentham (1788–1830). By second marriage, brother-in-law of David Elisha Davy (*q.v.*), with whom he shared antiquarian excursions.

BARTON or Burton, – . Colonel in Ipswich locality during the summer of 1826.

BATCHELOR, –. Longe visited him in London in 1798, and was still in contact in 1833.

BATHURST, the Rt Revd Henry (1745–1837), bishop of Norwich from 1805 to 1837. Noted for his age and his Whig views. He lived at 12 Bedford St, London, and in Cheltenham for the waters and seldom visited his diocese in later years. *ODNB.*

BAYLEY/Bailey, –, London friends of Mrs Catherine Longe (*q.v.*), and visitors to Mrs A. Broke (*q.v.*).

BAYNING, the Revd Lord –, see Townshend.

BECK, Edward Bigsby of Needham Market (1760–1845), long-time medical adviser and friend of Longe. In the diary as 'Mr Beck'. Many professional attendances on the family and servants.

BECK (Dr) Edward (1794–1862), physician son of E.B. Beck (*q.v.*). After partnership with his father, qualified MB and in 1832 MD. Practised in Northgate Street, Ipswich.

BECK (Mr) Henry of Needham Market (1799–1891), son of E.B. Beck (*q.v.*), after apprenticeship to his father, was in practice with him from 1829.

BELL, the Revd Dr (b.1758), chaplain to the Princess Amelia, the youngest of the fifteen children of George III. Rector of a Yorkshire parish from 1808. Friend and patron of John Longe's father. Longe visited him in London and hosted him. *ODNB.*

BELLMAN, the Revd Edmund (1819–29), rector of Pettaugh from 1807 and Helmingham from 1812. Friend of Longe, for whom he sometimes took services.

BERNERS, Charles (1767–1831) of Woolverstone Hall. Unmarried. High sheriff of Suffolk, 1818.

BERNERS, the Ven. Henry Denny (1769–1862), archdeacon of Suffolk from 1819 and rector of Harkstead and Woolverstone with Erwarton. Resided at Erwarton parsonage until he succeeded to the family estate on the death of his brother Charles. JP.

BERRY, Lady –, moved to Leverets Lodgings, Ipswich.

BETHAM, the Revd William (1749–1839) Suffolk antiquary, editor of *The Baronetage of England*, 5 vols (1801–5). Until aged eighty-four, master of Stonham Aspal school, just north of Crowfield. Took services for Longe when already old. *ODNB*. His daughter was a poetess of national renown and his grand-daughter a noted novelist.

BETHAM, Sir William (1779–1853), son of the above. As Ulster King of Arms from 1820 and one of four chief heralds at the College of Arms he proclaimed the new sovereign in Dublin in 1830 and 1837. *ODNB*.

BEWICKE, the Revd Thomas (*c.*1770–1842) lived in Bungay; related to the family at Hallaton Hall.

BIRD, John (1755–1818). Longe's farm tenant at Malt House Farm, Coddenham. He supplied him with hops and malt. Churchwarden, 1807–11. He hanged himself 'in a fit of phrenzy'.

BLAKE, Dr Robert (1789–1862), rector of Bradfield 1820–31 and of Shotesham (Norfolk). Antiquary interested in the Booths of Shrubland (to sixteenth century).

BLAKE, Henry W. (*c.*1797–1857) of Norwich, Fellow of Corpus Christi College, Cambridge. Curate to John Longe (1823–25). Rector of Thurning (Norfolk) from then until his death.

BLAKE family (Francis John and William). Norwich attorneys who acted for Longe's father and between the diarist and Mrs Catherine Longe (*q.v.*), including interest on his loan to her.

BLOFIELD, the Revd Thomas C. (1778–1855), vicar of Hoveton (near Wroxham), 1819–1851.

BLOMFIELD, Barrington, of Coddenham (1801–70), surgeon, with a special interest in optics. Longe's sons sent for him occasionally in 1827 for general medical advice.

BOHUN, The Misses, of Saltgate St., Beccles.

BRAND, John (1756–1803), of Hemingstone Hall. In 1796 a widower, with young children.

BRETT, the Revd John (*c.*1781–1836), curate at Dersingham, rector of Wolverton, near Kings Lynn.

BRIGGS, the Revd John (1771–1840), incumbent of enlarged Creeting St Mary parish from 1829.

BROKE, Sarah (1743–1817), of Coddenham, daughter of the rector of Hintlesham. Longe referred to her alone as Miss Broke, and jointly with her sister as both the Miss Brokes and the Misses Broke.

BROKE, Anne (1757–1835), of Coddenham for nearly thirty-eight years. Sister of the above. 'Universally and deservedly beloved'. Although unmarried, Longe sometimes refers to her as 'Mrs', as a courtesy.

BROKE, Sir Philip Bowes Vere (1776–1841), of Broke Hall, Nacton. Rear admiral, famous for his action in HMS *Shannon*, created baronet 1813, married Sarah daughter of William Middleton (*q.v.*). The name Vere was added through his wife's inheritance from John Vere of Henley. *ODNB*.

BROKE VERE, Sir Charles, knight, major general (1779–1843), brother of Philip (above). Added the name Vere in 1822. Candidate in December 1832, and MP for East Suffolk from 1835. *ODNB*.

BROKE, George Nathaniel (1812–87), 3rd baronet. Son of Philip. Inherited Shrubland Park estate from his maternal grandfather after two related deaths without issue, as Broke-Middleton.

BROME, Lord (1774–1823), of Culford Hall, Charles Cornwallis. From 1805 2nd Marquess Cornwallis. MP for Suffolk in three Parliaments from 1796 to 1805, Colonel of West Suffolk Militia 1803.

BROME, Miss –, regular visitor to the Longes from 1798 on.

BROMILY, Arthur. Minister of Congregational church in Needham Market from 1794 to 1834.

BROOK, James (1754–1834). Through earlier marriage to widow Ann Bedingfield, became Longe's lifelong tenant at Choppyngs Hill Farm. Churchwarden 1803–07. Also leased Malt Office Farm in 1827 for his son Robert.

BROOK, Robert (b.1804), son of James (above) by his second wife. Occupied Longe's farm at Malt House and then succeeded his father as tenant at Choppyngs.

BROOK, B., tax collector in Coddenham in 1796.

BROOKE, Charles (1765–1836), rector of Blaxhall from 1798 and of Ufford from 1803.

BROOKE, Francis Capper (b.1810), son of the above. George Capper (*q.v.*) was his maternal uncle. Longe at first wrote his name 'Cooper' Brooke. Noted antiquary.

BROOKSBANK family included Mrs Ward and Mrs Stracey (Frances Longe's mother and aunt).

BROUGHAM, Henry Peter (1778–1868), Lord Chancellor in Earl Grey's cabinet. *ODNB*.

BROWN, the Revd Thomas: resident rector of Hemingstone from 1824 for sixty-one years. He took services for Longe (1824–32) and was also curate at Gosbeck and Henley.

BROWNE, the Revd William, JP, resident curate of Marlesford and of Stonham Aspal (1803–33).

BROWNLOW, Lady, wife of the earl. Mother of Lady Anne Middleton (wife of the 2nd baronet).

BUCK, the Revd John (1787–1838), unbeneficed curate, died at Ipswich by drowning in a pond.

BUNBURY, Thomas Charles (d.1821), 6th baronet, of Great Barton and Mildenhall. MP for Suffolk for forty-three years from 1768 to 1812. High sheriff of Suffolk, 1788. *ODNB*.

BUNBURY, Henry Edward (1778–1860), nephew of the above, 7th baronet. MP for Suffolk from 1830 to 1832. High sheriff of Suffolk, 1825. *ODNB.*

BURDETT, Sir Francis (1770–1844), controversial radical politician. *ODNB.*

BURTON, –, valuer of tithes, Ipswich (1797).

CAMELL, Dr Robert (1752–1837) of Bungay, surgeon.

CAMPBELL, Frederick W. of Birkfield Lodge, Ipswich. *ODNB*.

CAPPER, the Revd George (1767–1847), rector of Little Blakenham from 1794, of Knodishall briefly, of Gosbeck from 1803, and vicar of Wherstead (where he lived) from 1815 to 1847. JP, chairman of Suffolk Quarter Sessions Eastern division. Sporting prowess. His father (1735–1818) was rector of Earl Soham (*ODNB*), and his sister married the Revd Charles Brooke (*q.v.*).

CARNAC, John, of Aldeburgh. Lt Col. of the Lifeguards, his father (1716–1800) had a distinguished military career in India.

CARTHEW, the Revd Thomas (1764–1831), a member of the noted Woodbridge clerical family, perpetual curate of Woodbridge from 1791 to 1831, after his father. Had been a Royal Marine. Longe's son Henry was his curate for a few years. His brother was rector of Little Bealings, near Woodbridge, and another Carthew acted for the Longes as barrister.

CHARLESWORTH, the Revd John (1782–1864), evangelical rector of Flowton from 1815 to 1844.

CHEVALLIER, the Revd Temple Fiske (1764–1816), of Aspall near Debenham. Rector of Mickfield (1788–1804) and Badingham (1800–16) and perpetual curate of Aspall (1805–16).

CHEVALLIER, the Revd Clement (1765–1830), brother of the above, whom he succeeded as rector of Badingham from 1816 to 1830. He held other livings. JP from 1820.

CHEVALLIER, the Revd Dr John, of Aspall Hall. JP (*c.*1774–1846), physician, clergyman and agriculturalist. Perpetual curate of Aspall, from 1817 to 1846 and vicar of Cransford from 1831. Concern for mentally ill at Aspall Hall, licensed for six inmates. *ODNB.*

CHURCH, the Revd Joseph (1765–1830), of Coltishall. Contemporary of John Longe and his life-long friend and correspondent.They were ordained priest in the same year. After a Cambridge fellowship until 1803 he held incumbencies in Norfolk.

CLUBBE, John, of Ipswich, physician (1741–1811). Attended the Revd Nicholas Bacon for some years. Chief witness in Doctor's Commons on his mental state.

COCKSEDGE family, of Bury St Edmunds. Thomas Cocksedge High sheriff of Suffolk, 1802.

COLCHESTER, B., land surveyor, of Ipswich and Woodbridge.

COLLYER, Mrs Catherine, of Northgate St., Ipswich, related to those below.

COLLYER, the Revd Daniel (1752–1819), vicar of Wroxham with Salhouse 1776–1801, vicar of Reydon and perpetual curate of Southwold, 1777–1819.

COLLYER, the Revd John Bedingfield (1777–1857) of Hackford Hall, Reepham. Succeeded his father (above) as vicar of Wroxham with Salhouse, 1801–57.

COLLYER, the Revd Thomas, vicar of Holy Trinity, Bungay from 1834.

COLUMBINE, the Revd Dr Paul (1732–1821). Norfolk cleric who in 1798 received under delegated powers Longe's resignation of the Henley living.

COLVILE, Richard (d.1784). Acquired Hemingstone Hall, near Coddenham vicarage, by his marriage into the Acton family of Bramford Hall (*q.v.*) in the 1760s.

COLVILE, the Revd Dr Nathaniel (b.1761), son of the above. Rector of Lawshall from 1810. Also held Actons' livings of Broome near Bungay (1810–28) (where Robert Longe was his resident curate in 1827) and Baylham (1795–1828). Chairman of Quarter Sessions, Bury division.

COLVILE, the Revd Nathaniel (b. *c.*1800), son of Nathaniel (above). From 1824 incumbent of the Actons' living of the Livermeres, following his uncle, A.A. Colvile.

COLVILE, the Revd William (1804–59), younger son of Nathaniel, above. Curate at Coddenham (1827–29) and then held livings of Baylham and Broome (Norfolk) for thirty-one years.

CONDER, James (1762–1823), linen draper of Ipswich, noted antiquary and numismatist. *ODNB.*

COOKE, the Revd John C. (1776–1842), his father's curate and then (from 1806) vicar at Swilland near Coddenham, for forty-four years in total. Briefly also Longe's second curate (1819–20). Lived in Ipswich.

COTMAN, John Sell (1782–1842), of Norwich. Architectural draughtsman, water-colourist and leading figure in the Norwich school of painters. *ODNB.*

CRESPIGNY, Philip Champion C., of Doctor's Commons, bought estates in and around the Creetings in 1753. Member of an Aldeburgh family, and friend of the Bacons of Shrubland.

CRICKITT, Charles Alexander (d.1802), banker. See section II.

CRICKITT, Robert Alexander, son of above. Followed him as MP for Ipswich (1807–20).

CROASDAILE, Mr Henry (d.1831), of Hargrave Place, Stanstead. Son-in-law of Mrs Sleorgin of Henley Hall (*q.v.*).

CROASDAILE, Henry (jnr), son of the above, who after service in India suffered mental ill-health.

CROASDAILE, Miss –, grand-daughter of Mrs Sleorgin (*q.v.*). Estranged from her father over the care of her mentally ill brother. Resident in Coddenham.

CROFT, the Revd Stephen (1794–1868), rector of St Mary Stoke for forty-eight years from 1820.

CROSSE, Dr John Green (1790–1850), medical practitioner in Norwich, from 1815. *ODNB.*

CROWE, Charles (1785–1855), retired army officer, living for thirty-three years from 1822 near the church in Coddenham. Charitable donor to the parish. As friend, witness to Longe's will.

CULLUM, Sir Thomas Gery, 7th baronet (1741–1831), surgeon, botanist, FSA, Bath and Gloucester King of Arms. *ODNB.*

CULLUM, the Revd Thomas Gery, 8th baronet (1777–1855), rector of Knodishall from 1801. Antiquary and botanist.

DASHWOOD, Capt. C. Armand, married Harriet, daughter of William Middleton, in 1797.

DAVY, the Revd Charles (1756–1836). Suffolk-born of clergyman father. Dean of Gonville and Caius College and then Master of the Perse School, Cambridge. In 1791 briefly Nicholas Bacon's curate and then rector of Creeting St Peter and vicar of Wickham Market (1803–27). From 1818 resident rector of Barking with Combs. JP. With his wife and three daughters, friends with the Longe family. In 1828 Robert Longe married his daughter Margaret and became his curate at Combs.

DAVY, David Elisha (1769–1851), deacon, but never entered priesthood. Antiquary who recorded observations on extensive Suffolk excursions. JP and colonel of Volunteers. *ODNB.*

DAY, the Revd George (1792–1865), minor canon of Norwich Cathedral from 1817, vicar of Eaton.

DIGGENS, Thomas (1774–1855), Longe's tenant at Valley Farm and later church-warden.

DILLINGHAM, Brampton Gurdon. See Gurdon.

DRAKE, the Revd Nathan (1808–83), newly ordained curate at Creeting St Mary from 1832.

DRURY, the Revd George (1754–1830), rector of Whitton (1780–1830) and Claydon with Akenham (1807–30). His descendant in the second, a family living, was notoriously involved in the fiasco that led to the Burial Laws Amendment Act of 1880.

DUCKETT. See Jackson.

DUPUIS, Colonel Richard of Westgate St., Ipswich. His wife (d.1827), daughter of S.H. Kilderbee (*q.v.*), was cousin of Longe's first wife.

DURRANT, Lady and Colonel, of Eaton Road, Norwich.

DYSART, the Earl of (1739–1821), Sir Wilbraham Tollemache, 7th and last baronet and sixth earl of Dysart. His sister the countess (1745–1840) succeeded him. Both of Helmingham Hall.

EDGAR, Mileson (1760–1830), widely known as Colonel Edgar. Lieutenant Colonel in the 1st Loyal Suffolk Yeomanry. Of the Red House estate just north of Ipswich, with other landed and manorial interests in and around Coddenham. Longe served with him as JP and turnpike trustee.

EDGAR, the Revd John (1762–1842), brother of above. After army career, vicar of Falkenham from 1796, and rector of Kirton from 1820.

EDGAR, the Revd Mileson Gery (1784–1853), of Whitton and then the Red House. Eldest son of Col. Edgar, priest in charge of St Nicholas, Ipswich (1811–53), and rector of Trimley St Mary (1814–53).

EDGAR, the Revd John Robert (b.1798), second son of Col. Edgar. Curate at Trimley St Mary.

EDWARDS, Edward. Treasurer of Helmingham turnpike trust.

EDWARDS, John of Bramford. Valuer of land and tithes, 1798.

EDWARDS, Thomas. Chapel warden at Crowfield.

ELLIS, Henry. Tenant in the 1790s of the Longes' farm at Tunstall.

ELOUGH (or Etough), the Revd Dr Richard (b. *c.*1780), rector of Claydon (1832–41).

ELWIN family. John Longe's mother Dorothy was an Elwin.

ELWIN, Peter (1730–98), squire of Thurning and Booton (Norfolk), Longe's maternal uncle, eldest brother of his mother Dorothy, née Elwin (*q.v.*).

ELWIN, Fountain (1737–1833), Longe's maternal uncle, of Enfield and Gray's Inn, who had served as private secretary to his uncle General Tryon, governor of New York (*q.v.*). Involved in 1796–98 in transmiting dividends to Longe. Died aged ninety-six.

ELWIN, Hastings (1742–1833), Longe's maternal uncle, also of Gray's Inn.

ELWIN, Hastings jnr, son of the above, Longe's cousin, barrister and later Attorney General in the West Indies.

ELWIN, Fountain John (1777–1864). Lieutenant in East Norfolk Militia (diary 27 April 1798), Longe's cousin, son of Thomas (1734–1803), another maternal uncle.

ELWIN, Marsham (1784–1831), Longe's cousin, eldest son of the second marriage of Peter Elwin (above), given the maiden surname of his paternal grandmother (*q.v.)*.

ERRINGTON, the Revd –, curate at Stonham Aspal from 1833. Possibly John Richard (1809–82).

FENN, Simon. Longe's tenant of Valley Farm before 1798. Churchwarden 1798–1803. His widow Elizabeth died in 1831 aged seventy-eight.

FENN, Robert (d.1827), churchwarden 1812–14. Longe's tenant from before 1798 at or near Malt House Farm, Coddenham, which in his old age was run by his daughter or daughter-in-law.

FENN, Richard. Longe's farm tenant at Hemingstone about 1826 to 1834.

FIELD, Edward. Tenant of Coddenham school's farm at Mendlesham from 1830.

FLOWER, Miss, of Cheltenham. Aunt of Caroline Warneford of Wiltshire. Matchmaker in her marriage (1829) to Longe's eldest surviving son John.

FONNEREAU family. Owned Christchurch Park, Ipswich, from 1735. The owner between 1817 and 1840 was the Revd Charles William Fonnereau, who held several incumbencies, including Ipswich St Margaret from 1805.

FOORD, the Revd Henry (*c*.1776–1847), Longe's curate for about fourteen years, coming in 1801 as deacon after Cambridge. While incumbent of Semer (1815–21), he took some services for Longe.

FORD, the Revd James, of Brook St., Ipswich. Curate of Ipswich St Lawrence from 1808.

FOX, John (1787–1870), noted farmer and miller of Coddenham. He also assisted his widowed sister Mrs Rushbrooke, of Lime Kiln Farm, Coddenham.

FRERE, William (1775–1836). Serjeant-at-Law, Recorder of Bury St Edmunds, Master of Downing College from 1812 and Vice-Chancellor of Cambridge University. Married Mary, daughter of Brampton Gurdon, Dillingham (*q.v.*). Arbitrated between Longe and Middleton. *ODNB.*

GAUNT, Mr and Mrs. Visitors to Miss A. Broke and London friends of Mrs Catherine Longe (*q.v.*).

GEAR, Mr and Miss, nephew and niece of the Revd William Kirby of Barham.

GEE, the Revd. Clergyman in Ipswich (1797). Member of SPCK.

GOOCH, Sir Thomas Sherlock (1768–1851), 5th baronet, of Benacre. MP for Suffolk 1802–1830. High sheriff of Suffolk, 1833.

GOODWIN, George (1772–1848), of independent means, lived near the church in Coddenham. His daughter married Robert Brook (*q.v.*), farmer of Coddenham.

GOWARD, Miss (1805–99), born in Ipswich, successful operatic singer with Covent Garden company.

GREENE, the Revd Thomas (*c*.1788–1868), educated at Eton and Cambridge. Longe's curate from 1818 to 1822, and later rector of Fulmodeston (Norfolk) and honorary canon of Norwich.

GURDON, Major Brampton (b.1740), of a well-known East Anglian family including several clergy and army officers. He added his mother's name Dillingham. High sheriff of Norfolk, 1789. Built Letton Hall, Sir John Soane's first country house.

HALL, George Blair, of Bosmere House near Coddenham, previously the Uvedales' residence.

HAMILTON, Dr Robert (1748–1830), Ipswich physician. Author of *Cure of Hydrophobia* (1786).

HARLAND, Sir Robert, bt (1766–1848), of Wherstead Park, which in 1814 he exchanged with his relative Admiral Vernon for Orwell Park, Nacton. High sheriff of Suffolk 1817.

HASTED, the Revd Henry (1771–1852), of 76 Northgate St., Bury St Edmunds. Preacher at St Mary's (1802–42) and also rector of Ickworth, Horringer and Bradfield Combust. Involved in founding of County Hospital at Bury. Published a collection of sermons.

HAYNES, the Revd C.M., curate to J.C. Cooke (*q.v.*) at Swilland from 1790s.

HEATH, the Revd Benjamin, rector of enlarged Creeting St Mary from 1803 to 1829 and vicar of Chattisham from 1811. JP.

HENNIKER, John (1752–1821), 2nd baron (an Irish peerage) from 1803. Died *s.p.*

HENNIKER, John Minet (added name of Major in 1822) (d.1832), nephew of above, 3rd baron.

HENNIKER-MAJOR, John, of Thornham, 4th baron. MP for Suffolk (Eastern Division) from 1832. Longe calls him 'Lord Henniker'.

HENNIKER DE VERE. See Vere.

HIBGAME family of East Anglian clerics. It was probably the Revd Edward (1777–1861) with a living in Cambridgeshire who was a close friend of Henry Longe (*q.v.).*

HOLMES, Mr T., attorney of Bury St Edmunds.

HOWARD, –, farm tenant of Longe.

HOWES, the Revd Thomas (d.1796), rector of Morningthorpe (Norfolk). He married Longe's paternal aunt (d.1822). His sister married Longe's paternal uncle. He had three clerical sons (*q.v.*).

HOWES, the Revd Thomas (b.1770), eldest of the three brothers, rector of Fritton and vicar of Tharston (Norfolk), 1796–1848.

HOWES, the Revd George (1772–1855), second son. Like Longe, educated at Norwich School and Trinity College, Cambridge. Longe's curate at Coddenham to 1799. Succeeded Longe's father in the Spixworth living (1808–1855), minor canon of Norwich.

HOWES, the Revd Francis (Frank) (1776–1844), third son of the rector of Morningthorpe, above.Vicar of Wickham Skeith 1809–44. *ODNB.*

HULTON, Thomas (d.1823). Colonel of 3rd Norfolk Militia from 1799. Baronet in 1815 under name of Preston, assumed in 1805.

HUMFREYS, –, of Wroxham and Coltishall. Longe visited him when in Norfolk.

HUNT, W. Powell, attorney and partner of Pownall of Ipswich.

IBBETSON, Miss Harriet (1774–1843), daughter of Sir Charles Ibbetson, 2nd baronet, of Denton Hall, Yorkshire. She was the Theobalds' long-time tenant at Henley Hall.

INGLISH, Mrs, niece of Hannah Archer (servant of Nicholas Bacon) and beneficiary in her small estate, of which John Longe was executor.

IVES, Jeremiah (1753–1820), of Catton Hall Norwich. Mayor of Norwich in 1786 and 1801.

JACKSON, Sir George bt, father of John Longe's cousin by marriage, Catherine Longe (*q.v.*). Longe dined with him when in London. He took the name Duckett in 1797. *ODNB.*

JACKSON, the Revd Stephen (1786–1838), rector of Nettlestead from 1815, curate of Little Blakenham (1821–38) and of Ringshall from 1830. Antiquary. Father owned *Ipswich Journal.*

JAMES, William Rhodes, of Barking Hall. Tenant from 1825 until 1833 and then at Tattingstone.

JENNEY, Miss –, friend of Miss Broke in 1798.

JOHNSON, Capt. –, in Warwickshire cavalry, stationed in Ipswich.

JOHNSON, the Revd Charles (1765–1849), rector of Bildeston from 1796.

JOHNSTON(E), Sir William (1760–1844), 7th baronet, brother-in-law of Nicholas Bacon. He sold to Longe some Coddenham property at the farm occupied by John Bird which his wife (*q.v.*) had received on Bacon's death. *ODNB.*

JOHNSTON(E), Mary (d.1802), sister of the Revd Nicholas Bacon and from 1783 wife of Sir William Johnstone (above). She alleged that her brother lacked mental capacity to make a valid will.

JOSSELYN, –, valuer of land and tithes for Longe from 1826. Lived in Sproughton.

KEDINGTON, –, Coddenham farmer of some substance.

KENNY, Mary, cook and then housekeeper to the Longes from their marriage in 1791 until 1813. She and her sister Elizabeth were legatees of the Revd Nicholas Bacon.

KERRISON, Col. Sir Edward, bt (1774–1853), of Oakley Park. After active military service, he finally rose to rank of general. Prominent Tory, MP for Eye (1824–52). *ODNB.*

KIDD, the Revd Thomas (*c.*1772–1850), high master of Norwich School after Valpy (*q.v.*). *ODNB.*

KILDERBEE, Samuel H., of Great Glemham, JP (1725–1813), attorney and town clerk of Ipswich (1755–67), the first owner of Great Glemham House. Friend of Thomas Gainsborough, who painted portraits of him and his wife. Conflict with John Longe over repayment of a bond. The mother of Longe's first wife was a Kilderbee.

KILDERBEE, the Revd Dr Samuel, of Gt Glemham, JP (1760–1847), son of the above. Rector of Trimley St Martin from 1787, of Campsea Ashe until 1817 and of Easton from 1817. Heavy debts.

KILDERBEE, Spencer, of Campsea Ashe (1790–1860), son of the above. Took his mother's name Horsey. Between 1829 and 1841, was MP for three different constituencies.

KIRBY, John Joshua (1716–74), son of the author of *Suffolk Traveller* (1690–1753), painter, author on architectural perspective, friend of Gainsborough. *ODNB.*

KIRBY, William (1720–91), of Witnesham Hall, attorney at law. Brother of the above and of Sarah Trimmer (*q.v.*), the famous Christian author.

KIRBY, John (d.1797), estate manager of Suffolk estates including Shrubland Park. As one of two executors, he wound up the affairs of the Revd Nicholas Bacon but his own death soon followed.

KIRBY, the Revd William (1759–1850), son of William (above). After Ipswich School and Gonville and Caius College Cambridge, he lived at Barham parsonage for sixty-eight years, first as Nicholas Bacon's curate in charge and then from 1797 as rector. Additionally curate at Coddenham, he resigned shortly after Bacon's death in 1796. He took private pupils, corresponded widely and his study of insects led to his international renown as an entomologist. *ODNB.*

KITSON, John, of Upper Close, Norwich, attorney and notary, secretary to the bishop in 1826–27. Still in post in 1845.

LAWRENCE, –, attorney acting for Mr Croasdaile.

LAWTON, the Revd Henry, vicar of Ashbocking from 1793 and also assisted at Gosbeck. Under delegated power from the archdeacon he inducted Longe into the Coddenham living.

LEAKE, Robert Martin (1782–1876), married Longe's daughter Charlotte (*q.v.*) in 1822. Longe was always distant with him. He inherited Woodhurst, Oxted (Surrey), on his father's death in 1833 and rose to the rank of lieutenant-general.

LEAKE, Charlotte. See Longe.

LEEDS (otherwise Leedes), William, of the family farming at Hemingstone for generations.

LEGGETT, William. 'Surveyor' and collector of assessed taxes.

LEVESON GOWER, Miss –, friend of Miss A. Broke. Related to Lord Granville (1758–1833), the tenant of Wherstead Park near Ipswich, who became 1st Duke of Sutherland.

LONGE, the Revd John (1731–1806), father of the diarist. Rector of Spixworth from

1756 and also Reymerston and Hackford, perpetual curate of Horsham St Faith (Norfolk) and royal chaplain from 1760. Married Dorothy Elwin (1738–1819).

LONGE, Francis (1748–1812). Longe's cousin (son of his father's elder brother) was estate owner at Spixworth (Norfolk) from 1776 but lived often in London. After the death of himself *s.p.* and of his wife, the estate passed to the diarist's son John.

LONGE, Mrs Catherine (1754–1828), wife and for sixteen years impoverished widow of Francis (above).

LONGE, the Revd John, the diarist (1765–1834), son of the rector of Spixworth (above), educated at Norwich Grammar School and Trinity College, Cambridge, ordained priest December 1789. Curate at Coddenham from January 1790, vicar of Henley 1793–98, inherited the advowson to become vicar of Coddenham-cum-Crowfield (1797–1834). Married (1) in 1790 Charlotte Browne (1761–1812), whose sister had been wife of the Revd Nicholas Bacon, (2) in 1817 Frances Ward (1773–1863). JP.

LONGE, Robert (1768–1846), of Catton Lodge and then Blofield. Younger brother of John Longe the diarist. Captain in the East Norfolk Militia, married but died *s.p.*

LONGE, Charlotte (1796–1876), daughter of John of Coddenham, married in 1822 Robert Martin Leake. Lived in London and Surrey. Died *s.p.*

LONGE, Francis Bacon (1798–1819), eldest son of John of Coddenham, died young *s.p.*

LONGE, John (1799–1872), second son of John of Coddenham, married Caroline Warneford, inherited Spixworth estate in 1828, died *s.p.*

LONGE, the Revd Robert (1800–90), third son of John of Coddenham, married Margaret Davy. They had four children. He succeeded his father as vicar of Coddenham-cum-Crowfield, 1834–90.

LONGE, the Revd Henry Browne (1803–83), fourth son of John of Coddenham, married Anne Nicholson. Vicar of Monewden from 1847. Four daughters born after death of his father.

LUCAS, –, Capt. Norfolk Militia. Friend of John Longe's brother in 1798.

LYNCH, William, needy Ipswich friend of Nicholas Bacon, who assisted him financially.

LYNN, Wall, of Woodbridge. Medical practitioner and numismatist.

MAITLAND BARCLAY, Capt. Charles, gentleman. Formed and led Ipswich troop of cavalry, 1798. Lived at Hill House, in east Ipswich. Part of the grounds later became public as Alexandra Park.

MANN, the Revd Thomas (*c*.1761–1847), Nicholas Bacon's curate 1786–7. At later times curate of Bramford, of Baylham and of Hemingstone.

MAPES, Major –, administered detail of 'defence of the realm', 1798.

MARRIOTT, the Revd Robert (*c*.1765–1819), of Needham Market, curate at Henley. After seeing in John Longe's successor in 1798, the Revd William Norford (*q.v.*), and being curate at Great Blakenham until 1812, he took a living in Dorset.

MARRIOTT, John, brother of the above, attorney, clerk to justices of the hundred. The brothers may be sons of the shop-keeper at Needham Market described by Woodforde as 'a very hearty man'.

MARSHAM, Robert (d.1797), of Stratton Strawless Hall (Norfolk), probably Longe's great-uncle, brother of his maternal grandmother Philippa, née Marsham. The family continued at the Hall (Diary 13 June, 8 Sept. 1831).

MARTIN, William (1761–1842), of Hemingstone Hall from about 1803. His wife was the daughter of Sir Joshua Rowley bt. Mr and Mrs Martin died within a year of each other. The Longe and Martin families were united by a marriage in 1856.

MATCHETT family. Owned the *Norfolk Chronicle*, Norwich.

METHOLD, Thomas, the Revd Canon (1765–1836), forty-six years rector of Stonham Aspal from 1789 and canon of Norwich cathedral (1804–36). As JP, a long-time chairman of Quarter Sessions for the Ipswich division of the county.

METHOLD, the Revd John William (1801–83), son of above, ordained deacon with Henry Longe in 1826. Curate of Henley to 1830. First living, in Norfolk, 1835.

MIDDLETON, William (1746–1829), 1st baronet from 1804. Lived first at Crowfield Hall, and then at Shrubland Park which he purchased from Nicholas Bacon. High sheriff of Suffolk in 1784. MP twice for Ipswich borough (1784–90 and from 1802). Later took the additional name of Fowle. The divided leadership in two parishes led him into conflict with Longe.

MIDDLETON, Henry (1755–1811), brother of William. In 1801 won £30,000 on the lottery.

MIDDLETON, Harriet (*c*.1756–1852), Sir William's wife, the daughter of Nathaniel Acton of Bramford Hall (*q.v.*), later Dowager Lady Middleton. She inherited from her godfather, Fowle.

MIDDLETON, William Fowle Fowle, the 2nd baronet (1784–1860), of Shrubland Park from 1829. High sheriff of Suffolk, 1830. His wife Anne (d.1867) was the daughter of Lord Brownlow.

MILLS, the Revd Thomas, rector of Stutton from 1821, antiquary and JP from 1828.

MOOR, Major Edward (1771–1848), of Great Bealings. Author, both on his oriental experiences and on Suffolk dialect. *ODNB*.

MORGAN, Benjamin, of Baylham, farmer, land and tithe valuer. Became a director of Barham house of industry in 1826.

MOSS, Richard, deputy diocesan registrar in Norwich, 1796–97.

NELSON, Admiral Horatio (1758–1805), bought a property for his wife's occupation at Roundwood, Ipswich. Honoured by Ipswich borough as high steward. *ODNB*.

NORFORD, the Revd William (*c*.1772–1807), incumbent of Henley from 1798 to 1807, after Longe.

NUNN, the Revd Thomas (1799–1877), the senior of two curates in Longe's old age. He later held livings, first of Claydon (near Coddenham) from 1841, and later of Stanstead.

OAKES, Orbell (1768–1837), of Bury St Edmunds, son of the diarist James Oakes, was (with the Revd Henry Hasted, *q.v.*) an executor of the will of Mrs Wayth (*q.v.*).

ONLEY, Charles Savill (1756–1843), MP for Norwich 1812–18. Captain RN, then colonel in the Volunteers. Formerly Charles Harvey, he changed name on succeeding to Stisted Hall, Essex.

ORFORD, the Revd James (1795–1859), of St Mary Elms, Ipswich, and Poor Law chaplain.

PARKER, the Revd Charles F. (1787–1870), rector of Ringshall from 1819 to 1870. Longe asked him to be a replacement trustee of his marriage settlement.

PASKE, Edwin P. Involved in business matters, valuing copyhold farm property and in the return of a Bacon picture (1798). Manager of Coddenham Saving Bank (1827).

PASKE, the Revd Edward (*c.*1790–1885). After Cambridge briefly Longe's second curate (1819–20). He held livings of West Creeting (1818–85) and Battisford (1827–85), both in Bosmere deanery.

PASKE, George A. (*c.*1798–1882), younger brother of Edward, was perpetual curate of Needham Market from 1828 for fifty-four years, in plurality with Willisham (1837–82), both in Bosmere deanery.

PAULET, – (d.1831), married to a relation of Mrs Frances Longe.

PENRICE, John, of King St., Great Yarmouth.

PENRICE, Thomas, surgeon and physician, of Great Yarmouth.

PETTIWARD, Roger (1754–1833), squire of Finborough, JP. High sheriff of Suffolk, 1811. Long-time friend of Longe.

PETTIWARD, the Revd Daniel (*c.*1762–1833), younger brother of Roger (above). His curacy at Coddenham ended when Longe became vicar, but they remained friendly. Then family livings of Onehouse and Great Finborough. He died suddenly at the Angel Hotel, Bury St Edmunds.

PHEAR, the Revd John (b.1794), rector of Earl Stonham from 1823. He took pupils.

PLEES, the Revd William (1781–1849), of Dutch descent. Vicar of Ashbocking from 1833.

PLESTOW, the Revd John D. (1759–1824), of Ipswich, local landowner and sometime rector of Harkstead. Also from 1791 to 1824 rector of Watlington (Norfolk).

POGSON, Col. Thomas, of Kesgrave House, near Little Bealings (1764–1835), JP. Henry Longe was briefly engaged to his daughter. Eight of his eleven children died under thirty-five.

POWNALL, Edward, Ipswich attorney in partnership with W. Powell Hunt.

PRESS, Edward (1774–1841), curate to Longe (1821–24), ordained twenty-four years earlier. He also served curacies at Henley and Hemingstone from 1822. He died suddenly in church in Norfolk.

PRESTON, the Revd George, JP (1771–1840), of Stanfield Hall near Wymondham (Norfolk). He later took the name Jermy. Friend of both the Longe and the Ward families.

PRESTON, Miss Lucy, daughter of the above. She was invited to Coddenham for extended visits by the Longes. Her friends in and near Ipswich included the Collyers (*q.v.*) and Edgars (*q.v.*).

PROBART, Dr Francis George (1782–1861), physician, of 5 Honey Hill, Bury St Edmunds.

RABETT, Reginald (1771–1810), of Bramfield Hall, member of an old East Suffolk county family.

RANSOME, Robert (1753–1830), iron-founder in St Margaret's parish, Ipswich, from 1789. *ODNB.*

RAY, Richard (1721–1811), of Haughley and Lincoln's Inn. His daughter married Charles Tyrell (*q.v.*).

READ/REED, Col. –. When stationed in Ipswich in August 1796 he had his wife and daughter with him.

REEVE, Admiral Samuel (1732–1802), of a well-known Ipswich family. At Shrublands, 1796. *ODNB.*

REEVE, the Revd Thomas (*c.*1745–1824), Ipswich school boy. Master from 1772 of Bungay Grammar School. Married the daughter of the Revd Ambrose Uvedale, rector of Barking. *ODNB.*

RENDLESHAM. See Thelluson.

RIPPER family included William Kirby's first wife.

ROBERTS, the Revd John (1766–1822), incumbent of Creeting St Mary (with St Olave and All Saints) from 1790 to 1803. In his time, All Saints Church, standing a few yards from St Mary's, was demolished after storm damage.

ROBERTS, the Revd William, Longe's curate in 1826 and 1827. Left voluntarily, without animosity.

ROBINSON family. When living by Coddenham church were victims of a nocturnal break-in, 1827.

RODWELL, William (1792–1878), of Holbrook. Ipswich solicitor in partnership with John Chevallier Cobbold. Acted in Sleorgin/Croasdaile trust. Members of the family were intermarried with Theobalds, Meadows, Kirbys and Moores.

ROGERS, the Revd T.E. (1781–1844), rector of Hessett (1813–44) and also of Lackford (1817–44), where the neglected state of the church and churchyard drew strong criticism from D.E.Davy.

ROSE, the Very Revd Hugh James (1795–1838), dean of Hadleigh. Host of the Hadleigh Conference in July 1833 at the start of the Oxford Movement, editor of *The British Magazine*, potential leader of the Tractarians. Ill-health led to his early death. *ODNB.*

ROWLEY, Sir William (1761–1832), 2nd baronet, of Tendring Hall, Stoke-by-Nayland. High sheriff of Suffolk in 1791, MP for Suffolk 1812–30. Married daughter of Admiral Sir Robert Harland bt (*q.v.*).

RUSHBROOKE, Lt. Col. Robert (*c.*1777–1845), of Rushbrook, MP for West Suffolk, 1835–45. Re-ordered the church there with his own wood-joinery and carving.

RUSHBROOK, George (1759–1821). Longe's tenant at Lime Kiln Farm, Coddenham, from at least 1798. Churchwarden from 1813.

RUSHBROOK, Mrs (1775–1832), widow of the above. She continued the farm and in 'the lime trade' with the help of her son John and of her brother John Fox who continued to act after her death.

RUSHBROOK, John. Longe gave him notice to quit Lime Kiln Farm at Michaelmas 1833 after the death of his mother, with a view to selling the major part.

RUSHBROOKE, George, butler to the Revd Nicholas Bacon from 1792 and legatee.

SANDBY, the Revd George, of Denton and Flixton, near Harleston. He owned farms at Otley and Swilland, near Ipswich.

SEAMAN, –, of Coddenham, rate-collector, treasurer of local association for prosecuting felons.

SELVIN, Mr –, of Bosmere Hall, near Coddenham, in 1826.

SETON/SEATON, –, disputed Longe's institution to Coddenham living, probably as agent.

SEWELL, –, of Blake, Keith & Blake, attorneys, St Stephen's, Norwich.

SIELY, the Revd Thomas Hurford (1783–1874), of Norwich and Cambridge. Ordained deacon in 1807, curate of Gosbeck (1807–16), of Coddenham (1815–17) and of Hemingstone, and then chaplain to the British Embassy in Lisbon from 1819. Later curate of Baylham 1841–53.

SIMPSON, the Revd Mallyward (1772–1829), rector of Mickfield, a family living, from 1804. His reception at Shrubland in 1798 suggests a previous friendship with the Middletons.

SIMPSON, the Revd Mallyward (1804–72), succeeded father (above) as rector of Mickfield (1829–72).

SINGLETON, the Revd Thomas (1783–1842), son of the governor of Landguard Fort. He left Suffolk after ordination in 1807. *ODNB*.

SLEORGIN, Mrs (d.1808), parishioner of Longe's when tenant at Henley Hall. As her trustee after her death he had a continuing relationship with her family. See Croasdaile.

SMITH, Samuel, tenant of Coddenham school trustees' farm at Mendlesham from *c*.1821 to 1830.

SMITH, the Revd William (*c*.1790–1850), rector of Brome and Oakley but also curate to Longe (1822–23). Later rector of Honingham (Norfolk). Godfather to Longe's grandson Francis.

SPARROW, John E., of the Ancient House, Buttermarket, Ipswich. Attorney, town clerk of Ipswich from 1828 and coroner for the county.

SPOONER, Capt. –, stationed in Ipswich with Warwickshire cavalry.

SPORLE or Spall, Henry, of New Road, Bungay. Auctioneer and appraiser.

STAFFORD, Lord George of Costessey Hall, Norwich. Replaced manor house with new hall.

STEWARD family. Edward and John Henry. Norwich attorneys, notaries, registrars to the archdeacon.

STEWART, Col. –, of Melton.

STIMSON, John (1754–1837), freehold farmer of Hall Farm, Coddenham.

STISTED, Col. –, of Ipswich, Provisional Cavalry, 1797.

STRACEY, Sir Edward, bt, of Rackheath Hall (Norfolk). Neighbour to the Longes at Spixworth.

STRACEY, John, of Sprowston Lodge, Norwich. Mrs Stracey (d.1827) aunt of Mrs F. Longe (*q.v.*).

SUTTON, the Revd Dr Charles (*c*.1756–1846), perpetual curate of St George's, Norwich, 1788–1841. Married the widowed daughter of William Kirby of Witnesham, 1793. He helped Longe in prolonged searches into the history of Coddenham advowson.

TAYLOR, the Revd George (1787–1847), Bungay Grammar School and St Johns College, Cambridge, Longe's curate from 1815 to 1818 and held a living in Norfolk (1814–47). Also rector at Clopton where he was succeeded by his son. Trustee of Longe's marriage settlement.

THELLUSSON, Peter Isaac. Purchased a farm at Tunstall from the Longes. Having bought Rendlesham estate, he was created Baron Rendlesham in 1806.

THEOBALD, John Medows (1749–1830), of Henley Hall and later Claydon Hall, JP. Major in 1st Suffolk Yeomanry Cavalry. Landlord to Longe in Henley (1793–97) and continued a colleague for many years. His father (d.1788) had been high sheriff.

THOMAS, George, medical practitioner of the Thoroughfare, Woodbridge, with extensive gardens to the River Deben. High sheriff of Suffolk, 1820.

TIMSON, William (1740–1818), gentleman residing at Moor Park, Farnham (1798), having an interest in Temple pictures and heirlooms.

TONYN, General –. Lived in Ipswich, 1796.

TOWEL, Mrs. Farmer in dispute with Longe over ownership of land in Coddenham parish.

TOWNSHEND, the Revd the Hon. Henry (1797–1866), became 3rd Baron Bayning of Honingham Hall in 1823. Rector of Brome with Oakley (1821–47). Interest in early Tithe Bill.

TREADWAY, the Revd John (1802–34), from Norfolk, a 'ten-year man' at

Cambridge. Curate at Pettaugh from 1825; curate to Longe from 1828 to 1831. He died young at Helmingham, a living which he probably held with Otley.

TRIMMER, Mrs Sarah (1741–1810), daughter of the artist Joshua Kirby (*q.v.*). Nationally renowned as pioneering writer of Christian publications for young people. *ODNB.*

TRYON, Mrs (d.1819), Longe's maternal great-aunt, sister of his Elwin grandfather. By 1796 she was the widow of General Tryon who had been governor of New York.

TURNER, the Revd George (1767–1839), rector of Kettleburgh and Monewden.

TURNER, Dawson (1775–1858), prominent resident of Great Yarmouth. Norfolk and Suffolk JP. Banker, widely known antiquary, botanist and patron of Norwich school of painters. *ODNB.*

TURNER, the Revd Richard, son of Dawson Turner. Vicar of St Nicholas, Great Yarmouth from 1800, vicar of Ormesby (Norfolk) and rector of Sweffling, both from 1813.

TURNER, Major –, of Ipswich, friend of John Longe junior in 1826/27.

TYRELL, Charles (1776–1872), of Gipping and Haughley. High sheriff of Suffolk, 1815, MP for Suffolk (and then Western Division) from 1830 to 1835. Obtained copy of public records.

UVEDALE family. Admiral Samuel (1725–1808) of Bosmere House, near Needham Market, and later of Ipswich. When still a captain, he hosted Parson Woodforde in May 1775. His widow died in 1814, so the Mrs Uvedale known to Longe was his daughter-in-law. Otherwise a clerical family.

VALPY, the Revd Edward (1764–1832), high master of Norwich School and brother of the headmaster of Reading School, rector of Thwaite and vicar of South Walsham. *ODNB.*

VERE, Sir Charles Broke: see Broke.

VERE, Henniker de, unsucceessful candidate for Parliament in 1831.

WALFORD, the Revd Ellis (1802–81), son of the rector of Long Stratton (Norfolk), himself curate and then rector of Bucklesham and Newbourne (1829–1872), a family living, and rector of Dallinghoo.

WARBURTON, the Revd William P. (1762–1821), briefly curate of Redenhall with Harleston (Norfolk). Domestic chaplain to John Moore, archbishop of Canterbury to 1805. Held three livings in Kent. His daughter Miss Warburton was in Norfolk in 1833.

WARD, Col. Richard (1730–99), of Salhouse Hall (Norfolk). Despite his age, stationed at Ipswich in 1798 with East Norfolk Militia. His daughter was later John Longe's second wife.

WARD, the Revd William, of Diss (1769–1835), son of the above. Curate of Swainsthorpe, Carleton Rode and Bunwell (Norfolk). His wife died in 1826. For others see family tree, above, pp.lx–lxi.

WARD, William (b. *c.*1795), of St Neots and Huntingdon, medical practitioner. His wife Lydia (1798–1833) was his cousin.

WARD, the Revd Dr James (1766–1842), unrelated to the above Wards. After a career as senior chaplain in Bengal with the East India Company he settled at Coltishall (Norfolk).

WARNEFORD, Col. Francis, of Wiltshire. His daughter Caroline married John Longe's son John in 1829. He and his wife first met the diarist at Spixworth in 1831.

WATSON, Sir Frances, bt, of Gipping Hall.

WAYTH, Mrs (d.1831), of Bury St Edmunds, widow (probably of county coroner of that name, earlier living in Eye). Links with the Rabett family (*q.v.*) and with Spencer Kilderbee (*q.v.*).

WENN, James, earlier clerk to John Kirby, Ipswich attorney, and then on his own account. In constant business contact with Longe for thirty-seven years, and a family friend.

WENN, James (1796–1867), son of the above. After a Salisbury post, curate to Longe (1828–30). Later, vicar of Wickhambrook, and Broome (Norfolk) (1859–67) with chaplaincy to the duke of Hamilton and Brandon (1853–67).

WILCOX, the Revd John, an evangelical. Lacked pastoral success as rector of Stonham Parva from 1816.

WILLIAM FREDERICK, Duke of Gloucester (1776–1834), great grandson of George II. He married his cousin Mary, sister of George IV and William IV. Known as 'Silly Billy'.

WILLIAMS, Mr –, recipient (or acting for recipient) of a Bacon/Temple picture, probably an heirloom.

WINDHAM, Major –, of the Windham family of Felbrigg Hall (Norfolk).

WINDUS, Dr –, Longe's advocate (civil lawyer) in Doctor's Commons, London.

WODEHOUSE, Lord (1741–1834), of Kimberley Hall, 1st baron, MP for Norfolk to 1797.

WODEHOUSE, Philip (1745–1811), prebendary of Norwich cathedral, received Longe's resignation.

WODEHOUSE, the Hon. John (1770–1846), succeeded to become 2nd baron in 1834. Colonel of East Norfolk Militia from 1792.

WYNNE, Sir William, distinguished civil lawyer practising in church courts, dean of the arches (1788–1809) and in old age Master of Trinity Hall, Cambridge.

II. Trade, Commerce and Workmen

D	in the Diary for the year stated
S	in the Servants' Wages Book
A	reference is in *other* archival material (not transcribed) SRO(I) HA24/50/19/4.5(18) and (21), /4.8(2) and (3) – 1830, unless stated otherwise
'local'	living in or near Coddenham

Abbott, Freeman	appraiser	Stowmarket	D 1827
Ablitt	jeweller, clockmaker	Tavern St., Ipswich	D 1831
Abel	midwife	Stowmarket	D 1796–98
Acfield	caterer	Coddenham	D 1798
Acfield, John	plumbing, glazing, painting[1]	Coddenham	D 1826–31, A
Aldrich, Henry	coal merchant	St Mary at the Quay, Ipswich	A
Alderson	hotelier or caterer	Ipswich	D 1796
Alexander	horse doctor?	?	D 1796
Alexander & Co.	bankers	Needham Market and Ipswich	D 1798

[1] At the 1841 census John Acfield was plumber, 55. He was church organist at St Mary's from 1 July 1819 to 2 February 1860: Lummis, 'Material for a History of Coddenham', para 76.

Bacon, Cobbold & Co	bankers[2]	Tavern St., Ipswich	D 1826–33
Baker, Simon	grocer	Old Buttermarket, Ipswich	A
Ball, Squire	music & piano tuner	Old Buttermarket, Ipswich	D 1826
Bamford	coffee house	Tavern Street, Ipswich	D 1798
Banyard, John	coal merchant	?	D 1826
Barker, James	bricklayer	Coddenham	D 1826–33, A
Barker, William	inn-keeper, pump-maker[3]	Coddenham	D 1826–33
Barton, John G.	earthenware & glass	Brook St., Ipswich	A
Beart	carrier[4]	St Margarets St., Ipswich	D 1831
Beatniffe, Richard	bookseller	Norwich	D 1796
Bedwell	farmer & coal carrier	local	
Betts	carrier[5]	Carr St., Ipswich	D 1826
Beynon	tobacco & snuff dealer	London	D 1827
Bickner, Otto	uniform & clothing	Soho Sq., London	D 1798–1826
Bingham & Richards	wine merchants	London	D 1826
Blake, Robert	fishmonger	Yarmouth	D 1827
Bradell	?	?	D 1826
Breckell	?	Haymarket, London	D 1796
Bristo, Thos. & Son	spirit merchants	Tacket St., Ipswich	A
Broderip	piano manufacturer	Haymarket, London	D 1798
Brooke	hirer of barouche	? Soane St., Ipswich	D 1827
Brown	boot-maker	Piccadilly, London	D 1798
Brown, Henry	furniture joiner	local	D 1826
Burgess	supplier of vinegar	London	D 1796
Burrows	plumber	Orwell Place, Ipswich	D 1831
Butcher, John	hatter	Old Buttermarket, Ipswich	S 1820–23
Byles, Jeremiah, & Co.	coal & corn merchant	College St., Ipswich	D 1827–33, A
Caske	brass-mounted harness	?	D 1826
Catt, Samuel	coach-builder	St Peters & St Margarets Ipswich	D 1831–33
Child	banker	London	D many
Churchman, Wm & Sons	tobacco & snuff dealer	Westgate, Ipswich	D 1826–27
Clarke	organ tuner	St Helens, Ipswich	D 1827
Cockrill, Samuel	cordwainer, boot repairer	Coddenham	S 1814–23, A
Cole, Richard	jeweller, silversmith, clockmaker	Cornhill, Ipswich	D 1833, A
Cook, A.	hatter	?	S 1815–19

2 Bacon's bank: see note 7 below.

3 Barker was landlord of the Crown Inn (Coddenham) from 1788 to 1837 (the year he died, aged eighty-four). As his wife co-managed the Crown with him, he was able to undertake 'groundwork' as a 'daymen': such as trenching, hedging and work in the plantations, not suitable for either Longe's gardener unaided, or his farm staff.

4 Beart's waggon plied from St Margaret's Ipswich to Norwich via Stowmarket and Scole, every Tuesday morning.

5 Betts & Bury's plied to the Saracen's Head, Aldgate, London every Sunday and Thursday and every Tuesday to the Ipswich Arms, Cullum St. (off Fenchurch St.). They also had weekly routes to Saxmundham and Halesworth.

Cook (Robert?)	groundworker	Coddenham	D 1826
Cooper, Benjamin	groundworker	local	D 1798
Cope	painter	local	D 1798
Cornwell	banker	?	D 1796
Crabb	rose grower	Stowmarket	D 1826
Crickitt	banker[6]	Ipswich	D 1798
Crosswell	wine importer	London	D 1831
Dawes	supplier of livery buttons	Covent Garden, London	D 1831
de Carle, John & Son	monumental masons	Bury St Edmunds	1819, A
de Carle, Lancelot	coachmaker	St Matthews St., Ipswich	A
Deck, Robert	bookseller & stationer	Cornhill, Ipswich	D 1827, A
Deck, John	bookseller & stationer	1 Crown St., Bury St Edmunds	D 1827
Dunningham	attorney & banker	Ipswich	D 1827
Dutton	*(Bury &) Suffolk Herald*	Bury St Edmunds	D 1827
Eaton, Thomas & Son	silk merchants	1 Gentleman's Walk, Norwich	D 1826
Elliston, John	tailor	Westgate St., Ipswich	A
Elmsley, Peter	bookseller	Strand, London	D 1796–98
Esdaile, Sir James & Co.	bankers	London	D 1798–1826
Everett, William	wool stapler, fellmonger	Magdelan St., Norwich	D 1827
Farr	clothing	Norwich	D 1796
Fincham, C.& E.	tea merchant	55 Charing Cross, London	A
Forsdike	carpenter	Coddenham	D 1796
Forster	clothing manufacturer	London St., Norwich	D 1796/98
Franklin, L. (Mrs Vinson's daughter)	shirtmaker	local	A
Freeman, William	picture framing	Norwich	D 1826–31
Gall	chymist	Bury St Edmunds	D 1826
Gardner, E.	bibles & prayer books	Paternoster Row, London	A
Gidney, John	fruiterer	Queen St., Norwich	D 1798
Gillman, Mrs	tobacco & snuff	Norwich	D 1798
Girling	nurseryman	Stowmarket	D 1831
Gooding	inn-keeper, Bear & Crown	Westgate St, Ipswich	D 1826
Goodwin, George	game, gamekeeper certificates	Coddenham	A
Goodwin, William	groundworker	local	D 1796–98
Gowers, Andrew	groundworker	Coddenham	D 1826–27
Gowers, Charles	groundworker	local	D 1827
Gray, William	furniture	Norwich	D 1831
Gray, William & John	organ-builders	Fitzroy Sq., London 1817	D 1826, A
Grimwood, Jno	bricklayer	local	A

6 Crickitt opened a bank with Truelove & Kerridge at 13 Tavern St., Ipswich, in 1786. From 1807, after the death of all three, Edward Bacon, the son of an Ipswich baker, owned the bank. He was joined in 1826 by two of the Cobbold family and Rodwell. It was the 'Blue' bank, and as such patronised by Longe. Charles A. Crickitt was one of the Ipswich MPs from 1784 until his death in 1802.

Gurney	banker	Charing Cross, Norwich	D 1826–31
Guy	bookseller	Chelmsford	D 1826
Haggar, Samuel	hires chaises, horses	Swan Inn, Needham Market	D 1827–31
Harcourt, Fredk	ironmonger	Old Buttermarket, Ipswich	A
Harcourt, John	gunsmith	Upper Brook St., Ipswich	A
Hare, Jabez	wire screens	Buttermarket, Ipswich	D 1831
Harmer, John D.	chymist	Northgate St., Ipswich	A
Harold (George?)	groundworker	Coddenham	D 1827
Hart, Joseph	organ builder	Redgrave	D 1826
Hawkes	military outfitters	London	D 1798
Hayward, Robert	wheelwright	Coddenham	A
Hearne	carrier	Stowmarket	D 1798
Hobart	groundwork	local	D 1826–31
Jackson, Postle	*Ipswich Journal*	Old Buttermarket, Ipswich	D 1826, A
Keeble, Nat	groundworker	Coddenham	D 1798–1827
Kerridge, Richard	groundworker	Coddenham	D 1826–27
Kerrison	banker[7]	Norwich	D 1798
Lake, John	builder & plasterer	St Margarets, Ipswich	D 1831,1832, A
Lincoln	groundwork, gardener	Coddenham	D 1831–33
Lines & Fisher	coal merchants	Ipswich	D 1831
Ling, Wm S.	tailor of academic gowns	Princess St., Norwich	D 1826
Mackie & Sons	nursery & seedsmen	Exchange St., Norwich	D 1826–27
Marshall	cheesemonger	Cambridge	D 1826
Matchett Stevenson & Matchett	*Norfolk Chronicle*	Market Place, Norwich	A
Mayhew, Francis	timber haulier	Baylham	D 1826
Miller, Henry	linen draper & undertaker[8]	Old Buttermarket, Ipswich	S 1815–20, A
Moniment	farrier	local	D 1796
Moore	clock-maker	Ipswich	Inventory
Nunn	cattle dealer	Whitton, Ipswich	D 1831
Orbell, J.	veterinary surgeon	Crown St., Ipswich	D 1827
Orford,	farmer, carted coals	local	various
Parker (John?)	groundworker	Coddenham	D 1796
Phelps	stationer	44 Paternoster Row, London	D 1833
Porter, Richard	draper & agent for livery	Queen St., Ipswich	S 1812–21
Pritty, Charles	draper, & general stores[9]	Coddenham	S 1814–23, D 1831

7 Kerrison's bank collapsed in 1808.

8 Miller: the Trade Directory for Ipswich shows the dual trades given above, stressing what a large part mourning clothes played in funeral custom even before Victoria's reign. The 1841 census shows four tailors as resident in Coddenham parish in three separate households: Henry Miller (then seventy) and his sons Henry (then forty-five), Lionel (then forty) and Thomas (then thirty). It is unclear whether the Coddenham Millers traded from the Buttermarket Ipswich.

9 Pritty, shop-keeper at Crown Corner, Coddenham, was primarily a draper but this was a general stores (stocking tobacco, gunpowder and hops). In the 1837 tithe records he both owned his house and shop and also farmed 126 acres at Walnut Tree farm. In the 1841 census, with him (aged fifty-five) and his wife were living their son Charles, plus a male 'draper's assistant' and three domestic servants.

Protector Fire Office (agent: Richard Porter)		Queen St., Ipswich	A
Rainbird, William	groundworker	local	D 1826–27
Ransome, J., R. & A.	ironfounders[10]	St Margarets, Ipswich	D 1831–33
Raw, John	bookseller & stationer	Buttermarket, Ipswich	D 1826–27, A
Riches	gardeners[11]	local	various
Ringrose	tailor	Carr St., Ipswich	S 1818–23, D 1827
Rundell & Bridge	jewellers & goldsmiths	Ludgate Hill, London	1800, 1817, A
Savage	groundworker	local	D 1796
Scoging, James	cooper[12]	Coddenham	S 1823, A
Scoging, Philip	thatcher	Coddenham	A
Scoging, Thomas	thatcher	Coddenham	A
Scott, Thomas	groundworker	Coddenham	D 1796–1833
Scrutton	groundworker	Coddenham	D 1826–31
Seaman	taxidermist	?	D 1831
Shalders, Edward	book-binder	Westgate St., Ipswich	D 1831, A
Shave, Thomas	coach proprietor	Coach & Horses, Ipswich	D 1796
Shemming, William	ironmonger	Needham Market	A
Smith, Moses	harness-maker, saddler	Coddenham	A
Shewell, Thomas	draper & tailor	Tavern St., Ipswich	D 1827
Shorten (-ing)	horse dealer	St Matthews St., Ipswich	D 1826–27
Shrimpling	wool agent, silk & yarn	Magdalen St., Norwich	D 1827
Smart, John	portrait painter, picture restorer	Elm St., Ipswich	D 1796–1831
Smart, J. Mrs	dressmaker	local	1806, A
Smith	groundworker, bled horse	local	D 1796–33
Smith	inn-keeper	Scole, Norfolk	D 1798
Sparrow, John S.	furniture dealer	Buttermarket, Ipswich	D 1798
Spratt, William	coach-builder	Chapelfield, Norwich	D 1826
Spurling, William	supplier of gaiters	?	S 1816–20
Stephenson	veterinary surgeon?	?	D 1796
Stodhart	coach-builder & painter	Norwich	D 1798
Suffield	wine merchant	Norwich	D 1796–98
Tovell, George	stone merchant	'Car' St., Ipswich	A
Townsend, William	fishmonger	New Market St., Ipswich	D 1826
Wegeman	portrait artist	Norwich	D 1831
Wells	farmer, carrier	Coddenham	D 1826–31, S 1815
Whiting, William	repair fire & garden-water engines	?	A

10 The Ransomes, later internationally famous, were from 1789 to 1837 in business from premises in the town ditches outside the medieval ramparts (now Old Foundry Road) in St Margaret's.

11 Riches: two brothers worked as gardeners for Longe from his arrival in the vicarage in 1797 until well into the nineteenth century, plus the son of one of them. In 1798 Samuel was on an annual 'salary' of 10 guineas and his services were shared by Longe with Sir Edmund Bacon, relative of the deceased vicar. Samuel died in 1823 aged seventy-four. John Riches, deaf and dumb (known as 'Dumby'), was in 1811 discharged by Longe as lame and ill. He lived until 1833, when he was seventy-nine.

12 Scoging: this long-established Coddenham family surname was variously spelt.

Wild	leather breeches	Piccadilly, London	D 1798
Woodd, Basil George	wine merchant	London	D 1826–31, 1828/30
Woods	vet?	?	D 1796
Woods, John	nursery	Cumberland St., Woodbridge	D 1827–33, A
Yarrington, Samuel C.	stained glass	King St., Norwich	D 1831

III. John Longe's Farm and Domestic Staff

Farm

F in the Farm Accounts Book

Cornish, William (1750–1818) long-serving farm bailiff at Vicarage Farm
Cornish, William (1810–1878) 16 years farm bailiff to the Longes, probably grandson of the above

Mayhew, James		F 1797–1801
Southgate, J.	husbandman	F 1797–1801
Scrutton, W.	husbandman	F 1797–1801
Parr, Gabriel, & wife		F 1797–1801
Crack	horseman & carter	D 1826–27
John	involved in haymaking	D 1796
Sam(uel)	servant involved in haymaking	D 1796
Molly	involved in haymaking	D 1796

Servants' Wages Book, January 1811 to December 1822

Butler	Samuel Barrell	there in Jan. 1811–April 1811
	John Allen	1811–1818
	Reuben Lord	1818–20
	Robert Taylor	1820; there at end 1822
Coachman	John Gowers (1766–1843)	there in Jan. 1811; there 1833
Footman/Groom	William Lambert	there in Jan. 1811–1815
	James Keeble	1815–1817
	James Brown	1817–18
	Charles Spall	1818–21
	Charles Offord	1821–22
Gamekeeper	James Scoggin(g) (1760 –1837)	there in Jan. 1811; there 1830 '37 years faithful servant to late John Longe'
Servant-boy	John Brunwin	there in Jan. 1811 to Sept. 1811
	James Keeble	1811, promoted 1815
	William Keeble	1814–17
	John Crooks	1817–18
	Charles Offord	1819, promoted 1821
	Henry Fenton	1821–23
Gardener	John Riches	there in Jan. 1811 to March 1811
	Edward Edwards	1811–1812
	Charles Crickmay	1812; there at end 1822
Housekeeper	Mary Kenney	1790–1813
	Ann Tomlinson	1812–13 & 1815–20
	Phoebe Caldwell	1813–14
	Amy Alldiss	1814–1815

Cook	Elisabeth Hammond	there in Jan. 1811–1812
	Ann Leggatt	1812–13
	Lucy Taylor	1813–18
	Frances Underwood	1818–20
Cook/Housekeeper	Lydia Cobb	1820–21
	Mary Feaveryeare	1821 & below
	Sarah Durrant	1821–22
Cook	Elizabeth Parish	1822
	Sarah Barrell	1822; there at end 1822
	Ruth Margery	1822
Nursery-maid	Elisabeth Garnham	there in Jan. 1811–13
Ladies-maid (Charlotte)	Elisabeth Christopher	1813–22
Ladies-maid (Mrs L)	Elizabeth Scolding	1820–21
	Mary Feaveryeare	Dec. 1821; there at Dec. 1822
Housemaid	Amy Mayhew	there in Jan. 1811–1813
	Charlotte Warren	1813–15
	Martha Frost	1815–20
	Ann Fair	1820–21
	Elizabeth Wade	1821; there at Dec. 1822
Kitchen-girls	Mary/Elizabeth Davy	1811
	Mary Gooch	1811
	Phoebe Davy	1811–13
	Sarah Girling	1813
	Elisabeth Waspe	1813–15
	Mary Farrow	1815–17
	Ann Bent	1817
	Elizabeth Scrutton	1817–18
	Ann Hill	1818–20
	Mary Jessup	1820–22
	Mary Gaskin	1822 on
Servant-girl	Elisabeth Shilcot	1822 on

Other Servants named in the Diary

Kerridge, Samuel	butler until 1827
Hales, William	butler succeeding Kerridge from 1827
Meek, Alexander	gardener until 1826
Cowles, Robert	gardener succeeding Meek from 1826 on
Read, John	gardener until 1833
Hynard, James	gardener succeeding Read from 1833 on
Gowers, John	coachman, in diary 1826–27, 1831, 1833 – see above
Bennet	diary 1833
Brown, Ann	diary 1833

IV. Some of the Authors from the Catalogue of Sermons (p.171) and the Artists and Others Named in the Inventory (pp.210–20)

ADAMS, William DD (1706–89). Mild and liberal, he argued for the credibility of the gospel miracles.

ATTERBURY, Francis (1663–1732), bishop of Rochester, brilliant High Tory.

BASSANO, Jacopo (*c.*1510–92), painter of peasants and biblical scenes, of Venetian family of artists.

BENNET, Thomas (1673–1728), defender of the liturgy and sacraments of the established church.

BLAIR, James (1656–1743), served in Williamsburg (Virginia). His four-volume work on the Sermon on the Mount was published in London in 1722.

CLAPHAM, Samuel (1757–1830), contemporary of John Longe. From 1803, he published abridged versions of the sermons of others in collections. His books were widely influential.

CONYBEARE, John (1692–1755), bishop of Bristol. To raise funds for his children two volumes of sermons were posthumously published and heavily subscribed.

COURAYER, Pierre Francois le (1681–1776). French Catholic divine, best known in England for book (1727) defending validity of Anglican ordination.

ELMER, Stephen (1715–96), still-life painter who was baptised and buried at Farnham (Surrey). Fashionable with the aristocracy, but unassuming. *ODNB.*

FLORIS, Frans (1520–70), of Flemish family of artists.

FOTHERGILL, Anthony (1685–1761). Westmorland landowner; published several theological works.

GAINSBOROUGH, Thomas (1727–88): landscape and portrait painter, Suffolk born, but moved to fashionable Bath in 1759.

GARDEMAU, Balthazar (1656–1739), vicar of Coddenham. His love of scholarship is visually exhibited in his memorial in the chancel at St Mary's there.

GILPIN, Bernard (1516–84). The reprinting in 1752 of some of his sermons brought this Tudor to Longe's notice, rather than his legendary reputation as 'apostle of the north'.

HEWLET, John (1762–1844), contemporary of Longe's, published both sermons and bible notes in monthly parts.

HORNE, George (1730–92), briefly bishop of Norwich, spiritual 'Hutchinsonian'. Sixteen of his sermons were published in 1793.

KENT, William (1685–1748). English architect and landscape gardener, also painter and draughtsman.

LELAND, John (1691–1766), a Presbyterian. His historical account of pre-Christian religion (published in 1764) concluded that civilised nations also needed a revelation of the supernatural.

LELY, Sir Peter (1618–80). Dutch born, court painter to Charles II after taking English name.

MARATTI, Carlo (1625–1713). Italian painter and draughtsman.

MONAMY, Peter (1681–1749), naval and marine painter.

PASSIGNANO, Domenico (1559–1638). Italian painter.

POTT, John Holden (1758–1847), efficient administrator within high-church 'Hackney Phalanx'. He published at least seven collections of sermons.

PRIESTLEY, Dr Joseph (1733–1804), polymath, Dissenting theological writer, and chemist noted for pioneering work with oxygen and other gases. His short career as assistant at Needham Market Independent chapel was not a success (1755–58). Fled England in 1794 with controversial views.

PYLE, Thomas (1674–1756), eloquent and impetuous preacher in west Norfolk, whose son published collections of his sermons in 1773–83.

RAPHAEL (1483–1520), Italian painter, including frescoes and cartoons for tapestries.

ROGERS, Thomas (1760–1832), evangelical Yorkshire headmaster. He published sermons and a two-volume work on the liturgy of the Church of England (1804).

RUBENS, Peter Paul (1577–1640), German-born painter and diplomat in several European courts. Came to the court of Charles I in 1629.

SASSOFERRATO (1609–85), Italian painter and draughtsman.

SHARPE, John (1645?–1714), archbishop of York and one-time dean of Norwich. Praised the virtues of the Church of England in simple but effective language.

SINGLETON, Henry (1766–1839), English painter.

SHERLOCK, William (1639–1707), prolific author. Reckoned a leading non-juror in 1688 although previously anti-Catholic.

SMALRIDGE, George (1662–1719), high church bishop of Bristol. Posthumous publication of sixty of his sermons (1724), with subsequent edition and reprintings.

STELLA, Jacques (1596–1657), French painter and draughtsman.

TAPPS. The prefix 'Mr' shows that he was a contemporary of Longe, but neither he nor his writings has yet been traced.

TILLOTSON, John (1630–1794), archbishop of Canterbury. Stylish sermons famed for advocating contentment and obedience.

TURNER, J.M.W. (1775–1851), landscape painter, in early years a watercolourist.

VELDE, William van de (the younger) (1633–1707), Dutch naval and marine painter, court painter at the Restoration.

BIBLIOGRAPHY

PRIMARY SOURCES

SUFFOLK RECORD OFFICE, Ipswich:
HA24/50/19/, archive of Longe family

The main collection studied was deposited by Mr A. Bacon Longe, great-grandson of Longe, the diarist. Only the items most significant for the present volume are here listed, a small proportion of the total archive. A few of the catalogue numbers are assigned to a single item, but other numbers cover one, two or three bundles, each containing scores of pieces.

1. *Documents transcribed in this volume*

		HA24/50/19/
Pocket-book diary	1796	/4.3(1)
Pocket-book diary	1798	/4.3(2)
Pocket-book diary	1826	/4.3(3)
Pocket-book diary	1827	/4.3(4)
Pocket-book diary	1831	/4.3(5)
Pocket-book diary	1833	/4.3(6)
Servants book: wages, discipline, start and end of service	1811/1822	/4.7(11)
Servants, wages	1830–34	/4.5(21) and /4.8(2)
Servants, mourning	1812	/4.8(2)
Servants, medical bill	1827–30	/4.8(2)
Catalogue of sermons	1787–1825	/4.5(2)
Inventory of contents	*c.*1797	/4.7(2)
Plate, Stable	1774–5	/4.7(2)
Cellar	1800,1811	/4.7(3)
Visitation return	1820 **NRO DN/VIS/55/7**	

2. *Documents from Longe archive, HA24/50/19/, not transcribed in this volume (arranged by section of the Introduction and the Diary)*

Introducing John Longe		HA24/50/19/
Counsel's opinion on finance	1826	/3.19
Episcopal documents: institution, induction and reading-in	1797	/4.5(14)
Summary will of Nicholas Bacon	1792	/4.5(16)
Tithe papers (bundles)	1797–1830	4.5(17)
Services		
State prayers on occasions of fast and thanksgiving	1801 to 1832	/4.5(1)
Sermons for thanksgiving: battles of the Nile and Trafalgar	1798, 1805	/4.5(3)
Confirmation numbers and ages	1811, 1822	/4.5(12)(20)
Armorial bearings for chancel east window	1832	/4.5(12)
Installation of church organ and music	1817	/4.5(18) and (19)
Bill for repairs to chancel	undated	/4.5(18)
Notes on heraldic glass in store	1831	/4.5(20)

Out in the parish

Returns under the Population Act 1816	1821	/4.4(7)
Abstract from returns under the Population Act	1801, 1811	/4.5(12)
Parish roads survey, including turnpike	1830	/4.5(20)

The poor

Longe's Will including legacy for parish poor	1834	/4.1(3)
Official directions for church briefs	1797	/4.5(11)
School trust, extracts of 1753 and 1791 charitable register	1813	/4.5(16)
Rules of Coddenham charity school	undated	/4.5(20)

The wider church

12th annual report: Suffolk Society for Education of Poor	1824	/4.5(1)
Directions for primary visitations	1801–13	/4.5(1)
Bills, including diocesan payments (bundle)	1827–30	/4.5(21)

Georgian gentleman

Estate account and bundle of papers		/4.1(4)
Letters (incoming and draft outgoing) (bundles)	1797–1829	/4.2(1)
Correspondence with Tyrell	1831–3	/4.4(7)
Antiquarian notes and draft article: *Gentleman's Magazine*	1823–4	/4.5(21)
Bills: tradesmen and taxes (bundle)	1827–0	/4.5(21)
Bills: professional advisers and tradesmen (bundle)	1806–34	/4.8(3) Bills:
schools and tradesmen (bundle)	1815–6,1830	/5.1

Conflict

Arbitration Award on land disputes Middleton/Longe	1820	/3.7
Valuation of Bacon farms and advowsons	*c.*1828	/3(20)
Litigation papers (bundle)	1807–29	/3(21)
Counsel's opinion on resigning living	1833	/3(22)
Papers on rating of tithes	1818–22	/4.4(4)
Papers on tithe of demesne lands in Barham parish	1833	/4.4(7)
Rating of tithes dispute	1822	/4.5(13) to (20)
Unconsecrated status of Shrubland chapel	1829	/4.5(13)
Glebe title dispute: correspondence	1796–1801	/4.5(15)
Historical researches and legal on Crowfield tithe (bundle)	1816–23	/4.5(16)
Solicitor's letters in Birch case on bond	1820	/4.5(16)
Tithe compositions: 6 bundles of lists and working papers	1798–1831	/4.5(17)
Memorandum on disputed closure of bridleway	undated	/4.5(19)
Tithe dispute, Crowfield (hay), historical research	*c.*1820	/4.5(22)
Correspondence: unconsecrated status of Shrubland chapel	1827	/4.5(29)
Correspondence on Spixworth inheritance	1829	/4.6(4)
Copy bond (1808) and assignment in Spixworth case	1812	/4.8(1)
Copy probate account of John Longe, partition valuation and vicarage delapidations	1833	/4.8(2)
Croasdaile dispute over lunacy and trust	1823–6	/5.1, 2, 3
Disputed easements – arbitration Middleton/Longe	1822	/5.2
Correspondence: (1) Spixworth estate (2) Birch bond	1828–31	/5.2

Party politics

Correspondence Longe /Tyrell MP on securing records	1831–3	/4.4(7)
Suffolk Pitt Club: lists, rules and correspondence	1820–3	/4.4(8)

Magistrate, houses of industry, turnpikes

Calendars of Prisoners with manuscript notes;		
Bury Assizes and Quarter Sessions (Ipswich)	1818–32	/4.4(2)
Papers on gaol committals, gaol alterations and treadmill	1796–1821	/4.4(3)
Alehouse keepers, weights and measures convictions	1821–3	/4.4(4)

Defence of the realm

Instructions on defence and Longe's drafts (bundle)	1803–30	/4.4(6)
Abstract of lists in preparation for invasion	1796	/4.5(20)
Short notes for thanksgiving sermon	1801	/4.5(20)
Notice on special constables	1801	/4.5(20)

Disturbances

Letter from Longe's wife at Salhouse (Norfolk)	1822	/4.2(1)
JPs' printed material on civil disturbances (bundle)	1819–30	/4.4(1)
Disturbances: instructions, and Longe's drafts (bundles)	1803–30	/4.4(6)
Draft political address, notice of meeting, signing	1821	/4.5(13)

Diary, appendices etc.

John Longe's Will (copy)	1834	/4.1(3)
Pocket-book diary (printed material)	1831	/4.3(5)
Historical researches and legal on Crowfield tithe (bundle)	1816–23	/4.5(16)
Printed transcript: trial as to testamentary capacity of Bacon	1797	/4.6(4)
Inventory of some household goods	1834	/4.7(3)
Sale catalogue on death of Robert Longe	1890	/4.7(4)
Estate of Hannah Archer (bundle)	1795–1803	/4.8(2)

3. *Documents in SRO(I) not in the Longe archive*

Tithe Apportionment (Coddenham parish)	1837	FDA 66/A1/1a
Barham House of Industry: Guardians Minute Book	1821–34	ADA/2/ /AB1/1
Act of Parliament	1833	FB37/G2/1
Barham parish poor record	1784–1839	FB35/3a/1
Census records, Coddenham and Crowfield	1841	J409/2A & B
Coddenham Copy Terriers	1794–1834	FB37/C5/1–6
Churchwardens' book	from 1798	FB37/E1/2
Churchwardens' bills	1806–35	FB37/E5/2–7
Overseers' book	1798–1835	FB37/G1/3,4
Valuation for rates	1823	FB37/G3/1
School accounts book	1754–1835	FB37/L2/1
Officer's letter: Discontent in north Suffolk	1822	HA 247/5
Davy, David Elisha: antiquarian record book (pp.191 to 260) including Coddenham church: fabric goods and ornaments heraldry, memorials and tombstones		J 400/3
Helmingham Turnpike trustees: Proceedings from April 1823		ENI/B/B1/1
Redeemed securities (bundles)		EN1/B3/11
Ipswich Literary Institution: Minute Book	from Jan. 1832	K13/1/3.1
Manuscript book of extracts from a MS of John Longe compiled by EPM (E.P. Martin?)	*c.*1930	HA13/G/1
Archdeaconry of Suffolk: General Court Books	1787–97 & 1798–1812	FAA/2/2/54, 55
Suffolk Quarter Sessions: Minute and Order Books (20)	1801–33	B105/2/ 52.1–/73
Treasurer's Account Book (Ipswich Div. Quarter Sessions)	1830–6	B111/2/1.2

Quarter Sessions records		
Turnpike trust: Ipswich/Helmingham, Ipswich/Debenham, Hemingstone/Otley Bottom	1811	B106/5A/1
Highway Orders Book	1816–35	B106/5B/1
Saving Banks, Friendly Societies	1818	B106/13/2
Militia and Volunteer records		
List of commissions, Deputy Lieutenants	1809–18	B505/1/2
Militia qualification rolls	1802–32	B505/5/1,3,5
Suffolk Volunteer Commissions	1804–25	B506/1/1
Minute Book of Suffolk Society for the Education of the Poor in the principles of the Established Church	from 1812	FAA/15/1

NORFOLK RECORD OFFICE, Norwich

Norwich Diocesan Records

Visitation Books and Returns to Bishop's Queries	DN/VSB/11 DN/VIS/34/1, 34a/8, 35/1, 38/8, 43/6, 49/3, 55/7, 60/6, 65/11
Register of Conventicles	DN/DIS/4/1, 4/2
Visitation Booklets, Fees Book and Consignation Books	DN/VSC/14/28, 15/30–31
Minutes of Consistory Court	DN/MIN
Ordination Book and Papers	DN/ORR/3/3, /ORD/13
Faculty Books	DN/FCB/6
Caveat and Sequestration Book	DN/SQB 1/4
Miscellaneous papers	DN/VSM 6/2
Licences of curates	Microfilm F505

PRINTED PRIMARY SOURCES

Joseph Hodskinson's Map of Suffolk 1783, ed. D.P. Dymond, SRS xv, 1972

Letter on Roman finds at Coddenham, *The Gentleman's Magazine*, April 1825

Longe's Diary of 1797 (extracts), *East Anglian Miscellany* re-print of passages from *East Anglian Daily Times*, vol.26 III and IV (Ipswich, 1932)

SECONDARY SOURCES

Except where otherwise stated, the place of publication is London.

BOOKS

Allen, David (ed.), *Ipswich Borough Archives: a Catalogue 1255–1835*, SRS xliii (2000)

Archer, J.E., *By a Flash and a Scar: Incendiarism, Animal Maiming and Poaching in East Anglia 1815–70* (Oxford, 1990)

Armstrong, Alan, *Farmworkers 1770–1980* (London, 1988)

Atherton, Ian, *et al.* (eds), *Norwich Cathedral: Church City and Diocese 1096–1996* (1996)

Ayres, Jack, *Paupers and Pig Killers – Diary of William Holland, a Somerset Parson 1799–1818* (Stroud, 1984)

Barney, J., *The Defence of Norfolk 1793–1815* (Norwich, 2000)
Bathurst, Henry, *Memoirs of Bishop Bathurst, Lord Bishop of Norwich*, 2 vols (1837)
Bentham, C. (ed.), *Melton and its Churches* (Ipswich, 1981)
Beresford, John (ed.), *Diary of a Country Parson 1758–1802*, 5 vols (Oxford, 1924)
Best G.F.A., *Temporal Pillars* (Cambridge, 1964)
Bettey, J.H., *Church and Parish* (1987)
Bishop, Peter, *The History of Ipswich, Triumph and Disaster (*1995)
Black, Jeremy and Gregory, Jeremy (eds), *Culture, Politics and Society in Britain 1660–1800* (Manchester, 1991)
Blatchly, John (ed.), *A Journal of Excursions through the County of Suffolk: David Elisha Davy, 1823–4*, SRS xxiv (1982)
Blatchly, John, *Some Suffolk and Norfolk Ex Libris* (2000)
Blatchly, John, *The Topographers of Suffolk* (Ipswich, 1988)
Bovill, E.W., *English Country Life 1780–1830* (1962)
Brown, A.F.J., *Prosperity and Poverty: Rural Essex 1700–1815* (Chelmsford, 1996)
Brown, C.K. Francis, *A History of the English Clergy 1800–1900* (1953)
Brown, Ford K., *Fathers of the Victorians – the Age of Wilberforce* (Cambridge, 1961)
Brown, Richard, *Church and State in Modern Britain 1700–1850* (1991)
Browne, John, *History of Congregationalism and Memorials of the Church in Norfolk and Suffolk* (1877)
Cannadine, David, *Class in Britain* (1998)
Cautley, H. Munro, *Suffolk Churches* (1937)
Chadwick, Owen, *Victorian Miniature* (1983 edn)
Chadwick, Owen, *The Victorian Church*, I, *1829–59* (1971 edn)
Christie, O.F. (ed.), *The Diary of the Revd William Jones 1777–1821* (1929)
Clark, J.C.D., *English Society 1688–1832* (Cambridge, 1985)
Clark, J.C.D., *The Language of Liberty 1660–1832* (Cambridge, 1994)
Clarke, G.R., *The History and Description of the Town and Borough of Ipswich* (1830)
Claydon, T. and McBride, I. (eds), *Protestantism and National Identity: Britain and Ireland 1650–c.1850* (Cambridge, 1998)
Cockayne, E.E. and Stow N.J. (eds), *Stutter's Casebook*, SRS xlviii (2005)
Colley, Linda, *Britons: Forging the Nation 1707–1837* (1992)
Collini, S., Whatmore, R. and Young, B. (eds), *History, Religion and Culture: British Intellectual History 1750–1950* (Cambridge, 2000)
Collins, Irene, *Jane Austen and the Clergy* (1994)
Coombs, Howard and Peter (eds), *Journal of a Somerset Rector 1803–1834: John Skinner* (Oxford, 1984 edn)
Corfield, Penelope J., *Power and the Professions in Britain 1700–1850* (1995)
Crossley, C. and Small, Ian (eds), *The French Revolution and British Culture* (Oxford, 1989)
Dewey, Clive, *The Passing of Barchester* (1991)
Ditchfield, G.M., *The Evangelical Revival* (1998)
Dyck, Ian, *William Cobbett and Rural Popular Culture* (Cambridge, 1992)
Dymond, David (ed.), *Parson and People in a Suffolk Village: Richard Cobbold's Wortham, 1824–1877* (2007)
Dymond, David and Northeast, Peter, *A History of Suffolk* (Chichester, 1995 edn)
Dymond, David and Martin, Edward (eds), *An Historical Atlas of Suffolk* (Ipswich, 1999 edn)
Eastwood, David, *Government and Community in the English Provinces 1700–1870* (1997)
Emsley, Clive, *Crime and Society in England 1750–1900* (1996 edn)
Evans, Eric J., *The Contentious Tithe 1750–1850* (1976)
Evans, Eric J., *Tithes and the Tithe Commutation Act* (1978)
Evans, Eric J., *The Forging of the Modern State, 1783–1870* (2001 edn)
Fendall, C.P. and Crutchley, E.A. (eds), *The Diary of Benjamin Newton 1816–18* (Cambridge, 1933)

Fiske, Jane (ed.), *The Oakes Diaries – Business, Politics and the Family in Bury St. Edmunds 1778–1827*, 2 vols, SRS xxxii–iii (1990–91)
Fitzgerald, John P., *The Quiet Worker for Good: John Charlesworth* (1865)
Fletcher, Ronald (ed.), *The Biography of a Victorian Village: Richard Cobbold's Account of Wortham, Suffolk* (1977)
Foss, P.J. and Parry, T. (eds), *A Truly Honest Man: Diary of Joseph Moxon, 1798–9* (Macclesfield, 1998)
Gascoigne, John, *Cambridge in the Age of Enlightenment* (Cambridge, 1989)
Gash, N., *Pillars of Government and Other Essays on State and Society c.1770–c.1880* (1986)
Gibson, William, *Achievement of the Anglican Church 1689–1800* (Lampeter, 1996)
Gibson, William, *Religion and Society in England and Wales 1689–1800* (1998)
Gilbert, Alan D., *Religion and Society in Industrial England 1740–1914* (1976)
Gilley, S. and Sheils, W.J. (eds), *A History of Religion in Britain* (Oxford, 1994)
Grace, Frank, *Rags and Bones: a Social History of a Working Class Community* (2005)
Gregory, J. and Stevenson, John, *Britain in the Eighteenth Century 1688–1820* (2000)
Gregory, Jeremy and Chamberlain, Jeffrey (eds), *The National Church in Local Perspective: the Church of England and the Regions 1660–1800* (Woodbridge, 2003)
Haakonssen, K. (ed.), *Enlightenment and Religion: Rational Dissent in Eighteenth Century Britain* (Cambridge, 1996)
Haig, Alan, *The Victorian Clergy* (1984)
Halevy, E., *England in 1815: a History of the English People in the Nineteenth Century* (1949 edn)
Hardy, S., *The House on the Hill: the Samford House of Industry* (Ipswich, 2001)
Harper-Bill, C. *et al.* (eds), *East Anglia's History* (Woodbridge, 2002)
Harris, Tim (ed.), *Popular Culture in England c.1500–1850* (1995)
Hay, Douglas and Snyder, Francis (eds), *Policing and Prosecution in Britain 1750–1850* (Oxford, 1989)
Hempton, David, *Religion and Political Culture in Britain and Ireland* (Cambridge, 1996)
Henriques, U., *Religious Toleration in England 1787–1833* (1961)
Hervey, Lord Francis (ed.), *Suffolk in the XVIIth Century: the Breviary of Suffolk by Robert Ryece,1618* (1902)
Hobsbawm, E.J. and Rude, George, *Captain Swing* (1969)
Hole, Robert, *Pulpits, Politics and Public Order in England 1760–1832* (Cambridge, 1989)
Horn, P., *The Rural World 1780–1850: Social Change* (1980)
Houghton, John, *Parsons through the Ages* (Milton Keynes, 2002)
Hylson-Smith, Kenneth, *Evangelicals in the Church of England 1734–1984* (Edinburgh, 1988)
Knight, Frances, *The Nineteenth Century Church and English Society* (Cambridge, 1995)
Langford, Paul, *Englishness Identified: Manners and Character 1650–1850* (Oxford, 2000)
Machin, G.I.T., *Politics and the Churches in Great Britain 1832–68* (Oxford, 1977)
Malster, R. and Salmon, Neil P. (eds), *Ipswich from the 1st to the 3rd Millennium* (Ipswich, 2001)
Malster, Robert, *A History of Ipswich* (Chichester, 2000)
Mann, E. (ed.), *An Englishman at Home and Abroad 1792–1828* (1930)
Mann, E.and Cane, H. (eds), *An Englishman at Home and Abroad 1829–62: Extracts from the Diaries of John Barber Scott of Bungay, Suffolk* (Bungay, 1996)
Mews, S. (ed.), *Religion and National Identity* (Oxford, 1982)
Mingay, G.E., *The Gentry: the Rise and Fall of a Ruling Class* (1976)
Mingay, G.E., *Rural Life in Victorian England* (1976)
Moir, Esther, *The Justice of the Peace* (1969)
Morris, Marilyn, *The British Monarchy and the French Revolution* (Yale, 1998)
Muskett, Paul, *Riotous Assemblies: Popular Disturbances in East Anglia 1740–1822* (Ely, 1984)
Newby, Howard, *The Deferential Worker* (1977)

Nockles, Peter B., *The Oxford Movement in Context: Anglican High Churchmanship 1760–1857* (Cambridge, 1994)
Norman, E.R., *Church and Society in England 1770–1970* (Oxford, 1976)
Obelkevich, James, *Religion and Rural Society: South Lindsey 1825–75* (Oxford, 1976)
Page, A., *Supplement to the Suffolk Traveller* (1844)
Park, Chris C., *Sacred Worlds: an Introduction to Geography and Religion* (1994)
Parsons, G. (ed.), *Religion in Victorian Britain*, I (1988)
Peacock, A.J., *Bread or Blood* (1965)
Perkin, Harold, *The Origins of Modern English Society 1780–1880* (1969)
Porter, Roy, *English Society in the Eighteenth Century* (1990 edn)
Porter, Roy, *Enlightenment* (2000)
Rowell, G. (ed.), *Tradition Renewed* (1986)
Rule, John, *Albion's People: English Society 1714–1815* (1992)
Russell, Anthony, *The Clerical Profession* (1980)
Russell, Anthony, *The Country Parson* (1993)
Scarfe, Norman (ed.), *A Frenchman's Year in Suffolk, 1784*, SRS xxx (1988)
Searby, Peter, *History of the University of Cambridge*, III, *1750–1870* (Cambridge, 1997)
Soloway, R.S., *Prelates and People: Ecclesiastical Social Thought in England 1783–1852* (1969)
Spater, George, *William Cobbett: the Poor Man's Friend* (Cambridge, 1982)
Swanson, R.N. (ed.), *Unity and Diversity in the Church*, Studies in Church History 32 (Oxford, 1996)
Sykes, Norman, *Church and State in the Eighteenth Century* (Cambridge, 1934)
Sykes, S. and Booty, J. (eds), *The Study of Anglicanism* (1988)
Thompson, F.M.L. (ed.), *Cambridge Social History of Britain 1750–1950*, 3 (Cambridge, 1990)
Timmins, T.C.B. (ed.), *Suffolk Returns from the Census of Religious Worship of 1851*, SRS xxxix (1997)
Tindal Hart, A., *The Country Priest in English History* (1959)
Tindal Hart, A., *The Curate's Lot* (1970)
Towler, Robert and Coxon, A.P.M., *The Fate of the Anglican Clergy* (1979)
Venn, J. and J.A. (eds), *Alumni Cantabridgienses Part II (1752–1900)*, 6 vols (Cambridge, 1922–4)
Vialls, C. and Collins, K. (eds), *A Georgian Country Parson: the Rev. John Mastin of Naseby* (Northampton, 2004)
Virgin, Peter, *The Church in an Age of Negligence: Ecclesiastical Structure and Problems of Church Reform 1700–1840* (Cambridge, 1989)
Walsh, John, Haydon, C. and Taylor, S. (eds), *The Church of England c.1689 to c.1833: Toleration to Tractarianism* (Cambridge, 1993)
Walters, S.M. and Stow, E.A., *Darwin's Mentor* (Cambridge, 2001)
Ward, W.R., *Religion and Society in England 1790–1850* (1972)
Ward, W.R., *Faith and Faction* (1993)
Wardle, David, *English Popular Education 1780–1970* (Cambridge, 1970)
Warnes, David and Blatchly, John, *Bribery Warehouse* (Ipswich, 1986)
Williamson, Tom, *The Landscape of Shrubland Park* (Clare, 1997)
Winstanley, R.L., *Parson Woodforde: the Life and Times of a Country Diarist* (Bungay, 1996)
Winstanley, R.L. *et al.*, *The Diary of James Woodforde*, 17 vols (to 2007)
Wolffe, John, *The Protestant Crusade in Great Britain 1829–60* (Oxford, 1991)
Woodward, E.L., *The Age of Reform 1815–70* (Oxford, 1938)
Young, Arthur, *General View of the Agriculture of the County of Suffolk, 1813* (1969 edn)

ARTICLES
(including essays and articles in books listed above)

Allen David, 'The Vanished Barrel Organ of Coddenham Church', *PSIAH* xxxviii, 4 (1996)
Archer, J.E., 'Rural Protest, 1815–51' in Dymond and Martin (eds), *Historical Atlas of Suffolk*
Avis, Paul, 'What is Anglicanism?' in Sykes and Booty (eds), *The Study of Anglicanism*
Barrie, Viviane, 'The Church of England in the Diocese of London in the Eighteenth Century' in Gregory and Chamberlain (eds), *National Church in Local Perspective*
Beattie, J.M., 'The Pattern of Crime in England 1660–1800', *P&P* 62 (1974)
Black, Jeremy, 'Confessional State or Elect Nation? Religion and Identity in Eighteenth-Century England' in Claydon and McBride (eds), *Protestantism and National Identity*
Black, Jeremy and Gregory, J., 'Introduction' in Black and Gregory (eds), *Culture, Politics and Society*
Blatchly, John, 'The Terra Cotta Trail' in Harper-Bill *et al.* (eds), *East Anglia's History*
Burns, R. Arthur, 'A Hanoverian Legacy? Diocesan Reform in the Church of England *c.*1800–1833' in Walsh, Haydon and Taylor (eds), *The Church of England c.1689 to c.1833*
Bushaway, Bob, '"Tacit Unsuspected but still Implicit Faith": Alternative Belief in 19th-century Rural England' in Harris (ed.), *Popular Culture in England c.1500–1850*
Clark, J.C.D., 'Eighteenth Century Social History', *Historical Journal* 27, no.3 (1984)
Clark, J.C.D., 'On Hitting the Buffers: a Response', *P&P* 117 (1987)
Claydon, Tony and McBride, Ian, '"The Trials of the Chosen Peoples": Recent Interpretations of Protestantism and National Identity in Britain and Ireland' in Claydon and McBride (eds), *Protestantism and National Identity*
Colley, Linda, 'The Apotheosis of George III: Loyalty, Royalty and the British Nation 1760–1820', *P&P* 102 (1984)
Colley, Linda, 'Whose Nation? Class and National Consciousness in Britain 1750–1830', *P&P* 113 (1986)
Cook, Raymond A., 'As Jane Austen Saw the Clergy', *Theology Today* 18 (1961)
Cookson, J.E., 'The English Volunteer Movement of the French Wars, 1793–1815', *Historical Journal* 32, no.4 (1989)
Corfield, Penelope J., 'Georgian England: One State, Many Faiths', *HT* 45, no.4 (1995)
Dymond, David, 'Parish and Hundred Workhouses before 1834' in Dymond and Martin, *Historical Atlas of Suffolk*
Eastwood, David, '"Amplifying the Province of the Legislature": the Flow of Information and the English State in the Early Nineteenth Century', *Historical Research* 62 (1989)
Emsley, Clive, 'The Impact of the French Revolution on British Politics and Society' in Crossley and Small (eds), *The French Revolution and British Culture*
Evans, Eric J., 'Englishness and Britishness: National Identities *c.*1790–1870' in A. Grant and Keith J. Stringer (eds), *Uniting the Kingdom? The Making of British History* (1995)
Evans, Eric J., 'Some Reasons for the Growth of English Rural Anti-Clericalism *c.*1750–*c.*1830', *P&P* 66 (1975)
Gascoigne, John, 'Anglican Latitudinarianism, Rational Dissent & Political Radicalism in the Late 18th Century' in Haakonssen (ed.), *Enlightenment and Religion*
Gatrell, V.A.C., 'Crime, Authority and the Policeman State' in Thompson (ed.), *The Cambridge Social History of Britain 1750–1950*, 3
Gibson, William, 'Tories & Church Patronage (1812–30)', *JEH* 41/2 (1990)
Gilley, Sheridan, 'The Church of England in the 19th Century' in Gilley and Sheils (eds), *A History of Religion in Britain*
Gilley, Sheridan, 'Nationality & Liberty, Protestant & Catholic: Robert Southey's Book of the Church' in Mews (ed.), *Religion and National Identity*
Grace, Frank, 'A Census of the Poor: Barham in 1830', *SR* 38 (2002)
Grace, Frank, 'Economy, Government & Society in Ipswich 1500–1830' in Malster and Salmon (eds), *Ipswich from the 1st to the 3rd Millennium*

Grace, Frank, 'Food Riots in the Eighteenth Century: Popular Disturbances in Suffolk', *SR* 5, no.1 (1980)

Grace, Frank, 'The Governance of Ipswich, *c*.1550–1835' in Allen (ed.), *Ipswich Borough Archives, c.1255–c.1835*

Gregory, Jeremy, 'Eighteenth-century Reformation: the Pastoral Task of Anglican Clergy after 1689' in Walsh, Haydon and Taylor (eds), *The Church of England c.1689 to c.1833*

Gregory, Jeremy, 'Archbishops of Canterbury, their Diocese and the Shaping of the National Church' in Gregory and Chamberlain (eds), *National Church in Local Perspective*

Gregory, Jeremy, and Chamberlain, Jeffrey S., 'National and Local Perspectives on the Church of England in the Long Eighteenth Century' in Gregory and Chamberlain (eds), *National Church in Local Perspective*

Haydon, Colin, '"I love my King and my Country, but a Roman Catholic I hate." Anti-catholicism, Xenophobia and National Identity in 18th-century England' in Claydon and McBride (eds), *Protestantism and National Identity*

Innes, Joanna, 'Jonathan Clark, Social History and England's "Ancien Regime"', *P&P* 115 (1987)

Jacob, W.M., 'Church and Society in Norfolk 1700–1800' in Gregory and Chamberlain (eds), *National Church in Local Perspective*

Knight, Frances, 'From Diversity to Sectarianism: the Definition of Anglican Identity in Nineteenth-century England' in Swanson (ed), *Unity and Diversity in the Church*

Mather, F.C., 'Georgian Churchmanship Re-considered: Some Variations in Anglican Public Worship 1714–183', *JEH* 36/2 (1985)

Muskett, Paul, 'The East Anglian Agrarian Riots of 1822', *Ag. Hist. Rev.* 32 (1984)

Nockles, Peter B., 'Church Parties in the pre-Tractarian Church of England, 1750–1833: the Orthodox, some problems of identification and identity' in Walsh, Haydon and Taylor (eds), *The Church of England c.1689 to c.1833*

Nockles, Peter B., 'The Oxford Movement: Historical Background 1780–1833' in Rowell (ed.), *Tradition Renewed*

Norman, E.R., 'Church and State since 1800' in Gilley and Sheils (eds), *History of Religion*

Norrington, Val, 'Peace at Last: Celebrations of Peace and Victory during and after the Napoleonic Wars', *SR* 40 (2003)

Northeast, Peter, 'Education in Suffolk in the Nineteenth Century' in Dymond and Martin, *Historical Atlas of Suffolk*

Northeast, Peter, 'The Provision of Elementary Education in Nineteenth-century Rural Suffolk', *SR* 5, no.2 (1981)

Obelkevich, James, 'Religion' in Thompson (ed.), *Cambridge Social History* 3

O'Day, R., 'Clerical Renaissance' in Parsons (ed.), *Religion in Victorian Britain*

Paine, Clive, 'Protestant Nonconformity' in Dymond and Martin *Historical Atlas of Suffolk*

Peacock, A.J., 'Village Radicalism in East Anglia' in J.P.D. Dunbabin (ed.), *Rural Discontent in Nineteenth-century Britain* (New York, 1974)

Phillips, John A., 'The Social Calculus: Deference and Defiance in Later Georgian England', *Albion* 21, no.3 (1989)

Robbins, K., 'Religion and Identity in Modern British History' in Mews (ed.), *Religion and National Identity*

Robertson, Alistair, 'Turnpikes and Stagecoaches' in Dymond and Martin, *Historical Atlas of Suffolk*

Smith, Alan W., 'Popular Religion', *P&P* 40 (1968)

Somerville, C.J., 'The Secularisation Puzzle', *HT* 44, no.10 (1994)

Stafford, William, 'Religion and the Doctrine of Nationalism in England at the Time of the French Revolution and Napoleonic Wars' in Mews (ed.), *Religion and National Identity*

Stone, M.J., 'Below Stairs, or the Servant Problem: the Vicarage at Coddenham in the Early Nineteenth Century', *SR* 39 (2002)

Stone, M.J., 'Diverting Drama', *SR* 32 (1999)

Stone, M.J., 'Some Comments on the Established Church in Suffolk (1800–35)', *SR* 44 (2005)

Stone, M.J., 'The Week's Good Cause? The Royal or Church Brief', *Parson Woodforde Society Quarterly Journal* xxxvii, no.3 (2004)

Stone, M.J., 'Where to be Buried? A Sequel', *SR* 41 (2003)

Stott, Anne, 'Hannah More and the Blagdon Controversy, 1799–1802', *JEH* 51/2 (2000)

Sydenham, G., 'Glimpses of Congregational Life during the 18th & 19th Centuries', *SR* 3, no.6 (1968)

Thomas, Gwyn, 'Parliamentary Constituencies' in Dymond and Martin, *Historical Atlas of Suffolk*

Walsh, John and Taylor, Stephen, 'The Church and Anglicanism in the "Long" Eighteenth Century' in Walsh, Haydon and Taylor (eds), *The Church of England c.1689 to c.1833*

Waterman, A.M.C., 'The Nexus between Theology and Political Doctrine in Church and Dissent' in Haakonsen (ed.), *Enlightenment and Religion*

Watling, A.F., 'St Audry's Hospital' in Bentham (ed.), *Melton and its Churches*

Williamson, Tom, 'Shrubland before Barry: a House with its Landscape 1660–1880' in Harper-Bill *et al.* (eds), *East Anglia's History*

Wilson, R.G., 'The Cathedral in the Georgian Period' in Atherton *et al.* (eds), *Norwich Cathedral*

Wolffe, John, 'A Transatlantic Perspective: Protestantism and National Identity' in Claydon and McBride (eds), *Protestantism and National Identity*

Woodcock, George, 'The Meaning of Revolution in Britain 1770–1800' in Crossley and Small (eds), *The French Revolution and British Culture*

Young, Brian, 'A History of Variations: the Identity of the Eighteenth Century Church of England' in Claydon and McBride (eds), *Protestantism and National Identity*

UNPUBLISHED WORKS

Lummis, W.M., 'Material for a History of Coddenham' (1933) (SRO(I) qs Cod 9)

Martin, Edward, 'Pedigree of the Longe Family' (1980) (in private hands)

Ridgard, J. *et al.*, 'Raphaels seven, Bings of Port five' (1993) (SRO(I) qs 92.LON)

Stone, M.J., 'Shrubland Farm Labour Book' (2000) (SRO(I) 305.560942649 O/S)

Stone, M.J., '"John Bull in a dog-collar"? John Longe (1765–1834): a Suffolk Gentleman-parson', MA dissertation for the University of Essex (2004) (SRO(I) 920.LON O/S)

Stone, M.J., 'Nacton House of Industry' (1994) (SRO(I) qs Nacton 362.5)

Stone, M.J., 'Poor in Tuddenham' (1994) (SRO(I) qs Tuddenham 362.5)

INDEX OF PERSONS

* Titles, including those of nobility, have been given in the index only to distinguish two names.
* For the same limited purpose, alternative information is given.
* 'Family': used where the diarist refers to more than one family member without individual Christian names, usually in a social context. This use has been extended to other cases.
* Where a person is known by two names in the Diary, for example before and after marriage, both are given, cross-referenced.

INDEX of PLACES

* All places are in Suffolk unless otherwise shown.
* Where Longe's spelling differs from modern usage, the latter is preferred.
* Those places included in the Notes on People are not included in this index.

INDEX OF SUBJECTS